This modern text is designed to prepare you for your future professional career. While theories, ideas, techniques, and data are dynamic, the information contained in this volume will provide you a quick and useful reference as well as a guide for future learning for many years to come. Your familiarity with the contents of this book will make it an important volume in your professional library.

EX LIBRIS

Managerial Economics: Analysis and Cases

Managerial Economics: Analysis and Cases

Thomas J. Coyne, Ph.D.

Professor of Finance
John Carroll University

Fifth Edition
BUSINESS PUBLICATIONS, INC.
Plano, Texas 75075

To: Pat
and
Kathleen, Karen, Kevin, Kenneth,
and Thomas, III

P R E F A C E

Courses in applied price theory, business economics, decision making, and/or managerial economics are relatively new to academe. Yet, the subject matter ranks among the most fascinating studies a person can undertake. The first serious, formal treatment of managerial economics was probably done by Joel Dean in 1951.[1] Since that time, many colleges and universities throughout the United States, Canada, and elsewhere have introduced courses designed to enable one to apply abstract economic theory to the daily operations of profit as well as not-for-profit institutions. Professors located in business and arts and sciences colleges applaud these efforts.

Economic theorists believed at one time that economic theory was not intended to be applied. They thought theory should be studied for the sake of theory. Such study broadens one's mind, thereby making him/her an educated, well-rounded individual. While retaining the strengths of sound theory, professional schools of business have demonstrated that formalized presentation of the tools and techniques contained in this volume, once mastered, cause the student to become the most proficient of persons functioning in the business world.

Several hundred colleges throughout the United States, Canada, and abroad teach formal courses in managerial economics. Judging by the quality of their graduates, they have been and are doing excellent work. One major problem remains, however, and this book is written in the hope that it will contribute in some modest way to alleviation of that situation. The problem is this: Unlike more conventional courses—such as algebra, French, chemistry, and so on—the model building associated

---

[1] Joel Dean, *Managerial Economics* (New York: Prentice-Hall, 1951).

vii

with managerial economics cannot be taught; yet, as Baumol reminds us, it can be learned.[2]

Many subjects can be learned but cannot be taught. Consider, for example, the dilemma of a professor who writes and a student who reads a book describing how to ride a bicycle. The probability is high that no one will ever so successfully reduce to writing an explanation concerning how to ride a bicycle that a student, having read the book, will be able to jump on the bike and pedal across town. The same general statement, of course, holds for swimming. One interested in learning to swim must jump into the water and practice again and again the few successful techniques that have worked for others. These techniques help the novice swimmer to overcome fear of the water, to develop breathing and timing, and to build self-confidence. The rest is up to the novice. In essence, the same principles hold when economic theory is applied to the real world of business. As with riding a bike or swimming, once managerial economics is learned, it cannot be forgotten.

This book is not a treatise on how to succeed in business by applying basic economic theories. It does, however, present in a methodical manner several theoretically sound economic principles, which taken together, constitute a tool kit of sorts. This kit contains various methodologies that one should employ when analyzing business problems. To the greatest extent possible, it provides the reader with explanations of how, when, and why certain applications are appropriate. The analysis is based on qualitative as well as quantitative data.

Responsibility for successful implementation of the tools and techniques contained in this tool kit rests with the student, not with the professor. Each student has a business background and work experience that is unique. As a student reads this text, insights and understanding of the materials presented are limited only by one's imagination and creativity.

The book is appropriate for upper division undergraduate students and potential M.B.A. degree holders, both traditional and executive-type programs. The book assumes the student has introduced himself/herself to the fundamentals of math, accounting, finance, economics, statistics, and marketing. It appeared initially in colleges and universities as the sole effort of the late William W. Haynes.[3]

Dr. Haynes served as Dean, College of Business Administration, SUNY–Albany. His numerous articles on economics and the state of many industries and our national economy benefited the business and

---

[2] William J. Baumol, "What Can Economic Theory Contribute to Managerial Economics?" *American Economic Review*, May, 1961, pp. 142–46.

[3] William Warren Haynes, *Managerial Economics, Analysis and Cases* (Homewood, Ill.: Dorsey Press, 1963).

private organizations for whom he was researcher and consultant. The anthology to which he was contributing at the time of his death is now in its third edition.[4]

Economics is not only fascinating, it is practical. When corporations find they cannot operate to the right of their break-even point, losses occur, heads roll; major confrontations within the firm and between the firm and its creditors, unions, organizers, governments, stockholders, managers, and so on, inevitably arise. When a family encounters financial difficulties, conflicts arise that might lead to marital problems. When a nation finds too large a segment of its population not prospering as it would like, major military conflicts often develop. Such conflicts and confusion could be avoided with a proper understanding and application of economic theory. This book helps one gain a proper understanding of applied economic theory. It combines textbook exposition with cases in a manner that avoids having the student develop the principles of economics on his/her own.

In using this book be reminded that it represents an integral set of concepts as opposed to a variety of divergent and independent ideas. It presents a cumulative flow of analysis, which reaches a higher degree of complexity as the learning proceeds. The book introduces basic ideas in the earlier chapters and uses and builds upon those theories in the later sections. This method of presentation requires constant application, for a failure to master the earlier material will create difficulties in understanding what follows. This method also involves some repetition; the same ideas crop up from time to time throughout the volume. The author considers repetition of this nature advantageous. By considering the same ideas in different settings, the student grasps their full significance. After all, a medical student does not become a brain surgeon by reading about one operation. The same statement holds true for other professionals. A college of business student does not become an economist who can manage scarce and costly resources by successful one-time exposure to crucial concepts.

Managerial economics is not merely another course in economic theory; it requires a different approach than found in a theory text. The understanding of a graph revealing the theoretical equilibrium in perfect competition, for example, is less important in managerial economics than are the marginal tools of analysis incorporated in the theory. An understanding of theory *is* mandatory; this book assumes at least elementary training in economic theory. But managerial economics is concerned with application of that theory, a special subject in itself. When theoretical analysis is presented in this book, its relevance to practice is developed.

---

[4] Thomas Joseph Coyne, *Readings in Managerial Economics* (Plano, Tex.: Business Publications, 1981).

Nothing may be more irritating to a student than to read a section on pure theory and then another on practice with little obvious connection between the two. The connection between theory and practice is the reason for being of this book. Every effort is made to make these connections as clear as possible.

The presentation of analysis without case material is inadequate for the purposes of managerial economics. The very nature of managerial economics is one of application, and the best way to learn application is to apply. Anyone should be able to learn a formula for calculation of the elasticity of demand. But the estimation of price elasticities in actual markets requires a variety of skills; moreover, application of the knowledge of such elasticities to decision-making problems is far from simple. Procedures for the treatment of risk and uncertainty (Chapter 12), for example, cannot displace completely the more subjective skills in determining the extent to which such analysis should be carried and the degree of refinement, if any, that is justified. A course in managerial economics without cases misses the point, misses some of the judgmental skills considered by the author as an essential, vital part of the subject.

Price policy, a major subject of managerial economics, is governed in part by antitrust and other government regulations. This book makes no effort to teach the intricacies of such legislation and its interpretations in the courts. The reader is reminded of the importance of the legal environment within which decisions are made. The case method is used for this reminder because, again, it is an excellent way of introducing such considerations. A good case is never exclusively concerned with economic variables but reveals how economic factors are mixed with other variables. Chapter 3 and the cases associated with it suggest the complexity of the "total situation" found in actual business practice.

Decision analysis, Bayesian statistics, quantitative methods, strategic planning, and management science are subjects that have a close relationship to managerial economics. In fact, in 1984, it is impossible to determine whether capital budgeting is in the field of economics or finance. The same statement is true of operations research, a field distinguished by its mathematical approach. But as managerial economics becomes more mathematical, these differences lose significance. This book introduces the student to a variety of econometric studies and approaches that move in the quantitative direction of modern management science; it also contains a number of models of the sort that are characterized by new developments. But this book cannot hope to go into the quantitative approaches as deeply and thoroughly as do volumes specializing in those topics. Many of the simplifying assumptions in quantitative models are like those in managerial economics, so that the overlap with books in management science is substantial.

Some generalizations of managerial economics seem quite obvious when stated simply but take on a different character when related to concrete reality. *The economist who can manage* is one who can mold fundamental analytical tools to meet the needs of a specific decision-making situation. The materials presented in this book (of course, including the cases) provide the training necessary for successful application of theory to solution of real-world problems.

Numerous persons have given generously of their time and talent in the development of this book. Bruce Allen of Michigan State University provided helpful suggestions in the very early stages of this volume's development. Chandra Akkihal, Marshall University, reviewed rough drafts of one chapter. John M. Trapani, University of Texas at Arlington; Michael Stoller, SUNY–Plattsburgh; and John Claire Thompson, University of Connecticut, reviewed the book and offered meaningful suggestions.

Herschel Heath, Marshall University; Donald Anthony, Kent State University; and Welden Welfling, Case Western Reserve University each had a hand somewhere in the preparation of this text.

David Krazewski and Glen Weber are former research assistants of the author. They were graduate students at the University of Akron and Carnegie-Mellon University, respectively, when most of the book was in its mimeographed form. David and Glen helped find research materials and contributed ideas for improving certain problems. Hundreds of graduate students have been subjected to most of the materials presented in the text in mimeographed form and have contributed ideas for improving the exposition.

Thanks are due to Alain Remly-Post and to John Michael of John Carroll University (JCU) for their encouragement. Colleagues at JCU have read parts of the manuscript and have made helpful suggestions. Thanks in general are expressed to V. Ray Alford, Dean, JCU, for creating an atmosphere and environment conducive to research, and in particular for giving support and having patience during the writing stages of this volume.

Margie Wasdovich, the faculty secretary, and her staff and Marge Mauk, Joan Milenock, and others of JCU, and Dianne Berecek of Economic Consultants Incorporated (ECI) were helpful in typing and in correcting mistakes. JCU honors student Jeff Linkler suggested a title for one case and Clayton Cerny helped with the index. The author is very grateful to all but takes full responsibility for the errors that remain.

The assistance of businesspeople who provided materials for many of the applications is also gratefully acknowledged. In addition, on-the-job experiences gained by the author while employed or otherwise affiliated with the J. C. Penney Company; The Baltimore & Ohio Railroad; Vanpelt and Brown, Inc.; Ross Laboratories; The Robinson Clay Products Company; The Chessie System; Tri-State Petroleum Corporation; Summit Petroleum Corporation, and ECI brought the kind of real-world perspective that is indispensable to the writing of a book intended to help an economist manage resources more effectively.

Thomas Joseph Coyne

Contents

**Part two
Demand**   **101**

**Part three
Costs, production,
and productivity**   **206**

Managerial Economics:
Analysis and Cases

P A R T

1

Introduction to managerial economics

1

The scope and method of managerial economics

For the future manager, few topics are more exciting than managerial economics. It is the study of why some businesses prosper and grow, why some simply survive, and why others fail at the marketplace and go under.

Managerial economics goes straight to the heart of the U.S. mixed capitalistic system. Its topics include: demand and determinates of demand, supply and determinates of supply, cost conditions, production functions, capital budgeting procedures and techniques, short-range and long-range forecasting, corporate profits, and the problems of pricing.

Managerial economics also investigates the firm: the place it holds in an industry or field of business, its contributions to the economy as a whole, and even its impact on international affairs.

The study of managerial economics offers major benefits for students willing to pursue it seriously. It is here that you can learn practical applications for concepts already studied in the more traditional courses of micro- and macroeconomic theory. What you master from this textbook will apply directly to your skills and reputation as a manager. How far you advance in management will depend, in large part, on your ability to apply economic theories in matters useful to the daily operations of the firms that employ you.

For instance, you may be asked to determine how a price change will affect a company's principle product. You may someday have to determine the effects of raises or pay cuts on the productivity of hourly workers. Shifting demands for your company's products may require you to make high-priced decisions regarding plant capacity. Or you may be called upon by a puzzled chief executive officer to explain how changes in the price of oil from Saudi Arabia can alter the quantity of steel exported from Japan.

Managerial economics is woven through the great fabric of business and is found at the heart of any firm. It affects the sole proprietor who sells bicycles in a neighborhood shop as well as massive multinational corporations.

Solid grounding in managerial economics helps one decide many things important to a company's daily operations and short-run and long-run plans. For instance: Which products and services should you produce? How much output can be achieved and at what prices? When should equipment be replaced? What are the best sizes and locations for new plants? How should available capital be allocated?

This textbook examines many aspects, topics, and examples of managerial economics. Some of the subjects to be covered include practical application of the concept of price elasticity, the alternative cost concept, the profit contribution concept, how to apply the principles that describe the inverse relationship between the value of an asset and the interest rate, the notion that all factors of production relative to their price should be equal, and the incremental cost/price/profit concept.

Managerial economics is economics applied in decision making. It combines abstract theory with everyday practice, emphasizing the use of economic analysis in clarifying problems, in organizing and evaluating information, and in weighing alternative courses of action.

Although managerial economics is sometimes known as business economics, its tools, techniques, and perspective are useful in managing nonprofit organizations, public agencies, and government-owned businesses as well.

Economics is the study of how scarce and costly social resources are allocated throughout the world. Managerial economics, on the other hand, focuses directly on the firm and on individual units of management. As a subject, it is closely related to finance and financial management. Managerial economics is goal-oriented—it aims for maximum achievement of objectives, and it is concerned with strategies and choices vital to a firm's survival and growth. In short, it deals with the total situation in which decisions are made.

Relation to other branches of learning

Managerial economics' relation to economic theory is much like that of engineering to physics, or medicine to biology. It is very closely linked to microeconomic theory, macroeconomic theory, statistics, decision theory, and operations research. It draws together and relates ideas from several functional fields of business administration, including accounting, production, marketing, finance, and business policy.

Microeconomic theory

Microeconomic theory—also known as the theory of firms and markets, or price theory—is the main source of managerial economics' concepts and analytical tools. This text makes many references to such microeconomic concepts as elasticity of demand, marginal cost, short runs and long runs, and market structures. It also makes frequent use of well-known models in price theory—such as those for monopoly price, the kinked-demand theory, and price discrimination.

Managerial economics is explored from a pragmatic point of view. Thus, some of the field's fine points, given considerable space in theoretical literature, are deliberately neglected. For instance, this book makes no use of isoquants or indifference curves, which are central in the modern theory of demand. Indifference curves have helped clarify some important conceptual issues in economics, such as the separation of income effects and substitution effects of price change. But so far, they have played no part in managerial decisions. Measuring the variables required in indifference analysis is simply not feasible in practical situations.

Macroeconomic theory

The techniques and models of forecasting are macroeconomic theory's main contribution to managerial economics. Part 4 of this text, and Chapter 13 specifically, deal with forecasting.

The prospects of an individual firm often depend greatly on the conditions of business in general. Therefore, an individual firm's forecasts often depend heavily on general business forecasts, which make use of models derived from theory. For instance, the most widely used model in forecasting—the gross national product model—is the result of theoretical developments since World War II.

To actually use forecasting models in everyday business situations, close attention must be paid to details, such as inventory in the automobile industry, excess capacity in chemical manufacturing, or measurements of consumer attitudes. The manager doing the forecasting must engage in demand analysis. This topic is explored in general in Part 2 of this textbook, and specifically in Chapter 5.

Statistics

Statistics is important to managerial economics in several ways.

First, statistical measurements provide the basis for empirical testing of theory. Deductive reasoning has made a central contribution to economics, but its concepts cannot be deemed valid until they have been checked thoroughly against data from the real world—the hard facts of statistics. In this text, the student will find statistical tests of some of the generalizations most important to managerial economics.

Second, statistical techniques provide the individual firm with methods of measuring the functional relationships vital to decision making. It is not enough, for example, to simply state that a firm should base its pricing decisions on considerations of demand and cost. To take effective action and make effective plans, the firm also needs statistical measurements that reveal the shape and position of the demand and cost functions.

But statistics, vital as they are, ultimately provide only part of the input needed in decision making. Information from other sources, such as accounting and engineering, and a manager's subjective estimates also are needed.

The theory of decision making

The theory of decision making is especially significant to managerial economics. Much of economic theory is based on two assumptions: (1) Individuals and firms strive toward a single goal—maximum utility for the individual and maximum profit for the firm. (2) There is certainty or perfect knowledge in the individual's or firm's situation.

The decision-making theory recognizes that managers in the real world face a multiplicity of goals, and the only certainty they can count on is that each new day will bring new uncertainties. The theoretical notion of a single, optimum solution is replaced by the view that solutions must be found to balance conflicting objectives. Motivation, the relation of rewards and aspiration levels, and patterns of influence and authority all are key factors in the theory of decision making.

The theory of decision making is concerned with how expectations form under conditions of uncertainty. It recognizes the costs of collecting and processing information, the problem of communication, and the need to reconcile the diverse objectives of people and organizations. It also requires that psychological and sociological influences on human behavior be considered in the decision process.

This book is based on the belief that economic analysis is useful in the achievement of better decisions. Economic theory and the theory of decision making are not viewed as being in conflict. However, although economic theory is easy to apply in simple, slow-moving situations with clear-cut objectives, actual decision making is much more complex. Managers frequently must make quick choices in the face of multiple problems, divergent goals, and high degrees of uncertainty.

Use of the case method in managerial economics can reveal the strengths and weaknesses of economic analysis in actual decision-making situations. One of the skills to be learned from this book is to evaluate the relevance of various conceptual tools available for solving management problems.

Operations research

Operations research is closely related to managerial economics. It is concerned with model building—the construction of theoretical models that aid in decision making. Economic theorists began constructing models long before the expression "model building" became fashionable. Managerial economists apply the models.

Operations research is also concerned with optimization, and economics has long dealt with the consequences of maximizing profits and minimizing costs.

Some writers have suggested that operations research is made distinctive by its team approach and pooling of talents. Operations researchers come from the natural sciences, statistics, and mathematics as well as economics. Because operations research relies heavily on mathematics, most of its best-known techniques are quantitative in character. Management, on the other hand, frequently uses techniques that are more subjective and qualitative.

Operations research is best described by identifying its major techniques and models. The best-known technique is linear programming, which is applied to a variety of problems of choice. Operations-research workers also have developed inventory models that indicate optimum quantities to order and optimum ordering times. Other common operations-research techniques include applications of probability theory, waiting-line (queuing) models, and bidding models. The logic behind these models is closely related to the logic of economic analysis. For example, incremental or marginal reasoning used in economics is also applied in operations research's inventory models. Economists have taken great interest in linear programming's relation to traditional theories of the firm, and some topics in operations research, such as replacement theory, stem directly from the work of economists.

In this study of managerial economics, it is not important to determine where operations research ends and managerial economics begins. The two fields are closely related, each makes contributions to the other, and the manager can draw from both.

Integrating the functional fields of business

Business students must understand how the managerial process combines and synthesizes ideas and methods from all of the functional fields of business administration. The chapters on cost analysis and production economics are rich with concepts and relationships from the fields of accounting and production management. The chapters on forecasting, demand, and pricing show their close relationship to the field of marketing. And the discussions of competitive strategy, long-range planning, and capital budgeting contain many topics from finance and business policy. Mastering managerial economics offers the opportunity to integrate ideas from many specialties into an overall point of view: the perspective of a general manager.

Profits: A central concept

Profit maximization is the central assumption in managerial economics. Profits are, after all, the one pervasive objective of business. A firm's survival depends on its ability to earn profits. Profits are its measure of success. Other objectives are more a matter of personal taste or social conditioning and vary from firm to firm, society to society, and time to time.

The techniques for maximizing profits, however, are also useful for efficiently and effectively managing nonprofit organizations and public agencies.

Focusing on profits makes analysis of operations more convenient. It is easy to construct models based on the assumption of profit maximization. It is more difficult to build models based on a multiplicity of goals. This is especially true when those goals are concerned with unstable and relatively immeasurable factors, such as the desire to be fair, the desire to improve public relations, the wish to perform a community service, and the aim to increase one's personal influence and power.

As long as the goal is profits, economics offers a systematic and sophisticated system of logic to help the manager. But one must be careful with concepts of profit. The amount called profit on a firm's profit-and-loss statement (or net income on an income-and-expense statement) is usually much larger than the economic profit of the firm. To determine economic profit, a competitive or normal rate of payment for services of capital supplied by the firm must be subtracted from the profit for the period determined by conventional accounting methods. This capital supplied by the firm is the market value of land, plant, equipment, and working capital, the net of amounts borrowed against the physical assets. Later, it will be shown that a normal or going rate of return on capital supplied by the firm is called the opportunity cost of capital. The opportunity cost of capital is part of the cost of doing business, not part of the economic profit.

Theories of profit

One difficulty managers face in defining profit is that no single theory explains it in a simple way. Profit is a mixture of many influences. Thus, there are a variety of profit theories, and they fall into four categories: (1) theories emphasizing profit as a reward for taking risks; (2) theories stressing the effect of luck, frictions, imperfections, and time lags in producing profits; (3) theories centering on monopoly; and (4) theories that relate profits to the flow of innovations in the economy.

The first group of profit theories is based on the bearing of uncertainty. Entrepreneurs are unwilling to assume risks unless there is the possibility of a reward to compensate them for the chances they take. The greater the risk, the greater the profit incentive required. Thus, one could expect emphasis on a higher rate of profit in unstable and unpredictable industries, such as electronics, than in those with steady, dependable rates of growth, such as electric utilities.

Good luck and imperfections in the market mechanism are at the heart of the second group of profit theories. Changes in tastes and preferences, technology or institutions—events not anticipated or initiated by the firm —generate the profits. In a purely competitive economy without lags, such profits would quickly disappear. The entry of new firms into the market and the expansion of existing firms would create a downward pressure on profits. And the excess profits would be wiped out. In the real world of imperfections and frictions, however, the squeezing out of excess profits takes time. So there may be many instances of substantial profits that are the result of pure luck.

The third group of profit theories focus on the gains created by having a monopoly. Having a monopoly means being able to restrict entry to a market. The monopoly firm can thus profit by cutting production and raising prices above the competitive level. Relative profit is a socially desirable guide for production in competitive industries, since profit stimulates expansion in those parts of the economy in which expansion is desirable. Monopoly profit, on the other hand, may be socially undesirable. It may be viewed as a reward for curtailing expansion where such expansion would have been socially beneficial.

But the fourth group, the innovation theory of profit, warns against condemning all monopoly profit too hastily. Innovation theories note that profits arise from the development of new products, new production techniques, and new modes of marketing. The theories contend that innovators who develop new products and methods deserve rewards for their contribution to progress. It is true that they earn excess profits from the monopoly which the superiority of their innovations provides. But this monopoly will be temporary. Old innovations are replaced by new ones in a constant process of "creative destruction."[1]

Innovation theories of profit break away from the static equilibrium analysis in traditional economic theory. Innovation profits result from change—from disruption of the equilibrium or status quo. Any theory that ignores innovation neglects the most important function of profits: to reward change and stimulate the replacement of less valuable and productive activities with ones that are more vital.

Managerial economics and alternative profit theories

One paradox of managerial economics is that although it makes use of the assumption of profit maximization, it makes little direct use of the theories of profit. Instead, managerial economics is concerned with alternative profit theories. These, too, are created by uncertainty, lags, frictions, and innovations. But most of the analysis is in terms of cost,

---

[1] Joseph Schumpeter, *Theory of Economic Development* (Cambridge, Mass.: Harvard University Press, 1934).

demand, revenues, and market structure, rather than directly in terms of profits. Thus, this study is concerned with measurements of the incremental revenues and incremental costs that lie behind incremental profits. Managerial economics considers how certain alternatives contribute to overhead and profits. One needs to compute future value from the present value of an estimated stream of profit. An economist must compare discounted rates of return, which are measures of profitability, with costs of capital. But none of this analysis involves direct application of a profit theory.

Consider the risk and uncertainty theory first. Businesses have coped with it over the years in a variety of ways, mostly subjective in character. Formal techniques for the analysis of uncertainty have developed under the titles of decision theory, decision trees, Bayesian statistics, the Monte Carlo method, and the Markov processes. Modern managerial economics recognizes these important ideas and has incorporated them as part of the complex apparatus required for economic analysis. It is no surprise, then, that a long list of textbooks dealing with probability, statistics, and management sciences use the language of economics in many places: incremental cost, incremental gain, marginal utility, opportunity cost, probability models, and so forth.

This textbook does not relegate the topics of risk and uncertainty to secondary positions, and there are several reasons for this treatment. One reason is that, as the student becomes familiar with the basic concepts of managerial economics, the analytical contributions to be made by statistical approaches should be appreciated. Some books on managerial economics tend to displace the important ideas of demand, cost, pricing, and capital budgeting with discussions of normal curves, Bayes's theorem, and Bernoulli processes. This book stops short of that approach. Yet, the concepts of managerial economics and statistics are complementary rather than competitive, and both deserve attention. Probability theory is covered in courses in statistics and operations research. A course in managerial economics should concentrate on fundamental economic analysis and apply statistics where necessary. However, the importance of risk and uncertainty as a source of profits will be discussed again in Chapter 12 of this book.

Behavioral theory of the firm

The behavioral theory of the firm is helpful in understanding the processes of decision making when there are multiple objectives and incomplete information. The theory views the organization as a coalition of individuals, and most of these individuals constitute subcoalitions. The goals of the organization are developed through more or less continuous negotiations among and between members of the subcoalitions, who are potential members of the coalition.

Organizational goals may be stated as aspiration levels (for example, "increase our market share to 25 percent"; "earn 12 percent after tax on total capital employed"; "spend 8 percent of our budget on research and 2 percent on executive development"). Yet the goals established at any one time may be inconsistent. It may be impossible for all of them to be fully and simultaneously realized.

According to the behavioral theory of the firm, an organization's decisions and resource allocations are based on information and expectations that usually differ appreciably from reality. The organization does not have, and does not attempt to acquire, complete information about alternatives that are open to it. Flexibility, the possibility of revoking or modifying decisions, is highly regarded. When there are gaps between aspiration levels and actual results, the firm searches for additional alternatives. In many instances methods for closing gaps are discovered. In other instances the firm's aspiration levels must be reduced.

In the behavioral theory, the firm is an adaptive organization. It learns from experience and has a memory, and organizational theory that works is incorporated into decision rules and standard operating procedures. Over the long run, experience may cause these rules and procedures to be modified. However, in the short run, the organization's decisions are dominated by its standard methods and rules of thumb.

The behavioral theory of the firm was developed as a basis for a theory of administrative behavior. But it is also useful for understanding managerial decision processes. It helps one understand how much approximation is involved in the microeconomic theory of the firm, which has the following basic assumptions: a single decision maker, a single objective, and conditions of certainty.

Models and suboptimization

The real economic world is very complex. A firm's decisions hinge on a great many technological and social factors—so many that only a few characteristics of the environment can actually be considered in decision making. And even these selected characteristics can be known only approximately rather than exactly. Managers must plan with models and simplifications and settle for local improvement of results, not global optimization.

Models

Suppose that in future months a manufacturer expects to sell quantities of a six-foot, color video system. The expected quantities have been drawn from equations. These equations relate sales quantities to price, unit cost (which increases as more features are added), per capita income, and the manufacturer's expenditures on advertising. Some other influences that will have less effect on sales or are difficult to estimate are disregarded in the above model. These influences include: competitors' prices, dealer markups, dealer advertising, changes in official rates of currency exchange with other countries. It is clear that the manufacturer's view of demand is an approximation.

Models are structures involving relationships among concepts. Since the concepts are often represented as symbols, their relationships can be expressed in mathematical form. The mathematical form allows quick determination of the expected results of changes in controllable variables. Using the demand equation or model of demand, the television manufacturer cited above could quickly estimate the effects on sales of changes in price or advertising outlay.

Chapter 5, which focuses on demand analysis, shows how its models are developed and used.

Models are abstractions from reality that capture important relationships. They allow the analyst to understand, explain, and predict. The purpose of a model is to represent characteristics of a real system in a way that is simple enough to understand and manipulate. Yet the model must be similar enough to the actual operating system that it provides satisfactory results when used in decision making. Thus, the test of whether or not a model is satisfactory cannot be the degree to which it corresponds to the real world. The appropriate test is whether or not it provides successful predictions.

Suboptimization

Few managers actually seek the greatest attainment of a single goal. They settle for partial achievement of a variety of goals. They recognize that pushing toward one objective may mean partial sacrifice of another. Even if a manager could specify a single goal, he or she could not achieve the "true" optimum. The number of relevant variables and the variety of interrelationships are too large and complex for any system of thought. Even the most elaborate models are still abstractions from reality. Any model or theory must necessarily simplify. In managerial economics, a paradox results. Managerial economics often assumes a desire to optimize a given objective. Then it sometimes must simplify in ways that assure failure to fully achieve the optimum.

Throughout this volume are models and principles based on three assumptions: a single objective (profit maximization or, at times, cost minimization or a given output), a single decision maker, and full information. Practitioners of managerial economics must adopt a mixed attitude toward such assumptions. The assumptions must be simplified to create order out of chaos, but as a description of actual managerial behavior, the assumptions are oversimplified and inaccurate.

Operations researchers use the term *suboptimization* to describe the process of decision making by abstraction from the total complexity of reality and from the wide variety of goals. They construct models that reflect only part of reality and face up to the bounds of human rationality. The results may be imperfect but superior to decisions based on crude rules of thumb or simple repetitions of past decisions. Rules of thumb and rigid formulas are replaced by the point of view that "it depends."

Learning

Use of models in daily decision making creates a learning process. Models that do not work well must be revised. Figure 1–1 illustrates the learning process. The original symbolic model may be one that has worked previously. Or it may be a new one that seems plausible to the user. In any event, the model contains parameters. These are symbols for measurable relationships among the major components of the model. Parameters can be estimated from real-world data. But it usually is not possible to determine their exact values.

By manipulating the quantified model, the user can obtain quantified predictions of outcomes for alternative lines of action. The user can choose among these alternatives and observe the actual outcome of his or her decision. If the actual experience is not as predicted or within a predicted range, the decision maker must revise the theoretical model

Figure 1–1
The two worlds of a decision maker

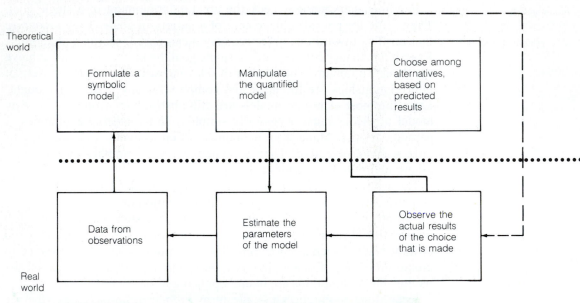

If prediction is not satisfactory, develop a better model.

and reestimate the parameters. This process of testing and revising a theoretical model is what is meant by "learning from experience."

The usefulness of managerial economics

Managerial decision making requires compromise between the need for simplification—to make the analysis manageable—and the need for complication—to consider a variety of objectives and influences. Costs of completeness must be weighed against errors of simplification. Large quantities, common sense, and good judgment are needed.

Managerial economics provides a rich body of tools and techniques that enable managers to become more competent model builders. Thus, they can capture the essential relationships that characterize a situation while eliminating cluttering details and peripheral relationships. Model builders cannot look at all aspects of an environment, but they can develop a clearer view of their problems, opportunities, and alternatives.

Normative economics

The main body of economic theory confines itself to descriptive hypotheses. Managerial economics, on the other hand, is prescriptive. Its concern is decisions that ought to be made. Economic theory attempts to generalize about the relations between and among variables, without making judgments of what is desirable or undesirable. For example, the law of diminishing returns is a generalization about what happens to output when variable inputs are added to fixed inputs. It involves no judgment of whether the outcome is good or bad. Managerial economics, however, goes at least one step further. It decides whether or not a probable outcome is desirable and whether or not management should pursue courses of action leading to it. This distinction may appear frivolous to those outside business. But it is of major consequence in managing a business.

Normative economics encompasses the branches of economics that attempt to reach specific policy conclusions by combining descriptive economics with value judgments. These value judgments include judgments about objectives, goals, and/or strategies designed to reach certain goals. Public policy—the economic policy of government—is one type of normative economics. Managerial economics is another form of normative theory.

One feature of normative economics has special significance to managerial decision making. Some of the main propositions of managerial economics are heavily deductive. For example, the statement that profits are at a maximum when marginal revenue is equal to marginal cost is entirely a matter of logic that requires no examination of the facts. A substantial part of economic analysis is of this character, providing a logic system that is self-contained. As stated earlier, it is necessary to fit the correct data into this logical framework to reach specific conclusions about what should be done. And the question of whether or not a particular line of logic is useful is an empirical issue. It has to be checked against the facts.

Summary

Managerial economics is a branch of normative economics that draws from descriptive economics (sometimes called positive economics) and from well-established, deductive patterns of logic. Managerial economics is, in addition, continually concerned with separating what will work from lines of thought that have not worked. The application of managerial economics is inseparable from considerations of values, or norms. It is always concerned with action—the achievement of objectives, the optimization of goals, or the implementation of strategies.

Managerial economics emphasizes the uses of economic analysis in decision making for business firms, nonprofit organizations, and public agencies. It attempts to maximize the achievement of objectives by allocating limited resources among alternative uses. Managerial economics integrates many concepts and techniques from economics, decision theory, and statistics, plus selected ideas and methods from the functional fields of business: accounting, production, marketing, finance, and business policy.

In managerial economic analysis, the usual approach is to begin by assuming that profit maximization is the only objective of the firm. After the consequences of that assumption have been derived, other objectives can be introduced, and their effects on profits can be estimated.

Typically, it is impossible to make a plan for overall, or global, profit maximization. The manager faces too many simultaneous choices and needs too much information to come up with the best possible combinations of resource-using activities. Instead, managerial economics focuses on partial, or local, profit improvement through incremental changes. Each decision involves only a portion of the firm's entire activity, and all decisions are based on models that are simplifications and approximations of reality.

Managerial economics provides an orderly, simplified, piecemeal approach to a complex environment, one presenting too many problems, opportunities, and alternatives to be handled in simultaneous, unrestricted, head-on confrontation.

PROBLEMS
The scope and method of managerial economics

1–1   Positive economics aims at understanding economic processes and systems. Normative economics aims at controlling economic processes to achieve objectives. Is managerial economics primarily an application of positive economics or of normative economics? Explain.

1–2   The intermediate course in microeconomics deals mainly with theories of firms and markets. Is managerial economics simpler or more complex than the microeconomic theory course? How do the objectives of the courses differ?

1–3   We say that managerial economics helps the business student in his or her effort to integrate knowledge gained in other courses. How is this integration accomplished?

1–4   How does an economic model differ from the ''reality'' to which it is related?

1–5   Analysis of economic matters with the aid of an economic model could be called theoretical analysis. Would it be better to carry out ''realistic'' analysis, in which no simplification or approximation would be permitted?

1–6   In the behavioral theory of the firm, objectives are stated as aspiration levels; in the economic theory of the firm, objectives are stated as profit maximization. Can these theories be reconciled?

C H A P T E R

Fundamental concepts: A case method approach

The case method is, perhaps, the most important and convenient way of acquiring skill in applying managerial economics—short of actual decision making itself. Case studies can reveal the complexity of the environment in which decisions are made and force the student to move away from elementary abstract theory and begin to recognize the uncertainties of the real world. Case studies demonstrate that many decisions must be made without the benefit of total, complete, and accurately quantified information, and they show that simplifications are often necessary if some semblance of order is to be made out of the multitude of facts and figures faced by most management persons.

College courses and textual materials in managerial economics that include the case method are more useful to a student than are textual materials devoid of the method. Decades of actual business experiences support this idea. Still, many readers of this book will be unfamiliar with the case method. Cases in a managerial economics book create an additional problem because they have a special character; they are not the same as cases in accounting, marketing, or policy. Consequently, special attention must be paid to them.[1] The cases in managerial economics provide an opportunity to apply the concepts of economics to the problems of management. Rather than being representative of all managerial decisions, they are chosen from those areas of management most amenable to economic analysis.

The initial effort in case-method analysis should go toward determining the problems or issues, with secondary regard to whether or not these are economic problems. Some students make the mistake of organizing a case analysis around economic concepts. Instead, they should use the

---

[1] The late W. W. Haynes may be the first person to have recognized this situation.

18

economic concepts as tools, where appropriate, in the analysis of the case. The objective is not to determine whether the case is an example of opportunity costs or demand elasticities or valuation but rather to determine the issues and then use whatever analysis is appropriate.

Some of the cases in this textbook, however, *are* intended as simple exercises in the use of economic analysis. Almost all of them are based on actual situations, and a few are synthesized from the experiences of several firms. Obviously, none of the cases supply all of the facts. Management never has all the facts during the decision-making process. Trying to make sense out of a situation without full knowledge may be frustrating, yet it is an essential part of management.

The best way to learn the case method is to use it, but a few introductory comments may be helpful.

Procedure in analyzing a case

The steps in analyzing a case can vary, so it would be wrong to claim that only one procedure is appropriate. The following outline of steps suggests one way to go about an analysis.

Subject Define the central issue or issues. A case may contain a variety of issues, from trivial to significant. The analyst must focus on the key problems and define the subject of inquiry.

Object All evidence must be organized in a manner that allows the analyst to choose a sense of direction, and to understand what the management team is attempting to achieve. After determining the central issue or issues, the analyst organizes the facts around topics related to those issues. This approach requires the separation of the unimportant from the significant, the irrelevant from the relevant. Often, it is necessary to arrange the facts in a new form, such as a break-even chart or flow-of-funds statement. Constructing effective charts and tables to clarify a situation requires imagination and is one of the chief tools of orderly decision making.

Present situation The existing situation must be clearly understood. If alternatives exist, what are they? In some cases the alternatives are obvious. In others the analysts must invent alternatives appropriate to the situation. Analysts cannot remain content with predetermined alternatives but must strive for new and better solutions.

Proposal If new alternatives are to be suggested, what are they? What is their real or potential impact on the price and output behavior of the firm? What does the analyst propose?

Advantages What advantages exist for the proposed action of alternative? Present all facts associated with the advantages and reveal the economic impact of each.

Disadvantages No matter how well the facts in a case are organized, and no matter how advantageous these facts are to the overall objectives of the firm, disadvantages exist. Look for the disadvantages associated with a proposal and cite them. Caution is in order here so as not to become overly negative. Yet, realistic disadvantages must be recognized and dealt with.

Action   Weigh the strengths and weaknesses of each alternative. Discard weak alternatives in favor of strong ones. Make a decision!

Most people are afraid to make decisions because they fear criticism. If 20/20 hindsight proves the decision wrong, the decision maker might be criticized. No one looks forward to criticism! Nonetheless, managers must not avoid choosing the alternative that seems best at that time. They must be decisive. Managers should be aware of the limitations, as well as strengths, of their choice and should beware of overstating their case. But managers must act, for inaction itself involves a choice.

Normally, there is no single correct solution to a case. Two managers of equal ability might select different alternatives. It is often difficult to say that one alternative is better than the other. Yet, some case analyses and some recommendations are superior to others. Criteria for making this determination include the following:

1. The extent to which the analysis and solution show an understanding of the real issues involved.
2. The extent to which the analysis is based on the particular facts in the situation.
3. The degree to which the solution appears to be workable under the circumstances.
4. The extent to which the analyst is able to support his or her position.

The fundamental concepts discussed in this chapter should be helpful when making decisions in all cases presented in this text. The student's objectives should be to size up each situation, to organize and analyze the facts, to evaluate the alternatives, and to reach a decision—using economic concepts when they are helpful.

As background for the remainder of the book, it is desirable to introduce seven fundamental concepts basic to all of managerial economics. These concepts are elementary—almost self-evident. But their application is not always so self-evident.

The incremental concept

Incremental reasoning is easier to describe than to apply. It involves estimating the impact of decision alternatives on costs and revenues, stressing the changes in total cost and total revenue that result from changes in prices, products, procedures, investments, or whatever may be at stake in the decision. The two basic concepts in this analysis are incremental cost and incremental revenue. *Incremental cost* may be defined as the change in total cost resulting from a decision. *Incremental revenue* is the change in total revenue resulting from a decision.[2] A decision is obviously a profitable one if:

1. It increases revenue more than it increases costs.
2. It decreases some costs more than it increases others.
3. It increases some revenues more than it decreases others.
4. It reduces costs more than it reduces revenue.

Before dismissing this analysis as too elementary for attention, consider some of its implications. Some businesspeople take the view that to make an overall profit they "must make a profit on every job."[3] The result is that they refuse orders that do not cover full cost (labor, materials, and overhead) plus a provision for profit. Incremental reasoning indicates that this rule may be inconsistent with profit maximization in the short run. A refusal to accept business below full cost may mean rejection of a possibility of adding more to revenue than to cost. The relevant cost is not the full cost but rather the incremental cost. A simple problem illustrates what is involved. Take a case in which a new order will bring in $10,000 additional revenue. The costs are estimated as follows:

Labor	$ 3,000
Materials	4,000
Overhead (allocated at 120 percent of labor cost)	3,600
Selling and administrative expense (allocated at 20 percent of labor and materials cost)	1,400
Full cost	$12,000

This order appears to be unprofitable. But suppose there is idle capacity with which this order could be produced. Suppose acceptance of the order will add only $1,000 of overhead (the incremental overhead, limited to the added use of heat, power, and light, the added wear and tear on the machinery, the added costs of supervision, and so on). Suppose also that the order requires no added selling costs, since the only requirement is a signature on the contract and no additional administrative costs. In addition, only part of the labor cost is incremental, since some idle workers already on the payroll will be put to work without added pay.

It is possible that the incremental cost of taking the order will be as follows:

---

[2] As is demonstrated in this chapter under "The Discounting Principle," the profitability of a decision is also often expressed in terms of net cash flows. In calculating cash flows, one adds depreciation to net income.

[3] The exact words of numerous managers in an interview. The cases that follow contain similar statements.

Labor	$2,000
Materials	4,000
Overhead	1,000
Total incremental cost	$7,000

Although it appeared at first that the order would result in a loss of $2,000, it now appears that the result is an addition of $3,000 in profit.

Perhaps a brief comment will minimize a common misunderstanding about incremental reasoning. Incremental reasoning does not mean that the firm should price at incremental cost or should accept all orders that merely cover incremental costs. In fact, "charging what the market will bear" is consistent with incrementalism, for it implies increasing rates as long as the resulting revenues increase. The acceptance of the $10,000 order in this illustration takes into account both the existence of idle capacity that would otherwise go unused and the absence of more profitable alternatives. Incremental reasoning never leads to acceptance of a less-profitable order in preference to one that is more profitable; in fact, it leads to the opposite.

To summarize the discussion in the form of a simple principle, which we can call the incremental principle: A decision is sound if it increases revenue more than it increases costs, or reduces costs more than it reduces revenue.

Do managers actually use incremental reasoning? Some do, and others do not. Managers of even the largest firms are not always fully aware of the reasoning behind their own decisions. Apparently, many of them unconsciously do apply incremental principles, as do managers of small firms. In any case, many firms are inarticulate in their decision-making processes, making it difficult to determine what logic they do apply.

Managers are often aware of the distinction between fixed and variable costs, and some managers make use of ad hoc cost analyses in applying incremental reasoning. Other managers reach decisions consistent with incrementalism by trial and error, or by experimentation.

Many, if not most, small firms do not have a programmed accounting method (a routine method automatically producing data period by period) to provide the kinds of cost figures required for decision making.[4] The item in the accounts that seems to have the greatest impact on decision making is the profit or loss figure on the income statement. If this figure seems low in relation to some predetermined standard, the manager often seeks ways to improve the situation. The income figure motivates the managers to make decisions, but it does not provide the analysis required

---

[4] Programmed techniques are routine, resulting in period statements of a standard form. The nonprogrammed methods involve ad hoc, or tailor-made, analyses (special studies) made for particular decision-making problems.

by those decisions. Accounting performs its stewardship function, supplying data required by the owners, creditors, or tax collectors. It also performs the control function, providing measurements of actual performance that could be compared with earlier experience or with standards. But accounting normally does not provide incremental data that would be useful for decisions.[5] This latter point is cruical to one's understanding of the incremental principle.

Although the failure of many accounting systems to supply incremental data is a deficiency, ad hoc analyses in many cases are less expensive than programmed accounting systems that must be maintained period after period. Furthermore, what constitutes an incremental cost varies from one decision to another. This variation makes it unlikely that a programmed incremental system would always produce the required information. A manager experienced in decision making may be able to make necessary adjustments in the regular accounting data with a few quick notes on the back of an envelope. Thus, the absence of marginalist accounting methods does not necessarily imply the absence of incremental reasoning.

A few illustrations should help the reader picture the variety of actual applications. Start with two firms that not only fail to maintain records consistent with incrementalism but also make decisions that appear to be inconsistent with incremental reasoning.

A laundry and dry-cleaning establishment　The managers of this firm rejected an opportunity to make use of idle capacity in the summer months when business was slack. A large motel wished to make a contract that would supply the laundry with business that would not cover full costs but would more than cover incremental costs, leaving a contribution to overhead and profit. Apparently, the managers were so certain that the full-cost figure, including allocated overhead, was the correct figure for decision making that they rejected a profitable order. They were unable to give any other reasons for rejecting the order. They did not believe that its acceptance would have any effect on their other business, either present or future.

An air-conditioning and sheet metal firm　The managers of this firm, like those of the laundry just mentioned, rejected a large order that would have filled excess capacity and would have made a contribution to over-

---

[5] The use of systematic incremental reasoning appears to be the exception rather than the rule in Japan and elsewhere. Traditional cost accounting, with its arbitrary cost allocations, appears to have confused far more managers than it has helped in the area of decision making. Still less than 20 percent, perhaps even less than 10 percent, of experienced managers in training programs in developing and some developed countries are able to see that the traditional accounting treatment of accountants fails to provide the kinds of incremental data required. Thus, the gap between "excellently managed" firms and the great majority of firms still remains, at least in the cost analysis area.

head and profits. Again, the reliance on full costs, including allocated overhead, appears to have confused the decision-making process.

Additional illustrations from actual practice present a different pattern: the absence of marginal accounting systems, but decisions consistent with incrementalism. The managers of a billboard advertising firm paid little attention to their regular accounting figures in making decisions on advertising rates. Instead, they made up ad hoc income statements for future periods under alternative assumptions about rates. By this method, they reached conclusions that appear to be fully in accord with incremental reasoning, even though the managers were unfamiliar with the economic jargon one might use to describe their analysis. They were successful in spite of, not because of, their accounting records. Other companies appear to approximate incrementalism by trial and error, learning from experience what policies are likely to be conducive to increased profits.

In studying business behavior, especially that of small business, one finds that most companies appear to fall between the extremes already discussed. Many managers are concerned with full costs (in retailing they emphasize wholesale costs) and use these costs as a starting point in pricing. However, they do not always adhere to rigid markups on costs but, instead, vary markups on different lines of goods and revise markups over time. Thus, the most common pattern may be one of "partial incrementalism," with either full cost or wholesale cost serving as a reference point or resistance point, but with considerable flexibility in adjustments to market conditions.

This approach to understanding incrementalism supports two conclusions:

1. It is impossible to generalize on the uses of incremental reasoning, actual practice being variable.
2. Most firms could profit by giving considerably more attention to incremental analysis, regardless of whether or not they revise their accounts to reflect this analysis.

Readers familiar with elementary economics are likely to recognize that incremental reasoning is closely related to the marginal costs and marginal revenues of economic theory. There are similarities and differences, and both require attention.

1. Marginal costs and revenues are always defined in terms of unit changes in output, but incremental costs and revenues are not necessarily restricted to unit changes.[6] If a one-unit increase in output results in an

---

[6] Strictly speaking, marginal concepts must be defined as derivatives of cost or revenue functions or, alternatively, as slopes of tangents to such functions.

increase in cost from $700 to $710 and an increase in revenue from $800 to $815, the marginal cost is $10, and the marginal revenue is $15. If a 10-unit increase in output increases cost from $700 to $790 and increases revenue from $800 to $940, one can speak of an incremental cost of $90 and an incremental revenue of $140. Or one can state that the average marginal cost over this range is $9, and average marginal revenue is $14.

If the cost function is curvilinear, the marginal cost may change for each unit change in output. The measurement of marginal costs and marginal revenues permits a microscopic examination of such unit-by-unit changes. The decision maker may wish to avoid such refinement, wanting only to know whether the decision as a whole is profitable and being willing to look at the entire increase in revenue to compare with the entire change in costs. The manager runs the risk of ignoring some other change in output within the range that might be even more profitable, but the cost of refinement may outweigh that risk.

2. Incremental concepts are more flexible than marginal concepts in another way. Marginal cost and marginal revenue are normally restricted to the effects of changes in output, but decision making may not be concerned with changed output at all. For example, the problem may be one of substituting one process for another to produce the same output. The problem is then one of comparing the cost of the first process with that of the alternative. The marginalist language is not particularly suited to this kind of decision.[7]

One way of comparing the marginal and incremental approaches is to draw a traditional cost diagram like those that appear in all principles-of-economics textbooks. Figure 2–1 shows marginal cost as a curve, rising over most of its range.

Let us consider increasing output from 2,000 to 3,000 units. What is the marginal cost of this change? In terms of this traditional diagram, it is rather dangerous to give a single answer. At first the marginal cost is low, but it rises rapidly. Even to speak of an average marginal cost over this range is to oversimplify and to ignore the dramatic change over the range of outputs.

But many studies of cost functions suggest that another pattern of costs is common in industry. The studies have found relatively constant marginal costs over a wide range of outputs, as in Figure 2–2. In this situation, no error results from using a single marginal cost figure over the whole range.

For the firm illustrated in Figure 2–2, assume that the total fixed costs

---

[7] It is possible to compare the marginal cost of one process with that of another but not of the marginal cost of the change. However, one can use the term *incremental cost* to refer to the change in cost brought about by the change in process.

Figure 2–1
Average and marginal costs as presented traditionally

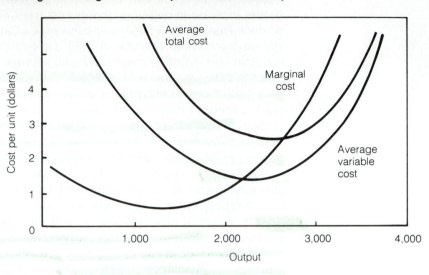

Figure 2–2
Cost curves with constant marginal costs

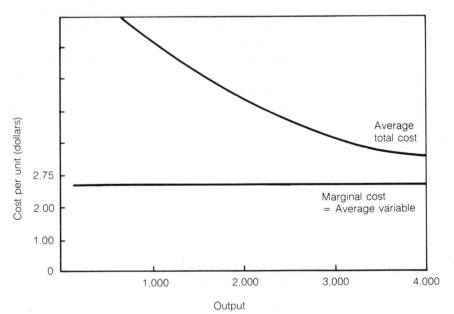

are $4,000 (per time period). The average variable cost is $2.75 per unit. The marginal cost is also $2.75 per unit. Suppose that the decision involves a choice between an output of 2,000 units and one of 3,000 units. In the language of marginal cost, there is no doubt about how to express the change in cost—it is $2.75 per unit. In the incremental language, however, it is perfectly appropriate to speak of an addition to total cost of $2,750. Even if the marginal cost curve were slightly curved, such a description of the change in costs might be precise enough for practical purposes.

The chief question here is whether or not marginal costs are in fact constant and justify the substitution of incremental cost measurements over large changes in output for measurements of cost changes for minute variations in output. If one could be certain of the universal linearity of short-run costs, the problem of decision making would be greatly simplified. At this point a general comment should suffice, but Part 3, devoted entirely to cost analysis, presents more detailed comments regarding this important distinction.

The empirical studies of Joel Dean were among the first to suggest the linearity of marginal costs. His early studies covered a hosiery mill,[8] a leather belt shop,[9] and a furniture factory.[10] They all indicated a pattern much like that shown in Figure 2–3—a straight-line total cost curve, which means a horizontal marginal cost curve and an L-shape average total cost curve. The reader should note how the curves were fitted to the dots representing actual observations (adjusted to remove some other influences).

Since the time of Dean's work, the preponderance of statistical studies has supported the conclusion that total costs are linear, and marginal costs are constant in the short run.[11] For example, Yntema's study of costs in the steel industry resulted in this equation:[12]

$$X_t = 182,100,000 + 55.73X_2$$

in which

X_t = Total cost in dollars.
X_2 = Weighted output, tons.

---

[8] Joel Dean, *Statistical Cost Functions of a Hosiery Mill* (Chicago: University of Chicago Press, 1941).

[9] Joel Dean, *The Relation of Cost to Output for a Leather Belt Shop* (New York: National Bureau of Economic Research, 1941).

[10] Joel Dean, *Statistical Determination of Costs, with Special Reference to Marginal Cost* (Chicago: University of Chicago Press, 1936).

[11] See J. Johnston, *Statistical Cost Analysis* (New York: McGraw-Hill, 1960), especially Chapters 4 and 5. Johnston's work is the most complete survey of cost studies.

[12] United States Steel Corporation, *T.N.E.C. Papers,* Vol. II (New York, 1940), p. 53.

Figure 2–3
Partial regressions of total, average, and marginal combined costs on output—leather belt shop

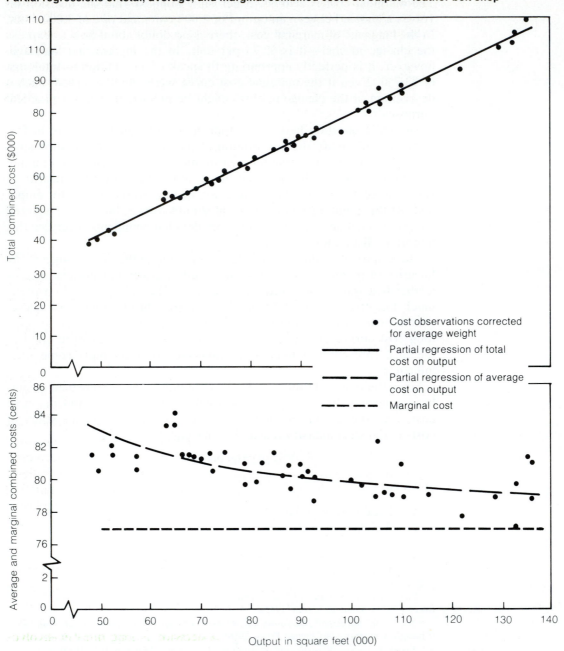

Source: Joel Dean, *The Relation of Cost to Output for a Leather Belt Shop* (New York: National Bureau of Economic Research, 1941), p. 27.

On a total-cost graph, this equation would appear as a straight line sloping upward to the right, intersecting the vertical (cost) axis at a positive figure. On an average-cost graph, the equation would take on an L shape, reflecting constant variable-unit costs and declining fixed-unit costs.

Several studies, including some before and some after World War II, fail to support the linearity hypothesis. For decades it has been recognized that it is dangerous to assume that the constancy of marginal costs is universal. A study of short-run fuel costs in steam electricity plants fitted the following curvilinear equation to the data.[13]

$$Y = 16.68 + 0.125X + 0.00439X^2$$

where

    Y = Total fuel cost.
    X = Output as a percentage of capacity.

Such an equation implies rising marginal costs.

The statistical studies are still a matter of controversy. First, on a priori grounds, limited short-run capacity would appear to be inconsistent with constancy of marginal costs at all levels of output. At some point diminishing returns must occur. Perhaps the statistical studies have failed to find data on cases in which output was pressing on capacity, at which point increasing marginal costs might have been experienced. In other words, the conclusion that costs are linear might apply only within the ranges of output for which the data were collected. An alternative conclusion is that marginal costs are constant up to capacity, at which point further increases in output are impossible (one might say that the marginal cost curve becomes vertical).

Other criticisms are that the statistical methods used may show a bias toward linearity and that the constancy of marginal costs is inconsistent with some observed market behavior. A fuller discussion of these criticisms appears in the chapter on costs. It is enough at present to indicate some misgivings about the widespread findings of linearity in statistical cost studies. Despite these misgivings, the evidence favors the conclusion that constant marginal costs are widespread, within the usually experienced, or relevant, ranges of output.

The concept of time perspective

So widely known are the economic concepts of the long run and short run that they have become part of everyday language. The economist uses these terms with a precision that is often missed in ordinary discussion. In the parlance of economics, a decision is long run if it involves

---

[13] J. A. Nordin, "Notes on a Light Plant's Cost Curves," *Econometrica*, July 1947, pp. 231–35.

possible variations in all inputs over the period being considered by decision makers. Such would be the case in building an entirely new plant. Decisions are short run if some of the inputs remain fixed and others may be varied over the period being considered. An illustration of this is the increase in the output of a department that requires variation in the quantity of labor and materials but not in the amount of floor space or number of machines.

It is not unusual in economic theory to express the distinction between the long run and short run by emphasizing different kinds of decisions. This procedure fits the purposes of managerial economics and shows clearly that there are a variety of short runs according to what is fixed and what is variable. The neat dichotomy between the short and long runs breaks down in actual practice. What remains is an estimate of those costs that will and those that will not be affected by the decision under consideration.

Managerial economists are concerned with the short-run and long-run effects of decisions on revenues as well as on costs. The line between short-run and long-run revenue (or demand) is even fuzzier than that for costs. The really important problem in decision making is to maintain the right balance between the long-run, short-run, and intermediate-run perspectives. A decision may be made on the basis of short-run considerations but may in time have long-run repercussions that make it more or less profitable than it first seemed. An illustration may make this clear.

Let us consider a firm with temporary idle capacity. A possible order for 10,000 units comes to management's attention. The prospective customer is willing to pay $2 per unit, or $20,000 for the whole lot, but no more. The short-run incremental cost (which ignores the fixed costs) is only $1.50. Therefore, the contribution to overhead and profit is $0.50 per unit ($5,000 for the lot), but the long-run repercussions of the order must be taken into account:

1. If the management commits itself to a series of repeat orders at the same price, the so-called fixed costs may eventually become variable. For example, it will someday become necessary to replace the machinery. In fact, the gradual accumulation of orders may require an addition to capacity, with added depreciation and added top-level supervision.

2. Acceptance of this order might have other kinds of long-run repercussions. Other customers may find out about this low price and demand equal treatment. Such customers may object that they are being treated unfairly and may transfer to suppliers with firmer "ethical" views on pricing. The shading of prices under conditions of excess capacity may undermine the company image in the minds of the clientele, giving a picture of a cutthroat competitor rather than a stable, dependable supplier.

Again, it is possible to summarize the discussion in the form of a principle, which we call the principle of time perspective: A decision should take into account both the short-run and long-run effects on revenues and costs, giving appropriate weight to the most relevant time periods. The real problem is determining how to apply this general principle in specific decision-making situations.

An illustration should indicate the rather complex interrelations between the short and long runs on both the cost and demand sides and how such considerations are important in decision making.

A printing company's refusal to price below full cost A large printing company in Boston maintains a policy of never quoting prices below full cost, despite the fact that it frequently experiences idle capacity. Management, aware that the incremental cost is far below full cost, has given considerable thought to the problem and has concluded that the long-run repercussions of going below full cost more than offset any short-run gain. First, the reduction in rates for some customers would have an undesirable effect on customer goodwill, especially among regular customers who would not benefit from the price reductions. Second, management argues that since the availability of idle capacity is unpredictable, by the time the order becomes firm the situation might change, causing low-price orders to interfere with regular-price business. Management wishes to avoid being perceived as a firm that exploits the market when demand is favorable and negotiates prices downward when demand is unfavorable.

It is difficult to demonstrate that management's reasoning on pricing is correct, but at least the argument is plausible. On the other hand, there is evidence that the management does not consistently enforce its policy. It admits that it regretfully breaks away from the policy, in special cases, and it sometimes performs special services (such as editing manuscripts) without charge, a practice that amounts to a hidden form of price reduction. Despite these reservations, this illustration reveals the need to consider the long-run as well as the short-run impact of price policy.

The discounting principle

One of the fundamental ideas in economics is that a dollar to be received tomorrow is worth less than a dollar received today. This appears similar to the saying that a bird in the hand is worth two in the bush. This analogy might be misleading, implying that the reason for discounting the future dollars is the uncertainty about receiving them. Even under conditions of certainty, it is still necessary to discount future dollars to make them comparable with present-day dollars.

A simple illustration should make clear the necessity of discounting. Suppose you are offered a choice between a gift of $100 today or $100 to be received next year. Naturally, you will select the $100 today. This is true even if there is certainty about the receipt of either gift, since today's $100 can be invested and can accumulate interest during the year. Suppose you can earn 5 percent interest on any money you have at your disposal. By the end of the year, it will accumulate interest to become a total of $105.

There is another way to bring out the discounting principle more forcefully. One might ask how much money today would be equivalent to $100 a year from now. Assuming a 5 percent interest rate, discount the $100 at 5 percent (divide it by 1.05). Thus:

$$V = \frac{\$100}{1+i} = \frac{\$100}{1.05} = \$95.24$$

where

V = Present value.
i = Rate of interest.

As a cross-check for those who are unfamiliar with the discounting principle, multiply the $95.24 by 1.05 to determine how much money will have accumulated during the year at 5 percent. The answer is $100.

$$\$95.24 \times 1.05 = \$100$$

This reveals that $95.24 plus the interest on $95.24 will accumulate to an amount exactly equal to $100. A person who can earn 5 percent on his or her money should be indifferent in choosing between the two bundles of money—$100 a year from now or $95.24 today. The present value of $100 is thus $95.24.

The same kind of reasoning applies to longer periods. A sum of $100 two years from now is worth:

$$V = \frac{\$100}{(1+i)^2} = \frac{\$100}{(1.05)^2} = \frac{\$100}{1.1025} = \$90.70$$

Again, one can check by computing how much the cumulative interest on $90.70 would be after two years.

One can now establish a general formula for the present value of a sum to be received at any future date:

$$V = \frac{R_n}{(1+i)^n}$$

in which

V = present value.
R = Amount to be received in the future.
i = Rate of interest.
n = Number of years elapsing before the receipt of R.

If the receipts are spread over a period of years, the formula becomes:

$$V = \frac{R_1}{1+i} + \frac{R_2}{(1+i)^2} + \frac{R_3}{(1+i)^3} + \ldots\ldots\ldots + \frac{R_n}{(1+i)^n}$$

Another form of the same formula is:

$$V = \sum_{k=1}^{n} \frac{R_k}{(1+i)^k}$$

when k can take on any value from 1 through n.

It will be necessary to refer to and elaborate on these formulas, especially in the chapters on investment decisions (see Part 5). For present purposes, however, the need is not so much to memorize formulas as it is to grasp a fundamental concept. The main point in this section may be summarized in a principle called the discounting principle: If a decision affects costs and revenues at future dates, it is necessary to discount those costs and revenues to present values before a valid comparison of alternatives is possible.

The practice of discounting is pervasive and observable in everyday business practice. The simplest case of discounting occurs when one borrows on a note at the bank. If the note is for $1,000, the borrower may not receive the full amount but rather that amount discounted at the appropriate rate of interest. If the discount rate is 6 percent and the note is for one year, the borrower will receive approximately $942. One might say that the present value to the bank of the borrower's promise to pay $1,000 in a year is only $942 at the time of the loan.

The bond market also illustrates the discounting principle in operation. The market price of a particular bond reflects not only the face value of the bond at maturity and the interest payments, but also the current discount rate. As the market discount rates vary, bond prices vary inversely in a definite mathematical relation to those discount rates. (One could say that the market discount rates reflect the changes in bond prices, for discount rates and bond prices move simultaneously with changes in the market conditions.) A small private foundation, for example, might have holdings similar to those presented in Table 2–1. The differences in cost and market value are due to changes in interest rates since the date of purchase.

Real estate prices reflect the discounting principle, though in a more complicated and less obvious way. The rational way to determine what one will pay for a piece of property is to estimate the future returns, which may in the case of a home be primarily subjective in character (i.e., the pleasure derived from living in the home). One will discount those future returns at the current cost of capital to reflect the sacrifice

Table 2–1
Schedule of cash receipts from riskless assets, if held to maturity (government investments)

Due date	Investments	Market value as of May 30, 1983	Cost or book value
7/7/83	U.S. Treasury Bills	$ 44,014.05	$ 45,000.00
7/31/83	U.S. Treasury Note	61,200.00	60,000.00
8/31/83	U.S. Treasury Notes	35,962.50	35,000.00
1/31/84	U.S. Treasury Note	52,250.00	50,000.00
2/29/84	U.S. Treasury Notes	41,950.00	40,000.00
3/26/84	Federal Home Loan Bank Bond	40,050.00	40,000.00
3/31/84	U.S. Treasury Notes	41,800.00	40,000.00
8/31/84	U.S. Treasury Note	41,000.00	40,000.00
12/31/84	U.S. Treasury Notes	29,812.50	30,000.00
1/31/85	U.S. Treasury Notes	143,550.00	145,000.00
2/28/85	U.S. Treasury Notes	149,250.00	150,000.00
5/15/85	U.S. Treasury Note	20,200.00	20,000.00
5/15/85	U.S. Treasury Notes	118,250.00	110,000.00
6/3/85	Federal Farm Credit Bank Bond	29,550.00	30,000.00
2/15/86	U.S. Treasury Note	19,925.00	20,000.00
8/15/86	U.S. Treasury Note	23,593.75	25,000.00
10/10/86	Federal National Mortgage Association	50,000.00	50,000.00
2/15/87	Government National Mortgage Association	29,126.46	44,131.59

of alternative earnings.[14] The market value of the real estate is determined by the interaction of such discounted present values set on the property by the various potential buyers and sellers. Even such rules of thumb as "an apartment house should sell at 10 times annual rentals" are only very rough approximations of the discounting principle.

The same principle of discounting should apply to the operations of an individual firm, although considerable uncertainty will exist over the future revenues and appropriate discount rates. If a firm is considering buying a new piece of equipment, it should estimate the discounted value of the added earnings from that equipment. (Chapter 11 covers this problem more fully.) If the firm is considering the purchase of another firm or a merger, the same principle of valuation applies. If a firm produces outputs that mature at varying ages, it cannot compare the profitability of changing the product mix without invoking the discounting principle.

The opportunity cost concept

The next concept, opportunity cost, is also self-evident when stated simply but sometimes becomes less obvious in practical application. Opportunity costs do not appear as such on traditional accounting statements. In fact, it may be impossible to devise a programmed system of accounting capable of routinely providing accurate estimates of opportunity costs.

---

[14] A full discussion of the cost of capital appears in Chapter 11.

The opportunity cost of a decision means sacrificing alternatives. Some specific illustrations of this concept are helpful to understanding its meaning:

1. The opportunity cost of the funds tied up in one's own business is the interest (or profits corrected for differences in risk) that could be earned on those funds in other ventures.
2. The opportunity cost of the time put into a business is the salary one could earn in other occupations (with a correction for the relative psychic income in the two occupations).
3. The opportunity cost of using a machine to produce one product is the sacrifice of earnings that would be possible from other products.
4. The opportunity cost of using a machine that is useless for any other purpose is nil, since its use requires no sacrifice of other opportunities.
5. The opportunity cost of using idle space is obviously less than that of using space needed for other activities.

It follows from the above that opportunity costs require the measurement of sacrifices. If a decision involves no sacrifices, it is cost-free. The expenditure of cash (for raw materials, for example) involves a sacrifice of other possible expenditures and is therefore an opportunity cost. Under this broad definition, the only costs relevant for decision making are opportunity costs.

The opportunity cost concept is in a sense the most fundamental cost concept. We should include in incremental cost or marginal cost only measurements of additional sacrifices required by a decision. If an increase in output requires no expansion of the factory but merely uses idle space, we make no sacrifice by using that space—we need not include a charge for its use; the opportunity cost of its use is nil; and therefore we exclude it from the estimate of incremental cost. Similarly, the rate of discount that we use to compute present values is really an opportunity cost rate.

Closely related to this discussion of opportunity costs is a distinction between explicit and implicit costs. Explicit costs are those recognized in the accounts, such as payments for raw materials and labor. Implicit (or imputed) costs are those sacrifices (such as the interest on the owner's own investment) not recognized in the accounts. Some writers use the term *opportunity costs* narrowly to refer only to the second category— the implicit costs. There are strong arguments, however, for our broader definition to include all sacrifices, implicit or explicit.

To complicate matters slightly, some explicit expenses may not involve sacrifices of alternatives. For example, a company may pay wages to idle labor in periods of slack activity. These wages are in the nature of a fixed cost and are not included in the opportunity cost in a decision to use that labor for a special order.

The discussion in this section can be summarized in another principle, which we shall call the opportunity cost principle: The cost involved in any decision consists of the sacrifices of alternatives required by that decision. If there are no sacrifices, there is no cost.

The question of whether managers actually use opportunity cost reasoning is not amenable to exact empirical test. Most managers are continually weighing alternatives, which means that they are at least resorting to rough, subjective evaluations of opportunity costs. Some modern mathematical models in use in large, progressive firms either implicitly or explicitly incorporate opportunity cost considerations. This is true of linear programming allocation models and of replacement models. However, even casual observations indicate strongly that some managers fail to make correct analyses of opportunity costs. Traditional accounting techniques are very poorly adapted to the reflection of opportunity costs. Cost accounting systems that allocate overhead on a predetermined basis, such as direct labor cost, fail to reflect varying availabilities of idle capacity. Standard cost systems avoid the extreme error of increasing overhead allocations when volume is down, which would run counter to opportunity cost reasoning. But even standard overhead allocations fail to reflect the true sacrifices required by decisions. For example, such a system would not apply a lower percentage allocation to direct labor cost in a department that is half idle, even though the sacrifice in increasing the use of that department would be small.

In short, the actual application of opportunity cost reasoning is variable. Perhaps the best that can be done here is to indicate a way in which the reasoning is applied by management.

Electric utilities that own hydroelectric dams also operate steam-generating plants. They face a choice of using hydro power or steam power or a combination of the two. It is relatively easy to measure the cost of generating power in a steam plant, although the correct handling of depreciation may present some difficulty; but the cost of producing hydro power is much more troubling. After all, the dams are already built; their costs of construction are sunk and are irrelevant in making decisions for the future. The same is true of the expensive generators, on which wear and tear is probably a small cost relative to the original machine price. Since water is a free gift of nature, why not run the water through the generators as rapidly as possible and minimize the use of the steam plants?

Merely posing the question should suggest the solution to the problem. The use of the water behind a dam is not cost-free, for it does require a sacrifice. Water used today cannot be used tomorrow; its use today involves an opportunity cost. Looking at the matter another way, the water behind a dam has value based on its capacity to produce power in the future.

Suppose a utility owns one hydroelectric dam and three steam plants. The three steam plants vary in efficiency, the new plant burning less coal per kilowatt-hour than do the old ones. To meet peak-load requirements, all three plants and the dam must operate near capacity. To meet lower loads, it is possible to cut off either the high-cost plants or the hydroelectric dam, or both. Running the water through the generators in off-peak periods would risk not having enough stored-up water for peak periods. The sacrifice (opportunity cost) would be a measure of the loss of revenue. Customer and public utility dissatisfaction might result. In addition, the operation of the high-cost steam plants involves a sacrifice in the inefficient burning of fuel. The flow of water should be regulated so as to minimize this sacrifice.

If the electric utility has additional objectives, such as flood control or maintenance of navigation (as is true of some public power systems), the analysis becomes more complex, but the basic principles are the same. The stored-up water has value, and its use involves an opportunity cost.

The equimarginal principle

One of the most widely known principles of economics is the proposition that an input should be allocated so that the value added by the last unit is the same in all uses. This generalization is called the equimarginal principle.

Consider a case in which a firm has 100 units of labor at its disposal. For purposes of simplicity assume this amount to be fixed, so that the total payroll is predetermined. The firm is involved in five activities requiring labor service: A, B, C, D, and E. It can increase any one of these activities by adding more labor but only at the sacrifice of other activities.

If one adds a unit of labor to activity C, an increase in output results. Call the value of this added output the value of the marginal product of labor in activity C.[15] Similarly, one can estimate the value of the marginal product in activities A, B, D, and E. It should be clear that if the value of the marginal product is greater in one activity than another, an optimum has not been achieved. It would be possible to shift labor from low-marginal-value to high-marginal-value uses, thus increasing the total value of all products taken together. For example, if the value of the marginal product of labor in activity A is $10 and that in activity B is $15, it is profitable to increase activity B and reduce activity A. The optimum is reached when the value of the marginal product is equal in all activities. Stated symbols:

$$VMP_{LA} = VMP_{LB} = VMP_{LC} = VMP_{LD} = VMP_{LE}$$

[15] We shall ignore certain refinements at this point, such as the distinction between the value of the marginal product and the marginal revenue product.

in which the subscript *L* indicates labor and the other subscripts identify the activities.

Several aspects of the equimarginal principle need to be clarified. First, notice that the values of the marginal products in the formula are net of incremental costs (the incremental costs do not include the cost of the input being allocated). In activity A one may add one unit of labor, with an increase in physical output of 100 units. Each unit is worth 25 cents, and the 100 units will sell for $25. However, since the increased production consumes raw materials, fuel, and other inputs, the variable costs in activity A (not counting the labor cost) are higher. Let's say that the incremental costs are $15, leaving a net addition of $10. The value of the marginal product relevant for our purposes is this $10.

If the revenues resulting from the addition of labor are to be in the future, it is necessary to discount those revenues before comparisons in the alternative activities are possible. Activity C might not produce its revenue for five years, but activity D will produce its revenue almost immediately. The discounting of these revenues will make them comparable.

Capital budgeting (to be taken up in Chapter 11) is based on the principles just reviewed. In capital budgeting the resource to be allocated consists of the funds available to the firm (rather than labor). The objective is to apply the funds where the discounted values of the marginal products are greatest, expanding the high-value activities and contracting the low-value activities until an equality of marginal values is achieved.

Implicit in the discussion up to this point are diminishing returns to the inputs being allocated. This point deserves closer attention. One of the most fundamental of all generalizations in economics is the law of diminishing returns (also known as the law of variable proportions), which states that as quantities of variable inputs are added to fixed quantities of other inputs, the marginal product eventually declines. To return to our earlier illustration, as more labor is added to activity A, we expect the value of the marginal product of labor to decline, as shown in Figure 2–4.

The value of the marginal product of labor is falling because the amount of capital equipment per worker is falling, as labor is increased with a fixed amount of capital.

One would expect the law of diminishing returns to apply to the other activities in the same way, though each marginal product curve will have a somewhat different shape, depending on technology.

Several complications are often important in practice, and should be briefly mentioned in this introductory chapter. One complication is that the measurement of the value of the marginal product may have to be corrected if the expansion of an activity requires a reduction in the price of the output. If activity A represents the production of radios, but it is

Figure 2–4
Diminishing returns to labor

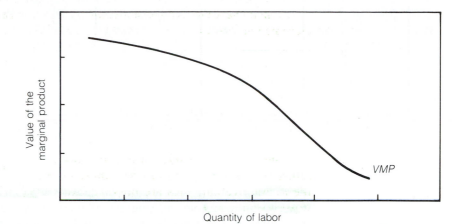

impossible to sell more radios without a reduction in price, it is necessary to adjust the value of the marginal product downward for the change in price. Another complication is complementarity of demand: An increase in the availability of one product stimulates the sales of another. Similarly, if products are complementary in production, a more involved analysis is required. But the equimarginal principle still applies after the necessary adjustments are made.

Constant marginal products

In many cases the law of diminishing returns may not operate exactly as described so far. It may be possible for a firm to increase the quantity of labor in one department without encountering diminishing marginal production—until some limit of capacity is reached or until all the labor is employed. The curve for the value of the marginal product is horizontal in such a case, up to full capacity, then it drops to zero. Figure 2–5 represents this situation for five activities.

In this case we do not reach the situation in which the values of the marginal products are equal in all activities unless there is labor to spare. Since the value of the marginal product is greatest in activity E, we prefer to use labor there rather than in the other activities. Why not shift all of the labor to E? Some constraint, such as a limit of the capacity in E, or limits on other variable inputs required, may set a limit on the amount of labor that can be used in E.

The outcome of the discussion is this: We may retain the equimarginal principle as long as diminishing returns are relevant; but when the values

Figure 2–5
Constant marginal products in five activities

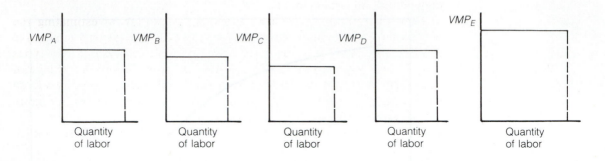

of the marginal products are constant (horizontal), we need an alternative form of the principle, making use of inequalities rather than equalities. This form of the principle can be stated as follows: Apply inputs first to activities with higher marginal product values before moving to lower values.

The equimarginal principle is an extremely practical idea (despite the abstract appearance of the preceding discussion) and underlies any rational budgetary procedure. The objective of budgeting is (or should be) to allocate resources where they are most productive, but it is productivity at the margin rather than average productivity that is relevant. Even when productivity is extremely difficult to measure, the equimarginal principle must be applied in at least a rough or general way if one wishes to avoid waste in useless activities.

One of the clearest examples of the application of the principle is seen in investment decisions. Whatever criterion is used in making such decisions—whether a crude measure, such as payback period, or a refined measure, such as the present value—the goal is to separate investments with high rates of return from investments with low returns so that the funds can be allocated accordingly.

At the opposite extreme is the allocation of research expenditures. The productivity of research is notoriously difficult to measure. In fact, some research organizations deliberately avoid measurements on the grounds that too careful a supervision and too great an eagerness to achieve results may actually interfere with fundamental research. One can never tell when highly theoretical and impractical research will pay off. Nevertheless, the equimarginal principle is relevant in research. After all, a company does not hire researchers indiscriminately. It selects people who promise to make a contribution to the company's line of activity. The company is likely to expand research activities that are beginning to pay off and to contract activities that appear to have passed their peak of usefulness. Mistakes can be made in this process, but the failure to make any comparisons of potential productivity can only lead to diffusion of expenditure on nonessentials.

Although one must not expect pinpoint precision in estimating the worth of alternative lines of research—and in many cases only qualitative estimates are possible—it is nevertheless possible to rank different types of research. Many companies budget research as a given percentage of sales, and others follow a rule of increasing such expenditures by a fixed percentage; but it makes more sense to evaluate each research program individually.

The same type of reasoning is (or should be) applied in budgeting for universities. It might be argued that universities are not operated for profit and that they are engaged in relatively immeasurable activities. Yet, expansion of the budget in any department is subject to diminishing returns, and rough comparisons of the value of the marginal product from department to department are surely possible. In one large state university, several departments have been expanded to the point that the marginal product must be close to zero. Some faculty members have virtually no teaching duties and negligible duties of any character, research or otherwise. In the same university, several other departments are in a decline because of an inability to retain key staff members. A casual observer could see that the marginal products are quite different from department to department and that the university's resources are being misallocated.

A great enemy of the equimarginal principle is the stress on averages. It is irrational, for example, to budget advertising expenditure on the basis of some average percentage of sales. Such a policy results in lower advertising in poor times than in times of prosperity, when the opposite practice might be more profitable. There is no reason to suppose that advertising expenditures on one product must hold the same ratio to sales as for another product, since the responsiveness may be quite different for one advertisement than for another. Similarly, the averaging of budget increases over all departments is unlikely to be consistent with the equimarginal principle. Some departments can make highly productive use of additional resources, and other departments may actually be due for cutbacks of less essential activities.

Other enemies of the equimarginal principle include a variety of sociological pressures. Inertia is one—activities are continued simply because they exist. Empire building is another—activities expand to fulfill the needs of managers for power. Unfortunately, departments already over-budgeted often use some of their excess resources to build up propaganda machines (public relations offices) to win additional support. Governmental agencies, less subject to constant tests in the market, are more prone to distortions in the allocation of resources because of an overstress on averaging, inertia, and bureaucratic self-perpetuation.

The contribution concept

The concepts presented so far are not independent of each other. It has already been shown how the opportunity cost concept overlaps several others. This is also true of the contribution concept, which is a convenient way of presenting ideas discussed earlier in this chapter. In fact, the expression "contribution to overhead and profits" has been used several times. Since one of the most important innovations in the language of management in recent decades has been the introduction of the idea of contributions, which deserves special attention despite the resulting duplication.

The simplest case to consider is that of a product whose price is determined by outside forces—by competition or by regulatory agencies. Let us assume this price is $95. Within the firm the total cost, including allocated overheads, is $103, but the incremental cost is only $75. The loss on the item appears to be $8, and the temptation is to drop the product. However, the contribution to overhead and profits is $20. Further analysis is in order.

The mere fact that the contribution is positive does not prove that the product should be retained. If the company has a backlog of orders on products requiring the same production time per unit, and if these products earn contributions of $50 or $40 or $30, one certainly would not wish to sacrifice these larger contributions in favor of a $20 one.[16] But it is the comparison of contributions that is important, not the comparison of profits or losses based on full costs.

Since most products vary one from another in production requirements, the simple comparison of contributions in the above illustration is inadequate in many cases. An item that contributes $50 may be less profitable than one that contributes only $20 if the $50 item uses up much more of the company's capacity. This suggests that the measurement of contribution per unit of output is inappropriate in most cases.

If a company has only one bottleneck in production, such as in machine-hours available, we can convert the contributions per unit of output into contributions per machine-hour. Table 2–2 presents such a situation in a company producing five products.

At first glance product B appears to be best; it produces a contribution larger than elsewhere and presumably deserves the first priority in allocation of capacity. But product B uses up more capacity for each unit

---

[16] Other factors will influence the decision, such as the desire to maintain a complete product line or to retain the goodwill of an old customer.

Table 2–2
Contributions on five products in a single plant

Product	Price	Incremental cost	Contribution per unit	Machine-minutes requirements
A	$15.00	$10.00	$5.00	60
B	14.00	8.00	6.00	80
C	13.00	9.00	4.00	40
D	12.00	7.50	4.50	30
E	6.00	2.50	3.50	15

produced. It is clear that we must convert the contributions to make them comparable. One way to do this is to convert them into contributions per hour of machine time. The results are as follows:

Product A	$ 5.00 per machine-hour
Product B	4.50 per machine-hour
Product C	6.00 per machine-hour
Product D	9.00 per machine-hour
Product E	14.00 per machine-hour

These results indicate that product E, which first appeared to be the lowest contributor, is, in fact, the largest. Therefore, the priorities should be almost the opposite of those that appeared at first glance. In practice, the order of contributions is frequently quite different from those suggested by casual observation.

Suppose, however, that more than one capacity bottleneck appears. If all five products pass through four processes, each of which can be the bottleneck, it is no longer possible to compute simple contributions in terms of one of the bottlenecks. The problem becomes one in linear programming.

The application of contributions to overhead and profits normally rests on an assumed linearity of revenues and costs. As in the above illustration, the price and unit cost are assumed to be independent of output. The unit incremental cost remains the same until the demand is satisfied or the capacity is used up. If the quantity demanded increases at lower prices, or if the incremental cost varies at different levels of output, the problem becomes more complicated, but the contribution idea is still useful. For example, one can compare product E's contribution of $3.50 at a price of $6 with its contribution of $3 at a price of $5.50. If sales at the higher price are 10,000 units and at the lower price are 30,000 units, the total contribution from product E increases from $35,000 to $90,000. It may be desirable to accept the lower unit contribution to obtain the higher volume, even if other lower contribution products are sacrificed.

When the author was an undergraduate student, the expression "contribution to overhead and profits" was almost unknown, although many managers were using the idea without giving it a name. Today the term has become part of the vacabulary of management, and a manager who does not understand contributions is probably not very proficient in modern cost analysis. The term is probably used most widely in product-mix decisions and pricing decisions, but it is also applicable to make or buy decisions and other choices. The cash flows estimated in financial management are closely related to the contribution concept, as will be seen in the chapter on capital budgeting.

The negotiating principle

Changes in costs and revenues, all commitments made in the short or long run, interest rates, net cash flows, the contribution margin that product X should (could) make to the overall profitability of company Y, and all other matters discussed in this chapter are negotiable. In fact, everything in life is negotiable.[17]

International borders are negotiable (Lebanon, West Bank, Israel, or the two Germanys, for example). Housing prices and terms and conditions of payment; automobile prices including terms and conditions of payment; equipment parts, specifications, and prices; jail and/or prison terms (i.e., plea bargaining and similar arrangements common in the U.S. justice system); where to spend one's vacation, how to get there, how long to stay—all are negotiable. No matter what the item, it is or can be made negotiable. Consequently, a businessperson contemplating merger, acquisition, consolidation, or other form of corporate takeover must not assume that all labor agreements and other seemingly long-term contracts are fixed. More than likely, each major commitment facing a firm can be, and at times should be, renegotiated. When negotiations are successful, both sides win and go away happy. The astute businessperson needs to understand the process by which this takes place.

To be successful all interested parties to the negotiation must desire and work toward a peaceful settlement or arrangement. If either side consistently bargains in bad faith, the process will fail. Failure of the process can be mildly disappointing or have catastrophic consequences. If one member of the family (wife) wants to vacation on the beaches in South Carolina, and another member (husband) is holding out for a trip to Denver, the "losing party" is pretty well assured of a nice vacation, once the initial sting of minor disappointment dissipates. On the other hand, if a Neville Chamberlain rushes from England to meet an Adolph Hitler in Germany (the meeting at Munich), the losing party (the world) could suffer for uncounted decades.

Negotiations refers to the art of coming to terms in as friendly a manner as possible with a party who represents interests that differ from one's

---

[17] As with every rule, there is an exception: student's grades.

own. If United States Steel Corporation decides it wants to own and operate Marathon Oil, for example, the management group at Marathon must be convinced that it is to Marathon's advantage, however defined, to allow U.S. Steel to win. Obviously, if the transaction is to Marathon's advantage, Marathon also wins. Win-win situations of this sort are possible through negotiations.

Without negotiations, there may be a winner and a loser. In such an event, the winner may get his or her way for a short time, but the entire process must eventually be started anew. Losers have been so resentful that they have created problems for hundreds of years (i.e., Ireland, Northern Ireland, and England). In the U.S. business world, if labor leaders consistently lose during the early 1980s, the full consequences might not be known until the 1990s and beyond.

Modern corporate executives are charged with the responsibility of properly applying economic theory as they manage the price and output behavior of their firms. To be successful, these managers must devise specific plans of action and then execute these plans properly. Proper execution often requires that the manager hire a professional negotiator to make the arrangements necessary for implementation of the plan. The negotiator takes instructions from the client-employer and goes about the business of attempting to have the client's side win, while simultaneously allowing members of the other side to consider themselves winners of the negotiations, too. Pulling this off properly may be a gift as well as an art.

Negotiation is a very challenging and interesting area of economic activity. It deals with human passions, feelings, temperaments, and various personality types. Success in negotiations is often based on subjective, sentimental, and/or emotional acts by one or more of the parties involved. The results of these acts (i.e., the sale by National Steel Corporation of its Weirton, West Virginia, facility to its employees via an employee stock ownership plan) are objective and, as such, are subject to precise quantitative measurement.

Although negotiations are often something less than perfect, as a process in resolving conflicts and/or implementing broad corporate strategies, there may be no better tool. Most certainly as an acceptable alternative to outright force (war in international affairs and riots in domestic affairs), negotiation must be mastered by the current generation of college students. The process can make significant contributions to one's success in business.

Unlike the other concepts covered in this chapter, neither specific chapters nor additional materials regarding negotiations are presented later in this book. It is hoped that the student will come to understand the flexibility that exists in real-world situations and, perhaps, formally study negotiations at a later date. Knowledge and skills in negotiating can lead to great business success.

Strategic planning

This book is not heavily concerned with negotiations, a process that permeates all areas of economic activity; instead, it is devoted to applications of the concepts presented earlier in this chapter. These applications involve a variety of decisions dealing with the overall goals, objectives, and strategies contemplated by management.

Strategic planning is involved in every aspect of management. It is a necessary and sufficient activity that cannot be separated from the overall management process. Strategic planning reviews the economic impact of current micro- and macroevents on the overall direction of a specific firm or other unit of economic activity. It considers alternative actions that could have been made and the probable change in outcome that might have occurred as a result of those actions. Alternatives that appear promising are seriously considered for future use. The strategic planning process is mastered by those who wish to be at the cutting edge of their discipline.

Strategic planning involves establishment of long-run objectives, specific short-run goals, and specific strategies for achievement of those goals. The process is systematic in that all steps taken by management are made intentionally. Each step has a purpose. To the greatest extent possible, nothing is left to chance. In successfully applying economic principles to the price and output behavior of a profitable corporation or in managing a hospital or other not-for-profit organization, one must realize that short-run budgets and such things as deciding whether to put on the third shift as opposed to working the second shift overtime must be part of the overall strategic plan if the results of those decisions are to be meaningful to the firm.

Strategic planning works something like this:

1. A manager or management group establishes an objective, something not easily definable and/or reachable.
2. Goals are designed to reach the objective and are reduced to writing. These goals can be defined and are within reach. If both of these conditions do not exist, the goals are unrealistic and must be reworked.
3. Strategies are designed to reach the specific goals. The strategies must be realistic in terms of achievement.

As the strategies are implemented and goals are reached, the objective comes closer to being achieved. But since objectives are not precisely defined, it is often difficult to know when they are achieved until after the fact.

Strategic plans operate for good or for evil. For example, Adolph Hitler had an objective—world conquest. His 1939 goal toward this objective—

conquer Poland; his strategy—surprise attack. Short-run budgets, logistics, food rationing, control of banking and other activities were considered necessary by him for achievement of his broad objective, his grand design.

One need not admire Hitler to admire his strategy. It was cold, calculated and, unfortunately for the human race, it almost worked. Please note: To be successful it is not necessary to have large numbers of people involved in the strategic-planning process. In fact, most Germans were not told of the Polish invasion until after the fact. The same general statement is true of Germany's "liberation" of Austria and the "liberation" of Afghanistan by Russia. Top management did the planning; lesser mortals administered the plan.

In the 1960s, a small group of Americans from the Deep South had an objective but did not call it by that name. The creative leader of this group, Dr. Martin Luther King, Jr., had a dream—to obtain equality and respect for the rights of black people in the United States. Respect is the state of being regarded with esteem, a vague concept and not one that is easily defined.

Dr. King's goal at one stage was to desegregate the public schools and universities in Mississippi and elsewhere. His strategy was to call public attention to the plight of blacks via the news media. He staged marches in Alabama and held rallies in Washington, D.C. His strategy of peaceful civil disobedience was superb, and he achieved one goal after another in a very impressive manner. Note: each step taken was designed to help him reach his broad objective.

Concepts covered in this chapter (including incremental costs, opportunity costs, the long and short runs, discounting, and the equimarginal principle) must be applied within the framework of a management plan, an objective or set of objectives. To the greatest extent possible, middle- and lower-level managers must be told of the objectives, as much as they need to know about specific goals, and how they are expected to act in implementing specific strategies.

A few years before the death of James Cash Penney, J. C. Penney stores numbered about 1660. Mr. Penney's objective was to be the number-one seller of soft goods (clothing, shoes, bedding, etc.) in the United States. Again note: *Number One* cannot be precisely defined. Penney's goal was to lease space for his stores in proper locations throughout the country. He was in the retail sales business, not the real estate business, and would not consider buying a location. Consequently, local J. C. Penney managers knew they were contributing to the broader objective when they did not waste their time or Penney's with shopping mall purchases, construction, or other real estate schemes. Penney's strategy was to sell only for cash (no credit ever while he was in control) and never to be undersold. If Sears or Ward's in a localized area had blue jeans for sale at a price lower than Penney's, the floor or department manager was expected to match or beat that price with no additional authority from, or discussion with, anyone.

Although one might question the wisdom of denying credit sales and of leasing all locations, the strategy worked. Penney's goal of establishing stores throughout the nation was achieved. Was his objective reached? The jury is still out on that question.

Product-line decisions

Within the framework of corporate objectives and goals, firms must sometimes decide whether or not to add new products, drop old products, change the relative proportions of products, or farm out part of the production to other firms. These issues concern the short run, in which capacity is fixed. A longer run analysis requires a discussion of investment analysis (this will be presented in a later chapter), but do not ignore the longer-run repercussions of short-run decisions.

The short-run problem itself includes a number of variations. Consider first the case in which a firm has excess capacity. Its present line of products is not absorbing its capacity. The question is whether or not to add another product. The first step is to compute the contribution of the new product to overhead and profits. This requires an estimate of the added revenue and of the incremental costs of the product. The normal overhead allocations should be avoided in such estimates. Instead, the estimates should measure the increase in each cost, direct or indirect, resulting from adding the product. If the contribution—the difference between the added revenue and the incremental cost—is positive, the analysis is favorable for adding the product.

However, a complete analysis must check for other considerations. For example, the management should not introduce the new product if an even better new product is available. A search for all the available opportunities should precede making the final decision. Another way of expressing this idea is to say that the opportunity costs of alternative uses of the excess capacity must be estimated. Another factor is the possible impact of the new product on the products already produced. In some cases the new product may complement or round out the product line, increasing the sales of the other products. In such a case, the contribution to overhead and profits of the new product is greater than the direct contribution of the product itself. In other instances the product may compete with items in the present line so that the initial contribution estimates must be adjusted downward. Such adjustments in estimates should recognize both immediate and longer-run impacts of the new product. For example, if the excess capacity is temporary, management must face the question of whether the new product can be abandoned when demand for the other products recovers or whether an expansion of facilities will be justified. It may often be preferable to accept temporary excess capacity than to create production bottlenecks when the excess disappears. In addition, management must determine whether it has the know-how to produce and distribute the new product.

If the situation is one of full use of capacity, the analysis becomes even more complex. In this case management must not only determine the contribution of each product (and of products that might be introduced into the product mix), but must also determine how much the opportunity cost of increasing the output of one product is in terms of the reduction of the contributions of the other products. This is the kind of estimate made in the simplex method of linear programming. A management that does not use linear programming must nevertheless run through estimates analogous to those in the simplex method, if it is going to approximate an optimal use of its resources.

Consider a more complex situation, one more closely related to the real world and the kind of application considered in this text: allocation of resources to a variety of slowly maturing products. An example is a garden nursery with a fixed acreage of land and a wide variety of planting opportunities. Such a nursery faces the problem of determining which plants to propagate and grow, what ages to assume in such choices, what future prices should be assumed, and what prices to charge now on plants that are already mature. In addition, the nursery must determine when to mark down prices on plants tying up land needed for other uses and when to destroy plant materials that are in the way. The solution to such a problem requires an estimate of the contributions of the various plants over time, which in turn, requires (1) estimates of revenues and incremental costs and (2) the discounting of future revenues, costs, and contributions to arrive at the present value of such contributions at the time decisions on the use of the land are to be made. Estimates of the present value of the contribution for all plants on an acre basis would provide a basis for rational decisions. These estimates would make it possible to compare the contribution from rapidly maturing plants with those of slowly maturing plants.

Such complex models for decision making are open to the criticism that they are impractical. Most managers do not have the data or the knowledge to apply the models. The trend, however, is toward a more systematic analysis of product-mix problems. And even in firms in which decisions continue to be qualitative and subjective, it can do management no harm to logically and rationally decide which products to expand, which to contract, and which to abandon.

Other applications of managerial economics

The principles in this chapter apply to many other decisions, some of which are listed briefly.

Decisions on allocation of space in a retail store The correct procedure would measure the contributions to overhead and profit above incremental cost for each commodity. The analysis is complicated by the fact that the space is not homogeneous. Because the space where more traffic flows is more valuable than space in remote parts of the store, the turnover of each product depends not only on its price, but also on its location.

Decisions on advertising expenditures   Many firms have applied simple rules of thumb in their advertising expenditures, but more refined techniques reflecting economic reasoning are coming into use. It makes no sense to budget advertising as a percentage of sales or on the level of the rival's expenditures. What is needed is a measure of responsiveness of sales to advertising along with measures of the added cost of production of a larger volume.

Figure 2–6 shows how sales and profits might respond to increased advertising outlays. This diagram assumes diminishing returns to advertising—a reasonable assumption. The problem of measurement is extremely difficult in this case, since advertising has effects spread out over time. Competitors may change their advertising, and consumer tastes may change independently of the advertising. Research techniques are being developed to overcome some of these problems, but even in the absence of exact measurements, it is clear that the principles outlined in this chapter provide a more flexible and rational basis for determining advertising expenditures than do the usual rules of thumb.

Summary

Incremental reasoning determines whether a change in business activity would be profitable by comparing the change in revenue with the change in cost. Change in revenue can be +, −, or 0; change in cost can be +, −, or 0. The net effect of the change in activity is change in revenue minus change in cost, with due regard to the signs of incremental revenue and incremental cost. Marginal analysis, a special case of incremental reasoning, focuses on the results of unit changes in some activity and is particularly useful in considering curvilinear trade offs.

Opportunity cost is the net revenue that a scarce resource would produce in the best alternative use from which it must be withheld in order to have it for a particular use. If the opportunity cost of an input exceeds its explicit cost, the difference is called implicit cost. Accounting profit must be decreased by implicit expenses in determining economic profit. A decision involving a transfer of a scarce resource can be made either by using incremental reasoning or by calculating the economic profitability of the proposed use of the resource.

Contribution of output is the amount given toward overhead cost and possible profit. It is calculated as incremental revenue less incremental cost. If the output can be produced without reaching the capacity of any limiting resource, the decision is easy—any contribution is better than

Figure 2–6
Relationship of revenue and profits to advertising outlays

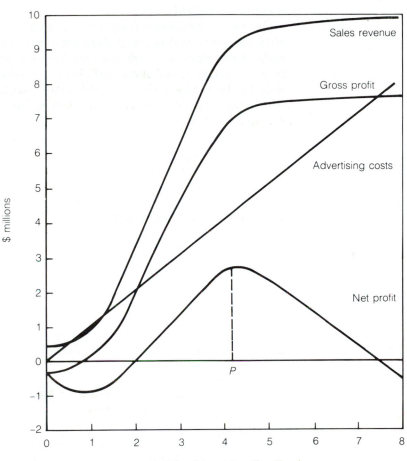

none. However, if the firm has an opportunity to produce any of several products and all of them require services of a bottleneck resource, each product's contribution should be converted to contribution per unit of scarce resource. The scarce resource should be allocated first to its best use, then to its next best use, and so on.

A decision is viewed in long-run perspective if it affects quantities of all inputs needed in production—if all costs are variable. A decision is viewed in short-run perspective if it affects quantities of some inputs but not of others—if some costs are variable but others are fixed. In many decisions, more and more items of cost become variable as the time perspective is extended. Revenue effects of decisions are also likely to change as the time perspective moves farther out. The usual approach is to begin with a short-run analysis and carry out a series of analyses, with the time perspective extending farther and farther until the long-run perspective is reached.

One of the fundamental ideas in economics is the principle that revenues and costs that occur at different times should be adjusted to their equivalent values at a common time before they are compared. For any given monetary amount at a given time, the equivalent value at any later time can be obtained by a process called compounding, and the equivalent value at any earlier time can be calculated by a procedure called discounting.

Virtually everything in business is negotiable. The items to be negotiated and/or renegotiated depend in large part upon the strategic planning, short-run goals, and long-run objectives of the firm.

CASES

Fundamental concepts: a case-method approach

Superior Quality Truck Repairs*

Shannon Smith is the manager of Superior Quality Truck Repairs, a business specializing in diesel engines. The business is a branch location of a chain of truck-repair shops scattered across the northeast quadrant of the United States. This chain of shops is a wholly owned subsidiary of a major oil company located in Houston, Texas.

Shannon has considerable autonomy in making decisions affecting the branch. The central office in Houston develops the accounting reports for each location and occasionally makes suggestions to individual managers.

In June 1983, the ratio of wages and salaries to sales at the branch was 46 percent. The company suggested that, as a rule of thumb, this ratio should never exceed 33⅓ percent. The home office in Houston recommended that Shannon discontinue the truck-washing service (a minor adjunct to the truck-repair business) to bring labor costs into line.

Shannon consulted the accounting reports he received from the central office in considering his decision. These financial reports provided broad aggregates that were not helpful in evaluating the profitability of the truck-washing service. Shannon made an estimate of costs and revenues resulting from truck washing in June and accumulated data on labor costs and supplies. He consulted Mr. Frederick, an accountant friend, who suggested the basis for allocating overhead. Exhibit 1 reveals the estimate of overhead costs and direct costs for the truck-washing operation. The result reveals a small loss on the truck-washing business:

---

* This case is adapted from William R. Henry, Ph.D. and W. Warren Haynes, "Newville Branch of Ajax Cleaners (Revised)," in *Managerial Economics* (Plano, Tex.: Business Publications, 1978), p. 49.

Revenue	$7,400
Full cost	7,450
Loss	$ 50

Mr. Frederick was not certain that the full-cost figure was the appropriate one for Shannon's problem. He had been reading some articles on marginal analysis and suggested that a variation on that approach might be helpful in clarifying not only the problem at hand but also future decision-making issues. It was thought that such an approach would have to be kept extremely simple and inexpensive to deal with Shannon's relatively small operation.

The steps used in establishing a system of incrementalism are as follows:

1. Segmentation of the business. Shannon Smith's business might be broken into two segments—truck repairs and truck washing.

2. Segregation of costs between fixed and variable costs. This would require that Shannon make qualitative judgments as to which costs were fixed and which were variable. A more elaborate statistical approach for segregating costs would be too expensive.

3. Separation of the fixed costs into assigned fixed costs and unassigned fixed costs. The assigned fixed costs would be those fixed for short-period fluctuations in activity but avoidable if the segment were permanently discontinued. Examples would be depreciation on specialized equipment and salaries of supervisors in the particular segment. The

Exhibit 1
Cost computations on the truck washing—June 1983
(including overhead allocation bases)

Manager's salary—average time spent in the department	$1,550
Advertising—sales	220
Telephone—sales	160
Heat, light, power—ratio of departmental heat, light, power costs	50
Employer's payroll tax—ratio of departmental salary costs	90
Rent—floor space	160
Amortization—floor space	230
Insurance—sales	240
	2,700
Add direct costs	
Salaries	2,000
Supplies	1,400
Heat, light, power	250
Payroll tax	100
Depreciation	1,000
	4,750
Total Cost	$7,450

unassigned fixed costs would be those that did not vary with output and that could not be avoided by discontinuance of the segment.

The result of such an analysis would be a chart of accounts similar to Exhibit 2. Such a system of accounts would break the data into four categories: revenue, variable costs, assigned fixed costs, and unassigned fixed costs. Shannon could easily prepare this report once the system had been established. The report indicated the contribution each segment was making to assigned and unassigned fixed costs and to profits.

Particular expenses might overlap several categories, requiring an allocation. For example, heat, light, and power would fall into both the variable-cost and unassigned fixed-cost categories. Shannon would have to determine which labor costs would in fact vary with output, which would be fixed as long as the segment was maintained, and which would be attributable only to the total operation. One danger of such a system is that it might not reflect the fact that a cost that had once been variable had become fixed, or vice versa.

Exhibit 2
Chart of accounts—marginal income analysis

Truck washing	Truck repairs
1. Sales revenue	1. Sales revenue
2. Variable costs	2. Variable costs
a. Salaries	*a.* Salaries
b. Supplies	*b.* Supplies
c. Heat, light, power	*c.* Heat, light, power
d. Employer's payroll tax	*d.* Employer's payroll tax
e. Repair and maintenance	*e.* Repair and maintenance
3. Assigned fixed costs	3. Assigned fixed costs
a. Depreciation of equipment	*a.* Depreciation of equipment

4. Unassigned fixed costs
   a. Salaries
   b. Advertising
   c. Repairs and maintenance of plant
   d. Taxes
   e. Telephone
   f. Heat, light, power
   g. Employer's payroll tax
   h. Rent
   i. Depreciation of building, fixtures
   j. Amortization of leasehold improvements
   k. Insurance

Frederick offered to assist Shannon without charge in preparing a report for June 1983 based on such a system of accounts because of his interest in the accounting problem presented. The result is shown in Exhibit 3.

Exhibit 3
Marginal income analysis report for June 1983

		Truck Repairs			Truck Washing
Sales			$28,000		$7,400
Variable costs					
Salaries		$ 7,900		$2,000	
Supplies		7,600		1,400	
Heat, light, power		1,500		250	
Employer's payroll tax		430	17,430	100	3,750
Contribution to assigned and unassigned fixed cost			10,750		3,650
Depreciation			2,000		1,000
Contribution to unassigned fixed cost		11,220	$ 8,570		$2,650
Unassigned Fixed Costs					
Salaries	$6,500				
Advertising	880				
Telephone	660				
Heat, light, power	350				
Employer's payroll tax	360				
Rent	1,000				
Depreciation	1,830				
Amortization	1,400				
Insurance	950	13,930			
Net Loss for the period		($ 2,710)			

Shannon was then faced with consideration of both the full-cost report and the incremental-income report in making his decision about abandonment of the truck-washing operation. Exhibit 4 presents a summary of the income statement for the entire operation in June.

Exhibit 4
Net income statements for June 1983

Sales		$35,400
Salaries	$16,400	
Supplies	9,000	
Heat, light, power	2,100	
Employer's payroll tax	890	
Advertising	880	
Telephone	660	
Rent	1,000	
Depreciation	4,830	
Amortization of leasehold improvements	1,400	
Insurance	950	
Total expenses		38,110
Net loss		($ 2,710)

1. Was the rule of thumb helpful? Why or why not?
2. Was the full-cost estimate helpful? Why or why not?

3. Did the incremental income analysis help in making the decision? Why or why not?
4. What is accomplished by separating fixed costs from variable costs? What is gained by separating assigned from unassigned fixed costs?
5. Are the allocation bases in Exhibit 1 reasonable? Do they contribute to decision making in this firm?
6. Which is relevant in this case: the contribution to the unassigned fixed cost or the contribution to the assigned and unassigned fixed cost? Explain.
7. What is the relation between the variable costs in this case and the incremental cost concept? What is the relation of assigned fixed cost to the concept of time perspective?
8. What considerations result from viewing truck-washing revenues in the light of a longer time perspective?
9. What considerations result from thinking about the possible effect on truck repairs of closing the truck-washing operation?
10. What decision was correct in the truck-washing business?

Selected tools and techniques of economic analysis

The following examples of practices, policies, and rules of thumb are taken from case studies of actual firms. Some of the examples may be consistent with the principles of managerial economics; others may represent a practical compromise with those principles; others may be difficult to reconcile with incremental reasoning.

1. Some firms follow the rule that the annual budget for the replacement of equipment should equal the annual depreciation charges on equipment. The vice president of one manufacturing firm, for example, was considering such a policy to accelerate the replacement of equipment she believed was lagging behind. Many of this company's machines were more than 10 years or even 20 years old.

2. The owner-manager of a small printing firm follows the rule: "To make a profit, you must make a profit on every job." By this he means that each job must be priced to cover all the costs, including allocated overhead, and return a profit above those costs.

3. A dry-cleaning and laundry operation at a hospital in Dallas considered the possibility of filling in its off-peak excess capacity with laundry service for motels. The hospital management, however, turned down this opportunity when it learned that the motels would not pay a high enough price to cover the overhead as well as the direct costs.

4. The plant manager of the Michigan Brass Company, a large, national firm, was faced with a decision on making or buying a component. Up to the time of the decision, the plant manufactured the part, but a potential supplier was willing to sell at a price below the plant's full cost. In spite of this low price, Michigan Brass decided to continue manufacture within the plant because:

a. The overhead presently absorbed by manufacturing the component would have to be reallocated to other parts manufactured within the plant.

b. The reallocation of overhead would result in higher unit costs for other parts.

c. These higher unit costs would require higher prices for the company's products, placing it in a less favorable competitive position.

5. One owner-manager of a furniture manufacturing company in North Carolina made the following statement: "Overhead must come first." By this he meant that price must cover the overhead costs and then cover as much of the variable costs as possible.

6. A garden nursery and landscaping firm in Pennsylvania refused to develop plants or trees that took more than eight years to mature. The management reasoned that the high prices of the slower-maturing plants didn't compensate for the longer period they tied up the land.

7. Many firms maintain a policy of not buying new equipment or replacing old equipment unless the investment will pay for itself in less than three years (or some other predetermined number of years). This rule is known as the payback criterion.

How do the tools and methods of analyses of these companies hold up under analysis in terms of the concepts in Chapter 2?

**PROBLEMS
Fundamental
concepts: A case
method approach**

2–1   The Promotion of Winning Warriors of Walsh (POWWOW), a booster organization that provides moral and financial support to the soccer program at the high school that won the state soccer championship in 1983, raises some money by selling programs at home games. They have been selling an average of 1,500 programs per game at a price of 50 cents per program. On the average, sales are one program for every five persons attending a game. The total cost of printing a run of 1,500 programs is $450; the printer has offered to increase the pressrun to 2,000 copies for a total cost of $575. This year, Walsh's big game will be against Copley/Hower High School. Tickets for the game are already sold out. Assuming good weather, attendance will be 9,500 people (2,000 more than average.) Should POWWOW increase the pressrun of programs for the Walsh-Copley/Hower game to 2,000 copies? Why or why not?

2–2   Comment on this statement: "Marginal analysis is always an instance of incremental analysis, but incremental analysis often is not an instance of marginal analysis."

2–3   Kathleen Grace worked hard to obtain her bachelor's degree in speech pathology and audiology but later decided she did not like the field. She is considering beginning a one-year program in gerontology at the University of Akron. If she does, she will give up a rather convenient full-time job in which she is earning $10,000 a year, and she will have to use $1,000 of savings (now earning 10 percent compounded annually) to pay tuition and fees. She believes she could earn $3,000 per year working part-time while she is in the program. Upon completion of her studies, she would expect to get a position with starting pay of $12,000 annually. She projects pay increases of $500 annually for her present job and also for the one she would get after finishing the gerontology program. Should she begin the program? How many years will it be before she breaks even?

2–4   For each of the following, which is more appropriate, incremental analysis or marginal analysis?

a. Deciding whether to drop a product that does not cover its full cost.

b. Deciding how much of input A to substitute for input B, where it is clear that input A replaces less and less of input B as more substitution is carried out.

c. Deciding upon the size of a new plant, given the knowledge that unit cost decreases with greater plant size.

d. Deciding whether to make a part inside the plant or send it out to be done to order.

e. Deciding whether to use process A or process B in a new production line to be added to an existing plant.

2–5   Diebold Inc. has assigned worker Smith to make product X, bank trays, and worker Jones to make product Y, bank-vault doors. The management is considering reassignment of both workers to make product Z, bank burglar-alarm devices. Smith is the only available worker who knows how to make product X, and Jones is the only one who knows how to make product Y. Both workers will be required to work full-time if the firm makes product Z. Revenues and costs per period for three products are as follows:

Product X		Product Y		Product Z	
Revenue	$850	Revenue	$1,000	Revenue	$2,150
Wages	400	Wages	300	Wages	700
Materials	100	Materials	400	Materials	650
Electricity	50	Electricity	100	Electricity	300

Calculate the economic profit per period from producing product Z (take into account the opportunity costs of the scarce skilled labor that will be required). Then apply incremental reasoning to this decision.

2–6   Suppose a student aiming for an MBA degree is taking a full load of courses (but works 20 hours per week in a part-time job) and is receiving veteran's educational benefits and support under the Social Security Act. How would you calculate the opportunity costs and full costs of the MBA degree?

2–7   How do the opportunity costs of a business firm enter into the determination of its taxable income?

2–8   When his daughter Megan was adopted from South Korea, Dr. Robert Elliot bought a life insurance policy to provide money for her college education. The policy paid Dr. Elliot $10,000 on August 15, 1984 (Megan's 18th birthday). Megan planned to begin college on September 1, 1984, at an institution requiring prepayment of the tuition and fees amounting to $2,500 for the first year. Dr. Elliot believes the sophomore year will cost $2,600, the junior year will cost $2,700, and the senior year will cost $3,000. The proceeds of the insurance policy have been deposited in a savings account at 6 percent interest compounded annually. How much additional money will Dr. Elliot need to pay for his daughter's tuition and fees?

2–9   A project manager at General Motors is attempting to determine the incremental cost of proposed new product A. In making this product, machine X, already fully utilized, will be needed. Is the opportunity cost of machine X part of the incremental cost of new product A? Explain.

2–10   In producing a unit of product A at Chrysler, two units of input Z will be required. What is the role of the unit price of input Z in calculating the unit contribution of product A?

2–11   How can one determine whether a given decision is being viewed in long-run or short-run perspective? Can every decision be classified as a short-run or a long-run decision?

Selected references

Brown, Rex V. "Do Managers Find Decision Theory Useful?" *Harvard Business Review* 48 (May–June 1970).

Dhalla, Nariman K. "The Role of Business Economists in Marketing." *Business Economics* 13, no. 3 (May 1978), pp. 47–51.

Hazledine, Tim, and Scott R. Moreland. "Population and Economic Growth: A World Cross-Section Study." *The Review of Economics and Statistics* 59, no. 3 (August 1977), pp. 253–63.

Heller, Walter W. "What's Right with Economics?" *American Economic Review* 65, no. 1 (March 1975), pp. 1–26.

Jones, Sidney L. "Are We Giving Answers to the Right Questions?" *Business Economics,* January 1975, pp. 19–22.

Kimball, James N. "The Price Elasticity of Demand and Its Effect on Public Utility Revenues." *Public Utilities Fortnightly* 106, no. 12 (December 1980), pp. 53–54.

Klein, Lawrence R. "The Supply Side." *American Economic Review* 68, no. 2 (March 1978), pp. 1–7.

Lieberman, Charles. "Inventory Demand and Cost of Capital Effects." *Review of Economics and Statistics* 62, no. 3 (August 1980), pp. 348–56.

C H A P T E R

3

Applications in not-for-profit operations

A major thesis of this volume is that the tools and techniques of managerial economics are applicable to all forms of economic activity and, as such, are not confined solely to private business ventures designed to generate normal profits. An introductory section to managerial economics is not complete until the reader has an opportunity to consider these areas in which the materials learned in Principles of Economics can be applied.

Government has a major role in modern economic systems. Many people believe that the government interferes in the economy to an extent far greater than intended or justified by framers of the Constitution of the United States. Nonetheless, the interests and activities of business firms and public agencies are becoming even more closely intertwined. The government is the regulator, the rule maker for much of the conduct of business. Also, federal, state, and local governments are major customers for business and industrial outputs. Businesses supply most of the non-labor inputs used in public sector production but are in turn major demanders of public services. Clearly, the profit and nonprofit sectors of the economy are important to each other from the points of view of both supply and demand.

The importance of government agencies and nonprofit enterprises relative to the private sector has been growing rapidly. At least one fifth of the labor force is employed in the public sector, and not-for-profit enterprises also have substantial numbers of workers. Many students either are or will be employed in public and nonprofit organizations during part or all of their careers. Thus, a need exists for attention to applications of managerial economics in the public sector.

The chapter begins by showing that the objectives of government agencies and nonprofit organizations are broader than those of profit-oriented firms. The chapter reveals some of the topics to be covered in subsequent chapters. Included, of course, is a discussion of demand, analyses of production, and costs in the public sector. Pricing decisions are considered at some length. Attention turns also to longer-run decisions involving investment. A discussion of the many (possibly conflicting) goals of public activities in a democratic society brings the chapter to a close.

Role of the public sector in the economy

Externalities, public goods, and options

In general, a market economy uses resources efficiently.[1] However, governmental intervention is thought necessary by some observers to oppose over- or underallocations of resources to particular activities because of externalities.[2] Externalities are costs imposed upon, or benefits provided to, third parties as the result of production and consumption decisions. Examples of externalities are all around us. A person who decides to drive a poorly tuned auto using leaded fuel pollutes the air, possibly leading to health problems for others. Because the health costs of others are not borne directly by the driver, the effects may not be considered in the decision of whether or not to have the engine tuned. Similarly, when one person is immunized for polio, the probability that other nonimmunized persons will contract the disease is reduced. The person with immunity conveys some of the value of this benefit to others, but it may not be a factor in deciding to get the vaccination.

The first of the above examples is a negative consumer externality (the decision maker imposes costs upon others), and the second example is a positive consumer externality (benefits are conferred upon others). Producers also create externalities. A firm that pollutes a river causes downstream users of water to have additional costs of cleaning the water before using it. On the other hand, a firm that carries out research often produces benefits much more than the returns realized on the research.

From the social welfare point of view, activities that yield external costs are overproduced and overconsumed because the producers and consumers take into account only the variable costs they must bear. On the other hand, activities that have external benefits are underproduced and underconsumed because the decision makers give no weight to the

---

[1] This section is a brief summary of certain aspects of the field of public finance. For comprehensive treatments, see Richard A. Musgrave and Peggy B. Musgrave, *Public Finance in Theory and Practice,* 2d ed. (New York: McGraw-Hill, 1976); or John F. Due and Ann F. Friedlander, *Government Finance—Economics of the Public Sector,* 6th ed. (Homewood, Ill.: Richard D. Irwin, 1977).

[2] Public intervention may also be needed to prevent inefficiencies resulting from noncompetitive behavior of firms. How to correct for inefficiencies in the allocation of scarce and costly resources that are caused by governmental intervention is beyond the scope of this book.

third-party gains from the activities. To attain a socially optimal level of an activity that has externalities, the third-party benefits or costs must somehow be reflected in the outcome for the decision maker. In other words, the government must deal with the externalities so that a socially desirable resource allocation is achieved. Taxes and subsidies are often used to "internalize" the external costs or benefits. For example, an additional tax on leaded gasoline may be an incentive for drivers to use unleaded fuel and thus to cut down on pollution. Or a subsidy on health care (free immunization) may be an incentive for citizens to protect against polio and thus to decrease the disease hazard for others.

In some activities, externalities are so great in relation to internal benefits and costs that the activities will be undertaken only by the government. Such activities are called public goods. Public goods are available to everyone in a given area, and no one can be excluded for reasons of nonpayment. The classic example of a public good is national defense. If one person is made safer because of an MX missile, that may not detract from another person's welfare. Furthermore, the Pentagon could not deprive any person of the benefits if he or she refused to buy a share. City planning, pollution control, consumer product testing, and many other services have the characteristics of public goods. The taxing power of the government is used to pay for public goods, since users (who realize that they cannot be individually excluded from benefits) do not make voluntary contributions equal to the value of the goods.

Finally, there are some public activities that have benefits even less direct than those from pollution control or national defense. Persons who do not visit Yellowstone Park, or ride the Bay Area Rapid Transit system, or swim in the Santa Barbara Channel may place some value on the knowledge that the facilities are available for possible future use. Nonusers may be willing to pay something for such options that are created and preserved by public action.

How public agencies differ from private firms

Although there are many similarities between public agencies and private firms, there are several major differences that should be noted. First, the constituency of the public agency is much larger than that of the business firm. A private enterprise may either confer benefits or impose costs upon the general public, but its responsibilities to employees, customers, and stockholders are given priority if the firm is to continue producing and investing. Interests of stockholders and the general public may diverge, as in the case of pollution-creating processes. The pressures of competition do not usually allow a business firm to assume more social responsibility than the law requires. On the other hand, in the case of a public agency, the well-being of those indirectly helped or harmed by its activities may be as important as that of the direct users of the agency's services. For example, the highway department is as responsible to those whose lives are disrupted by highway construction as it is to potential travelers of the route. Decision making and investment analysis for government agencies take into account and weigh the interests of all individuals and groups who are or will be affected.

A second peculiarity of public management is that many products and services are not sold directly for a price, and many others are priced at less than average cost. Those principles of pricing that are applicable to public agencies must be tailored somewhat to the public viewpoint. Furthermore, the guides to production and investment decisions that businesspersons obtain from market prices are not fully available to public managers.

Despite the distinctions between private and public enterprise, both kinds of organizations can use profit as a test of efficiency in resource allocation. In public decisions, it is necessary to redefine the concept of profit, and it is perhaps useful to rename it "net social benefit." In order to maximize public profit, or net social benefit, a public service is expanded until decreasing marginal benefits become equal to marginal costs. The concept of social benefit is quite similar to that of private revenue—it is the value of agency output to the various beneficiaries. Owing to the public viewpoint, the concept of social cost embraces the value of all opportunities foregone by the constituent population as a result of the agency's activities.

Third, please note that public decisions often involve equity considerations. That is, at times public decisions are made partially on the basis of who derives the benefits and who bears the costs, in addition to the determination of whether or not net social benefit is increased. Since equity appraisals involve subjective judgments, little can be said about them in the context of optimizing. Nevertheless, equity criteria need to be examined as does benefit and cost estimation, pricing, and benefit-cost analysis.

Finally, it is worthy of note that government agencies at the federal, state, and local level are tax takers, not the taxpayers they would be if their good or service were produced by private enterprise. A municipal power plant (or similar organization) owned and operated by the city of Cleveland, Ohio, for example, can exist without paying property taxes and without paying federal, state, or local income taxes. In fact, it can lose money routinely and receive a cash subsidy from the city of Cleveland. On the other hand, a privately owned Cleveland Electric Illuminating Company (or similar organization) may compete for the same electric business as its municipal counterpart, incur roughly the same operating costs but, in addition, be held liable for property taxes and for federal, state, and local income taxes.

Estimating demand and evaluating benefits

Public sector activities in the modern economy are nearly as diverse as those of the private sector. Governments provide cradle-to-grave services ranging from prenatal medical advice to burial in public cemeteries. They make and sell goods and services ranging from water to works of art. Estimating the demands for some public activities is very difficult. However, many functions performed by governments are similar to activities in the private sector, and the demands for these functions are analyzed by similar methods.

Demands for public services

The value of services provided by a public agency derives ultimately from citizen demands, which some agencies can determine in essentially the same ways used by private sellers. The postal service, water departments, and agencies renting campsites provide services for fees assessed on a partial or full-cost, pay-as-you-go basis.

However, many government agencies produce nonpriced products or services. Demand for nonpriced outputs is a meaningful concept, but special methods are required in demand estimation. Basically, proxy variables must be substituted for prices of the service and its substitutes. Consider outdoor recreation. A ''free'' recreation or park area actually has a price per visit in the form of extra costs (travel time, meals and lodging, vehicle operation, and so on) that must be borne by the user. The price would vary with the distance traveled by each prospective visitor, so that the rate of visits as a proportion of total population would tend to vary with distance from the park. Analysts have used this relationship to derive estimates of demand for outdoor recreation. The demand curves are constructed by relating visit rates of the population in each (distance) zone to estimated differences in cost.[3] The accuracy of such demand estimates depends upon proper estimation of all costs that would not have been incurred except for the visit to the park. In addition, just as prices of other goods and levels of income are important determinants of demands for privately produced goods, such factors as the availability of other parks and income variations within the region are taken into account.

Marginal value versus total benefit estimation

A public agency manager may have great difficulty in estimating the entire demand function for one of the agency's services, especially if

[3] See Jack L. Knetsch and Robert K. Davis, ''Comparison of Methods for Recreation Evaluation,'' in *Water Research*, ed. A. V. Kneese and Stephen C. Smith (Baltimore: Johns Hopkins University Press, 1960).

there are no charges for them or there are no good proxy variables that can be substituted for prices. However, it may still be practical to estimate the maximum amount users would be willing to pay for additional service. This approach is framed in marginal terms. For decisions involving small changes in the level of an ongoing activity, marginal valuations may be sufficient. The city water department would have to carry out a sophisticated analysis if the value of its total output were needed. On the other hand, the marginal value of additional water may be easy to estimate for most users, and this is the relevant value in decisions about additions to capacity of the system.

In the case of proposed new programs, evaluations of total benefits are needed. Such analyses may be quite difficult. They are necessary if rational decisions are to be made.[4] Total benefit estimation is described below.

Enumerating benefits

The first step in evaluating a particular government program is to enumerate specific ways in which various groups are benefited, whether these are direct uses, externalities, options, or public goods. In this undertaking, the pitfalls to avoid are (1) counting benefits to some individuals or groups that are offset by costs imposed upon others and (2) counting the same benefits twice.

Suppose the objective is to list the benefits of a new highway. The primary benefit is time and expenses saved by those who travel the new road, net of possible increases in costs to others who use only feeder roads that have become congested. External benefits may accrue to travelers using parallel routes that have become less congested because of the diverting of traffic. These motorists may also place some value on the option of an alternate route.

There is no net benefit from those effects that simply alter resource or goods prices without changing physical production or consumption possibilities. For example, a new highway will improve the profitability of service stations, restaurants, motels, and the like along the new route; however, much of this improvement is offset by reduced incomes to other facilities affected by traffic reductions along previously existing roads. A new highway will also increase values of adjacent land suited for facilities rendering services to travelers, but these increases are simply capitalizations (present values) of the potential additions to future income production on the sites. Listing both the current increases in land values and the current increases in incomes would be double counting.

---

[4] For an extensive discussion of benefit-cost analysis, see E. J. Mishan, *Cost-Benefit Analysis* (New York: Praeger Publishers, 1976). The topic is also discussed in Harley H. Hinrichs and Grahame M. Taylor, *Program Budgeting and Benefit-Cost Analysis* (Pacific Palisades, Calif.: Goodyear Publishing, 1969).

It is sometimes difficult to make a clear distinction between benefits and costs. To do so, an agency must specify a target population for which the program is intended. Benefits often fall to persons outside the target group—construction contractors, for example—at the expense of those within it—the region's taxpayers. A similar point of view applies to increased employment, at possibly higher pay, of local construction workers. Their gains are also at the expense of the area's taxpayers. In both examples, the payoff from the program is the difference between the value of the services and the cost of producing them.

Ideal evaluation of benefits

Simple enumeration of benefit categories and their incidence is only a beginning. Choice of the best level for a program and choice among competing programs require measurement of benefits, usually in terms of money. The ideal measurement would be monetary value of total utility to all beneficiaries of a program. This value may be illustrated conceptually by means of Figure 3–1. Curve D represents demand of all beneficiaries for the output of a program—it indicates at every level of the program the marginal value of the program to beneficiaries. Now, suppose it is proposed to expand the program in a large "jump" from Q_0 to

Figure 3–1
Consumers' surplus in comparison of programs

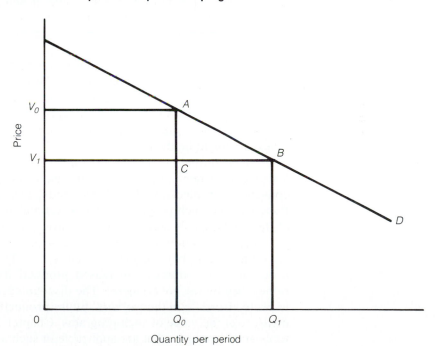

Q_1. The value of marginal units will fall from V_0 to V_1. Total monetary value of the expansion of services to the users is Q_0ABQ_1. However, if output is priced at V_1, revenue is less than the increase in monetary value of benefits provided (by the amount ABC). Area ABC is an increment in the total, called consumers' surplus. Consumers surplus is the summation of differences of marginal valuations from price. Note that the price, QV_1, which just rations the increased output, is below the consumers' marginal evaluations of those quantities acquired in moving from Q_0 up to the greater output at Q_1.

To illustrate the implications of the consumer's surplus approach to benefit evaluation, suppose an analyst attempts to put a value on the use of a congested facility by measuring the amount (and value) of time that users will voluntarily sacrifice by waiting in line to receive government benefits. Expansion of the facility by some sizable amount would reduce the waiting time price paid by all users. However, to value all output of the facility at the new lower price would be to overlook the fact that some users of the service would be willing to wait longer (pay a higher price) than they actually do.

Direct estimation techniques

Estimation of consumers' surplus may be impractical. It requires estimation of the entire demand curve. Consumer expenditure (value of the last unit times all units) is much easier to estimate and will not be a serious underestimate of monetary value of benefits if demand is highly elastic or if the project adds only marginally to the amount of service available. Estimation of ''expenditure'' is easiest when the output of the project is an intermediate good used in production. For example, if one of the outputs of a dam is irrigation water that will be used to increase output of agricultural land, the value of the increased agricultural output is a good estimate of the value of the irrigation portion of the project. The concepts provided in succeeding chapters will help the managerial economist solve these and similar public sector problems more easily than otherwise might be the case.

Often the output of a public program is a capital good expected to yield a stream of benefits over a period of years. Such is the case with major construction projects, such as dams, roads, and rapid-transit rail systems. Benefits from such programs must be estimated over the expected lives of the capital goods created. In some programs, such as vocational training and rehabilitation of disabled workers, benefits are expected to extend over time spans beyond the program's life. The final product of such programs is the trainees' increased productivity (sold by the workers rather than by the government). The discounted, or present, value of the expected increase in the workers' future productivities is the appropriate measure of the value of such programs. Chapter 11 discusses the various tools and techniques that are applicable in such a situation.

Indirect estimation techniques

External benefits, public goods, and unpriced direct benefits must be evaluated through indirect estimation of consumer demands. The three most common techniques of indirect estimation are: (1) to observe changes in prices of land (or other complementary goods) affected by the project, (2) to obtain prices paid for close private substitutes for the benefit in question, and (3) to estimate reductions in cost that are made possible by the project.

The demand for land is affected by external costs and benefits. For example, buyers may be willing to pay a premium to live near a neighborhood park. On the other hand, the value of land directly under the final approach to an airport is likely to be depressed. One indirect measure of the benefits or costs of a public program is the difference in land values between the affected properties and otherwise similar land not affected by the program.[5]

Prices of close private substitutes are sometimes available when a public project duplicates private facilities already operating in other locations. An example is electricity generated at a publicly owned dam. The value of the electricity can be estimated by using prices of privately produced power. The value of public education, at times, may be estimated by comparing the tuition charged at state universities to prices at private institutions of higher learning.

Reduced costs to direct beneficiaries or to society as a whole may be a large part, even all, of a program's output. Thus, a program to reduce the number of school dropouts may do more than increase lifetime incomes of students; society may also benefit from decreased costs of crime and welfare.[6] The most important benefit of a rapid-transit system may be the reduced cost of commuting time.[7]

Each of these indirect estimation techniques can be illustrated by reference to Rothenberg's study of urban renewal projects.[8] The principal efficiency objective of urban renewal is to improve productivity of land in and around the renewal site. Assembly of a number of separately

---

[5] For discussions of the use of property values in indirect measurement of benefits of public programs, see Roy W. Bahl, Stephan P. Coclen, and Jeremy J. Warford, "Land Value Increments as a Measure of the Net Benefits of Urban Water Supply Projects in Developing Countries: Theory and Measurement," in *Government Spending and Land Values,* ed. C. Lowell Harriss (Madison: University of Wisconsin Press, 1973).

[6] Burton A. Weisbrod, "Preventing High School Dropouts," in *Measuring Benefits of Government Investments,* ed. Robert Dorfman (Washington, D.C.: The Brookings Institution, 1965), pp. 117–71.

[7] For a discussion of valuation of travel time, see James R. Nelson, "The Value of Travel Time," in *Problems in Public Expenditure Analysis,* ed. Samuel B. Chase, Jr. (Washington, D.C.: The Brookings Institution, 1968), pp. 78–126.

[8] Jerome Rothenberg, *Economic Evaluation of Urban Renewal* (Washington, D.C.: The Brookings Institution, 1967).

owned parcels into one large tract allows a developer, public or private, to build better housing that is not exposed to the value-depressing effect of a surrounding slum district. Increased rentals (net of increased costs) are capitalized in higher land values for those sites that are sold to private interests for highest bids. Thus, increases in land values provide a dollar measure of part of the direct benefits of an urban renewal project.

A typical urban renewal project will also increase the attractiveness of real estate in adjoining neighborhoods. Hence, increases in market values of land surrounding the project provide partial measures of external benefits of the project. Another type of external benefit that may result is reduction in fire hazard to nearby neighborhoods. This benefit can be measured in the form of lower costs of fire protection services and lower insurance premiums—an example of a benefit measured as a reduction in associated costs.

Finally, there may be a problem of estimating the value of public housing built as part of the project where this property is not sold at competitive market prices. If such housing does not constitute a large portion of the total supply in the community, its value may be estimated on the basis of values of nearby private housing with similar characteristics.

This illustration does not give a complete accounting of benefits from urban renewal. Actual estimates of changes in values and costs due to a program and the identification of appropriate private substitutes for unpriced publicly provided benefits may require a great deal of ingenuity.

Problems in estimating benefits

Benefit estimation encounters several difficulties: (1) risk associated with project outcomes; (2) valuation of lives saved; and (3) measurement of intangibles. When project outcomes are uncertain, the best approach is to attach probabilities to the alternative outcomes, as is discussed in later chapters in relation to the decision-tree approach. The expected value of a project becomes the probability weighted average of the dollar values of net benefits of each of the possible outcomes.[9]

Transportation projects, health care projects, and other public activities may be expected to reduce the likelihood of accidental or premature death. Benefits of life saving cannot be estimated without estimates of the "value of life." One method of assigning financial value to life is based on expected lifetime incomes of persons expected to live longer as a result of the project.[10]

---

[9] Uncertainties are prominent in John M. Vernon, "Benefits and Costs of Developing Advanced Nuclear Power Reactors," *Applied Economics* 1 (January 1969), pp. 1–16.

[10] See Thomas C. Schelling, "The Life You Save May Be Your Own," in *Problems in Public Expenditure Analysis*, ed. Chase, pp. 127–76.

Finally, some programs have benefits that defy monetary valuation. As examples, increased beauty of the environment and increased prestige of the nation are difficult to translate into monetary terms. In such cases managerial economists often provide a list of intangible benefits to inform decision makers that these benefits do exist and should be considered.

Production and costs in the public sector

Public sector production and cost can be analyzed in essentially the same ways used in the private sector.[11] Part three—Costs, Production, and Productivity—is devoted to this subject. However, it may be important to distinguish between the outlays for the project (dollar amounts that appear in the budget) and the project's true economic costs. Only the latter costs are relevant in benefit-cost analysis.

Project outlays

Estimates of program costs take the form of projections of outlays for each year of the project's life on the basis of current market prices of inputs. General increases in input prices need not be considered, since they affect all alternatives alike, but changes in the relative prices of inputs should be taken into account.

True economic cost (social cost) may be substantially different from the explicit outlays. Social cost is the opportunity cost of all resources used in the project. Many social costs do not show up in the budgets of public agencies, since these agencies may use underpriced services of other agencies, use agency-owned lands and facilities without showing the corresponding costs of capital, and impose external costs upon other persons or groups.

Estimating true economic costs

As an example of the estimation of a project's relevant costs, consider an urban highway project. The immediate explicit costs are site acquisition, planning, and construction. Future explicit costs include operation and maintenance of the facilities over their estimated useful lives. If a portion of the right-of-way is already under government ownership, the value of this land in its next most productive use is an opportunity cost.

The highway project may have external costs. Construction involves disruption of established travel patterns and dislocation of residents along the right-of-way. Moreover, to the extent that it encourages an increase in vehicle-miles of auto travel within the jurisdiction, there are future

---

[11] For a discussion of productivity in the public sector, see John P. Ross and Jesse Burkhead, *Productivity in the Local Government Sector* (Lexington, Mass.: Lexington Books, 1974).

increases of air pollution and noise. Unless reimbursements of affected individuals are specifically required by law or by agency policy, external costs are not borne by the agency, but they are still relevant costs from the point of view of the welfare of a target population.

Project outlays that are based upon market prices of inputs may need to be adjusted for effects of unemployment, monopoly elements, government controls, price supports, or other conditions that cause market prices to diverge from marginal social costs of the resources. For example, consider the case in which some unemployed people (resources) are expected to gain employment as a result of a project. The social cost of such resources is much less than their price, since they would otherwise produce nothing. Note that adjustments for unemployment are appropriate only if the condition would be expected to exist at the time the resource is to be used. Project analysis usually concerns some future period, and it is probably not reasonable to assume that mass unemployment will persist year after year.

Monopoly prices and government-supported prices may overstate the opportunity cost of resources required by a project. Unfortunately, there are no reliable rules of thumb for making the necessary adjustments in such cases. Since the unadjusted market prices do represent marginal evaluation of those resources (at inefficient usage levels), they may be the best estimates available to the analyst.

An illustration of the need for careful handling of implicit cost is given by a study of graduate education in management in India.[12] From the student's point of view, the largest private cost of management education is the value of foregone earnings from postponement of full-time employment. Of course, his or her projected gross earnings would be reduced by indirect taxes, sales taxes, property taxes, and excise taxes to obtain the net private sacrifice. Under assumptions of competition in the labor market and full employment, the student's gross earnings represent social cost of the sacrifice of his or her contribution to production. On the other hand, if there is a pool of educated underemployed, as was found in Paul's study of India, there may be little social cost of the student's withdrawal from the labor force. In this case, a series of workers move to better jobs, and most of these are about as productive as the person they replace.

Prices, charges, and subsidies

Public agencies produce a wide variety of outputs, some of which might properly be termed *private goods*. These are goods that, in contrast to public goods, can be enjoyed independently and exclusively by individ-

[12] S. Paul, "An Application of Cost-Benefit Analysis to Management Education," in *Benefits, Cost and Policy Analysis*, ed. W. A. Niskoven et al. (Chicago: Aldine Publishing, 1973).

uals. That is, one person's use reduces the amount available to others but does not otherwise affect their well-being. Such goods can be divided and offered to individuals in varying amounts. Among such services commonly provided by governments are parking, water, recreation facilities, and limited-access highways. It is feasible for public agencies to impose direct charges for private goods.

Pricing of public services helps in the efficient rationing of scarce supplies. Demand for a private good that is provided free is likely to outrun the available supply. This is so because the good will be consumed up to the level at which marginal units are worth nothing to users, without regard to the additional cost of providing increased service. For example, on warm summer days there never seem to be enough free public swimming pools. As a consequence, such facilities are usually rationed by exclusion rules, such as time limits or residence requirements, and/or by queues. More efficient price rationing of such goods can be achieved by using the rule that price should equal marginal cost. Considerable discussion follows in Part 4 of this book regarding price behavior.

Marginal-cost pricing

Marginal-cost pricing can be illustrated by the example of a congested highway. Variable costs of highway transportation include highway maintenance, traffic control, vehicle maintenance and operating costs, and the travel time, effort, discomfort, and safety hazard incurred by travelers. Most of these costs (per vehicle) increase as the traffic flow increases. A toll set equal to marginal cost (in place of the present system of gas taxes set at levels that cover average costs) would cause each user to compare the value of benefits from use of a congested highway with all costs of the addition to traffic, including those costs imposed on others. If the toll exceeds marginal benefit for a particular trip, then the trip will not be made (at least not by this route), thus reserving the highway for others who value their trips more highly. Hence, a system of tolls that vary with changes in traffic levels could potentially improve economic well-being of highway users.[13] This is the same concept of peak-load pricing that is discussed in Chapter 10.

User charges do not just ration scarce facilities; they also provide guides to decisions about investment in additional capacity. In the simplest case wherein expansions may be made in small increments and production exhibits constant returns to scale, expansion is justified whenever total revenues exceed total costs. In other words, positive net revenue is evidence that expansion will yield benefits in excess of additional

---

[13] William Vickrey, "Pricing in Urban and Suburban Transport," *American Economic Review, Papers and Proceedings*, (May 1963), pp. 452–65.

costs. In the absence of user charges, there are no such direct measures of the benefits of expanded facilities.

A more general rule for expansion of a program that has direct user charges is that expansion should continue until long-run marginal cost equals demand price. An agency that wished to apply this rule would need to estimate marginal cost for a variety of program sizes and then estimate the number of users at a charge equal to marginal costs. If scale economies are present (Chapter 6), the optimal solution would result in losses, so that the profitability test does not hold. Conversely, decreasing returns to scale imply that total charges would exceed costs even at optimum program size. These are the same problems of marginal cost pricing that are discussed in Chapter 10, and elsewhere in Part 4.

In some cases, it may be appropriate for an agency to deliberately charge less than marginal cost. Recall that many public services are of the type which have important external benefits to nonusers. Such nonusers might reasonably be said to have demands for (that is, place value upon) the services. A user charge that decreases the frequency of residential trash collection increases the unsightliness and health hazard that must be tolerated by those who are passing by. A charge on direct users that completely covers costs will result in an undersupply of services to the indirect users. Since indirect benefits accrue to taxpayers collectively (as public goods), subsidization of services to the fee-paying direct users by appropriations from general tax revenues can raise the total community well-being as compared with full-cost pricing.

Indirect charges

A number of public outputs have not normally carried direct charges, despite their basically private character, because of the high cost of collecting from users. This condition holds for most streets and highways and many recreation facilities. However, indirect methods of charging may be feasible. These may take the form of licenses or of taxes on private goods that are complementary with the public outputs. For example, hunting and fishing license fees can finance wildlife conservation programs; taxes on gasoline can pay for transportation facilities. Another example of an indirect price commonly used by local government is the basing of sewage charges on usage of water. This arrangement may be considered reasonable to the extent that increased water consumption means greater output of sewage.

Since the tax is tied to use of the service, these benefit levies serve some rationing function as well as providing revenue. On the other hand, such charges do not follow the principle of marginal cost, since the user pays nothing for additional units of the associated government service. In particular, taxes on complementary goods do not ration efficiently if the public output is subject to peak-load congestion. For example, marginal costs of highway use fluctuate widely among locations and hours of the day. These differences cannot be reflected in the amount of gasoline tax, since gasoline purchase is largely independent of the time and place of highway use. Likewise, using water consumption as a basis for sewage charges does not differentiate between users. One user may be using large amounts of water to sprinkle lawns (with no resulting load on the sewer system), and another user may be washing clothes and dishes (which does impose a load on the system).

Penalty prices

A type of government-administered "price" that has been receiving increased attention is the penalty for damage to the environment. Examples are proposed taxes on leaded gasoline and sulfurous fuels. These would be incentives to reduce production of underpriced, or unpriced, products. As another example, suppose the waste from a plant were tested periodically for concentration of a harmful chemical, and suppose a charge equal to the value of damages were levied per unit of discharge of this effluent. A profit-maximizing firm would respond to this charge according to its cost of controlling the waste. Allen V. Kneese has shown the effect of this policy (see Figure 3–2). Costs associated with waste disposal are minimized at point *E* rather than at point *D,* where the latter represents the level of waste disposal when use of the stream is free to the firm. The institution of the charge induces the firm to adopt socially optimal waste disposal methods, reducing but not eliminating pollution. Notice that further treatment would require resources (equipment, location changes, or processes) that outweigh in value the additional improvement.

Subsidies

In a similar way, subsidies may be used to encourage increased production of goods that are overpriced in private markets because the suppliers cannot collect the value of externalities. Higher education, low-income housing, and commuter railroads are among the goods which may be produced privately and sold to direct users, but also provide significant benefits to others. One means to improve social welfare in such cases is to leave production in private hands, but to provide a public subsidy that will allow the private firm to set the price to direct users below the average cost.

Pricing and efficiency

Charges and subsidies will usually increase efficiency of resource use as compared with rationing by prohibitions, regulations, or other direct controls. Consider again the case of water pollution. The natural capacity of water to cleanse itself is an important resource. This resource can be

Figure 3–2
Industrial plant's response to effluent charges

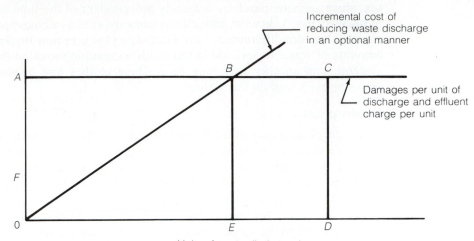

OD: Units of waste discharge if no charge levied on effluent.
OA: Damages per unit of waste discharge and effluent charge per unit.
OACD: Total damages associated with unrestricted waste discharge, i.e., no effluent charge levied.
OE: Reduction of waste discharge with effluent charge OA.
OFBE: Total cost of reducing effluent discharge to ED.
OFBCD: Total cost associated with waste disposal with ED waste discharge, i.e., residual damage costs plus cost of reducing discharge.
OABE: Total damages avoided.
ABF: Net reduction in waste disposal associated costs by reducing waste discharge by OE, i.e., OABE minus OFBE.

overused, and it almost certainly will be if it is entirely free, but outright prohibition of its use would require some waste treatment with cost in excess of benefits. Cost of control varies widely among effluent-producing activities, and efficiency requires that any given level of water quality should be attained at the lowest possible total cost. Rules restricting the absolute quantity of effluent from each source do not take into consideration the varying costs of waste treatment. By contrast, effluent charges leave the choice of type and level of waste treatment to the polluting firm. As shown above, each firm would expand waste treatment up to the point at which marginal treatment cost is just equal to the effluent charge. Any desired level of water quality can be achieved by this method, depending upon the level of the effluent charge. The choices of the individual firms then minimize the total social cost of achieving any given level of water quality. Pricing in the public sector is no longer simply an academic topic. In order to receive federal construction grants, local sewer systems will be required to use rate structures that reflect the loads each of the users is imposing.[14] Although strict marginal cost pricing is not mandated, the prices must be tied to costs so as to come closer to the desired efficient allocations of resources.

Since we have been stressing the importance of the pricing mechanism in properly allocating resources, it is appropriate to review the situations under which charges are justifiable or questionable. The following list is by Professors John F. Due and Ann F. Friedlander.

Use of the pricing mechanism where possible instead of free distribution with financing by taxation is regarded as most justifiable when:

1. Benefits are primarily direct, so that charges will not cause significant loss of externalities.
2. Demand has some elasticity [Chapters 4 and 5], so that the use of prices aids resource allocation and eliminates excessive utilization.
3. Charges do not result in inequities to lower-income groups, on the basis of accepted standards.
4. Costs of collection of charges are relatively low, or alternate taxes measured by use can be employed.

Use of charges is more questionable when:

1. Externalities are significant and will be lost in part if charges are made.
2. Demand is perfectly inelastic, so that resource allocation is insensitive to the pricing system. Even so, charges may be regarded as warranted on equity grounds.
3. Equity standards require that the lower-income groups be assured of obtaining the services.
4. Collection costs are relatively high and alternative tax measures related to usage cannot be devised.[15]

Benefit-cost and cost-effectiveness analyses

Benefit-cost analysis is a set of techniques for comparing alternative programs or projects that are expected to yield returns over a period of years. To a considerable extent benefit-cost studies follow the same principles of cost and return estimation that are used in private investment decisions (Chapter 11). They are intended to provide for the public sector the kinds of guides to investment policy that are given to private firms by market prices and considerations of competition.

[14] This is required by Section 204 of the Federal Water Pollution Control Act Amendments of 1972.

[15] Due and Friedlander, *Government Finance*, p. 101. For an excellent discussion of the economics of pricing services of public agencies, see Alice John Vandermeulen, "Reform of a State Fee Structure," *National Tax Journal* 17, no. 4 (December 1964), p. 394.

Competition can be simulated in decisions about public projects by the specification of a number of alternative production techniques, levels of service, and combinations of output. This list of alternatives will also probably include the possibility of no additional government program at all (the status quo alternative). The purpose of systematic analysis is not only to justify government expenditure to advance a certain objective, but also to find the most efficient means to that objective and to determine the best level of service to provide. Comparisons among alternatives may be largely technical, having to do with alternate types of equipment, or they may involve more fundamental questions of priority, such as whether to build more job training centers or more research libraries.

Definition of the outputs or objectives of the project is the first necessary step in any benefit-cost analysis. These may be simple and obvious, as in the case of a bridge, or quite complex, as in the case of multiple-purpose water resources projects. In the latter case the outputs could be electric power, recreation, irrigation water, domestic and industrial water, flood control, and pollution control. Each of these outputs can be produced at different levels, but their production cannot be considered independently. In other cases, project objectives may be quite intangible. Consider the problem of defining outputs of a correctional institution.

After objectives are stated and feasible alternative means and program levels are formulated, the goal of benefit-cost analysis is to estimate net improvement in the well-being of the target population for each of the alternatives.

Discounting benefits and costs

In practice, most studies of this type deal with durable projects from which benefits and costs will accrue over a period of years. However, investment in intangibles that are expected to yield a stream of future benefits (for example, Head Start programs for preschool children or, more generally, any educational programs) can also be subjected to benefit-cost analysis. Any such investigation requires that evaluation of both costs and benefits take account of timing as well as absolute amounts of dollar magnitudes. The methods for dealing with time streams of costs and returns are discussed in Chapter 11. The risks associated with these income streams are covered in Chapter 12. The same type of reasoning applies to government projects. For example, building a dam will require government financing, which—either by raising resource prices or increasing taxes—will take resources away from other public investment (such as roads) or from private sector investment (such as factories). Since the time streams of costs and returns will be different for these competing alternatives, discounting is required so that the projects can be compared in terms of present values.

The appropriate rate of discount is the estimated rate of return on alternative investment that must be foregone in order to carry out the project under evaluation. The importance of correct choice of a discount rate may be shown by the following example.

Consider two potential government housing projects. The first, alternative *A*, would be built over two years at a level annual cost of $100,000 and is expected to produce benefits worth $30,000 per year beginning in year 3 and ending after 10 years of use, whereupon it would be replaced by a more productive land use. Alternative *B* would take three years to build at $100,000 per year but would generate benefits of $30,000 per year for 20 years before it, too, became obsolete. The following table compares the net present values (NPV) for these two projects under three different discount rates.

Project	NPV discounted at 5 percent	NPV discounted at 7 percent	NPV discounted at 10 percent
A	$25,383	$ 3,465	$ − 23,300
B	29,661	− 3,205	− 62,474

Notice that the choice of the discount rate is crucial in determining (1) whether a public project is warranted as compared with private investment or other uses of public funds and (2) whether long-term or short-term investments will be favored. At 10 percent, neither project is justified. At 7 percent, project *A* is justified, but *B* is not. At 5 percent, both projects are justified, but *B* is preferable to *A*. Increases in the discount rate simultaneously improve the relative position of shorter-term alternatives and disqualify a greater number of projects.

Choosing the discount rate

Public agencies should use a discount rate that assures that public investments at the margin yield at least the opportunity rate of return on marginal private alternatives. The most common measures of ''opportunity cost of capital'' are the various market borrowing and lending rates. Which of these is most relevant to public investments? Actual government practice of recent years has favored using the rates the governments must pay to borrow funds. Since public and private securities compete for the same lenders, these rates are related to private investment opportunities. However, a private investment that used the same resources would pay corporate income taxes; total social return is greater than the net private yield. In addition, the rate paid on government bonds is subsidized by granting personal income tax advantages to lenders. For these reasons, governments are able to borrow at rates that are well below marginal social return on private investments. Commercial rates, on the other hand, include the effects of financial risks that are relevant for investment by individual firms but not for the expected return from all private investment taken together.

Considering these factors, suppose that corporations are paying 8 percent to obtain capital, using their optimal blend of debt and equity financing. Because of risk, a private firm might be willing to pay this rate to finance a project only if its expected return after taxes were substantially greater than the cost of capital. Corporate profits are taxed at approximately 50 percent in the United States, but (depending upon the proportion of debt finance) this tax is partially offset by deductibility of interest. For example, a before-tax return of 15 percent with a 50–50 ratio of 6 percent bonds to new equity would be an aftertax yield of 9 percent.[16] If firms regard this as sufficient return to offset risk, then the 15 percent before-tax return would represent the contribution of the marginal private investment to the value of national output. Using this as the discount rate for government investment decisions, would equalize marginal returns in the public and private sectors.

Although the above approach yields a reasonable estimate of the cost of capital for the public sector, there is not a definitive method of obtaining such costs.[17] Actual benefit-cost studies often show benefits and costs under alternative discount rates, so that decision makers can see how sensitive the results are to changes in the rates.

Now suppose that benefit and cost streams are quantified as accurately as possible in dollar terms for each feasible alternative, and a discount rate is chosen. Estimated net benefits in each year may then be discounted to present values and a total discounted net benefit may be determined for each project

In the simplest case, all projects under consideration would be independent of one another (in terms of the resources to be used or the outcomes expected) and funds would be available for all worthy projects. In this case, all projects with net discounted benefits greater than zero should be undertaken. This is equivalent to recommending adoption of any "lumpy" project whose internal rate of return exceeds the discount rate, or increasing size of any continuously variable project with marginal rate of return above discount rate. Under this criterion, if marginal private investments are yielding a 10 percent before-tax return, any public project (or incremental increase in a project) that promised a greater return would be adopted, and revenues would be raised to finance it.

But real public agencies are seldom able to undertake every project and every expansion that they can justify on net benefit grounds. Usually the budgetary limitation will be expressed in maximum dollars available rather than as a required rate of return. These conditions complicate the

---

[16] An investment of $1 returns 15 cents in Year 1 and (with half of total capital obtained by borrowing) incurs an interest charge of 3 cents (6 percent on 50 cents). Taxable profit is therefore 12 cents, and taxes are 6 cents, leaving a 9-cent profit after taxes.

[17] For discussions of the choice of discount rates, see Mishan, *Cost-Benefit Analysis*.

choice process. A foolproof choice criterion can still be simply stated: Approve that set of independent projects that maximizes discounted net benefits without exceeding the budget constraint. However, if the list of projects is long and the number of mutually exclusive sets is large, project ranking requires mathematical programming techniques.

Examples of benefit-cost studies

This section provides two examples of benefit-cost studies that show the following: (1) Benefit-cost techniques can be used to determine whether investing in "human capital" is efficient, as well as in appraisals of tangible capital projects. (2) The approach can be applied in an ex post evaluation of old projects, as well as in decisions on whether or not to undertake new ones.

The first study is an analysis of benefits and costs of a rapid rail and bus transit system for the metropolitan Atlanta, Georgia, area.[18] Quantifiable and nonquantifiable benefits are listed in Table 3–1, and estimated

Table 3–1
Benefits of the proposed Atlanta Marta System

Nonquantifiable benefits:
  Facilitation of regional growth.
  Retention and enhancement of existing urban areas.
  Broadening educational opportunities.
  Increasing the accessibility of cultural and recreational sites.
  Reduction in emission of air pollutants.
  Reduction of traffic accidents.

Quantifiable benefits:
  Time savings to "constant" transit users.
  Benefits to motorists using transit (diverted auto drivers and
    riders).
      Time savings.
      Operating cost savings.
      Insurance savings.
      Additional vehicle savings.
      Parking cost savings.
  Time savings to motorists not using transit (nondiverted auto
    drivers and riders).
  Benefits to the business community.
      Time savings to the trucking industry.
      Parking facility savings to suburban employers.
  Other benefits
      Savings from termination of present bus system.
      Highway accident savings.

Source: Development Research Associates, "Benefits to the Atlanta Metropolitan Area from the Proposed Regional Transportation Program" (Metropolitan Atlanta Transit Authority, 1971), p. 2.

---

[18] Development Research Associates, "Benefits to the Atlanta Metropolitan Area from the Proposed Regional Transportation Program" (Metropolitan Atlanta Rapid Transit Authority, 1971).

values of the quantifiable benefits are shown in Table 3–2 under the assumptions that the value of time of commuters would average $2.75 per hour from 1971 through 2020. Benefits of future periods should be discounted at 6 percent. Table 3–2 shows that more than one quarter of the value of benefits is in the form of expected time saved by highway users making no direct use of the rapid transit system (an example of a project's external benefits). The second largest category of benefits is the expected decrease in costs of highway accidents due to reduced congestion. These examples show that estimation of indirect benefits often has a major role in a benefit-cost study.

Part A of Table 3–3 shows the sensitivity of estimated benefits to changes in prices (in this example, prices of time saved) and to changes in discount rates. A doubling of the discount rate reduces the value of benefits by more than half. Part B of Table 3–3 is the estimate of the present value of the projected future costs of the system, and Part C shows benefit-cost ratios resulting from various combinations of prices of time saved and discount rates. The ratios vary from 1.85 to 4.19.

The second example of a benefit-cost study is an analysis of investment in human capital—an Upward Bound program.[19] This program attempted to identify "high school students who would be unlikely to go on to college because of poverty or because of low perceptions of probable success associated with race or socioeconomic status."[20] The program,

Table 3–2
Monetary values of the quantifiable benefits of the proposed Marta System (Cumulative benefits by 2020, discounted to constant dollars)

Constant transit commuters	$ 321,650,000
Diverted motorists	
Time savings	219,770,000
Operating costs savings	217,930,000
Insurance cost savings	22,540,000
Additional vehicle savings	160,170,000
Parking cost savings	103,840,000
Nondiverted commuters	1,052,990,000
Business community	
Time savings to trucking industry	685,040,000
Parking facilities savings to employers	7,990,000
Other benefits	
Termination of present bus system savings	58,000,000
Highway accident savings	745,410,000
Total	$3,595,330,000

Source: Development Research Associates, "Benefits to the Atlanta Metropolitan Area from the Proposed Regional Transportation Program," (Metropolitan Atlanta Rapid Transit Authority, 1971), p. 36.

---

[19] Walter I. Garms, "A Benefit-Cost Analysis of the Upward Bound Program," *Journal of Human Resources,* Spring 1971, pp. 206–20.

[20] Ibid., p. 206.

Table 3–3
Benefits-costs analysis, proposed Marta System

A. Total quantified benefits:

Discount rate (percent)	Value of time in 1971 ($ millions)		
	$2.25	$2.75	$3.25
4%	$5,496.48	$5,989.75	$6,555.62
6	3,305.44	3,595.33	3,885.23
8	2,105.43	2,286.37	2,467.30

B. Present-value total costs, 1971

Discount rate (percent)	Present value ($ millions)
4%	$1,566.0
6	1,325.0
8	1,139.0

C. Benefit-cost ratio under alternative assumptions

Discount rate (percent)	Value of commuter time		
	$2.25	$2.75	$3.25
4%	$3.51	$3.83	$4.19
6	2.50	2.71	2.93
8	1.85	2.01	2.18

Sources: Development Research Associates, "Benefits to the Atlanta Metropolitan Area from the Proposed Regional Transportation Program" (Metropolitan Atlanta Regional Transit Authority, 1971), pp. 36, 38, and 40.

operated by the U.S. Department of Education, consisted of enrolling such students in local colleges during summers after their sophomore year in high school, so as to introduce them "to skills and attitudes that are helpful in college and to remedy those subject matter areas in which the student is weak."[21] Stipends were paid to the participants.

The estimated internal benefits and costs (that is, benefits and costs to the participants in the program) are shown for two rates of discount in Table 3–4 for students of different sexes and races. The principal benefit was the expected increase in lifetime earnings after having attended college. It was not necessary to include foregone earnings as a cost, since the benefits were estimated as of age 16. Estimated benefit-cost ratios for participants varied from 1.49 (nonwhite males and a 10 percent discount rate) to 10.18 (nonwhite females and a 5 percent discount rate).

The above analysis of Upward Bound is based on internal benefits and costs alone. Table 3–5 shows an analysis that also includes costs borne by persons who were not participants in the program. From the larger point of view, the program was not a clear-cut success. Although benefit-

---

[21] Ibid.

Table 3–4
Benefits and costs from the individual's viewpoint*

	White		Nonwhite	
Discount rate 5 percent	**Male**	**Female**	**Male**	**Female**
Benefits:				
Lifetime income differentials				
(after taxes)†	$5,209	$3,549	$3,943	$5,843
Upward Bound stipend‡	210	209	224	224
Scholarships and grants§	454	394	683	498
Total benefits	$5,873	$4,152	$4,850	$6,565
Cost differentials‖:				
Tuition#	370	319	537	378
Extra living costs**	260	225	379	267
Total costs	$ 630	$ 544	$ 916	$ 645
Net benefits:	$5,243	$3,608	$3,934	$5,920
Discount rate 10 percent				
Benefits:				
Lifetime income differentials				
(after taxes)†	$ 770	$1,152	$ 354	$1,902
Upward Bound stipend‡	202	201	214	214
Scholarships and grants§	373	324	561	410
Total benefits	$1,345	$1,677	$1,129	$2,526
Cost differentials‖:				
Tuition#	308	264	446	314
Extra living costs**	215	185	312	220
Total costs	$ 523	$ 449	$ 758	$ 534
Net benefits:	$ 822	$1,228	$ 371	$1,992

* All figures shown as present value at age 16, the approximate age at which a decision is made to include a student in Upward Bound.

† Differentials are calculated by multiplying the proportion of Upward Bound students in each educational category by the present value of lifetime income for that category, and summing over all four categories. The same is done for siblings, and the difference between those figures is the raw differential. The raw differential is reduced by 25 percent on the assumption that only 75 percent of income differentials are caused by education.

‡ Stipends averaged $45.36 per month during the summer and $5.60 per month during the school year. For the whole program, stipends ranged from $218 for white females to $233 for nonwhite females. Figures shown are present values of these amounts.

§ Scholarships and grants ranged from $739 to $793 per year for Upward Bound students and were assumed to be identical for siblings. Differentials shown arise because of differential rates of college attendance between Upward Bound students and siblings.

‖ Because present values are computed at age 16, the income series automatically shows foregone income as a reduction in benefits, and it is not included separately as a cost. This is also true of the reduced receipts of unemployment and welfare payments by educated individuals.

Based on average 1968–69 tuition of $602 for all U.S. institutions.

** Assumes an average of $425 per year in extra living cost while in college.

It should be noted that the benefits of a higher education include advantages other than higher lifetime income.

Source: Walter I. Garms, "A Benefit-Cost Analysis of the Upward Bound Program," *Journal of Human Resources*, Spring 1971, p. 216.

Table 3–5
Benefits and costs from society's viewpoint*

	White		Nonwhite	
Discount rate 5 percent	**Male**	**Female**	**Male**	**Female**
Benefits:				
Lifetime income differentials (before taxes)†	$7,020	$4,777	$5,491	$7,942
Cost differentials‡:				
Upward Bound cost to the government§	$1,811	$1,798	$1,922	$1,919
Upward Bound cost to colleges‖	260	257	275	275
Cost of education#	1,057	872	1,424	1,028
Extra living costs**	260	225	379	267
Total costs	$3,388	$3,152	$4,000	$3,489
Net benefits:	$3,632	$1,625	$1,491	$4,453
Discount rate 10 percent				
Benefits:				
Lifetime income differentials (before taxes)†	$1,066	$1,560	$ 598	$2,609
Cost differentials‡:				
Upward Bound cost to the government§	$1,737	$1,724	$1,845	$1,842
Upward Bound cost to colleges‖	249	247	264	264
Cost of education#	852	724	1,183	856
Extra living costs**	215	185	312	220
Total costs	$3,053	$2,880	$3,604	$3,182
Net benefits:	− $1,987	− $1,320	− $3,006	− $ 573

* All figures are present values at age 16.
† Differentials are calculated as in Table 3–4, including the assumption that only 75 percent of differentials are caused by education, but excluding the reduction for taxes paid. The effect of decreased receipts of unemployment and welfare benefits by educated individuals has been removed because in the social context these are transfer payments.
‡ As in Table 3–4, foregone income is included in lifetime income differentials as a reduction in benefits.
§ Excludes cost of stipends paid students, which are transfer payments. Cost calculated from data furnished by OEO.
‖ Calculated from data furnished by OEO.
Based on total economic cost of education, estimated at $623 per pupil in high school and $1,470 per pupil in college.
** Extra living cost is estimated at $425 per year while in college.
Source: Walter I. Garms, "A Benefit-Cost Analysis of the Upward Bound Program," *Journal of Human Resources,* Spring 1971, p. 219.

cost ratios greater than one were calculated using a 5 percent rate of discount, benefits were less than costs when both were discounted at 10 percent.

Cost-effectiveness analysis

Cost evaluation is usually considerably easier than evaluation of benefits, since inputs are more often subject to pricing in the market than are public outputs. It is sometimes feasible to make explicit dollar comparisons among alternative programs only in terms of costs, thus bypassing the difficult problems of benefit estimation. If the programs to be compared are alternative ways of reaching the same objective, this procedure obviously yields useful results. The alternative that has lowest cost is judged most effective. Notice also that both explicit and implicit costs that are common to all alternatives can be disregarded in cost-effectiveness analysis.

This type of approach is commonly used in highway planning. A variety of alternate routes between origin and destination may result in similar benefits, and the major categories of benefits are time saving and safety improvements, both of which are difficult to evaluate in dollars. Common standards can be set in terms of average speeds, lives saved, and property damage avoided; comparison of alternatives can then be based only upon quantifiable costs.

Even in cases in which performance specifications of alternatives are not identical, comparison of costs may be useful in clarifying the issues involved in choice. For example, an increase in average speed of two miles per hour may be shown to be attainable on route A, which will cost $1 million more than alternate route B. These values can be combined with traffic projections to derive an estimate of the value that must be placed on each hour of time saved in order to justify the additional cost of route A. An example of an especially useful type of cost-effectiveness analysis is comparison of costs of public operation of garbage collection with costs of contracting with a private firm. Outputs (benefits) of the two modes of operation may be identical, so the relevant analysis is limited to the cost comparison. The method that costs the least is deemed to be cost effective.

Note that cost-effectiveness analysis cannot indicate the efficient level of a particular program, nor is this technique useful in choosing among programs with dissimilar benefits. Nonetheless, because it requires less information than benefit-cost analysis and is less demanding of the time and expertise of agency personnel, it has become a regular part of the planning process in most federal agencies and in many states and localities.

Appraisal of benefit-cost analysis

Users of the benefit-cost approach should be aware of both the strengths and weaknesses of the technique.[22] Perhaps the most important strength of benefit-cost analysis is its firm basis in economic theory.

---

[22] More complete evaluations of benefit-cost analysis are provided in Jesse Burkhead and Jerry Miner, *Public Expenditure* (Chicago: Aldine Publishing, 1971), pp. 246–49; and Alan Williams, "Cost-Benefit Analysis: Bastard Science? And/or Insidious Poison in the Body Politick?" *Journal of Political Economy*, August 1972, pp. 199–226.

It emanates from a consistent and well-defined set of principles. Second, the technique is systematic. Alternative projects are compared according to common assumptions about prices of benefits realized and inputs used. Finally, the emphasis upon measurement of outcomes tends to decrease the effects of preconceived notions and pure rhetoric upon the final decisions made.

Although the strengths of the benefit-cost approach are impressive, the weaknesses lay the technique open to several criticisms. One line of criticism attacks benefit-cost analysis on the pragmatic grounds that it is difficult to carry out. Determination of shadow prices and appropriate discount rates, specification of target populations, the importance of nonquantifiable benefits, price adjustments needed when there is unemployment or noncompetitive market structure, and the handling of uncertainty about outcomes are not standardized practices. The examples earlier in this chapter showed that results of benefit-cost studies may be quite sensitive to the assumptions and judgments that the analyst makes about these matters. Some observers have suggested that a reasonably imaginative analyst can produce positive benefits for any project without violating generally accepted practices.

A second line of criticism is that benefit and cost estimates are solemnly totaled and compared regardless of what individuals or groups stand to gain and what persons are expected to bear the costs. For example, a recreation area accessible mainly to higher-income families and designed to accommodate their motorized campers may outrank neighborhood playgrounds in ghetto areas. This is the result of dollar evaluations of benefits that depend upon the purchasing power of the beneficiaries as well as their relative preferences among goods and services. For completeness, benefit-cost studies should always be accompanied by studies of the incidence of benefits and costs upon various groups of people.

Another line of criticism is that a target population which is not also the funding population has a very strong incentive to make the benefit-cost ratio look better than it actually is. For example, a local project that will be funded primarily from federal tax dollars can have large local benefits in relation to local costs, even though the true overall benefit-cost ratio is negative. Local sponsors of a proposed project may exaggerate benefits and understate costs in order to establish a higher priority for federal funding.

A final criticism is that benefit-cost analysis is seldom applied to the problem of choosing the best level of programs. Choosing among whole programs on the basis of their benefit-cost ratios is based on comparisons of averages. It would be desirable to pay more attention to estimates of the marginal benefit-cost ratios for incremental changes in program sizes. Planning-programming-budgeting (PPB) is an attempt to apply incremental analysis across the total expenditure plans of a governmental unit, scaling the various programs up or down as indicated by comparisons of benefit-cost estimates for incremental changes. Zero-base budgeting is PPB with the added feature that whole programs must be justified from the ground up (in addition to being evaluated for incremental changes in program size), and consideration is given to the possible elimination of programs.

Multiple objectives and group decisions in the public sector

Most of this chapter's discussion of government decision making has dealt with the problems of increasing efficiency of resource use. Except for the brief consideration of intergroup equity in the preceding paragraph and in the first section of the chapter, one assumes here that all parties to any decision regard efficiency as the primary goal. In reality, efficiency may not be the only, or even the most important, concern, and it may not be fully compatible with other objectives. In fact, in government spending, it is often not considered at all.

A full listing of objectives perceived by public agencies would include: (1) efficient allocation of resources; (2) equitable distribution of costs and benefits; (3) prosperity, growth, and stability of the overall economy; (4) economic development of particular regions or sectors of the economy; and (5) the country's relations with other nations. The last three of the above goals are particularly important in the decision making of federal agencies.

There is often conflict among the first two of the above goals.[23] For example, consider the decisions related to energy policy. From a pure efficiency point of view, it might be desirable to allow all energy prices to rise as supply and demand conditions change. Yet such a policy would produce windfall gains for firms holding reserves of energy sources and would impose hardships upon consumers generally and upon low-income groups especially.

To understand how all five of the above goals enter into public decisions, consider the analysis of a federal program aimed at encouraging increased exploration for domestic sources of petroleum. A benefit-cost study would be aimed at answering whether federal dollars would generate more valuable benefits in this or some other use. However, even if net benefits are positive, some people may object that benefits accrue narrowly to producers and marketers of oil and to large oil consumers at the widely distributed expense of typical taxpayers. In addition, many people will have an interest in the impact of the employ-

---

[23] For an interesting essay on the choice between efficiency and equity, see Arthur M. Okun, *Equality and Efficiency, The Big Trade-off* (Washington, D.C.: The Brookings Institution, 1975).

ment-and-income-generating effects of the program. Still others will be interested in which regions of the country are helped most (and which, if any, are hurt). Finally, there will be concern for the effect of increased domestic oil capacity on national military preparedness, international political power, and the balance of international payments. Benefit-cost analysis alone is not suited to considering all these objectives at one time.

Conceptually, an optimal decision in the case of multiple goals requires that those goals be given explicit decision weights. Suppose, for example, that efficiency is measured in terms of net dollar benefits, equity in terms of the number of dollars transferred from those above the median family income to those below it, regional development as the dollar addition to the gross product of a region (e.g., the Southwest), and international affairs impact by net change in the domestic trade balance. If weights can be assigned according to the relative importance of each goal, and the weighted outcomes can be regarded as additive, it is possible to produce a single number with which to compare alternative programs. For example, one might have as the overall objective to maximize

$$0.4E + 0.3Q + 0.1R + 0.2I$$

where E stands for efficiency, Q for equity, R for regional development, and I for international affairs as measured above.

A somewhat more sophisticated and realistic procedure for dealing with problems of this type is given by goal programming. Goal programming is an extension of linear programming which allows the setting of target minimum values for each goal, with relative priorities specified among them. For example, goals for a program might be to achieve $5 million of priority net benefits, $2 million of redistribution, $1 million of regional development, and $2 million of improvement in the balance of payments. The priorities are then simply the relative importance of the targets in case they are not all simultaneously attainable. The advantage of this method is that the setting of target values may be easier or more politically feasible than explicit determination of relative weights of goals categories.

In the public agency, perhaps more so than in private business, the decision analyst must be aware that economic consequences will not entirely rule the final choice. The decision models described in this chapter handle economic variables imperfectly, and other variables—such as political costs—are not dealt with at all. Nevertheless, benefit-cost analysis and related techniques provide systematic organization of available economic information and some guide to the relative importance of information that is not yet at hand. The chapters that follow should put much of this information in perspective.

Summary

In general, an economy in which actions of private firms are determined by self-interest as regulated by competitive markets will use resources efficiently. Intervention by public agencies may be needed to prevent inefficiencies resulting from noncompetitive behavior and from externalities. The chapter dealt only with cases of externalities.

Externalities are costs imposed upon or benefits provided to third parties as the result of private producer and consumer behavior. From the social welfare point of view, activities that have external costs are overproduced and overconsumed. Activities that have external benefits are underproduced and underconsumed.

Where externalities are small in relation to private costs and benefits, the activities may well be left to the private sector; the externalities can be offset by imposing taxes on activities that have external costs and by providing subsidies to those that have external benefits. However, a good or service cannot be profitably produced by the private sector if nonpayers can receive the same benefits as payers; if they are to be available, such goods and services must be produced by public or nonprofit agencies.

The constituency of a public agency is much larger than that of a private firm. Decision making by a public agency should take into account the interests of all individuals and groups that will be affected. Estimation of the values of public agency outputs may be more difficult than for products and services of private firms, since many of these outputs are provided to users at zero prices or at prices well below average cost. Nevertheless, public agency managers should attempt to maximize public profit (net social benefit). They should expand public activities only so long as the marginal value of social benefits is greater than the marginal social cost.

Steps in benefit estimation include: (1) enumeration of specific ways in which various groups are benefited, (2) estimation of monetary values of total tangible benefits (in the case of proposed new programs) or of incremental tangible benefits (in the case of evaluation of expansion or contraction of ongoing programs), and (3) enumeration of any intangible benefits, such as beautification or prestige. Direct estimation of monetary values can be carried out only for goods and services sold at prices reflecting their value in marginal applications. Indirect estimation techniques must be used for unpriced goods and services; these techniques include: (1) observation of changes in land values affected by public programs, (2) use of prices of close substitutes produced in the private sector, and (3) estimates of reductions in private cost resulting from the public programs.

Costs of public production are estimated in essentially the same ways as in the private sector. However, opportunity costs of resource services used by a public agency may be different from the explicit outlays in the agency's budget; the social cost of services of a monopoly-produced or government price-controlled resource may be well below prices paid by the agency. On the other hand, the agency may use some services of resources owned by the agency (or by other agencies) that have no budgeted agency cost but do have social opportunity costs.

Benefit-cost techniques are useful in analyzing public investment. The values of future benefits and costs are discounted, and the ratio of present value of benefit to present value of cost is formed. Marginal social opportunity costs of capital should be used in discounting. Assuming full employment and capacity production, the marginal social cost of capital is the marginal pretax return on total capital in the private sector. Marginal social cost of capital may be zero or close to zero in periods of considerable unemployment and excess capacity.

CASES

Applications in not-for-profit operations

Government's role in cost-benefit analysis: The profit and the not-for-profit situation[1]

It is too early in the text to expect serious application of the numerous concepts touched upon in this and the two preceding chapters. In fact, the temptation was great to place this chapter as the final one in the book. To do so would have allowed each student an opportunity to achieve some greater degree of familiarity with the techniques of analysis presented in the text. In addition, it would have allowed the author to present a cost-benefit case at this point. However, the chapter might not have been read with the same interest and intensity it receives in this seemingly illogical location.

This "Little Red Hen" material is presented as a humorous, almost flippant case. It is intended, and may be used at the professor's option, to generate serious classroom discussion concerning, generally, the extent to which government involvement in economic matters is helpful or harmful in the short- or long-run (The Time Perspective), the impact it has on interest rates (The Discounting Principle), the contribution it makes to proper allocation of scarce and costly resources (The Equimarginal Principle), and the pricing structure it pursues (The Incremental Concept and The Contribution Concept).

When the case and classroom discussion of it is concluded, the student should look for tools and techniques in subsequent chapters that are applicable to innumerable government and not-for-profit operations.

---

[1] Not completely original with the author; initial source unknown.

A little red hen scratched about the barnyard until she uncovered some grains of wheat. She called her neighbors and said, "If we plant this wheat, we shall have bread to eat. Who will help me plant it?"

"Not I," said the cow.

"Not I," said the duck.

"Not I," said the pig.

"Not I," said the goose.

"Then I will," said the little red hen, and she did. The wheat grew tall and ripened into golden grain.

"Who will help me reap my wheat?" asked the little red hen.

"Not I," said the duck.

"Out of my classification," said the pig. "You are trying to get me into trouble. You know I am on Social Security and not allowed to work."

"I'd lose my seniority," said the cow.

"I'd lose my unemployment compensation," said the goose.

"Then I will," said the little red hen, and she did.

At last, it came time to bake the bread. "Who will help me bake the bread?" asked the little red hen.

"That would be overtime for me," said the cow.

"I'd lose my welfare benefits," said the duck.

"I'm a dropout and never learned how," laughed the pig.

"If I'm to be the only helper, that's discrimination," said the goose.

"Then I will," said the little red hen. She baked five loaves and held them up for her neighbors to see.

They all wanted some—in fact, demanded a free share. But the little red hen said, "No, I can keep the five loaves myself, or I can give you a loaf in exchange for something of value."

"The duck simply quacked. The goose grunted. "Unfair" picket signs were painted and the malcontents marched around shouting obscenities.

The government agent came and said to the little red hen. "You have so much more than any of the others. You don't want to be a troublemaker. You don't want to be greedy. You must give some of your loaves to me." In addition, "you must report to me each time you bake an additional loaf."

"But I earned my bread," pleaded the little red hen.

"Sure," said the agent. "The wonderful free-enterprise system allowed it. As with the others, you are free here. Anyone in the barnyard can earn as much as he wants. But, under government regulations, the productive workers must divide their product with the idle."

And they lived happily ever after. But the little red hen's neighbors wondered why she never again baked bread.

What would you tell the little red hen?

The not-for-profit sector: Pricing problems

Education.   Pricing problems are not confined to the private sector of the domestic American economy. Much economic activity undertaken in a mixed capitalistic society is conducted by some segment of the federal, state, or local government or by not-for-profit corporations. For everything a business unit buys, a price must be paid; for most things sold, a price is received. This price is often expressed as a cost. A public or not-for-profit private school district having 5,590 students and a total operating budget of $6,900,000, for example, has a cost per student of $1,234.35 per year. This cost, in effect, is the price per student enrolled in the district. This price must be paid if the district is to survive in the long run.[1]

The alleged wastes of a monopolist do not disappear simply because the firm is located in the not-for-profit as opposed to the private sector. The monopolist in education, for example, charges a price higher than would be charged if some competition existed; in addition, it serves a smaller number of students.[2]

The examples cited here are in terms of education, but numerous other examples could be cited. The U.S. Post Office could be used for illustrative purposes. The U.S. Post Office monopolizes the price and distribution of all first-class mail in the United States. Were it not for its monopolist structure, the real price of a first-class postage stamp could be expected to decrease, and the volume of mail moved and the speed at which it is moved could be expected to increase. As with monopolists in the private sector, the Post Office wastes and otherwise misallocates resources.

Via taxation, households and businesses have paid the price of generating a large number of school teachers. These teachers are resource inputs for the educational system. The structure of the not-for-profit educational system is such that the taxpayer subsidizes the public teacher-education colleges. (This subsidy may be considered necessary when teachers are in short supply.) The educational system continues the subsidy by passing bond levies after the teacher is graduated. (The bulk of all school money generated by operating levies is used to pay teachers.) When a public university uses public money to produce a product for which there is little demand, is this expenditure an appropriate allocation of tax revenues?

Formal schooling today at the elementary and secondary level is paid almost entirely by governmental units. Has the government nationalized the largest industry in the United States, education? Has the quality of the U.S. educational program(s) been changing in direct proportion to

---

[1] These costs are synonymous with price and if collected from students on an individual basis could as easily be called tuition.

[2] Average costs (price) per student tend to increase as the student population decreases. Two reasons for this development may be: (*a*) A relatively large percentage of total costs incurred by a public school district are fixed in nature, and (*b*) in spite of the serious oversupply of elementary and secondary school teachers, teacher's unions have been able to gain and then maintain salary increases. Often these increases exceed average annual rates of inflation as revealed by changes in the consumer price index.

this governmental intervention?[3] Simultaneously, have educational prices (costs) risen?

The quality of many programs declines in direct proportion to the degree of governmental involvement in these programs. The areas of national defense, water and air pollution control, regulation of some public utilities and other natural monopolies notwithstanding, is there justification for governmental intervention into the affairs of private households and businesses within the domestic American economy?

On the one hand, through establishment of the Justice Department and its antitrust division, the government is opposed to monopolization. But, in the area of education, government has allowed a near monopoly to be created. The desirability of such monopolization is something that is not questioned often.

Can you build a case to reveal how prices (costs) per pupil would decline and the quality of education rise if the government would loosen its authority over the educational function?

The pricing of municipal services

Rapid transit   That unclear thinking exists in the public sector regarding the need for some public services to recover their costs (to earn a normal profit) becomes obvious when one reviews the price charged per ride on the rapid transit system in any of our larger cities. For example, assume the city of New York increases its subway fares at a time when New York is threatening to default on outstanding bond issues. The increase in price is expeditious and designed to increase cash flows to the city.

Precisely what concepts should be considered by transit authorities before the price (fare) increase goes into effect?

The price of garbage   The short- and long-run economic impact of a change in the price of one or more municipal service is too great to allow a price change to be undertaken in a whimsical manner for expeditious reasons. In addition to studying the cost and demand functions for the goods or services and considering whether peak-load pricing practices might alleviate the problem, a manager must look carefully at the rudiments of the problem. A creative, deep-thinking not-for-profit executive might be quick to see that a change in structure or business organization could lower the price (cost) of a service being provided while, simultaneously, increasing the quality of that service.

At least 1 billion pounds of solid waste is generated in the United States each day. To haul this waste away may cost the American people $6

---

[3] Make a list of the 10 best institutions of higher learning in the United States, however defined. How many state (government) schools are on your list?

billion annually. Approximately 75 percent of this cost could be allocated directly to the collection process. Although this collection of garbage is one of the major problems confronting American cities, it receives relatively little formal attention, and virtually no imagination has been applied to coping with it.

The general method of collection utilizes a three-person crew consisting of a driver and two collectors. Each collector takes one side of the street and fills a container before returning to the packer (garbage truck) to dump the container contents. The packer is driven slowly while collections are in process. The four main types of collection systems are (1) curb-side collection, (2) backyard collection, (3) refuse set-out system, and (4) alley collection. The collection method used depends largely on the physical layout of the city.

A University of California study states that most people prefer municipal collections to private garbage haulers; yet, they prefer a combination of private and municipal collection in cities having total populations of about 300,000 to 500,000 persons. In addition, households express a strong preference to one- or twice-a-week collections in the cities sampled. The sample questions assumed that municipal collection would be paid by the city out of its general fund, whereas private collections would be paid directly by the household using its service.[4]

Studies have shown that one-person crews are more efficient at curb-side collections than multiperson crews when route-person hours per ton is the criterion of efficiency. The U.S. Department of Health, Education, and Welfare states that units costs (prices) of a one-person crew are 25 to 35 percent less than those of two-person crews and 35 to 40 percent less than three-person crews. Multiperson crews use less equipment per person than one-person crews, but the resulting cost reduction is often offset by higher operating expenses, amortization, and labor costs attributable to multiperson crews. A reduction in size of the collecion crew results in increased efficiency of the operation.[5]

The price households and businesses should pay for garbage removal and the mechanism by which it should be paid are unresolved at this writing. Most large cities have huge numbers of municipal employees, hired for the express purpose of collecting the city's garbage. The operating expenditures for these sanitation service workers include wages, salaries, employee benefits, supplies and materials, debt service, repayments, contractual maintenance on personal and real property, garages, and mechanics. The total cost of garbage collection for a particular mu-

---

[4] The U.S. Department of Health, Education, and Welfare, "A Study of Solid Waste Collections Systems Comparing One-Man with Multi-Man Crews," Washington, D.C., 1969.

[5] Ibid.

nicipality could be calculated with relative ease. In addition, the approximate number of pickups per day and the subsequent cost per ton of garbage collected are statistics that could be made available for each city. The question then becomes: Can costs per ton of garbage collected by the municipality in question be reduced and the quality of the service improved by a change in structure?

PROBLEMS
Applications in not-for-profit operations

3–1   An activity that has external costs will be overproduced and overconsumed, whereas an activity that yields external benefits will be underproduced and underconsumed.'' Explain. What can be done to bring activities that have externalities closer to their socially optimal levels?

3–2   What are the distinguishing or unique characteristics of pure public goods?

3–3   What is a target population? How is specification of the target population helpful in a cost-benefit analysis?

3–4   Explain the difference between consumers' surplus and consumers' expenditure. How do these two concepts fit into the ideal evaluation of benefits from a program or project?

3–5   What is social cost? In what ways might social cost vary from the budgeted outlays for a program or project?

3–6   How could you determine whether a particular public program should be expanded or cut back?

3–7   What do penalties and subsidies have in common?

3–8   How could you determine the discount rate (or rates) that should be used in calculating present values of a program's future benefits and costs?

3–9   List the strengths and weaknesses of benefit-cost analysis.

Selected references

Adelman, M. A. ''The Two Faces of Economic Concentration.'' *The Public Interest* 21 (Fall 1970).

Allen, Robert D. "Meet the New Bell System." *Telephony* 201, no. 3 (July 1981), pp. 64, 69–70.

Austin, Douglas V. "The Evolution of Commercial Bank Merger Antitrust Law." *Business Lawyer* 36 (January 1981), pp. 297–396.

Brito, Dagobert L., and William H. Oakland. "On the Monopolistic Provision of Excludable Public Goods." *American Economic Review* 70, no. 4 (September 1980), pp. 691–704.

Brokaw, Alan J., and William E. Barstow. "Purchasing and the Antitrust Laws." *Journal of Purchasing & Materials Management* 15, no. 4 (Winter 1979), pp. 24–32.

Burns, Michael E., and Cliff Walsh. "Market Provision of Price-Excludable Public Goods: A General Analysis." *Journal of Political Economy* 89, no. 1 (February 1981), pp. 166–91.

Chang, Semoon. "Multiple-Listing Services: The Antitrust Issues." *Real Estate Law Journal* 10, no. 3 (Winter 1982), pp. 228–46.

Cole, Roland J., and Paul Sommers. "Business and Government Regulation: A Theory of Compliance Decisions." *Journal of Contemporary Business* 10, no. 1 (First Quarter 1981), pp. 143–53.

Cook, Peter. "Ottawa versus the Private Sector." *Executive* (Canada) 23, no. 6 (June 1981), pp. 38–39.

Coyne, Thomas J. "Financial Proposals for Alleviation of Price Inflation: A Beginning." *Carroll Business Bulletin* 21, no. 4 (1982), pp. 4–7.

———. "A Manufacturer's View of the Akron Metropolitan Area." *Akron Business and Economic Review* 10, no. 1 (1979), pp. 46–49.

Dewey, Donald. "Information, Entry, and Welfare: The Case for Collusion." *American Economic Review* 69, no. 4 (September 1979), pp. 587–94.

Edwards, R. D. "Interstate Banking: The Debate Begins." *Bankers Magazine* 163, no. 5 (September-October 1980), pp. 64–70.

Fox, Eleanor M. "From Antitrust to a Trust-In Business." *Across the Board* 18, no. 10 (November 1981), pp. 59–67.

Globerman, Steven. "Canada's Changing Merger Environment." *Antitrust Bulletin* 24, no. 3 (Fall 1979), pp. 519–33.

Hay, George A. "Whither Antitrust?" *Cornell Executive* 8, no. 3 (Summer 1982), pp. 12–15.

Heien, Dale. "The Cost of the U.S. Dairy Price Support Program: 1949–74." *The Review of Economics and Statistics* 59, no. 1 (February 1977), pp. 1–8.

Hibner, Don T., Jr. "Antitrust Compliance." *Credit & Financial Management* 81, no. 4 (April 1979), pp. 30–31, 40.

Johnson, M. H., and J. T. Bennett. "Increasing Resource Scarcity: Further Evidence. *Quarterly Review of Economics & Business* 20, no. 1 (Spring 1980), pp. 42–48.

Kohlhepp, Daniel B., and Charles A. Ingene. "The Effect of Municipal Services and Local Taxes on Housing Values." *AREUEA Journal* 7, no. 3 (Fall 1979), pp. 318–43.

Lovell, Michael C. "Are Treble Damages Double Damages?" *Journal of Economics & Business* 34, no. 3 (1982), pp. 263–68.

Mann, Richard A., and Barry S. Roberts. "Comment: The Overlooked Effect of Antitrust Law Upon Small Business." *Business Law Review* 13, no. 2 (Winter 1980–81), pp. 33–39.

Mishan, Ezra J. "The Postwar Literature on Externalities: An Interpretative Essay." *Journal of Economic Literature* (March 1971).

Newhouse, Joseph D. "Toward a Theory of Nonprofit Institutions: An Economic Model of a Hospital." *American Economic Review* 60 (March 1970).

Paul, Chris W., II. "Competition in the Medical Profession: An Application of the Economic Theory of Regulation." *Southern Economic Journal* 48, no. 3 (January 1982), pp. 559–69.

Ragan, James F., Jr. "Minimum Wages and the Youth Labor Market." *The Review of Economics and Statistics* 59, no. 2 (May 1977), pp. 129–36.

Rider, K. L. "The Economics of the Distribution of Municipal Fire Protection Services." *The Review of Economics & Statistics* 61, no. 2 (May 1979), pp. 249–58.

Schelling, Thomas C. "On the Ecology of Micromotives." *The Public Interest* 25 (Fall 1971).

Schmalensee, Richard. "Another Look at Market Power." *Harvard Law Review* 95, no. 8 (June 1982), pp. 1789–816

Smith, Vernon L. "Experiments with a Decentralized Mechanism for Public Good Decisions." *American Economic Review* 70, no. 4 (September 1979), pp. 584–99.

Stanbury, W. T. and G. B. Reschenthaler. "Reforming Canadian Competition Policy: Once More into the Breach." *Canadian Business Law Journal* 5, no. 4 (September 1981), pp. 381–437.

"The State Enterprises Can't Simply Be Handed over." *Euromoney* (UK, Turkey Supplement, February 1982).

Waldman, Don E. "Economic Benefits in the IBM, AT&T, and Xerox Cases: Government Antitrust Policy in the '70s." *Antitrust Law & Economics Review* 12, no. 2 (1980), pp. 75–92.

Wetzel, James N. "Congestion and Economic Valuation: A Reconsideration." *Journal of Environmental Economics & Management* 8, no. 2 (June 1981), pp. 192–95.

White, Lawrence J. "Vertical Restraints in Antitrust Law: A Coherent Model." *Antitrust Bulletin* 26, no. 2 (Summer 1981), pp. 327–45.

2

Demand

CHAPTER

4

Demand theory

An understanding of demand for a firm's product requires identification of those factors that determine or influence sales volume. After a firm defines as precisely as possible why its product is selling at current levels, it is in a better position to consider what might be done to cause changes in demand. Alterations may be feasible in production functions, cost schedules, prices, advertising, and/or other variables. These adjustments may allow profits to increase.

Economists study demand because it is the basis upon which all other decisions are made. Why should anyone invest time, effort, and money in manufacturing Chrysler Newports, for example, if there is no demand for them? A firm needs to describe the factors that cause households, government, or businesses to desire a particular product. An understanding of the theory of demand is helpful in this regard.

Demand theory is one of the manager's essential tools in short- and long-range planning. Prospective growth of demand in various market areas is taken into account in choosing sizes and locations of new plants. If demand is expected to fluctuate, plants with flexible design (but higher average unit costs at the most likely rate of output) may be desirable. Considerable capital may be needed to carry inventories of finished goods. If demand is sufficiently responsive to advertising, heavy investment in market development may be justified.

Demand considerations affect day-to-day financial, production, and marketing management. Sales forecasts provide some of the key assumptions used in projecting cash flows and net incomes by periods. Demand expectations affect production scheduling and inventory planning. Probable reactions of competitors and customers are taken into account before changes in prices, advertising, or product design. Managers can and should make good use of the concepts and techniques of demand theory.

Law of demand

A fundamental concept in the study of economics is the law of demand. This law describes the relationship that exists at a particular time between the dependent and independent variables. It explains the inverse relationship between price per unit and quantity demanded of a product. As price declines, quantity demanded increases.

If price declines for product A, apples, quantity demanded of apples will increase, but demand may decrease for product B, bananas. The law of demand often implies substitutability between products.

To some people, demand means one quantity sold or to be sold. For example, one often hears an expression such as this: "The demand for domestically made automobiles may be 7.25 million in the coming year." To the economist, however, demand is a specific relationship of various quantities per period to such variables as price, consumer incomes, prices of substitutes, expected future conditions, season, and availability of credit, to name a few.

Demand quantities are rates; that is, amounts per unit of time. Demand relationships can be estimated for whole industries or for single firms. The basic concepts in this section are applicable to either type of demand, industry or firm.

The law of demand can be explained graphically as a line, curve, or function. This curve describes a relationship between the price of a good or service and the quantity demanded of that item. It is traditional to express the demand curve for a product on a two-dimensional graph in a manner similar to Figure 4–1. This curve also represents the average

Figure 4–1
Demand curve

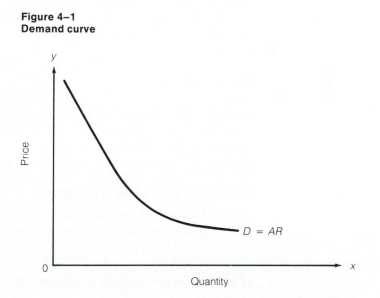

Figure 4–2
Change in quantity demanded

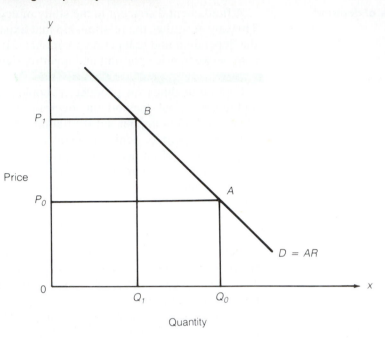

revenue function for the product. The demand curve generally slopes downward and to the right; its slope is negative because quantity demanded, x, increases if price, y, decreases.

A change in quantity demanded refers to movement along an existing demand curve from, say, some point A to a point B as depicted in Figure 4–2. Movement from A to B causes quantity demanded to decline from Q_0 to Q_1 as price climbs from P_0 to P_1. Note: If the product is sold, total revenue is price times quantity demanded. But one does not know from Figure 4–2 whether total revenue increases or decreases because (1) the elasticity of the demand curve has not been identified, and (2) neither the x nor the y axis has been expressed in units. All that can be stated with certainty from Figure 4–2 is that quantity demanded declines as price rises.

Quantitative expressions of demand

Knowledge about demand can be expressed in several ways. At the most abstract level, the functional relationship can be stated:

$$Q = (X_1, X_2, X_3 \ldots X_n)$$

in which Q is the quantity purchasers are willing to buy, and the Xs are the influences on Q. The Q in such an equation represents the quantity per unit of time (such as a week or year) of a particular product (baby shoes or all shoes) in a particular market (Boston or the United States), and the Xs represent values of the specified influences (price, advertising, credit availability, and other factors).

For decision making, the manager needs quantified estimates of the relationships of quantity to each of the other variables. A demand equation is a convenient way to express quantified relationships. An example is:

$$Q = b_0 - b_1 P + b_2 A + e$$

in which

Q is quantity and is the dependent variable.

P (price) and A (advertising) are independent variables.

b_0, b_1, and b_2 are symbols for the parameters to be estimated. For example, b is the change in sales for each dollar change in price.

e is error, assumed to be normally and independently distributed with a mean of zero and constant variance.

The above example assumes linear relationships of Q to the independent variables. Although the underlying relationships are usually believed to be curvilinear, linear approximations may be satisfactory over the limited range of available data and expected future experience.

A frequently used curvilinear model of demand has the form:

$$Q = b_0 P^{b_1} A^{b_2} e$$

in which the variables and parameters are as defined above.

The second equation assumes that the marginal effects of each variable are not constant but rather are dependent upon the value of that variable and of all other influences represented in the demand equation. An equation of the second form has constant elasticities; these elasticities are the exponents of the variables. The equation transforms to become linear in logarithms; the transformation is

$$\log Q = \log b_0 + b_1 \log P + b_2 \log A + e$$

Quantified demand relationships can also be presented in the form of demand schedules, which are tables showing the associated values of quantity and the variables that influence quantity. Table 4–1 is a demand schedule that illustrates some assumed relationships of quantities to two variables, price and income. Demand schedules are specific only at selected points on the demand function, and they become unwieldy if effects of three or more influences upon quantities are to be handled.

Table 4–1
Demand schedule

	Units per month by income (dollars per year)		
Price	$2,400	$3,000	$3,600
$10	100	125	150
9	120	150	180
8	150	187	224
7	200	250	300
6	260	325	390
5	340	425	510

The information in Table 4–1 could be represented in the form of a graph, a depiction of the relation of quantity to one, or at most two, of the influences, as in Figure 4–3. Graphs are useful when attention is focused upon just one relationship, especially the important relation of quantity to price. Each price-quantity relationship is called a demand curve and shows the various quantities that would be demanded at alternative prices, with other influences held constant. Figure 4–3 represents the effect of changes in income by shifts in the position of the price-quantity curve.

Demand curves are usually drawn with price on the vertical axis, as if

Figure 4–3
A family of demand curves

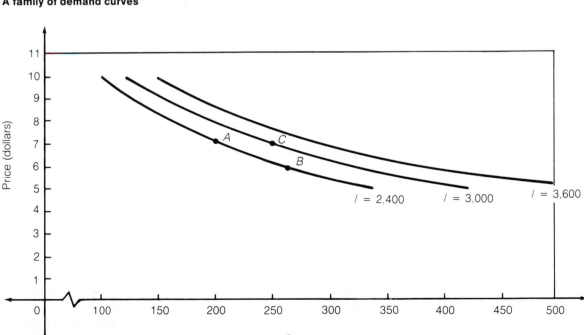

Quantity per month

price, rather than quantity, were the dependent variable in the relationship. In some instances, price is actually a function of quantity. For example, the wheat harvest quantity in a given year depends upon weather during the spring and summer as well as upon acreage planted. The harvest must then clear the market at whatever price it will bring.

In other industries, such as automobile manufacturing, it appears that prices are set by producers, leaving quantities to be determined by prices and other market forces. In such cases quantity is the dependent variable. In statistical estimation of demand, it is of some importance to have the correct variable specified in the dependent position of the demand equation.

Changes in demand

There is an important distinction between quantity change due to price being different and quantity change due to a shift of the demand curve. This distinction is illustrated in Figure 4–3. The quantity increase from point *A* to point *B* is entirely the result of a price reduction; it is movement along a demand curve similar to what we saw in Figure 4–2. On the other hand, the quantity increase from point *A* to point *C* is entirely attributed to the effect of a change in income; it is the result of a shift in demand. Influences other than price are conceived as demand curve shifters—forces that move the price-quantity relationship left or right. "Changes in demand" means such shifts of demand curves.

If demand is a function of price, $D = f(p)$, changes in quantity demanded are brought about by changes in price only; changes in demand are brought about by changes in factors other than changes in price of the product.

Determinants of demand

If changes in quantity demanded are caused by changes in price, and changes in demand are caused by factors other than price, what are these factors? Changes in quantity demanded refer to movement along a curve. Changes in demand refer to a shifting of the curve. Changes in demand for consumer products are thought to be related to (1) changes in wages, salaries, and supplements plus changes in rental income and/or interest income, if any; (2) changes in the size of the total population; (3) changes in government rules, regulations, policies, and procedures concerning products they consider to be harmful, illegal, and so on; (4) changes in the kinds and types of products that appeal to households.

Changes in demand on the part of business and government buyers are affected by all factors mentioned here plus changes in corporate and/or unincorporated business profits.

This chapter on the theory of demand establishes the groundwork necessary for presentation of demand estimation techniques in the chapter that follows. Demand theory is important, and much time and effort should be devoted to its description and analysis. Yet, one must remember to consider demand only in connection with supply.

Normal goods

Generally speaking, the demand for most goods and services within the aggregate economy increases as income increases, as depicted in Figure 4–3. If income is defined as disposable personal income, the demand for a good or service is said to be normal if greater quantities of the product are sold as disposable personal income increases.

Over the course of a business cycle, the demand for a particular good manufactured by a corporation might rise at increasing rates and/or actually fall a little. The business economist of that firm should make some effort to relate changes in income to changes in demand for all major products of the corporation. By doing so, she/he may be able to identify rather early—before expensive new capital equipment is acquired and major expansion of existing capacity is undertaken—those products for which demand decreases when income increases. Products whose demand functions decrease when income(s) increases are thought to be inferior goods. If an economy prospers and incomes rise, the consumer will discontinue purchasing inferior goods in the long run. Aggregate demand and long-run profitability of the product can be expected to decline for inferior goods.

Inferior goods

An inferior good, by definition, is one for which demand decreases relative to income increases. Demand for such a good may at times be increasing but doing so at rates less rapid than increases in income. Examples of inferior goods include such things as potatoes and small apartments. As incomes rise households consume fewer potatoes than had been the case when their incomes were relatively low. Also, as incomes rise people tend to move out of small apartments into larger private residences. If income rises and the demand for large autos declines, full-size Chryslers, Buicks, and so on should be considered as inferior goods (despite the improved quality of American product construction).

Elasticity of demand   Elasticity is a relative measure of the responsiveness of changes in quantity demanded, the dependent variable, to changes in price, the independent variable. Use of the concept in business, labor, and government enables one to determine the sensitivity of changes in quantity demanded to changes in price. Application of the concept is possible after calculation of an elasticity coefficient.

The degree of elasticity for a product is influenced heavily by a number of factors. Generally speaking, the elasticity of demand coefficient increases: (1) if the product represents a relatively large percentage of the total budget, (2) if purchase of the product can be postponed (most luxury goods fall into this category), or (3) if the product is one for which numerous substitutes exist.

Elasticity can be calculated as an average value over some range of the demand function, in which case it is called arc elasticity; or it can be calculated for a point on the demand function, so as to be called point elasticity. To determine arc elasticity, we need price and quantity values corresponding to the end points of the range. Often these end points consist of a present price-quantity combination and an estimate of the quantity that could be sold at a higher or lower price.

Here is the formula for calculating arc elasticity:

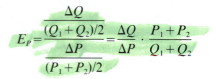

$$E_P = \frac{\dfrac{\Delta Q}{(Q_1+Q_2)/2}}{\dfrac{\Delta P}{(P_1+P_2)/2}} = \frac{\Delta Q}{\Delta P} \cdot \frac{P_1+P_2}{Q_1+Q_2}$$

in which

E_P is arc elasticity of quantity with respect to price.
P_1 and Q_1 are the original price and quantity.
P_2 and Q_2 are the final price and quantity.
ΔP is the change in price, observing sign of the change.
ΔQ is the change in quantity, observing sign of the change.

Note that the signs of ΔP and ΔQ are usually opposite, so that the calculated value for elasticity usually has a negative sign.

The demand relationship of Table 4–1 may be used to illustrate how to compute arc price elasticity. Suppose income is constant at $3,000 per year, present price is $10, and present quantity is 125 units per month. At a lower price of $9, a greater quantity of 150 units per month is expected. What is the arc price elasticity over this range of the demand curve? Substituting values into the arc elasticity equation, we have:

$$E_P = \frac{25}{-\$1} \cdot \frac{\$10+\$9}{125+150} = -1.73$$

The calculated elasticity coefficient, -1.73, indicates that quantity expands 1.73 percent for each 1 percent of price reduction over the relevant range of the demand curve. The negative sign of the coefficient shows that quantity moves up if price moves down, and vice versa.

Figure 4–4 depicts the demand curve for teenage labor as a negatively

Figure 4–4
Equilibrium in factor market

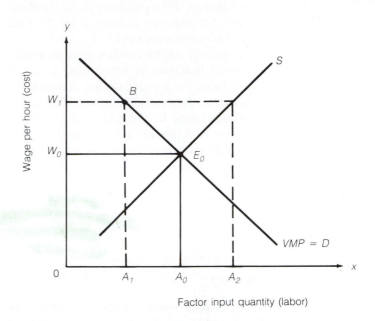

Factor input quantity (labor)

sloped downward and to the right function of changes in the price of
labor, wages. An average elasticity of demand coefficient over some
range of the downward-sloping demand curve may be calculated by using
an arc elasticity formula. An example of one of the more commonly used
formulas is as follows:

$$E_d = \frac{\dfrac{\Delta A}{A_1 + A_2}}{\dfrac{\Delta W}{W_0 + W_2}}$$

Assume the vertical axis (y) represents wage rates; the horizontal axis
(x), the quantity of labor demanded. W_0 in Figure 4–4 equals \$2; W_1 is
\$2.50. A_0 represents 15,000 teenagers; A_1 is 10,000 persons. The elasticity
of demand coefficient between E_0 and B on demand curve, D, could be
calculated as follows:[1]

---

[1] Application of the elasticity of demand formulation results in a negative coefficient.
However, this negative is often not revealed in economic studies. The negative sign is useful
if it reminds the user of the inverse relationship that exists between the price of a good or
service and the quantity demanded.

$$E_d = \frac{\dfrac{A_0 - A_1}{A_0 + A_1}}{\dfrac{W_0 - W_1}{W_0 + W_1}}$$

$$= \frac{\dfrac{15,000 - 10,000}{15,000 + 10,000}}{\dfrac{2.00 - 2.50}{2.00 + 2.50}}$$

$$= \frac{\dfrac{5,000}{25,000}}{\dfrac{-.50}{4.50}}$$

$$= \frac{.20}{-.11}$$

$$= -1.82$$

Elasticity of demand measures the sensitivity of the percentage changes in quantity demanded to percentage changes in price. Its interpretation is along the following lines: (1) if E_d is greater than one, the demand curve is said to be elastic; (2) if E_d is equal to one, demand is said to be unitary; and (3) if E_d is less than one, demand is said to be inelastic.

An elasticity of demand coefficient of -1.8 could be interpreted to mean that over the range of the demand curve studied a 1 percent increase in wages may be expected to be associated with a 1.8 percent decrease in the number of teenage workers hired; a 10 percent increase in wages would be associated with an 18 percent decrease in the quantity of labor demanded. Conversely, a 1 percent decrease in wages would be expected to bring about a 1.8 percent increase in the number of teenage persons employed; a 10 percent decrease in wage rates would be expected to bring about an 18 percent increase in the number of such workers hired.

Point price elasticity

The responsiveness of quantity demanded to price can be determined for a point on the demand function if the slope of the function is known. If the changes in price and quantity are made smaller and smaller, at the limit, $\Delta Q/\Delta P$ becomes $\partial Q/\partial P$, the partial derivative of the demand equation with respect to price.

Use the partial derivative to calculate elasticity by the formula for point elasticity:

$$e_P = \frac{\partial Q}{\partial P} \cdot \frac{P}{Q}$$ (4–1)

in which

e_p is point elasticity of quantity with respect to price.
P and Q are price and quantity at any point we choose.[2]

To demonstrate how to calculate point elasticity, use an equation relating the number of passengers per year on a rapid-transit system to the fare charges. The equation, from an actual study, is:

$$Q = 2,207 - 52.4P$$ (4–2)

in which

Q = number of passengers per year in millions.
P = fare in cents.

The partial derivative of the function with respect to price is:

$$\frac{\partial Q}{\partial P} = -52.4$$

To calculate elasticity at a student-subsidized price of 10 cents, for which the quantity is 1,683 (millions), substitute values into Equation (4–1):

$$e_p = -52.4 \cdot \frac{10}{1,683} = -0.3113$$ (4–3)

The elasticity coefficient of -0.31 says that passenger traffic would decrease by 0.31 percent for each increase of 1 percent in fares. Here one is dealing with a straight-line demand function, and the elasticity would be different at any other point on the function. For example, at an assumed subsidized price of 15 cents, for which quantity is 1,421 (millions), one obtains by substituting values into Equation (4–1):

$$e_p = -52.4 \cdot \frac{15}{1,421} = -0.5531$$

---

[2] Many functions are defined for a single independent variable, but more often than not, two or more independent variables are required to define a particular function. In such a situation, if all variables are held constant except one and that one is allowed to vary, the rate of change in the dependent variable is the same as the rate of change in this single variable. The value produced by this calculation is called the partial derivative. This function may be generalized as follows; for example, let price (p) depend upon cost (c), time (t), and market structure (s).

$$dp = \frac{\partial p}{\partial c}dc + \frac{\partial p}{\partial t}dt + \frac{\partial p}{\partial s}ds + \ldots$$

It is the partial derivative that is used in point price elasticity of demand calculations.

From the examples above, it should be clear that slope and elasticity are not the same thing. Slope does enter into the determination of elasticity. The ratio dQ/dP is the reciprocal of the slope of the demand curve, dP/dQ. However, the ratio P/Q also enters the calculation of elasticity as a multiplier, and this ratio falls steadily as we move down and to the right on a straight-line, constant-slope demand curve. Thus, the absolute value of the elasticity coefficient becomes smaller and smaller as price falls, point by point, on a straight-line curve.

Marginal revenue is the rate of change in total revenue as output changes by one unit. When depicted on a two-dimensional graph with price expressed on the y, or vertical axis, and quantity on the x, or horizontal axis, the marginal revenue function is lower than the demand or average revenue function for all units produced except the first. In order to increase quantity sold, price must be lowered. Therefore, the marginal revenue of the additional units must be lower than their price. A formula for determination of marginal revenue at some point on the curve is:

$$MR = \frac{dR}{dQ}$$

where the dR with respect to dQ is the first derivative of the total revenue function.

For all market structures other than purely competitive ones, marginal revenue will be less than average revenue because $\dfrac{\partial P}{\partial Q} < 0$; marginal revenue must be less than price.[3]

Marginal revenue may be calculated also by:

$$MR = p(1 - \frac{1}{E_d})$$

where

MR = Marginal revenue.
p = The price per unit of output.
E_d = The price elasticity of demand for the product.

A typical linear marginal revenue curve and its position with respect to the demand curve may be as depicted in Figure 4–5.

---

[3] Inasmuch as $\dfrac{dP}{dQ}$ equals zero for a purely competitive product market, the marginal revenue curve is equal to the average revenue curve and also equals the price curve and the demand curve. There is more on this subject later.

Figure 4–5
Marginal revenue curve, imperfect competition

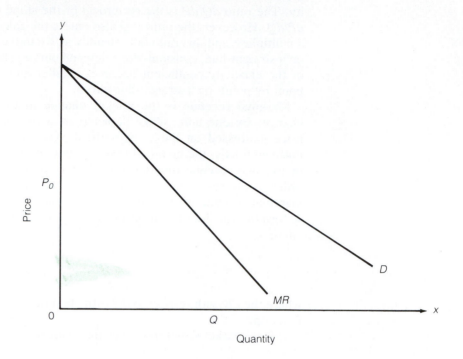

Relationship of marginal revenue to price and elasticity

Marginal revenue is, roughly, the addition to revenue by the last unit added to sales quantity. In precise terms, marginal revenue is the ratio of increase in revenue to increase in quantity, and it has meaning in terms of a point on the demand function as well as in terms of a discrete change in quantity. Managers need to know the value of marginal revenue when making decisions about price and rates of output.

Consider the relation of marginal revenue to price for the case of a demand curve that slopes down and to the right as in Figure 4–5. Price must be reduced as quantity per period is increased. In this circumstance, marginal revenue must be less than revenue received from the last unit added to sales. Revenue received from the last unit is, of course, the price per unit. The explanation of the difference between price and marginal revenue is simple: In adding the last unit to sales quantity Q, the firm accepts a reduction in price that applies to all units in sales quantity $Q - 1$.

Marginal revenue can be calculated for a one-unit increase up to quantity Q by the following formula:

$$MR = P - (|\triangle P| \cdot Q - 1) \qquad\qquad (4\text{--}4)$$

in which

MR = Marginal revenue.
P = Price at quantity Q.
$|\triangle P|$ = The absolute value of the small reduction in price resulting from adding one unit to quantity.

To illustrate the difference between price and marginal revenue, we shall use data points from demand Equation (4–2) and calculate marginal revenue at an assumed price of 10 cents, for which the quantity is 1,683 million passengers annually. The equation, restated in individual quantity units, is:

$$Q = 2,207,000,000 \text{ passengers} - 52,400,000 \cdot \text{Price in cents}$$

Reduction of price enough to increase Q by one unit would be 1/52,400,000 cent. By substituting values into the Equation (4–4), we ascertain:

MR for the one unit increase $= 10¢ - (1/52,400,000¢ \cdot 1,682,999,999)$
$\qquad\qquad\qquad\qquad\qquad = 10¢ - 32.1¢$
$\qquad\qquad\qquad\qquad\qquad = -22.1¢$

   In the above example, marginal revenue is negative; total revenue would be reduced by 22.1 cents for each passenger added to quantity through price reduction. A price cut as small as the one used in the example would not be feasible. But we know what we need to know. Any price reduction that is made, multiplied times initial quantity, will subtract more from total revenue than the corresponding addition to revenue, the added quantity multiplied by the final price.
   The following formula allows calculation of marginal revenue at a point if elasticity is known:

$$MR = P\left(1 + \frac{1}{e_p}\right)$$

With the aid of the above formula, let us again calculate marginal revenue for the transit system at the price of 10 cents, where elasticity was found to be -0.3113 in Equation (4–3). We obtain:

$$MR \text{ at the point} = 10¢\left(1 + \frac{1}{-0.3113}\right) = -22.1¢$$

The formula relating marginal revenue to price and elasticity is especially useful if the demand function has a known, constant price elasticity.

Relationships of total revenue to output and elasticity

Generally speaking, the demand for a given good or service is thought to be price elastic if total receipts increase when price per unit decreases. Demand is inelastic if total revenue increases as price increases.[4]

A perfectly elastic demand curve may be depicted as in Figure 4–6. This situation is one in which the seller of the product believes he/she can sell any quantity of the good or service at the prevailing market price, P_0. This kind of demand curve is often used to depict the price and output behavior of the purely competitive market and is mentioned later in connection with discussions of all four market structures: oligopoly, monopoly, monopolistic competition, and pure competition. It is used in Figure 4–6 for purposes of revealing the completely elastic point and/or arc price elasticity of demand.

Since $\frac{dy}{dx} = 0$, the graphing of y in terms of x as in Figure 4–6, for example, has a slope of 0. This demand curve is perfectly elastic.

Perfectly inelastic demand

Rarely, if ever, should one expect the quantity demanded of a particular good or service to be perfectly elastic or inelastic with respect to price. Nonetheless, for illustrative purposes only, it is convenient often to present demand functions similar to those depicted in Figures 4–6 and

Figure 4–6
Perfectly elastic demand curve

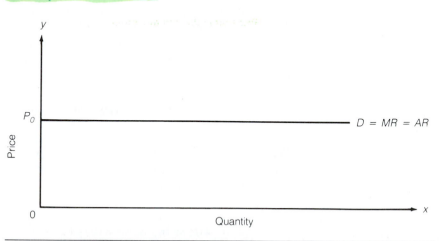

---

[4] If the demand curve does not shift to the right as the price of, say, gasoline increases and total receipts increase, the quantity demanded for gasoline may be said to be price inelastic. Additional increases in price would not cause a reduction in demand unless it provided someone with incentive enough to develop an alternative fuel, in which case the demand curve would shift to the left.

4–7. Figure 4–7 depicts a perfectly price inelastic demand function. This curve assumes a specified quantity, Q_0, of products that can be sold regardless of whether the price is very low, P_0, or relatively high, P_1. Cigarettes, beer, and liquor may be examples of products the demand for which is price inelastic. Significant decreases in quantity demanded do not occur when the price of these products increases. Knowing this to be the situation, government often imposes additional taxes on one or more of these products, and the tax is passed to the ultimate consumer via increased price(s).

As indicated in this section, values of price elasticity can be in the range 0 to $-\infty$. Values from 0 to -1.0 are said to be in the inelastic range. In this range, percentage increases in quantity (which work toward elevating revenue) are not as great as the corresponding percentage decreases in price (which work toward lowering revenue). Total revenue falls as price is reduced.

Marginal revenues, viewed as the effects of adding one more unit to rate of output, under the assumption that production is sold in the same period, are reckoned for a few elasticities in the inelastic range as follows:

For $e_p = -0.999$, $MR = P(1 + 1/-0.999) = -0.001 \cdot P$
For $e_p = -0.5$, $MR = P(1 + 1/-0.5) = -1 \cdot P$
For $e_p = -0.001$, $MR = P(1 + 1/-0.001) = -999 \cdot P$

In the inelastic range, the effect upon revenue of increasing sales by one unit per period ranges from $-0.001\,P$ at the barely inelastic $e_p = 0.999$ to

Figure 4–7
Price inelastic demand curve

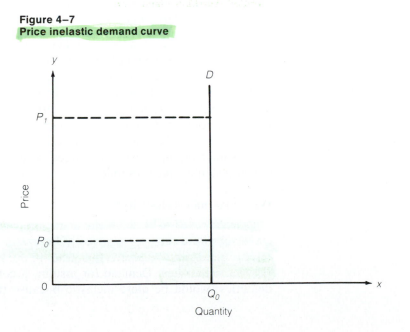

$-999\,P$ at the highly inelastic $e_p = 0.001$. On the other hand, decreasing the rate of sales by one unit would increase revenue, and it would also cut cost of production. An informed firm facing inelastic demand would not voluntarily decrease price. Instead, it would stand to gain from raising the price and lowering the rate of output. Firms do not knowingly sell at prices where demand is inelastic.

The price elasticity value of -1.0 is called unitary elasticity. Percentage change in quantity is equal to percentage change in price in the opposite direction. Total revenue is not affected by a small price change. Note:

$$\text{For } e_p = -1.0, \; MR = P\left(1 + \frac{1}{-1.0}\right) = 0 \cdot P = 0$$

Although a firm facing unitary elastic demand would not gain revenue from a price boost, it would benefit from cost reduction as output fell. Therefore, a firm facing unitary elastic demand would also wish to move price up and bring down the rate of output.

Elasticity values in the range of -1.0 to $-\infty$ are said to be elastic. For these values, percentage expansion of quantity is greater than percentage contraction of price. Total revenue rises if price is reduced.

The impact upon revenue by reduction of price so as to sell one more unit per period is shown below for a selection of elasticities in the elastic range:

For $e_p = -1.001, \; MR = P(1 + 1/-1.001) = 0.001 \cdot P$
For $e_p = -2.0, \; MR = P(1 + 1/-2.0) = 0.5 \cdot P$
For $e_p = -\infty, \; MR = P(1 + 1/-\infty) = 1 \cdot P$

Addition of one more unit to the rate of output increases total revenue by amounts ranging from 0.001 times price for the barely elastic $e_p = 1.001$ to the full value of price for the completely elastic $e_p = -\infty$ (where no price reduction is necessary when output is increased). A firm that has elastic demand may or may not gain from cutting price and increasing quantity. Increasing output does increase revenue, but cost is also greater. The decision about price and output depends on comparison of marginal revenue with marginal cost; techniques of making such comparisons are developed in chapters to follow.

What determines elasticity?

Demand tends to be more elastic as goods (1) face a greater number of close substitutes at similar prices, (2) make up greater percentages of the total expenditures of purchasers, and (3) are regarded as luxuries rather than as necessities. Demand for insulin, a compound vital to the life of diabetics, would be quite inelastic because there are no substitutes, it comprises a small part of total expenditure of buyers, and it is certainly regarded by the buyers as a necessity.

On the other hand, motor homes would have highly elastic demand because there are good substitutes at comparable and even lower annual costs (truck campers, travel trailers, motels and eating out, tents and camping gear), they compose a large part of total expenditure for most prospective buyers, and most of the prospective purchasers regard motor homes as luxuries. We would expect shoppers in the motor home market to be very aware of prices of various brands and models and of substitutes for motor homes. We would also expect sales of motor homes to increase with reductions in their prices.

Income elasticity of demand

We will see in the next chapter that the typical business economist devotes much time and effort to analysis of demand. This attention given to demand and changes in demand is necessary because of the firm's need to know more about its own product and the product manufactured and sold by its competitor(s). In addition, if the firm is to remain viable, it must investigate new areas of potential profitable operation. It may not matter whether a firm has the technological ability to produce a product at a low cost per unit of output if, alas, there is no demand for the finished good.

Demand analysis is needed if the firm is to do forecasting of a meaningful nature and if its marketing people, through various advertising and public relations campaigns, are to be able to manipulate (increase) demand for their company's product. Once an analysis of future demand is available, a firm can determine whether existing plant capacity is capable of producing enough units at a low enough cost to provide a profit margin and a turnover of assets that will make additional sales of the particular good profitable to the firm.

We have seen the responsiveness of changes in quantity demanded to changes in price. Look briefly now at changes in quantity demanded associated with changes in income so as to measure income elasticity.

Income may refer to national income, personal income, disposable income, per capita income, and so on. Any or all of these income variables may be legitimate in demand-analysis work so long as they are identified and defined with some degree of precision. In determining the price and output behavior of demand for beef, for example, and when determining the price per pound, the price may be adjusted for changes in at least two variables: (1) changes in population and (2) changes in disposable personal income. It is the latter variable that is relevant to this discussion and may be the variable that is of greatest significance in determining the responsiveness of changes in quantity demanded of virtually all consumer durable goods.

The demand for some goods may be price inelastic but income elastic or price elastic and income inelastic. It is alleged by some observers, for example, that the demand for automobiles is price inelastic but income elastic. If they are correct, a decrease in the price of an automobile does not cause an increase in the quantity of cars demanded, whereas an increase in income would be associated with an increase in the number of cars demanded. Other analysts argue that the price elasticity of demand for automobiles is quite high (highly price elastic), whereas the demand for automobiles is unitary insofar as changes in income are concerned. If this latter group is correct, a reduction in auto prices should give rise to an increase in the quantity of autos demanded. This increase would be noticeable regardless of whether the economy is in a contractionary stage (recession) or expansionary stage (prosperity) of a business cycle.

Early in 1975, the auto industry was faced with huge inventory stockpiles. To alleviate this condition, cash rebates were offered for the first time to persons ready, willing, and able to buy an automobile. Cash rebates, of course, represent price cuts, and, to the extent that automobile inventories were depleted as a result of this practice, it would appear the demand for autos early in 1975 was somewhat price elastic. This practice tapered off substantially by 1983, at which time the price elasticity of demand for automobile debate remain unresolved.

Income elasticity of demand may be measured along lines similar to determination of price elasticity of demand coefficients. The difference is the denominator. It contains information pertaining to income and changes in income as opposed to containing information regarding price per unit of product sold. Income elasticity coefficients may be "arc" or "point," as is true in calculating price elasticity. The interpretation is the same. If point income elasticity is used, measurement is being made of the responsiveness of quantity demanded at a particular point on the demand curve resulting from a change in income, with prices constant. If arc elasticity is used, one is measuring the elasticity over a range, or small part of the demand curve, with prices remaining constant. An arc formulation for determining income elasticity of demand coefficients may be as follows:

$$E_d = \frac{\dfrac{\Delta Q}{Q_1 + Q_2}}{\dfrac{\Delta I}{I_1 + I_2}}$$

where

Q = Quantity demanded.
I = Income.

Remember: income may be total income, per capita income, disposable personal income, and so on, so long as the variable is defined precisely.

A formula for average income elasticity over a discrete change in volume also is:

$$e_I = \frac{\dfrac{Q_2 - Q_1}{(Q_2 + Q_1)/2}}{\dfrac{I_2 - I_1}{(I_2 + I_1)/2}}$$

in which I_2 and I_1 represent the new and old incomes.

The point income elasticity of demand may be calculated as follows:

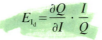

$$E_{I_d} = \frac{\partial Q}{\partial I} \cdot \frac{I}{Q}$$

where

$\dfrac{\partial Q}{\partial I}$ = *The partial derivative of quantity with respect to income.*

I = Income at some specific point on the curve.

Q = the quantity demanded at that level of income.[5]

Income elasticity is the major tool used for separation of ''normal'' from ''inferior'' goods. If the income elasticity coefficient is positive, the good is normal; if negative, it is inferior.

Knowledge of income elasticities is useful in determining the effects of changes in business activity on particular industries. If one has made a forecast of national income or disposable personal income, one can then apply income elasticities in estimating the changes in the purchases of individual commodities. Such forecasting is limited by the same difficulties to which the price elasticities are subject: Sales are influenced by other variables not covered by the elasticity measure, and past relationships may not persist in the future.

Cross-elasticity of demand

Cross-elasticity of demand measures one of the most important demand relationships, the closeness of substitutes or the degree of complementarity of demand. The quantity of sales of one commodity or service is influenced by the prices of substitutes; the lower the prices of substitutes, the lower the sales of the commodity under consideration. The formula for cross-elasticity is:

---

[5] $\partial Q/\partial I$ is the first derivative of the demand equation with respect to income.

$$e_c = \frac{\dfrac{Q_2 - Q_1}{(Q_2 + Q_1)/2}}{\dfrac{P_{o2} - P_{o1}}{(P_o + P_{o1})/2}}$$

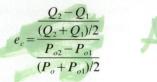

in which P_{o1} and P_{o2} represent the new and old prices of the other commodity.

Point cross-elasticity is calculated by the formula:

$$e_c = \frac{\partial Q}{\partial P_o} \cdot \frac{P_o}{Q}$$

in which

$\partial Q/\partial P_o$ = The first derivative of the demand equation with respect to price of the other good.

P_o = Price of the other good.

Q = Quantity of the own good.

A high positive cross-elasticity means that the commodities are close substitutes. Butter and margarine are examples of commodities that are close substitutes. Competing brands of many consumer goods, such as foods and toiletries, are close substitutes. A cross-elasticity of zero means that the goods are independent of each other in the market. A negative cross-elasticity means that the goods are complementary in the market—a decrease in the price of one stimulates the sales of the other. An example would be the sale of high-fidelity components and the prices of records. Reduced prices of records in recent years have no doubt stimulated the sale of high-fidelity components.

This ends the discussion of demand elasticity concepts. The concept of elasticity is a flexible tool that may be used to measure the influence of changes of any variable on another. The reader probably can work out the formulas for other elasticities that may be useful. Two examples are market share elasticity (responsiveness of the percentage share one firm has of the market to changes in the ratio of its prices to industry prices) and promotional elasticity (responsiveness of sales to changes in advertising or other promotional expenditure).

Two common demand models

Many forms of equations could be used in estimating demand relationships, but only two of these forms—the arithmetically linear form with varying elasticity and the log-linear form with constant elasticity—are commonly used. These two forms are closely examined in this section.

Arithmetically linear model

If only two variables are involved, the arithmetically linear form is simply an equation for a straight line. An example of a straight-line demand curve is shown in Figure 4–8 along with the corresponding marginal revenue curve. Below these, the total revenue curve is depicted.

A straight-line demand curve has an equation of general form, $P = a + bQ$. Parameter a is the intercept of the price axis (corresponding to a quantity of zero), and parameter b is the slope that determines how much price change there is for each unit of increase in quantity per period (b nearly always has a negative sign). The quantity axis can be marked off in any convenient units (individual units if desired, but hundreds, thousands, or millions can also be units of quantity).

The slope of any marginal revenue function that corresponds to a straight-line demand function is twice as steep as the slope of the demand function. The intercept of the marginal revenue function is the same as that of the demand function. Given a demand function, $P = a + bQ$, then total revenue TR is the function

$$TR = P \cdot Q = aQ + bQ^2$$

and marginal revenue, MR, is the function

$$MR = dTR/dQ = a + 2bQ$$

in which the slope is twice the slope of the corresponding demand equation. The above relationships are depicted in Figure 4–8, where the marginal revenue function has the same intercept as the demand function, $10, but has a slope twice as steep, −$4 compared with −$2 per unit of quantity.

At that price that restricts sales quantity to zero, total revenue is also zero. As quantity increases above zero with reductions in price, there is an initial range in which total revenue grows at a decreasing rate. The explanation of the decreasing rate is this: Total revenue at any given quantity is the summation of marginal revenues for each of the units added to a quantity up to the given rate, and these marginal revenues are steadily falling as quantity increases. Total revenue reaches its maximum at the sales quantity for which marginal revenue is zero. As quantity expands beyond the point that produces maximum revenue, revenue falls off at an increasing rate. The explanation for the increasing rate is that marginal revenues continue to fall steadily as the effect of price decreases outstrips increases in quantity demanded in moving down the demand curve. At the point at which sales quantity is so great that price is down to zero, total revenue again has a value of zero.

Price elasticities change from $-\infty$ to -1.0 to 0 with movement down and to the right along any straight-line demand curve. The elasticity value

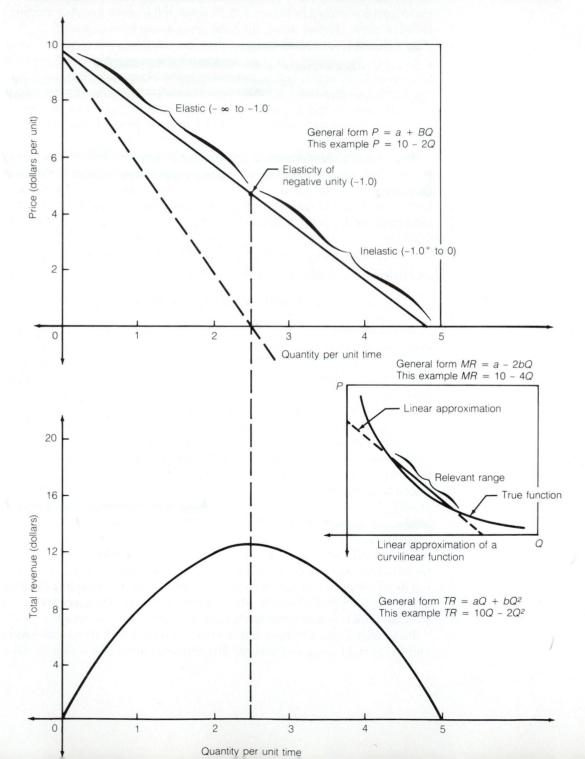

Elastic (– ∞ to –1.0)

General form $P = a + BQ$
This example $P = 10 - 2Q$

Elasticity of
negative unity (–1.0)

Inelastic (–1.0+ to 0)

General form $MR = a - 2bQ$
This example $MR = 10 - 4Q$

Linear approximation

Relevant range

True function

Linear approximation of a
curvilinear function

General form $TR = aQ + bQ^2$
This example $TR = 10Q - 2Q^2$

of -1.0 corresponds to the quantity for which total revenue is maximum and marginal revenue is zero, and this set of values is always at the midpoint of an arithmetically linear demand curve.

For the example straight-line curve in Figure 4–8, we can calculate elasticities at selected points, using $\partial Q/\partial P = 1/(\partial P/\partial Q) = 1/-\$2 = -\$0.5$ and Equation (4–1), as follows:

At price $10, quantity 0, $e_p = -\$0.5 \cdot \$10/0 = -\infty$ (perfectly elastic).
At price $8, quantity 1, $e_p = -\$0.5 \cdot \$8/1 = -4.0$ (elastic).
At price $5, quantity 2.5, $e_p = -\$0.5 \cdot \$5/2.5 = -1.0$ (unitary).
At price $2, quantity 4, $e_p = -\$0.5 \cdot \$2/4 = -0.25$ (inelastic).
At price 0, quantity 5, $e_p = -\$0.5 \cdot \$0/5 = 0$ (completely inelastic).

If their entire ranges were depicted, many real demand curves would be curvilinear and convex to the origin, resembling the curve in the inset diagram of Figure 4–8. However, a relatively short range of prices and quantities often includes all the alternatives that are feasible to consider —perhaps all that the firm is likely to face or all those for which data have been obtained. Because it is often a good approximation along the short relevant range, easy to estimate by statistical methods, and easy to use in analytical calculations, the arithmetically linear curve is frequently used by managerial economists as a model of demand.

We have been discussing the form, $P = a + bQ$, which is an equation for a demand curve drawn in conventional position with price as the dependent variable. The same data points could be traced with an equation of form, $Q = c + dP$, with quantity being dependent. In the latter case, parameter c would be the value of Q when price is zero (the intercept of the horizontal axis for a demand curve drawn in conventional position), and parameter d would be $\partial Q/\partial P$ (the reciprocal of the slope, $\partial P/\partial Q$, of a demand curve drawn in conventional position). For example, the following equations trace the same data points:

$$P = 42.12¢ - 0.01908¢ \cdot Q$$
$$Q = 2207.5 - 52.4 \cdot P$$

Log-linear model

Several constant-elasticity, log-linear forms of demand equations are shown in Figure 4–9. Curve A, the solid trace, has a constant elasticity of -1.0. It is a rectangular hyperbola—all rectangles with one corner on the function and the opposite corner at the origin have the same area, and this area is $P \cdot Q$, or total revenue. So total revenue is the same at all price-quantity combinations on the function. The marginal revenue function corresponding to curve A, and to any demand curve with constant unitary elasticity, is a straight line at value zero. Observe:

$$MR = P\left(1 + \frac{1}{e_p}\right) = P\left(1 + \frac{1}{-1}\right) = 0$$

Curve B, the dashed trace, has a constant elasticity of -2.0, from the elastic range. Total revenue increases at a decreasing rate as quantity per period increases. Marginal revenues corresponding to constant-elasticity demand curves are the product of price times some constant, where the constant is a function of elasticity. For curve B, the marginal revenues are positive and are one half of price:

$$MR = P\left(1 + \frac{1}{e_p}\right) = P\left(1 + \frac{1}{-2}\right) = 0.5P$$

Curve C, the dotted trace, has a constant elasticity of -0.5, from the inelastic range. Total revenue falls at a decreasing rate as sales quantity expands. Marginal revenues are negative for elasticities in the inelastic range, and they are the product of price times some constant, where the constant is a function of elasticity. For curve C, the marginal revenues are simply the negatives of prices, since:

$$MR = P\left(1 + \frac{1}{e_p}\right) = P\left(1 + \frac{1}{-0.5}\right) = -1 \cdot P$$

Note that constant elasticity demand functions have the general form $Q = a \cdot P^{e_p}$ in which the exponent, e_p, represents elasticity. The effect of the elasticity exponent is, roughly, to determine the slope and rate of bending of the curve. Compare curves A, B, and C to see that the demand curve bends faster as the absolute value of the elasticity exponent is raised. The effect of the coefficient a is roughly to shift the function farther from the origin as the value of the coefficient is made larger.

Any smooth single-bending curve in the quadrant can be closely tracked by some equation of the constant elasticity form. It is necessary to find an appropriate combination of positioning coefficient a and the slope-and-bend exponent e_p. Finding values for these parameters is a task in statistical estimation.

There are no convenient statistical methods for estimating constant elasticity demand equations in their original form. However, constant elasticity curves transform to straight lines if the price and quantity values are replaced by their logarithms. This result is shown in Figure 4–9. Linear regression statistical techniques, with their well-known properties, can be used in estimating the parameters of the log-transformed functions. The transformation works like this:

Original form: $Q = a \cdot P^{e_p}$
Log transformation: $\log Q = \log a + e_p \cdot \log P$
Example of original form: $Q = 20 \cdot P^{-1.0}$
Example of transformation: $\log Q = \log 20 - 1.0 \cdot \log P$

Figure 4–9
Constant-elasticity demand curves and their log-linear transformations

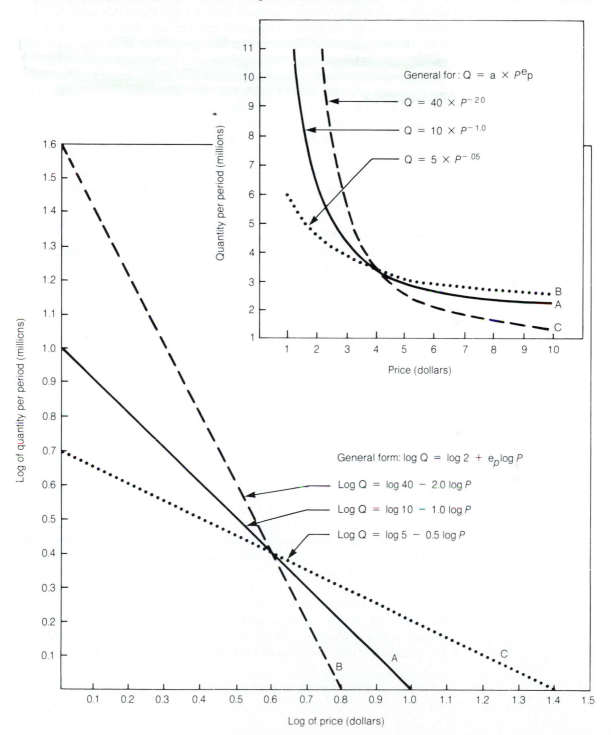

Market structure   It is time to note the differences between two kinds of demand schedules or curves: the industry (market) demand and the firm's demand. It is possible to compute price elasticities and income elasticities for either kind. In general, one would expect price elasticity of an individual firm's demand to be greater than that of industry demand, since the company faces competition from the similar products of rival firms, but the industry usually has few if any close substitutes from other industries. The firm's demand function could include variables related to prices charged by competitors and their promotional activity; such variables often take the form of a ratio of the firm's price to an industry average price and a ratio of the firm's outlay for promotion to the estimated industry total outlay. The precise relationship between industry demand and the firm's demand depends on the nature of competition within the industry—on the structure of the market.

A classification of markets

Based on the relationship of firm demand to industry demand, there are four categories of market structure:[6]

1. Monopoly.
2. Pure competition.
3. Monopolistic competition.
4. Oligopoly.

The case of single-firm monopoly is rare. It is approximated in public utilities, such as electric utilities, which are usually granted a monopoly privilege within a specified market area by government franchises. Even an electric utility faces some competition from substitutes (gas, fuel oil). Thus the concept of monopoly is not a neat one. If a single firm actually controls an entire industry, the company demand curve and the industry demand curve are the same.

The case of pure competition is equally rare. The conditions for pure competition are: (1) a homogeneous commodity for all firms in the industry; (2) numerous sellers and buyers, so that none has a perceptible influence on the total market; and (3) free entry into and exit from the industry. The theory of pure competition also assumes perfect knowledge of the prevailing price on the part of buyers and sellers. Under these conditions the product of one firm is indistinguishable from that of another. Advertising, patents, brand names, and other features that separate one firm's product from that of another do not exist. Although cases that meet all of these requirements are exceptional, some markets approach pure competition closely enough that the theory is a useful approximation. Under such conditions the demand for the individual firm's

---

[6] These market structures are discussed in somewhat greater detail in Chapter 8.

product approaches perfect elasticity. A perfectly elastic demand implies that the firm can sell all it wishes at the market price. It can sell nothing at a price that is higher, for buyers will transfer to other sellers.

Monopolistic competition refers to markets in which (1) the sellers are numerous and (2) the product of each firm is differentiated from that of the competitors. In such a situation the firm's demand curve slopes downward to the right, with an elasticity greater than that of the industry demand. There is some question whether one may refer to the industry demand curve at all in such a case, for the product of each firm is to some degree different from that of the next. Nevertheless, it is useful to retain the concept of the industry as long as one recognizes its limitations.

Oligopoly refers to markets with small numbers of firms; the Greek base of the word means few sellers. The markets for steel and cement approximate the conditions of homogenous oligopoly, for most buyers of standardized products care little about who the supplier is but are interested in minimizing the cost of an approximately standard product. Differentiated oligopoly is more widespread (automobiles, machinery, household appliances). In such conditions products are differentiated physically; advertising, sales practices, trade names, and other devices also distinguish the product of one firm from that of another. It is more difficult to generalize about the shape or elasticity of the demand curve in oligopoly than in the preceding market situations. In fact, the interdependence of the price policies of competing firms in oligopoly may preclude drawing a simple demand curve, showing the relationship between a firm's own price and the quantity it sells.

Other influences on demand elasticities and demand levels

The preceding section dealt with the influence of market structure on demand. It is now appropriate to review a variety of other influences affecting demand. Most of these affect industry demand, but some operate directly on company demand.

Derived demand

Some commodities and services are final goods, ready for direct use by consumers. Others are producer goods: materials, parts, services, or components that are to be used in further production. Demand for producer goods is derived from demand for ultimate consumer goods and thus is known as derived demand. Demand for steel is a derived demand; consumers do not buy steel directly, but rather they buy finished products that combine steel with labor and other inputs. Similarly, demand for labor services is usually derived from demand for the final products resulting from combining the labor with other inputs.

In general, derived demands are less elastic than final demands. The less costly the component in relation to the total cost of the final good, the more likely this is to be the case. For example, demand for glue used in binding books is probably quite inelastic, since a large percentage change in the price of glue will have little effect on the total cost of production. Some labor unions may try to take advantage of this "principle of unimportance" in demanding high wages for special skills that are a small proportion of total cost of products. However, a derived demand can still be subject to competition from close substitutes. If it is easy to replace a certain type of labor with machinery, for example, the elasticity of demand for that labor may be high.

Another factor distinguishes demand for producers' goods from that for consumer goods. Buyers of producers' goods are usually experts, less influenced than lay people by promotional activity and more influenced by a careful evaluation of the characteristics of the commodity. Expert buyers are often sensitive to small price differences.

If the demand for a final good increases, the derived demand for the durable producers' goods may rise more rapidly. The reason is that the demand for increased capacity is likely to be large in proportion to the normal replacement demand. This effect is called the acceleration principle. Operation of the acceleration principle is best explained by an example. Producers of coal by open-pit methods use power shovels that have expected lives of about 20 years. In other words, the annual replacement of shovels amounts to about 5 percent of the total shovels in use. Suppose demand for coal, after having been stable, increases by 5 percent. Now the derived demand for power shovels will consist of replacement demand (5 percent of the shovels in use) plus expansion demand (another 5 percent of the shovels in use). Thus, a 5 percent increase in demand for final product affects the producer's good as a 100 percent increase in derived demand.

Attitudes and expectations

Demand for a durable good, consumers' or producers', is likely to be more volatile than demand for nondurable goods for two additional reasons: (1) It can be stored, and (2) its replacement can be postponed.

Storability of durable goods makes possible the expansion or contraction of inventories. In each recession since World War II, Korea, and Vietnam, the decrease in the size of inventories in billions of dollars has been almost the same magnitude as the decrease in the entire gross national product. Those industries dependent upon the buildup of inventories as an important part of total demand suffer disproportionately in recessions. If a producer of durable goods wishes to forecast demand, he or she must give some attention to the probability that inventories of the product will be increased or decreased. This may require an evaluation of the current inventory-sales ratio and of buyers' attitudes toward increases in inventories.

Storability of the commodity also affects the short-run price elasticity of demand. If buyers believe that a reduction of price is temporary, they will tend to build up inventories. A price increase believed to be transitory may have the opposite effect. If, on the other hand, buyers forecast that the price decrease is merely a beginning of a trend, they may wait for even lower prices and use up their inventories, whereas a price increase viewed as the start of a trend would stimulate stocking. Expectations are a central influence on demand for durable goods. Customers buy not for the past or present but for the future and must make predictions of the state of future markets.

Another influence on demand for durable goods is the postponability of replacement. In periods of recession, consumers postpone the replacement of automobiles, furniture, and other durable consumer goods. In the Great Depression of the 1930s, especially in 1932 and 1933, there was little replacement of producers' goods, as is indicated by the fact that the net investment was small or even negative. Expressed in 1972 dollars (real dollars), consumer expenditures for durables declined from 147.2 in 1979 to 137.1 in 1980 (billions of dollars). In periods of expected shortages, such as the period just after the beginning of the Korean War, replacement demand took an upward leap. A similar event did not take place at the outset of the Vietnam War, a reason being that entry into that conflict was gradual over a period of years.

Long-run and short-run demand

In general, the short-run elasticity of industry demand is less than the long-run elasticity (unless the change in price is considered to be temporary). The reasons are:

1. It takes time for buyers to become familiar with the new price and to adjust to it and to make the required changes in their consumption habits.
2. It may take time to wear out durable items that are not to be replaced. For example, reduced fares for mass transit systems may not have full effects until some private automobiles have worn out.

Product improvements

Changes in the product itself will bring a change in its demand. In many industries, firms are constantly improving products. A large part of research and development activity is devoted to modifying products that already exist.

In the modern world, the constant flow of innovation—the development of new products, new distribution and selling techniques, and new modes of production—has a tendency to create new substitutes for old products. The result is what Schumpeter has called "creative destruction," which includes the destruction of demands for old goods and services. No evaluation of demand is complete until the analyst has examined the possible encroachment of new products on old markets. Since forecasting of technological change may go quite wide of marks, innovation is another factor creating uncertainty in predictions of demand.

Promotional activity

Management does not necessarily take the demand as given. It can act to shift the position and shape of the demand curve. A sales force can promote the product through personal selling. Advertising can create a greater awareness of a product and its attributes; it may develop tastes that were formerly unknown and unexpressed. Changes in distribution channels or in the service provided may help shift the demand curve upward.

Managers can sometimes manipulate the closeness of substitutes or degree of differentiation to some extent through advertising and other forms of sales promotion. The objective is to increase the degree of differentiation, with an increase in the monopoly power of the firm. But maximization of differentiation is not, and should not be, the objective of every firm. Many firms indeed profit from imitating competing products. Some furniture firms, for example, send representatives to furniture shows to copy the designs of leading firms. The objective in such cases is to minimize the degree of differentiation so that the imitating firms can take advantage of the resultant high elasticity of demand with somewhat lower prices. In such cases advertising may be aimed at demonstrating similarities to products of competitors rather than emphasizing differences from these products.

Population changes and shifts

Population growth, including illegal immigration, is another important influence on demand. Shifts in the age distribution of population bring about substantial changes in markets for a wide range of products. In most parts of the world, the proportion of the population below 20 years of age and over 65 years of age is increasing sharply. The proportion of income under the control of these age groups is increasing even more rapidly. Demography, the study of population, will become increasingly significant in demand studies in the future.

Summary

A product's demand function explicitly specifies relationships of various quantities per period to values of such variables as price, incomes, prices of other goods, season, credit availability, promotion, expectations, and perhaps still more influences. A product's demand curve is the relation of various quantities per period to various prices, other influences being held constant. A change in some influence other than price can shift the demand curve, whereas a change in price causes a change of quantity along the curve itself.

Price elasticity is the ratio of percentage change in quantity to percentage change in price. Arc price elasticity, E_p, is calculated by the formula $E_p = \Delta Q/\Delta P \cdot (P_1 + P_2)/(Q_1 + Q_2)$, in which ΔQ and ΔP are the signed changes in quantity and price, respectively; P_1 and P_2 are the initial and final prices, respectively; and Q_1 and Q_2 are the initial and final quantities, respectively.

Marginal revenue (MR) is the ratio of change in total revenue to change in sales quantity. It can be calculated at a point, if elasticity at the point is known, by the formula $MR = P(1 + 1/e_p)$, in which P is the price at the point and e_p is the elasticity of demand with respect to price.

Elasticity of 0 to -1.0^- is said to be in the inelastic range. In this range marginal revenue is negative, and total revenue is decreased by a price reduction. An elasticity of -1.0 is called unitary elasticity; marginal revenue is zero, and total revenue is not affected by a price reduction. An elasticity of -1.0^+ to $-\infty$ is in the elastic range; marginal revenue is positive, and total revenue is increased by price reduction. A firm facing elastic demand may or may not gain from price reduction; revenue is increased, but so is cost. The net result, obtained by comparing marginal revenue and marginal cost, is what counts.

If $P = f(Q)$, then total revenue $TR = f(Q) \cdot Q$, and $MR = dTR/dQ$. In words, if we have a demand function, we can multiply it by the quantity to get a total revenue function. We can then get the marginal revenue function as the first derivative of the total revenue function with respect to quantity.

Income elasticity is the ration of percentage change in quantity to percentage change in income; it is positive except for the few commodities known as inferior goods. Knowledge of income elasticity is very helpful in forecasting demand. Cross elasticity is the ratio of percentage change in quantity of one good to percentage change in price of another good; it is positive for a substitute good, negative for a complement, and zero for an independent good.

Two forms of demand equations will meet most needs. Arithmetically linear models are often good approximations over the limited relevant range. Price elasticities change with movements point to point along a linear demand curve; elasticity of unity and marginal revenue of zero are found at the midpoint. If we have an arithmetically linear demand curve, the corresponding marginal revenue curve has the same intercept on the vertical axis but has a slope twice as steep. A constant-elasticity, log-linear model becomes linear if we use logarithms of prices and quantities in place of the original values. This form is theoretically appealing, and the constant elasticity feature makes it convenient to use.

The relation of a firm's demand to the industry demand depends upon industry structure. In a monopoly, industry demand is the firm's demand.

In pure competition the industry has a sloping demand curve, but the firm's demand appears to be horizontal at the prevailing price. Demands for monopolistically competitive and differentiated oligopolistic industries cannot be rigorously defined, since each firm has a somewhat different product. Demand for the output of a monopolistically competitive firm slopes down and to the right, but is likely to be quite elastic. Demand for the output of any oligopolistic firm can be defined only in conjunction with specification of the reactions of competitors to the firm's price changes.

Derived demand is less elastic than the demand for the final good. Derived demand for a durable producer good is likely to be cyclically volatile because of the acceleration principle.

Data for use in estimating demand functions can come from experiments, household consumption surveys, or time series. In time-series analysis, multicollinearity and autocorrelation pose problems so serious that this method probably should be used only by econometricians—and only with the greatest care even by these skilled professionals. Demands for durable goods are particularly difficult to estimate because of problems in finding a suitable common unit of quantity, changes in the nature of the products over time, inadequacy of available price data, and difficulties in estimating wear-out (which is use or consumption) in any given period of time.

CASES

Demand theory

Bausch & Lomb, Inc.[1]

Bausch & Lomb, one of the oldest and strongest names in the American optical industry now stands on the threshold of one of the most important developments in its corporate life—the introduction of soft contact lenses. These lenses, made from materials sublicensed under patents originating from work done in Czechoslovakia, are now being gradually introduced to professionals across the country.

In 1971, B&L was the nation's second largest producer of ophthalmic products, ranking behind the American Optical Division of Warner-Lambert.

B&L had experienced reasonably satisfactory growth from this market, although it lost some share of the market to American Optical in the late 1960s. The market for frames and lenses increased at least 6.4 percent and 14.3 percent, respectively, in the 1963–70 period; this pattern of growth slowed somewhat in the 1967–70 period. However, at that time gains were relatively better maintained in frames than in lenses, reflecting

---

[1] This case was initially prepared at Georgia State University by Eric Tweedy under the direction of Dr. William R. Henry. It is based upon hearings of the Senate Select Committee on Small Business in connection with soft contact lenses.

a trend toward higher-priced products, stimulated by a greater emphasis on the fashion aspect of eyeglasses.

Eyeglass sales had been hurt by the poor economy in early 1970. As the economy turns upward, and particularly as the consumer becomes interested in discretionary medical spending, B&L is expected to experience a strong surge in its ophthalmic business. The leverage in this operation should be substantial and, on a 10 percent sales move, earnings could increase by 25 percent or so.

Soft lenses, trade named Soflens®, constituted significant advance over the traditional hard contact lenses, due mainly to a high degree of comfort obtained with the lens even in the initial wearing stages as well as a closer fit with the eye which reduced the possibility of losing the lens or of having dirt particles lodge under the lens. In addition, and obviously most important, the lenses provide excellent vision correction—fully satisfactory in the substantial majority of patients.

The lenses were unique in 1970, and the market was relatively uncrowded. Significant bars to competition included the following:

1. The lens is covered by both product and process patents. These patents may not guarantee the total absence of competition but, on the other hand, as the patents are enforced they will at least hinder the development of alternate products.
2. B&L has made a number of improvements in both the lens itself and in the manufacturing process.
3. The lenses were judged to fall under the Food and Drug Act, and it was therefore required that they go through elaborate premarketing testing procedures and ultimately governmental approval; passage through this process took B&L more than four years.
4. The name and reputation of Bausch & Lomb—both at the consumer and professional levels—supports a preference for B&L's products even in a strongly competitive market.

Competition Bausch & Lomb's major competition in the soft contact lens market comes from Naturalens®, a product of Griffin Laboratories, a subsidiary of Frigitronics. The Griffin lenses are composed of basically the same material as the Soflens®, but they are more hydrophilic, somewhat harder and thicker, and come in a wider range of fitting parameters. Additionally, the Griffin Naturalehs® has been shown in clinical studies to have better optical properties, to be better suited as a bandage lens and drug dispenser, and to have other valuable therapeutic uses. The Naturalens® has FDA approval for therapeutic use only.

Pricing The B&L lenses were priced initially at $65 per pair. This price compared with a typical price from a hard lens manufacturer of $15–20 per pair. However, the price to the dispenser was a relatively minor portion of the price of the fitted lens to the patient. The price of the soft lens to the patient, at least at the outset, was $300 per pair or so, compared with about $200 for the hard lens. In time, dispensers—particularly optometrists who had been losing share of the contact lens market to ophthalmologists—reduced prices to the patient. This price change was facilitated by the relative ease with which the soft lens is fitted to the patient, particularly compared with the hard lens, as well as the probability that the time involved in fitting the soft lens was substantially reduced.

B&L sold the lenses to the dispenser in a kit containing: 72 lenses, each pair costing $65; five sterilizers, each costing $21; a professional-size sterilizer; and a film projector. The kit was priced at $2,905. The extent of the initial acceptance of the kits influenced the development of sales from B&L to the dispenser for the next year or so. For example, 20 percent of the nation's 18,000 dispensers—roughly 3,600 dispensers—ordered kits during 1971, resulting in sales to B&L of about $10.5 million. This also placed about 130,000 pairs of soft contact lenses in the hands of the dispenser and acted as a brake to additional sales in subsequent months. The extent of this restraint depended on the relationship of the size of the pipeline to the consumer acceptance rate. For example, 130,000 pairs of lenses was equal to only about three months sales when the market for soft lenses reached 500,000 pairs per year.

Apart from the pipelining consideration, B&L shipped lenses to dispensers as they were sold to the consumer. As the dispensers fitted each patient, they recorded the specific lenses used in the fitting, thus maintaining a relatively complete inventory of most popular sizes. In this way, B&L's sales reached a close relationship to detail demand, but this relationship was warped initially by the pipelining.

Industry demand   The following table shows the total number of people, distributed by age groups, wearing corrective lenses as of June 1966 in thousands:

	Persons 3 years or older	No corrective lenses	With corrective lenses		
			Total	Eyeglasses only	Contact lenses
Total 3+	178,907	92,693	86,020	84,247	1,773
3–16	55,037	46,652	8,263	8,110	153
17–24	22,393	13,039	9,310	8,474	835
25–44	45,185	26,250	18,914	18,314	599
45 and over	56,292	6,743	49,533	49,348	185
45–54	21,850	4,112	17,732	17,636	97
55–64	16,864	1,337	15,526	15,469	57
65+	17,578	1,294	16,275	16,244	—

Source: National Center for Health Statistics.

As indicated, the use of corrective lenses increases proportionately with age. Furthermore, the proportion of people wearing contact lenses is centered primarily in the 17–24 age group, where about 10 percent of all corrective lens wearers used contact lenses, and in the 25–44 groups, where 3 percent (of a far larger group) wore contact lenses at that time.

The number of people wearing contact lenses in 1970 reached 3 million, somewhat less than double the number of four years earlier. Although not shown in the table, traditionally, the usage rate of contact lenses among females is more than twice as frequent as among males. The usage of contact lenses, relative to eyeglasses, is relatively heavy in the western part of the United States, among people with higher incomes, and among white-collar workers. These segments of the population are growing as a percentage of the total.

The table below includes both new patients—those purchasing a pair of contact lenses for the first time—and patients reordering a pair of lenses either due to a change in vision or loss of the initial pair. The number of people who have purchased a pair of contact lenses is in excess of 10 million. Some people think that about 3 million continue to wear the lenses with a high degree of regularity and 7 million people either wear them infrequently or not at all, out of each 10 million pairs sold.

Year	Contact lenses sold (millions of pairs)	Eyeglass lenses (millions of pairs)
1965	0.8	36.0
1966	1.0	37.0
1967	1.2	38.0
1968	1.2	44.0
1969	1.3	45.0
1970	1.0	44.0

Sources: Bureau of the Census, Optical Goods Manufacturers Association and FD&S.

Assume about 42 percent of all people 17 to 24 years of age wear glasses; similarly, 42 percent of all people 24 to 44 wear glasses. The onset of vision defects is typically at a relatively early age. The following table shows the age at which each segment of the population first obtained corrective lenses (000 omitted):

Present age		Age when first obtained corrective lenses*			
		Under 17	17–24	25–44	45+
All ages	86,020	—	—	—	—
3–16	8,263	8,263	—	—	—
17–24	9,310	6,533	2,531	—	—
25–44	18,914	6,778	4,654	6,571	—
45+	49,533	4,400	4,021	15,550	22,592

* Totals may not add due to small number of people in categories above age 17 who did not recall when they first obtained correction.
Source: National Center for Health Statistics.

Of the 86 million people wearing glasses at the date of the 1970 census, 30 percent of these obtained vision correction before the age of 17, and another 13 percent before the age of 24. The substantial majority of these people were nearsighted, a vision defect well suited to the use of contact lenses. Based on this data, it appears that about one out of seven people under the age of 17 and two out of five people in the 17–24 age category wear some type of corrective lens.

The following table presents the age of the population of the United States at the end of 1969 and the likely distribution of the population by 1975 and by 1980 (000 omitted):

Year	Total	Under 5	5–14	15–24	25–44	45 +
1969	203,216	17,960	41,345	35,054	47,994	60,863
1975*	217,557	19,968	38,565	40,011	53,928	65,086
1980*	232,412	23,245	38,104	41,736	62,302	67,024

* Assumes fertility rate of 2,775 per 1,000 women of childbearing age (known as series C in census projections).

This study of industry demand assumes that contact lens usage has increased modestly as a percentage of all corrective lenses worn over the years cited and, furthermore, that contact lens usage will continue to increase in future years. Specifically, contact lens usage might conform to the following usage rate:

Year	Percent of all corrective lenses
1966	2.1
1969	2.4
1975	7.2
1980	12.2

1. Assume that about 6 million people wearing eyeglasses or not yet wearing any type of corrective lenses converted to contact lenses between 1969 and 1975 and another 6 million converted between 1975 and 1980. Assume the conversion rate to soft lenses will start slowly but build up significantly as the decades proceed:

Year	Soft, as percent of total
1971	16.7
1972	50.0
1973	63.3
1974	70.0
1975	73.7
1976	76.3
1977	78.7
1978	81.1
1979	85.8
1980	85.3

These estimates assume that about 4 million people a year are passing age 24, approximately half of whom are wearing some type of corrective lens. Of these, probably half will be attracted to contact lenses, producing a new market of 1 million pairs of contact lenses per year. The balance will be derived from the substantial group of eyeglass wearers attracted to contact lenses for the first time.

2. Assume that the conversion of existing contact lens wearers to the soft lenses will probably be relatively minor. The only reasons for switching from a reasonably acceptable product would be either due to the high discomfort associated with dirt and grime lodging under the lens, typically in a city environment, or due to the ability of the wearer to use the soft lens on a less regular schedule, not available to the hard lens wearer due to the discomfort normally associated with readapting to the lens. The barrier to conversions from hard lenses to soft lenses will be the substantial price of being refitted with soft lenses. About 5 percent per year of the existing hard lens population might be attracted to the soft lens—or roughly 150,000 pairs per year. This will build up gradually over the next few years.

3. A substantial number of people who had purchased hard lenses and subsequently dropped out of the market will purchase a pair of soft contact lenses.

The primary reason for not using the pair of hard lenses, even after spending something in the area of $200, is the high degree of difficulty which most people encounter in adapting to the lens. Many people—probably half—eventually give up this effort and revert to eyeglasses. However, all of these people were motivated at one time to wear contact lenses. If the adaptation period is eased—as it is with the soft lenses—a significant number may come back to the market. Roughly 5 percent per year of the dropout population, or about 350,000 people, could be attracted back to the market.

1. Did price decline for soft lenses between 1977 and 1982?
   a. For B&L?
   b. For the industry?
   c. By how much, if any?
2. Did the soft lens price reduction, if any, affect the quantity demanded of soft lenses?
   a. For B&L?
   b. For the industry?
   c. By how much, if any?
3. What is the industry demand for soft lenses? The B&L demand?
4. Is the demand for soft lens price elastic? Income elastic? How do you know? Be specific.

5. Has the age distribution of people wearing corrective lenses changed, 1966 through 1982? Be specific!

6. Using 1975 and 1980 as points of reference, estimate the number of people, by age, by sex, who purchased a pair of contact lenses in 1980. In 1985. Of these people, how many persons will wear them infrequently or not at all?

7. Reveal the share of the soft lens market enjoyed by Bausch & Lomb in 1981. In 1985?

8. How elastic is demand for their product, and why do you believe this to be the case?

"Best Looking Men at OSU"[1]

The "Best Looking Men at OSU" is a calendar published in Ohio, depicting the best looking men at The Ohio State University in Columbus. A group of ambitious undergraduate students (female) from nearby Ohio University published the calendar in the fall of 1982. The publication was priced at $8.50, and sales were estimated at a relatively modest 1,800 copies. After discounts by distributors, the publishers expected to receive about $5.70 per copy—barely enough to cover its unit costs.

The manager of a retail store claimed that the price of $8.50 was too high and believed that at a price of $5 the publishers could expect substantial gift sales of the calendar, with perhaps a doubling or tripling of volume. The editors believed, however, that sales would be only 50 percent higher at the lower price.

The costs of publishing the calendars are shown in Exhibit 1. These costs were accumulated after publication but include some estimates. A prepublication forecast of costs had estimated them at $4,881. The higher actual costs resulted from a substantial number of changes in the galley proof and page proof stages, some of which occurred because several would-be male students withdrew permission to use their photo.

1. Estimate the elasticity of demand, incremental revenue, and marginal revenue under the following assumptions: (*a*) a doubling of sales at the lower price, (*b*) a tripling of sales, (*c*) a 50 percent increase in sales. (Assume that the proportion of the retail price going to the publishers is about the same at various prices.)

2. Assuming that the demands can be approximated by straight lines and sales will double at the lower price, estimate the marginal revenue at a number of prices between $8.50 and $5—for example, at $8, $7.50, and $7. Is the assumption of straight-line demands reasonable?

3. Estimate the marginal cost or incremental cost per calendar for quantities exceeding 1,800. For this purpose assume that the publishers' pressrun would be increased upward from 2,000 to take care of the

[1] See *Newsweek*, May 23, 1983, pp. 48–51.

Exhibit 1
Estimated Cost of Calendar (publication date,
September, 1982; quantity, 1,000 bound copies plus 1,000
unbound sheets)

Text:
Stock	$ 774.50	
Composition (354.8 hours)	2,305.90	
Press (106.9 hours)	740.40	
Ink	22.34	
Art	40.00	
Cuts	64.66	
Miscellaneous	36.50	
Overhead (15% of above)	597.00	
Total text costs		$4,581.30

Jacket, glossy:
Stock	$ 28.50	
Composition (2 hours)	13.00	
Press (8.3 hours)	58.30	
Ink	7.26	
Art	107.00	
Cuts	39.00	
Overhead (15% of above)	38.00	
Mailing	3.94	
Total jacket covers		$ 295.00
Binding (1,000 copies)		724.00
Freight (estimated)		120.00
Total cost		$5,72X.30

extra demand at the lower prices. Note that the composition costs are
fixed for a single run. Binding costs include a fixed element of $150
per lot, but the remaining binding costs are proportional to volume.
Make any other assumptions that seem appropriate. (A full discussion
of costs appears in Chapters 6 and 7, but the incremental reasoning
presented in Chapter 2 should suffice for this purpose.)

4. Would a price of $5 be sound? Discuss.
5. Would a price of $5 be sound for these publishers, recognizing that
   the objective is maximum profit? Heavy losses on this calendar would
   cut down on funds available for similar projects at other universities,
   (i.e., Oklahoma State University, etc.)

PROBLEMS
Demand theory

4–1   If average demand daily for tennis balls at the Hilton Key pro
       shop in terms of canisters is expressed by the equation:

$$D = f(P)$$
$$= 100 - 40P$$

a. What would you calculate the average daily sales of tennis
balls to be at a price of $1.35 per canister of 3 balls? How
many cans would be sold?

b. If the resident pro wanted to sell 60 cans of tennis balls daily, what price would the pro have to charge?

c. Assuming the demand function remains valid and a can of tennis balls was given away free to all players, how many cans of balls would be given away?

d. How high a price would the tennis pro have to charge to assure that no cans of tennis balls were sold?

e. Using a two-dimensional graph with *price* on the vertical axis and *quantity* demanded of tennis balls on the horizontal or *x* axis, plot the demand function of these cans of tennis balls.

f. Determine the price at which total revenue is maximized for the tennis pro.

g. Determine the price elasticity of demand for the tennis pro when price is established at $1.25 per can.

h. Interpret the coefficient obtained in *g* above.

4–2   Distinguish between a change in demand and a change in quantity demanded.

a. What factors bring about a change in quantity demanded?

b. What factors bring about a change in demand?

4–3   Firestone Bowling Alley charged 70¢ a game. On average, 10 lanes were in use all the time. In an effort to raise total revenue, Firestone lowered rates to 50¢ a game and now averages 20 lanes in use at any given time.

a. Calculate Firestone's price elasticity of demand.

b. Approximately how many lanes will be used if Firestone establishes a price of 60¢ per game? (Assume the same price elasticity as found for question *a*.)

c. If Firestone has 60 lanes, what price should it charge to fill them all? (Assume the price elasticity in *a* is valid.)

4–4   Demonstrate your understanding of the concept of elasticity by fully explaining the following:

a. Arc and point price elasticity of demand. How do these formulas differ when determination is made of elasticities of supply?

b. Present a formula for calculation of (1) point price elasticity and (2) arc price elasticity.

c. Under what conditions is demand said to be (1) elastic, (2) inelastic, and (3) unitary?

4–5   The average annual income in Youngstown has decreased from $13,000 to $11,000 due to the closing of a steel plant. Since the decline in income, Larry's Meat Market has sold only 1700 pounds of steaks per year, as opposed to the 2300 pounds sold yearly before at the same price.

   a. Determine Larry's income elasticity of demand.
   b. An airplane parts factory is to open in Youngstown, and average annual per capita income should be $17,000. Assuming the income elasticity figure obtained in *a* is valid, calculate Larry's steak sales after the parts plant opens.

4–6   By definition, a demand function is unitary if changes in price and quantity demanded leave total revenue unaffected. In other words, the elasticity of demand coefficient would be equal to one. Calculate the elasticity of demand coefficient for the demand function assumed in Exhibit 1, and interpret your calculations.

Exhibit 1
Unitary demand curve

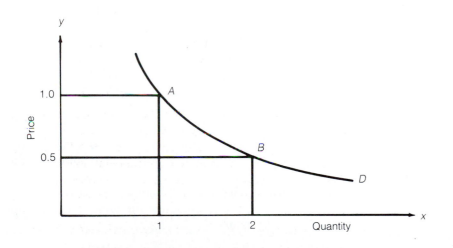

4–7   The University Deli sold 160 cups of frozen yogurt daily. A local A&P supermarket cut its yogurt price from 65¢ to 55¢; subsequently, the University's sales are at 140 cups.

   a. Calculate the cross-price elasticity of demand. Interpret your answer.
   b. If A&P cuts price to 45¢, how many cups will the University Deli sell?

4–8   Assume a least-squares estimation of a regression based on 88 observations of two independent variables resulted in the following equation:

$$Od_b = 1940 - .166Pb + .867Yd$$
$$\quad\quad (0.043) \quad (0.244)$$

Standard error terms are in parenthesis; $r^2 = .86$; where Qd_b is the quantity demanded of butter, Pb is the price per pound of butter in dollars, and Yd is disposable personal income expressed in tens of thousands of dollars. Assume the price per pound of butter is $1.40, quantity demanded is 2,000 pounds.

a. Explain the r^2.
b. Calculate the point price elasticity of demand coefficient.
c. Calculate the income elasticity of demand coefficient.
d. Is butter a normal good?
e. What relationship, if any, is revealed between butter and margarine?
f. How much confidence could an analyst have in the equation as presented?

4–9   Income elasticities may be calculated by an arc formula

$$E_I = \frac{\dfrac{\triangle Q}{Q_1 + Q_2}}{\dfrac{\triangle I}{I_1 + I_2}}$$

How can your knowledge of income elasticities be used to identify and distinguish between *(a)* "normal" goods and services and *(b)* inferior goods and services? In what way(s) can identification of normal goods be of use to the corporate economist?

4–10   A price and quantity-demanded relationship is revealed in Table 1. Complete the table. Plot the total and marginal revenue curve.

Selected references

Barnett, William A.; Kenneth J. Kopecky and Ryuzo Sato. "Estimation of Implicit Utility Models." *European Economic Review* (Netherlands) 15, no. 3 (March 1981), pp. 247–59.

Cosimano, Thomas F. "The Incentive to Adopt Cost-Reducing Innovation in the Presence of a Nonlinear Demand Curve." *Southern Economic Journal* 48, no. 1 (July 1981), pp. 97–104.

Table 1
Demand, total, and marginal revenue

Price	Quantity	Total revenue	Marginal revenue
$15	0		
14	1		
13	2		
12	3		
11	4		
10	5		
9	6		
8	7		
7	8		
6	9		
5	10		
4	11		
3	12		
2	13		
1	14		
0	15		

Harris, Frederick, H. "Value-Maximizing Price and Advertising with Stochastic Demand." *Southern Economic Journal* 48, no. 2 (October 1981), pp. 296–311.

Heady, Earl O.; H. C. Madsen; K. J. Nicol; and S. H. Hargrove. "National and Interregional Models of Water Demand, Land Use, and Agricultural Policies." *Water Resources Research,* (August 1973), pp. 777–91.

Holliday, Clifford R. "Competitive and Regulatory Changes in the Telephone Industry, or 'Who Wants Service at $100 a Month?' " *Public Utilities Fortnightly* 110, no. 8 (October 1982), pp. 23–29.

Holthausen, Duncan M. "Kinky Demand, Risk Aversion, and Price Leadership." *International Economic Review* 20, no. 2 (June 1979), pp. 341–48.

Ippolito, Richard A. "Welfare Effects of Price Discrimination when Demand Curves Are Constant Elasticity." *Atlantic Economic Journal* 8, no. 2 (July 1980), pp. 89–93.

Leibenstein, H. "Bandwagon, Snob, and Veblen Effects in the Theory of Consumers' Demand." *Quarterly Journal of Economics* 64 (February 1950), pp. 183–207.*

Lester, Tom. "Why Black and Decker Takes the Lion's Share." *Marketing* (UK, May 1979), pp. 23–26.

Mann, Jitendar S. "A Dynamic Model of the U.S. Tobacco Economy." *Agricultural Economics Research,* (July 1973), pp. 81–92.

Reddy, Nallapu, N. "Japanese Demand for U.S. Coal: A Market-Share Model." *Quarterly Review of Economics and Business* 16, no. 3 (April 1978), pp. 51–60.

Taylor, Lester D., and Daniel Weiserbs. "On the Estimation of Dynamic Demand Functions." *The Review of Economics and Statistics* (November 1972), pp. 459–65.

Telser, L. G. "A Theory of Monopoly of Complementary Goods." *Journal of Business* 52, no. 2 (April 1979), pp. 211–30.

Working, E. J. "What Do Statistical 'Demand Curves' Show?" *The Quarterly Journal of Economics* 41, no. 2 (February 1927), pp. 2–35.*

* This article is included in Thomas J. Coyne, *Readings in Managerial Economics,* 3d ed. (Plano, Tex. : Business Publications, 1981).

5

Demand analysis

This chapter focuses upon market demands and the firm's market share. Industry, market, and firm demands are defined as follows. Industry demand is nationwide demand for a given product or service, including net exports. Market demands break down national demand by classes of purchasers or by geographic market areas, or both. A firm's demand is the sum of its projected shares of the various market demands.

In this chapter's approach to demand, the firm's pricing is assumed to have some given relationship to an industry average, and the analysis focuses upon prospective future changes from current sales rates. In other words, demand shifts are forecast as changes in quantity per period assuming no change in pricing.

Demand theory is explained nicely by utilization of two-dimensional graphs and the assumption that quantity demanded is a function of price —nothing but price. But total demand is often a function of numerous variables, only one of which is the price per unit of product sold. For this reason, somewhat more complicated demand functions must be understood. These functions may be linear or multiplicative. Regression analysis may be used to describe the interrelationships that exist between the independent and dependent variables. Functions of this nature, described and interpreted properly, are very helpful to the business economist. Such functions plus some psychological factors and other factors that influence demand are discussed here.

Psychological and sociological concepts of consumer behavior

Traditional demand analysis takes price, income, and the availability of substitutes as the independent variables, and the quantity purchased as the dependent variable. Although aware that human beings are involved in this relationship, economists usually give little attention to the

147

psychological and sociological motivations of these human beings. The question is whether the behavioral sciences are helpful in the analysis of demand. In this book it is possible only to list some major propositions along with some recent findings and some directions of research.

A few major propositions

1. One of the basic propositions of psychology is that there is much more to human choice than the careful evaluation of alternatives. People make choices for a great variety of reasons, some of which are observable (such as a reaction to a change in price), some of which the individual may not wish to reveal in an interview, and some of which even the decision maker may not realize.

2. Behind patterns of consumer behavior that appear on the surface to be straightforward are deeper causes and motives that are difficult to observe and to measure. Accordingly, research into such behavior is a difficult task, involving techniques that go behind and beyond the simple correlation of prices, incomes, and quantities purchased.

3. Consumer behavior is socially conditioned. Economists themselves have long recognized the inadequacies of the traditional approach of adding together individuals' demand curves to obtain market demand curves. This approach implicitly assumes the independence of each individual's demand for a product. Such an assumption ignores such notions as the following:

    a. Veblen's "conspicuous consumption," which views people as buying not merely to satisfy inner wants but also to impress others.

    b. Duesenberry's "demonstration effect," which portrays individuals coming under the influence of the consumption patterns of those with whom they come into contact. A family moving into a wealthy neighborhood is running the risk that higher consumption patterns there will set a higher goal of family spending. Studies have shown, for example, the major importance of neighborhood influence in the purchase of central air-conditioning units.

    c. The notion that commodities serve as status symbols. The drop in automobile sales and the introduction of compact cars in the late 1950s and again in the early 1980s were attributed by some to the reduced prestige value of the automobile. Some observers argue that homes have taken the place of automobiles as status symbols.

4. Interviews may reveal shifts in consumer expectations and attitudes that help explain changing consumption patterns. In particular, it is claimed that optimism or pessimism about the future will determine the level of purchases of durable consumer goods, such as furniture, appliances, and automobiles.

Some hypotheses

There are at least two competitive approaches to consumer behavior. One approach tries to avoid the rather undefined areas of psychology and sociology by relating purchasing outcomes to relatively measurable variables, such as income or price. The other approach makes a more direct attack on the intervening psychological and sociological variables. The managerial economist takes an interest in these alternative attacks on the problem despite the inconclusive state of the research, for these studies should eventually increase one's ability to predict changes in demand.

Chapter 4 developed measures (such as income elasticities) that related purchases to the absolute level of income. Two alternatives to the absolute income hypothesis have been proposed: the relative income hypothesis, which stresses the relative position of the consumer on the income scale, and the permanent income hypothesis, which suggests that consumption is related to average income or anticipated income over a number of periods.[1]

The permanent income hypothesis has important implications for the purchase of durable consumer goods. It separates current income into two components: transitory income and permanent income. Transitory income includes any fluctuations in short-run income that are not expected to persist in the long run. An increase in transitory income, according to this hypothesis, is more likely to flow into durable goods purchases that are intermittent in character. Transitory income appears to be closely related to the concept of discretionary income, which has long been used in studies of the demand for durable goods. Discretionary income is that part of income left over after deduction of regular, recurrent expenses; it is available for the purchase of durable goods. One weakness in this approach is the difficulty of drawing the dividing line between the part of income that is permanent and the part that is transitory or discretionary. Nevertheless, the permanent income hypothesis promises to lead to a deeper understanding of consumer behavior.

Other studies are attempting to relate consumption to recent changes in income, to increases in household wealth, and to the size of liquid assets. The heavy purchases of durable goods after World War II, for example, are claimed to relate not only to the difficulties of purchasing such goods during the war, but also to the high levels of liquid assets.

Another approach focuses on expectations, attitudes, and other psychological and sociological variables. George Katona has long argued that such attitudes as optimism about the future and the willingness to buy are important determinants of consumer behavior. These changes in attitudes may bring about shifts in consumption patterns long before in-

---

[1] Robert Ferber, "Research on Household Behavior," *American Economic Review*, March 1962, pp. 19–63.

come and wealth changes take place. Data on attitudes provide an insight into underlying motives and thus lead to a deeper understanding of behavior.

At the same time Katona and his associates at the Survey Research Center were collecting attitudinal data, they were also surveying consumer intentions to buy, which are on a somewhat different plane from the underlying psychological motives. Close relations between intentions to buy and actual purchases were discovered. Some observers have argued that success of predictions based on intentions to buy makes deeper probing into motives unnecessary, since the data on expectations and attitudes appear to add little to the predictive power of this type of analysis.

Other research workers are focusing attention on consumer decision-making processes. For example, attention is being devoted to the extent to which consumers deliberate on the purchase of durable goods. Deliberation appears to be more frequent among consumers with more education and higher incomes.

Such a wide variety of hypotheses and research approaches is confusing to the practitioner. In time this type of analysis should lead to a deeper understanding of consumer behavior and a higher predictive power in dealing with broad consumption aggregates and with the demand for individual commodities.

Estimating demand equations

The exact nature of relationships of various influences to the quantity sold per period cannot usually be determined. It is not feasible to set up conditions under which each of the influences is varied, one at a time, as the others are held constant. A manager cannot hold weather constant, keep the selling effort of competitors from changing, increase or decrease prices of competing goods, or change consumer incomes. Information about demand relationships is necessarily limited to estimates of the demand equations.

Models

An assumed relationship of quantity per period to price and other variables becomes a model when it is expressed in a mathematical form. One example of a model of demand is:

$$FHA = a + bI + cP + dCCF$$

When the parameters of the above model were estimated, the following demand equation was obtained:

$$FHA = 1.63 + 1.15I - 0.74P - 0.34CCF$$

in which

> *FHA* = The log of the deflated average acquisition cost of FHA-insured new one-family houses (a measure of quantity of housing per purchaser).
>
> *I* = The log of the deflated effective average income of home buyers.
>
> *P* = The log of the deflated price for a standardized house.
>
> *CCF* = The log of the composite credit factor (an index of monthly payments, reflecting changes in average mortgage amounts, interest rates, and lengths of mortgage amortization periods).

The above equation is a constant-elasticity, linear-in-logs form. The equation should be understood to specify that the average acquisition cost of new one-family houses increases by 1.15 percent for each 1 percent increase in average income, decreases by 0.74 percent for each 1 percent in deflated price of a standardized house, and decreases by 0.34 percent for each 1 percent increase in the composite credit factor.[2] The equation has some obvious uses in forecasting that might be carried out by home builders and credit agencies.

In order to estimate the parameters of a demand equation, data are necessary, and experiments provide such data.

Experiments

Experiments can be carried out either in a laboratory or in the marketplace. Laboratory experiments allow good control over the experimental conditions. Participants in the experiment can be carefully selected to have demographic characteristics of the population of interest. The form of the experiment usually provides a limited amount of money to the participants; they are then allowed to choose between brands of a product, and they get to keep both the product selected and the remainder of the money. The prices of the brands can be deliberately varied to determine the price elasticity of the brand of interest and its cross-elasticities with competing brands.

Results of laboratory experiments cannot be extrapolated to provide forecasts for the marketplace unless the participants in the experiment are actually representative of the target population. Further, the experiment must be carried out in such a way that participants do not alter their behavior because of knowledge that they are under observation.

Experiments can also be carried out in actual markets. This is often done in connection with new products, where there may be interest in consumer responses to different packages and different advertising ap-

---

[2] L. Jay Atkinson, "Factors Affecting the Purchase Value of New Houses," *The Survey of Current Business,* August 1966, pp. 20–34.

proaches as well as in effects of price changes. Test marketing is experimentation in a few selected market areas with the objective of obtaining estimates of demand relationships for a total market that contains many areas.

An excellent example of market experimentation is a study of demand for fresh oranges by University of Florida researchers in 1962.[3] Grand Rapids, Michigan, believed to be representative of the Midwest market, was the test market. Valencia oranges from two Florida areas (Indian River district and Florida interior) in two sizes (200 and 163) were evaluated against California size 138.

Nine supermarkets cooperated. Prices per dozen were systematically varied plus to minus 16 cents from a base price, in 4-cent increments. The base price was the average retail price of each type prior to the experiment. Thus, each of the types of oranges was offered at nine different price levels. The experiment ran 31 days and involved sales of more than 9,250 dozen oranges.

The researchers estimated price elasticities for each type of orange and were also able to estimate cross-elasticities between the different types. Several of these estimates are shown in Table 5–1.

Experimentation in actual markets is very expensive. Retailers must be compensated for their cooperation and for any losses that they may have. Many observers are required to make counts of purchases and to relate these to such circumstances as customer traffic, time of day, and location. Costs also include possible permanent losses of customers who switch to competing products during the experiment and possible loss of information to competitors who may also monitor the experiment. Furthermore, competitors sometimes sabotage market tests through unusual price changes, sudden changes in advertising, special offers to consumers (coupons), and so forth.

Table 5–1
Elasticities of demand for oranges (Florida Valencia sizes 200 and 163 and California Valencia size 138)

At 1 percent change in the price of	Produces these percentage changes in quantities of		
	Florida (Indian River)	Florida (interior)	California
Florida Indian River	−3.07	+1.56	+0.01
Florida interior	+1.16	−3.01	+0.14
California	+0.18	−0.09	−2.76

[3] Marshall B. Godwin, W. Fred Chapman, Jr., and William T. Hanley, "Competition between Florida and California Valencia Oranges in the Fruit Market," *Bulletin 704*, December 1965, Agricultural Experiment Stations, Institute of Food and Agricultural Services, University of Florida, Gainesville, Florida, in cooperation with the U.S. Department of Agriculture and Florida Citrus Commission.

Because of the expense and administrative and logistical problems of running a market test, along with the danger of revealing information to competitors and the vulnerability of the test to competitive sabotage, such experiments are usually carried out only for brief periods of time and only in a few markets. The brevity of the experiments tends to assure constant incomes and unchanging tastes and preferences, but it also precludes estimates of long-run effects of changes in price, package, advertising, and so on. Only short-run elasticities can be estimated.

Another limitation of market experimentation is that test markets must be selected very carefully to be representative of the whole market. Some cities have been favored for test marketing to the extent that there is concern that their populations have been overtested (i.e., subjected to so much experimentation that their reactions to variations in influences on demand are no longer representative of the larger market).

Household consumption surveys

Household consumption surveys provide data that are especially helpful in estimating relationships of incomes and demographic characteristics to the quantities of goods purchased per week. A consumption survey begins with selection of a sample of households that is representative of the population in the market or markets of interest. For example, the national market could be stratified into regions, then into rural and urban populations, and finally into income groups within each degree of urbanization.

A survey is usually designed to determine consumption of a selected set of commodities in a cross section of households during a short period, perhaps one week. Measurement of consumption involves going into the home and making an initial inventory of the amounts of each item that are on hand, obtaining the cooperation of the homemaker in keeping a diary of total purchases during the week, and returning to the home to make a final inventory of quantities on hand at the end of the period.

An excellent example of a household consumption survey is the study that obtained detailed data on a week's consumption of about 250 commodities for households in four regions, with three urbanizations within each region, and by income group within each urbanization.

Table 5–2
Income elasticities for food as estimated cross-section data

	Income elasticity			
Item	All U.S.	Urban	Rural nonfarm	Farm
1. Per person use of purchased farm foods	0.24	0.14	0.26	0.15
2. Value of food marketing services bought with food per person	0.42	0.33	0.46	0.26

Some results from the Household Consumption Survey are shown in Tables 5–2 and 5–3. These results, as summarized by one of the principal investigators, suggest the following:

1. The quantity of all food per se, excluding marketing services, consumed per person varies with the level of income within each urbanization but has a quite low income elasticity (item 1, Table 5–2).

2. The value of food-marketing services per person bought with food per se, both in retail stores and eating places, varies with the level of income two to three times as much as the quantity of food per se consumed among families within each urbanization category (item 2, Table 5–2).

3. Income elasticity of food expenditures is less among families with higher real incomes than for lower-income groups (Table 5–3).[4]

Household consumption survey data pertain to a very short period and may not permit adequate estimates for commodities with consumption that varies markedly from season to season. Quantity data cannot be obtained for consumption away from home; this consumption can be measured only by expenditures. If there are regional price differences, it is not usually possible to separate the regional demographic influence from the price effects. (It would be possible if reliable estimates of price elasticities were available, such as those from experiments.) In spite of the above problems, household consumption surveys are the best sources of data for estimates of the influences of income and demographic factors. The principal drawback related to this method is the great expense involved.

Time-series data

Time-series data are observations of economic variables at various points through time. Such observations can be especially useful in estimating the influences of price changes on quantity sold per unit of time.

Table 5–3
How expenditures on food increase as
real income of higher-income families
increase

Income above mean (percent)	Expenditures per person (percent)
25	8
50	17
100	22
200	51

[4] Marguerite C. Burk, "Ramifications of the Relationship between Income and Food," *Journal of Farm Economics,* February 1962, p. 115.

However, great care must be taken in making and using estimates based on time-series data.

An example that illustrates several problems encountered in time-series analysis is a study of U.S. demand for coffee.[5] The demand model was

$$Q = F(Yd, rP)$$

where

Q = The quantity of unroasted coffee beans annually deflated by population.

Yd = Aggregate real disposable income deflated by population and consumer price index.

rP = A weighted average of prices of regular and instant deflated by consumer price index.

Estimates of the demand parameters are revealed in Table 5–4 for the total populations for post World War I and post World War II.

One problem encountered by the investigator was the postwar introduction of instant coffee. This product uses less green coffee beans per cup than regular coffee because of greater efficiency of extraction, but the price also reflects the cost and the value of extra convenience built into the product. Instant coffee gradually increased its share of the market over the postwar period. The investigator estimated Equation 3 in Table 5–4 with quantities of green beans adjusted to what they would have been if the instant coffee consumed had been regular coffee, but effects of the introduction and gradual acceptance of instant coffee are not clear. The form of the product changed over time. Change of products is a major problem in making estimates from data collected over any long period.

Table 5–4
Demand equation for coffee

Equation*	by†	Ey‡	brp†	Erp‡	R^2	DW
1. Post World War I, total population	4.21	0.338	−0.084	−0.302	0.758	7.25
2. Post World War II, total population	−5.05	0.556	−0.030	−0.143	0.74	1.86
3. Post World War II, Q', total population	−2.72	0.290	−0.033	−0.150	0.51	2.10

* The means of the Qs for Equations 1 through 3 are: 17.6, 16.1, and 17.0. The Qs are per capita pounds in green (unroasted) beans annually.

† *by* and *brp* are regression coefficients for Yd and rP.

‡ *Ey* and *Erp* are the elasticities of quantity with respect to income and relative price, respectively, evaluated at the means.

[5] John J. Hughes, "Note on the U.S. Demand for Coffee," *American Journal of Agricultural Economics*, November 1969.

Another problem facing the investigator was the apparent switch of income elasticity from positive in the prewar period to negative in the postwar period. It is possible that coffee became an inferior good as incomes rose and consumption of distilled wines and spirits increased. However, the role of alcoholic beverages in the demand for coffee could not be determined. Their consumption over time is highly collinear with disposable income; as a result, per capita wine and spirit consumption and incomes could not be used as independent variables in the same equation. If the investigator attempted to do so, both of the coefficients relating income to coffee quantity and alcoholic beverage consumption to quantity would be unreliable estimates. The only really satisfactory way of coping with two-variable multicollinearity is to remove the effect of one of the collinear variables. For example, if the effects of income upon consumption of coffee were already known (through household consumption surveys, for example), these could be removed, and there would be no need to have income as a variable in the demand equation. Consumption of alcoholic beverages could then be used as a shift variable in the demand equation, thus picking up the effect of a specific trend in consumer tastes and preferences.

A third problem often encountered in deriving estimates from time-series data is autocorrelation, in which the residuals (unexplained variations in the dependent variable) are serially correlated when plotted in the order of occurrence. The effect of autocorrelation is to make the standard errors unreliable. Autocorrelation was apparently not a problem in the study of the demand for coffee, since the tests for autocorrelation with the Durbin-Watson statistic were close to or above 2.0. This value indicates absence of serial correlation in the residuals.

A study of demand for durable goods

Durable goods offer an especially difficult challenge to the researcher, since consumers are able to build up or contract their stocks of durables at various rates over time. The problem is one of determining the major influences on rates of change in purchasing. It must be decided at the outset whether one is going to measure the influences on the consumption of the services produced by durable goods or is going to try to measure influences on the goods proper. In addition, the researcher faces the following problems:

1. There are no well-defined units in which the quantity of durable goods can be measured. The quantity of wheat is measured in bushels, but in what units do we measure the quantity of automobiles?

2. Great differences exist in the quality of durables at a given time and quality changes over time, complicating the measurement problem.

3. Related to the preceding problems is the difficulty of obtaining adequate price data for durables. What is the price of an automobile? The

problem is compounded by the fact that the published suggested price is rarely the price at which the car is sold.

4. The existence of a secondhand market for durable goods creates a problem of relating the demand for new units to the demand for old units. It is necessary to consider both the "stock demand" (such as the demand for automobiles both new and old) and the "flow demand" (the demand for new automobiles). But the data on the stocks of durable goods are usually inadequate.

5. The most difficult problem in measuring the stock of existing durable goods is that of depreciation. Only rough approximations of depreciation are possible. The possibility of repairing the durable good means that there is more than one way to increase the stock.

Studies of automobile demand both before and after World War II indicate that its price elasticity is not much more than 1.0, a fact that helps explain the reluctance of automobile manufacturers to reduce price to offset declines in demand.[6] The evidence is overwhelming that the elasticity of demand for cigarettes is extremely low in Western countries. In Great Britain, for example, enormous tax and price increases on cigarettes have done little to curtail the volume of purchases.[7] Both the price elasticity and the income elasticity of demand for public utility services are low, as one might expect. The income elasticity of demand for clothing and furniture is probably slightly greater than unity; the income elasticity of expenditures upon rent is probably less than unity.[8]

The best known of the U.S. demand studies of the 1960s was that of H. S. Houthakker and L. D. Taylor.[9] Their findings are not easily summarized, since they applied a variety of approaches to the different commodities in their study. Their results are considered as accurate in the mid1980s as when they were written. In most cases they tried to apply a dynamic model that recognizes that current expenditures depend upon preexisting inventories and upon habit formation. The short-term effect of price or income changes is distinguished from the long-term result. For durable commodities for which inventories are maintained, the short-

[6] See, for example, C. F. Roos and V. von Szelski, *The Dynamics of Automobile Demand* (New York: General Motors Corp., 1939), pp. 21 ff.

[7] A statistical study of the demand for tobacco in 14 countries found low price and income elasticities, but a high response to population growth: A. P. Koutsoyannis, "Demand Functions for Tobacco," *The Manchester School of Economic and Social Studies,* (January 1963).

[8] Summaries of the demand elasticities for these and other commodities appear in Aaron W. Warner and Victor R. Fuchs, *Concepts and Cases in Economic Analysis* (New York: Harcourt Brace Jovanovich, 1958), pp. 144–69.

[9] H. S. Houthakker and L. D. Taylor, *Consumer Demand in the United States, 1929–1970* (Cambridge, Mass.: Harvard University Press, 1966).

term effect of a change in income will be greater than the long-term effect. For habit-forming commodities, the long-term effect is larger than the short-term effect, and income changes have a smaller effect than they do on durable commodities.

One illustration of the Houthakker-Taylor study is the demand for new cars and new purchases of used cars. The equation reached after considerable experimentation was:

$$f_t = 0.5183 f_{t-1} + 0.1544 \triangle y_1 + 0.0148 y_{t-1} - 0.4749 \triangle p_t$$
$$- 0.0457\ p_{t-1}\ +\ 14.0725 d_t$$

in which

f_t = Per capita personal consumption expenditures on new and used automobiles in the year t (1954 dollars).

y_t = Total per capita consumption expenditure in year t.

p_t = Relative price in year t of the good in question (1954 = 100).

d_t = Dummy variable used to separate post-World War II years from earlier years; takes a value of 0 for 1929–41 and 1 for 1946–61. The results are dated, but the method is as fresh as it was more than 20 years ago.

According to this equation, the short-run relative price elasticity was -0.9578, and the long-run relative price elasticity was -0.1525. The short-run total expenditure elasticity (somewhat like the income elasticity) was 0.1937, and the long-run total expenditure elasticity was 0.0308. An attempt to include consumer credit as a variable did not improve the equation.

The Houthakker-Taylor study covered 83 commodities. The authors do not claim a high degree of accuracy for many of their equations and suggest some ways in which research methods could be improved. It is clear that the study of consumer demand is still in the developing stages.

These various measurements of demand are all subject to error. Obviously, they do not have the degree of precision and accuracy of prediction sometimes achieved in the physical sciences. The difficulty of conducting controlled experiments in which one could test consumer responses to given changes in price or income is a great handicap. Furthermore, statistical methods suited to available data on quantities and prices are still under development. One British study that measured predictive accuracy of demand analysis came to rather negative conclusions on the subject.[10] Future improvements in the statistical methods used in

---

[10] Mark B. Shupack, "The Predictive Accuracy of Empirical Demand Analysis," *The Economic Journal,* September 1962, pp. 550–75.

measuring demand will undoubtedly increase the usefulness of demand analysis.

Industry demand and capacity

Industry demand and capacity are important to the firm for several reasons. First, it is from industry demand that market demand and the firm's demand can be derived. Second, expected relationships of industry demand to industry capacity are needed in estimating profit margins. Third, determinations and/or estimates of demand and capacity in other industries are needed in projecting their pricing and rates of production; the outlook in other industries is important if these industries supply inputs used by the firm or if they are markets for the firm's products. Fourth, near-term prospects for another industry may be basic considerations in timing an entry into it.

The following discussion provides brief treatments of survey methods of analyzing demand.

Surveys

Surveys used in analyzing industry demand range from informal to sophisticated. A common technique, especially for describing the current level and estimating potential changes in sales, is polling of the sales force. Sometimes selected outside consultants are asked for estimates of future industry demand. For some industries, consumer anticipation surveys of the Survey Research Institute or the Census Bureau can be used. For example, a supplier who needs to know intentions of consumers to build houses during the next three months can obtain the Census Bureau's *Current Population Reports,* "Consumer Buying Indicators," to obtain an extremely low-cost estimate. For a firm concerned only with regional markets, this approach may not be sufficient. Finally, there are surveys of consumers or retailers that incorporate random-sample designs and pretested, sophisticated questionnaires.

Major problems with sample surveys are their cost plus some conceptual problems in handling nonrespondents and evaluating the true intent of those who do respond. Nevertheless, surveys are and will continue to constitute an important research tool in studying and analyzing demand.

Statistical analysis

This rather vague heading includes wide spectrum of somewhat mechanical methods based upon various statistical techniques. Probably the most naive method of statistical projection is to assume the future will behave in a manner similar to the past, to assume constancy—either no changes, constant absolute changes, or constant rate of change. A stationary-state forecast in period t of the level of the variable X in period $t+1$, denoted X_{t+1}, would specify:

$$X_{t+1} = X_t$$

where X_t denotes the values of X during the forecast period. A stationary state means things don't change. Thus, $x_{t+1} = X_t$ means: The value of X in period of $t+1$ is the same as the value of X in period t.

Constant absolute change can be predicted using the formula

$$X_{t+1} = X_t + (X_t - X_{t-1})$$

That is, the expected next period change in the value of X is equal to the past period's absolute change in this variable. Constant absolute change means something changes by the same amount each period. For example, a cereal manufacturer, (i.e., Kellogg's), might observe that sales are rising by 500 cartons of Special K each week.

Finally, a constant relative change can be forecast as

$$X_{t+1} = \frac{X_t - X_{t-1}}{X_{t-1}} \cdot X_t$$

Thus, if the variable grew at 5 percent during the past period relative to period $t-1$, this growth rate will continue during the next period.

The above methods of forecasting have one overriding advantage—a low cost. Their weakness is the rigidity in assumptions about the nature of changes over time. Because of this rigidity, they are not capable of predicting turning points in a series of data. However, for certain purposes they may be quite useful.

A more complex method of describing demand is time-series analysis. "Decomposition of time-series data" is described in many business statistics textbooks and will not be detailed here. Basically, it breaks the changes in values of a time series into seasonal movements, cyclical movements, trends, and erratic events. Differences among the various decomposition methods are mainly in the assumption about how the various components interact, e.g., multiplicatively or additively. Chisholm and Whitaker review several of these methods and provide a list of further references, which could be studied before choosing any of these methods.[11] The technique called exponential smoothing is particularly useful in assuming future sales of an item will be based only on its own past sales history.[12] Finally, some sophisticated techniques for analysis of time series are available. These tools could possibly provide useful information in industry demand forecasting.[13]

[11] Roger K. Chisholm and Gilbert R. Whitaker, Jr., *Forecasting Methods* (Homewood, Ill.: Richard D. Irwin, 1971), pp. 16–27.

[12] Robert G. Brown, *Smoothing, Forecasting, and Prediction of Discrete Time Series* (Englewood Cliffs, N.J.,: Prentice-Hall, 1963).

[13] G. E. P. Box and G. M. Jenkins, *Time-Series Analysis, Forecasting and Control* (San Francisco: Holden-Day, 1970); or Charles R. Nelson, *Applied Time-Series Analysis for Managerial Forecasting* (San Francisco: Holden-Day, 1973).

Forecasts of demand can be made with the aid of correlation and regression techniques. Correlation analysis implies no causal relationship, but specifies the direction and strength of association between two variables. Such a measure can be of use if the variable of interest is highly correlated with some other variable for which there is a forecast. For example, if demand for building materials is found to be highly correlated with housing starts during the previous quarter and there is a major drop in such starts, it is reasonable to forecast that demand for building materials will fall.

Regression analysis requires more detailed a priori assumptions than correlation analysis. In regression analysis, an explicit functional relationship between one or more independent variables and the dependent variable is hypothesized and estimated. Given this estimated relationship and forecasts of values for the independent variables, values of the dependent variable can be projected. For example, assume that the forecaster has specified that the level of total quarterly sales of a particular product in the building materials industry, D, is a linear function of housing starts in the previous quarter, S, and the level of GNP, Y. Using past observations of these variables, the forecaster can estimate the regression coefficients. Assume the following regression equation is estimated:

$$D = 40.35 + 50.13S + 0.000000045Y \qquad R^2 = 0.943$$

The coefficient of determination, R^2, indicates the percent of the total variation in the dependent variable that can be attributed to variations in the independent variables. Thus, in this example, it appears that the two chosen variables account for more than 94 percent of the changes in industry demand—an encouraging sign when one wishes to use regression analysis for predictive purposes.[14]

If the analyst has values of the independent variables for the prediction period, the values are "plugged in" to determine predicted or projected value for the dependent variable. For example, in the regression equation above, if the value of housing starts in the current period were $3,000, and if the predicted value of GNP for the next period were $1,200 billion, then the forecast value of the dependent variable would be $204,430. Two practical points are illustrated in the above example. First, the use of lagged values, when appropriate, makes forecasting easier; observed values from an earlier period do not have to be predicted. Second, if one must use predicted values, it is helpful if these values are already being forecast by others (e.g., GNP).

Success in using regression techniques for prediction depends upon the

---

[14] Note that the absolute size of R^2 may not be important in other uses of regression analysis. For example, if the primary purpose of the technique were to test hypotheses about the theorized relationships between the independent and dependent variables, one would be more concerned with the sizes of the standard errors of the coefficients relative to values of the coefficients themselves.

constancy of the structural relationship between the independent and dependent variables. Also, several assumptions about the nature of the variables must hold for the estimated coefficients to have desirable properties and for the predictions to be accurate.

One of the real advantages of regression analysis for describing and analyzing demand is that the technique allows a more "scientific" or systematic approach to the problem. By starting with those variables that theoretically influence the dependent variables, the analyst is building upon a somewhat more solid foundation than if he or she were simply looking at the situation and making ad hoc prognostications.

Formal econometric models are coming into increasing use. Table 5–5 presents the range of opinions expressed by various model builders throughout the United States.

Industry capacity   Consider now the potential rate of real output (capacity) in an industry and how it may be constrained by various factors. Industry capacity forecasts are compared with demand projections to make judgments about an industry's short-term prospects for pricing and profits.

If labor is readily available (i.e., there exists a pool of unemployed within the labor market area), it cannot be a constraint on capacity, and capital is the relevant restriction. However, in cases of full or nearly full employment in the labor market, increased employment in an industry can occur only via three paths, all of which might increase costs. First, current workers may be employed for longer hours per week. Second, workers currently employed in other industries may be attracted away from their position. Finally, individuals not in the labor force may be attracted into the labor force. The first two possibilities, of course, involve higher labor costs, either overtime rates or higher wages to attract mobile workers. The third, an increase in labor force participation, often requires higher wages and may involve new labor force entrants who are likely to be less productive than the general labor force.

Capital (plant and equipment) is important in determining an industry's potential output. In the very short run, plant and equipment cannot be increased except in the rare cases in which there are both unoccupied floor space and new equipment available for stocks. Thus, for industries using specialized capital equipment, the forecaster should usually not expect an immediate increase in new capital even if the firms are willing to invest. However, one possibility for short-run increase in capital levels is utilization of previously unemployed capital, such as putting into service older machines retired before they were worn out. Of course, the productivity of such machinery is likely to be lower than currently used machines or newly produced machinery, and costs are likely to be higher.

In the slightly longer run where it is physically possible to increase capital through investment, one must consider the willingness of firms to

Table 5–5
Range of opinion (1983 economic forecasts)

	Percent change over 1982			Housing starts (millions)	Interest rates (percent)	
	Real GNP	Inflation (CPI)	Industry production		Short term*	Long term†
Econoviews International	5.9	6.6	4.5	1.70	9.0	12.0
Bostonian Research Associates	4.6	5.6	7.4	1.50	8.5	12.6
Harris Trust & Savings Bank	4.4	5.4	4.6	1.50	8.6	12.3
Morris Cohen & Associates	4.0	4.9	5.0	1.45	8.1	11.0
Eggert Economic Enterprises	3.8	5.1	5.8	1.38	8.2	12.0
Wayne Hummer	3.7	4.9	6.7	1.42	7.8	11.8
W. R. Grace	3.5	5.3	3.2	1.43	7.5	10.8
University of Michigan, M.Q.E.M.	3.4	5.6	4.8	1.62	6.9	11.2
Citibank	3.4	5.6	3.5	1.50	8.3	12.0
Dean Witter Reynolds	3.4	5.4	3.2	1.40	6.9	12.0
Metropolitan Insurance	3.3	5.6	2.5	1.40	7.3	11.4
First National Bank—Chicago	3.2	4.5	3.0	1.49	7.3	12.6
Brown Bros. Harriman	3.1	5.4	4.1	1.35	—	—
National City Bank—Cleveland	3.1	5.0	4.1	1.40	9.0	13.3
Chamber of Commerce, U.S.A.	3.1	4.9	4.4	1.40	7.7	10.7
Cahners Publishing	3.0	5.5	5.5	1.40	9.3	—
Goldman, Sachs	2.9	4.7	4.1	1.53	—	—
Arthur D. Little	2.8	6.0	4.5	1.50	7.5	12.0
Wharton Econometric	2.8	5.0	1.5	1.45	7.8	11.1
Irving Trust	2.8	5.0	2.7	1.32	7.6	12.4
Peter L. Bernstein	2.8	4.7	4.5	1.50	6.9	11.4
Arnhold & S. Bleichroeder	2.7	4.0	3.0	1.20	8.0	11.0
Conference Board	2.6	5.6	2.7	1.40	7.5	10.4
LaSalle National Bank	2.6	4.5	5.0	1.33	8.6	12.3
Bank of America, N.A.	2.5	5.2	2.5	1.40	—	—
Equitable Life Assurance	2.4	5.4	1.9	1.36	8.4	11.5
Chase Econometrics	2.4	5.1	1.6	1.37	7.9	12.1
Morgan Guaranty	2.4	4.8	2.2	1.52	—	—
Shearson/American Express	2.3	5.6	3.5	1.44	7.8	11.0
Manufacturers Hanover Trust	2.2	5.2	2.5	1.41	7.9	13.0
Philadelphia National Bank	2.2	5.0	0.9	1.50	7.6	12.0
Bankers Trust	2.2	5.0	1.7	1.45	—	—
Monsanto Company	2.1	5.5	3.0	1.40	9.4	13.2
UCLA Business Forecast	2.1	4.3	1.4	1.44	6.4	10.5
Pennzoil	2.0	5.5	2.6	1.39	7.6	12.3
Security Pacific National Bank	2.0	5.2	2.2	1.38	6.7	11.9
U.S. Trust Company	2.0	5.5	1.0	1.30	7.7	12.0
Business Economics, Inc.	2.0	5.5	4.3	1.35	6.3	12.7
E.I. du Pont de Nemours & Co.	1.9	4.6	4.2	1.30	7.0	11.0
Prudential Life	1.8	5.3	2.2	1.38	—	—
Chase Manhattan Bank	1.5	4.3	0.4	1.30	—	—
Siff, Oakley, Marks	1.4	5.5	3.7	1.25	7.8	11.9
Evans Economics	1.4	5.2	0.0	1.21	8.6	13.5
1983 CONSENSUS	2.8	5.2	3.3	1.41	7.8	11.9

* Three-month Treasury bills.
† AA utility bonds.
Source: Eggert Economic Enterprises, Inc.
    Robert J. Eggert, Sedona, Arizona
    Reprinted with Permission.
    December 1982 Survey.

add to capital. Expected profitability is the underlying motivation for such expenditures. A final point, closely tied to the concept of capital expansion, is the ease of entry into the industry. For certain industries in which there are few unique real-capital requirements (e.g., management consulting), firms may spring up very rapidly in response to increased demand, thus making capacity constraints very weak. On the other hand, in cases where inputs are unique and require time for production (e.g., the lumber industry) new firms may not find entry easy.

Forecasting of industry capacity requires certain kinds of data. For information about current situations in labor markets, one can consult various documents by the U.S. Department of Labor, especially the publication titled *Employment and Earnings Statistics in the United States and Selected Labor Market Areas.* Current levels of industrial production in various industries are compiled by the Board of Governors of the Federal Reserve System. Also, McGraw-Hill periodically publishes in *Business Week* an index of production compared to capacity in various industries. This index is based on surveys of manufacturers. Finally, an analyst interested in a particular industry will do well to consult industry trade publications, which often provide valuable insight into the current state of the industry and may report plans for expansions by individual firms that will substantially change industry capacity.

Market demand versus the firm's share

Having discussed some of the more global approaches to studying and describing demand and the factors that influence it, attention is turned now to the individual manager's objective, namely, determining demand for a product or service. The discussion begins with estimates of market potential, first for producer's goods, then for consumer's goods. Next it moves to forecasts of market share for an individual firm.

Quite often firms obtain forecasts of industry shipments from outside consultants. The major problem then is to predict their share of that market. At other times the firm will make its own estimate of industry demand.

Market potential for producer's goods

Producer's goods are goods that will be used by other firms in their production process. One common technique of predicting demand for such goods is the "buildup" approach to market potential.[15] The method includes these steps: (1) determining the industries that purchase the product and the percent of the total market that is attributable to each of these industries; (2) adjusting these percentages to account for changes or trends in market structure; (3) ascertaining the importance of an indus-

---

[15] Francis E. Hummel, *Market and Sales Potentials* (New York: The Ronald Press, 1961).

try in a particular geographic area relative to that industry nationwide—this involves construction of weights based on published data; and (4) calculating weighted market potentials for specific areas. Such steps are carried out for a machine tool manufacturer in Table 5–6.

This method of describing and estimating market potential can be used for markets defined in ways other than spatially. For example, the buildup approach could be based on types of customers, demographic groups, and types of outlets.

Probably the greatest weaknesses of the method are the importance of judgments in adjusting the weights and the problems with lack of data.

Market potential for consumer's good

Techniques similar to the method discussed above can also be used for forecasting market potential for a consumer's good. One approach to consumer goods market potentials is through the use of consumer "buying power" estimates. Probably the best-known generally available index of buying power is published by *Sales Management* magazine in its "Annual Survey of Buying Power." Indexes of buying power are estimated for all counties and larger cities in the United States. Each index is a weighted average of three factors, and the relative weights are 0.5: 0.3: 0.2 for the area's percentage of total national income, percentage of total

Table 5–6
Market area buildup method of estimating a producer's goods market potential (hypothetical example)

Industry*	SIC†	SIC weight un-adjusted‡	SIC weight adjusted §	Percent SIC‖	Weighted pro-portion #
Mining machinery	3532	40	30	0.080	2.40
Industrial furnaces and ovens	3567	45	50	0.035	1.75
Truck and bus bodies	3713	15	20	0.60	1.20
			100		5.35

Market potential: 5.35% of national market

* Industries in area that might purchase goods.
† Standard industrial code of industry.
‡ Past relative importance of industries as purchasers of product.
§ Expected relative importance of industries as purchasers.
‖ Relative importance of area in U.S. market. May be found as:

$$1. \quad \frac{\text{Number production workers in SIC in area.}}{\text{Number production workers in SIC in United States}}$$

$$2. \quad \frac{\text{Value added in SIC in area.}}{\text{Value added in SIC in United States}}$$

or by some other weighing method.
SIC weight adjusted times percent SIC.

national retail sales, and percentage of total national population, respectively. The index numbers range from 6.5438 in New York City and 3.9719 in Chicago to such levels as 0.0005 in Issaquena County, Mississippi, and 0.0002 in Arthur County, Nebraska. After estimating total national consumer sales potentials for a product, the forecaster would simply multiply this total by a given area's index of buying power to get its market potential.

Market share forecasting   After forecasting market potential for the nation or for a regional market, a firm must estimate what share of this total it will obtain. Probably the approach used most often conceives the firm's market share as depending upon various decision variables, such as advertising expenditures, other distribution policies, price, and "effectiveness" of marketing effort. Upon hypothesizing the variables of importance in this process, the forecaster sets up the general behavioral equation $S_i = f(X_1 \ldots X_n)$, which "explains" the ith firm's share. Of course, an explicit functional form with parameters that specify exactly how the Xs act to determine S_i is hypothesized. The parameters can then be estimated from market data by statistical methods.

Some useful ideas

A number of interesting ideas that deserve attention include the following.

Population changes   The demand for some goods and services is closely related to population growth and demographic changes. The producer of baby foods profits from projections of increased birth rates. The publisher of textbooks studies the potential changes in college enrollment in the near future. Real estate investors pay attention to the growing proportion of the population over 65 in age and the special housing needs of this group. Forecasters use estimates of the rate of family formation to help determine the potential market for residences. Bureau of Census publishes population projections periodically.

Discretionary income   Some business economists make use of measurements of discretionary or supernumerary income rather than the usual measures of GNP or disposable personal income. There is evidence that the sale of consumer durables relates more closely to income after the deduction of certain regular expenses than it does to total income. Discretionary income is disposable personal income (personal income after income tax but including transfer payments) less necessary living costs (such as food and clothing) and less fixed commitments (payments on debt). The National Industrial Conference Board has developed a discretionary income series.

Discretionary buying power   Indexes of discretionary buying power start with discretionary income and add cash balances, near liquid assets, and new consumer credit. Obviously, a wide variety of such measurements is possible. (The purist may raise questions about the addition of flows, such as income, to stocks, such as cash, but both stocks and flows are sources of liquidity that may influence consumption.)

Consumer credit outstanding   An economist may wish to consider the status of consumer debt outstanding before estimating the demand for a durable consumer good. A high ratio of outstanding consumer debt to current income may suggest a slowdown of purchases based on new debt for two reasons: Lenders will become more cautious about risks, and the consumers themselves will reduce additions to debt. The manager may also take into account any changes in the regulation of installment debt by the Federal Reserve Board.

Saturation levels   Some economists give attention to the concept of a limit or saturation level in the particular market. This consideration is especially important for durable consumer goods, such as automobiles or household appliances. When almost 100 percent of households have refrigerators, the potential market for additional refrigerators becomes limited; the demand becomes mainly a replacement demand (which is bolstered by planned obsolescence through the use of new designs and colors).

Size and age distribution of existing stocks   For many consumer durables the size of existing stocks must have a considerable influence on additions to stocks. This statement repeats the point made about saturation levels. The age distribution of the outstanding durables may be of particular importance. For example, the automobile market in 1980–81 was depressed by the existence of a large number of unsold automobiles. Auto manufacturers knew the average age of autos in use was significantly higher than that to which U.S. citizens had become accustomed. The manufacturers could only hope that the older autos would eventually have to be replaced with the higher cost, smaller models being offered at the time.

If auto demand did not recover to "pre-OPEC" levels of demand, only low growth was thought possible for the aggregate economy. Conversely, if auto demand would increase to the point that the age of existing auto stocks would decline, high economic growth was thought possible. Figure 5–1 depicts the difference between low and high growth and its potential impact on real GNP.

In attempting to determine the level of demand for a specific good or service, the managerial economist often establishes a statistical demand function.

Statistical demand functions

It is desirable to derive a statistical demand function for each major good or service produced by one's firm or industry. But reliable raw data needed for such a determination are not always available, and demand

Figure 5–1
Real GNP

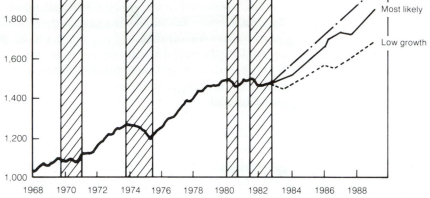

functions may have to be approximated. Once developed, these demand functions enable a firm to describe with some degree of preciseness the influence that factors operating within the economy have on the firm and its products. The firm then (1) may attempt to manipulate one or more of these factors, perhaps through advertising campaigns, and/or (2) may attempt to forecast changes in demand and the impact of these changes on the employment, output, and income of the firm.

These demand functions may be for manufactured goods or for commodities. If regression analysis is used, certain statistical criteria must be met before the regression model results can be used with any degree of confidence. An in-depth discussion of those criteria are beyond the scope of this text.

In each instance, one factor affecting the quantity demanded of a particular good or service is its price. However, rarely will quantity demanded be a function of anything other than price. Yet, simple relationships of this nature—ones that explain quantity demanded to be dependent upon price—are permissive of many generalizations necessary for an understanding of basic concepts concerning elasticity.

Large quantities of data about agricultural products are available from public sources. For the most part, these products represent finished goods often associated with purely competitive product markets. Beef is such an agricultural product, and the demand for it has been obtained from information provided in Table 5–7.

Quantity demanded in Table 5–7 is expressed in millions of pounds of

Table 5–7
Demand for beef

(1) Year	(2) Quantity § (millions of pounds)	(3) Price of beef per pound* (dollars)	(4) Yd‡ (millions)	(5) Population (millions)	(6) Price of pork per pound† (dollars)	(7) Col. 4 ÷ col. 5 Yd ÷ Pop = Per capita Yd	(8) Col. 3 ÷ col. 7 Price of beef per capita Yd	(9) Col. 6 ÷ col. 7 Price of pork per capita
1950	7,718	.475	206,900	152.3	.466	1358.50	.000350	.000343
1951	7,014	.578	226,600	154.9	.486	1462.88	.000395	.000332
1952	7,808	.552	283,300	157.6	.493	1797.59	.000307	.000274
1953	10,249	.420	252,600	160.1	.518	1577.76	.000266	.000328
1954	10,612	.420	257,400	163.0	.532	1579.14	.000266	.000337
1955	11,098	.410	275,300	165.9	.444	1659.43	.000247	.000268
1956	11,992	.392	293,200	168.9	.433	1735.94	.000226	.000249
1957	11,580	.412	308,500	171.9	.479	1794.65	.000230	.000267
1958	10,773	.467	318,800	174.9	.523	1822.76	.000256	.000287
1959	11,037	.473	337,300	177.8	.448	1897.07	.000249	.000236
1960	12,065	.451	350,000	180.7	.471	1936.91	.000233	.000243
1961	12,612	.427	364,400	183.7	.479	1983.67	.000215	.000241
1962	12,559	.464	385,300	186.5	.475	2065.95	.000225	.000230
1963	13,649	.417	404,600	189.2	.443	2138.48	.000195	.000207
1964	15,643	.398	438,100	191.9	.443	2282.95	.000174	.000194
1965	15,995	.433	473,200	194.3	.532	2435.41	.000178	.000218
1966	16,710	.442	511,900	196.6	.569	2603.77	.000170	.000219
1967	17,252	.451	546,300	198.7	.515	2749.37	.000164	.000187
1968	18,270	.473	591,000	200.7	.509	2944.69	.000161	.000173
1969	18,874	.492	634,400	202.7	.575	3129.75	.000157	.000184
1970	19,489	.490	691,700	204.9	.569	3375.79	.000145	.000169
1971	19,697	.547	746,400	207.0	.498	3605.79	.000152	.000133
1972	20,511	.576	802,500	208.8	.645	3843.39	.000150	.000168

* Price of beef = Dollars per pound wholesale price of beef, fresh steer carcasses, choice cut, New York.
† Price of pork = Dollars per pound, wholesale price, fresh loins, 8–14 pounds average, New York.
‡ Yd = Disposable personal income.
§ Quantity of beef = Beef and veal production.
Source: Business Statistics, 1973, *The Biennial Supplement to the Survey of Current Business,* January 1975, pp. 7, 68, 138, 139.

beef. The price of beef per pound is expressed in dollars (column 8), which have been adjusted for changes in both population and disposable personal income, yearly from 1950 through 1972. In other words, disposable personal income in millions of dollars is divided by total population in millions of persons so as to obtain per capita disposable personal income. This figure is divided into the price of beef per pound (column 3) to obtain the adjusted price (column 8). This price per pound of beef in column 8 is used in Figure 5–2 where beef demanded is presented as a function of price, $Q_d = f(p)$.

Figure 5–2 reveals (1) demand for beef and (2) the inverse relationship that exists between price and quantity demanded for beef, using the time-series data presented in Table 5–7. Price is on the vertical axis (y), and quantity demanded is on the horizontal axis (x).

A review of Figure 5–2 indicates the demand for beef was more price inelastic from 1953 through 1963 than it was from 1964 through 1972. A

Figure 5–2
Demand for beef—$Q_d = f(p)$

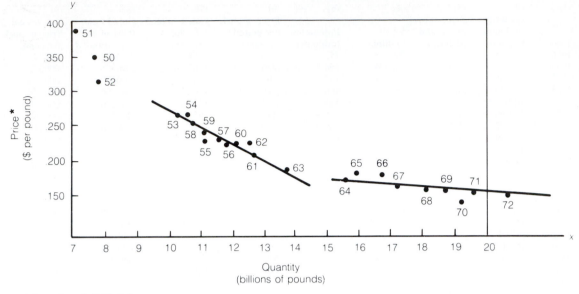

* See column 8, Table 5–7.

freehand regression line drawn through the data points from 1953 through 1963 is steeper than a similar line drawn through the data points from 1964 through 1972. The latter freehand regression line is relatively flat, indicating almost perfect price elasticity of demand for beef. The years 1950, 1951, and 1952 appear to stand alone in this figure. Many observers are willing to ignore these three data points, explaining that they are not representative of the price and output behavior of beef for many reasons, at least one of which is the Korean War. The Korean conflict started in June 1950, and the shooting did not cease until July 27, 1953. The three data points represent activity that transpired during warlike economic conditions and for that reason are not representative and are not considered.

A review of Figure 5–3 reveals a goodness of fit in the regression equation. Testing of the relationship via regression analysis reveals that 87 percent of the variation in quantity demanded, the dependent variable, is associated with changes in price per pound, the independent variable. The validity of this finding is confirmed by the standard error of measurement, which in this case is 1,490 (millions of pounds). This standard error provides a measure of confidence that one may place in the r^2.[16]

---

[16] The equation is not presented at this time.

Figure 5–3
U.S. beef demand: Actual and predicted values—$Q_d = f(p)$

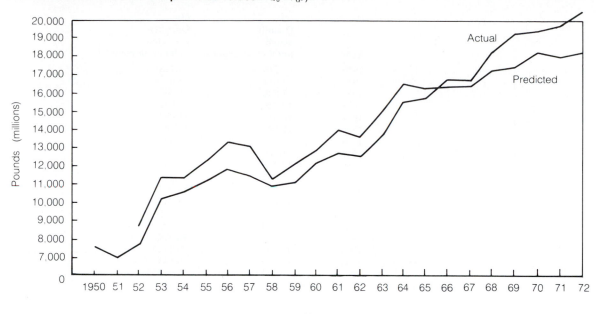

Years

Assuming a normal distribution of the errors, one can reject, at the 95 percent confidence level, the hypothesis that there is no relationship between quantity demanded and the price of beef. Sixty-eight percent of the time the predicted value revealed in Table 5–8 and Figure 5–3 will be equal to the actual value, plus or minus one standard error (1,490); 95 percent of the time, the predicted quantity of beef in Table 5–8 will be within plus or minus two standard errors ($2 \times 1,490 = 2,980$); and 99 percent of the time, the predicted value will be within three standard errors ($3 \times 1,490 = 4,470$).

This kind of demand analysis is conducted conveniently by "calling" one of the many canned regression subroutines available on home computers, on time-sharing devices, and in computer rooms everywhere.

Interpretations of statistical demand functions

Demand analysis often relies heavily upon statistics in general and simple or multiple regression analysis in particular. The demand study of beef, for example, uses regression analysis as a tool needed for explanation of the variation in quantity demanded that may be traced to changes in prices per pound of beef. Important for the purpose here is that time-series data are used. A word of caution is in order, otherwise demand analysis might evolve into nothing other than regression without theory, the cardinal sin.

Table 5–8
Demand for beef: Actual and predicted values

(1)	(2) Quantity actual (millions of pounds)	(3) Quantity predicted (millions of pounds)
Year		
1950	7,718	6,218
1951	7,014	3,612
1952	7,808	8,708
1953	10,249	11,082
1954	10,612	11,082
1955	11,098	12,182
1956	11,992	13,398
1957	11,580	13,167
1958	10,773	11,661
1959	11,037	12,066
1960	12,065	12,993
1961	12,612	14,035
1962	12,559	13,456
1963	13,649	15,193
1964	15,643	16,409
1965	15,995	16,178
1966	16,710	16,641
1967	17,252	16,988
1968	18,270	17,162
1969	18,874	17,394
1970	19,489	18,088
1971	19,697	17,683
1972	20,511	17,799

When using regression analysis, one may rely upon an expression between price and total demand that might say:

$$Y = a + bx$$

where

Y = the predicted value.
a = some constant, the Y intercept.
b = the slope.

The regression coefficient b, measures the degree by which the dependent variable is expected to change if a unit change takes place in the independent variable, x. If r^2 is 87 percent, 87 percent of the change in the dependent variable is explained by the changes in the independent variable. A statistical purist might worry about such an explanation for several reasons, including:

1. Only one explanatory variable may be used in this kind of analysis, and rarely, if ever, is one variable standing alone sufficient.

2. Movements in price and quantity demanded may have simply accompanied one another, and one cannot be absolutely certain whether or not movement in one caused movement in the other.

3. Time-series data reveal price and/or outputs that have moved uniformly. The data may have been selected over a 10-year time span as opposed to a longer or shorter period of time. These data may by their nature tend to conceal more information than they reveal. Unintentional concealment is made possible when wide amplitude fluctuations occur within the period covered by the data within, say, one year; these fluctuations may not be revealed when annual data only are used.

4. The "normal" downward slope in the demand curve is obtained and presented as Figure 5–4; this curve reveals the average relationship among the price-quantity observations. The demand curve in Figure 5–4 is obtained by drawing line segments between data points on a static two-dimensional graph. The assumption of a continuous function is present when, in fact, such a function may not exist.

5. "Average" quantities and "average" prices are used with no statement concerning the standard deviation, if any, that is associated each year with these averages. Without having some notion of the standard deviations that take place during each year about the mean, one may

Figure 5–4
Changes in elasticity of linear demand curve

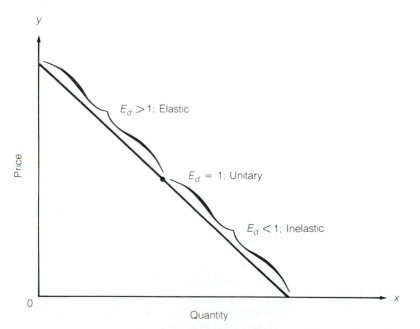

not have confidence enough in the figures presented to recommend changes in corporate policy.

6. The inference of a demand function obtained from price and quantity data is somewhat uncertain unless one has a high degree of confidence in the data source(s). Acquisition of reliable raw data with which to work is almost always a problem.

This abbreviated list cannot exhaust all of the problems that may exist when regression analysis based upon time-series data are used in demand analysis. The list is primarily intended to serve as a word of caution—to guard the analyst against overstatement, against claiming too much for his or her results.

Linear Functions

A linear demand function may take the form of

$$Q = a + bY + cP$$

where

Q = The quantity demanded (say, the number of students expected to enroll at a large institution of higher learning located in Milwaukee, Wisconsin).

a = A constant in the multiple-regression equation that has no economic meaning for the moment.

Y = Disposable personal income.

P = The price per semester hour enrolled or, more commonly, tuition.

The dependent variable is Q, and the independent variables in the equation are disposable personal income and tuition. If b equals 6.89 and c equals -15, then interpretation of the function is that enrollment will increase by almost seven students for every \$1 increase in disposable personal income, and enrollment will decrease by about 15 students for every \$1 increase in tuition per semester hour.[17]

Multiplicative functions

Capital budgeting (Chapter 11) relies heavily upon compound interest formulas, at least one of which is:

$$P_n = T_o(1 + i)^n$$

where

T_o = The principal investment.

i = the riskless interest rate.

---

[17] This interpretation assumes other factors affecting enrollment, if any, remain unchanged in the short run.

n = The number of periods over which the cash flow is expected to continue.

P_n = The value of the principal after n number of years.

In effect, this equation could be referred to as a multiplicative form of regression and is often referred to as a growth or power equation; it may be expressed as:

$$Y = ab^x$$

The least-squares technique may be applied in calculating its coefficients. This power function presented in logs is:

$$\log Y = \log a + X \log b$$

A somewhat more complex power function could be:

$$Y = aX_1^{b1}X_2^{b2}$$

This form could be used to explain, for example, the demand for some consumer durable, say, a refrigerator, clothes dryer, or similar item. Or it could be used to describe the demand for domestic automobiles, such that

$$Y = 0.00009058X_1^{1.089}X_2^{0.439}$$

where

X_1 = The number of households in the economy.
X_2 = Disposable personal income in billions of constant dollars.

Studies of the demand for consumer durables in general and of automobiles in particular have caused considerable serious inquiry by Gregory C. Chow and Arnold C. Harburger, two authorities in the field.[18]

The exponents of multiplicative functions are the elasticities; consequently, the exponent 1.089 is the elasticity of Y with respect to the number of households in the economy. The interpretation of this exponent is: A 1.0 percent change in the number of households in the domestic American economy is associated with a 1.089 percent change in Y, the total demand for domestic-made automobiles, all other factors remaining constant. Following that same logic, a 1.0 percent change in disposable personal income in billions of constant dollars would be associated with a 0.439 percent change in the number of automobiles demanded, all other factors remaining constant.

This demand function, $Y = aX_1^{b1}X_2^{b2}$ could be expressed also in logs as

$$\log Y = \log a + b_1 \log X_1 + b_2 \log X_2$$

[18] Gregory C. Chow, *Demand for Automobiles in the United States* (Amsterdam: North Holland Publishing, 1957); and Arnold C. Harburger, *The Demand for Durable Goods* (Chicago: University of Chicago Press, 1960).

One transforms a power function into logarithms because a power function is linear in logs.

Cross-elasticity of demand: Beef and pork

Cross-elasticity of demand refers to the relationship that may exist between the price of one product and the demand for a different product. Cross-elasticity of demand coefficients, E_c, may be positive or negative. If the E_c is positive, the products are thought to be substitutes, and a negative E_c indicates complementary products. Zero cross-elasticity of demand coefficients are possible and indicate that the two products are independent of one another.

Substitute goods are ones for which demand increases as the price of a competing good or service increases. If a certain Chevrolet model and a certain Ford model are substitute goods, the demand for the Chevrolet model will increase as the price of the Ford model increases.

Complementary goods are ones for which demand decreases as the price of a related good increases. If the price of automobiles declines and the demand for automobile tires increases, the two products are thought of as complements.

If changes in the price of pork are related to changes in the demand for beef and the cross-elasticity of demand coefficient is positive, one would interpret the coefficient to mean the two products are substitutes for one another. Figure 5–5, panel A, for example, reveals the price of pork to have increased from point A to point B. This increase in the price of pork causes the quantity demanded of pork to decrease from X_0 to X_1. Because of the substitutability of beef for pork, the demand for beef increases from D to D' in panel B. Note: the price of beef remains constant as pork increases from P_0 to P_1.

In this example, changes in the price of pork are related to changes in the demand for beef. To establish this relationship the cross-elasticity of demand between the two products should be calculated. If the coefficient is positive, then one interprets this coefficient to mean the two products are substitutes for one another. Using data provided in Table 5–7, a demand curve may be established relating the quantity demanded of beef (the dependent variable) to the price per pound of pork (the independent variable). It is based on the equation:

$$Q_{d_b} = a + bx$$

where

$a =$ Some constant that currently has no economic significance.
$b =$ The regression coefficient.
$x =$ The price of pork (1972).

Figure 5–5
Price of pork and demand for beef

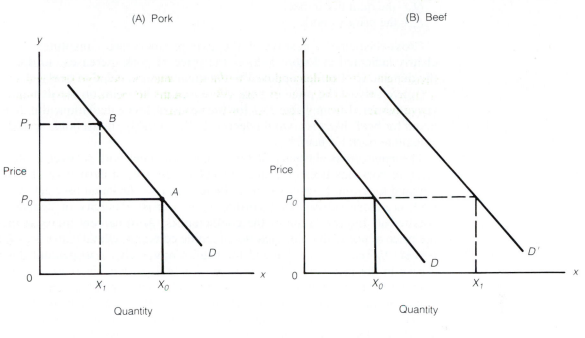

(A) Pork   (B) Beef

$$Q_{db} = a + bx$$
$$= -8,903 + 44,867.23 \cdot .645$$
$$(13,964.94)$$
$$= -8,903 + 28,939.36$$
$$= 20,036.36 \text{ (millions of pounds of beef,}$$
$$\text{predicted value)}$$

The figure in parentheses beneath the regression coefficient is the standard error term.

The calculation for point cross-elasticity of beef and pork is given by this equation:

$$E_c = \frac{\partial Q_b}{\partial P_p} \cdot \frac{P_p}{Q_b}$$

$$= 44,867.23 \cdot \frac{.645}{20,036}$$

$$= \frac{28,939.36}{20,036}$$

$$= 1.44$$

where

Q_b = the quantity of beef.
P_p = the price of pork.

Cross-elasticity is positive if the two products are substitutes. As clearly indicated in Figure 5–5, as the price of pork increases, so does the demand for beef (as opposed to the quantity demanded of beef).

Conversely, if the price of pork decreased at the point on the demand curve assumed from Table 5–7 for purposes of this calculation, the demand for beef, likewise, would decrease. Presumably, households would substitute pork for beef.[19]

The point cross-elasticity of the demand for beef with respect to the price of pork has been calculated by taking the partial derivative of the demand function. It results in a coefficient of 1.44. Demand for beef and pork are close substitutes according to this cross-elasticity of demand coefficient. Interpretation of the coefficient is: A 10 percent increase in the price of pork, all other factors remaining constant, would cause a 14.4 percent increase in the demand for beef. Conversely, a 10 percent decrease in the price of pork would cause a 14.4 percent decrease in the demand for beef. In other words, we are able to measure the degree by which a change in price of one good may cause a change in quantity demanded of that good. Simultaneously, we can estimate the direction and degree by which the demand curve for a different good will shift.

Beef and pork as complementary goods

About 89.9 percent of the variation in the dependent variable, quantity of beef, is explained if one uses prices of beef and pork as the independent variables. These data are taken from Table 5–7, where each price has been adjusted for changes in disposable income and changes in population. The function, generally, is as follows:

$$Q_d = f(P_b, P_p)$$

where

P_b = the price of beef.
P_p = the price of pork.

A linear function presenting the demand for beef as the dependent variable and the prices of beef and pork, as adjusted, as independent variables is as follows. The quantities in parentheses beneath the regression coefficients are standard error terms. The prices of beef and pork are X and X_1, respectively, as revealed in Table 5–7.

---

[19] This statement assumes all other factors in the economy, such as population and income, remain constant.

$$Q_d = a + bx + cx_1$$
$$= 27{,}974 - 37{,}758{,}256 P_b - 25{,}006{,}052 P_p$$
$$(9{,}759{,}317) \qquad (10{,}814{,}910)$$
$$= 27{,}974 - (37{,}758{,}256)(.000150) - (25{,}006{,}052)(.000168)$$
$$= 27{,}974 - 5{,}663 - 4{,}201$$
$$= 18{,}109 \text{ pounds of beef (millions)}$$
$$r^2 = 89.9$$

The point cross-elasticity of demand for beef with respect to the price of pork is calculated by taking the partial derivative as follows:

$$E_{Q_{db}} = \frac{\partial Q_{db}}{\partial P_p} \cdot \frac{P_p}{Q_b}$$
$$= -25{,}006{,}052 \cdot \frac{.000168}{18{,}109}$$
$$= -.23$$

Demands for beef and pork are not very close substitutes according to this cross-elasticity of demand coefficient; in fact, they are complements.[20] In other words, when the prices of beef and pork are adjusted for changes in population and changes in disposable personal income, the point cross-elasticity of demand coefficient is such that as the price of pork increases, the demand for beef decreases. In the example used here, if the price of pork were to increase by 10 percent, beef demand would decrease by 2.3 percent. This explanation of beef and pork as complements may not be a very plausible set of circumstances, yet it could happen. If the prices per pound of beef and pork, as adjusted, decrease at rates less rapid than the general population desires, the public may, quite simply, reduce their overall consumption of meat.[21] In other words, the demand for beef and pork may decrease as the households substitute other foodstuffs (i.e., fish, vegetables, poultry, and so on) for meat productions, generally.

The concept of cross-elasticity of demand is clear enough for most persons, yet it is rather hard to apply because of difficulties associated with obtaining reliable raw data with which to work. The concept is used often in antitrust matters when the U.S. Justice Department attempts to determine whether a change in price by one manufacturer can bring about a shift in demand for the finished good or service of a competing corporation. If Roadway Express, a trucking company, competes with the

---

[20] Under conditions of *ceteris paribus* (other things being equal) a negative cross-elasticity of demand coefficient indicates complementarity. To the extent that *ceteris paribus* conditions do not exist, it can be argued that these two products are not complements.

[21] Beef prices, column 8 of Table 5–7, decreased at an annual rate of 3.62 from 1950 through 1972; pork prices, column 9, decreased at an average annual rate of 3.06.

Chessie System, a railroad, for the shippers' transportation dollar and if their demand functions are such that the cross-elasticities are positive, Chessie could cause a decrease in Roadway's demand curve by changing its (Chessie's) price. The Interstate Commerce Commission exists because of this possibility.

High cross-elasticities of demand coefficients, either real or imagined, caused the Justice Department to disallow the takeover of The B. F. Goodrich Company by Northwest Industries. The federal government filed an antitrust suit to block the merger.[22] The major method of analysis in the case: cross-elasticity of demand.

The concept is useful. An effort should be made to understand it thoroughly.

Empirical demand analysis

Hogarty and Elzinga in a note published in the *Review of Economics and Statistics* analyzed the demand for beer using the ordinary least-squares method and expressed all variables in logarithmic form:

$$\log_n Q_{it} = b_o + b_1 \log n P_{it} + b_2 \log n Y_{it}$$

where

Q_{it} = Number of cases of beer (quantity demanded) consumed per adult in the ith state in year t.
P_i = Real price of a case of beer in the ith state in the year t.
Y_i = Per capital real income in the ith state in the year t.
i = 1, 2, 3, . . . , 45.
t = 1,2,3,4.

The authors presumed constant price and income elasticities initially. When tested they found price elasticity to be at or near unity. Experimentation with subsamples of states having high or low incomes per capita demonstrated a tendency for the income elasticity of beer to vary inversely with the level of income. Hogarty and Elzinga believe lack of price data for beer over the past decade made prediction impossible, but they noted that from 1962 to 1969 per capita beer consumption of adults increased by 16 percent while the real per capita income rose by 27 percent. Assuming stable prices for beer, they considered the implied price elasticity of demand for beer to be 0.59 for the 1962–1969 period and estimated income elasticity for that period to be 0.37.[23] Assuming these elasticity of demand coefficients to be correct, one would conclude

[22] "Goodrich's Four-Ply Defense," *Fortune*, July 1969, pp. 110, 184–90.
[23] Thomas F. Hogarty and Kenneth G. Elzinga, "The Demand for Beer," *The Review of Economics and Statistics*, May 1972, pp. 195–198.

the demand for beer to be price and income inelastic. Is beer an inferior good? Is it a normal good? How do you know?

Demand for marijuana

Nisbet and Vakil have estimated price and expenditure elasticities of demand for marijuana among UCLA students.[24] Their approach was quite simple: analysis of an anonymous mail questionnaire, which was answered by 926 respondents, approximately 52.8 percent of whom claimed to have never tried marijuana.[25] These persons were classified as non-smokers and were compared with the remaining 47.2 percent of the sample who said they had tried marijuana; anyone admitting to having tried marijuana (even once) was classified as a smoker. The intent of the questionnaire was to obtain data with respect to how many ounces of marijuana a consumer (student) would buy from a given income and whether the purchaser would be willing to continue purchasing if the price per ounce (lid) were to rise. Consequently, the authors hoped to trace the demand function for an individual user.

Two alternative functional forms were used in estimating an individual's demand curve for the product. Equation 1 was:

$$\log (Q_m) = b_o + b_1 \log(P_m) + b_2 \log(E) + b_3 \log(S) + e$$

where

Q_m = Quantity of marijuana in ounces per month.
P_m = Price of marijuana in dollars per ounce.
E = Mean monthly expenditure in total dollars.
S = Expenditure dispersion measure.
bs = parameters to be estimated.
e = Error term.

They decided upon a double log function. The price elasticity of demand is b_1, and the expenditure elasticity is b_2.

Nisbet and Vakil concluded: (1) the individual college student's demand curve for marijuana exhibits all of the characteristics one would expect to find in traditional economic theory, a so-called normal demand curve; (2) estimates of price elasticity of demand ranged from -0.40 to -0.151; (3) the expenditure elasticity is very close to zero; and (4) the price elasticity data suggest that any policies designed to restrict supplies of marijuana may not be effective in reducing the quantity demanded. Restrictions in supply would serve to increase price. However, rising prices of marijuana caused by reductions in supply could encourage stu-

---

[24] Charles T. Nisbet and Variouz Vakil, "Some Estimates of Price and Expenditure Elasticity of Demand for Marijuana Among U.C.L.A. Students," *The Review of Economics and Statistics,* November 1972, pp. 473–75.

[25] Reliable raw data from secondary sources were not available.

dent to substitute more harmful drugs than the one to which they have become accustomed.

Demand for cigarettes

James Hamilton concluded that the ban on cigarette advertising was designed to lower the quantity demanded of cigarettes, but the ban "disconnects the cigarette industry from the Fairness Doctrine, which offered government the most effective and least fiscally expensive channel for promulgating health warnings and reducing smoking. Any future policy action must be either less effective or more expensive."[26]

Hamilton's study (1) presents econometric estimations of the demand function for cigarettes, (2) gauges the comparative effects of advertising and the health scare on the quantity demanded of cigarettes, and (3) evaluates whether the congressional ban on cigarette advertising will, in fact, promote public health by reducing cigarette consumption. His conclusions include the notion that policymakers in the future should evaluate their policy models more carefully. Cigarette demand functions estimated by him indicate that intensification of the health scare would have been a more productive approach if one wanted quantity demanded to decline. Moreover, he reminds government officials that action taken by them based on wishful thinking is seldom as effective as action they could have taken based on carefully specified models "accurately depicting the forces influencing the policy objectives and the connections between forces and proposed policy actions." That is, the impact upon the demand for cigarettes caused by advertising, the health scare, and the cigarette advertising ban must be quantified and their elasticities determined before governmental action is taken if maximum public benefit is to be expected.

Summary

Statistical derivations of demand functions should be made, if possible, before the elasticity of demand coefficient, E_d, of that function is measured. But data are not always available, and the curve may have to be estimated. An equation for the demand curve is not needed before an arc price elasticity of demand determination can be made.

Derivation of the demand function has been explored, but before leaving the concept of demand and demand elasticity, one should consider the value of this information to top management. Ask what piece(s) of data is available or could be collected for purposes of calculating E_d. Ask where this kind of information would be invaluable. For example, if the mayor of New York City knew the elasticity of demand coefficient for

[26] James L. Hamilton, "The Demand for Cigarettes: Advertising, the Health Scare, and the Cigarette Advertising Ban," *The Review of Economics and Statistics,* November 1972, 401–9.

subway travel, he would be able to comment intelligently concerning whether fares should be increased, decreased, or remain the same. If demand for subway travel in New York City is highly price elastic, a decrease in price would cause ridership to increase, total revenue to the system to increase, the number of automobiles coming into the city daily to decrease, the availability of parking spaces within the city to increase, parking rates to decrease, and pollution associated with heavy automobile traffic to decrease. Generally speaking, residents of New York City might expect the quality and quantity of life within the city to improve—and all becuase E_d is highly elastic.

When the 58,850-seat stadium was constructed in Atlanta, Georgia, for purposes of housing the Atlanta Falcon football team, did top management give consideration to the price elasticity of demand for ticket sales? Do the public utility commissioners located in each state in the United States consider elasticity of demand in determining whether or not to allow increases in rates to consumer and industrial users of natural gas and electricity? Do colleges and universities, both public and private, concern themselves with this relative measure of sensitivity to quantity demanded when they explore the tuition and other fees charged to graduate and undergraduate student bodies? Do labor unions consider the elasticity of demand for the product they help to produce when they request higher wage rates? Do movie theatres consider E_ds when they charge $4 per seat and complain when fewer people seem to go to movies anymore? Referring to minimum wage legislation, do members of the U.S. Congress consider the elasticity of demand for unskilled labor and ask themselves, in effect, if one would rather be fully employed at $3 per hour or unemployed at $4 per hour? Unfortunately, for the employment, output, and income of the aggregate economy and for the dividends and capital growth per share to many common stockholders, the answer in each instance may all too often be no.

This chapter has attempted to delineate some of the tools and techniques available to the managerial economist as she/he contributes to the overall goals and objectives of the firm. In addition, two approaches to industry demand analysis were given brief attention.

Surveys may be useful in determining attitudes or plans of retailers and consumers, and these may in turn be helpful in describing and determining demands for discretionary goods and services. Statistical analysis, in order of increasing sophistication, include: (1) projection and (2) time-series analysis, both techniques aimed at analyzing a variable using only information about its own past behavior; (3) correlation and (4) regression analysis, both aimed at viewing one variable on the basis of measured or forecast values of one or more other variables; and (5) econometric models, aimed at reviewing values for a set of endogenous variables based on values of a set of exogenous variables and a structure of relationships specified by an economic model.

Industry capacity forecasts are needed for comparison with demand forecasts in determining the outlook for industry pricing and profitability. Possible short-range constraints on industry expansion include labor (skilled workers in a full-employment economy) and capital (specialized machines and equipment under order backlog conditions). In a slightly longer-range perspective, constraints may be willingness to expand and ease of entry.

Analysis of market demand is derived from industry forecasts by using indexes of relative buying power that have been estimated for various market areas and classes of buyers. The market potential for a particular firm is established by adding the total purchases that have been projected for the various markets served by the firm. Once the forecasts of market potential are in hand, the firm can estimate the share that it will get on the basis of current position and expected effects of its marketing policies —product quality variations, promotion, and pricing.

Cases

Demand analysis

Five elasticity of demand situations*

The five short cases presented here provide an opportunity to evaluate the significance of the elasticity concept in a variety of actual business decisions. In some of the cases the objective is to estimate the demand elasticity and to use this estimate in arriving at a decision on price. The other cases supply information on the actual decisions on price made by management; the question is whether the managers made a sound analysis of their particular demand situations.

Senior citizen's bowling alley   In 1980, a limited partnership was formed at a senior citizens apartment building, the idea being to provide a tax shelter for the partners, while simultaneously providing a form of exercise and recreation for the building's occupants. One of the problems the partners faced before the alley opened was establishment of an appropriate price policy. Bowling alley charges are established on the basis of the lines played. The price is expressed as so much money per line.

The partners made a survey of the several hundred occupants living in the high-rise complex and in nearby surrounding retirement neighborhoods. It was determined that senior citizens would use the lanes at a price somewhere in the neighborhood of 65 to 85 cents per line. The survey indicated the price could vary from 60 cents per line at the minimum to $1 at the maximum, and 70 cents per line would be the most

---

* These cases are altered versions of materials presented as 'Five Cases in the Elasticity of Demand,'' W. W. Haynes, *Managerial Economics* (Plano, Tex.: Business Publications, 1969), pp. 177–86.

common figure. Certain capital equipment and fixed costs of installation would be paid by a Housing and Urban Development (HUD) grant; consequently, the limited partnership could generate a profit with a price in the 75-cent area.

This particular alley would have some advantages. It would be the first alley in the housing complex area and would thus hold a monopoly position. The high-rise apartment buildings in the complex appeared to be large enough to support a 16-lane alley, but not so large as to attract competition. Because no location within 20 miles was large enough to support an alley, customers would be attracted from a fairly large area.

A survey of other alleys suggested that 75 cents per line was a viable rate—high enough to cover the costs and return a profit but not so high as to discourage customers. The question was whether a higher rate would be even more profitable.

Telecommunications Since 1962, when the Federal Communications Commission turned its attention to the problem of interstate telephone rates, American Telephone & Telegraph Company has paid special attention to "after nine" rates.

The after-nine rates incorporate an extra reduction in telephone rates between 9 P.M. and 4:30 A.M., beyond the reductions in effect at 6 P.M. The aim of this extra reduction has been to stimulate more nonbusiness use of telephone facilities in off-peak hours. It was estimated that between 10 percent and 15 percent of total interstate long-distance calls were made between 9 P.M. and 4:30 A.M. The reduced rates have increased this percentage.

An experiment with after-nine rates was tried in 1962 in 10 states on an intrastate basis. An AT&T vice president reported little response to the reduced rates. A study of 800,000 messages from 20 central offices provided no clear-cut evidence of the stimulation of calls after 9 P.M. AT&T thought evidence was inadequate in estimating the long-range effect of the after-nine plan, since customer calling habits change slowly, and the publicity given the rates could have been inadequate.

One effect of the after-nine rates was to transfer some traffic from the "after-six" discount period to the after-nine discount period, with a consequent reduction in revenues. Another effect was a transfer from person-to-person calls, which formerly had been underpriced in relation to cost, to station-to-station calls.

After a series of meetings, the Bell System and the FCC announced plans for an after-nine nationwide interstate plan, along with increases in person-to-person rates up to 800 miles. The new rates became effective April 1, 1963. The maximum charge for the initial period of a call was $1 anywhere in the continental United States. At the same time a slight increase in interstate person-to-person rates up to 800 miles made up for some of the loss in revenue. The estimated reduction in station-to-station revenues to the Bell System was $55 million per year. The 5- and 10-cent increases in person-to-person calls increased revenues by $25 million, leaving a net loss of $30 million on the 1962 traffic base.

The interstate rates resulted in reductions of from 8 percent to 43 percent. In terms of mileage bands, the after-nine rates were 60 cents for 221–354 miles, 65 cents for 355–600 miles, 70 cents for 601–800 miles, 75 cents for 801–1,050 miles, 80 cents for 1,051–1,360 miles, 90 cents for 1,361–1,910 miles, and $1 for all continental calls above 1,910 miles. Some comparisons with earlier years were dramatic. A call from the East Coast to the West Coast would have cost $4.25 in 1940 but cost only $1 under the new rates.

The Chairman of the House of Representatives Interstate and Foreign Commerce Committee gave his approval to the rates. He suggested that the increased utilization at the lower rates might be so great as to permit a reduction of rates at other hours of the day. He doubted the rates would result in the reduction of $30 million revenues indicated above. His position implied an increase in revenues.

Automobile rebates and other price adjustments   In 1958, the president of the United Automobile Workers (UAW) suggested a reduction in the price of automobiles averaging $100 a car. The automobile market was weak in 1958, with resultant unemployment; lower prices would lead to greater sales and would stimulate employment. UAW leadership believed that a $100 reduction in prices, about 4 percent, would increase sales by 16 percent. A similar situation existed in 1980 with respect to depressed automobile sales.

Prices were not reduced or otherwise adjusted in 1958 as suggested by the UAW; however, by 1980 the automakers appeared a little more desperate. They had just doubled the list price of most makes and models over the 1970 prices. They were still reluctant to cut these new prices, but they agreed to price rebates. The rebates represented a system whereby the consumer paid whatever price she/he was able to negotiate with the dealership, and the manufacturer would then kick back something in the neighborhood of $300 to $1,000 to the buyer.

In testimony before the Senate Subcommittee on Antitrust and Monopoly, a vice president of the Ford Motor Company cited studies that indicated price elasticities ranging from 0.5 to 1.5.[1] Another study found elasticities ranging from .65 to 1.53 Many such E_d interpretations fall within the range of .65 to 1.53.

A Department of Commerce study of automobile demand resulted in several estimating equations, one of which was:

---

[1] Statement before the Subcommittee on Antitrust and Monopoly, Committee on the Judiciary, U.S. Senate, February 4–5, 1958. Extracts from this statement appear in A. W. Warner and V. R. Fuchs, *Concepts and Cases in Economic Analysis* (New York: Harcourt Brace Jovanovich, 1958), pp. 147–48.

$$Y = 0.0003239 \, X_1^{2.536} \, X_2^{2.291} \, X_3^{-1.359} \, X_4^{0.932}$$

where

Y = New private passenger car registrations per million households.

X_1 = Disposable personal income per household in constant dollars.

X_2 = Current annual disposable income per household as a percentage of the preceding year in constant dollars.

X_3 = Percentage of average retail price of cars to consumer prices measured by consumer price index.

X_4 = Average scrappage age in years.

Similar equations based on slightly different assumptions resulted in price elasticities close to the one implied by the above equation, as do studies by Chow.[2] The values of the independent variables have changed somewhat, but the elasticity of demand coefficient remains almost the same, 1958 through 1980.

Price cutting: The retail store case The U.S. Supreme Court of 1951 freed many firms from the restriction of "fair trade" legislation and opened the way to more aggressive price policies.[3] This decision freed firms that had not signed state fair-trade contracts on merchandise that had been transported in interstate commerce. R. H. Macy and Company was a nonsigner firm and was also a proponent of free pricing. Macy's slogan was "We endeavor to save our customers at least 6 percent for cash, except on price-fixed goods." Therefore, it is not surprising that Macy's proceeded to cut prices only eight days after the decision. Macy's ran a two-page advertisement announcing 6 percent price reductions on 5,978 items that had been fixed in price under the fair-trade legislation.

Macy's faced strong competition from other department stores, including Abraham and Straus, Bloomingdale's, Namm's, and Gimbel's, whose motto was "Nobody—but nobody—undersells Gimbel's." These stores took retaliatory action against Macy's. One hour after the Macy's reductions took effect, Gimbel's began to cut prices. Abraham and Strauss followed a few hours later with cuts of 10 percent or more. As Macy's learned of this retaliation, it proceeded to cut to 6 percent under the new low prices of competitors. By the end of the day, all the other stores mentioned were engaged in a full-scale price war. Some price cuts were as much as 30 percent in the first day.

The price cuts involved well-known branded items to include big-ticket consumer durables, such as typewriters and suits. Only a small percentage of the original 6,000 items on which Macy's had originally cut price became involved in the deeper price cuts. A few items were cut below

---

[2] G. C. Chow, "Statistical Demand Functions for Automobiles and Their Use for Forecasting," in A. C. Harberger, ed., *The Demand for Durable Goods* (Chicago: University of Chicago Press, 1960).

[3] *Schewegmann Bros.* v. *Calvert Distilleries Corporation*, 314 U.S. 384 (1951).

wholesale cost (Bayer asprin slipped in price to 4 cents a bottle). The tempo of price cuts varied from item to item. Price cuts in the competing stores were not identical but tended to be similar.

The volume of business done by the stores engaged in price cutting increased sharply. Macy's normally sold less than 3.5 percent of Sunbeam Mixmasters sold in New York, but its proportion rose to 56 percent in the 10 weeks following the beginning of the price war. Abraham and Straus increased its share of Brooklyn sales from 2.5 percent to 60 percent. In June the total sales of 13 New York and Brooklyn department stores were 14 percent above those of the previous June, and one store recorded a 33.4 percent increase. The largest increases in volume were in major appliances and housewares.

The Fifth Avenue stores did not participate in the price cutting. Many neighborhood hardware stores did cut prices, and price reductions spread to the Bronx and to Jersey City. But the price war came to a close about six weeks after it started. The impact of the price cuts on volume began to diminish rapidly, and the stores wished to bring the war to an end. Prices were gradually restored to their former levels. One way this was done was for the aggressor to run out of stock until competitors restored the old price.

The chief question raised by these events is whether or not the Macy executives made a correct evaluation of the elasticity of demand in initiating price reductions. Some observers have suggested that Macy's might have done better to cut price-fixed items by 6 percent without publicizing this cut.

Elasticity of demand: Commuter services   Assume that on Sunday, January 6, 1983, the Boston and Maine Railroad instituted a new rate schedule for certain commuters into Boston. A federal subsidy of $2.2 million, part of a program to aid mass transportation, made this experiment with reduced fares possible. The objective of the federal program of subsidies was to determine whether lower commuter rates for routine travelers would relieve the problem of congestion on highways. The Boston and Maine experiment was to last one year, unless the railroad became discouraged with the results and terminated the program in six months.

The Boston and Maine could carry 40,000 commuters a shift to and from branches to the west, north, and east of Boston. In recent years it had modernized commuter equipment but had steadily lost passengers. It raised fares to cover the higher costs per passenger, with the result of further reductions in traffic and the curtailment of schedules. Expressways into Boston had stimulated commuting by automobile but had also accentuated traffic and parking problems in downtown Boston. By January 1983, the Boston and Maine passenger count had fallen to 11,000 per shift, and the passenger deficit had reached $3.8 million.

The subsidies made possible the reduction of fares from 25 percent to 40 percent and the increase in the number of daily trains from 187 to 391.

The railroad spent hundreds of thousands of dollars cleaning and refurbishing diesel cars and setting up a canopy at North Station in Boston. The railroad hoped to reduce passenger revenue deficits despite the reduction of fares and the improvement in service.

Exhibit 1 presents passenger counts for comparable weeks in 1982 and 1983, before and after the fare reduction. Each passenger is counted both on the inward and the outward trip; this explains the fact that the totals for 1982 are about double the figure of 11,000 passengers mentioned above.

Exhibit 2 shows some of the fare changes from selected points on the Boston and Maine. The rates are quoted for 20-ride commuter books.

Exhibit 1
Day Shift passenger counts, Boston and Maine Railroad (comparable weeks in 1982–83)

New Hampshire District (Boston to Woburn)					
Week ending February 15, 1982			**Week ending February 14, 1983**		
Day	**Number of trains**	**Passenger count**	**Day**	**Number of trains**	**Passenger count**
Friday	37	2,758	Friday	55	2,833
Saturday	29	794	Saturday	36	1,132
Sunday	21	285	Sunday	19	397
Monday	37	2,616	Monday	55	3,163
Tuesday	37	2,660	Tuesday	55	3,186
Wednesday	37	2,627	Wednesday	55	3,280
Thursday	36	2,325	Thursday	55	2,981

Portland District (W) Reading					
Week ending February 15, 1982			**Week ending February 14, 1983**		
Day	**Number of trains**	**Passenger count**	**Day**	**Number of trains**	**Passenger count**
Friday	54	6,765	Friday	112	7,535
Saturday	36	1,575	Saturday	36	1,846
Sunday	24	447	Sunday	20	808
Monday	54	6,625	Monday	112	8,121
Tuesday	54	6,693	Tuesday	112	7,872
Wednesday	54	6,939	Wednesday	112	8,087
Thursday	54	6,830	Thursday	112	8,022

New Hampshire District					
Week ending February 15, 1982			**Week ending February 14, 1983**		
Day	**Number of trains**	**Passenger count**	**Day**	**Number of trains**	**Passenger count**
Friday	25	3,159	Friday	46	3,868
Saturday	22	1,080	Saturday	27	1,467
Sunday	16	1,052	Sunday	18	1,199
Monday	25	2,543	Monday	46	3,699
Tuesday	25	2,478	Tuesday	46	3,876
Wednesday	25	2,686	Wednesday	46	4,978
Thursday	25	2,450	Thursday	46	3,703

Exhibit 1 (*concluded*)

Fitchburg Division					
Week ending February 15, 1982			**Week ending February 14, 1983**		
Day	**Number of trains**	**Passenger count**	**Day**	**Number of trains**	**Passenger count**
Friday	24	2,221	Friday	42	3,112
Saturday	10	449	Saturday	22	1,060
Sunday	8	200	Sunday	8	331
Monday	24	2,456	Monday	42	3,368
Tuesday	24	2,318	Tuesday	42	3,419
Wednesday	24	2,426	Wednesday	42	3,414
Thursday	24	1,380	Thursday	42	3,175

Portland District—Eastern Route					
Week ending February 15, 1982			**Week ending February 14, 1983**		
Day	**Number of trains**	**Passenger count**	**Day**	**Number of trains**	**Passenger count**
Friday	41	5,169	Friday	92	6,855
Saturday	33	1,299	Saturday	35	1,969
Sunday	21	644	Sunday	19	1,188
Monday	41	4,690	Monday	92	6,939
Tuesday	41	4,841	Tuesday	92	6,803
Wednesday	41	4,991	Wednesday	92	6,924
Thursday	41	4,526	Thursday	92	6,786

Portland District—Western Route					
Week ending February 15, 1982			**Week ending February 14, 1983**		
Day	**Number of trains**	**Passenger count**	**Day**	**Number of trains**	**Passenger count**
Friday	26	2,817	Friday	40	3,221
Saturday	25	1,212	Saturday	27	1,813
Sunday	15	869	Sunday	13	870
Monday	26	2,590	Monday	38	3,041
Tuesday	26	2,518	Tuesday	38	2,786
Wednesday	26	2,528	Wednesday	38	2,909
Thursday	26	2,282	Thursday	38	2,836

1. What is your estimate of the elasticity of demand in the bowling alley case at prices from 70 cents to 75 cents per line? From 75 cents to 90 cents per line? From 90 cents to $1 per line? What reasoning underlies your estimates?
2. Is there great uncertainty about your elasticity estimates?
3. What are the implications of your elasticity estimates for pricing in the bowling alley? Explain.
4. In what way is the elasticity of demand involved in the telephone case?
5. On the basis of your impressions of consumer behavior, estimate the elasticity of demand for after-nine telephone services.

Exhibit 2
Commuter fare changes, selected points Boston and
Maine Railroad

	1982	After January 6, 1983
New Hampshire District		
North Chelmsford, Mass.	$16.80	$11.13
Lowell, Mass.	15.82	10.72
Woburn	9.83	7.70
Portland District (Reading)		
Reading	10.69	8.12
Portland District—Eastern		
Salem	12.75	8.88
Portland District—Western		
Andover	14.85	10.13
Fitchburg Division		
Fitchburg	23.60	15.47
Concord	14.20	9.70

6. What considerations other than the elasticity of demand would influence the impact of the after-nine rates on company profits?

7. In the automobile case, what is the significance of the UAW demand estimate? Of Ford Motors demand estimates?

8. What is the price elasticity of the demand for automobiles according to the Department of Commerce estimating equation?

9. Did Macy's make a sound evaluation of the elasticity of demand in its pricing decisions? Was the analysis of competitors' reactions an essential part of elasticity estimates?

10. Would a nonpublicized price cut of 6 percent have resulted in a different elasticity of demand? Discuss.

11. What were the sources of uncertainty about the elasticities of demand facing Macy's?

12. Was the short-run elasticity of demand greater or less than the longer-run elasticity of demand in the case of the price war? Explain.

13. Estimate the elasticity of demand for the commuter services of the Boston and Maine Railroad.

14. Do the reductions in rates on the Boston and Maine appear to be profitable? Discuss in terms of the demand elasticities.

15. Do the data in Exhibits 1 and 2 provide a sound basis for estimating the elasticity of demand? Discuss.

The Indian County Dairy*

The executives of the Indian County Dairy, near New Delhi, India, were concerned about the losses the dairy had been incurring during the

*This case is an altered version of material presented as "Mahanagar Municipal Dairy (D)" W. W. Haynes, *Managerial Economics,* (Plano, Tex.: Business Publications, 1969) pp. 669–80.

previous few years. Their consensus was that the dairy could show better results by increasing the demand of milk and by cutting back on the conversion of milk into ghee and butter. Some of the executives were of the opinion that the existing distribution system presented many opportunities for improvements, both in terms of service to the consumers and of sales volume to the dairy. They were also concerned whether or not the dairy should continue to sell both bottled and loose milk. This matter was, therefore, discussed in a meeting of the executives.

Sales and distribution   At times the dairy purchased more milk than could be sold as fluid milk, and the excess was converted into butter and ghee on which the dairy typically did not recover even the cost of the milk.[1] This problem was intensified during the monsoon and winter months when the dairy, by the terms of purchase agreement, had to accept more milk from its suppliers than it did in the summer months (see Exhibit 1). On the other hand, the demand for milk in the monsoon and winter months was considered to be lower than it was in the summer months. However, in the winter and monsoon months of the year 1983–84, the suppliers of milk were not offering as much excess milk as they had in the previous year (see Exhibit 2).

The dairy sold whole milk,[2] cow milk, and toned milk[3] in half liter and 200 milliliters bottles. Whole milk and toned milk were also sold in unbottled form; such loose milk sales constituted 46.8 percent of the total sales volume in the year 1983–84 (Exhibit 3). In addition, the dairy sold double-toned milk[4] in amounts limited by the commitment between the municipal corporation and UNICEF.

The purchases of the dairy's milk fell into two categories—institutions that made bulk purchases (such as hospitals, schools, hotels, and cafeterias) and individual consumers. The milk supplies to institutions accounted for 15 percent of the dairy's total volume of milk in terms of value.

---

[1] To describe the situation:

Average purchase price of 100 liters of cow-cum-buffalo milk in 1983–84	Rs. 64.30
Less credit for skimmed milk computed at the rate of equivalent price for skimmed milk powder	9.60
Cost of fat recovery, i.e., 6.5 kg. fat	54.70
Average realization for fat	40.62
Loss on 100 liters of milk	14.08

[2] Whole milk was any milk that contained a minimum of 6 percent fat and 9 percent SNF. Most of it was buffalo milk, since milk from this source contained solid ingredients in those approximate proportions.

[3] Toned milk contained a low percentage of fat (3 percent fat and 9 percent SNF). It was prepared by adding skimmed milk powder and water, or skimmed milk to the fresh milk, and was sold at a cheaper rate.

[4] Double-toned milk contained roughly 1.6 percent fat and was distributed free to municipal school children who were between the ages of 7 and 12, and to nursing and pregnant women. The municipal corporation paid a subsidy to the dairy for the free distribution of milk and for the reduced price distribution to low-income families.

Exhibit 1
Indian County Dairy (sales of milk by seasons and type* in thousands of liters)

1982–83	Summer	Monsoon	Winter	Total	Percent of total
Whole milk					
Loose †	574	454	343	1,371	13.9%
Bottled	738	935	812	2,485	25.2
Toned milk					
Loose	1,548	1,526	1,072	4,146	42.2
Bottled	128	143	124	395	4.0
Cow milk, bottled	83	78	113	174	2.8
Doubled-toned milk	47	512	608	1,167	11.9
Total	3,118	3,648	3,072	9,838	100.0%

1983–84	Summer	Monsoon	Winter	Total	Percent of total
Whole milk					
Loose †	356	360	329	1,045	10.8%
Bottled	871	1,130	1,099	3,100	31.8
Toned milk					
Loose	927	1,321	1,253	3,501	36.0
Bottled	128	161	170	459	4.7
Cow milk, bottled	118	136	139	393	4.0
Doubled-toned milk	81	507	649	1,237	12.7
Total	2,481	3,615	3,639	9,735	100.0%

* The dairy also sold small amounts of syrup milk, cold coffee milk, and higher-fat milk in 1983–1984.

† The dairy sold excess loose cow milk to another dairy; such sales amounted to 558,000 liters in 1982–83 and 210,000 liters in 1983–84, at approximately 50 paise per liter.

The rating committee usually set the purchase price for the procurement of milk at a fixed price for an entire year. In the year 1982–83, it fixed the rate for buffalo milk (containing 6 percent fat and 9 percent SNF) at 57.8 paise per liter. For additional fat content, a premium was payable at the rate of 0.77 paise per 0.1 percent fat content over 6 percent. In the year 1983–84, the base rate was reduced to 56.7 paise per liter. However, the premium payable for additional fat content was fixed at 0.94 paise per 0.1 percent on excess over 6 percent up to a figure of 7 percent and 0.77 paise for every 0.1 percent thereafter. The committee had fixed the purchase price for the year 1984–85 at 56.1 paise per liter. The premium for additional fat content was set at 1.05 paise per 0.1 up to 7 percent and at 0.77 paise per 0.1 percent thereafter. During the year 1983–84, the fat content in buffalo milk received by the dairy averaged 7 percent.

The purchase price for cow milk in 1982–83 was fixed at 46.4 paise per liter for 12 percent solid content (3.5 percent fat and 8.5 percent SNF). A premium for additional solid content in the cow milk was set at 0.39 paise per 0.1 percent. In the year 1983–84, the base price was reduced to 44.5 paise per liter. However, the premium was payable at the same rate as in the year 1982–83. In the year 1984–85, there is expected to be no change

Exhibit 2
Indian County Dairy (quantities of milk purchased and milk converted into butter and ghee in thousand liters)

	Fresh milk purchases			Sour milk purchases (both cow and buffalo)	Converted to ghee and butter
	Buffalo	Ratio	Cow		
1982–83					
Summer:					
April	497		93	NA	—
May	398		81		—
June	375		87		—
July	446		115		—
Total	1,716	3:0	376	NA	—
Monsoon:					
August	586		135		2
September	601		83		19
October	635		82		133
November	640		100		189
Total	2,462	4:3	400	NA	343
Winter:					
December	759		129		372
January	755		149		379
February	631		131		268
March	694		147		244
Total	2,839	4:9	556	NA	1,263
Grand total:	7,017	—	1,332	506	1,606
1983–84					
Summer:					
April	554		127	56	173
May	462		121	55	91
June	352		111	43	1
July	361		86	36	—
Total	1,729	3:0	445	190	265
Monsoon:					
August	455		94	42	3
September	502		84	45	—
October	540		75	48	7
November	515		71	45	9
Total	2,012	3:5	324	180	19
Winter:					
December	611		73	40	—
January	634		77	13	3
February	524		62	34	2
March	472		90	51	—
Total	2,241	3:9	302	138	5
Grand total:	5,982		1,071	508	289

Exhibit 3
Indian County Dairy (realization, direct variable costs, and contribution per liter of milk)

| Type of milk | Realization | Direct variable costs of milk sold | | | | | Contribution |
		Milk and milk powder*	Power, coal, and chemicals†	Bottle breakage and aluminum foils	Commission‡	Total	
Whole							
Bottled	80.9	60.6	1.2	2.8	3.8	68.4	12.5
Loose	76.0	60.6	0.6	—	2.2	63.4	12.6
Cow, bottled	70.0	47.5	1.2	2.8	3.8	55.3	14.7
Toned							
Bottled	58.5	36.3	1.2	2.8	1.6	41.9	16.6
Loose	51.8	36.3	0.6	—	1.6	38.5	13.3
Double-toned							
For schools	40.0	15.2	0.6	—	1.3‡	17.1	22.9
For low income families	40.0	25.0	0.6	—	1.3‡	26.9	13.1

* Cost of milk and milk powder includes process and handling losses with adjustment for fat and SNF content.
† This refers to power, coal, and chemicals consumed in washing and filling of bottles and cans.
‡ Expense incurred on selling double-toned milk through self-operated centers.
Source: Casewriter's calculation based on information supplied by the dairy's executives.

in the base rate, but the premium for the additional solid content was raised to 0.5 paise per 0.1 percent. Cow milk purchased by the dairy during 1983–84 contained an average 12.8 percent solids (4.2 percent fat and 8.6 percent SNF). The dairy purchased a large quantity of cow milk, although sales of such milk were meager. The unsold cow milk principally utilized for standardization of whole milk.

The main sources of buffalo milk supply to the dairy were two milk producers' unions. Purchases from these two unions represented roughly 70 percent of the dairy's total purchases of milk (both buffalo and cow). Cow milk was supplied mainly by the Gopalak Sangh, an organization for the protection of cows.

The dairy experienced a shortage of milk supplies in the summer season and on many occasions was not in a position to cope with the demand.

Individual consumers received milk through a network of nine depots and 226 centers.[5] The depots were run by the dairy employees on a permanent basis at a monthly salary of around 50 to 100 rupees per month. For home delivery from the depots, the dairy employed delivery boys on a commission basis. In April 1984, there were 32 such young men employed. The dairy sale of milk from these depots on an average

---

[5] The depots and centers served an area of 36 square miles and a population of about 1.3 million. The majority of the population drank tea regularly. There were no official statistics on the numbers of persons in various income groups, their milk consumption, etc. However, the third five-year plan estimated the all-India per capita daily consumption of milk at roughly 0.14 liters.

was 700 liters. In contrast to the depots, centers were run by individuals, who operated them under terms laid down by the dairy and received a commission calculated on sales (see Exhibits 4 and 5). The dairy ran some centers on a temporary basis when people could not be found to run them on a commission basis. In such cases, the dairy employed temporary workers at a daily wage of Rs. 1.50 for running the center; in case the center also undertook home delivery, they were paid Rs. 3 per day. The daily average sales of the temporarily self-operated centers were in the range of 20 to 30 liters. The number of temporarily self-operated centers and centers on commission basis is shown in Exhibit 6.

Most of the persons operating centers on a commission basis took up milk distribution work as a part-time job. They got help from their children or hired people (generally at a salary of Rs. 30 to 40 per month) to run the center. These operators were responsible for the maintenance of cabins, for keeping accounts of the milk supplied, and for arranging home delivery of bottled whole and cow milk. The dairy required a cash secu-

Exhibit 4
Indian County Dairy (selling prices of the dairy's milk in paise per liter)

Milk	August 20, 1980 to August 19, 1982	August 20, 1982 to April 14, 1983	April 15, 1983 to July 14, 1983	July 15, 1983 to March 31, 1984
Whole				
Bottled*	77	80	80	80
Loose	70	76	76	76
Cow, bottled*	66	70	70	70
Toned				
Bottled*	53	56	62	56
Loose	44	50	60	50
Double-toned	34	40	40	40

  * The bottled milk prices were for half-liter filling. For 200 milliters filling the diary charged slightly higher prices.

Exhibit 5
Indian County Dairy (commission rates for center operators*)

1. For home delivery of whole and cow milk in bottles.	75 paise for 20 liters
2. For whole milk and cow milk in bottles sold along with straw and ice, if required by the consumer for drinking at the spot.	80 paise for 20 liters
3. For selling whole milk and cow milk (loose and bottled both) at the center.	44 paise for 20 liters
4. For selling toned milk (loose and bottled both) at the center.	31 paise for 20 liters

  * Delivery boys attached to the depots were paid a commission of 75 paise per 20 liters on bottles actually delivered by them.

Exhibit 6
Indian County Dairy (number of centers selling dairy's milk in April, 1984)

Centers	On commission basis	Temporarily self-operated centers	Total
Selling whole loose milk	24	1	25
Selling toned loose milk	92	11	103
Selling double-toned loose milk	—	22	22
Selling toned bottled only	6	1	7
Selling both loose and bottled milk	12	—	12
Selling bottled milk of all types	41	16	57 *
	175	51	226

* Of these centers, 26 also sold milk to be drunk on the spot from the bottle. The persons in charge of such centers were required to supply ice and straws at their own cost to the consumers without additional charge. The ice box was, however, supplied by the dairy free of charge on a returnable basis. The commission on such sales was 80 paise for 20 liters.

rity of Rs. 250 (repayable without interest) and a surety bond for Rs. 500 from these operators. The monthly earnings ranged between Rs. 20 and 500, the average being about Rs. 60.

The dairy had constructed approximately 100 wooden cabins of five-foot size for the depots and centers at an average cost of Rs. 700 each. The rest were open-air centers, generally shaded by a tree and reached by footpaths. If the demand for milk in a particular place was expected to be greater than 30 liters per day, a new center was opened. It was the general practice of the dairy to separate distribution of bottled and loose milk in the centers, in order to minimize the chances of fraudulent practices by the operators of the centers (Exhibit 5). The nine depots operated by the dairy sold only bottled milk.

The depots and centers sold milk at the cabins or at fixed distribution points. In addition, bottled whole and cow milk was sold (at the same price as in the depots and centers) by home delivery. The bottled, toned milk was also delivered to homes and 1 paise per bottle was charged for delivery regardless of size.[6] The 1 paise was retained by the delivery boys. The sale of milk was on a cash basis, and the consumer was required to pay the money at the time of delivery. The consumer had to return the bottles immediately. This meant that most consumers had to transfer the milk into their own vessels at the point of buying. However, the consumer could purchase empty bottles (at 50 paise each), which could be exchanged for the filled ones at the time of delivery.

Between 2 A.M. and 5 P.M. daily the dairy dispatched five trucks and

---

[6] For the supply of toned milk, the dairy had fixed the commission (payable to persons operating centers on commission and to their own employed delivery boys) on the basis of sales at the cabins/fixed-distribution points. The dairy, therefore, allowed them to charge 1 paise extra per bottle if the consumer wanted home delivery.

17 autorickshaws to deliver milk to fixed distribution points. There the milk was sold between 5 and 7 A.M. and 5 and 6:30 P.M. Home delivery was also made during these hours. The delivery boys generally used bicycles and carried 15 to 30 liters of milk in bags at a time.

The loose milk was supplied to the centers in sealed cans. The seal of the lid was to be opened only by the person in charge of the center and in the presence of at least three customers. Although the capacity of a can was 40 liters, the center could order a smaller quantity down to a minimum of 20 liters in a can.

The empties and unsold bottled milk were collected by the dairy vehicles after sales hours in the morning and evening. The dairy did not accept unsold loose milk from the centers. The returns of unsold milk varied in different seasons. In the summer months such returns were hardly 1 to 2 percent of bottled milk sales, whereas in the winter months they ranged between 5 and 8 percent. The returned milk was reused by the dairy as its condition warranted. Milk in good condition was redistributed as it was or after reprocessing. Milk that was sour or showed signs of becoming sour was converted into butter or ghee.

The dairy had appointed eight people to collect cash daily from the centers between 8 A.M. and 12:30 P.M. The cash collected at each depot, however, was deposited with the dairy's cashier at the dairy by the depot in charge.

The dairy had two inspectors and six subinspectors to supervise the milk distribution and to attend to the complaints of the public as well as of the centers and depots. These inspectors made frequent rounds of the centers and depots and visited each cabin at least twice a week. They also checked to ensure that hygienic conditions were maintained. The depots and centers were required to maintain a book on which consumers recorded their complaints.

Pricing the dairy's milk   In the past the authorities had adopted a policy of uniform selling prices for the whole year for each variety of milk. However, the executives believed that the dairy could charge a higher price for the summer season when there was an overall shortage of milk supply and when local milk carriers and milk vendors generally charged higher prices. Selling prices prevailing in the years 1982–83 and 1983–84 are set out in Exhibit 4.

The nature of competition   Besides the sale of pasteurized milk by the dairy, a very large number of milk carriers and milk vendors sold milk in the city. The milk carriers either had their own cattle or purchased milk from villages and sold it directly to consumers or to milk vendors who, in turn, sold it to consumers in their own shops. Most of the milk vendors also arranged home delivery to their regular customers. Virtually all of these vendors held licenses for sale of cow milk; the fat content in such milk ranged between 3.5 percent and 5 percent. Either through deliberate oral misrepresentation or the general ignorance of the average customer, most of this milk was accepted as "buffalo milk." The prices charged depended on the demand and supply position. In the summer, the milk prices shot up to 82 paise per liter. In the winter months the prices dropped to 55 paise per liter. Practically all milk carriers and milk vendors sold their milk on a credit basis to their regular customers, and payment was collected at the end of the month.

Highlight of the April meeting   In the April 15 meeting, the executives of the dairy considered in detail the distribution practices being followed in order to determine whether improvements were possible. The highlights of the deliberations are summarized below:

The scope for penetrating demand in the middle- and upper-middle-class market was quite impressive inasmuch as these consumers in the higher brackets of income would buy quality milk at prices even slightly higher than the existing rates. But a penetration of this kind could hardly be achieved with the existing distribution arrangements.

The delivery boys did not make *home delivery* in the real sense of the term. The consumers living in the first and second floors were required to take delivery of the milk at the foyer of the house on the ground floor. This caused considerable hardship to the customers.

The delivery schedule was not strictly adhered to by the delivery boys. It was also not uncommon for the delivery boys to skip over regular customers. When a delivery boy came to a customer's house, he would shout or ring his bicycle bell once or twice, and if the homemaker did not answer immediately, he would leave.

The daily payment system had its own aspects of practical inconvenience. There was not only the problem of keeping money on hand daily but not having exact change sometimes resulted in considerable inconvenience. Moreover, there was no guarantee of getting additional milk in adequate quantities, since the delivery boys carried only a small quantity of milk in excess of regular ordered amounts and since they were rarely willing to make a second trip from the cabin to meet the additional requirement of a customer.

In regard to loose milk, the centers ordered only that quantity that could definitely be sold to prevent having leftover loose milk.

Besides causing inconveniences to the customers, the delivery boys indulged in such unhygienic practices as opening a half-liter milk bottle and pouring part of it into a 200-milliliter bottle for a customer who wanted 200 milliliters of milk.

Some of the executives suggested the discontinuance of centers on a commission basis and recommended the setting up of self-owned depots, roughly 50, from which milk could be distributed throughout the day. The operating time of two hours in the morning and one and a half hours in the evening was considered to be inadequate. It was also suggested that a coupon system or monthly card system[7] could be introduced along with the cash system. Some of the persons operating these centers had already started their own system of issuing coupons privately. But the executives were not in favor of such private arrangements for which the dairy did not assume any responsibility whatsoever.

A few executives believed that selling whole milk in loose quantity prevented the dairy from having effective control on the checkpoints for maintaining hygiene and purity of the milk supplied and wanted to stop the sale of loose milk. However, one of the senior executives favored no change in the present pattern of the distribution system. He did concede that changes might be desirable to provide additional facilities to consumers but was nevertheless against the implementation of these measures while the dairy was running at a loss. He believed that the dairy's efforts to increase sales would not bear any fruit until the dairy could assure regular and adequate supplies of milk throughout the year. Under the present circumstances, he thought that the only solution was the installation of an ice cream plant so that the excess supply of milk to the dairy could earn a profit. Moreover, the suggested changes in the distribution system at this juncture would make the system unwieldy, giving rise to innumerable complaints from the public. His comments to the various suggestions were:

If the delivery boys supplied the milk on the first or second floor, they would have to leave the bicycle and milk bottles in the bags on the foyer of the ground floor, where chances of theft could not be ruled out. Besides, mischievous small children could play tricks like taking air from the bicycle's wheels and thereby put the delivery boy to a great inconvenience.

The coupon or card system would mean maintenance of innumerable accounts by the dairy. Unless the dairy installed an effective system of checks and audit, it would lead to frauds, manipulation and counterfeiting of coupons, etc. To set up such a system would be both costly and cumbersome.

The dairy's own shops would not be economical in the current state of affairs. Depots would increase the administrative difficulties, but could not be expected to perform better services to the consumers. The incentive of a person on commission should be greater than that of an employee getting fixed monthly salary.

The executive also pointed out the problem of the dairy's location in the milk-producing tract wherein local milk carriers could supply raw

---

[7] Under the coupon system, customers can purchase coupons of various denominations in advance according to their requirements for a certain period. The milk is then supplied daily against these coupons, and in this way the daily handling of cash is eliminated. Under the card system, instead of issuing coupons, a monthly card is issued (against cash payment in advance) for the daily milk supply. For any ''extra'' milk on any particular day, the consumer is required to pay cash on delivery. A consumer who does not want to draw milk supply on a particular day is required to inform the center/depot in advance; money for such nondelivery is refunded at the end of the month.

milk at cheaper rates. However, he was optimistic about the future and believed that the problem would be automatically solved in a year or so with the coming of another cooperative dairy in the adjacent district. That dairy would then purchase milk that currently competed for the customers within the municipal limits. He also believed that the county dairy would also be in a position to purchase milk in the summer months from that dairy, thereby affecting a seasonal adjustment in the milk supply. This would lead to an increased sales volume and removal of the dairy's loss.

1. The dairy continued to lose money in 1983–84, despite an increase in sales to Rs. 7.25 million. The loss amounted to Rs. 250,000. How do you explain these losses?
2. In 1983–84 the dairy's fixed costs were to be about Rs. 1.35 million and variable costs about Rs. 6.15 million. Construct a break-even chart. Would it be difficult for the dairy to reach the break-even point? Explain.
3. Why were the dairy's sales far below capacity? Could anything be done to improve demand and, if so, should the dairy take such action?
4. Why were losses in 1983–84 below those in 1982–83?
5. Are there other ways the dairy could reduce losses?
6. What is the significance of Exhibit 3?
7. Some nutritional experts claim that toned milk is preferable to whole milk because of its lower fat content. What is the significance of this claim in this case?
8. What recommendations would you make to the dairy's management? to the municipal commission?

PROBLEMS
Demand analysis

5–1   Demand for one of The Rochester Ceramic Tile Company's industrial chemical products has been estimated as $Q = 360 - 0.8P$, in which Q is weekly demand in thousands of tons, and P is price in dollars per ton.

a. The firm wished to sell 100,000 tons per week. What price should it set?
b. At a price of $300 per ton, how many tons per week will be sold?
c. Calculate arc price elasticity for a change from a sales quantity of 100,000 tons per week to a sales quantity of 120,000 tons per week, where the sales increase is entirely due to price reduction.
d. Derive the equations relating total and marginal revenue to weekly sales.

e. Calculate marginal revenue at a price of $300 per ton, using the marginal revenue function just derived.

f. Calculate point price elasticity at the price of $300 per ton, and then calculate marginal revenue at the $300 price by using the formula $MR = P(1 + 1/e_p)$.

g. Assume that the marginal cost of production is constant at $100 per ton (in other words, each ton added to the weekly rate of output adds $100 to the firm's weekly cost). How high should the firm set the weekly rate of production?

5–2   What would be the expected sign of the cross-elasticity of demand for the following:

a. Fords relative to the price of Chevrolets?
b. Autoalarm systems relative to the price of CB radios?
c. Automobile tires relative to the price of gasoline?
d. Eight-track tape players relative to the price of cassette players?
e. Eight-track tape players to a specific firm relative to the price of eight-track players, in general?

5–3   Long-run price elasticity is greater than short-run elasticity. Explain.

5–4   If you have elasticity at a point on a demand function, how can you calculate marginal revenue at that point? Illustrate by an original example.

5–5   If you have the equation for a demand function, how can you get the corresponding total and marginal revenue functions? Illustrate by an original example.

5–6   Rank the following items in the order of their income elasticities, highest first:

a. Fresh whole milk.
b. Insulin for control of diabetes.
c. Travel for pleasure.
d. Fresh fruit for home consumption.
e. Works of original art for interior decoration of homes.

5–7   What is the difference, exactly, between a demand function and a demand curve? Between a shift in demand and a movement along a demand curve?

5–8 Would a knowledgeable firm voluntarily establish a sales rate in the inelastic range of its demand curve? Explain.

5–9 Consider the following demand equation:

$$Q = 163I^{1.15}P^{-0.74}C^{-0.34}$$

where

Q = Quantity of a durable good per customer.
I = Average income of buyers.
P = Price of a standardized unit of the durable good.
C = An index of cost of credit.

Assume that the number of customers per year is constant. What is the price elasticity of demand? Reveal all calculations, if any. Interpret your answer.

5–10 What is income elasticity? How is it used? When is it used?

5–11 Explain fully the concept of cross-elasticity of demand. Explain the condition necessary for products to be:

a. Complements.
b. Substitutes.
c. Independent.

5–12 What problems, if any, are associated with using time-series data in demand analysis?

5–13 The San Juan Fish mart sold about 33 pounds of turbot daily. Due to a modest increase in Puerto Rican industries in 1981 and 1982, the average income for the market area rose from $7,000 to $8,000. As a result, The San Juan's sales declined to 22 pounds of turbot.

a. Calculate the income elasticity of demand coefficient.
b. The San Juan's turbot sells at 90¢ per pound. If its price elasticity of demand coefficient is −0.6, what price must it establish to bring sales up to 33 pounds?
c. Calculate The San Juan's *TR* at all three points.

5–14 Imperial Imports, Inc. of Baltimore, Maryland, sells radios for $30 each. A competitor in Washington, D.C., sells a similar model of radio, manufactured by the same Japanese company. The Washington, D.C., firm reduced its price from $32 to $28.

Each firm has branches in Baltimore and in Washington, and competition between them is keen in most areas of activity.

Imperial Imports, Inc. has a price elasticity of demand coefficient of -0.84; a cross-price elasticity of demand coefficient of 0.625.

a. Imperial's CEO wants sales of this model of radio to increase to 2,700 units per month. What price should be charged per radio? Reveal all calculations.
b. If Imperial wanted to eliminate all competition by selling 4,000 radios per month, what price should be charged per radio?
c. Under the conditions specified in paragraph b, will any total revenue (*TR*) be lost? How much, if any? Note: Calculate *TR* at $Q_d = 2,700$; 4,000.

5–15   The severe winter of 1983 battered the U.S. West Coast, washing many oceanfront cottages and permanent residences into the ocean. Much of this area has been or is being rebuilt. One construction effort under way near Carmel, California, faces the following demand function:

$Q_d = 250 - 2P$.
P = Price in thousands of dollars.

a. Calculate marginal revenue at $P = 30$; $P = 60$; $P = 90$; $P = 120$.
b. At what price is marginal revenue equal to zero?
c. Calculate point price elasticity of demand at $P = 60$; $P = 65$.
d. What is the maximum total revenue (*TR*) possible in this equation?

Selected references

Anderson, Kent P. "Residential Demand for Electricity: Econometric Estimates for California and the United States." *The Journal of Business*, October 1973, pp. 526–53.

Carlson, Rodney L. "Seemingly Unrelated Regression and the Demand for Automobiles of Different Sizes, 1965–75: A Disaggregate Approach." *Journal of Business* 51, no. 2 (1978), pp. 243–62.*

Chow, G. C. *Demand for Automobiles in the United States, A Study in Consumer Durables.* Amsterdam: North Holland Publishing.

Drucker, Peter. "The New Markets and the New Capitalism." *The Public Interest* 21 (Fall 1970).

---

* This article is included in Thomas J. Coyne, *Readings in Managerial Economics*, 3d ed. (Plano, Tex.: Business Publications, 1981).

Fraser, Donald R. "The Impact of Holding Company Affiliation on Deposit Growth at Commercial Banks." *Review of Research* 12, no. 1 (Fall 1976), pp. 19–31.

Gerking, Shelby D., and William J. Boyes, "The Role of Functional Forms in Estimating Elasticities of Housing Expenditures." *Southern Economic Journal* 47, no. 2 (October 1980), pp. 287–302.

Halvorsen, Robert. "Residential Demand for Electric Energy." *Review of Economics and Statistics* 57, no. 1 (February 1975), pp. 12–18.

Harberger, Arnold C., ed. *The Demand for Durable Goods* Chicago: University of Chicago Press, 1960.

Hogarty, Thomas F., and Kenneth G. Elizinga, "The Demand for Beer." *The Review of Economics and Statistics* 54 (May 1972).*

Houthakker, H. S., and L. D. Taylor. *Consumer Demand in the United States, 1929–1970, Analyses and Projections.* Cambridge: Harvard University Press, 1966.

Katona, George. "Consumer Behavior: Theory and Findings on Expectations and Aspirations." *The American Economic Review* 58 (May 1968).

Makin, John H. "Demand and Supply Functions for Stocks of Eurodollar Deposits: An Empirical Study." *The Review of Economics and Statistics,* November 1972, pp. 381–391.

Mandell, Lewis; George Katona; James Morgan; and J. Schmiedeskamp. *Surveys of Consumers 1971–1972, Contributions to Behavioral Economics* (Ann Arbor, Mich.: Institute for Social Research, 1973).

Nelson, Glenn, and Tom H. Robinson. "Retail and Wholesale Demand and Marketing Order Policy for Fresh Navel Oranges." *American Journal of Agricultural Economics* 60, no. 3 (August 1978, pp. 502–9.*

Steigmann, A. John. "A Partial Recursive Model of Automobile Demand." *Business Economics,* September 1973, pp. 28–30.

Woud, Herman. *Demand Analysis, A Study in Econometrics.* New York: John Wiley & Sons, 1953.

3

Costs, production, and productivity

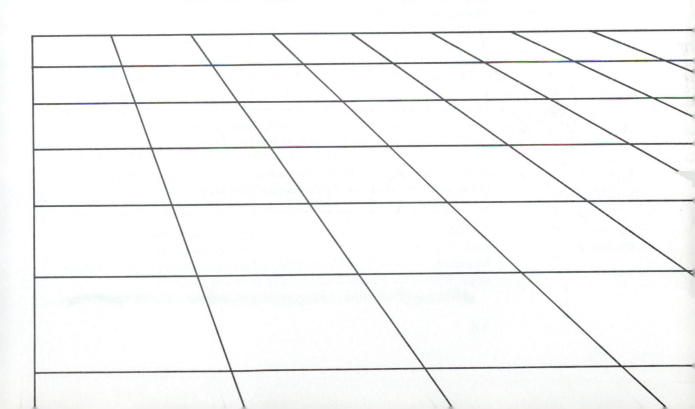

CHAPTER

6

Cost theory

The word *cost* means different things to different people, and business people are prone to overwork this word at times. (The words *production* and *productivity* appear to be no less susceptible to the same problem.) Yet mastery of cost concepts places the formally trained economist in a position to make a large contribution to the overall goals and objectives of his/her firm.

The central focus of this chapter is cost theory, a theory developed from an underlying theory of production. Economically feasible production is any economic activity that transforms resource inputs into outputs having a greater value. Resource inputs (i.e., management know-how, land, labor, capital) carry a price a firm must incur if it is to have use of the resource(s). These prices are the explicit and implicit costs of producing that firm's goods or services. Therefore, the level of resource inputs a firm decides to use, combined with the price of each, determines the cost of that firm's finished product. However, even with the payment of fixed and variable explicit costs, production may at times not be at levels high enough to allow an organization to break even. This chapter explains the connection between production and cost theory.

A brief overview of production, followed by a theoretical production function and some important cost concepts, helps one understand costs in the short and long run. Let's take a closer look.

An overview of production

Production of goods and/or services exists for all public agencies, non-profit organizations, churches, schools, police and fire departments, and households—as well as for proprietorships, partnerships, and corporations. It involves domestic and foreign economic activity.

The principles of production concern efficient uses of inputs in obtain-

208

ing desired outputs. Production theory applies to activities that yield tangible goods (such as construction and manufacturing), enterprises that provide raw materials (mining and agriculture), operations that make personal services available (health care and police protection), businesses that provide facilities (storage and equipment leasing), activities related to financing and risk management (banking and insurance), operations centering on information and education (publishing and schools), ventures that provide entertainment and recreation (concert booking and park operation).

Production processes

Production processes are integrated sets of activities that combine and transform inputs into desired outputs. Inputs needed in a production process may include materials (raw materials, supplies, parts made by others); labor (various skills); capital; and management (know-how, planning, organizing, motivating); and, of course, land.

Outputs of production processes are the goods and/or services produced. Some processes yield more than one output. Petroleum refining, for example, produces a variety of fuels, oils, greases, and other products. Products emanating from the same process are called joint products. The cream substitute marketed under the brand name *Pream* was initially a joint product with the baby milk substitute marketed under the brand name of *Similac*. Both products were very profitable for the company producing them.

Pream is made from an extract of powdered Similac. The extract was thrown away, buried underground near Sturgis, Michigan, before biochemists and marketing people got involved. Once Pream's commercial potential was realized—first as a food substitute for geriatric patients in India, later for coffee drinkers in the United States—the production process was changed so as to ensure optimum utilization of all inputs. Not all joint products are as compatible and desirable.

Pineapple juice was at one time considered to be a waste product. It had negative value, which means that time, effort, and other resources had to be spent to get rid of it in an acceptable manner. Other products of negative value are brine from oil and gas wells and nuclear wastes. Undesirable joint products increase internal costs of production as producers compensate persons adversely affected by the products. Today, pineapple juice is a highly marketable joint product, one capable of generating substantial revenues; nuclear power producers continue to seek acceptable burial grounds for nuclear wastes; brine disposal is now mandated by law, but an acceptable and economically feasible disposal method does not appear to exist at this writing.

The technology in existence at a given time determines the relationship of inputs to outputs. The best technology might be one that produces the greatest rate of output from a given rate of input at the lowest possible cost. Inputs can be combined inefficiently, but it is assumed here for our purposes that firms are using the best technology.

Inputs and outputs are measured as rates, or quantities per unit of time. When inputs and corresponding outputs are compared, a common unit of time is selected. Accounting periods of weeks, quarters, or years are often used as time periods in production analysis, but shorter periods (hours, shifts, or days) are at times more appropriate.

Production function

A production function expresses in words or numbers the relationship of inputs to outputs. The maximum output attainable from a given combination of resource inputs could be expressed in a general sense as

$$Q = f(X_1, X_2, X_3, \ldots, X_n)$$

where

Q = The quantity produced.
Each X = A resource available as part of the technology used.

If K and L are used as symbols representing capital and labor input levels, respectively, the function may be specified as

$$Q = f(K, L)$$

Table 6–1
Total productions: Tennis balls

(1) TPP, Q (000)	(2) X (labor Input)	(3) APP Q/x $APP_x = b + cx - dx^2$	(4) MPP dQ/dx $MPP_x = b + 2cx - 3dx^2$
18	5	3.6	6.6
63	10	6.3	11.3
128	15	8.5	14.6
206	20	10.3	16.3
288	25	11.5	16.6
369	30	12.3	15.3
440	35	12.6	12.6
492	40	12.3	8.3
520	45	11.6	2.6
515	50	10.3	−4.7
470	55	8.6	
378	60	6.3	

$Q = TPP$ (Quantity = Total physical product)
$TPP = bx + cx^2 - dx^3$; where $b = 0.3$, $c = 0.7$, $d = 0.01$, and x = factor input (labor).

An example using one variable input may help clarify the situation and serve to explain the relationship between production and cost theory.

Production with one input variable

Assume a manufacturer of tennis balls can obtain the output specified in column 1 of Table 6–1 by using the quantities of labor specified in column 2, so the number of tennis balls produced (Q) is a function of the level of the variable input labor, X.

Firms want that combination of factor inputs that enables them to produce a product of quality at the lowest possible cost. *Lowest cost, least cost of production*, and *optimal level of economic output* for the firm are synonomous. These terms are used also in conjunction with economies and diseconomies of large-scale operation, for tennis ball manufacturers and other manufacturers.

Law of variable proportion, total, marginal, and average physical product

Marginal product, the ratio of increase in rate of output to increase in rate of input, is defined in incremental terms as: $MPP_x = \triangle Q / \triangle X$, in which MPP_x is marginal physical product of input X, $\triangle Q$ is a discrete change in rate of output, and $\triangle X$ is a discrete change in rate of input.[1]

Instances of varying marginal productivity of an input are commonly observed, and this relationship has been laid out in a formal statement: "the law of variable proportions." This law says that if the rate of one input is increased and the rates of other inputs are held constant, the marginal productivity of the one input may increase at first, but it will eventually begin to decrease; it will reach zero at a point of maximum total output and will thereafter be negative in a range where total output is actually falling.

In other words, the law of variable proportion states that if a manufacturer holds all the factors of production (inputs) constant save one and increases that factor, total physical product for the firm will increase at an increasing rate, increase at a decreasing rate, and ultimately decrease absolutely. The law of variable proportions exists because the size of the plant cannot be changed in the short run; instead, only the rate of output from the already existing plant can be changed. The law of variable

---

[1] By making the changes in input and output smaller and smaller, the ratio $\triangle Q / \triangle X$ can finally be measured at a point on the input-output function, as the slope of a line tangent to the function at that point. Thus, marginal productivity at a point is $\alpha Q / \alpha X$, the first derivative of the production function with respect to input X.

proportions is the law of diminishing returns applied to production theory. Since the size of the tennis ball factory is fixed in the short run and since the manager of that plant cannot change its size, control with reference to the number of balls produced is limited to changes in the level of resources. The plant manager may utilize more efficiently and/or effectively available resource inputs, nothing else. The plant should operate in stage II.

Figure 6–1 illustrates the law of diminishing returns, which generalizes that as the quantity of the variable input is increased, holding other inputs constant, the marginal product and the average product must eventually decrease. The law of diminishing returns may be called the law of eventually diminishing marginal productivity. A simple example is the addition of labor to land in producing a farm commodity. As more and more labor is added, the total product must eventually decline and may even drop to zero as workers get in each other's way.

Stage II is the area of diminishing returns to the resource input, and it is rational to operate in this area because, although diminishing, the marginal physical product of labor remains positive. Besides, consider the alternatives. No one would want to operate in stage III, since marginal productivity there is negative. In other words, the factory receives a loss (decline) in *TPP* for each additional worker hired.

Stage I is not rational because in that area of operations the factory receives increased output (in terms of tennis balls produced) disproportionately in excess of the units of labor employed. Consequently, it should hire more units. Therefore, stage II remains as the rational and only remaining place to function. It must be noted, however, that only when factor input prices and demand conditions are given can the firm select this "best level of input."

The *TPP* of the tennis ball plant plotted on the static two-dimensional graph in Figure 6–1 reveals: (1) the point of inflection on the *TPP* curve, (2) the interrelationship between the *MPP* and *APP* curves, (3) the rational stage in which one should utilize the services of input *X,* stage II, and (4) the irrational stages of production, stages I and III. It is a curve permissive of many generalizations about production functions for products. (An excellent project for students is to have them calculate, plot, and interpret a *TPP, MPP,* and an *APP* curve[s] from actual data for a specific firm and product.)

Quantity produced in Figure 6–1, total physical product, is a function of resource inputs called labor. Put differently, changes in the total number of tennis balls produced is dependent upon the level of labor used, assuming all other factors of production than that remain constant.

Referring to Figure 6–1, part *(a),* increasing returns to the variable resource input called labor exists in stage I; decreasing returns to the

Figure 6–1
Tennis ball production

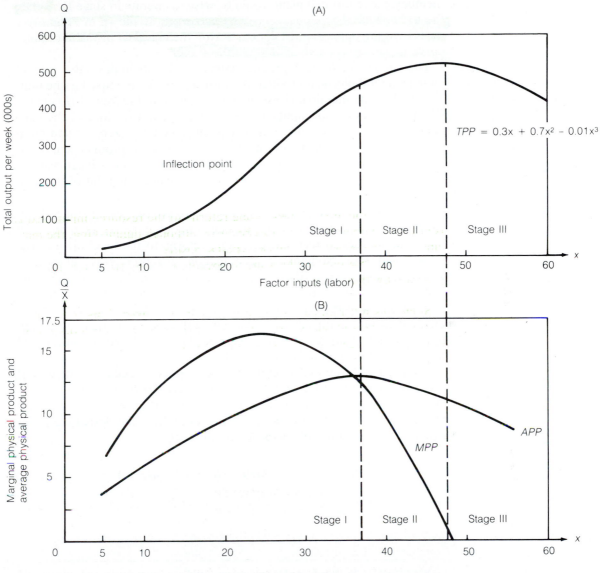

$TPP = 0.3x + 0.7x^2 - 0.01x^3$

variable resource input called labor exists in stage II; and negative returns to the variable resource input called labor exists in stage III. (Remember, the tennis ball plant would be wise to operate in stage II.) When the total physical product reaches its maximum M shown in Figure 6–1 part *(a)* at the point that its slope is zero—the marginal physical product curve in part *(b)* is crashing through the x axis.

The marginal physical product curve is, by definition, the rate of change in total physical product as factor inputs *(X)* increase by one unit. The peak of the marginal physical product curve in Figure 6–1 *(b)* occurs when 25 units of labor inputs are being employed. The slope of the marginal physical product curve at that point is equal to zero. When compared with Figure 6–1 *(a)* of the total physical product curve, it corresponds to the point at which that *TPP* curve changes its curvature. This change in curvature is referred to as the inflection point of the total physical product curve.

Where the marginal physical product curve crosses the average physical product curve from the top, the beginning of stage II, the tennis ball factory continues to receive decreasing returns to the level of resource input called labor. Nonetheless, marginal physical product is still positive although falling.[2] From the beginning of stage II to the point where the marginal physical product curve passes through the x axis, the rate of change in total product associated with hiring additional factor inputs diminishes but is still positive. Consequently, assuming demand conditions warrant it, additional units of labor should be hired. Labor should not be hired beyond the end of stage II.[3]

The maximum rational level of resource inputs, x, occurs at the end of stage II where the slope of *TPP* is zero, where *MPP* = 0. This point, 47 units, is revealed graphically in Figure 6–1 *(b)* but may also be found by utilization of the general quadratic equation, where the derivative is set equal to zero and one solves for X, as follows:[4]

$$MPP_x = b + 2\ cx = 3dx^2 = 0$$
$$.3 + 2cx - 3(.01)x^2 = 0$$
$$.3 + 2(.7)x - 3(.01)x^2 = 0$$

---

[2] Were it not for the law of variable proportions, MPP would not decline and output could increase indefinitely as changes in X were made.

[3] To the extent that Equal Employment Opportunity regulations and other governmental hiring requirements cause firms to overlook negative MPPs, stage III, costly misallocations of resources occurs.

[4] The subscripts in the quadratic do not follow the subscripts in the formulation of MPP$_x$; instead, they follow the subscripts one would expect to find in the general quadratic equation. Remember: $b = .3$, $c = .7$, $d = .01$.

$$x = \frac{-b \pm \sqrt{b^2 - 4ac}}{2a}$$

$$= \frac{-1.40 \pm \sqrt{1.96 - 4(.03)\,(.3)}}{2(.03)}$$

$$= \frac{-1.40 \pm \sqrt{1.96 + .036}}{.06}$$

$$= \frac{-1.40 \pm \sqrt{1.996X}}{-.06}$$

$$= \frac{-1.40 - 1.41}{-.06} = \frac{-2.81}{.06}$$

$$= 46.83, \text{ or } 47 \text{ units}$$

Compare the marginal and average physical product curves to the total physical product curve. (Some observers argue that of the two curves, the marginal is more important because of its close relationship to the marginal cost curve—but more on this matter later.) The average product curve is output divided by input:

$$APP_x = TPP \div x; \text{ or, } b + cx - dx^2$$

The average physical product curve peaks in this example at 35 units of labor input, or the point at which the rate of change in the average physical product curve is equal to zero—the point at which $APP_x = MPP_x$. As indicated in connection with the total physical product curve, the slope of the average curve at 35 units of input is equal to zero. It is the peak of the average physical product curve that marks the beginning of stage II in the traditional production function. In addition, it is the point at which one notices diminishing average returns to the resource input.

The minimum rational level of labor inputs (X) occurs where $MPP_x = APP_x$. This point, 35 units, is revealed graphically in Figure 6–1 (a) but may be found also by solving for X as follows:

$$MPP_x = APP_x$$

$$b + 2cx - 3dx^2 = b + cx - dx^2$$

$$cx - 2dx^2 = 0$$

$$.7x - 2(.01)x^2 = 0$$

$$.7x - 0.02x^2 = 0$$

$$.7 = \frac{x(0.02x)}{x}$$

$$.7 = .02x$$

$$x = \frac{.7}{.02}$$

$$= 35, \text{ minimum level of resource inputs}$$

Productivity interrelationships, elasticity of production, and stages of production

The marginal physical product curve reveals the rate of change in total physical product resulting from a unit change in the variable input. As long as this ratio is increasing—as long as the marginal physical product curve is rising, the total physical product curve is increasing at an increasing rate. The point at which the total physical product curve changes its curvature is the point of inflection, and this point corresponds vertically with the peak of the marginal physical product curve. At this point the law of variable proportions becomes evident. The peak of the marginal physical product curve is the point of diminishing marginal returns to the resource input called labor in Figure 6–1. Over all ranges of the marginal physical product curve prior to this point, there are increasing marginal returns to the variable resource input called labor; beyond this point there are decreasing marginal returns to the input called labor. The astute reader may deduce that although the marginal physical product curve is declining, the total physical product curve and costs of production continue to rise. Therefore, even though the firm is getting decreasing marginal and average returns to the resource input called labor, total product is expanding. If one can assume this product will be sold at some constant or rising price and demand stays constant or rises, total revenue to the firm will rise.

Average physical product has been defined as total output divided by total input. The average physical product curve represents the changes in average output that takes place as technology and all other factors of production are held constant, except labor, and labor is increased as indicated along the *x,* or horizontal axis.

When the marginal physical product curve is higher than the average physical product curve, the average physical product of the variable resource input called labor is increasing; when the marginal physical product is less than the average physical product, the average physical product is declining. Interrelationships between average, marginal, and total physical product curves enables one to delineate stages of production.

Marginal revenue product

A firm facing a downward-sloping demand curve must reduce price as sales quantity per period is expanded. Under this condition, the output's marginal revenue is below its unit price at every rate of output and, like price, drops off as quantity increases. As the output's marginal revenue falls, the monetary value of additional output per unit of added input must also fall, even though the increase in physical output per unit of added input may hold constant. (Some students may benefit from a quick review of the section that deals with marginal revenue in Chapter 4.)

In dealing with constant marginal product and falling marginal revenue, we calculate marginal revenue product as follows:

$$MRP_x = MPP_x \cdot MR_y; \quad MR_y = f(Q); \quad MRP_x = f(Q)$$

In words, input xs addition to the value of output per additional unit of x used, MRP_x, is obtained by multiplying the marginal physical product of x, MPP_x, times the output's marginal revenue, MR_y. Since marginal revenue varies as a function of rate of sales, the input's marginal revenue product is also a function that varies with rate of sales.

Elasticity of production is the term used to explain the percentage change in total physical product that results from a percentage change in resource input which, in Figure 6–1, we are calling labor. It may be calculated as:

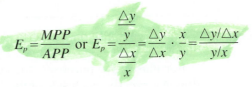

$$E_p = \frac{MPP}{APP} \quad \text{or} \quad E_p = \frac{\dfrac{\Delta y}{y}}{\dfrac{\Delta x}{x}} = \frac{\Delta y}{\Delta x} \cdot \frac{x}{y} = \frac{\Delta y / \Delta x}{y / x}$$

where

   y = Output or quantity produced.
   x = Resource inputs.

This ratio of the marginal physical product curve to the average physical product curve is known as elasticity of production or elasticity of productivity. The tennis ball plant manager can look at Table 6–1 and corresponding Figure 6–1 and know this elasticity of productivity measure is such that a 1 percent increase in the factor input called labor will cause greater than a 1 percent increase in output of the labor. Elasticity of productivity is greater than one only during stage I.

It is irrational to produce in stage I because changes (increases) in total physical product are taking place at a rate more rapid than changes (increases) in resource inputs. Consequently, additional resources should be employed.

In stage II marginal physical product is less than average physical product, $MPP < APP$, and for that reason a 1 percent increase in the use of factor inputs will result in less than a 1 percent increase in tennis balls. However, the ratio of MPP to APP, although falling, is still positive, and total physical product continues to rise, although at a lesser rate. It may be profitable to continue the use of factor inputs throughout stage II.

In stage III, total physical product is falling, and the rate of change in output is negative when additional resource inputs are hired. No production should take place in stage III. A 1 percent increase in resource input in stage III would be associated with negative marginal physical product.

Producers of tennis balls could (would) be labeled irrational if they should decide to continue hiring inputs beyond the point at which the marginal product curve crashes through the x axis.

If at all possible the firm will want to produce a *TPP* somewhere within stage II. It is necessary for a firm to know precisely where stage II is located. However, it is not sufficient for the firm to make a policy decision along lines that would require it to always operate at the same point within stage II. As indicated in Chapter 5, the demand potential for the product being produced must be calculated. Also, the firm must consider the overall impact on its business, adverse or otherwise, of equal employment opportunities hiring guidelines and/or laws. As a practical matter, a firm might at times be required to hire resources into stage III in order to comply with political, as opposed to economical, considerations.

Production and cost theory: the relationship

Putting quantity on the vertical axis for a moment and resource inputs and cost on the horizontal axis, Figure 6–2 can be drawn.

For illustrative purposes, the cost of each unit is assumed to be $1. If drawn correctly, each side of the curve should reflect the other side. With no production, there are no costs. Remember: The production function determines the *TPP* curve and its slope.

Using Figure 6–2 rotate the axes a quarter turn to the right and obtain the results in Figure 6–3.

Figure 6–2
Relationship between production and cost curve*

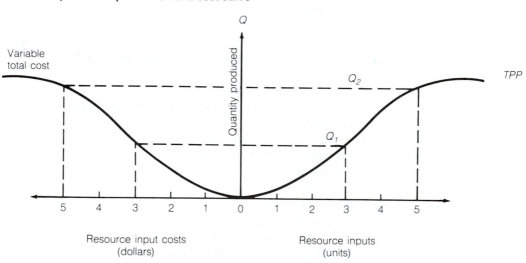

*Inspired by Evan J. Douglas, *Managerial Economics* (Englewood Cliffs, N.J. (Prentice-Hall, 1979), p. 204.

Figure 6–3
Graphic depiction of average variable and marginal cost curves from total variable curve

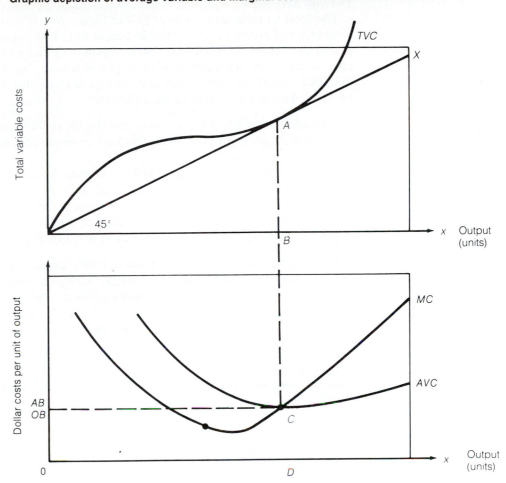

Another way of viewing this relationship between production and cost is to picture Figure 6–1 upside-down and envision the *TPP* curve in panel *(a)* from that perspective. Consider it the mirror image of total variable costs. In a similar manner imagine panel *(b)* of Figure 6–1 upside-down and inside-out, and notice two curves similar to the marginal cost and average variable cost curves presented in Figure 6–3.

Label the x and y axes as before and, mark the upside-down, inside-out *MPP* curve marginal cost, *MC;* mark the *APP* curve average variable cost, *AVC*. Average variable cost is equal to the price of labor divided by its average physical product $(AVC = P_L/APP_L)$; marginal cost of the resource input is equal to the price of labor divided by its marginal physical product $(MC = P_L/MPP_L)$. Place these two curves on the same two-dimensional graph with the average total cost curve, *ATC*, from Figure 6–3, and you have Figure 6–4.

The total variable cost curve *(TVC)* in Figure 6–3 is derived from the total physical product curve *(TPP)* in Figure 6–1. It is obtained by multiplying each level of variable resource input(s) by the explicit financial cost of each unit and plotting it in graphical format. Average variable, marginal, and other cost curves (average fixed costs, for example) may be derived from TVC. Assume the following:

1. The addition of one worker is associated with an increase in output of 4,000 units per eight-hour shift. The worker would cost the firm $8 per hour.
2. The same increase in output (4,000 units) could be obtained during the same time span by acquiring additional units of capital equipment. This equipment could be leased at a cost to the firm of $250 per week. The worker and the equipment are resource inputs to the firm.
3. This plant works one shift only per 24 hours, five days weekly.

The marginal physical product of labor, MPP_L, could be compared with the marginal physical product of capital, MPP_K, to determine which change in cost, *MC*, provides the greater change in total physical product, *TPP*, per dollar spent. *MC* is MPP_L/P_L and MPP_K/P_K. Under the circumstances, the MPP_L is equal to 4,000 units divided by eight hours, or 500 units per hour of labor $(4,000 \div 8 = 500)$; the increase in output per dollar

Figure 6–4
Short-run costs: Average total cost, marginal cost, and average variable cost curves

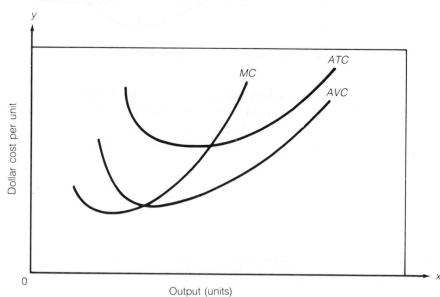

cost of input is 500 units divided by $8 per hour, or 62.5 units
($500 \div \$8.00 = 62.5$).

The MPP_K over the time interval described is 4,000 divided by $50, or
80 units per dollar spent on equipment rental.

Capital equipment provides the greatest increase in output per dollar
of resource input. In fact, one who wanted no increase in output but
wanted to hold output constant would add the piece of leased equipment,
thereby increasing output by 4,000 units per shift and increasing costs by
$250 per week. However, simultaneous reduction of the work force by
one person would decrease output by 4,000 units per shift and decrease
cost by $320 per week. Total physical product for the firm would remain
unchanged, but total costs would be reduced by $70 per week. Consid-
erations of this sort allow one to combine production and cost theory in
the allocation of scarce and costly resources.

Total cost curves for a given plant

For any given set of input prices, there is an expansion that defines the
least-cost combinations of variable inputs and thus specifies the lowest
total variable cost attainable at each rate of output. A variable cost function is depicted in Figure 6–5. Total variable cost curves derive their
form from the production function and from the possibilities for economic
input substitution(s) that may exist. Variable cost functions with gentle S
shapes similar to the one depicted in Figure 6–5 are often found in practical situations. Near the point of origin, variable cost is increasing at a
decreasing rate; whereas near the point of maximum output, variable cost
is increasing at an increasing rate.

By adding fixed costs per period to variable cost, one obtains a function
that relates total cost per period to the plant's output. To illustrate, assume fixed costs of $300 per day have been added to the total variable
cost function in Figure 6–5. The presence of fixed costs per period is
explained by inputs that must be treated as fixed. Call the bundle of fixed
inputs a plant. In regarding some inputs as fixed, one views production
in the short-run perspective, a short-run cost curve.

Unit cost curves for a given plant

Marginal cost at any given rate of output is the ratio of change in cost
per period to change in output per period, the increase in total cost per
period due to the addition of the last unit to the rate of output. Marginal
cost at point A on the total variable cost curve in Figure 6–5 is approximately the ratio $390/130, or about $3. Marginal cost is the slope of the
variable cost function; so marginal cost is the rate of output. Note that
the slope of the total cost function in Figure 6–5, at any given rate of
output, is the height of the marginal cost function in Figure 6–6 at that
same rate.

Figure 6–5
Total fixed, total variable, and total costs per period at various rates of output in hypothetical plant

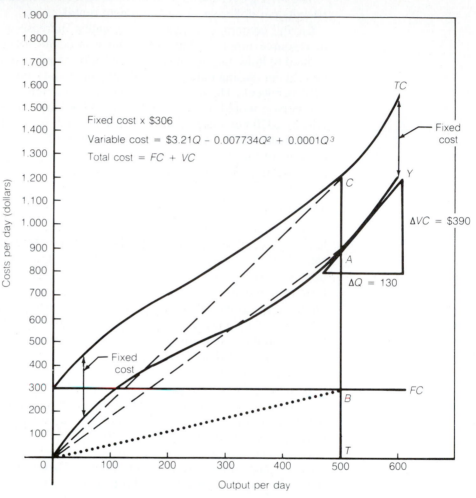

Marginal cost is of special interest to the managerial economist because of its use in determining the optimum rate of output. There is contribution from each unit added, and it is profitable to increase the rate provided marginal revenue equals or exceeds marginal cost. The profit-maximizing optimum rate is found where the marginal cost function cuts the marginal revenue function from beneath, point B in Figure 6–6. At point B, $MR = MC$, and a condition of equilibrium exists.[5]

---

[5] *MC* crosses *MR* from above at point A in Figure 6–6. This intersection is at approximately 7.67 units of output and is not a condition of equilibrium. At point A, *MC* continues to decrease as output increases.

Figure 6–6
Marginal, average variable, average fixed, and average total cost at various rates of output

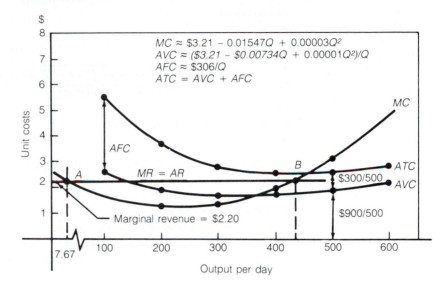

Assume the price of a finished good or service is constant at $2.20, so that marginal revenue is also constant at $2.20, as shown in Figure 6–6. By inspection, the rising marginal cost curve becomes equal to the constant marginal revenue at a production rate of approximately 440 units per period.

If the equation for the cost function is known, the optimum rate of output can be determined analytically by the approach demonstrated by the following example. Using the least-square estimation technique, a polynomial of third degree is fitted to the total cost and output rate combinations plotted in Figure 6–5. The total cost *(TC)* curve is found to be approximately:

$$TC = \$306 + \$3.21Q - \$0.007734Q^2 + \$0.00001Q^3$$

The corresponding marginal cost *(MC)* function is the first derivative:

$$MC = \frac{\partial TC}{\partial Q} = \$3.21 - \$0.01547Q + \$0.00003Q^2$$

Set the marginal cost function equal to marginal revenue, and obtain

$$\$3.21 - \$0.01547Q + \$0.00003Q^2 = \$2.20$$

After combining terms and rearranging, the equation in general quadratic form is:

$$0 = ax^2 + bx + c \qquad \text{(general quadratic form)}$$
$$0 = -\$0.00003Q^2 + \$0.01547Q - \$1.01 \qquad \text{(our example)}$$

The solution is:

$$X = \frac{-b + \sqrt{b^2 - 4ac}}{2a} \qquad \text{(solution for general form)}$$

$$Q = \frac{-\$0.01547 \pm \sqrt{\$0.0002393 - [4 \cdot (-\$0.00003) \cdot (-\$1.01)]}}{2 \cdot (-\$0.00003)} \quad \text{(example)}$$

The two values of the solution are:

438.95, the optimum rate.
7.67, the *other* rate at which *MC* also equals *MR*.

Average cost functions

Average variable cost at any given rate of output is total variable cost divided by the rate of output. At point A on the variable cost function in Figure 6–5, average variable cost is \$900/500, or \$1.80. Average fixed cost at any given rate is total fixed cost divided by the rate of output. At point B on the fixed cost function in Figure 6–5, average fixed cost is \$300/500, or \$0.60. Average total cost at any given rate is the sum of the average variable cost and the average fixed cost. At point C on the total cost function in Figure 6–5, average total cost is \$1.80 + \$0.60, or \$2.40.

If the equation for the total cost function is known, equations for the average cost functions may be derived to demonstrate using Figure 6–5:

$$\text{Total cost} = \text{Fixed cost} + \text{Variable cost}$$
$$TC = \$306 + \$3.21Q - \$0.007734Q^2 + \$0.00001Q^3$$

Average variable cost, *AVC*, is *VC/Q*, so for the above example:

$$AVC = \$3.21 - \$0.007734Q + \$0.00001Q^2$$

Average fixed cost. *AFC*, is *FC/Q*, so:

$$AFC = \frac{1}{Q} \cdot \$306$$

Average total cost, *ATC*, is *AVC + AFC*, so

$$ATC = \$3.21 - \$0.007734Q + \$0.00001Q^2 + \frac{1}{Q} \cdot \$306$$

How flexibility affects costs

Managers prefer to maintain at least four types of cost flexibility. The first consists of adjustments for seasonal and year-to-year changes in sales rates. Adjustment of costs for seasonal variations often involves changing the hours of operation per day. If raw materials and finished products can be stored, annual and seasonal flexibility can be achieved through changes in plant operating time per year. Another way of obtaining annual and seasonal flexibility of costs is to use a number of small but identical machines rather than use one large unit (the large machine may have a lower average cost under conditions of full utilization). Labor-intensive firms stay flexible by laying off workers as sales fall. Capital-intensive firms are not as flexible, since costs of durable inputs are committed regardless of sales volume.

Changes in the relative prices of inputs through substitution of one input for another is possible at times and, in addition, one can make changes in the nature of the product. This kind of flexibility is made possible by using general-purpose, rather than specialized, machinery and equipment.

Ability to quickly and economically contract or expand the designed rate of output of the plant in response to changes in the sales rate may be achieved by reserving space for expansion, using easily expandable and contractable layout and construction, and installing service facilities (utilities, sewer, drives, and so forth) that can adjust to loads other than those initially imposed.

Figure 6–7
Short-run cost curves for plants differing in flexibility

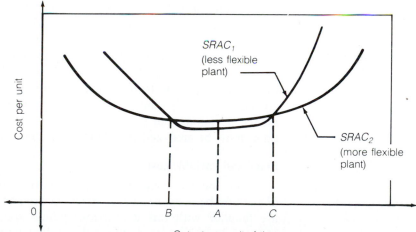

Short-run costs

Regardless of whether costs are explicit or implicit, they exist in either a short- or long-run period. However, it is a mistake to think in terms of short run or long run in connection with some specified number of days, weeks, or months. Short- and long-run considerations have to do with the firm's ability (1) to change its rate of output, based on existing operating capacity of the plant(s) or (2) to change the size of its plant(s). In differentiating the short- from long-run time period, one must consider what influence, if any, the firm is able to exert on its fixed and variable explicit financial costs.

In the long run, all costs are variable. Variable costs are ones that change as output changes; fixed costs remain at a specified level regardless of whether the firm produces output. The shorter the short run, the more likely it is that all costs are fixed.

Interpreted narrowly, short-run cost analysis deals exclusively with the relationship of total costs to output, the way total costs increase as more variable inputs are added to provide greater output. But this chapter is concerned with more than cost-output relationships. It covers the cost effects of a wide variety of decisions under conditions in which some inputs are fixed and others variable.

Short-run cost analysis incorporates, perhaps, the most useful bag of tools in managerial economics. It provides the logic for determining the impact of a variety of decisions on costs. Short-run cost analysis is indispensable in the discussions of pricing that come later in this book. It is necessary for rational decisions regarding abandonment of a product line or establishment of a new product line while using existing facilities. It is useful in determining whether to increase the volume of specific outputs, to use idle capacity, to rent facilities to outsiders, and so on. Short-run cost analysis is also important in decisions regarding new capital investments, decisions that would appear to be long-run ones but that sometimes must be analyzed in a short-run framework.

Fixed and variable costs

At the most elementary level, short-run cost analysis starts with a distinction between fixed and variable costs. Most readers of this chapter are familiar with this distinction, which separates costs unrelated to changes in volume from those dependent upon volume. However, because several misunderstandings may exist, a few warnings are provided:

1. The dividing line between what is a fixed and what is a variable cost

is not the same for all decisions. Elementary treatments include material costs and direct labor costs in the variable cost category; they relegate the depreciation expense and, usually, the indirect labor and administrative charges to a fixed cost category; and they leave little scope for judgment. Such an approach may be far too simple. Consider direct labor costs. It makes a difference whether a decision to accept a particular order requires the addition of overtime or can be managed with the use of available idle time. It is often assumed that depreciation is entirely a fixed expense, continuing regardless of the level of output. A little reflection on this subject suggests that the wear-and-tear component of depreciation is related to output; this component of depreciation may be known as user costs.

Depreciation expense is peculiarly difficult to analyze. It may be that in some industries the assumption that is completely fixed is a helpful simplification. It is also possible that the decision under consideration may increase depreciation not only by increasing user cost, but also by requiring the purchase of additional machinery on which additional depreciation will be incurred.

A variety of "short-runs" exist, each depending on the decision under consideration at the time. It follows that there must also be variety in the way in which expenses are segregated into fixed and variable categories. The decision maker must select the classification suited to his/her purposes.

2. The second warning has to do with the assumption that an expense must be either fixed or variable. Some expenses are a mixture of both fixed and variable elements, and for decision-making purposes it may be desirable to recognize this complication. The case of depreciation has already been noted in this respect. The obsolescence component of depreciation is a function of time and thus continues regardless of decisions about the level of output from the plant and equipment already on hand. This element of depreciation is "sunk"; it involves an investment already made and thus an expense that will continue regardless of the decision (ignoring salvage value that might be gained from the sale of such an asset). The wear-and-tear element of depreciation is related at least in part to output, often in a very complicated way. Depreciation may be accelerated by the use of overtime or extra shifts. Some types of equipment, on the other hand, may actually deteriorate faster when not in use. It is claimed, for example, that an automobile left in a garage for a long period of time suffers depreciation. A similar claim exists for lightweight, Cessna-type private airplanes. It appears, therefore, the only way to recover cost of some items (i.e., the car or airplane) is to "run the wheels off it." The railroad industry in the United States has understood this concept for years and, as a result, almost never shuts down diesel locomotives in the yard during numerous, consecutive 24-hour work shifts.

Other expenses are also a mixture of fixed and variable components. Such costs may be called semivariable expenses. Utility bills, for example, frequently include both a fixed charge and a charge based on consumption; the telephone system charges a flat amount of money for having the unit in a place of business and assesses a second charge for each time the phone is used. Using the phone for long-distance calls magnifies this second charge considerably.

Salespeople are often paid a straight salary plus commissions based on volume. Supervisors often receive bonuses based on output, in addition to their fixed salaries.

3. Experience with misunderstandings in the past suggests other elementary warnings are in order. Some students interpret the expression "variable cost" to mean any cost that varies over time. For example, they take the fact that a machine may cost more to purchase today than five years ago as evidence that depreciation on such machines is variable. This is a complete misinterpretation of *variable*. The term does not refer to variations in prices over time; instead, it refers to cost-output (or decision-cost) relationships at given moments in time. In classifying costs into the variable and fixed categories, the issue is whether a change in output affects the cost.

4. The expression "completely fixed expense" is open to numerous interpretations. One needs to distinguish among the following kinds of costs:

a. Costs that are fixed only so long as operations continue, but are escapable if and when operations shut down. An example might be salaries of some staff members.
b. Costs that continue even if production is halted but that are escapable if the company is liquidated. Such costs are inescapable in the short run but escapable in the long run. An example might include the wages of a guard or the minimum heating expense required to prevent the freezing of pipes in a nonoperating plant. Such expenses may be referred to often as standby fixed costs.
c. Costs that cannot be escaped even if the company is dissolved and its assets sold. An example is depreciation on equipment that has no market value. Strictly speaking, of course, these costs are *not* economic costs at all (the opportunity costs are nonexistent), but they may appear on the books.
d. Costs that are not the result of output but are incurred at the discretion of management. Examples are advertising expenses, research expenses, and consultants' fees. This category of costs may at times include a substantial portion of the wages-and-salaries component. Such expenses go under the name *programmed fixed costs* or *discretionary expenses*.

Even this classification is incomplete, for it does not cover the depreciation expense that is fixed over a range of output but increases when facilities are expanded to permit increases in capacity.

Cost classifications

It will become increasingly clear as we proceed that the fixed-variable classification is inadequate to deal with all cost relationships involved in managerial decisions. It is appropriate at this point to review a wider range of cost terminology. Throughout the study of managerial economics, the following classifications are useful, and each classification reveals a different aspect of the decision-making problem.

Sunk versus escapable costs

Sunk costs refer to expenses incurred by the firm during some previous time. These costs are fixed in nature and exist for the firm regardless of whether the facility is used. Chapter 2 introduced the incremental cost concept, but it is of such central importance to decision making that it must be reviewed here. A cost is incremental if it results from a decision; costs not arising from a particular decision but continuing to exist regardless of that decision are excluded from incremental costs. For example, suppose that after a major snowstorm United Airlines management must decide whether or not to put on an extra flight from Boston to Chicago. Managers should consider the extra fuel costs, wear and tear on tires, the out-of-pocket costs associated with ground crews in both locations, wages, salaries and expenses associated with the flight itself, and landing fees, if any. They should overlook the portion of depreciation that continues regardless of whether or not the extra flight is added. In a like manner, a salesperson deciding whether or not to drive an extra 1,000 miles should consider the extra fuel costs and wear and tear on tires but can ignore the portion of depreciation that continues. A decision to buy a second aircraft or to buy a second car, in contrast, must consider the added depreciation expenses resulting from having two airplanes and/or two cars rather than one. The point is this: Sunk costs may be ignored in the short run. It is mandatory that one determine for each decision which costs are actually incremental. If the importance of this distinction in costs is not apparent to the reader in this chapter, he/she will have an opportunity to see its application in Part 4, entitled "Pricing."

On the other hand, costs are escapable if the decision frees the enterprise from an outflow of funds that would have been required otherwise. If cutting back production by 10 percent will free the firm fom material costs of $10,000 per month and labor of $5,000 per month, those costs are escapable. But if no line supervisors can be laid off as a result of the decision, their salaries do not enter into the escapable-costs calculation.

Whether certain costs are escapable or inescapable varies according to the decision. Some costs are inescapable. Some costs that cannot be escaped as a result of reduction in output may be escaped only by closing the department. The part of depreciation relating to wear and tear (the user costs) is escaped by reducing output, but the part that continues regardless of output is escapable only if the machine or building is sold, and even then only if there is a market for the asset(s).

The opposite of the escapable cost is the inescapable or sunk cost, the cost that continues regardless of whether or not an alternative is chosen. Again, what is or is not sunk depends on the decision being considered. If I am considering leasing my house during the summer while on sabbatical leave, I must consider the depreciation on the house (exclusive of wear and tear), the payment for mowing the lawn, and the fixed charge in my telephone and other utility bills to be inescapable. But I can escape from all those expenses by selling the house, at the cost of incurring considerable inconvenience and expenses of other types.

Common versus separable costs

A distinction needs to be made between common and separable costs. Many, if not most, firms produce more than one product and thus run into the problem of common costs. It is often difficult to attribute costs to particular products, since they result from the mix of products rather than from one product taken at a time. In decision making much of the confusion of trying to determine which costs are common and which are traceable to a particular product can be resolved by applying incremental reasoning. It is often easier to determine how much a change in output of a single product brings a change in a particular kind of cost than it is to determine a product's fair share of that cost. In any case, it is the change in cost rather than the traceability of cost that is relevant. But it is necessary to recognize more complex situations in which an increase in the output of product A results in an increase (or decrease) in the marginal cost of product B. Such problems are important in determining the product mix in the oil industry or other industries in which the same raw materials or processes result in a variety of end products.[6]

A barrel of oil contains 42 U.S. gallons of gasoline. Less than one pint of aviation gasoline (Avgas) can be obtained from each barrel of crude oil. If additional Avgas is to be obtained, fewer gallons of regular, un-

---

[6] If a German or Japanese conglomerate owns steel mills and automobile manufacturing companies, a relationship exists between its common costs and its common goods. This relationship is such that careful allocation of costs can result in one product—say, steel—being made to bear the largest share of total fixed costs. Autos could incur lower fixed costs and, consequently, could be sold at lower prices without interfering with the firm's profit margin on autos. Under such circumstances, charges of "dumping" autos on United States markets may be without foundation—more of this subject in Chapter 10.

leaded, and premium unleaded gasoline may be available; in addition, diesel fuel, home heating oil and other by-products of the refinery may be affected. The price of each petroleum product mentioned here differs significantly from the price of every other product mentioned. Yet, the costs of producing these various products may be common.

Shutdown versus start-up costs

To be complete it is desirable to introduce a few additional terms that appear in business literature. Frequently businesspeople and the news media refer to shutdown costs, but their interpretation of the term may be incomplete. Both implicit and explicit costs are incurred in the short run when a firm decides to shut down, to close its production facility. In the case of an automobile manufacturer or a steel mill, the banking of furnaces and the cost incurred in otherwise protecting the plant and equipment while it is temporarily in a period of disuse must be calculated. In the event the plant is one day supposed to reopen, implicit and explicit short-run start-up costs associated with the reopening must also be calculated. The explicit portion of shutdown and start-up costs will be accounted for by the firm; the implicit portion often goes unreported. These implicit shutdown and start-up costs must be recognized by economists as they analyze the financial impact on the firm in the short run of the shutdown and/or start-up decision. The cost to the firm of certain salaries and other fringe benefits plus funded, unfunded, or partially funded pension commitments of the firm are examples of implicit costs that may go unnoticed by the firm in the short run. Traditional accounting statements and schedules do not normally call the analyst's attention to these costs.

Opportunity costs

From the point of view of applied price theory, the subject being studied at this time, a cost is not really a cost unless it requires a sacrifice of alternatives, unless it is an opportunity cost. Determining what is an opportunity cost or, more important, determining the level of opportunity costs, requires the measurement of what is given up by the decision. The use of idle space that has no alternate use is cost-free for a particular purpose, regardless of the amount of depreciation being charged on that space. If the output of a steel mill, auto plant, or rubber factory cannot be sold profitably, there is no opportunity cost associated with letting the plant sit idle. Only if the decision maker can find a legitimate, profitable use for the space that had been sitting idle can a so-called user cost be assigned to the previously idle work space. The use of a factory or a machine that has been completely written off the books involves a cost if its use for the purpose under consideration requires the giving up of alternative opportunities.

The opportunity cost of attending class for a college student is the amount of money he/she could be earning if gainfully employed. If no opportunities for income exist and if one values his/her leisure time at or near zero, no opportunity cost exists for attending school. For an airline that owns one airplane, the opportunity cost associated with flying to Boston from Chicago is the amount of income and, therefore, profit that could have been derived by flying to some other location with that plane at the same time.

Opportunity costs are implicit by nature. They are costs incurred by using resources to accomplish objective A as opposed to using those same resources to accomplish some other goal, objective B. Rarely, if ever, is it true that resources have no other use.

Long-run costs

This book devotes less space to long-run costs than to short-run costs analysis, since the relevance of long-run cost analysis for decision-making purposes is less clear than it is for short-run analysis. Technological considerations are more important in the long run; the economics of choice among alternative technologies falls under the heading of "capital budgeting," to which an entire chapter is devoted later. Besides, as John Maynard Keynes said: "In the long run we are all dead."

Long-run cost analysis is concerned with the economies or diseconomies of scale facing a single firm.[7] In some industries the economies of scale may be insignificant past a minimum size, in which case it is possible for large and small firms to compete on relatively equal terms. This situation is apparently the case in much of agriculture and retailing, in which the survival of small firms is at least partial evidence that their average costs are not sharply different from those of larger firms. In other industries the inability of small firms to persist suggests they do not benefit from the same cost advantages made available to larger firms. An example is the automobile industry in which the past 70 years have marked the disappearance of dozens of small firms unable to compete with giants located at home and abroad.[8] In still other industries the situation may be a combination of economies of scale at low levels of output and diseconomies at large sizes, with the optimum at some intermediate size.

---

[7] By "economies of scale," we mean the savings in unit costs that result from larger size plants or from larger size firms.

[8] These firms were not considered small at the time (e.g., Packard, Hudson, Studebaker, to name a few).

Relations of short-run cost functions to long-run functions

If production planning is viewed in long-run perspective, all inputs can be varied as the rate of production is changed. Machines and equipment can be changed. Methods and processes can be changed as desired. New plants can be built in whatever sizes and locations are advantageous. The firm can even change its business. Long-run planning reaches to a horizon that is far away.

With no inputs considered fixed in relation to rate of output, there is no fixed cost per period. Variable cost is total cost per period. Consider a long-run average cost curve such as the one shown in Figure 6–8. This curve would define the lowest total cost per period and the lowest average cost per unit, respectively. For various rates of output, each cost is conceived as being established for continuous production at only the given rate.

At each point on the long-run curve of Figure 6–8, there is conceptually a plant—a bundle of inputs that, once put in place, would be fixed in relation to variations in rate of output. Corresponding to each such plant, there would be short-run total and average cost curves defining the behavior of costs with respect to changes in the rate of output of that plant. Of the innumerable short-run cost curves that could be depicted in Figure 6–8, only six have been drawn. These curves correspond to just six of the many, many plant sizes among which management can choose so long as it has the long-run, or planning, perspective.

It can be seen that the long-run curve is an envelope—it goes around a family of short-run curves. So long as the firm is in a long-range planning posture, it has the full range of possible combinations of costs and rates of output as defined by the long-run curve. Once any one of the plants is actually in place, the firm's range of possible combinations of costs and rates of output will be defined by the plant's short-run curves.

Figure 6–8
The long-run planning (envelope) curve

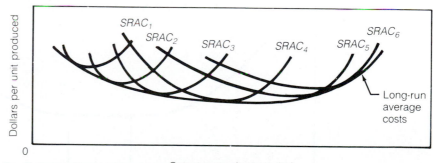

The average total cost curve is U-shaped in both the short and long run. The curvature of *ATC* is explained in the short run by the law of diminishing returns, in the long run by economies and diseconomies of scale.

Figure 6–9 depicts the behavior of the long-run average total cost curve over time. The curve tends to decline as the overall scale of the firms operation expands; it reaches a period during which costs tend to be constant and, ultimately, the curve rises slowly. This long-run average total cost curve is referred to by some economists as the envelope curve, since it envelopes or includes successive changes within the firm from short-run cost conditions. It is known also as the planning curve. In the long run, a firm can plan to build any number of plants needed, and each plant may be to whatever scale the firm desires.

In the long run, accounting and statistical cost analysis is beneficial to the economic analyst; however, reliable results are rather difficult to obtain when time-series analysis is used. Fortunately for the analyst, it is neither necessary nor desirable to calculate long-run cost functions with the same degree of precision as that required for short-run cost analysis.

In Figure 6–9 average total costs per unit decline from zero to x_1 units of output along the horizontal axis. Over this range of output, cost decreases are attributable to large-scale operations entered into by the firm. Large-scale operation enables the firm to generate a larger output per unit of resource input. In other words, since large firms are more specialized in every department than are small firms, the larger firms can operate more efficiently. Specialization of labor, capital equipment, finance personnel, and so on provide the larger firm with cost-saving techniques not

Figure 6–9
Long-run average total cost curves

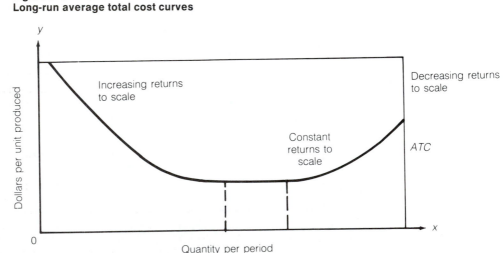

available to smaller counterparts. In addition, the larger firm can acquire raw materials in huge quantities and at relatively low prices. In fact, many of the larger firms may be integrated vertically to the extent that one or more of their wholly owned subsidiaries provide as a finished product the raw material input needed by the larger firm. In the rubber industry, for example, it is common for a large rubber manufacturer to own rubber plantations. Large electric utility generating companies often own coal mines. Large automobile manufacturers may own steel companies, plastic companies, brake shoe manufacturing plants, and so on. Additional economies of large scale are realized by the larger firms in the sale of their finished product (i.e., sales personnel may be more specialized, better educated, more productive). And last but not least, large companies enjoy tremendous political advantages.

In fact, a wide variety of reasons for the downward slope of the curve in the initial stages are available. The reasons cited here are no doubt incomplete. Large firms may be in a better position to employ highly skilled top management and may have greater negotiating powers, causing greater advantage in the market place. Most of the advantages of scale can be explained in terms of indivisibilities of some of the inputs. If large machines were divisible into equally efficient smaller parts, or if skilled labor or management were divisible into equally skilled units, these economies of scale would disappear. In fact, some economists take the position that economies of scale are entirely a result of indivisibilities, a position too extreme for some other economists.

This is an appropriate point at which to introduce the distinction between the plant and the firm. Economic theory often concerns itself with the firm as a whole and with economies and diseconomies of scale for the firm. The internal management of the firm must also consider economies of plant size and distinguish between those economies available to the firm as it increases in size, regardless of the number of plants, and those available to the plant as it increases in size.

Within the individual plant, economies of scale may result from lower unit costs of maintenance or the lower costs of moving products from one operation to another. A larger plant may be able to take advantage of the line (product) principle of plant layout, with its greater specialization of equipment and shorter lines of transportation; the smaller plants may be dependent on the functional principle of layout with its greater flexibility but with more complex problems of transportation and production control.[9]

Reasons for increasing returns to scale realized in Figure 6–9 between

---

[9] Discussions of line versus functional layout appear in most production management textbooks. A line layout is one planned around a single product (or group of closely related products); a functional layout is one planned around various types of equipment.

zero and x_1 units of output along the horizontal axis include: (1) technological advantages enjoyed by the firm and (2) highly skilled and highly
specialized labor. But keep in mind that although the average total cost
curve is in a state of decline and the firm is enjoying increasing returns to
scale, total costs are increasing. Total costs almost always increase when
output increases. During increasing returns to scale, these total costs
increase at a rate less rapid than the increase in output being enjoyed by
the firm.

The advantages to the firm of specialization within departments and on
various management committees reaches the point at which no additional
decreases in average total costs per unit of output are possible. The same
statement is true for additional benefits to be derived from technological,
political, and negotiating advantages inherent in the large company. The
result is a period of neither increasing nor decreasing returns to scale, a
period of constant returns.[10]

Diseconomies of large-scale operation exist in Figure 6–9 for all levels
of output to the right of x_2 on the horizontal axis. These decreasing
returns may occur and be seen more rapidly in some industries than in
others. For example, it is unlikely that operation to the right of point x_2
is noticeable as quickly in the railroad industry as it might be in the
manufacture of color television sets. Maintenance of the right-of-way for
railroads is a high and rising operating expense. However, it differs significantly from the capital cost associated with initial construction of
bridges, tunnels, prestressed concrete ties, and so on. Once incurring the
costs associated with this kind of an expenditure, the railroad can expect
to benefit from the expenditure for many years to come.

Electric utilities have much in common with railroads in that their long-
run average total cost curve tends to decrease over a relatively long range
of outputs. Replacement costs of capital assets for railroads and electric
utilities are exceedingly high, so much so that new private capital information may not be available quickly enough and in sufficient quantity to
prevent the death of one or more firms within an industry. No firm knowingly allows itself to enter into a level of output that, in the long run,
causes decreasing returns to scale.[11]

Diseconomies of large-scale operation may occur and become highly
probable when a business conglomerate allows its management group to
be spread too thinly. There are limits to the decision-making process. As
an organization becomes larger, it becomes more difficult to coordinate

---

[10] Constant returns to scale may exist more in economic theory than in practice. Constant
returns may imply homogeneous production functions.

[11] Studebaker Corporation made its long-run adjustment in a period of diseconomies of
scale when it moved to Canada; the Baltimore & Ohio Railroad made it when the firm
merged with the Chessie System; Seiberling Rubber was burdened with diseconomies of
scale prior to merger with Firestone Tire & Rubber Company.

the activities of the firm's overall operation. As a result, important decisions are not made quickly enough for profitable implementation by the firm; or (more likely) decisions are postponed by top managers because they have too many other things on their minds already, and lower and/or middle managers are reluctant to make a decision for which they might be criticized later. The net result: indecision and/or no decision. Meanwhile, smaller firms with whom this conglomerate competes are able to take advantage of the situation.

But are there diseconomies of scale for the firm? The economist points to one important bit of indirect evidence that such diseconomies exist— the fact that more than one firm is able to survive in most industries. If economies of scale persisted throughout all ranges of output, one firm would drive out all others to gain advantages of lower unit costs. Such persistent economies apparently prevail in the public utilities, for which the public grants monopoly privileges in recognition of the economies of the scale that are available. Public utilities are often known as natural monopolies in recognition of the inability of small firms to compete against the low cost of large enterprises. Even if the long-run cost curve were to become perfectly horizontal, it would appear that the horizontal portion of the curve would be lower for some firms than for others, resulting in a tendency toward monopoly. Thus, from the absence of monopoly in most industries, some economists deduce that most cost curves must eventually rise.

Economies and diseconomies of multiplant firms

The shape of the long-run average cost curve and the relation of average cost per unit to the rate of output is determined by the technological and institutional economies of scale of the industry. Economies of scale of plants result from combinations of scale effects and economies of input substitution as rate of output is increased with all inputs variable.

A firm that has expanded a plant to optimum size at a given location may still find economies in bringing several plants under a single management. Some economies of size in multiplant firms take the form of reductions in administrative cost per unit of product or service. Efficiencies of specialization of labor and equipment in the administrative function are similar to those in production. And a large organization can take advantage of skills of economic forecasters, industrial psychologists, and other highly trained staff members that cannot be efficiently utilized in smaller businesses. Nelson found in a study of life insurance companies that the relation of total administrative cost per $1,000 of insurance in force to the total amount of insurance in force was as shown in Figure 6–10. The output scale in the figure is logarithmic, so the largest companies are on the order of 1,000 times as large as the smallest. Although there are variations in administrative cost at each size of insurance firm, the under-

Figure 6–10
Economies of scale in administration of life insurance companies

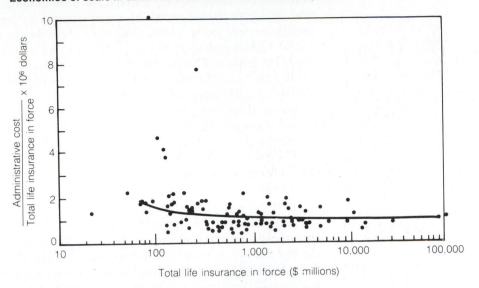

lying economies of size appear to benefit most the largest firms in the study.[12]

Multiplant operations can have economies of size in selling the output. The Chevrolet Division of General Motors Corporation might spend $20 million a year on advertising at a cost of only $20 each on more than 1 million units sold, whereas a similar level of advertising for an American Motors model would cost close to $100 per unit on sales of perhaps 200,000 units. There are also economies of size in financing that may benefit multiplant firms. Larger companies may be able to attain blue-chip status, which lowers the cost of equity capital as well as the interest rate on borrowed money. Such retailers as Sears Roebuck & Co., J. C. Penney Company, Inc., and many smaller chains, have economies of purchasing as a result of their multiplant retail locations.

Finally, vertical integration that is not economic even for the largest size of a single-plant firm may be advantageous to a multiplant company. For example, a multiple-plant petroleum refiner may be able to integrate the crude oil production function. Or a national retailer may be able to integrate factories that make a variety of consumer goods. A company that publishes a number of daily newspapers in large cities may be able to integrate a paper mill. Such automobile assemblers as General Motors

---

[12] Edward A. Nelson, "Economic Size of Organizations," *California Management Review*, Spring 1968.

Corporation and Ford Motor Company are able to set up their own divisions to supply components—batteries, radiators, starters, alternators, and so forth.

Diseconomies of size of multiple-plant firms exist. Management difficulties have traditionally been proposed as limits to company size. Management groups spread themselves too thinly. However, the successes of General Motors, Sears, General Electric Co., and numerous other giants reveal, as some economists might think, that management need not be as limiting a factor. Management probably does limit the size of firms in cases in which day-to-day operations require the personal attention and creative talent of a particular person. Examples may include: manufacture of high-style women's wear; development of urban real estate; production of crops and livestock; operation of fine restaurants; booking of live entertainment; many types of retailing; and provision of such professional services as medical care, legal advice, high-level negotiations, and some aspects of strategic planning.

The survivor technique

The optimal level of economic output for most firms is difficult to determine in the long run for a variety of reasons, not the least of which is scarcity of data. Stigler developed the survivor theory and acknowledges that it suffers from inadequate information; however, it suffices.[13] Quite simply, an efficient size of firm is one that survives. An efficient firm is capable of inventing and/or innovating when necessary; it can adjust to federal, state, and local governmental regulations; it can sustain the onslaught of foreign competition; it can adjust to any number of imperfectly competitive factor markets; and it can generally survive in an industry at a time when seemingly better firms failed.

Application of the survivor technique is along the following lines:

1. Stratify all firms in an industry by size of output.
2. Calculate the percentage of total output controlled by each firm in the industry.
3. Plot over time the percentage of total economic output accounted for by each firm; those firms with increasing percentages are more efficient than their counterparts within the industry who will have decreasing percentage shares. Firms with decreasing percentage shares are, by definition, less efficient.
4. The firm with a relatively high and rising percentage share of total output over time is the most efficient member of the industry. This latter firm comes closest to operating at the minimum point of the

---

[13] George J. Stigler, "The Economies of Scale," *Journal of Law and Economics*, October, 1958, pp. 54–71.

average total cost curve. This firm, it is thought, will survive in its industry.

The survivor principle or technique is "more direct and simpler than the alternative techniques for the determination of the optimum size of firm, it is also more authoritative." [14]

The engineering technique

An interesting alternative to the survivor technique and to statistical long-run cost functions is what has come to be known as the engineering technique. Engineering studies assume various (different) levels of capacity for the firm while holding constant all other variables (i.e., factor input prices, market structure, technology, plant site, and so on). [15]

Referring to Figure 6–9, the astute reader will notice that it is the slope of the long-run average total cost curve that determines the rate of increasing returns to scale, constant returns to scale, decreasing returns to scale. The slope, not the level of the curve, may be the most important factor to consider when studying economies of scale. The engineering approach, dwelling as it does upon capacity, concerns itself primarily with the slope of the curve. And it is just as well, because engineering studies that allow for different assumptions concerning the percentage of rated operating capacity at which the firm will operate often result in inaccurate long-term cost projections. These inaccuracies, if and when they occur, do not nullify a technique designed to assist in determination of the long-run optimal level of economic output for the firm.

Considerable additional empirical research will be conducted before one will be able to say whether the survivor or the engineering technique is the more reliable. The probability is high that each approach will continue to possess certain unique characteristics that will prove useful in helping to determine the slope and level of long-run average total cost curves for a variety of firms and industries in a growing, dynamic economy.

Break-even analysis

Up to this point we have been mainly concerned with the classification of particular expenses (salaries, depreciation, etc.). We now turn to the aggregation of these expenses for the firm as a whole or for departments in the short run. Again, it is possible to examine these costs as totals or as averages. Our objective is to compare total cost of output with ex-

---

[14] Ibid.

[15] Innovation is possible in the engineering studies whereas new invention is not; in other words, production techniques may alter but technology remains constant.

pected revenue at various rates of production. Analysis of this sort often uses linear break-even charts.[16]

Figure 6–11 illustrates a typical break-even chart. The horizontal axis represents output; the purpose of the chart is to reveal the effects of changes in output on changes in profit. The analysis, of course, cannot be completed without cost data. It should be noted that revenues as well as expenses are shown on the *y*, or vertical axis, usually with total revenue drawn as a straight line through point of origin. The linear revenue function assumes price is unrelated to output. This assumption may be appropriate under conditions of pure competition, in which a firm may sell any quantity of its product at the market price. This linear assumption is not suitable when the demand curve slopes downward and to the right.

Figure 6–11
Break-even analysis*

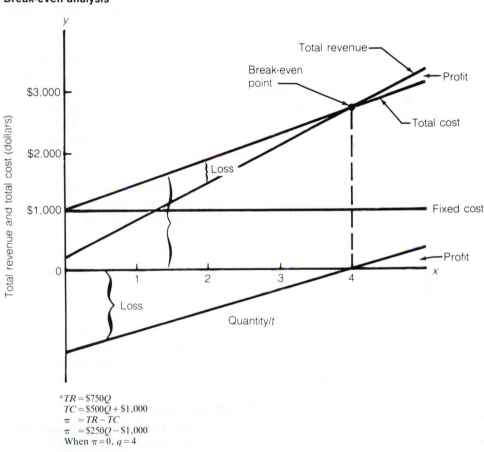

$$*TR = \$750Q$$
$$TC = \$500Q + \$1,000$$
$$\pi \;\; = TR - TC$$
$$\pi \;\; = \$250Q - \$1,000$$
$$\text{When } \pi = 0, q = 4$$

---

[16] Curvilinear break-even analysis is included in Part 4.

Total cost is revealed as a straight line; it is the sum of fixed costs, which are horizontal in Figure 6–11. One other point: Variable costs are assumed to rise in a linear fashion. Assume variable costs of $500 per unit; fixed cost per period of $1,000. Each unit is sold at a price of $750.

Inasmuch as we are dealing here with break-even analysis, a reader might be tempted to assume the purpose of the analysis is to determine where the firm can break even. Wrong. The point at which the firm breaks even is of interest, but the primary purpose of the analysis is to reveal the impact on profits and/or losses that occurs when the firm fails to reach or exceeds its break-even point. The objective of the graph is to reveal the relationship between total costs and total revenues as output changes from one level to another.

The total cost function in Figure 6–11 is revealed as a straight line from an intercept on the vertical axis. Sometimes the information is presented in an alternative form, with the variable costs revealed first on the vertical axis, and with the addition of the fixed costs to the variable costs. Such a form is revealed in Figure 6–12, which has the advantage of allowing one to read the contribution to overhead and profits quite readily. Decision making in the short run is more concerned with the contribution to both overhead and profits than it is to the profit figure alone. This form presented in Figure 6–12 is closely related to the incremental reasoning concept discussed in Chapter 2. Emphasis here is on changes in total revenue and changes in total cost as output varies. Fixed costs under such an approach appear in a subordinate position. The interesting point about a change in output and sales of, say, 10 percent is the additional contribution to overhead and profit that results; this involves a simple comparison of the increase in revenue with the increase in cost. It involves financial and operating leverage, two concepts discussed in greater detail in Chapter 9.

It is highly desirable to calculate one's break-even point in terms of units as well as dollars so as to be sure the break-even point does not occur at some output greater than the ability of the firm to produce. In other words, without calculating the break-even point in terms of units, one might find belatedly that the capacity of the firm is not great enough to break even, given its cost and price structure. Analysis of the sort presented here alerts the firm to the possibilities of profits and/or losses associated with the expenditure of monies before these monies are contractually committed by the firm.

Construction of break-even charts

Where does one obtain the information necessary for plotting a break-even chart? Two common methods exist, each based on the profit and loss summary as provided by the accountant.

Figure 6–12
Profit contribution analysis

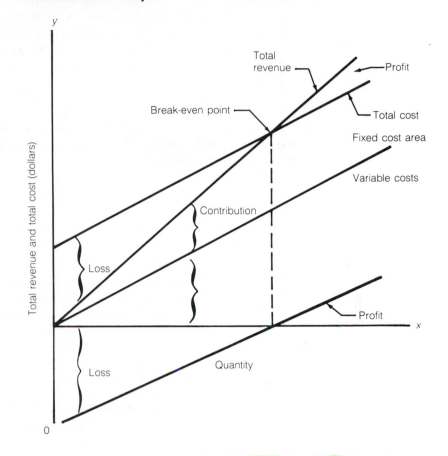

1. One approach, called the analytical, or engineering, approach, is to take a single income statement of the firm (or department) and to use considerable judgment in the classification of costs into those that are fixed and those that are variable. A manager of a small firm who is intimately familiar with the output-expense behavior should not have much difficulty with classifications of this sort, but even for such a person numerous borderline problems exist, as in the case of semivariable expenses. Managers ask themselves whether they would actually increase this expense if output were to increase. They may find it necessary to abandon the linearity assumption upon which break-even charts are usually constructed and introduce in its place a stair-step cost assumption with other semivariable expenses. Such line managers might make several assumptions about which costs are fixed and which are variable,

Figure 6–13
Estimating the total cost line from a scatter diagram

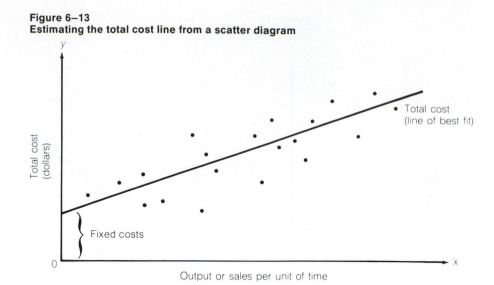

changing their assumptions until they have a range of fixed and variable costs. Final analysis would reveal a range of break-even points, and instead of having a precise point at which the operation breaks even, they would face a range of break-even points. Assuming they would feel comfortable at the lower as well as the higher break-even point within this range of possible points, the manager might go ahead with the project.

2. A second approach, the statistical or historical approach, compares a series of income statements for succeeding periods that reflect varying levels of output and costs. By plotting the output-cost relationship on a scatter diagram, one can estimate the position of the total cost line. If one assumes that costs are linear, one can extrapolate the total cost line back to the vertical axis (at which output is zero), thus determining the level of fixed costs.

Figure 6–13 illustrates this approach and could be used to lead one into application of an often overworked tool, that of simple regression analysis.

Precautionary considerations in break-even analysis application

Because break-even analysis is widely used in decision making and in projecting financial results of business operations, one should consider some of the limitations of the technique.

1. If a break-even chart is based on past data, those data should be adjusted for changes in wages and in prices of raw material. Such adjustments are always cumbersome.

2. The price and output information on the break-even chart is usually

assumed to be given; that is, the assumption is made of a horizontal demand curve that is realistic only under conditions approximating pure competition. A simple way of attempting to overcome this limitation is to draw a series of total revenue lines on the chart, each based on the assumption of a different price. One can then estimate the volume that will be sold and produced at each price and can read from the diagram the expected profits.

3. The charts often ignore other influences on profits. They assume profits are a function of output, neglecting the obvious fact they are also a result of technological change, improved management, changes in the scale of fixed inputs, and many other forces.

Break-even charts are static. They are drawn on the assumption of given relationships between costs and revenues on one side and output on the other. However, costs and revenue may shift over time in such a way that projections based on past data may be misleading.

4. As has already been indicated, break-even charts are based on rather arbitrary assumptions as to the relative importance of different products in multiproduct firms. A change in the sales mix may mean that the revenue-output relationship revealed on the chart is no longer applicable.

5. When break-even charts are based on accounting data (and they are almost always based on accounting data), they suffer from all the limitations of such data. These limitations include neglect of imputed cost, arbitrary depreciation estimates, and inappropriate allocations of overhead costs. This limitation may be the most serious one for decision makers to consider.

6. The carryover of inventory from one period to another presents another difficulty. What is the value of output produced in one period to be sold in another? Accountants have long struggled with this issue, but their solution is usually one related to past rather than future transactions. Managerial economics concerns itself always with future transactions. Normally, this difficulty is glossed over in break-even analysis, though it is possible to make adjustments that will correct the error. Watch especially when dealing with inventory for changes from FIFO to LIFO, or vice versa.

High and rapidly rising price inflation during the late 1970s and early 1980s caused many firms to shift from FIFO to LIFO in accounting for their inventories. This shift on their part resulted in major tax advantages to their respective firms and was done for that purpose. The economist using accounting data for break-even analysis purposes may find a small series of years of inventory reported under FIFO and a subsequent number of years reported under LIFO. Serious judgmental and financial errors await the analyst who ignores these adjustments in his/her analysis.

7. Selling costs are very difficult to handle in break-even analysis.

Selling costs are not a result of output changes; they are a cause of changes in sales and output. Furthermore, the relationship between output and selling expenses is unstable over time, reducing the accuracy of the projection of past relationships into the future.

8. Costs in a particular period may not be a result exclusively of the output in that period. Maintenance expenses, for example, are especially hard to attribute to a given time period, being a result of past output or a preparation for future output. Maintenance costs are usually not perfectly matched with output, resulting often in an error in profit projections.

9. The simple form of the break-even chart reveals no provision for federal, state, or local taxes. Particularly conspicuous by its absence is the corporate income tax. One may develop the chart to show part of the profit going to the government via taxation and the remainder going to stockholders or being retained by the firm. If the company suffers alternating years of profit and loss, or if it falls into varying tax brackets, this adjustment for taxes is sometimes difficult to show on the chart. The major difficulty with taxation in this analysis is not computational; instead, it is to remember that it must be done.

It is easy to build a formidable list of precautionary steps to be used in applying break-even charts. Some authors are skeptical of their usefulness unless they are made much more complex than a practitioner considers necessary. Simultaneously, break-even analysis is simple, easy to use and understand, and very inexpensive. It would be unthinkable for a managerial economist to recommend acceptance or rejection of a new or continuing project without giving some consideration to the break-even point of that project.

Usefulness of break-even analysis undoubtedly varies from industry to industry. Those industries experiencing frequent changes in input prices, rapid improvements in technology, and many shifts in product mix will profit to a lesser extent than other firms from break-even charts. In other industries, break-even analyses may be quite useful to managers who are familiar with their limitations. Management depends heavily on analytic tools that cut through the complexity of reality and focus attention on fundamental relationships. In actual business practice one finds that regardless of how sophisticated the number crunching methodology employed by the analyst may be, the numbers, per se, are not nearly as important as the logic underlying why and to what purpose the analysis will be put.

Summary

This chapter develops the theory of cost directly from the theory of production. It presents an overview of production and a hypothetical production function from which cost conditions and curves are developed. There is a direct relation between production and costs, and this relationship is explained for short- and long-run time frames.

The U-shape of the short-run average total cost curve is explained by the laws of diminishing returns. In the long run the U-shape curve is explained by economies and diseconomies of scale. The long-run average total cost curve goes through three distinct phases: (1) increasing returns to scale, (2) constant returns to scale, and (3) decreasing returns to scale. Each phase of this long-run *ATC* is explained.

The long-run average total cost curve may be explained qualitatively with relative ease, but due to the scarcity of reliable raw data with which to work, it seems virtually impossible at times to quantify it for a particular firm or industry. To alleviate problems associated with acquiring reliable data, Stigler developed the survivor technique; a brief explanation of his approach is included. An alternative to the survivor technique is what has become known as the engineering technique. Enough information is presented dealing with each technique to enable the reader to develop them further.

The shorter the short run, the more likely it is that virtually all costs are fixed; in the long run all costs are variable. The short run may be considered a period of time sufficient to allow a plant (firm) to change its rate of output—the assembly line may be speeded or slowed—but not enough time to change the capacity of the plant.

The long run is a period of time sufficient to allow the plant (firm) to change not only its rate of output, but also the size and, therefore, the capacity of the plant. It is often true that the long-run adjustment, if made, may not be noticed until some period after it is too late to avoid having the event take place. The Studebaker-Packard Corporation may have made its long-run adjustment when it left South Bend, Indiana, to set up operations in Canada; the Penn-Central Railroad may have made its long-run adjustment when it declared bankruptcy.

Under no circumstances should one think of the short or long run in connection with some specified period of time. Changes in costs over time are much too subtle for that kind of thinking. By the same token, it may be inconsistent with the definition of short run, and it is an overstatement to suggest that all costs are fixed rigidly in the short run. They are not. It is recognized that variable costs such as direct labor charges to the firm may be reduced by laying off workers if and when demand for the finished product and/or service of the organization declines. Total short-run direct labor costs may be flexible in a downward direction at times. This condition existed and was noticeable during the late 1970s and early 1980s. If changes in the cost function take place, they do so at irregular intervals over the course of a business cycle. These changes may represent only a small fraction of total costs and may have little or no impact on the short-run price and output policies of many oligopolistic companies.

Determination of a firm's break-even point is presented in this chapter, which assumes that total costs can be broken into two distinct components: fixed costs and variable costs. If substantially all costs are fixed in the short run, no meaningful distinction between these two kinds of costs can be made. Any calculation of a firm's break-even point in terms of the number of dollars of sales needed to break even or in terms of the number of units the firm needs to produce in order to break even may be subject to a considerable degree of error. Nevertheless, the break-even example and concept is sound but difficult at times to apply.

Short-run and long-run cost analysis is appropriate in a variety of problem-solving situations. The cases that follow require such a cost analysis in pricing decisions, decisions of product mix, decisions on abandonment of activities or expansion of activities, and the establishment of new branches.

It is not possible to find cases that isolate cost considerations from all other economic variables. The cases in this chapter require some attention to the demand concepts covered in Chapters 4 and 5. Some of the cases foreshadow the discussions of pricing and capital budgeting treated more formally later in this book. Marketing considerations are also important throughout. No attempt is made here to isolate one aspect of the analysis from other business considerations.

CASES

Cost theory

Robertson Products Company

The Robertson Products Company is a partnership engaged in clay sewer-pipe manufacturing. The company sells primarily to state and local governments; its sewer pipe is purchased by various state and local governments, including sewage authorities in the state of Pennsylvania for installation in various parts of the state.

The company owns and operates five small clay-pipe manufacturing facilities located within 100 miles of each other. In addition, it owns a paving operation in the same vicinity.

The plants are generally profitable, returning on average a book profit of from 10 to 20 percent of the book value of the partners' property. Occasionally, one of the plants operates at a loss, though this results partly from the fact that special repairs at one of the plants may be charged off as a current expense.

The most unstable part of the business is the paving operation. Its instability results from the variations in road construction activities of the state government involved. In election years paving activity is high; in other years it tapers off. The result is that the paving activities of the firm fluctuate sharply from high to low profits. Exhibit 1 covers data on paving revenues and expenses for the years 1978 through 1983.

1. Classify the expenses into fixed expenses and variable expenses based on the 1983 profit and loss statement. Use judgment in determining

Exhibit 1

ROBERTSON PRODUCTS COMPANY
Statement of Profit and Loss
For the Years Ended December 31, 1978 through 1983

	1978	*1979*	*1980*	*1981*	*1982*	*1983*
Net Sales	$131,758.71	$248,025.45	$404,037.72	$196,432.41	$84,574.65	$433,658.51
Operating expenses:						
Salaries and wages	19,186.50	35,196.48	41,484.90	24,543.03	17,379.57	46,598.01
Travel expense	114.00	529.26	308.79	171.96	54.90	204.60
Stationery and office supplies	67.35	126.12	78.18	78.66	.36	94.14
Auditing and legal	1.89	469.50	226.14	40.50	4.20	4.59
Dues and subscriptions	325.32	1,541.10	2,248.77	582.39	439.92	1,499.40
Repairs of equipment	2,157.24	2,933.19	7,496.79	4,475.01	1,294.83	9,559.09
Freight, in	8,104.29	13,779.39	10,270.02	5,315.64	2,763.69	12,542.07
Hired truck expense	13,513.08	27,204.21	39,039.69	15,553.44	7,897.17	42,546.69
Miscellaneous expense	508.41	424.59	1,621.26	569.10	4.65	606.00
Truck repair expense	207.42	456.24	1,981.56	1,082.22	317.94	1,814.10
Gas, oil, and lubricants	8,127.39	6,222.00	12,842.70	5,502.57	3,135.36	6,805.20
Stone purchased and sand	26,895.42	46,092.93	94,143.48	58,066.53	16,924.95	134,154.18
Oils and asphalt	29,425.35	53,740.89	80,837.55	22,336.02	11,076.18	46,041.87
Rent	514.29	—	6,972.51	6,804.60	2,345.34	3,682.26
Insurance expense	300.27	1,135.08	8,874.36	4,402.89	245.19	1,057.95
Utilities	814.38	1,706.19	2,123.79	464.82	245.55	333.18
License and fees	90.66	471.00	739.14	1,033.71	563.25	766.98
FICA expense	342.54	763.98	1,004.40	670.38	451.05	1,375.62
State unemployment contributions	344.01	831.39	1,345.29	744.48	452.91	1,249.77
Interest expense	1,592.01	4,795.50	4,852.20	3,533.55	1,863.54	1,350.84
Bonding expense	520.35	1,156.05	256.89	713.64	371.19	2,420.46
Depreciation of equipment	6,075.39	12,144.33	15,988.59	17,354.13	17,221.83	31,498.68
Telephone and postage	—	84.69	36.99	42.42	15.39	6.00
Taxes	—	3.81	33.15	263.55	15.75	315.00
Commissions	—	750.00	—	—	—	—
Advertising	—	—	402.15	440.43	37.50	52.89
Federal unemployment insurance	—	—	74.16	80.94	73.35	91.77
Sales tax	—	—	—	2,260.89	2,319.72	6,926.25
Bad-debt expense	—	—	—	1,042.41	42.18	274.80
Road construction supplies	—	—	—	—	—	911.81
	119,227.56	212,557.92	335,283.45	178,169.91	87,557.46	354,783.72
Net profit (loss)	$ 12,531.15	$ 35,467.53	$ 68,754.27	$ 18,262.50	$(2,982.81)	$ 78,874.79

whether the expense is fixed or variable. Some expenses, such as advertising and rent, may be classified in a separate category, since they are more in the nature of programmed or manipulable expenses that are neither fixed nor a result of changes in output.

2. On the basis of your answer to question 1, construct a break-even chart.
3. Plot a scatter diagram relating total cost to sales. Complete a break-even chart based on this approach.
4. Compare your two break-even charts (the one based on the classification of accounts, the other on a rough statistical analysis). Do they

provide approximately the same estimate of fixed costs? How do you account for the differences in the two charts?

5. What limitations would a statistician find in the statistical chart constructed as an answer to question 3?

The Minerva oxygen vent valve[1]

H. R. Deming, president of Dem-A-Lex Dynamics Corporation of Lexington, Massachusetts, called a meeting of the executive committee to consider a proposal which would establish improved quality control over an item produced by Dem-A-Lex as subcontractor for several prime contractors. The item was an oxygen vent valve used in the U.S. missile program.

This valve had been adopted by several large missile-manufacturing companies for use in a recently developed missile. The Department of Defense announced that the Minerva missile had been designated as an operational, first-line weapon and that all prime contractors of the Minerva missile were to enter crash production programs. Because of the increased urgency of the program and the importance of the oxygen vent valve to the Minerva's proper functioning, an executive committee meeting had been called to consider a proposal submitted by Mr. Massey, the company's production manager. Massey's proposal recommended the utilization of a newly introduced piece of testing equipment which would greatly reduce the number of defective vent valves delivered by Dem-A-Lex to the various prime contractors.

Company History   Since 1958, the company had grown rapidly, and net sales in 1984 should exceed $6 million (see Exhibits 1, 2 and 3). As the company had expanded, Deming decided to devote his time and energy to research and development of new products and turned the actual operating management of the business over to his son, Stephen Deming, a former Air Force jet pilot and a recent graduate of a well-known business school. Deming, Sr., had developed several unique and commercially salable products since 1958, among which were: metal and fabric strain gauges which signaled a condition of overload on the material; special high-pressure intensifiers and pressure transducers; solenoid-triggered butterfly valves; ultralow-temperature liquid pumps and flow regulators; high-tension circuit breakers; and most recently the oxygen vent valve. Patents had initially been obtained on each of these items, but after they had been a few years on the market, similar devices, but different enough to avoid patent infringement, had been developed by the larger manufac-

---

[1] This case was prepared by Andrew McCosh under the direction of Stanley I. Buchin of the Harvard University Graduate School of Business Administration as a basis for classroom discussion rather than to illustrate either effective or ineffective handling of administrative situations. Copyright © 1965 by the President and Fellows of Harvard College. Dates have been altered to make the case more meaningful to the 1980s.

Exhibit 1

THE MINERVA OXYGEN VENT VALVE
Balance Sheet
For the Year Ended December 31, 1984
($000)

Assets

Current assets:
Cash and marketable securities	$378	
Accounts receivable (net)	954	
Inventories	685	
Notes receivable (employees)	126	
Total current assets		$2,143

Fixed assets:
Land and buildings (net)	360	
Machinery and equipment (net)	680	
Prepaid expenses	6	
Other assets..	13	
Total fixed assets		1,059
Total assets		$3,202

Liabilities and Net Worth

Current liabilities:
Accounts payable....................................	$250	
Notes payable to bank @ 6%..........................	700	
Dividends payable	35	
Other accruals......................................	315	
Total current liabilities		$1,300

Fixed liabilities and net worth:
Mortgage payable on real estate	120	
Long-term bonds (7% coupon)	500	
Common stock (40% owned by Deming, Sr., and his son)..	410	
Earned surplus	872	
Total fixed liabilities and net worth................		1,902
Total liabilities and net worth		$3,202

turing companies in the industry. Because of their size and volume-production methods, these companies could generally produce the item more cheaply than could Dem-A-Lex.

As a result of this, Dem-A-Lex did not attempt to compete on a volume-price basis with the larger firms in the industry but exploited each product as fully as possible before the larger concerns developed a similar item. After the loss of the high-volume customer to the larger producers, Dem-A-Lex then concentrated its efforts on modification and adaptation of the item to the customer with unique or special requirements who could not obtain the special adaptation from the high-volume producer, or whose requirements were too small to interest such a producer.

Flexible production scheduling and the ability of the research department to modify standard production models to meet unusual product specifications have given Dem-A-Lex the ability to capture a specialized

Exhibit 2

THE MINERVA OXYGEN VENT VALVE
Statement of Profit and Loss
For the Year Ended December 31, 1984
($000)

Gross sales	$6,193	
Less allowances given for defective valves	143	
Net sales		$6,050
Cost of goods sold:		
Direct labor	1,010	
Materials	2,030	
Factory burden	1,362	
Cost of goods sold		4,402
Gross profit		1,648
Operating expenses:		
Selling expense*	332	
Administrative expense*	198	
Research expense*	350	
Interest expense	93	
Total operating expenses		973
Net profits before tax		675
Federal taxes (52%)		350
Net income after tax		325
Dividends on common stock		30
Net addition to retained earnings		$ 295

* See Exhibit 3 for analysis of this expense.

portion of the total market for most of its products. H. R. Deming commented, "We are not trying to butt heads with the big boys. Our policy is to sell our real assets—our research and development skills, and our productive flexibility."

Sales of vent valves accounted for nearly 25 percent of Dem-A-Lex's total sales during 1984, while the other 75 percent was made up of the sale of strain gauges, pressure gauges, intensifiers, and transducers, various types of electrically and hydraulically operated valves, regulators, circuit breakers, and other electrical and mechanical devices. Sales revenue from these items had been increasing at an annual rate of 8 percent since 1977. All of these items were manufactured in the general production department with general-purpose equipment, while the vent valve was produced in a separate department on specialized equipment. This specialized equipment had been purchased or built by Deming himself during 1983 and 1984 at a cost of about $525,000. However, Deming commented that if he had to replace all this equipment today by purchase from outside vendors, it would probably cost him over $950,000.

Oxygen vent valve   In November 1982 H. R. Deming had begun work on the development of an improved oxygen vent valve. He had been moti-

Exhibit 3
Analysis of selling, administrative, and research expenses for year
ending December 31, 1984 ($000)

Selling expense:
    Advertising — $ 33
    Sales staff's salaries and commissions — 251
    Traveling expenses — 24
    Supplies — 7
    Heat, light, and power (allocated on basis of floor space
        utilized by sales department) — 2
    Samples — 13
    Depreciation (allocated on basis of floor space utilized
        by sales department) — 2
Total selling expense — $332

Administrative expense:
    Officers' salaries (included half of Deming, Sr.'s salary) — $ 62
    Office wages — 81
    Office expenses — 14
    Legal and accounting — 6
    Telephone and telegraph — 3
    Miscellaneous expenses — 7
    Depreciation (allocated on basis of floor space utilized
        by the office. Also included direct depreciation
        computed on various articles of office equipment) — 4
Bad-debt losses — 16
Heat, light, and power (allocated on basis of floor space
    utilized by the office) — 5
Total administrative expense — $198

Research expense*:
    Officers' salaries (included half of Deming, Sr.'s, salary) — $ 25
    Laboratory supplies and expendable equipment — 45
    Depreciation (allocated on basis of floor space utilized
        by the research laboratory) — 4
    Heat, light, and power (allocated on basis of floor space
        utilized by the research laboratory) — 4
    Salaries of research personnel — 186
    Materials used in development of operational prototypes — 79
    Machinery and equipment depreciation — 4
    Liability insurance — 3
Total research expense — $350

    * During 1984, the research staff spent approximately 75–80 percent of its time on the development and testing of an oxygen vent valve constructed of ''Berylitt,'' a metal alloy recently perfected by Dem-A-Lex.

vated to experiment with this type of valve because of the high number of failures (nearly 60 percent defective) of valves which were then being used by missile producers. By January 1984 he had designed a valve which was lighter in weight and more resistant to extreme temperature and pressure than any valve then on the market. A new missile, designated the Minerva, was also introduced in early 1984, and by coincidence Dem-A-Lex's new vent valve met the missile's more rigid technical requirements. Because of this, Dem-A-Lex received subcontracts from several missile manufacturers to produce the oxygen vent valve for the Minerva missile.

The oxygen vent valve was a critical component to the proper functioning of any liquid rocket engine. A liquid rocket engine was basically a very simple mechanism. It consisted of a fuel tank, an oxygen tank, a pressure tank, a combustion chamber, and a number of valves for regulating the flow of material from the various tanks into the combustion chamber. Nitrogen gas from the pressure tank was used to force liquid oxygen and a liquid fuel (generally alcohol or kerosene and LOX) through propellent control valves into injector nozzles and thence into the combustion chamber where the mixture was ignited to provide the rocket's thrust.

Most missiles had four vent valves located on either side of the airframe just below the nose cone or warhead; the Minerva missile, however, had eight vent valves. In order to fill the oxygen tank, these vent valves were opened, and liquid oxygen at −220°F. was pumped into the oxygen tank through filler valves at the base of the tank until the tank was full. When the tank was completely filled, liquid oxygen spewed out

Exhibit 4
Analysis of projected factory burden for fiscal 1984 ($000)

	Budgeted for 1985 assuming no change in production procedures	Budgeted for 1985 assuming plating-polishing operation added for 2,000 vent valves	Budgeted for 1985 assuming testing equipment rented *
Fringe benefits†	$ 354	$ 358	$ 359
Supervision	213	213	213
Inspection	147	150	149
Purchasing and receiving	123	128	128
Repair to tools and equipment	99	102	100
Clerical, trucking, and cleanup	90	90	90
Maintenance	43	43	48
Valve replacement parts	17	0	5
Small tools	41	43	40
Spoiled work	69	65	67
Supplies	83	84	85
Department indirect	52	54	54
Heat, light, and power	23	26	26
Test machine rental	—	—	24
Depreciation (allocated on basis of floor space utilized by the production facilities)	44	44	44
Total factory burden	$1,398	$1,400	$1,432

* These budgeted figures did not include any expected change in overhead costs associated with the addition of the plating-polishing process to the vent valve production operation.

† This item was composed of the cost of unemployment compensation, social security, a company-sponsored health insurance plan, and vacation payment, for all direct and indirect labor. It averaged 20 percent of labor costs annually.

the four vent valves in heavy white streams. These valves then had to be closed before the system could be pressurized. Pressurization was accomplished by pumping nitrogen gas through a second chamber of the oxygen vent valve into the oxygen tank. If the vent valves did not close (because of the very low temperature), all pressure would be lost, and no oxygen could be forced into the combustion chamber.

These valves had to withstand not only temperatures of $-220°F.$, but also those of $+500°F.$ generated by the missile in flight as well as the great pressure caused by the expansion of nitrogen gas as it was forced through the valve chamber into the oxygen tank. Deming had developed an alloy of beryllium and titanium, referred to as "Berylitt," which was designed to withstand both extreme temperature and pressure. Deming felt the vent valves had been quite successful because only 450 vent valves had proved defective out of the total 1984 sales of 1,500 valves. Previous valves had failed, on the average, 60 percent of the time.

Under the terms of various subcontracts which Dem-A-Lex held, the prime contractor was permitted to charge Dem-A-Lex $300 for each vent valve which was found defective. Of this, $250 was the cost of removing the defective valve from the missile and the installation of a new valve, while $50 was allowed for repairing the defective valve with parts supplied by Dem-A-Lex. These repair parts had cost Dem-A-Lex an average of $25 per defective valve in 1984 and had been charged to the burden account (Exhibit 4) by the accounting department, while the charge of $300 for each defective valve was recorded as a deduction from gross sales (Exhibit 2). Thus, each defective valve cost Dem-A-Lex an additional $325. Because of the urgency of the missile program, the prime contractor repaired the valves at the missile site, rather than sending them back to Dem-A-Lex for replacement.

The standard price Dem-A-Lex received for each oxygen vent valve was $975. The cost accounting department computed the factory cost of each vent valve as follows:

Direct materials		$139
Direct labor:		
Machining time	$175	
Assembly time	100	
Inspection and packing time	25	
Total direct labor		$300
Overhead—135 percent of direct labor		405
Total product cost per valve		$844

The 135 percent overhead rate was based on the relationship of overhead costs to direct labor costs in 1984 (Exhibit 2). The factory cost accountant itemized the costs charged to the factory burden account as shown in Exhibit 4.

Quality control of the oxygen vent valve   Dem-A-Lex, in early 1985, would have no way of subjecting a vent valve to operational temperatures and pressure before the valve was assembled into the missile. Each component part of the valve was carefully inspected for size, required tolerances, and surface before assembly, and the assembled valve was hydraulically tested before shipment to the missile manufacturer, but this did not prevent valve failure when the rocket engine was statically fired at the launching site (a test firing with the missile securely fastened to its launching pad).

One of the two types of failure might occur when the engine was statically fired: First, the valve might freeze in the open position because of the frigid temperature of the liquid oxygen, or second, after it was closed, a butterfly valve (inside the vent valve) might freeze in the closed position and, as the nitrogen gas was forced into the chamber of the vent valve, pressure would build up until the vent valve ruptured, thus depressurizing the oxygen tank. If either of the above conditions occurred, the valve had to be removed and rebuilt by the replacement of tension springs, the butterfly valve, and various pressure seals and diaphragms. Both types of valve failure were caused by a common factor, the expansion or contraction of the metal components in the valve as it was subjected to operational temperatures. Even the most accurate measurement of specified tolerances could not eliminate these failures, since the internal molecular structure of the metal in each valve was slightly different, and thus each valve would be affected differently by the operational temperatures. Stephen Deming stated that it was much cheaper to have the prime contractor repair the defective valve than it was to junk it and that the cost of a valve failure ($300) charged by the prime contractor did not depend upon the type of defect that occurred. The subcontract did not permit the prime contractor to charge Dem-A-Lex $300 for the failure of a valve which had been rebuilt by the prime contractor. Thus, Dem-A-Lex could never be held financially responsible for more than one failure on each valve produced.

Stephen Deming pointed out, however, that the research department had developed a vanadium electroplating and polishing process which, if used, would guarantee that every vent valve would function perfectly. This process would eliminate all defects by reducing the expansion or contraction of any metal surface which had been treated with vanadium. The plating and polishing procedure would require $110 of material and three hours of labor at $3 per hour for each valve produced.

The company currently had excess capacity on the electroplating and polishing equipment located in the general production department and thus would not have to purchase additional equipment to perform this operation. However, there was no excess labor time available in the department, and Deming estimated that two or three new employees would have to be hired to run the plating and polishing equipment. Massey stated that this equipment was currently being used by the general production department about 20 hours per week and that the processing of the vent valves on this equipment would consume another 14 to 15 hours per week, thus loading the equipment to nearly 90 percent of its total capacity. These pieces of machinery occupied approximately 800 square feet of the total factory space of 20,000 square feet and were being depreciated at the rate of $2,100 per year. This equipment would be fully depreciated by December 31, 1989. However, Deming, Sr., commented that he did not feel the additional cost was justified, since he thought it was cheaper to "let your customers do your testing for you, and then all you have to do is pay for just those valves that have to be repaired. It's nonsense to incur the cost of plating when we don't have to!"

Massey, on the other hand, was in favor of renting a "revolutionary" piece of testing equipment which had just been put on the market. He had recently been approached by the National Machinery and Testing Equipment Co., of Zanesville, Ohio, about newly developed testing equipment which could be used to test each valve before its shipment to the prime contractor. Massey had loaned National Machinery 100 vent valves to test on this new equipment and had been told that 40 of these valves were defective while 60 were operationally perfect. The 60 valves which had tested "good" were especially marked and sent to one of the prime contractors by Dem-A-Lex. Later this prime contractor informed Dem-A-Lex that 12 of the valves which had tested "good" failed to operate and hence had to be rebuilt. The 40 vent valves which tested defective were sent to the general production department for electroplating and polishing. The National Machinery and Testing Co. stated that they could not guarantee complete accuracy in that a few valves which tested good would prove defective, while some that tested bad would in fact be operationally perfect. However, the equipment was reliable in that it would produce consistent readings on successive tests for any given valve. Massey was very much in favor of renting the testing equipment because he stated, "It's obvious that it's going to save us money. By testing the valves we had only 12 rejects in a hundred, while if these same valves had been shipped directly to the prime contractor we would have incurred the cost of making good on about 42 (30 + 12) rejects. Thus, you see, the testing equipment would reduce our number of rejects by 70 percent; this would mean a cash saving of $300 as well as a reduction in the cost of repair parts for each potential reject which would be detected before shipment."

The testing equipment would cost Dem-A-Lex $24,000 a year for rental, and this figure would be a flat rate. There would be no additional installation charge, and the shakedown testing that would be required would be done at the expense of National Machinery. Massey proposed that the testing equipment be installed in a room recently vacated by the office staff. "If we do this," he said "we won't have to charge any overhead to the testing operation, since the space was vacant anyway." The office staff had just recently moved to quarters (2,400 square feet) which rented for $250 per month, across the street from the factory in order that the supplies storeroom could be expanded for the purpose of increasing its operational efficiency. The space which was vacated by the office staff consisted of 2,000 square feet of the total factory area of 20,000 square feet. The valve department occupied approximately 5,000 square feet of the total factory area. However, expansion of the storeroom was not critical and thus could be delayed for an extended period of time. This testing equipment would require the addition of two employees to the payroll who would operate and load the equipment as a team. Because of union regulations these workers would not be permitted to perform any other operation in their slack time. These specially trained employees would be paid $3.50 per hour. The National Machinery and Testing Equipment Co. estimated that the testing equipment could handle 2,500 vent valves annually working a 40-hour week. The machinery was also capable of operating under overtime conditions. The period of the initial rental contract would be one year, though this could be extended at Dem-A-Lex's option. The company also estimated that an annual expense of $3,500 could be expected for normal maintenance of the testing equipment including bimonthly replacement of the Freon gas used in the equipment. Massey had also been informed that National Machinery was working on an improved testing machine which would probably be put on the market in 1987 or 1988.

Neither H. R. Deming nor his son, Stephen, was at all convinced of the advisability of renting the special testing machine. H. R. Deming did not feel that the anticipated volume of vent valve production would be enough to justify the rental charge and further was concerned over the possibility that one of the large manufacturing companies might develop an improved oxygen vent valve which would replace Dem-A-Lex's valve. Sears (sales manager) did not feel that any competitor would be interested in spending a lot of time and money developing an improved oxygen vent valve unless specifically requested to do so by a major prime contractor. She did not think that any competitor was working on an oxygen vent valve at that time, and she estimated it would take at least two years and $400,000 for a competitor to develop an improved valve. Sears further pointed out that the increased urgency of the missile program might encourage missile manufacturers to look elsewhere for more reliable vent valves, but she did not think this too likely as long as the number of defective valves did not exceed a "reasonable" level. Dem-A-Lex was well liked by its prime contractors and had built up good rapport with them in past associations. Sears estimated that 2,000 oxygen vent valves would be demanded annually through 1990. Because of the complexity of the vent valve and because of expected increases in labor and material costs, Sears could foresee no reason for the biannually negotiated price of the valve to fall below the current contract price of $975. All of Dem-A-Lex's vent valve two-year subcontracts came up for renewal in January to April 1986.

Stephen Deming was not sure whether the rental of the testing equipment could be justified, but he felt very strongly that all vent valves should be vanadium plated and polished by the newly developed production process. He commented, "Why should we spend $2,000 a month on fancy testing equipment when all we really need to do to solve our problem is to just plate the valves on existing equipment with only a small additional cost per valve?"

After extensive discussion of each of the above points of view, Deming adjourned the executive committee meeting until the afternoon of the following day, when he expected Swen's (the company controller) return from an out-of-town trip. He instructed Stephen Deming to fill Swen in on the discussion which had taken place at the committee meeting and to ask him to be prepared to submit his recommendations relative to quality control of the vent valve to the executive committee the following afternoon.

1. Calculate the cost of continuing with payments of $300 plus $25 for parts for each failure.

2. Calculate the cost of the vanadium process.

3. Calculate the cost of renting the new equipment.

4. Which of the above alternatives is preferable?

PROBLEMS
Cost theory

6–1   A Budweiser Brewing Company supervisor has estimated that output of his department can be increased by 4,000 bottles each eight-hour shift if one more employee is added. Without an increase in the work force, he estimated output could be increased by 4,000 units per shift by adding another piece of leased equipment. The equipment would cost $250 per week. The plant works one shift every 24 hours, five days per week. The wage rate is $8 per employee-hour.

a. What is the marginal physical product of labor over the interval described above? What is the increase in output per $1 spent for labor?

b. What is the marginal physical product of capital over the interval described above? (Hint: Capital input can be measured in dollars per shift.) Does labor or capital give the greatest increase in output per $1 spent on the output?

c. Assuming output is to be held constant, suggest a substitution of inputs that will reduce cost. Calculate the cost reduction.

6–2   The marginal physical product of an input is roughly the increase in rate of output per unit of added input. For a Cleveland, Ohio, car-washing firm, it is $MPP_x = \dfrac{\Delta Q}{\Delta X}$; where, Q is the rate of output, X is the rate of input, and MPP_x is marginal physical product. Assuming constant marginal product, if the number of cars washed increases from 0 to 420 and variable units of labor increase from 0 to 70, what is the marginal physical product of labor?

6–3   Assume constant marginal physical product of labor for each of three activities as follows:

Exterior car washer, per employee-hour

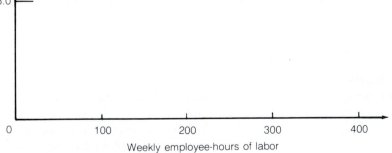

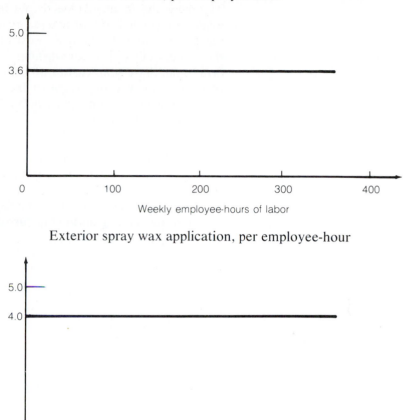

Interior car washes, per employee-hour

Weekly employee-hours of labor

Exterior spray wax application, per employee-hour

Weekly employee-hours of labor

If the price received by the car-wash firm is as follows:

Exterior car wash, per unit	$2.00
Interior car wash, per unit	$4.00
Exterior spray wax application	$3.25

a consumer may purchase each activity (i.e., exterior wash or interior wash, or exterior spray wax) separately.

a. Calculate the value to the car-wash firm of each activity.
b. Graphically illustrate the value to the car-wash firm of each activity.
c. Ranked by order of priority, how would a profit-maximizing car-wash firm prefer to allocate labor?

6–4   A profit maximizing firm should allocate resources to the activity where the input's value to the firm is greatest. After the quality demanded of that activity reaches its limit, the firm allocates resources to the next most profitable activity. Assume the activity of exterior car washing in problem 6–3 requires the firm to purchase soap costing 10 cents per car, and the activity of interior car washing requires the firm to purchase cleaning materials worth 25 cents per car ($0.25). Calculate the value to the firm of each activity.

6–5   Summit Petroleum Corporation (SPC) is limited to no more than $80,000 of new investments during the current period. In subsequent periods, funds are expected to be adequate to support all profitable projects. Each of the following projects has been proposed for funding during the current period:

Project	Amount	Percent annually
Expand inventory of gasoline	$30,000	8.0%
Expand accounts receivable	20,000	9.0
Expand heating oil storage	10,000	8.0
Market research	30,000	10.0
Product development	20,000	9.5
Replace tank truck	30,000	8.0
Install burner in boiler	10,000	8.5
Make investments outside the firm	Unlimited	7.0

a. What projects should be undertaken this period?

b. What is the change in value to SPC this period?

6–6   Suppose the rate of silicone produced by Union Carbide, Q_t, is related to the amount of labor used per period, X_t, by the following input-output function:

$$Q_t = 6X_L + 0.03X_L{}^2 - 0.0006X_L{}^3$$

Further, suppose silicone's price is a constant $3 per ton, and labor's wage is constant at $8 per hour. The sales rate is the same as the production rate.

a. How much labor should be used?

b. What is the optimum rate of production?

6–7   Given that total cost per period, *TC*, for a particular product is related to the product's rate of output, *Q*, as follows:

$$TC = \$264 = \$3.03Q - \$0.006Q^2 + \$0.00002Q^3$$

a. How much is the fixed cost per period?

b. Derive the relation of average fixed cost, *AFC,* to rate of output, *Q.*

c. Derive the relation of marginal cost, *MC,* to rate of output, *Q.*

d. Derive the relation of variable cost, *VC,* to rate of output, *Q.*

e. Derive the relation of average variable cost, *AVC,* to rate of output, *Q.*

f. Derive the relation of average total cost, *ATC,* to rate of output, *Q.*

6–8   In Ohio it is assumed the total cost of operating a maternity floor at most hospitals depends upon the number of beds available as follows:

$$TC = \$960Q - \$0.402Q^2 + \$0.00012Q^3$$

where

    TC = Total cost per maternity floor per calendar year.
    Q   = Average number of women using the maternity facility.

a. Are there economies of scale in maternity-floor operation? Diseconomies? What size of maternity floor would give the lowest cost per woman (minimum *AC*)?

b. The solution to part *a* takes into account only the maternity floor's internal costs. Costs of feeding the women and radiology and lab costs imposed on women are not considered. Consolidation of hospitals to take advantage of the internal economies of scale usually increases radiology and other similar costs. How much is the reduction in the maternity floor's internal costs per woman when the average number of women using the facility is increased from 800 to the number that gives the lowest cost per person as determined in part *a* above?

c. If a maternity facility has 1,000 women using the hospital, what is the estimated increase in cost per calendar year if one more woman is added to the maternity floor?

Selected references

Alchian, Armen A., and Harold Demsetz. "Production, Information Costs, and Economic Organization." *American Economic Review* 62 (December 1972).*

---

* This article is included in Thomas J. Coyne, *Readings in Managerial Economics,* 3d ed. (Plano, Tex.: Business Publications, 1981).

Anthony, Robert N. "What Should 'Cost' Mean?" *Harvard Business Review* 48 (June 1970).*

Appelbaum, Ellie. "On the Choice of Functional Forms." *International Economic Review* 20, no. 2 (June 1979), pp. 449–58.

Arvan, Lanny, and Leon N. Moses. "Inventory Investment and the Theory of the Firm." *American Economic Review* 72, no. 1 (March 1982), pp. 186–93.

Berndt, Ernst R., and Mohammed S. Khaled. "Parametric Productivity Measurement and Choice among Flexible Functional Forms." *Journal of Political Economy* 87, no. 6 (December 1979), pp. 1220–45.

Bopp, Anthony, and John Kraft. "A Note on Cost-Push versus Demand-Pull Inflation: Analysis of the Petroleum Industry." *Review of Business & Economic Research* 15, no. 2 (Winter 1979–1980), pp. 94–100.

Carlin, Alan, and R. E. Park. "Marginal Cost Pricing of Airport Runway Capacity." *American Economic Review*, June 1970.

Caves, Douglas W.; Laurits R. Christensen; Michael W. Tretheway. "Flexible Cost Functions for Multiproduct Firms." *Review of Economics and Statistics* 62, no. 3 (August 1980), pp. 477–81.

Colenutt, D. W. "Economies of Scale in the United Kingdom Ordinary Life Assurance Industry." *Applied Economics* (September 1977), pp. 219–25.

Cotterill, Ronald. "Economies of Size and Performance in Preorder Food Cooperatives." *Journal of Retailing* 57, no. 1 (Spring 1981), pp. 43–64.

De Vany, Arthur, and N. G. Frey. "Stochastic Equilibrium and Capacity Utilization." *American Economic Review* 71, no. 2 (May 1981), pp. 53–57.

Ho, Thomas S. Y.; Anthony Saunders; and Eugene Lerner. "The Determinants of Bank Interest Margins: Theory and Empirical Evidence/ Discussion." *Journal of Financial & Quantitative Analysis* 16, no. 4 (November 1981), pp. 581–602.

Johnson, Manuel H.; Frederick W. Bell; and James T. Bennett. "Natural Resource Scarcity: Empirical Evidence and Public Policy." *Journal of Environmental Economics & Management* 7, no. 3 (September 1980), pp. 256–71.

McRae, James J. "An Empirical Measure of the Influence of Transportation Costs on Regional Income." *Canadian Journal of Economics* 14, no. 1 (February 1981), pp. 155–63.

* This article is included in Thomas J. Coyne, *Readings in Managerial Economics*, 3d ed. (Plano, Tex.: Business Publications, 1981).

Murray, J. D., and R. W. White. "Economies of Scale and Deposit-Taking Financial Institutions in Canada—A Study of British Columbia Credit Unions." *Journal of Money, Credit and Banking* 12, no. 1 (February 1980), pp. 58–70.

Nooteboom, Bart. "A New Theory of Retailing Costs." *European Economic Review* (Netherlands) 17, no. 2 (February 1982), pp. 163–186.

Slade, Margaret E. "An Economic Model of the U.S. Secondary Copper Industry: Recycling versus Disposal." *Journal of Environmental Economics & Management* 7 no. 2 (June 1980), pp. 123–41.

Soyster, A. L. "An Objective Function Perturbation with Economic Interpretations." *Management Science* 27, no. 2 (February 1981) pp. 231–37.

Stigler, George J. "The Economies of Scale." *The Journal of Law and Economics* 1 (October 1958).*

Thomas Christopher R. "A Theory of the Vertically Integrated Input Monopolist with a Depletion Allowance." *Southern Economic Journal* 47, no. 3 (January 1981), pp. 799–804.

Wilde, L. L. "Information Costs, Duration of Search, and Turnover: Theory and Application." *Journal of Political Economy* 89, no. 6 (December 1981), pp. 1122–41.

Zelenitz, Allan. "Below-Cost Original Equipment Sales as a Promotional Means." *Review of Economics and Statistics* 59, no. 4 (November 1977), pp. 438–46.

---

* This article is included in Thomas J. Coyne, *Readings in Managerial Economics,* 3d ed. (Plano, Tex.: Business Publications, 1981).

C H A P T E R

7

Empirical cost analysis

Empirical analysis often deals with explicit accounting data regarding production costs essential to the continued operation of the firm. Production costs are often used for pricing decisions (a topic covered in Part 4), and understanding these costs is essential for setting output determination levels.

Analysis of the sort presented here was relied upon by Bethlehem Steel as it decided to all but close its huge upstate New York facility in 1983. National Steel in Pittsburgh used this kind of empirical cost analysis when it mandated in 1982 the closing or sale of its profitable Weirton, West Virginia, operations. Apple Computers combined this analysis with some fancy income tax interpretations when it proposed to provide a computer, free of charge, to every elementary and secondary school in the United States. Cost analysis is simple but effective, and very important.

Firms generally rely for decision-making purposes upon short-run, explicit costs. These costs are often expressed on a per-unit basis and may be explained by using the tennis ball manufacturing data revealed in Table 7–1.

Table 7–1 and corresponding Figure 7–1 use a production function with one fixed and one variable resource input; moreover, the price (cost) paid for the variable input remains unchanged, constant at $10 per unit as output expands. If the resource input costs were assumed to change instead to remain constant, diminishing returns to the input would be noticed more quickly. The result would be a sharper and earlier increase in the *AVC* and *MC* curves. Fixed costs are $500.

Average variable costs

Average variable cost is total variable cost divided by quantity. Using Table 7–1 and 18 units of output, for example, the average variable cost

Table 7–1
Short-run costs: Tennis Balls

(1) Quantity	(2) Fixed cost	(3) Variable costs $VC = \$10 \cdot X$		(4) Total cost $TC = FC + VC$	(5) Average final cost $AFC = \dfrac{FC}{Q}$	(6) Average variable cost $AVC = \dfrac{VC}{Q}$	(7) Average total cost $ATC = \dfrac{TC}{Q}$, or $AFC + AVC$	(8) Marginal cost* $MC = \dfrac{\Delta TC}{Q}$, or $= \dfrac{\Delta VC}{Q}$
18	$500	5	$ 50	550	$27.78	$2.78	$30.56	
63	500	10	100	600	7.94	1.59	9.52	$\dfrac{\$50}{45} = 1.11$
128	500	15	150	650	3.91	1.17	5.08	$\dfrac{\$50}{65} = .77$
206	500	20	200	700	2.43	.97	3.40	$\dfrac{\$50}{78} = .64$
288	500	25	250	750	1.74	.87	2.60	$\dfrac{\$50}{82} = .61$
369	500	30	300	800	1.36	.81	2.17	$\dfrac{\$50}{81} = .62$
440	500	35	350	850	1.14	.80	1.93	$\dfrac{\$50}{71} = .70$
492	500	40	400	900	1.02	.81	1.83	$\dfrac{\$50}{52} = .96$
520	500	45	450	950	.96	.87	1.83	$\dfrac{\$50}{28} = 1.79$

* Technically, this column represents incremental cost; marginal cost is the first derivative of the total cost function, $MC = \dfrac{dTC}{dQ}$.

per unit calculation is simple: $50/18 = $2.78. At 63 units of output, AVC is determined by dividing $100 by 63, $1.59, and so on. AVC is therefore total variable cost divided by quantity produced:

$$AVC = TVC/Q$$

It may also be expressed as the reciprocal of average physical product, APP, multiplied by average resource price (cost) per unit:

$$AVC = P(1/APP)$$

where P equals average price per unit of resource input.

For example, if APP is equal to 3.6 and resource price is $10, AVC is:

$$\$10 \times (1/3.6) = \$10 \times .2773 = \$2.78$$

at 18 units of output. This amount is consistent with the $2.78 found in line 1, column 6 of Table 7–1.

Since there can be no production without incurring some costs, average costs are a reflection of average production. As revealed in the chapter on cost theory, average physical product usually rises in the short run, reaches a maximum, and then declines; conversely, average variable cost usually falls, reaches a minimum, and rises. This curvature reflects the law of diminishing returns. *AVC* and *MC* are inversely related to the *APP* and *MPP* curves.

Average fixed cost

Average fixed cost, *AFC*, is total fixed cost divided by quantity produced. *AFC* declines as output increases, coming closer to zero along the horizontal axis in Figure 7–1, but never quite reaching it.

A fundamental distinction between *AFC* and *AVC* lies in the slope of the curves in Figure 7–1; *AFC* has a negative slope throughout, whereas after declining and reaching a minimum point, *AVC* increases. *AVC* as illustrated in Figure 7–1*a* would not decline before rising as in the case normally if marginal cost were constant throughout this illustration; instead, *AVC* would rise continuously.

Marginal cost

Marginal cost, *MC*, is the change in total cost associated with a change in output. In Table 7–1, *MC* is revealed in column 8. It is the amount by which total cost changes when output moves in increments of 10 units. In a dynamic cost function, *MC* is the first derivative of the total cost function. In this presentation, marginal cost is determined by subtracting

Figure 7–1a
Short-run average variable cost and marginal cost curves.

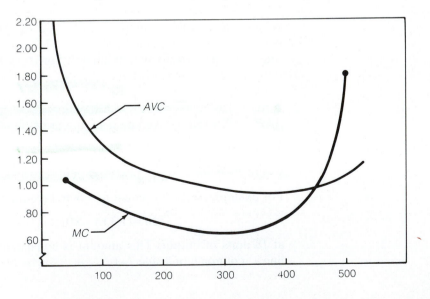

Figure 7–1b
Average fixed cost

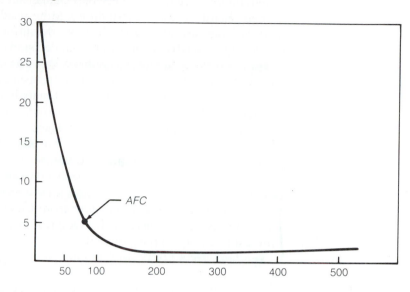

each successive entry or increment in the total cost column from the entry that preceeded it. Inasmuch as total fixed costs are constant in the short run, the calculation of *MC* may also be made by measuring the incremental changes in the total variable cost column, column 3.

Relating *MC* to the chapter on cost theory, the calculation may be made as follows:

$$MC = P(1/MPP)$$

where MPP equals marginal physical product.

More traditionally, however, it is expressed incrementally as:

$$MC = \Delta TC/\Delta Q$$

where Δ equals average change.

A noticeable distinction between *AVC* and *MC* is the respective rate of increase and/or decrease in the curves. *AVC* declines, reaches its minimum point, and subsequently increases in a relatively gradual manner. On the other hand, *MC* usually responds more quickly to the law of diminishing returns. *MC* usually declines rapidly, reaches its minimum, and rises sharply, cutting the AVC curve at its minimum and from the bottom. In Table 7–1, *AVC* reaches its minimum point at 440 units produced, $0.80; *MC* hits minimum earlier, at 288 units, $0.61.

Semifixed–semivariable costs

From the preceding discussion, one might be tempted to assume total costs can be broken neatly into fixed and variable component parts.

Nothing could be further from the truth. Considerable confusion exists often among various members of a management team's executive committee regarding specific definitions to be used by the firm for its fixed and variable cost allocation. Specific definitions of these costs must be agreed upon in advance if meaningful decisions are to be made.

Fixed costs, by definition, are ones that do not change in the short run. In the long run, these costs do not exist; instead, all costs are variable. If this is the Chicopee, Massachusetts, tennis ball manufacturing plant for Spalding tennis balls, and if the company has committed a specified sum of money for plant and equipment, wages, salaries and supplements, and if this commitment is contractual so that payments cannot be altered for a specific period of time, the cost may be defined as fixed. Examples of semivariable-semifixed costs fitting this description include fixed interest charges, certain depreciation allowances, average utility charges, certain labor and freight costs. Remember from Chapter 2, however, that most economic issues are negotiable. Often, if not always, a seemingly fixed interest rate may be renegotiated.

Variable costs are costs that change as output changes. These costs exist in the short and long run. Examples of short-run variable costs include certain depreciation expenses, some administrative charges, some labor costs, and other items listed in a typical profit and loss summary. In this short run, these are costs for which no contractual agreements exist to the extent that the cost could not be negotiated and would not be allowed to fluctuate upward or downward with changes in output. Unfortunately, many if not most of the examples cited under variable and fixed costs are neither variable nor fixed; instead, they are semivariable and semifixed. It is for this reason that a management team must decide and define in advance how each cost incurred by the company will be treated for pricing and output decisions.

Costs appearing at times to be fixed are, in fact, made variable by successful renegotiation(s). If the Chrysler Automobile Corporation survives, it may be due largely to its success in changing, via negotiations, what appeared to be fixed costs into variable ones. As we enter the 21st century, this same general statement holds true for many firms in the rubber, steel, glass, chemical, and other industries. Through negotiations many, if not most, of these firms will change fixed costs into variable ones, or they may not survive.

Cost functions   A cost function is a line or curve that depicts the cost-output relationship for a particular product at a specified time. Graphically, it could be as depicted in Figure 7–2.

Some assumptions implicit in Figure 7–2 include the following:

1. When no output is produced, total fixed cost is equal to total cost. Moreover, the shorter the short run, the greater the degree of certainty

Figure 7–2
Linear cost function: Tennis balls

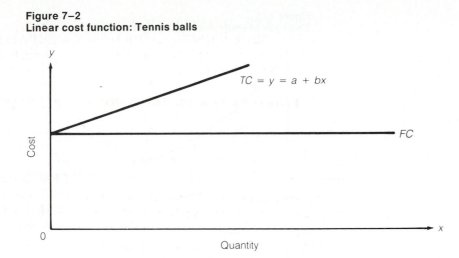

that these fixed costs are sunk costs by definition. With total fixed costs constant, regardless of the level of output, any increase in total cost is traceable to changes in total variable costs. More precisely, if resource input prices are constant over the relevant range of production, a doubling of resource inputs would be associated with a doubling of product produced, output.

2. Diminishing returns to the variable resource inputs do not occur. The linear cost function depicted in Figure 7–2 depicts the short-run cost condition of the firm. In the short run, the firm can change its rate of output within the existing plant but cannot change the capacity of its plant. The equation used in preparing the total cost curve in Figure 7–2 has no bends. It does not allow for an increase in total costs as the maximum operating capacity of the firm is reached.

3. Average total cost declines as output increases. A formula for its calculation is:

$$AC = y/x$$
$$= (a/x) + b$$

where

x = Output.
y = Cost.

Marginal cost is:

$$MC = \Delta y/\Delta x$$
$$= b$$

or, with a continuous cost function, marginal cost is:

Figure 7–3
Short-run average cost and marginal cost curves

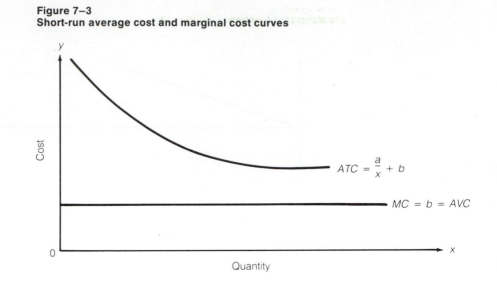

$$MC = d(TC)/dQ$$
$$= b$$

In any event, marginal cost is equal to b, which in a linear cost equation is constant as output increases. On a two-dimensional graph, a constant marginal cost curve appears as a horizontal line, parallel to the x axis for all levels of output (see Figure 7–3).

The shorter the short run, the higher the probability that statistical cost functions will have a bias toward linearity. This bias may be justifiable and, in fact, reasonably valid if it occurs over the relevant range of a firm's total physical product curve. Extrapolation of linear cost functions requiring output beyond the relevant range in either direction and used for predictive purposes will generate misleading and statistically insignificant results.

Applied to the tennis ball example, this cost curve assumes the existence of a linear production function. If a linear cost function exists, output of this tennis ball plant in Chicopee would expand indefinitely and in a one-to-one relationship with increases in total costs. Diminishing returns to the variable resource inputs would not set in. Such a function could exist for the tennis ball factory only if the relevant range over which it was being considered were very small.

Quadratic cost function

Quadratic cost functions behave in a manner similar to that depicted in Figure 7–4.

1. In contrast to the linear function, the quadratic function allows for the existence of diminishing returns to variable resource inputs. There is

Figure 7–4
Quadratic cost function: Tennis balls

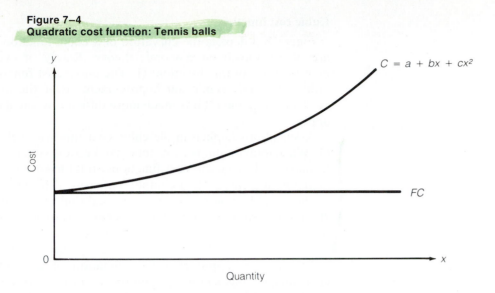

a point beyond which additional increases in output cannot be made. Costs can rise beyond that point, but output cannot.

2. The quadratic function has one bend, one bend less than the highest exponent of x.

3. Total cost is equal to fixed cost when output is zero. As one moves outward and to the right along the horizontal axis—as output increases —increases in cost are traceable to changes in variable cost; as output increases, the fixed cost area remains constant.

The astute reader will notice the major difference between the linear and quadratic cost functions is the area of diminishing returns to the variable resource inputs. In the quadratic cost function, Figure 7–4, variable cost increases at an increasing rate; whereas in the linear example, Figure 7–2, variable cost increases at a constant rate. It is unreasonable to assume that linear cost functions exist regardless of the current level of operating capacity at which the firm is producing; instead, it must be recognized that as output reaches the physical capacity limitations of the plant and equipment, in the short run, variable costs rise because of the law of diminishing returns.

Linear cost functions as presented in Figure 7–2 are valid over the relevant range of output for the firm. Over this relevant range, "no statistically significant improvement on the linear hypothesis is achieved by the inclusion of second or higher degree terms in output;" also, "supplementary tests, such as the examination of incremental costs ratios, usually confirm the linear hypothesis."[1]

---

[1] J. Johnston, *Statistical Cost Analysis* (New York: McGraw-Hill, 1960), p. 170.

Cubic cost function

Figure 7–5 depicts the curvature of a cubic function. These functions are of use mostly in economic theory. Rarely, if ever, does one see empirical use of this function: (1) The cubic cost function does not provide statistically significant improvements over the linear or quadratic cost function; and (2) it is much more difficult to calculate, interpret, and apply.

Assumptions implicit in the cubic cost function include the following: (1) When total output is zero, total fixed cost is equal to total cost. (2) As in linear and quadratic cost functions, total fixed cost remains constant as output increases. (3) As output increases, there are increasing returns to the variable inputs; a point is reached (inflection point) at which constant returns to the resource input occur; and there are eventually diminishing returns to the resource input. In essence, the cubic cost curve has two bends, one bend less than the highest exponent of x.

Two general approaches to estimation of cost functions include: (1) economic-engineering, an approach consisting of designing least-cost combinations of durable and variable inputs and (2) statistical approach, an approach applying accounting data to statistical procedures and techniques. The economic-engineering approach is closest to the long-run perspective on costs, in which all inputs and the rate of output are treated as variable. The statistical approach is closest to the short-run perspective, in which some inputs and the rate of output are regarded as variable. Let's look first at the statistical method.

Figure 7–5
Cubic cost function: Tennis balls

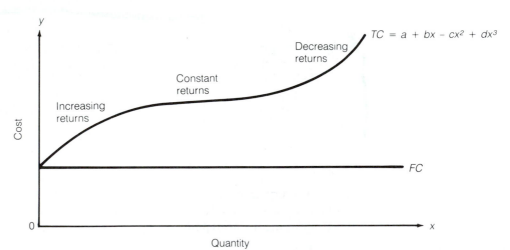

Statistical estimates of cost functions

Cost functions can be estimated from accounting data by statistical methods. The statistical approach starts with specification of a model of cost behavior. Careful adjustment of data may be necessary where they do not conform to explicit or implicit assumptions of the model. Statistical techniques are used to estimate parameters of the model and to establish ranges above and below each of the estimates that will allow specified levels of confidence.

Data used in statistical estimation consist of observations of each of the variables in the model for a single firm over a number of time periods in which the firm had various rates of production. Observations of this type are called time-series data. The data may also come from observations of each variable over a number of firms during a single time period in which the firms were producing at various rates. Observations of this type are called cross-sectional data.

The objective of statistical analysis is to estimate a relation of physical rate of use of one or more variable inputs. These statistical studies may have as an objective the estimation of a short-run cost curve. They attempt to determine the relation of cost to changes in rate of output of a plant or service. Other statistical studies have the objective of estimating a long-run cost curve. Such studies attempt to determine the relation of cost to rate of output, with each rate being produced in a plant designed for least-cost production.

Statistical models are approximations of reality, expressed in symbols. They attempt to explain the behavior of a dependent variable, when that behavior is believed to depend on the values of independent variables. Useful models are consistent with the economic theory of production and cost and with what is known about technological and institutional influences. Models are often deliberately simplified out of necessity. Simplification may consist of using linear approximations of functions believed to be curvilinear. The model may consist of omission of explanatory variables believed by the analyst to have only slight effects upon the dependent variable. Simplified models may provide a better fit over the limited range of available data.

Linear forms Linear-form statistical cost models may contain a single explanatory variable. Consider this cost function:

$$C_i = b_0 + b_1 Q_i + U_i$$

where

C_i = Observed cost per period in the ith period.
Q_i = Observed rate of output in the ith period.
U_i = Sum of the disturbances in the ith period.
b = Parameters.

Linear-form statistical cost models may contain two or more explanatory, independent variables. An example of a multivariate model is this cost function:

$$C_i = b_0 + b_1 Q_i + b_2 X_{2i} + \ldots + b_n X_{ni} + U_i$$

where

C_i = Observed cost in the ith period.
Q_i = Observed rate of output in the ith period.
Xs = Observed value of some other influence on cost in the ith period.
U_i = Sum of disturbances in the ith period.
bs = Parameters.

Other forms   In the linear forms presented herein, marginal productivities of inputs and marginal costs of the output are assumed to be constant. Curvilinear models, allowing changes in marginal productivity and marginal cost, are often desirable. Such changes are accommodated by the quadratic and cubic cost functions.

A quadratic cost model might be:

$$C_i = b_0 + b_1 L_i + b_2 L_i^2 + U_i$$

where

C_i = Observed total cost in the ith period.
L_i = Observed cost of labor used in the ith period.
U_i = Sum of disturbances in the ith period.
bs = Parameters.

The use of the squared value of an input as one of the variables of the model allows the marginal productivity of the input to increase (or decrease, but not both) as the rate of output goes up. This model and the one following are said to be additive because the effects of the various explanatory variables in any given period are algebraically summed to obtain their net effect upon the dependent variable.

A cubic model of cost:

$$C_i = b_0 + b_1 Q_i + b_2 Q_i^2 + b_3 Q_i^3 + U_i$$

in which

C_i = Observed cost in the ith period.
Q_i = Observed rate of output in the ith period.
U_i = Sum of disturbances in the ith period.
bs = Parameters.

Using both the squared and the cubic values of rate of output allows marginal cost first to decrease and then to increase as the rate of output expands. Thus, this form can accommodate scale economies and diseconomies in a cost function.

Curvilinear multiplicative form   The following form (often called a Cobb-Douglas function) has been of assistance in many studies of cost and production:

$$TC_i = L_i^{b_1} \cdot C_i^{b_2} \cdot U_i$$

in which

TC_i = Observed total cost in the *i*th period.
L_i = Observed labor use in the *i*th period.
C_i = Observed use of capital services in the *i*th period.
U_i = Sum of disturbances in the *i*th period.
bs = Parameters.

A sometimes useful characteristic of this form is that the parameters b_1 and b_2 are constant percentage changes in rate of output, for each 1 percent of change in labor or capital, respectively. Another useful characteristic is that the effects of the explanatory variables are multiplicative in terms of their net effect upon the dependent variable. This form allows any input to have increasing, constant, or decreasing marginal productivity. ($b > 1$, $b = 1$, and $b < 1$, respectively). It allows increasing, constant, or decreasing returns to scale ($\Sigma bs > 1$, $\Sigma bs = 1$, and $\Sigma bs < 1$, respectively). To allow estimation of this model by multiple regression methods, the data are transformed to their logarithms, and the model is stated as:

$$\log TC_i = \log b_0 + b_1 \log L_i + b_2 \log C_i + \log U_i$$

Other inputs could be added to labor and capital in the above model, or inputs other than labor and capital could be used as explanatory variables in the model.

Data problems

Available data often do not conform to the explicit and implicit assumptions of the models that have been specified and the statistical methods that will be used. Careful adjustments of data may be needed prior to estimation of parameters.

General data problems   Measured cost may be above or below actual cost, or it may need movement in time to match it to the corresponding output. Depreciation is treated as fixed cost per period in most accounting systems, but the wear-and-tear component does vary with changes in the rate of output. Thus, the depreciation statistic in a given period may be either too high or too low. Maintenance in a given period may consist largely of repair of accumulated wear resulting from heavy use in an earlier period, or it may contain costs of preparing for intensive use in a period to follow. Bonuses, paid in one period at the end of a fiscal year, may be the result of services during the entire year.

Output may also need adjustment to make it comparable from observation to observation. A product may have changed over time, or it may differ somewhat from plant to plant. And a product mix may have the added problem that proportions of products in the mix are not constant from one observation to another. It may be necessary to measure output in terms of labor contents or percent of plant capacity used, or in terms of an index based on these variables.

Time-series data problems.   Time-series cost data usually contain effects of price inflation. Cost can be restated in constant dollar terms with the aid of a price index. The data may contain effects of technological change, such as introduction of new materials, new processes, or new machines and equipment. Effects of technological change during adjustment periods may be different from long-run effects. Cost data can be standardized for technology by adjustments based on engineering estimates, or the adjustment can be made statistically by using dummy variables in the regression equation.

Cross-section problems   Cross-section data usually contain effects of differences in ages of factories. Older factories may not be up-to-date technologically, so some items of cost are higher than they would be in a more modern plant. On the other hand, depreciation costs of older plants may be based on original costs that are far below present replacement costs of the same items. Costs may need adjustment to remove effects of regional differences in wage rates, prices of raw materials, utilities rates, local property taxes and insurance, and so forth. Also, data may need adjustment to remove effects of other differences in accounting practices.

Problems revealed during statistical estimation

Further problems may become apparent after the process of statistical estimation begins. Multicollinearity, a high degree of correlation between two or more of the explanatory variables, may make standard errors of regression coefficients so large relative to values of the coefficients that the estimates are useless. The only satisfactory solution of the multicollinearity problem is to do the following: (1) obtain independent estimates of the effects of all except one of the collinear explanatory variables, (2) adjust the values of the dependent variable so that these effects have been removed, and (3) leave the collinear explanatory variables out of the model when it is reestimated.

The residuals from time-series analyses should be plotted against time to determine whether there is evidence of serial correlation. The desired appearance of the residuals is as shown in Figure 7–6a. A pattern like that of Figure 7–6b is due to serial correlation. The effect of serial cor-

Figure 7–6
Effects of serial correlation upon residual

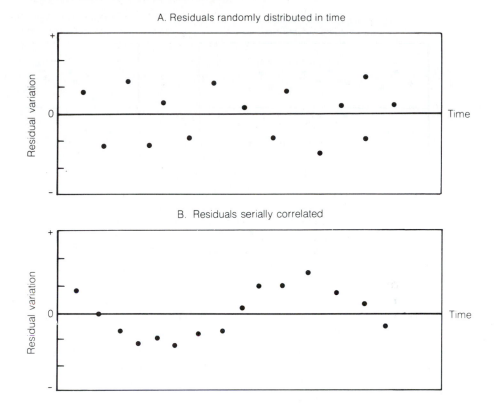

A. Residuals randomly distributed in time

B. Residuals serially correlated

relation is to cause standard errors of the regression coefficients to be underestimated.

The residuals should also be plotted against the values of each of the explanatory variables to show any evidence of correlation. If there is correlation, the estimates of the regression coefficients will be biased. The desired appearance of residuals in a plot against an explanatory variable is as shown in part *A* of Figure 7–7. If the residuals appear as in part *B*, the explanatory variable has a curvilinear effect that has not been picked up; the model may be improved by adding the square of the variable and reestimating. If the residuals have a pattern like that of part *C*, their variance is proportionate to the values of the explanatory variable; the model can be reestimated with the logarithms of the explanatory variable substituted for its original values. If the residuals make a pattern like that of part *D*, their variance is more than proportionate to the values of the explanatory variable; the model can be reestimated with the square roots of the explanatory variable substituted for its original values.

Figure 7–7
Other methodical disturbances of residuals

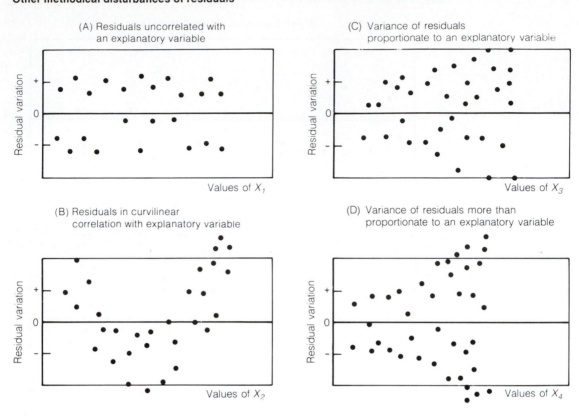

(A) Residuals uncorrelated with
an explanatory variable

(B) Residuals in curvilinear
correlation with explanatory variable

(C) Variance of residuals
proportionate to an explanatory variable

(D) Variance of residuals more than
proportionate to an explanatory variable

**The economic-
engineering
approach[2]**

The economic-engineering approach outlined here is designed for studies that compare the efficiency of alternative technologies, derive short-run cost functions for plants of specific sizes, and derive long-run functions that are envelopes for the cost functions of the individual plants. This section begins with the engineering view of plant costs and long-run costs, then surveys sources of data and procedures used in estimating cost-output relationships.

The nature of plant operations

A stage consists of all productive services that cooperate in performing a single operation. The production process begins with receipt of some

[2] See B. C. French. L. L. Sammet, and R. G. Bressler, "Economic Efficiency in Plant Operations," *Hilgardis* 24, no. 19 (July 1956), pp. 547–721.

basic material, either in raw or partially processed form. Receipt of the material is the first stage in plant operations. The material then moves to a second stage, where it is in some way transformed. Transformation can take the form of melting, pulverizing, washing, sorting, milling, stamping, assembling, inspecting, painting, or whatever. The material then moves to another stage, where another transformation occurs. By-products, if any, are removed at the third stage and flow in another direction.

At various points other materials are received, transformed in various stages, and finally fed into the main line of flow, where they are combined with the partially completed product. Various partially completed products may be split off at different stages and given their own individual series of further transformations so as to emerge as final products.

The various stages are connected by transportation links. Between-stage transportation is in a sense a stage itself, in which the only operations performed are to move the product from one place to another. Storage plays an important role in leveling out the flow of materials and products. Materials may be received at irregular intervals, but a fairly continuous flow is maintained by feeding materials into, and then withdrawing them from, storage. Storage also compensates for irregularities or differences in rates of activity in the various stages. And in batch-type production, storage is an integral part of the planned production process. Storage is in a sense a stage, too, in which the only operation performed is to hold the product for some period of time.

Variations in rate of output

Technical requirements limit rate variations of some processes. The rate at which a product passes through a stage is very narrowly defined, (i.e., sterilizing, pasteurizing, cooking, baking, drying, freezing, and so forth). Such limitations are overcome by organizing plants in multiple units—in effect, several plants within a plant. A four-unit plant might operate at instantaneous rates that are one fourth, one half, three fourths, or all of the designed capacity of the plant.

Total plant output within any given period can also be varied by changing hours of operation per day or, for seasonal operations, per season. An automobile plant, for example, can produce the year's output in less than a year. It can shut down for a considerable time to retool for the next model and continue sales from inventories of finished product. The retooling period can be shortened or expanded as the demand situation may warrant.

For some kinds of production, storage possibilities are limited, and production rates must match consumption. Electric power must be produced as it is used because there is no method of storing mass-produced electricity, but storage is possible for most products manufactured. The output used to satisfy a given demand can be produced over a fairly wide time range. In such cases, output per year can be varied by changing the number of hours of plant operation.

There are many kinds of production in which the instantaneous rate of output can be varied. Such variation requires changes of operating speeds and cycling rates of machines and repositioning and reassignment of worker tasks. Assembly processes, packaging, order filling, freight handling, and clerical work are some examples of production in which the instantaneous rate of output is varied by changing the intensity of use of variable inputs. As these changes occur, costs change.

Effects upon marginal cost as output is varied

If instantaneous rates of plant output are held constant and total output in a sales or accounting period is varied by changes in the number of hours worked per day or per week, the inputs are being combined at constant rates and in a constant proportion despite the changes in output. In such situations, marginal cost can be expected to be constant (unless the firm has to pay higher wages for overtime or night work, or fatigue of workers diminishes output per employee-hour). The scale effect, the effect of the law of variable proportions, and the effect of input substitutions cannot enter into the behavior of cost as output is varied.

If total output in a sales or accounting period is varied by successive additions or subtractions of the services of identical machines and workers performing identical tasks, the resulting total cost function will be discontinuous, but cost will tend to increase by constant increments as output is increased by constant increments. Thus, marginal cost—calculated discreetly as an increase in total cost divided by an increase in output per period—can be expected to be constant in this situation, too.

In the case of output per sales or accounting period being varied by changes in the instantaneous rate of production, through changes in the proportioning of inputs (through changes in intensity of use of variable inputs relative to use of services of durable inputs), marginal cost is expected to change as output is varied.

The long-run cost function

The long-run cost function is not determined directly; instead, it is approached from the short-run perspective by comparing costs of plants of different sizes and technologies and then combining these into a function showing the least cost of producing at each instantaneous rate of output for various numbers of hours per sales or accounting period. The long-run cost function appears as an envelope to the many individual plant cost functions. Just as the individual plant functions contain both a rate-of-output element and a time-of-operation element, so does the long-run function.

An efficient approach to estimating long-run functions is: (1) select several rates of output, (2) determine the least-cost method of maintaining each of these rates of output at each of the numerous stages, and (3) aggregate stage costs into long-run total cost functions.

Cost measurement

Cost measurement should begin at the stage level. Because measurement problems differ somewhat among the major types of inputs, they are discussed under four headings: labor, materials, other operating inputs, and durable goods.

Labor   Two main sources of data can be used to estimate basic physical and cost relationships of labor to output: (1) plant payroll and output records and (2) engineering studies of actual operations. Plant payroll records usually show hours of labor per day or week and the pay rates for each worker in the plant. The disadvantage of payroll records is that because they usually reveal little of the specific details of many of the plant jobs, they may be inaccurate in classifying workers as to actual work performed.

Engineering studies are means of obtaining labor data not readily available from accounting records. These studies consist of detailed descriptions of plant operations (description of each job, number of workers employed in each job classification in each stage of plant operations, and the route and rate of flow of materials through the plant) plus performance standards derived from time studies, work-sampling studies, or analysis of standard work data. It is desirable to compare standards based on engineering studies with actual rates of performance.

The physical performance standards for labor are transformed into estimates of labor cost, stage by stage, at the selected rates of production. Performance standards determine the number of workers needed at each rate of production, and the number of workers times the wage rate determines the hourly labor cost at each rate of output.

Materials   The costs of materials in the final product are probably the easiest of the inputs to measure, for the materials commonly enter in rigidly fixed proportions. Costs of the materials are obtained by simply multiplying the physical quantities by their prices, which may be constant or may be some function of the quantity purchased. Price data are usually readily available from supplies.

An alternative source of material cost data is plant accounting records. An advantage of data from this source is that they reflect loss due to breakage or damage that may be normal in the course of ordinary handling. A disadvantage is that costs of materials obtained from plant records may be based on past purchase prices that are out of line with the prices that should be used in planning future operations.

Other operating inputs   Power, fuel, water, and similar costs may be estimated from accounting records or by engineering studies of production processed. If these costs are a sizable part of the total, engineering studies are desirable. Physical measurements can be made on such components as the power load of each large motor, the fuel-use rate required for each heat process, and so on.

Such miscellaneous supplies as office stationery, and janitorial materials are likely to be related to the size of the plant rather than to its rate of operation, and accounting records may be a good basis for estimating these.

Administrative costs are the salaries of managers and executives. Accounting records are the chief source of these. Frequently, these accounts are inaccessible to outsiders, and if they are available, the salaries may be related to profits in such a way that the figures for a particular year do not indicate long-run levels. Discreet inquiries and careful adjustments may be advisable.

Durable Goods   Three main sources of durable goods data are: plant accounting records, engineering-architecture estimates of building costs, and data supplied by manufacturers of machines and equipment. Values and period charges found in accounting records will usually be of limited value, since they reflect not future costs of replacement, but past purchase prices at varying dates and price levels. Moreover, book charges for depreciation may be out of line with actual costs. The engineering-architecture approach consists of estimating the physical inputs required to build a plant of a given size and multiplying these requirements by an appropriate set of prices to obtain estimates of replacement costs. Estimates of repair costs and depreciation rates are derived from plant records and engineering judgments. Insurance, taxes, and costs of capital are based on going rates for these items.

Using estimated cost functions

Managerial uses of emperical cost curves

Estimates of cost curves enter into many important decisions. These include short-run choices of rates of output and prices and long-run decisions about numbers, sizes, and locations of plants.

In the case of decisions about rates of output for competitive firms, the optimum rate is the one that makes marginal cost equal to price. Firms with sloping demand curves can choose an optimum combination of price and output at the rate that makes marginal cost equal to marginal revenue. Pricing decisions are discussed in more detail in Chapters 8 through 10.

Decisions about output and pricing are so important to the firm that reliable estimates of cost functions are worth considerable effort and expense, and managers obviously cannot make these decisions without using some kind of estimates or assumptions about the short-run cost functions. Case 7–1, Toronto Edison Company, is designed to stress the importance of statistical procedures in cost function estimation. Particular attention is given in the case to the use of regression analysis to estimate the cost function; in addition, the case provides an opportunity to interpret the estimated cost function coefficients.

A firm considering plant construction or expansion also needs estimates of long-run cost functions to determine whether or not to make the investment and what size plant to build. In a situation with unchanging demand and constant structure of factors affecting cost (factor prices, technology, etc.), this decision rule would be simple: Build the size of plant that makes long-run marginal cost equal to marginal revenue. Under actual conditions, the decision is more complex because demand can be expected to shift over time; the structure of factors affecting cost also may be expected to shift. There are construction economies that make it advisable to build or expand plants in substantial increments of capacity. Thus, the plan for expansion of capacity should be optimal through time in the face of dynamic changes; simulation of projected results under alternative expansion plans may be the best approach.

Decisions about plant construction or expansion are especially difficult in multiplant firms. The problem of simultaneously determining the number, size, and location of plants to minimize the combined transportation and processing costs for raw material produced in varying amounts and at scattered production points may be handled by a model. The following data could be used as input: [3]

1. Estimated or actual amount of raw material to be assembled from each point or origin.
2. Cost of transporting a unit of material between each point of origin and each potential plant site.
3. A plant-cost function that permits determination of the cost of processing any fixed total quantity of material in a varying number of plants.
4. Specification of potential plant locations.

The form of each plant's total cost function may be assumed initially to be linear with respect to total output. It should have a positive intercept. Equal factor costs could be assumed for all locations.

A note of caution! Remember that past production and cost relationships may not be relevant to decisions about future investments in plant and equipment. Statistical estimates may require adjustments to reflect changes expected to affect costs of future periods. Such changes may involve relative prices of inputs and combinations used, conversions of inputs to output and the amounts of inputs used, nature of the product, mix of products, scale of output, scale of plant, and so forth. The future

---

[3] See John F. Stollsteimer, "A Working Model for Plant Numbers and Locations," *Journal of Forum Economics* 45 (August 1963), pp. 631–45.

does not necessarily behave in a manner identical or even similar to the past.

Summary

Estimation of cost functions is part of the managerial process. An understanding of costs is imperative to the decision-making process. This chapter discussed estimation of cost functions by the statistical and the economic-engineering approaches.

The economic-engineering approach consists of design of least-cost plants for various rates of output on the basis of current technology and prices of inputs. Steps in the engineering approach are:

1. Select instantaneous rates of output for which the various plants are to be designed.
2. Break the production process into transformation stages, transportation links, and storage points.
3. Determine least-cost combinations of labor, materials, and equipment for each of the design rates of operation in each of the stages.
4. Combine optimally designed stages into complete plants for each of the instantaneous rates of output.
5. Estimate total and unit costs for each plant at the design rate and at other rates, so as to obtain short-run cost curves for each of the plants.
6. Estimate the long-run total and unit cost curves, treating costs of the various plants at their design rates as points on the long-run curves.

The engineering approach has the following advantages: (1) It standardizes technology, prices of inputs, plant efficiency, operating rates, and other factors affecting costs so that effects of changes in instantaneous rates and in hours of operation can be isolated. (2) Effects of changes in any of the other factors affecting cost can also be estimated. (3) Overall costs under any assumed future condition can be synthesized. The disadvantages include the large amount of time required and the high cost involved. The engineering approach is the only recourse in cases involving new products, new processes, or new plants.

The statistical approach consists of estimating parameters of cost models so as to get best (or least-squares) fits of the models to accounting data. The source of the accounting data may be a series of observations on a single firm, operated at different rates over a sequence of time periods (time-series data), or it may be a set of observations across a group of firms operating at various rates during the same period of time (cross-section data).

Cost models should be consistent with economic theory and with what is known of the technology and institutional setting of production. Models are often deliberately simplified. Linear models are appropriate if rates of output per sales or accounting period are varied by changes in hours of operation or by changes in multiples of identical machines and work crews. These methods tend to result in constant marginal productivities of inputs and constant marginal costs. Curvilinear models are appropriate if instantaneous rates of output are varied by changes in the relative intensities, or proportions, of various inputs.

Considerable adjustment of accounting data may be advisable before statistical estimation. Either the costs or the outputs of a given period may be too high or too low as they stand. Depreciation, maintenance, and bonuses are examples of cost items that may not be matched with the corresponding output. An output may need revision to remove effects of changes in products or in the mix of products over time, or from plant to plant in cross-section data. In time-series data, effects of price inflation and changes in technology may need to be removed. In cross-section data, costs may need adjustment to take out the effects of differences in ages of plants, regional differences in prices of inputs, and differences in accounting practices.

During statistical estimation certain problems may appear. One problem is multicollinearity, a condition in which there is a high degree of correlation between two or more of the explanatory variables. The condition makes estimates of the model parameters useless. The only satisfactory method of handling multicollinearity is to obtain independent estimates of effects of all except one of the collinear variables. Adjust values of the dependent variable to correspond to standardized values of the collinear variables. Leave the collinear variables out of the model when it is reestimated.

Another problem is serial correlation of the residuals, which causes underestimation of standard errors of the regression coefficients. This condition can sometimes be overcome by substituting first differences of the observations in place of the original data. Another problem is variance of residuals proportionate or more than proportionate to values of one of the explanatory variables. Either condition causes bias of the estimates of the regression coefficients. The latter problems can sometimes be overcome (1) by substituting logarithms of the explanatory variable for the original values if variance is proportionate and (2) by substituting square roots of the variable if variance is more than proportionate.

CASES

Empirical cost analysis

Toronto Edison Company

I. Introduction   Since all electric utilities in the United States and Canada are regulated by state and federal agencies, records of output, prices, and costs are maintained by these firms. All these utilities have the necessary information from which to construct short- or long-term statistical cost functions. Firms able to construct cost 197 functions can use them (1) to forecast changes in total costs, (2) to forecast changes in one or more of the independent variables associated with total costs, (3) to study the elasticities associated with specific variables, and (4) to gain and maintain a better understanding of causal factors associated with cost changes.

II. Given   Accounting data for the period 1966 to 1984.

III. Assume   Specific cost categories are known to us. These categories are the ones that explain total operating costs for this utility and are as follows:

1. *Total coal used in generation (W_t)*   Fuel expense; total coal used in generation equals coal from system mines plus purchased coal, measured in thousands of tons.
2. *System heat rate (H_t)*   Heat rate expressed as BTU's per kilowatt-hour of net generation (a measure of efficiency).
3. *System load factor (L_t)*   Load factor indicates the degree of utilization of the demand imposed by consumers on a utility. It is obtained by dividing the total kilowatt-hours produced by the average demand multiplied by the hours in a year. It is an indication of efficiency and is measured as a percentage.
4. *Number of customers (C_t)*   Total electric customers (includes residential, industrial, commercial, municipal, cooperatives, and other electric utilities).
5. *Energy used by all customers (E_t)*   Energy use measured in millions of kilowatt-hours.
6. *Energy delivery (M_t)*   Energy delivery measured in total circuit-miles (includes all transmission and distribution lines).

IV. Required

1. Test the assumption. Demonstrate the use of statistical analysis to determine a long-run cost function that explains the operating costs of this elective utility. Develop a least-squares regression for the cost functions. Linear cost function of the form:

$$O_t = b_0 + b_1 W_t + b_2 H_t + b_3 L_t + b_4 C_t + b_5 E_t + b_6 M_t$$

where

O_t = Total operating costs (millions) and is the dependent variable.
W_t = Total coal used (thousands of tons).
H_t = System heat rate (BTU/KWH).
L_t = Load factor (percent).
C_t = Number of customers (thousands)
E_t = Total energy use by customers (millions of KWH).
M_t = Energy delivery (circuit miles).

where

> W_t, H_t, L_t, C_t, E_t, M_t are independent variables.

2. Eliminate the variables that are not statistically significant, if any.
3. Use the adjusted function you develop to project (forecast?) future operating costs for this electric utility.
4. Depict your results on a two-dimensional graph.
5. Reveal the relevant elasticities associated with your cost function.
6. Present marginal cost.
7. Discuss the specific contributions and limitations of this analysis to an electric utility.

V. Data provided (see Exhibit 1).

Exhibit 1
Toronto Edison Company

Year	W_t ($ millions) X_2	O_t (thousands of tons) X_2	H_t (BTW/KWH) X_3	L_t (percent) X_4	C_t (000's) X_5	E_t (millions of KWH) X_6	M_t (circuit miles) X_7
1966	248	12,008	9725	63.3	1387	25,866	76,105
1967	259	12,292	9619	69.6	1405	27,206	77,311
1968	268	12,924	9363	68.6	1419	28,552	77,924
1969	284	13,907	9420	70.2	1437	31,287	78,881
1970	296	15,031	9457	69.1	1456	33,244	80,321
1971	314	15,939	9478	71.9	1477	36,218	81,112
1972	335	16,933	9476	70.0	1500	39,503	81,897
1973	369	18,298	9543	71.0	1523	44,625	86,160
1974	390	19,912	9487	72.2	1547	50,119	87,027
1975	440	21,139	9560	72.8	1594	54,460	89,077
1976	470	22,873	9620	72.7	1625	58,185	91,343
1977	504	24,254	9689	72.4	1662	60,114	92,653
1978	562	25,073	9654	70.4	1702	62,435	93,869
1979	634	28,436	9484	69.9	1745	68,540	95,159
1980	692	31,406	9526	75.1	1784	74,912	96,545
1981	1030	31,938	9641	71.7	1822	75,858	97,787
1982	1227	31,897	9686	66.7	1883	75,917	98,595
1983	1387	35,810	9717	67.7	1917	84,913	99,508
1984	1558	35,855	9763	71.1	1946	81,865	101,552

Charles R. Grewy Associates

The Charles R. Grewy Company retained Economic Consultants Incorporated (ECI) for purposes of obtaining some advice regarding use of the company's accounts in decision making. ECI presented the accounts of Grewy Associates in the form of marginal income accounting (also known as differential accounting, cost-volume-profit analysis, and incremental analyses). The method is closely akin to direct costing but does not require the tie-in with the day-to-day financial accounts or the change in inventory valuation required by direct costing.

ECI thinks marginal income accounting would help achieve the following objectives:

1. Separation of the results of the Charleston and Huntington operations. There has already been a tendency to mix the Charleston and Huntington accounts in such a way that the results are confusing and misleading. It is imperative for a businessperson to know how much each operation is contributing to the business.

2. Separation of the results of poster, paint, and commercial departments. One can neither tell presently whether any of these departments is contributing adequately to the business to justify its existence, nor which branches are the most profitable and thus the most appropriate for expansion.

3. Determination of the incremental costs of each activity. Although at present it seems that the variable costs are much less than the fixed costs and that the incremental costs are perhaps only 30 to 40 percent of the billings, that such is the case has not been determined in a systematic way. The incremental costs vary from one activity to another. In fact, they vary from one type of decision to another. Any system that helps to determine incremental costs should assist the executives in future decisions about the business.

Marginal income accounting tries to avoid arbitrary allocations of overhead. If some costs are common for the company as a whole (Charleston and Huntington) and not a result of any particular activity, these costs are marked as company overhead. Other costs related to Charleston activities or Huntington activities but not clearly a result of a particular department (poster, paint, or commercial) are marked as Charleston overhead or Huntington overhead. One of the primary objectives of marginal income accounting is to determine how much Charleston and Huntington separately contribute to the company's overhead and profits and how much poster, paint, and commercial departments contribute to local overhead, company overhead, and profits. Thus, a central concept throughout is the contribution to overhead and profits.

Arrangement of the accounts   Each of ECI's major account classifications is self-explanatory. The classes are shown in Exhibit 1. A code has been established for each class.

Marginal income analysis for July through December 1983   The operational results for the six months from July through December 1983 appear in Exhibit 2. These results are based on a close study of each individual expense item to determine whether it is fixed or variable, sunk or escapable, and attributable to Charleston, Huntington, or the company as a whole.

All information necessary for Exhibits 1 and 2 can be stored (filed) and calculated easily by use of a small, personal computer. IBM and/or Apple are easy and useful for this type of work.

Exhibit 1
Marginal income—classification of accounts

C–PO–1	Charleston income from poster plant.
C–PO–2	Charleston variable costs in poster plant.
C–PO–3	Charleston poster plant contribution to poster fixed costs, local and company overhead, and profit.
C–PO–4	Charleston poster plant fixed costs.
C–PO–4A	(Part of C–PO–4) Charleston poster plant sunk costs.
C–PO–4B	(Part of C–PO–4) Charleston poster plant escapable fixed costs.
C–PO–5	Charleston poster plant contribution to local and company overhead and profit (after deduction of poster plant fixed costs)

C–PA–1
C–PA–2
C–PA–3
C–PA–4   The same for the Charleston paint plant.
C–PA–4A
C–PA–4B
C–PA–5

C–C–1
C–C–2
C–C–3
C–C–4   The same for the Charleston commercial plant.
C–C–4A
C–C–4B
C–C–5

H–PO–1	H–PA–1	H–C–1	
H–PO–2	H–PA–2	H–C–2	The same for the Huntington poster
H–PO–3	H–PA–3	H–C–3	plant, Huntington paint plant, and
H–PO–4	H–PA–4	H–C–4	Huntington commercial plant,
H–PO–4A	H–PA–4A	H–C–4A	respectively.
H–PO–4B	H–PA–4B	H–C–4B	
H–PO–5	H–PA–5	H–C–5	

In addition there are three overhead accounts, two local contribution accounts, and one company profit account.

C–OH	Charleston overhead.
H–OH	Huntington overhead.
C–6	Charleston contribution to company overhead and profit.
H–6	Huntington contribution to company overhead and profit.
O	Companywide overhead.
P	Company profit.

Break-even charts: Charleston   The results can also be shown in the form of a series of break-even charts. Rather than construct a break-even chart for the company as a whole, it makes more sense to construct individual charts for each segment of the business. An overall break-even chart would add together differing elements, thereby obscuring the outcome of particular operations.

The special break-even chart required is the profit/volume chart. On it is first plotted the fixed costs (both sunk and escapable) resulting from the particular segment. Then is plotted the P/V line (profit-volume line), which is the incremental income at various volumes of sales—in other words, the added income minus the added (variable) costs. The slope of

Exhibit 2
Operational results—six months (July–December)

C–PO–1	$355,230.92	C–PA–1	$206,261.48	C–C–1	$81,361.56
Less C–PO–2	107,621.19	Less C–PA–2	72,305.19	Less C–C–2	54,718.73
Equals C–PO–3	247,609.73	Equals C–PA–3	133,956.29	Equals C–C–3	26,642.83
Less C–PO–4A	96,155.16	Less C–PA–4A	32,343.98	Less C–C–4A	—
Less C–PO–4B	89,651.49	Less C–PA–4B	51,502.33	Less C–C–4B	2,299.83
Equals C–PO–5	61,803.08	Equals C–PA–5	50,109.98	Less C–C–5	24,343.00
H–PO–1	$ 99,898.50	H–PA–1	$ 23,318.21	H–C–1	$ 14,514.51
Less H–PO–2	40,619.18	Less H–PA–2	3,866.94	Less H–C–2	9,883.79
Equals H–PO–3	59,279.32	Equals H–PA–3	19,451.27	Equals H–C–3	4,630.72
Less H–PO–4A	13,608.73	Less H–PA–4A	4,068.32	Less H–C–4A	—
Less H–PO–4B	15,937.68	Less H–PA–4B	5,517.93	Less H–C–4B	591.66
Equals H–PO–5	29,732.91	Equals H–PA–5	9,865.02	Equals H–C–5	4,039.06

Total Charleston contributions to local and company overhead and profits ($61,803.08 + $50,109.98 + $24,343.00)	$136,256.06
Less C–OH (Charleston overhead)	89,482.10
Equals C–6 (Charleston contribution to company overhead and profits)	$ 46,773.96
Total Huntington contribution to local and company overhead and profits ($29,732.91 + $9,856.02 + $4,039.06)	$ 43,636.99
Less H–OH (Huntington overhead)	31,011.46
Equals H–6 (Huntington contribution to company overhead and profits)	$ 12,625.53
Total contribution to company overhead an profits	$ 59,399.49
Less O (companywide overhead)	100,011.60
Equals company's loss	(40,611.11)

the P/V line is the P/V ratio—the added contribution per unit of sales. Where the P/V line crosses the zero horizontal line is the break-even point. At this point, the income less the variable costs is enough to cover the segment's fixed costs. But at this point the segment makes no contribution to the company's overhead and profits.

Exhibit 3 gives the specific fixed costs of the Charleston poster department as $185,806.65. The P/V ratio is 0.70, which means that every $1 of Charleston poster sales adds $0.70 more income. It takes billings of $266,580 in each six-month period to break even in the poster plant—that is, to cover the specific fixed costs. Beyond that point the contribution to profit increases rapidly, reaching a level of $61,803.08 at billings of $355,230.92. At billings of $450,000, it would appear that the contribution would be more than $127,500.

However, one qualification is necessary. Exhibit 3 probably exaggerates the added profits beyond present level of sales in one respect. Remember that the sales representatives' earnings have been treated as a fixed cost and partly as a variable cost. As billings push on past present levels and the salespeople become relatively more dependent upon commissions, the proportion of variable costs will rise, with a reduction in

Exhibit 3
P/V (break-even) chart, Charleston poster department (July–December 1983)

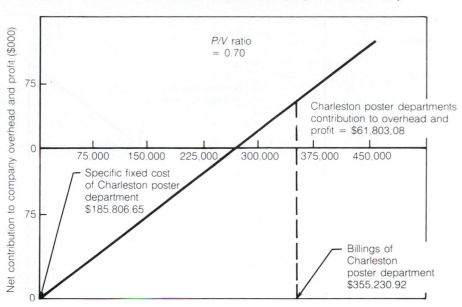

the P/V ratio line somewhere beyond the present level of sales. This error is probably not serious—it may reduce the ratio from .70 to .65 beyond the sales level of $420,000 (or something of that magnitude).

Which of the three Charleston departments is most profitable? The paint department made the largest contribution in ratio to its revenue in the six months under study. (See Exhibit 4.) The contribution of $50,109.98 on sales of $206,216.48 appears to be more favorable than the poster department's contribution of $61,803.08 on revenues of $355,230.92. This comparison is misleading, however. The results for the poster department are for its poorest six months. It will make a much larger contribution in the other six months, and the paint department will remain relatively stable. In addition, the poster department's P/V ratio is somewhat higher, which means that its contribution will respond rapidly to sales increases.

The Charleston commercial department's high ratio of contribution to sales certainly indicates that it is a desirable adjunct of the business. (See Exhibit 5.) Its main advantage is its low proportion of fixed costs. Its main disadvantage is its low P/V ratio, which would preclude it from over making the kind of profit possible in the poster department.

The fact appears to be that all three Charleston operations are profitable in every sense of the word—even though the overall company

Exhibit 4
P/V (break-even) chart, Charleston paint department (July–December 1983)

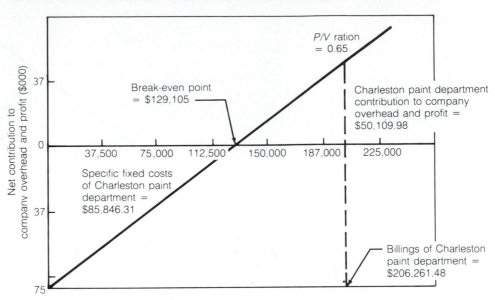

Exhibit 5
P/V (break-even) chart, Charleston commercial department (July–December 1983)

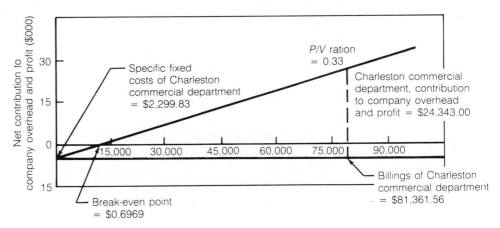

income statement shows a loss for the six months from July through December 1983.

Break-even charts: Huntington

The analysis for the Huntington operation runs along similar lines. For some reason the poster department P/V ratio is lower (0.59) in Huntington than in Charleston—its variable costs are proportionally higher than in

Charleston (Exhibit 6). But the billings are high enough to give a high ratio of contribution ($29,732.91) to billings ($99,898.50). Of course, the contribution should be considerably higher in the summer months.

The Huntington paint department's P/V ratio of 0.83 is extremely high (Exhibit 7). One wonders whether or not all the variable costs for this segment have been discovered. Perhaps some of the poster department's variable costs should be shifted to the paint department. In checking over the original worksheets, it is found that Charles R. Grewy's accounts show $12,714.21 of labor for the poster department but only $1,181.56 for the paint department. Perhaps this allocation of labor cost should be rechecked.

If the present allocations are correct, the Huntington paint department is extremely profitable in relation to sales and would be fantastically profitable if volume could be increased.

The Huntington commercial department also makes a satisfactory contribution to overhead and profit (Exhibit 8). In this case the contribution results from the high volume in relation to fixed costs rather than to the P/V ratio, which is relatively low. The low P/V ratio of 0.32 results, of course, from the fact that commercial work lacks proportionally more labor and materials (outright sales cost).

ECI believes companies of this sort, between the Charleston and Hun-

Exhibit 6
P/V (break-even) chart, Huntington poster department (July–December 1983)

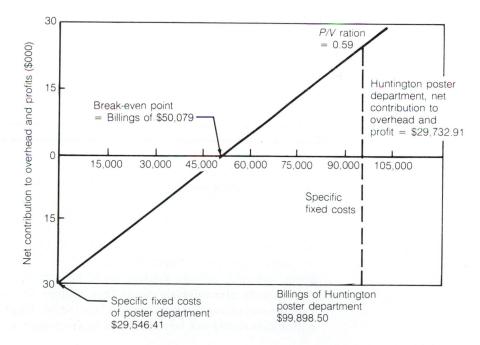

Exhibit 7
P/V (break-even) chart, Huntington paint department (July–December 1983)

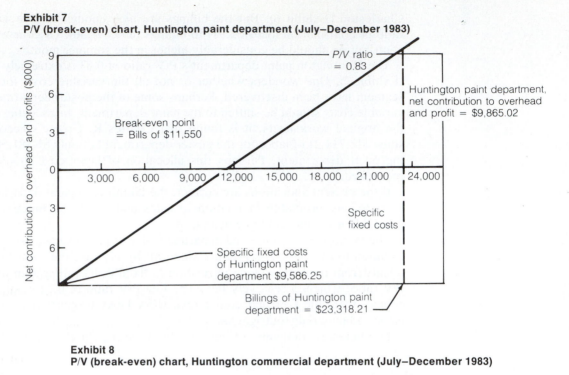

Exhibit 8
P/V (break-even) chart, Huntington commercial department (July–December 1983)

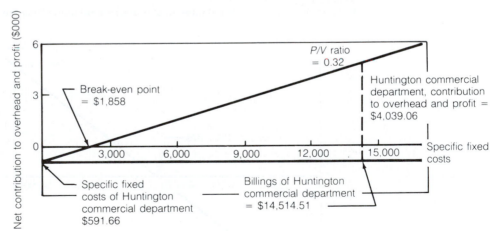

tington operations, can be maintained with relative ease via proper use of modern, low-cost computers. The analysis could be simplified so that future marginal income reports could be constructed with less effort. Accountants often use shortcuts that assume all costs of one type are variable and of another type are fixed and so on. ECI thinks that such simplifications would not be appopriate in this business for several reasons:

1. It is desirable to separate specific fixed costs from local overhead and companywide overhead. It is unlikely that any simple formula will do this exactly.
2. Costs that are fixed in one period may become variable and vice versa. Therefore, a period review of each classification is desirable.
3. As you change your business (buying new property and perhaps selling off old property), you will need flexibility in changing the classification.

ECI returned the original worksheet showing the classification of accounts. It will serve as a useful guide for future marginal income reports. It will not provide automatic answers to all problems of classification that might arise.

1. What is the purpose of separating sunk fixed costs from excapable fixed costs? What is the meaning of these terms? How is this breakdown relevant?
2. What is the meaning of the term *specific fixed costs* as used here?
3. Would a break-even chart for the company as a whole serve the purpose just as well as the individual P/V charts?
4. What are the meaning and significance of the break-even points shown on the P/V charts?
5. Three types of "contribution" are shown in Exhibit 2. What is the significance of each?
6. What purposes could be served by this type of analysis?

PROBLEMS[1]
Empirical cost analysis

7–1   A cross-sectional cost study attempting to simultaneously estimate the relationship of cost to changes in output rates (short-run cost curves) and the relationship of cost to changes in design capacity of plants (long-run cost curves) used the following function estimated from a score or more of individual plants:

$$C = 10,018 + 6.8193V + 0.3051K$$

where

C = Annual cost in dollars.
V = Annual volume (tons).

---

[1] Some of these problems are concerned with the use of costs in pricing, a subject raised in Part 4. Consideration of the role of costs in pricing at this point helps the reader get more out of the later pricing material. A source for Problems 1 and 2 is J. F. Stallsteimer, R. G. Bressler, and J. N. Boles "Cost Functions from Cross Section Data—Fact or Fantasy?" *Agricultural Economics Research*, July 1961, p. 84.

Exhibit 1
Plant curves and envelope curve

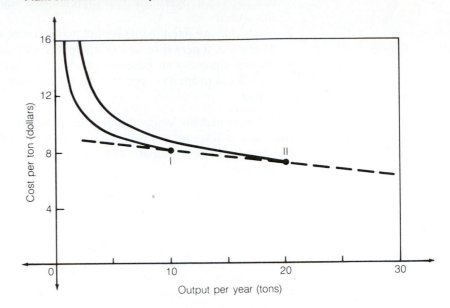

$K =$ Designed annual capacity of each plant (tons), where K is 10,000 tons per year. Unit cost varies with V as in curve I of Exhibit 1. When K is 20,000 tons per year, unit cost varies with V as in curve II.

By connecting the low points of the various plant curves, which are at design capacities of the plant, the long-run (envelope) curve is obtained. This long-run cost curve is illustrated by the dashed line in Exhibit 1.

The R^2 statistic for this estimate is 0.98. Parameters of seven other cost models using the same data from the score or more of plants obtained the results depicted in Exhibit 2.

1. As measured by R^2, are the estimates of total cost a "good fit?"

2. On a two-dimensional graph, plot the range of forms among the estimated seven long-run average cost curves.

3. What multicollinearity, if any, exists for this cost function(s)? Explain fully.

7–2   In your own words, what is multicollinearity? What statistical problems result from multicollinearity? Exhibit 2 in problem

Exhibit 2
Alternative cost equations derived from identical annual data on total costs, plant volume, and plant capacity

Equation	Total cost equation	R^2
1	$C = 70.042V^{0.8} + 0.30140(K - V)$ (16.80) (1.86)	0.96
2	$C = 22.702V^{0.9} + 0.30001(K - V)$ (20.53) (2.25)	0.98
3	$C = 2.229V^{1.1} + 0.41178(K - V)$ (18.10) (2.83)	0.97
4	$C = 10{,}018 + 6.8193V + 0.3051K$ (15.05) (2.27)	0.98
5	$C = 7.1080V + 0.4458K - 0.00000182VK$ (15.16) (3.22) (1.75)	0.98
6	$C = 5{,}799 + 6.5445V + 0.2578K + 0.00000083K^2$ (6.22)oo (0.43) (0.32) $+ 0.00000365VK - 0.000000000012VK^2$ (0.61) (0.73)	0.98
7	$C = 0.004122K^{1.4} + 109.3V/K^{0.27} - 6.01)$	0.94

7–1 is illustrative of multicollinearity in cross-section data and reveals what happens when annual volume and design capacity, highly related with each other, are used as variables in the same equation for determination of cost. How could the problems in Exhibit 2 be resolved?

7–3   In making statistical estimates of cost functions, influences on cost other than changes in the instantaneous rate and the running time must either be removed from the data or be included as variables in the economic model of cost.

Describe the best way of handling the following influences on costs appearing in the time-series data for a single plant: (*a*) general price inflation, (*b*) changes in relative prices of inputs, which may have resulted in input substitutions.

Describe the best way of handling the following factors affecting costs in cross-section data for a number of plants: (*a*) variations of the actual operating rates from the designed rates, (*b*) differences in the ages of the plants, which may mean that they were not all designed at the same state of technology, (*c*) locational variations in the prices of inputs.

7–4   John Carroll University Press produces scholarly books and monographs, for which the demand is relatively limited. The objective is not profit. The press operates within the limits of its budget, including subsidies from outside foundations. It must control costs.

One important decision affecting costs is the length of run for each publication. If the first run of a book is too small, the press takes the risk of running out of stock and losing sales and must also meet the extra setup costs required by a second run. But if the run is too large, the press encounters storage costs and losses from unsold books.

Before publication of each book, one of the press's editors makes an estimate of costs based primarily on past experience with similar books. For example, the cost of publishing 1,000 copies of a monograph in business administration planned for November 15, 1985, is estimated at $1,300 for composition and printing, $550 for binding, and $50 for freight.

Sometimes estimates are considerably in error, especially if the author's alterations are numerous (The estimates tend to be low.)

The stock cost is completely variable. The composition and press costs are a mixture of direct labor costs and allocations of equipment and space charges.

A second run of 1,000 copies would be considerably cheaper than the first run (see Exhibit 3). A second run of the text would require 11 offset plates, costing $18 per plate. The stock would cost about $138. The offset pressrun would take about 11 hours at only $9 per hour. The ink is $3.10. The jacket requires $10 for stock, $2 for ink, $18 for one offset plate, $9 for one offset pressrun, and $7 for one letter-pressrun. Binding costs would be approximately $507. If the second run were less than 1,000

Exhibit 3
Costs on monograph (Publication data—November 15, 1985)

Text		
Stock	$138.00	
Composition	638.00 (98 hours)	
Press	141.40 (20 hours)	
Ink	3.10	
Miscellaneous	10.00	
Overhead (15% of above)	140.50	
Total cost of text		$1,071.00
Jacket		
Stock	$ 10.00	
Composition	39.20 (5 hours)	
Press	37.80 (5.4 hours)	
Miscellaneous	1.50	
Ink	2.00	
Overhead (15% of above)	13.50	
Total cost of jacket		104.00
Binding		506.83
Freight		40.72
Total cost (est.)		$1,722.55

copies, the costs would be about the same except for the stock and binding costs. The stock costs would be proportional to the run, but the binding costs include a fixed element of about $100 per run.

Sometimes the press prints extra sheets of a book in the first run, postponing binding the sheets until the first batch of bound copies are sold. For the business monograph under discussion, no extra sheets will be printed.

Decisions on the length of run are influenced by the shortage of storage space. No one has made an estimate of storage costs, but one could assume the space used for storage would be $1,000 per annum. The space has a capacity for about 16,000 volumes and is overcrowded. Copies of some old books are stored in a basement room.

The retail price of the monograph is set at $3. The press expects to receive an average of $2.10 per copy after discounts to distributors. The greatest uncertainty concerns sales. One purchaser has agreed to buy 500 copies. The press has no previous experience with monographs in the business area and thus has little basis for estimating sales beyond 500 copies. Sales of monographs in other subject matter areas usually run below 500, sometimes as low as 200. The press makes fairly accurate estimates of sales of books on historical subjects and of monographs in archaeology and anthropology because it has published a number of works in those areas. Estimates on other books are subject to considerable error.

1. Construct a model for the determination of the economic length of run on books.
2. What economic principles are incorporated in your model?
3. Apply your model as best you can to the problem of the business monograph.
4. Does the press make a sound decision by running 1,000 copies? Explain. Should it run some extra sheets?
5. Is a formal analysis of uncertainty helpful in this case? Discuss.

7–5   The owner-manager of a small printing firm in Atlanta, Georgia, maintains a policy of cost-plus pricing. He computes the full cost of each order by adding an overhead allocation to the direct labor and material expenses. When asked what he did during the 1982 recession when sales declined sharply—with a resultant increase in overhead costs per unit of production—he replied that he increased price to meet the higher overhead costs.

He insists he intends to maintain this policy in subsequent years. His firm began operations just after the Vietnam War, and 1982 was the first year he faced such a serious decline in sales. Is this decision concerning cost a sound one?

7–6   Firms who follow a full-cost policy of pricing may be prompted to do so because of:

a. The desire to be fair, however defined.
b. Ignorance of demand and marginal revenue conditions.
c. Uncertainty about the potential reaction of competitors.
d. Belief that responsiveness to price decreases is low.
e. Belief that higher prices would encourage new entrants.
f. Administrative difficulties of a more flexible price policy.

One full-cost firm in Dallas refuses to supply anything below full cost. It computes average overheads on the basis of conventional output (output under normal business conditions.) It adds a margin for profit that is smaller on competitive lines and higher on specialties and novelties. This add-on is necessary because of the firm's research and development activity. The managers believe experience shows that price cuts below full costs do not pay. Demand is inelastic, they think. Furthermore, price changes are thought to be a nuisance to distributors and an annoyance to customers.

A trade association set minimum prices on a few lines. In the severe recession of the 1980s, management found that demand shifted to more popular, competitive lines. Timely price reductions on such lines alone were successful in increasing revenue. They survived the recession. Does this firm have a good understanding of its costs?

7–7   A cereal box manufacturing firm in Michigan owns five printing presses to print labels on boxes. These presses vary in size and in the capacity to print multicolored labels. Some presses are better suited to the printing of large volumes than are others. In the past, management was uncertain about the allocation of orders to the presses. In many cases it was clear that a certain large order or a certain multicolored label would go on a particular press. However, there was and is uncertainty about the desirability of printing some small, simple orders on the large, complex presses when those presses are idle, especially when there is a backlog of small orders. A "Big Eight" accounting firm advised the firm to compute an hourly rate for each press and to include an allocation of overhead. The hourly rate on the large, complex presses is higher because of the higher labor costs (more press operators per press), the higher depreciation charges on the press, and the higher allocation of plantwide overhead. These hourly rates help prevent the use of expensive presses on low-value jobs. Discuss.

7–8   The B. F. Goodrich Company abandoned a machining operation in its main plant. The machine was used to make and/or repair unique office furniture. The four spindles that had been used were now idle. The four employees who had done the machining for the company had rented a shed in another part of Memphis and had rented four second-hand spindles. They were supplying the parts formerly produced by the company at a lower price but were earning more money. They were able to provide the same quality of product at a lower cost because the overhead costs in their shed were far below the overhead rate in the main plant. The overhead costs in the main plant were allocated on the basis of direct labor cost. The direct labor cost on this operation was especially high because the machinists were highly skilled and the job less mechanized than other jobs in this plant, or at other plant locations (i.e., Akron). What do you think?

7–9   A trade association official, who for the moment at least is best left unnamed, said the pricing practices of association members lacked uniformity and objectivity. Many of the members made their pricing decisions in a highly subjective way, he said. The trade association should convert its members to a "scientific approach," to a pricing system based on costs. What do you think?

7–10   The owner-manager of the largest garden nursery firm in Detroit claims he cannot determine the cost of his individual plants; therefore, he cannot price on the basis of costs. Some costs are attributed to individual items; for example, although labor cost of digging up the plants could be measured, and it is easy to compute the labor and transportation costs of a landscaping job, the costs of propagating and growing a plant are uncertain. What is the cost of the occupied land? How are the general expenses of the company to be charged against particular items? The variable weather and plant diseases create uncertainty about losses and damage that occurs before some plants mature. Can and should this Detroit Nursery allocate its costs? Would this cost information be useful in pricing decisions?

7–11   The cost of eastbound and westbound traffic on the Chessie
System and all other railroads is a joint cost. Every freight car
hauled eastward must eventually be hauled west, even if it is
empty. The railroads are therefore faced with the problem of
determining the costs to be attributed to the return trip. A similar problem exists for United Airlines and other commercial
carriers when they face less than a full load on return flights
from some airports.

It is not uncommon for revenue ton-miles hauled for the railroad to be 20 billion going east and 10 billion going west.

a. In each case evaluate the use of costs in the decisions with
which the firm or firms are faced.

b. Which cost concepts are most pertinent in these case situations?

Selected references

Allen, P. Geoffrey; Thomas H. Stevens; and Scott A. Barrett. "The
Effects of Variable Omission in the Travel Cost Technique." *Land
Economics* 57, no. 2 (May 1981), pp. 173–80.

Bawa, Vijay S., and David S. Sibley. "Dynamic Behavior of a Firm
Subject to Stochastic Regulatory Review." *International Economic
Review* 21, no. 3 (October 1980), pp. 627–42.

Dirlam, Joel B. "Marginal Cost Pricing Tests for Predation: Naive Welfare Economics and Public Policy." *Antitrust Bulletin* 26, no. 4 (Winter 1981), pp. 769–814.

Graddy, Duane B., and Reuben Kyle III. "The Simultaneity of Bank
Decision Making, Market Structure and Bank Performance." *Journal of Finance* 34, no. 1 (March 1979), pp. 1–18.

Haldi, J., and D. Whitcomb. "Economies of Scale in Industrial Plants."
Journal of Political Economy 75 (August 1967).

Just, Richard E., and Wen S. Chern. "Tomatoes, Technology and Oli-
gopsony." *Bell Journal of Economics* 11, no. 2 (Autumn 1980),
pp. 584–602.

Kast, Ronald S., and David A. Walker. "Short-Run Cost Functions of a
Multiproduct Firm." *Journal of Industrial Economics* 18 (April
1970).

Kennan, J. "Pareto Optimality and the Economics of Strike Duration."
Journal of Labor Research 1, no. 1 (Spring 1980), pp. 77–94.

Longbrake, William A. "Statistical Cost Analysis." *Financial Management* 2 (Spring 1973).*

* This article is included in Thomas J. Coyne, *Readings in Managerial Economics,* 3d
ed. (Plano, Tex.: Business Publications, 1981).

Maxwell, W. David. "Production Theory and Cost Curves." *Applied Economics* 1 (1969).

McGee, John S. "Economies of Size in Auto Body Manufacture." *Journal of Law and Economics* 16 (October 1973).

Munashinghe, Mohan. "Costs Incurred by Residential Electricity Consumers Due to Power Failures." *Journal of Consumer Research* 6, no. 4 (March 1980), pp. 361–69.

Roth, Timothy P. "Empirical Cost Curves and the Production-Theoretic Short Run: A Reconciliation." *Quarterly Review of Economics and Business* 19, no. 3 (Autumn 1979), pp. 35–47.

Williamson, Oliver E. "Hierarchial Control and Optimum Firm Size." *Journal of Political Economy* 75 (April 1967).

4

Pricing

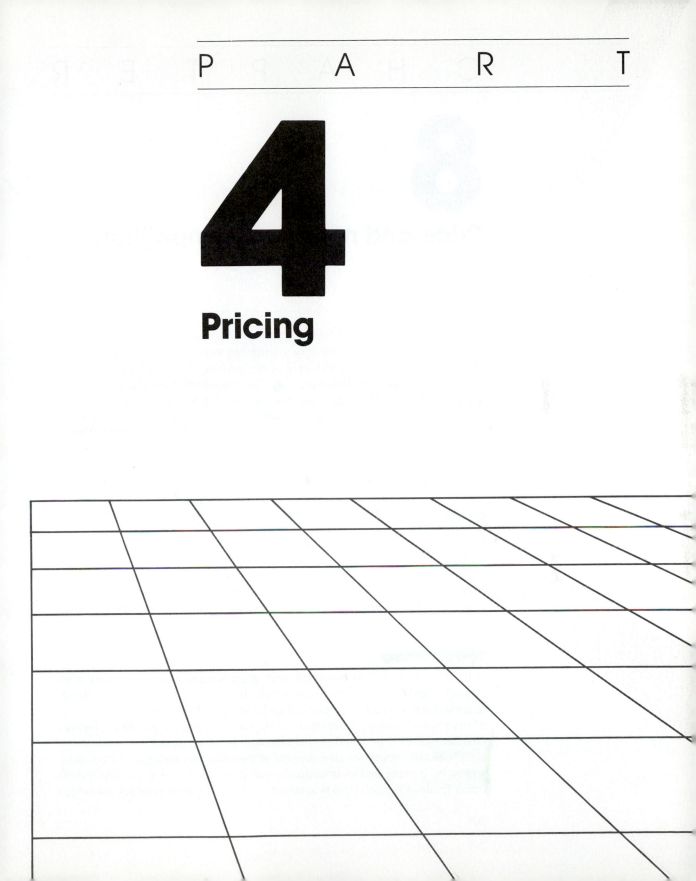

CHAPTER

8

Price and nonprice competition

Business firms are presumably attempting to maximize something. This chapter establishes the rudiments of the pricing problem and places emphasis upon some basic facts: (1) All firms must sell their particular product at some price; (2) all firms must decide with some degree of precision how many units to produce; and (3) all price and output decisions made by firms take place within one of four basic market structures. Each market structure is broadly defined and has characteristics unique to that structure.

The four market structures into which all firms and industries operating within the United States may be classified are: (1) pure competition, (2) monopoly, (3) monopolistic competition, and (4) oligopoly. By definition, certain conditions must exist within the firm and industry for the business to be called purely competitive. These conditions are important to the numerous generalizations that may be made when the model is applied. Then, as one or more of these conditions are relaxed, the purely competitive market model allows for somewhat more specific conclusions than can be drawn from the three remaining "imperfectly competitive" models.

Basic assumptions

In this chapter it is assumed that management wishes to maximize tangible profits over a period for which the analysis is being made. Sales and production rates are assumed to be identical, so there are no effects of inventory buildup or depletion to be taken into account: (1) The firm's structure of cost is based on an assumption of continuative production. (2) Costs and revenues of subsequent periods are assumed to be unaffected by pricing and output during the period for which the analysis is being made. (3) Each firm is assumed to have a single product for which there is a single market. Under these simplifying assumptions, this chapter concentrates upon decisions about pricing, product quality, and promotion under various market structures.

Determinants of market structure

There are two major determinants of market structure. The first is number of firms in the industry. There are many firms, and if any one producer's decisions and activities cannot have perceptible effect upon any other firm's profits, in which case competition is diffused and firms pay little or no attention to each other, any seller can take independent action without appraising the possible reactions of competitors. There are few firms if one producer's behavior can cause a noticeable change in another company's profits, in which case competition becomes personal and adversaries closely watch and react to each other—each firm must consider possible responses of rivals in determining its own actions. There is only one firm in a monopoly industry; such a seller obviously does not need to weigh possible reactions of present competitors, but potential competition may be a relevant consideration if the monopoly structure is not permanent.

The second major determinant of market structure is the extent to which products of the various firms are differentiated. Products are homogeneous if they are standardized or identical—buyers have no reasons to prefer one supplier's product over that of another, and differences in prices cannot be maintained. The products of the various firms are differentiated if they are perceived by consumers as being different from each other—buyers have preferences among the products, and continuing differences among their prices can be maintained. A monopoly firm has a unique product with no close substitutes—pricing of a unique product can be changed without noticeable effects upon sales of any other product, and sales of the unique product are not perceptibly affected by changes in the price of any other product.

Behavior of producers within the above market structures may be influenced by the ease of entry of new firms. Entry is easy if a new company would have little or no disadvantage compared with established firms—the structures of pure and monopolistic competition permit easy entry. There are barriers to entry if a new seller would have substantial disadvantages compared with established firms. Oligopoly structures typically do have barriers to entry, but the barriers are greater for some oligopolistic industries than for others. Entry of a new firm is precluded in a monopoly structure, although some monopolies are temporary.

Theory of pricing with demand taken as given

In the traditional theory of pricing under pure competition, monopoly, and monopolistic competition, demand is taken as given. Optimum output-sales rates are found at the points at which marginal cost and marginal revenue are equal, and optimum prices are found on the demand functions at the best output-sales quantities.

Pure competition

In pure competition there are many sellers of a homogeneous product. Information about cost, prices, and quality of product is readily available to both buyers and sellers. Any one producer's maximum sales are a small part of the industry total, and variations in any supplier's output and sales have no perceptible effect upon the product's market price. Entry into the industry is easy.

The economist uses pure competition to describe a particular kind of price and output behavior that is unique to certain firms operating within the economy. The purely competitive firm is one that exists in a rather large industry. It is so small relative to the industry that, acting individually, it has no control over the price charged for its finished product. The firm cannot establish a price policy for itself. Prices charged by the firm for products are "given" by the market place. The purely competitive firm is a price taker instead of a price maker.

Assumptions implicit in pure competition include the following:

Smallness   Each producer is so small relative to the number of firms in the industry that, acting alone, the producer cannot influence the price paid for factors of production. When hiring a carpenter, for example, the producer expects to pay the going rate for carpenters. Likewise, when borrowing money at the bank, the producer will have to pay whatever interest rate the bank charges. Unlike the larger oligopolistic firms, the purely competitive operator does not have an in-house staff of carpenters and is often unable to negotiate and thereby receive the prime rate at the bank. The firm is so small that if it were to leave the industry, it would not be missed.

Ease of entry   Another characteristic of the purely competitive model is that virtually anyone in society can enter and/or leave the industry. Entrance requirements, if any, are so minimal that they could not be considered barriers. Producers of agricultural products are examples. Anyone who can find enough land to plant some tomatoes is free to plant them, take them to market when they are ripe, and obtain the going market rate for home-grown tomatoes.

Unsophisticated technology   The technology required for satisfactory operation within the industry is easily obtainable and can be mastered by virtually any member of society.

Homogeneous product   As with the tomato grower, all producers in a purely competitive product market manufacture or otherwise provide for sale a product that is not differentiated in the mind of the consumer. A bushel of winter wheat is, by definition, the same whether grown in southern Canada or northern Nebraska.

Perfect knowledge   Generally speaking, the model assumes that producers, consumers, resource suppliers, and other persons interested in the market have a perfect knowledge of all that takes place within that market. For example, they are aware of all prices and changes in prices. They know how many additional suppliers exist. All persons know whether or not short-run economic profits are being made and whether or not economic losses are occurring.

Few industries have a market structure of pure competition. Farmers sell their crops and livestock in markets closely approaching pure competition, and the market in which money is lent to businesses at the prime rate is a close approximation. Each supplying firm in pure competition perceives its demand and marginal revenue functions as horizontal at the market price. The firm cannot vary product quality, nor can it gain from product promotion. A company in pure competition can produce and sell any quantity up to its capacity at the market price, but at a higher price it can sell nothing. Thus the competitive firm cannot make a decision about price, but it can choose a rate of output and sales.

Figure 8–1 illustrates the choice of output and sales rate under pure competition. Optimal rate is at O_0, the rate at which marginal cost equals marginal revenue. Figure 8–1 depicts marginal cost rising (in the relevant range) with rate of output and sales. Nearly all agricultural production has rising marginal cost in the short run, and funds allocated to business loans by financial institutions would have rising marginal opportunity costs. Graphic and analytic methods for quantitative determination of optimum rates of output under the structure of pure competition are discussed in Chapter 9 (see Figure 9–7 and the corresponding explanation).

The average total cost curve in part *B* of Figure 8–1 includes the opportunity cost of capital provided by the firm's owners; it is conceived as a curve of full economic cost of all outputs used. The price in part *B* is well above the average total cost at the optimum rate of output and sales, so the firm is earning economic profits. The condition shown would be short run if all firms in the industry were earning economic profits because entry of new sellers and expansion of established suppliers would increase total industry output and exert downward pressure on price. In a competitive industry forces of supply press against demand and push price down in relation to costs of production. A competitive market structure tends to squeeze out economic profits as producers adjust capacities over the long run.

A well-managed company in a purely competitive structure may in the short run be able to maintain above-average returns on investment in the face of the steady pressure of market forces upon profits. If the industry has developing technology, astute innovation can keep the firm's costs well below those of the industry's marginal producers (the least profitable ones).

The theory of pure competition has limited relevance to a discussion

Figure 8–1
Pricing and output under pure competition

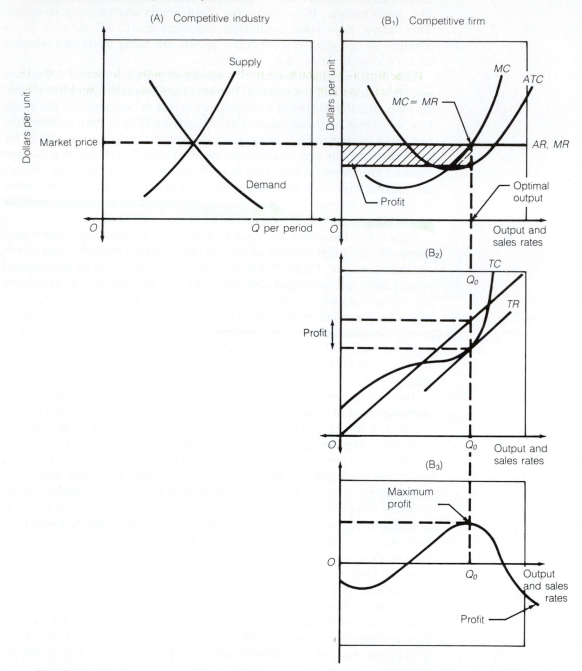

Note: Parts *B–1*, *B–2*, and *B–3* are alternative views of the same thing, namely, the determination of optimum output-sales for a firm under pure competition.

of pricing. It does illustrate the role of impersonal market forces in any structure into which entry is easy. However, a chapter on pricing and other competitive tactics must emphasize market situations in which firms have some control over price.

Equilibrium: Pure competition

If the firm is to maximize profits and/or minimize losses, it must produce where marginal revenue (MR) and marginal cost (MC) are equal. This condition of equilibrium is the same regardless of whether the market structure is purely competitive or is one of the three imperfectly competitive models. Moreover, the short-run and long-run cost curves will generally have the same slopes and for the same reason, regardless of whether perfect or imperfectly competitive market models are used.[1]

Figure 8–2a depicts the price and output behavior of a hypothetical purely competitive firm, which operates in the purely competitive industry depicted by Figure 8–2b. In each instance price is on the vertical axis and quantity demanded is on the horizontal, or x, axis.

Equilibrium for the firm in Figure 8–2a is at E_F, the point at which marginal revenue equals marginal cost. Equilibrium for the industry is at E_I, where total industry supply equals total industry demand.

Figure 8–2a
Normal profit equilibrium for the firm: Pure competition

Figure 8–2b
Normal profit equilibrium for the industry: Pure competition

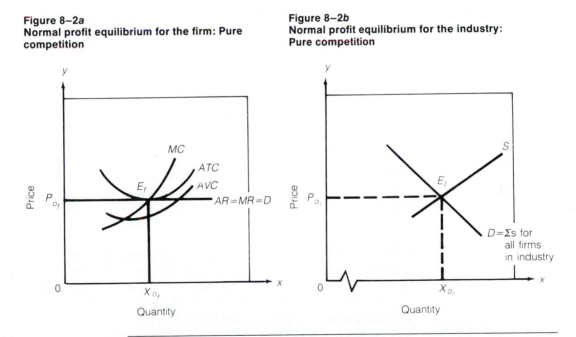

---

[1] U-shape average total cost, average variable cost, and marginal cost curves exist in the short run because of diminishing returns; in the long run because of increasing and decreasing returns to scale. Differences in the four market structures are confined to differences in the slopes of the demand and marginal revenue curves.

The assumption implicit in the demand function represented in Figure 8–2a is that the firm thinks it can sell any quantity it can supply at the price, P_{of}. That is, the market has given a price for this product, and the firm believes it can sell whatever quantity of the product it can obtain at that price. The price is equal to the average revenue, marginal revenue, and demand function for the firm. If the demand curve is tangent to the minimum point of the average total cost curve, the firm is said to be in short-run equilibrium, making a normal profit.

Although firm managers think they can sell any quantity of the good being demanded, the industry cannot. The industry demand curve, Figure 8–2b, is a summation of the individual demand curves represented by all firms similar to the one in part A of Figure 8–1. The summation of the demand curves for all firms in the industry will be normal; it will slope downward and to the right reflecting, in the short run, the law of diminishing returns. The demand curve for the industry falls because product price falls within the industry as total industrial output increases. The individual firms remain as price takers, but until price falls they continue to think that they can sell any quantity at the prevailing price.

Equilibrium price per unit of output is the same in Figure 8–2a as in Figure 8–2b. The quantity made available differs significantly. Figure 8–2b could represent a quantity, X_{of}, of say, 100 million bushels of wheat, whereas X_{of}, the quantity supplied by the firm, could equal 1,000 bushels of wheat. If all firms in the industry were of equal size, one could assume from this difference in quantity that 100,000 wheat farmers exist and sell their product in this purely competitive market.

Economic profits

Figure 8–2a reveals the firm to be in short-run equilibrium making a normal profit. Figure 8–3 is the same as Figure 8–2a except demand for the product has increased in the short run when all costs remained constant. The price, P', is higher for this firm than it was initially; consequently, MR' intersects MC at E'. E' designates the new short-run output position for the firm. It is a position that generates economic profits. The magnitude of economic profit is equal to the area under the average revenue curve represented by $E'ABP'$. In Figure 8–3 it is revealed as a shaded area.

If cost conditions remain constant while demand increases, all firms within the industry may realize a short-term economic profit. However, in the long run they will not be able to continue with economic profits because new firms will be enticed into the industry. These new entrants will take a share of the expanded market for themselves. Since they, too, will be price takers, they will provide their product at the prevailing market price. Should that price be higher than the minimum point of the newcomers' average total cost curve, the newcomers will also earn an

Figure 8–3
Economic profits for the firm: Pure competition

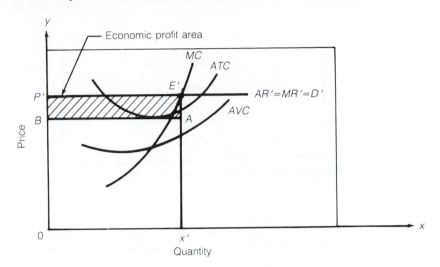

economic profit. Still more new entrants will be enticed into the industry. When market price becomes equal to the minimum point of the average total cost curve, all firms in the industry will once again be earning a normal profit. At that point, there is no incentive for new firms to enter the industry; likewise, there is no reason for existing firms to leave. All firms can exist together making a normal profit.

Economic losses

As even the most casual observer of the American economy would be quick to note, not all business firms generate normal or economic profits in the short run. Some firms incur losses. In a purely competitive market structure, if a firm is unable to maximize its profit, it attempts to minimize its loss. Loss minimization is depicted in Figure 8–4a for the purely competitive firm. This firm is assumed to have the same cost curves as in Figure 8–2a. But instead of assuming an increase in demand as was done for Figure 8–3, the assumption is that demand for the finished product dropped quickly and the firm was either unwilling or unable to reduce its costs. The question that begs itself in Figure 8–4a is: If the firm is unable to make normal profits, at what point does it shut down?

Total cost to the firm is broken into two components: fixed costs and variable costs. Likewise, average total costs for the firm is the summation of the average variable and average fixed cost curves at each point of output along the horizontal, or *x*, axis. Minimization of loss means that

Figure 8–4a
Economic losses for the firm: Pure Competition

Figure 8–4b
Short-run supply for the firm, obtained from marginal cost curve: Pure competition

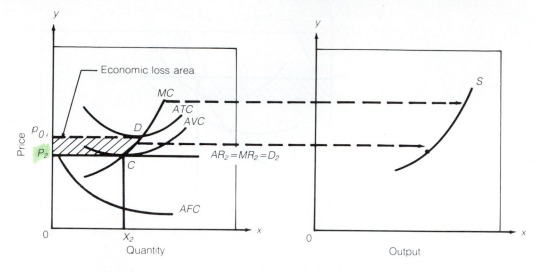

the firm will continue operations so long as its average price per unit of output covers at least the average variable cost of producing the unit.

In Figure 8–4a both the average fixed cost and average variable cost curves are revealed. The average fixed cost is total fixed costs divided by quantity. As one would expect, this curve decreases as output increases, coming closer and closer to the horizontal axis without touching it.

If demand drops from P_{of} (as in Figure 8–2a) to P_2 (as in Figure 8–4a), the firm will find itself producing where MR_2 equals MC—in other words, at the minimum point of the average variable cost curve. At this point, C, the firm is covering its wages, salaries, supplements, and other costs that vary with the level of output for the firm. It is unable to cover the wear and tear on its capital equipment and/or its average fixed costs. Should the firm decide to operate at a price of P_2 and an output of X_2, the time will come when its capital equipment is no longer useable. It will find itself with no money with which to replace that capital equipment. Inasmuch as it has not been earning a normal profit, the firm may have no borrowing power at the commercial bank. Being a small, perfectly competitive product market firm, as defined, the bond and stock markets are closed to it. Quite simply, the firm goes out of business.

The shaded portion of Figure 8–4a depicts the area of economic loss for this firm. It is represented by $CP_2P_{of}D$. The firm would be able to minimize its loss by taking any price between P_2 and P_{of} on the vertical axis. Prices lower than P_2 would result in (1) no coverage of fixed costs and (2) only partial coverage of variable costs, per unit of output. In other words, on a per-unit basis, the firm would be charging a price less than its unit costs. Under such a set of circumstances, the firm would be paying for the privilege of staying in the industry, and such a firm could not correct its condition by making it up on large volume. Such a firm should close its plant.

The short-run supply curve

If the firm cannot maximize its profits, it will attempt to minimize its losses. It will do so by taking a price lower than that necessary to produce a normal profit but higher than the minimum point on its average variable cost curve.

Referring to Figure 8–4a, the firm would accept a price somewhere between P_{of} and P_2, if it wanted to stay in business and minimize its losses. If it had to take a price lower than P_2, th manager of the place would be derelict if he or she did not pick up the phone and shut down the plant immediately. The output of this firm, therefore, should be zero if it were required to take a price somewhere between zero and P_2 on the vertical axis in Figure 8–4a.

A company will continue to operate only so long as it receives a price equal to or greater than the minimum point of the average variable cost curve. Inasmuch as the marginal cost curve must cut the average variable cost curve at its minimum point, the supply curve for the firm and/or the plant is that segment of the marginal cost curve that happens to lie above the minimum point of the average variable cost curve. In other words, that portion of the firm's marginal cost curve that happens to lie above the minimum point of the average variable cost curve is the supply curve for the firm just as surely as if it had been picked from the paper and plotted on a normal, positively sloping supply curve as in Figure 8–4b. This situation is a one-to-one relationship between the marginal cost curve and the supply curve for the firm in a purely competitive market structure only. Companies operating in imperfectly competitive product markets have price policies. They are price makers and not price takers.

Monopoly

Pure competition is characterized by the existence of an extremely large number of relatively small competing producers; conversely, monopoly is characterized by no competition. The firm is the industry. Examples of pure monopoly in the private sector may be found in small markets (i.e., small towns). In addition there are a few monopolists in the public sector: The U.S. Post Office monopolizes all first class mail. Monopoly in education exists in many parts of many states. If private and parochial schools fail financially, for example, the drive for monopoly of education within the United States will have been completed.

Absolute barriers to entry, temporary or more enduring, are the foundations of monopoly structures. Barriers have included (1) control of known supplies of low-cost raw materials, such as Alcoa's control of bauxite ores prior to World War II; (2) patents, such as Polaroid's patents on many forms of instant photo devices and materials; (3) franchises, such as the rights granted in the past to single air carriers and currently to single television stations to provide exclusive service to smaller market areas; and (4) economies of scale so great that a single supplier has a notable cost advantage, as in the cases of the electric, gas, and telephone utilities.

A monopoly's demand curve slopes down to the right. The marginal revenue function lies below the demand curve. The firm can choose the most profitable combination of price and output-sales rate. Figure 8–5 illustrates optimal pricing and output for a monopoly in the short run—the cost curves are short-run (operating) curves for a plant, which must be taken as given. Figure 8–6 shows optimal pricing and output for a monopoly in the long run—plant size can be changed, and the cost curves are long-run (envelope) curves, which may have decreasing costs as in the figure or may have eventually increasing costs. The principle that determines optimal price and output is the same, whether the decision is short run or long run and whether long-run marginal cost is increasing, constant, or decreasing. It pays to increase output and sales if marginal revenue is greater than marginal cost, so the optimum rate is at the point at which marginal cost becomes equal to marginal revenue.

Optimal rates are at Q_o in Figures 8–5 and 8–6, and optimal prices are found on the respective demand curves at P_o, corresponding to the optimal rates of output sales. Graphic and analytic methods for quantitative determination of pricing and output that maximize profit for a monopoly are explained in Chapter 9 (see Figure 9–8 and the corresponding text).

The long-run perspective on monopoly is actually somewhat more complicated than the view provided in the preceding paragraphs. Both the monopoly firm's demand and its cost structure may be shifting over time, so that the firm's management faces a dynamic optimization problem in making decisions about changes in plant size.

A monopolistic firm can make one of two decisions: (1) It can determine its level of output, or (2) it can determine its price. Under no set of circumstances can it simultaneously determine price and output. If it selects the price at which it wants to sell, output will be determined by guiding off the demand curve. If it determines the level of output at which it wants to operate, price is determined by guiding off the demand function.

A firm wanting to maximize its profits will have to operate at a level that will allow it to draw the largest possible area under the demand function. In Figure 8–5 the firm would produce where marginal revenue

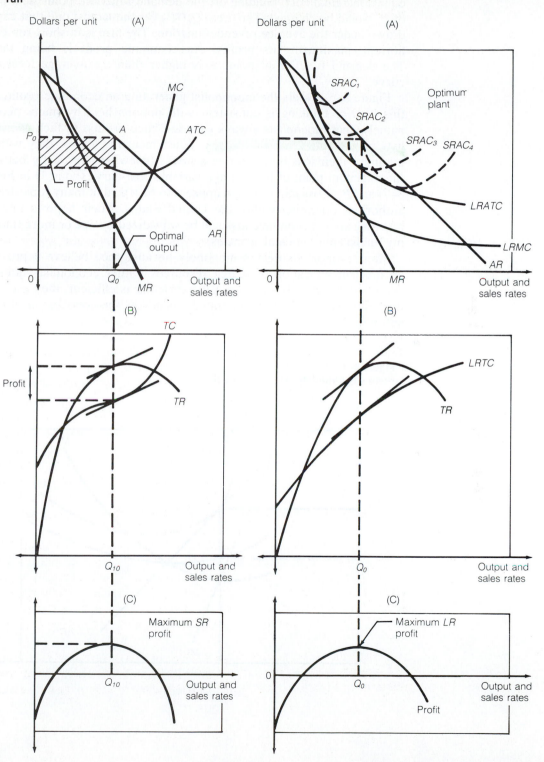

Figure 8–5
Pricing and output under monopoly—short run

(A)

Dollars per unit

P_0

Profit

MC

A

ATC

AR

Optimal output

0   Q_0 MR   Output and sales rates

(B)

TC

Profit

TR

Q_{10} Output and sales rates

(C)

Maximum *SR* profit

Q_{10} Output and sales rates

Figure 8–6
Pricing and output under monopoly—long run

(A)

Dollars per unit

$SRAC_1$

Optimum plant

$SRAC_2$

$SRAC_3$ $SRAC_4$

LRATC

LRMC

AR

0   MR   Output and sales rates

(B)

LRTC

TR

Q_0 Output and sales rates

(C)

Maximum *LR* profit

0   Q_0 Output and sales rates

Profit

equals marginal cost. Guiding off the demand function, point A, a price of P_o would be charged. The area, $Q_o O P_o A$ is the largest one that can be drawn under the average revenue function. The firm is in short-run equilibrium, maximizing its profits. An economic profit is being made. The demand function at point A is higher than the average total cost curve.

Figure 8–5 reveals the monopolist generating an economic profit, and this kind of thinking is consistent with notions held by many people, namely, that monoplists always generate huge profits. In fact, monopolists may at times generate losses. When incurring losses, they want to minimize their loss by accepting a price somewhere vertically between the minimum point of the average variable cost curve (point D in Figure 8–7) and P_o. Loss minimization appears to be a goal of many rapid-transit authorities operating within the United States. Their hope is that the resulting area of economic loss will be subsidized by one or more (matching funds) governmental agencies.

Many economists defend monopoly because they believe it provides an efficient allocation of scarce resources. Other economists question such "efficiency." If a monopolistic structure is efficient, they ask, why do government-owned and operated businesses (monopolies) need to be subsidized?

Figure 8–7
Price and output behavior: Monopoly

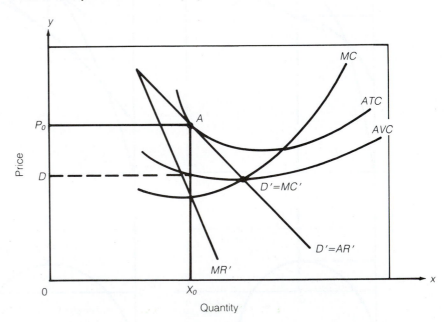

Monopolistic competition

Monopolistic competition is the term used to describe the relatively large number of firms operating within the domestic American economy that do not fit very neatly into the pure competition or pure monopoly market models but possess characteristics of each. For the most part, monopolistically competitive firms have a pricing policy. They determine for themselves the price they expect to receive for each unit sold. They are price makers and not price takers. In addition, their industry is one characterized by a large number of relatively small firms, each one of which sells a slightly differentiated product. Unlike their counterparts in the purely competitive market structure, monopolistically competitive firms do not sell a homogenous product. It may be true that winter wheat is winter wheat, by definition, regardless of where it is grown and harvested. It is untrue that a 16-ounce loaf of Wonder Bread cannot be differentiated from a 16-ounce loaf of Betsy Ross Bread.

As soon as product differentiation is introduced into the model, the perfectly price elastic demand curve of the purely competitive producer develops into a slightly price-inelastic downward-sloping demand curve. The curve is more price inelastic than can be found in the purely competitive market structure but is not nearly as price inelastic as one might expect in cases of monopoly. It is the ability of competing firms to differentiate their product that causes price inelasticity to creep into the curve. Further, entry of new products is easy. Differentiation gives each seller some control over price. Each producer can make decisions about pricing without considering possible reactions of competitors. Since each supplier is small in relation to total industry output and sales, the impact of any one firm's marketing tactics is spread over many competitors and becomes too small to be identified. Thus, no other seller will react with countermeasures.

It is not easy to find industries in which all firms can behave as monopolistic competitors. Canned foods, carpets, clothing, and furniture may be examples. Also, the small firms in some differentiated oligopolies do not expect reactions of competitors to their decisions about prices. Banking, insurance, retailing, and some kinds of manufacturing are oligopolistic at the center (which is composed of the larger firms) and monopolistically competitive (among the smaller firms) on the periphery.

A firm in monopolistic competition can determine optimum price and output-sales in the manner of a pure monopoly, as discussed above. The firm selects an output-sales rate that equates marginal cost with marginal revenue and maximizes profit, as depicted in Figure 8–8. Graphic and analytic techniques for quantitative determination (depicted in Chapter 9, Figure 9–8) can be used.

The competitive aspect of monopolistic competition enters through

Figure 8–8
Pricing and output of a profitable firm under monopolistic competition

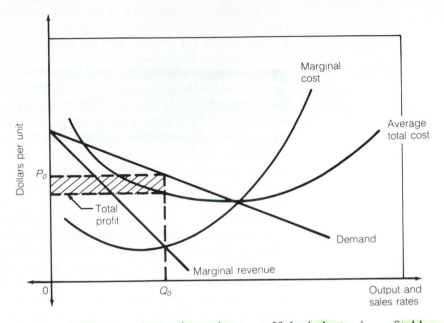

long-run adjustments of capacity and output. If the industry is profitable, new producers enter and existing suppliers expand. With each firm facing greater competition from close substitutes, its demand curve is shifted to the left and may be tilted so as to become more elastic. Profits of marginal firms are eliminated as their demand curves are pushed back to tangency with the average cost curves, as illustrated in Figure 8–9.

Well-managed companies in monopolistic competition may earn good returns on investment, year after year, despite the steady pressure of competitive forces. Wise choice of new technology can hold costs below those of marginal firms, and skill in nonprice competition (quality improvement and promotion) can push demand to the right, away from the tangency position (and perhaps tilt it so it becomes less elastic), so that profitability is maintained.

The firm is in short-term equilibrium at point A in Figure 8–9. This condition of equilibrium will continue so long as there is: (1) no upward or downward change in the demand curve or (2) no change upward or downward in the cost curves. However, at point A certain alleged wastes exist.

Alleged wastes

Example of monopolistically competitive firms include barbershops, most retail stores, the neighborhood bar, most grocery stores, most gas-

Figure 8–9
Pricing and output of a marginal firm under monopolistic competition

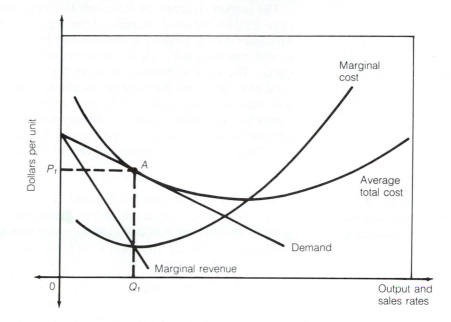

oline stations, small accounting firms, small law offices, and so on.[2] A feature these firms generally have in common is that households and other businesses will not demand services from them if their business is not idle at the time the household wants to be served. How long is the average consumer willing to wait in line for a haircut? The oil embargo of 1973 notwithstanding, how long would the average U.S. consumer wait in line to fill a gas tank? In urban areas of the United States, if the area around the gasoline pump is not empty or about to become empty, the consumer simply refuses to enter the situation and, instead, drives away not to consider filling the tank until sighting an empty gas pump in an uncrowded station. The gasoline station owner and/or pump must be available for purposes of providing gasoline throughout the day. If gasoline station services are going to be utilized only when it is obvious they are not busy, the cost of maintaining this idle capacity must be borne by those persons who ultimately use the service. The same is true for similar down time incurred by barbers. Many barbers sit in their own chairs longer than the combined time of all customers because customers are reluctant to get haircuts unless the barber is not busy. The economy is

---

[2] This statement does not include the oil companies who own the gasoline stations. The oil companies may belong more properly in the oligopolistic market structure.

alleged to be wasting the downtime incurred by these barbers, bartenders, beauty salon operators, and retail clerks.

The market structure of monopolistic competition is such that equilibrium can be obtained at point A in Figure 8–9, the point where the demand curve is tangent to the average total cost curve. Note that this equilibrium does not occur at the minimum point at the average total cost curve. The vertical distance between the minimum point of the average total cost curve and the equilibrium point, point A, as measured on the *y* axis represents the wastes in dollars per unit of this market structure. In a purely competitive structure, similar wastes do not exist because equilibrium occurs at the point of tangency between a perfectly elastic demand function and the minimum point of the average total cost curve.

Theory of deliberate demand shifting, with price taken as given

The discussion thus far has focused on the choice of price and output-sales rate, taking demand as given. But demand can be shifted by the seller's changes in product quality and promotion. The possibility of deliberately shifting the firm's demand curve introduces additional choices and decisions:

1. There is usually some least-cost combination of inputs for any given promotion activity or for any given improvement in product quality.
2. There is some least-cost combination of spending on promotion and spending on product quality that will minimize the total cost of any given shift in demand.
3. Demand becomes less and less responsive as spending for demand shifting is increased, so that there is some optimum total outlay for nonprice competition at any given price.
4. As demand is shifted, the best price may also change—in the final analysis, pricing, promotion, and product quality are variables to be determined simultaneously.

This section asks the reader to assume: (1) The total revenue function is a straight line because price remains constant as the sales rate is increased; (2) total cost at various sales rates is the sum of production costs for the basic or minimum salable product; and (3) the cost of demand shifting is determined by sales expansion.

The optimum output-sales rate at the given price is found in part A of Figure 8–10, at the point at which total revenue exceeds total cost by the greatest amount. This is the point in part B at which marginal cost is equal to marginal revenue (price). Notice that part B of the figure depicts demand as shifting to the right as the total cost increases due to product improvement and greater promotion. The optimum output-sales rate, to which there corresponds some optimum total outlay on product quality and promotion, cannot be determined graphically or analytically unless the firm has knowledge of the sales expansion path. Nevertheless, the

Figure 8–10

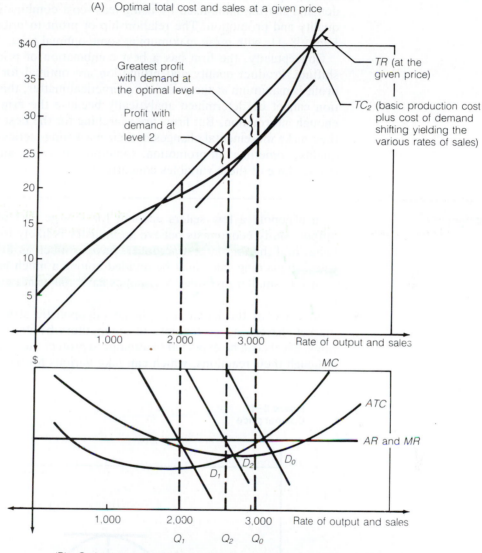

(A) Optimal total cost and sales at a given price

Greatest profit
with demand at
the optimal level

Profit with
demand at
level 2

TR (at the
given price)

TC₂ (basic production cost
plus cost of demand
shifting yielding the
various rates of sales)

Rate of output and sales

MC

ATC

AR and MR

D₂

D₀

D₁

Rate of output and sales

Q₁   Q₂   Q₀

(B) Optimal average and marginal cost and sales at a given price

concept depicted in Figure 8–10 shows what the firm is trying to do as it
makes incremental changes in its total outlays for demand shifting—to
get closer to the optimum output-sales rate for the given price.

The best combination of product quality, promotion, and price

Imagine for a moment that we have been able to carry out the above-
described analysis for each of several different prices. Thus, we are able

to plot a relationship of profit to price, with the total outlay for demand shifting optimal at each price and with outlay for any given amount of demand shifting minimized by using least-cost combinations of product quality and promotion. The relationship of profit to price will look like Figure 8–11, with profit maximum at some optimal price.

Conceptually, the firm has a best combination of price and demand shifting. Product quality and promotion are optimal for the price, and profit is maximum at the price. As a practical matter, this best combination cannot be determined analytically because the firm does not have enough information. But firms are searching for the best combination as they make incremental changes in their marketing tactics—sometimes in quality, sometimes in promotion, sometimes in price, and sometimes in two or three of these variables concurrently.

Oligopoly

In oligopoly a few sellers account for a large part of total industry output. Many economists believe an industry is likely to have oligopoly behavior if the four largest producers have as much as 40 percent of total sales. Remaining sales may be divided among a much larger number of relatively small firms; some oligopolies have 100 or more smaller producers.

Any one of the larger firms in an oligopolistic structure can affect market shares and profitability of competitors by its decisions and actions. Rivals can be expected to attempt to protect their market positions, although their reactions, which can take various forms, may be difficult

Figure 8–11
Optimal price

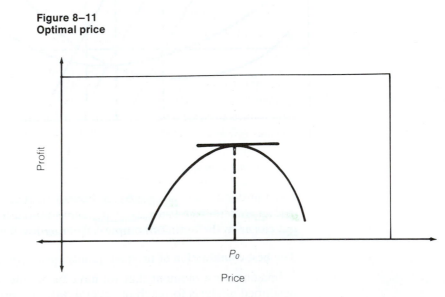

to predict. Competition among the larger firms is personal and volatile and increases the uncertainty surrounding decision making. The need to consider possible reactions of competing sellers in making decisions about pricing and other marketing tactics is a distinguishing feature of oligopoly structure.

There are two forms of oligopoly. In pure oligopoly the various firms sell a standardized product. Buyers of homogeneous or standardized products care little about who the supplier is, but they are interested in minimizing their procurement costs. They are usually very well informed about available supplies, pricing of recent transactions, and qualities of products. No supplier can do business at delivered prices higher than those of competitors, and any suppliers who beat competitive prices are deluged with more orders than they can fill. In most pure oligopolies the products have large costs of transportation in relation to value; as a result, suppliers have rising costs of delivery over increasing distances from plants. Thus, sellers in most pure oligopolies tend to develop geographically concentrated shares of the national market because prices are usually too low to cover variable costs of supplying to distant points. Some examples of pure oligopoly are aluminum, cement, copper, explosives, industrial fuels, red meat in bulk forms, steel, sugar, sulfur, and tin cans.

In differentiated oligopoly, each seller offers a particular combination of design, features, packaging, service, warranties, credit, promotion, and price. Buyers have preferences among products, and there can be continuing differences among prices of various suppliers. Each product has a market share, given the current prices, and each has a sloping demand curve that is quite elastic and shifts perceptibly with changes in prices or other marketing tactics of any of the larger firms. Some examples of differentiated oligopoly are automobiles, beer, breakfast cereals, canned soups, cigarettes, computers, farm machinery, gasoline, home laundry equipment, household refrigerators, razor blades, soaps and detergents, soft drinks, and television sets.

Entry into oligopolies is usually difficult. These industries usually have economies of scale continuing out to plant sizes that are large in relation to total industry output. A firm attempting to enter a pure oligopoly at a production rate great enough to have costs comparable to those of other firms may increase total industry outputs so much that prices are driven below costs for a considerable period of time. A producer attempting entry into a differentiated oligopoly may be at great disadvantage initially because established firms already have a wide distribution of products preferred by buyers. Thus, the new contender has higher unit costs at its lower rates of production and has heavy promotion costs in attempting to gain distribution and acceptance of the new product.

In some industries with differentiated products, there are a few large rivals and a much larger number of smaller firms in any given geographic area. These industries may have an oligopolistic structure from the point of view of the larger firms, although they have a monopolistically competitive structure from the viewpoint of the smaller firms, permitting independent changes in pricing or other marketing tactics without considering reactions by other firms. In these mixed-structure industries, economies of scale and the degree of product differentiation are not great enough to put smaller sellers at a definite disadvantage. Entry into such industries is relatively easy. Examples of industries in which large firms must operate as oligopolies and smaller ones can be monopolistically competitive are banking, insurance, and retailing.

Competitive behavior of firms in oligopolistic market structures can fall into several different patterns, and behavior in a given industry can shift from one pattern to another. No single theory of oligopoly pricing is sufficient. We shall look at several theories, each having some value in this discussion.

"Kinked" demand and "sticky" prices

The price and output behavior of the typical oligopolist is "sticky." When demand changes, prices and outputs change for all firms in the industry, but these changes are relatively slow in occurring. When the change does occur, all firms in the industry tend to adjust price by a similar amount, in the same direction, and at about the same time. For example, when General Motors announces a 5 percent or similar price increase on automobiles, Ford Motor and Chrysler Corporation can be expected to make similar announcements within a matter of days and, at times, within a matter of hours. In contrast, a campus pub might not increase its price of 12-ounce bottles of Michelob until many weeks after a competitor down the street had done so.

Suppose management of an oligopoly firm believes competitors will not follow a price increase but will promptly match any price decrease. Under these assumptions about reactions of rival firms, the oligopoly firm's demand curve is "kinked," with an abrupt change in slope at the current price and sales quantity. Quantity reduction for a small price increase is much greater than the quantity expansion for a comparable cut in price.

A kinked demand curve for an oligopolistic firm with a differentiated product is shown in Figure 8–12. Because of the sharp change at the kink in the response of quantity to a small change in price, the seller's marginal revenue function has two sections. The upper section defines marginal revenues at alternative prices above the current price, and the lower section specifies marginal revenues at alternative prices below the current price. The two sections of the marginal revenue curve are separated by a vertical gap at the current rate of output and sales.

**Figure 8–12
A kinked demand curve**

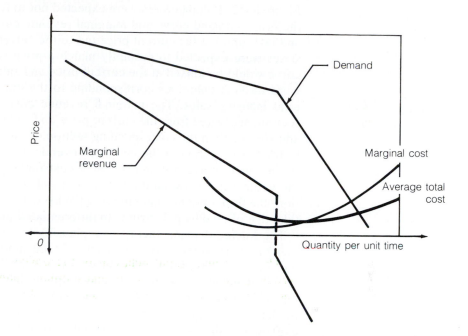

In the example depicted by Figure 8–12, the producer's average and marginal cost functions are positioned in the gap between the upper and lower sections of the firm's marginal revenue function. Thus, marginal revenue is higher than marginal cost at any output and sales rate less than the current level, whereas marginal revenue is lower than marginal cost at any rate more than the current quantity. The firm will be made worse off—contribution will be decreased—by any change in price.

Notice in Figure 8–12 that the producer's average and marginal cost functions could shift up or down for a considerable distance before marginal cost would become equal to marginal revenue at some price different from the current value, but shifting costs would eventually make it advantageous for the seller to change price. Note also that the seller's demand curve could make considerable shifts left or right, with the kink remaining at the current price, before the firm would stand to gain from a price change, although shifting demand would eventually lead to price adjustment. The producer's optimal output and sales quantities would shift with any movements of the demand curve. Assuming a kinked demand curve, the firm's pricing would be sticky, holding steady in the face of shifts of cost or demand over considerable ranges; the firm's output would be sticky in the face of cost shifts but would be immediately responsive to demand shifts.

An oligopolistic company selling a standardized product could perceive its demand curve as kinked but somewhat different from the curve in Figure 8–12. If competitors were expected not to follow a price increase, the firm's demand curve and marginal revenue curve would be identical and horizontal at the current price out to the current sales rate. If adversaries were expected to promptly match a price reduction, the demand curve would be kinked at the current price and sales rate, sloping downward through quantities corresponding to the firm's share of increasing total industry sales. The marginal revenue curve would have a lower section, separated from the current price and sales rate by a vertical gap and steeper than the corresponding section of the demand curve, similar to the lower section of the marginal revenue function in Figure 8–12. If the producer's average and marginal cost functions were positioned in the vertical gap between the two sections of the marginal revenue function, the firm's pricing and output behavior would be as described above (like that of an oligopoly firm with differentiated products).

The kinked-demand theory is a plausible model for an oligopolistic industry with some excess capacity shared among various producers more or less proportionately to their sales with a current price that is modestly profitable to most or all sellers, and with the larger companies having similar costs. However, kinked-demand theory is a short-run model. It can explain stickiness of prices at a given level, but it cannot explain how the industry got to that level or how it may move to another.

If all firms have similar shifts in cost or demand or both, a time may come when one of the larger producers believes that competitors will follow a price increase. The probability that they will follow is greatest if both costs and demand have increased—reducing profitably and increasing output until most firms are producing at or close to capacity. If other competitors are expected to follow a price increase, a theory of price leadership becomes useful.

Price leadership

Suppose management of an oligopoly firm believes its rivals will promptly follow a price increase within some range. The demand curve of the firm in question will be seen as smoothly sloping through the current price and sales quantity, with the quantities at higher or lower prices being the firm's share of total industry sales. It might at first appear that the seller can act as a monopolist, selecting a price and sales rate at which its own marginal cost and marginal revenue are equal and its own profits are maximum. However, other firms may not be willing to follow a price increase as great as the price leader would like to make.

A little thought suggests that the price increase by the price leader will not hold unless the other large firms perceive their own demand curves as being rekinked at the new price and also estimate that their marginal cost functions are positioned in the new gap between the two sections of their marginal revenue functions. If the price leader tries to set the price too high, one of the rivals may estimate that its marginal cost function passes through the lower section of the new marginal revenue function. If so, the rival will initiate a price reduction back to the level that it prefers. And other firms will follow the price down.

It appears that an oligopolist wishing to exercise price leadership is more effective if the following tactics are used:

1. The leader makes price changes infrequently, foregoing possible gains from small adjustments to avoid risks that the changes will be misinterpreted or opposed.
2. The company announces changes only in response to significant changes in cost and demand that are perceived by all firms in the industry.
3. Management prepares rivals for the forthcoming price change by speeches, interviews with the trade press, and general news releases.
4. The leader tries to select a new price that compromises conflicts of interest among various rivals; it pays particular attention to the short-run interests of larger producers that have low costs and excess capacity.

If (1) entry into an industry is quite difficult because of economies of scale, (2) there is little differentiation of products, and (3) the industry has a high concentration ratio with few small competitors—a pattern of collusion may replace the price leadership form of industry behavior.

Price wars

In a price war, price reduction by one rival is immediately undercut by another. The price level is driven well below the average cost of even the most efficient producers and may go even below the marginal cost of some firms that continue supplying the market because of long-run benefits from maintaining distribution and product acceptance. A condition of excess capacity combined with a large buildup of product inventory may lead to a price war. A price war eventually makes every firm weaker than it would have been at higher price levels, and all firms become willing to follow a leader in a price increase.

Price wars are usually limited to particular geographic areas. Companies with wide regional or national distribution are unlikely to undercut a price reduction by a rival, although they will often meet a price cut. If sellers with wide distribution undercut prices of a rival in a local market, without making similar reductions in all of their pricing, they are engaging in price discrimination that may injure a competitor—an action that is illegal. On the other hand, firms that serve only a small area can systematically undercut prices of regional or national companies because the small suppliers are reducing all of their prices. A price war is usually a mistake on the part of a small producer. These producers may believe that rivals will stop meeting their price reductions and thus leave room for the small firm to earn greater contributions on substantially increased output and sales, utilize excess capacities, and sell burdensome inventories. But the opponents usually continue to match the price cuts of the small contender.

The cartel

The price and output behavior of all businesses is determined in large part by profit expectations. Some firms have been known to fix price or market areas with other members of the same industry in order to maximize total profitability for each firm. This is a cartel, and it works something like this: A Cleveland-based manufacturer of sewer pipe might say, "I'll stay out of Chicago with my products if you, a Chicago-based manufacturer of sewer pipe, will stay out of Cleveland with your products."

By fixing prices and territories in which products will be sold, the cartel agreement causes the consumer to pay a higher price than would be paid under competitive conditions. Also, it provides the manufacturers with a smaller output. In an "I'll stay out of your market area and you stay out of mine" arrangement, each manufacturer can charge a noncompetitive price for products, and expects total profitability to increase. The only loser in such an arrangement is thought to be the ultimate consumer.

Cartel arrangements are out of the question in purely competitive product markets.[3] It is not so with imperfectly competitive ones. If a cartel exists, almost always it was formed during the expansionary phase of a business cycle. Almost always, the cartel will be profitable for at least some of its members during the short run. During the contractionary stage of a business cycle, the cartel is almost certain to fall apart, with or without government intervention.

Honesty among thieves may be a great theme in some old movies, but in real life it does not work. During the expansionary phase of the business cycle, business is good. All parties to the arrangement are operating at or near full capacity, and there may be little incentive to cut price or to invade another's territory. When economic conditions tighten, during the downturn in a business cycle, corporate profits (a leading U.S. economic indicator) drop dramatically, and the cartel dissolves. A shakeout takes place in the industry as the situation quite literally becomes one of "survival of the fittest."

An interesting cartel dissolution to watch in the early 1980s is the oil cartel started by certain Arab states and supported heavily by Iran, Venezula, and Mexico. The so-called OPEC nations did well financially

---

[3] Do you know why?

during the early 1970s expansion of the domestic American economy but were teetering on the brink of economic bankruptcy in the early 1980s. Their sorry financial condition and the cartel leading to it may one day be treated as a causal factor in yet another world war.

Collusion is based on recognition by each firm that both short-run and long-run interests are served by coordinated industry pricing above the level resulting from simple price leadership. Collusion involves agreement among rivals on pricing, market sharing, and/or other aspects of their interdependency. Collusion may be profitable for a time, but it is unwieldy because of the necessity for trust in setting up the agreements, the considerable conflicts of interest among the various participants with respect to market shares and plant capacity, and the difficulty of preventing concealed price cuts and other forms of cheating. Collusion also involves considerable personal risk to participants in the United States because it is illegal.

Cartels are illegal in the United States because, in effect, they charge monopoly prices. The price and output behavior of a monopolist is thought to be wasteful of scarce economic resources. Cartels are not only legal but, in fact, encouraged in many foreign nations because these nations believe that competition between and among firms is wasteful of scarce and costly resources. One should wonder if both arguments can be correct.

Nonprice competition

In differentiated oligopoly and without collusion, deliberate demand shifts through quality improvement and increased promotion are likely to receive more emphasis than are price reductions as the various producers strive for increased sales. Although competitors sometimes react to an oligopoly firm's changes in product and promotion, their responses may not be immediate, and they are unlikely to be head-on. Some or all competitors may wait to see the market response to the new tactics. If they do decide to mount a frontal counterattack against product changes or a new sales campaign, it takes time for them to make similar changes in their own products or promotion. On the other hand, they may elect to proceed with their own long-run marketing strategy rather than setting up a direct challenge to the new activities of the firm in question. Nonprice competition among the major adversaries in an oligopoly industry is not nearly as personal and direct as their price competition. Yet, it is very effective. Johnson and Johnson's promotion of its new, safer TYLENOL package is a nonprice example of a firm attempting to regain and maintain what it considers to be its proper share of a given market.

Under the assumption that there will not be immediate, head-on reaction by competitors, the economic analysis of deliberate demand shifting by an oligopolistic firm is very similar to the analysis for a monopoly.

Costs of any product improvement should be minimized by input substitution; costs of any increase in promotion should be minimized through substitutions among selling activities. Costs of demand shifting, to increase sales at a given price, should be minimized by substitution between product quality improvement and increased promotion. Optimal total outlay for demand shifting, at a given price, is found at the point where the marginal cost of production plus demand shifting becomes equal to price-marginal revenue (see Figure 8–10 and the corresponding discussion). Demand shifts to the right with a kink maintained at the current price, and the marginal revenue from increased sales is the current price.

Decision-tree analysis of an oligopoly firm's marketing alternatives

At the outset of the discussion of oligopoly structure, it was noted that: (1) The outcome of any change in an oligopoly firm's marketing behavior depends upon the responses of rivals; and (2) these reactions can take various forms, and there may be great uncertainty about them. A firm in an oligopolistic industry may benefit from a decision-tree approach to its complex choices among marketing tactics. Decision trees provide efficient organization of the firm's estimates of the payoffs or outcomes of various tactics, taking each of the possible response patterns as given, and the firm's subjective estimates of the probability of each of the response patterns. One major point to remember: The numbers used are not nearly as important as the methodology employed.

Constructing a basic decision tree

Suppose a medium-size firm in a differentiated oligopoly is considering whether or not to follow a price increase, which has just been announced by a competitor. Most firms in the industry are modestly profitable, and there is some excess capacity. The industry does not have an established pattern of following the company that has just raised its price. Management of one firm is concerned that the remaining producers in the industry may not follow this particular price hike.

If the firm in question promptly follows the attempted price leadership of the larger competitor, management believes that there is a 40 percent probability that other sellers will not follow, the price increase will have to be rescinded, and the firm will have some loss of business because of its participation in an abortive price increase. On the other hand, if the firm does not follow the larger company's price action but rather adopts a wait-and-see posture, management believes there is an 80 percent probability that none of the remaining suppliers will raise prices.

Outcomes of the firm's decision are as follows. If all firms match the price increase of the one large company, the firm in question expects net earnings of $1.2 million over the relevant planning period. If the firm in question follows but subsequently rescinds with a loss of business, management expects net earnings to be $800,000. If the firm waits to see what others will do and none follow, management projects net earnings of $1 million.

Figure 8–13 reveals how this problem is specified in a decision-tree format. The tree is composed of a series of nodes and branches, and it runs from left to right. At the extreme left, a square node represents a decision point—a point at which the firm may choose among alternatives. The branches leading to the right from the decision point are labeled to correspond to the various action alternatives; the alternatives in the example are "immediately follow" and "wait and see."

At the right end of each branch representing an action alternative, there is a round node representing a chance event point—a point at which there may be alternative "states of nature"—events that the firm in question cannot control. In the example, the chance events are the reactions of the other firms in the industry, and the branches leading to the right from the chance-event points are labeled to show the alternative response patterns. The alternatives in the example are "no other firms follow" and "all other firms follow."

At the extreme right of the decision tree are the firm's payoffs. Each payoff is an outcome resulting from a combination of a particular posture of the firm in question with a particular chance event. In the example, the firm's payoffs are measured in terms of net income. In other applica-

Figure 8–13
An oligopolist's decision tree

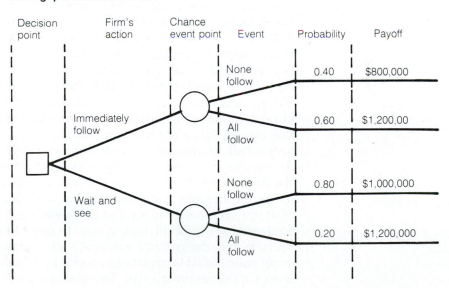

tions of decision trees, net cash flow, net worth, discounted present value of future net cash flows, or some other measure of payoff could be more appropriate.

Let us calculate the expected values of each of the alternative marketing tactics under consideration. The calculations begin at the payoffs on the extreme right. For the chance-event point at the top of Figure 8–13, there is 40 percent probability of a payoff of $800,000 and a 60 percent probability of a payoff of $1.2 million. The expected value of a posture at the upper chance event node is calculated as follows:

$$
\begin{array}{r}
0.40 \times \$\ \ 800{,}000 = \$\ \ 320{,}000 \\
0.60 \times \$1{,}200{,}000 = \underline{\$\ \ 720{,}000} \\
\$1{,}040{,}000
\end{array}
$$

Note that the expected value of an action or a decision is the average result that would be expected if this action or decision were carried out many times under the same conditions. The outcome of a single trial or the marketing tactic in the above example would be either $800,000 or $1.2 million.

The expected value of a posture at the lower chance event node can be calculated as:

$$
\begin{array}{r}
0.80 \times \$1{,}000{,}000 = \$\ \ 800{,}000 \\
0.20 \times \$1{,}200{,}000 = \underline{\ \ \ \ 240{,}000} \\
\$1{,}040{,}000
\end{array}
$$

If the firm in the above example is a simple odds player, willing to take its chances on averaging out over the long run, it will be indifferent as to which tactic is chosen. Management can simply flip a coin to determine what the firm will do. However, when management acts as an odds player, there are implicit assumptions that: (1) The game will go on and on, and (2) the final outcome of the game will be maximized if every decision is based on the greatest expected value. In other words, the worst possible outcome of any decision cannot stop the game; nor can it change the nature of the game in subsequent plays. In risky decisions that involve only a portion of the activity of a diversified firm, it may be appropriate to approach each decision as a simple odds player. However, the payoffs in the above example make up the entire operating results of the firm for whole accounting periods, and management may not feel indifferent between one tactic that has a downside potential as low as $800,000 and another tactic that has a minimum outcome of $1 million. Management is probably risk averse. In order to make proper use of the decision tree, the expected values of each posture of the firm at a chance event node should be replaced by a new set of values that reflect management's attitudes toward risk. The next section indicates how one might measure attitudes toward risk and incorporate them in a decision-tree approach.

Risk adjustment

Always attempt to measure management's attitudes toward risk as of a current, specified date.[4] One could begin by setting up the axes of a preference curve, as revealed in Figure 8–14. The horizontal axis is a scale of monetary value of payoffs. This scale should have a range at least as great as that of the outcomes of any decisions that are to be made. A range of $600,000 to $1.2 million is established for this example. The end points of the range of payoffs are called reference consequences. Label the lower end point R_0 and the upper end point R_1.

The vertical axis of the preference curve is used as a scale of relative preferences. Assign a preference value of 0 to R_0 and a preference value of 1.0 to R_1. Having established two points on the preference scale by definition, obtain several other points by assessment.

Pose the following questions to management. "Suppose you have placed your firm in a position in which there is a 50 percent chance of a $600,000 profit for the next period and a 50 percent chance of a $1.2

Figure 8–14
A preference curve

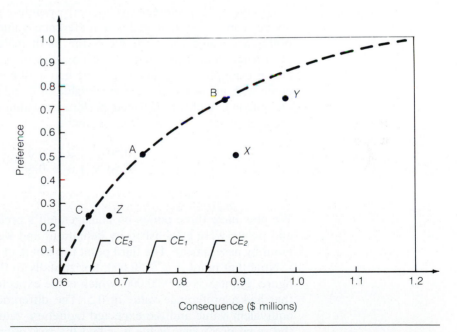

<hr>

[4] The explanation of risk adjustment in this text is based on John S. Hammond, "Better Decisions with Preference Theory," *Harvard Business Review*, November–December 1967.

million profit. Suppose a very wealthy person comes along and offers to pay you cash for the rights to receive your firm's net earnings during the period. You will have no risk whatsoever. If the person offers you $700,000, will you accept the offer?''

Management immediately replies, in chorus, ''No!'' It is saying in effect, that a certainty equivalent value of $700,000 is not worth as much as a gamble that has a 50 percent chance of $600,000 and a 50 percent chance of $1.2 million. Expected value of this particular gamble is $900,000.

Next ask management if it would accept an offer of $800,000. The quick response is ''Yes, of course.'' This answer reveals the management team to be risk averse (most are), since it will accept a sure thing of $800,000 in place of a gambling posture that has an expected value of $900,000.

Follow by asking management if it will accept $750,000. The query leads to considerable discussion, a discussion very similar in style, content, and substance to discussions that take place during merger and/or acquisition negotiations. The group appears to be almost equally divided. After a time, there is consensus on acceptance of the offer. The value of $750,000 can be regarded as a certainty equivalent of the assumed gamble. (A certainty equivalent is a value barely acceptable in lieu of a gamble.) This is the first certainty equivalent obtained by assessment, label it CE_1 on the horizontal axis.

To obtain the preference value corresponding to the gamble assumed above, use a rule that yields a preference value for any gamble: The preference value for a gamble is the mathematical expectation of the preferences corresponding to the consequences of the gamble. In the above example, the assumed gamble had a 50 percent chance of an outcome with an assigned preference value of 0 and a 50 percent chance of an outcome with an assigned preference value of 1.0. Therefore, the preference value for the assumed gamble is:

$$
\begin{array}{r}
0.50 \times \quad 0 = 0.0 \\
0.50 \times 1.0 = \underline{0.5} \\
0.5
\end{array}
$$

We now have three points on management's preference curve. The two end points were established by definition, and we have obtained a third point by assessment. The third point is point A in Figure 8–14.

Note that point A is $150,000, horizontally to the left of point X in the figure. Point X is at $900,000, which is the expected value of this gamble that had a preference value of 0.5. The difference between a certainty equivalent value and the expected monetary value of a gamble that has the same preference value is called the risk premium. In the above example, the risk premium is $900,000 − $750,000, or $150,000.

To obtain another point on management's risk preference curve, set up a hypothetical gamble with a preference value of 0.75. This gamble will have a 50 percent chance of an outcome with a preference value of 0.5 (in the example, $750,000 has just been determined by assessment to have a preference value of 0.5) and a 50 percent chance of an outcome with a preference value of 1.0 (in the example, $1.2 million has been assigned a preference value of 1.0). By a series of questions similar to those used in obtaining the first certainty equivalent, bracket and then pinpoint a certainty equivalent value that has the same preference value as the hypothetical gamble—eventually obtaining $875,000, shown as point B in Figure 8–14. This value, labeled CE_2 on the horizontal axis, is a certainty equivalent of a gamble with an expected value of $975,000 and a preference value of 0.75, as shown in the figure by point Y.

Next set up a hypothetical gamble with a preference value of 0.25. Remember that the preference value of a gamble is the mathematical expectation of the preference values corresponding to the outcomes of the gamble. The next gamble will have a 50 percent chance of an outcome with a preference value of 0 (in the example, $600,000 as initially assigned) and a 50 percent chance of an outcome with a preference value of 0.5 (in the example, $750,000 as determined by assessment). By a series of questions, one may eventually obtain CE_3, $650,000, as the certainty equivalent of a gamble that has an expected monetary value of $675,000 and a preference value of 0.25, a gamble represented in the figure by point Z.

Notice what has been done. We began by assigning preference values of 0 and 1.0, respectively, to the outcomes $600,000 and $1.2 million. Then we asked a series of questions to elicit a certainty equivalent value (CE_1) to a gamble with a preference value of 0.5 (that is, a gamble with a 50 percent chance of an outcome with a preference value of 0 and a 50 percent chance of an outcome with a preference value of 1.0). By similar techniques, we obtained certainty equivalent value CE_2 for a gamble with a preference value of 0.75 and certainty equivalent value CE_3 for a gamble with a preference value of 0.25.

The assessment process can be continued to obtain certainty equivalent values corresponding to preference values of 0.375, 0.625, 0.875, and so on, until enough points are estimated that a smooth curve can be sketched, as revealed in Figure 8–14.

Now see how the preference curve is used in obtaining risk-adjusted values to replace the expected values at the chance event nodes of a decision tree. Begin with the upper chance-event node of the decision tree in Figure 8–13. First, replace the payoff of $800,000 by the corresponding preference value of 0.6 from management's preference curve, and replace the payoff of $1.2 million by the corresponding present value of 1.0. These changes are shown in Figure 8–15. Next, calculate the mathematical expectation of the preferences:

$$0.40 \times 0.6 = 0.24$$
$$0.60 \times 1.0 = \underline{0.60}$$
$$0.84$$

Finally, use the preference curve to find the monetary certainty equivalent of a preference value of 0.84. From the curve in Figure 8–14, this is $970,000. The expected monetary value of the gamble at the upper node of the decision tree is $1,040,000, so there is a risk premium of $70,000 for this particular gamble.

By the method described above, a certainty equivalent value can be determined for the lower chance event node of the decision tree in Figure 8–13. Replace $1 million by the corresponding preference value of 0.87, and replace $1.2 million by the corresponding preference value of 1.0. These changes have been made in Figure 8–15. Then calculate the mathematical expectation of preferences for the lower chance event node:

$$0.80 \times 0.87 = 0.70$$
$$0.20 \times 1.00 = \underline{0.20}$$
$$0.90$$

From the preference curve in Figure 8–14, the certainty equivalent corresponding to a preference value of 0.90 is $1,030,000. Since the gamble

Figure 8–15
A risk-adjusted decision tree

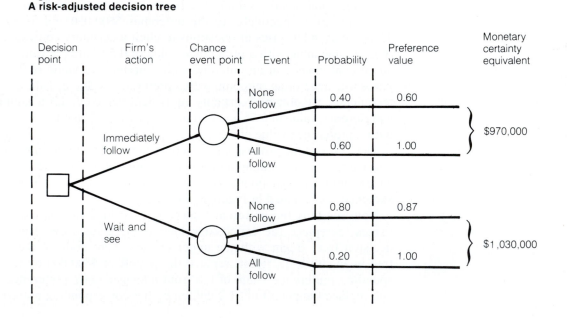

at the lower chance event node had an expected monetary value of $1,040,000, the risk premium is $10,000.

It can be seen that the certainty equivalent value of the lower chance event node of the decision tree in Figure 8–13 is greater than the certainty equivalent value of the upper chance event node ($1,030,000 is greater than $970,000). So the marketing tactic that places the firm in the posture at the lower node is the best choice.

Other applications of decision trees

Decision trees can be constructed for any decision about marketing tactics that must be made by an oligopoly firm. Decisions about pricing, quality changes, or promotion can be handled, whatever the possible responses of rivals may be. Decisions involving discounting costs and revenues of future periods (to take the time value of money into account) are not difficult. A special strength of the decision-tree approach is that decisions involving action—chance event—action chains can be structured. Space allows no further discussion of the technique at this point, but additional explanation can be found in Chapter 11 on capital budgeting.

Pricing strategies and an appraisal of several shortcut approaches in pricing

The market structures of monopoly, monopolistic competition, and oligopoly belong in the category known as imperfectly competitive market structures. Pure or perfect competition as a structure stands alone. Within the imperfectly competitive market structures there exists an extremely large number of firms that, when taken together, have a multiplicity of goals and objectives. These imperfectly competitive firms are able to achieve one or more of their short- and long-term objectives by relying upon a particular pricing strategy. A closer look at some of their pricing policies is in order.

In pricing to be competitive, neither oligopolists nor monopolistically competitive firms allow their prices to be too far out of line from those of their competitors. The time lag needed to bring prices in agreement with one another may vary considerably from firm to firm and industry to industry; yet, if the firm in an imperfectly competitive market structure expects to exist in the long run, retaining for itself its fair share of the business conducted in that industry, its prices will have to be more or less in line with those of everyone else. A truly unique product or service may be able to command a price higher than that obtained by competing firms within the industry, but this higher price will prove to be available in the short run only.

Some companies may find it advantageous not to charge a price in excess of that being charged by everyone else in the industry, even if market conditions allow it. A firm hoping to achieve normal profits in the long run may try to do so by charging a price low enough to prevent the entrance of new firms into the industry. Combining this tactic with min-imization of cost curves may, in both the short and long terms, help assure the continued existence of profitable operations.

Lanzillotti found that The Goodyear Tire and Rubber Company and the National Steel Company both had as primary pricing goals the match-ing or meeting of competitor prices.[5] Although American Can considered meeting or matching competitor prices as important, it was of secondary importance to them. American Can's primary pricing goal was and con-ceivably still is that of maintaining their share of the total market for all types of cans produced.

Pricing strategies designed to match, meet, or prevent competition appear to be commonplace in American business and industry. Specific short- and long-term pricing plans for a larger number of specific corpo-rations are difficult if not impossible to obtain. For that reason, they are not cited here.

Any one among us could easily find the name of the chief executive officer of any major corporation in the United States. We could likewise find the name of the person in charge of production, marketing, finance, and so on. But most firms do not have a vice president in charge of pricing. Pricing decisions are made by committees, which are composed of one or more top-management officials from the functional areas of law, finance, production, and so on. When attempting to determine the pricing strategy of a particular corporation, one must speak with one or more of the persons who serve on the pricing committee. This person's response may or may not be the official corporate policy on pricing but, instead, what she/he as a committee member thinks the pricing situation ought to be. The committee member may be revealing what the situation could be or what the pricing situation will be one day if she/he becomes chief executive officer of the corporation. Consequently, specific pricing objec-tives, goals, and strategies of specific firms can be acquired and relied upon with certainty only after those pricing practices have been put into effect, and even then, one would know only the pricing policy actually followed by the company, not necessarily the pricing policy the company had intended to follow. For example, on paper the J. C. Penney Company has a pricing policy on its soft goods that is determined independent of prices charged by Sears and Wards. In practice, however, managers of one or more of the 1,600 J. C. Penney stores throughout the nation have a store policy of not allowing Sears or Wards to sell similar products at lower prices. Policy at the local level appears to be one of not allowing individual departments within the store to be undersold because prices at

---

[5] Robert V. Lanzillotti, ''Pricing Objectives in Large Companies,'' *American Economic Review,* December 1958, pp. 305–6.

the competing Sears and Wards stores are slightly less than those charged by Penney's. In each instance, the Penney manager may lower price to match the competitor.

Percent of total market

Some firms follow a pricing policy that is designed to give them a certain share of the total market for a specific product. If four, five, or six firms do 80 to 85 percent of the total business conducted in a given industry, it is conceivable that each firm would like to have approximately 25 percent or so of the total industry for itself. One of these firms having only 13 or 14 percent of the market might be expected to pursue a very aggressive pricing policy that would be designed to increase its share. A corporation that has gained and maintained an almost monopolistic position in the industry and has become the price leader might follow a pricing policy that would cause its market share to decline to something in the neighborhood of 50 percent or less. In the case of this dominant firm in the industry, a pricing policy designed to reduce market share could serve to increase long-term profitability for the firm. Profit improves if the reduction in market share causes the antitrust division of the Justice Department not to enact certain provisions of the Sherman Act. Monopoly, per se, is illegal; and court costs, attorney fees, blemished reputations, and the resultant impact on the corporate image, to cite a few reasons, may cause a firm to intentionally decrease its share of a given market.

A primary pricing objective of Kroger, Standard Oil of Indiana, and Swift appears to be following pricing practices that allow them to maintain market share. On the other hand, A&P has apparently pursued a pricing policy designed to increase its market share. Each firm must determine its price after giving serious consideration to its current and anticipated percentage of total business available in the industry.

Return on investment: Benchmark figures

During the expansionary phase of a busienss cycle, the typical oligopolistic firm may be operating at or near 85 percent of rated capacity. During this period the price charged for finished products depends in large part on (1) the internal rate of return the corporation hopes to earn on all new business and (2) the target rate of return it hopes to achieve for all business. A new business investment is profitable to the firm so long as the finished product can be sold at a price that results in the internal rate of return (IRR) being equal to or greater than the firm's marginal cost of capital (MCC). This matter is discussed in greater detail in Chapter 11.

The average rate of return on investment may be expressed as the ratio of the firm's profit after tax *(PAT)* to its investment cost *(I)*. In other words,

$$\text{Average rate of return} = PAT/I$$

It is the average rate of return that many firms attempt to maximize when they establish price for their product.

If a McDonalds, Burger King, Wendys, or similar drive-in–restaurant franchise originally cost $150,000, and each establishment earned an annual income after taxes of $33,000, the average rate of return could be calculated as follows:

$$
\begin{aligned}
\text{Average rate of return} &= PAT/I \\
&= \$33,000/\$150,000 \\
&= 22 \text{ percent}
\end{aligned}
$$

A corporation owning one or more outlets might decide to buy additional franchises (1) if it is satisfied with a 22 percent rate of return on investment after tax and (2) if it were reasonable to assume that this average rate of return could be used as a target for subsequent investment decisions.

Libbey-Owens-Ford (LOF) is a large manufacturer of plate glass windows for the automobile industry. It might be willing to acquire new pieces of capital equipment for purposes of manufacturing glass windows that would meet the specifications of the smaller American-made automobiles, such as GM's Cadillac Cimarron, if the price to be charged would allow an average rate of return on that investment equal to or greater than the target returns established internally by the company. The LOF decision regarding the price of windshields for the Cimarron would be heavily influenced by (1) the target rate of return established by LOF, (2) the historical average rate of return it has been able to earn on GM business to date, (3) the probability of losing the Cadillac windshield order to Pittsburgh Plate Glass or another competitor after having made the capital investment necessary to manufacture the equipment and after having quoted a price. The possibility of losing business to another firm within the same industry almost always exists and is one reason for the stickiness of prices in all oligopolistic models.

In deciding what price to quote and establishing the target rate of return on new investment, LOF in this example and oligopolistic firms in general must consider the adverse impact on average rate of return caused by losing a valued customer to a competitor. Conscientious executives also consider the impact on the local community in terms of employment, taxes, schools, streets, sewers, and so on. These factors are affected, adversely or otherwise, by pricing decisions. In this windshield example, if LOF lost a major contract because of faulty pricing decisions, the city of Toledo, Ohio, and its suburbs (i.e., Northwood Local School District) might suffer.

The actual return on a particular investment may be somewhat lower than the target returns initially specified by the firm. Since amplitude fluctuations about the target mean returns take place, many firms establish relatively high targets. If the most pessimistic of events takes place, they may earn a rate of return on investment considerably less than anticipated. But this lower return must exceed the firm's marginal cost of capital, on average, so that the firm is able to make a profit even if the most pessimistic of events occurs.

Target rates of return on investment are often lower than actual returns. Reasons for this occurrence include: (1) management's desire to report profits to stockholders that are greater than those initially targeted, (2) price inflation that proceeds at rates more rapid than anticipated by management, and (3) perhaps not adjusting the targeted rate of return for probable changes in the overall price level.

Target rates of return on investment are relatively easy to calculate, and they provide management with another analytic device against which to (1) measure returns on investment with respect to plans for progress (how returns compare with past and projected returns), (2) compare returns with similar data for other oligopolistics within the same industry, and (3) compare returns with other oligopolistics in other industries. This latter comparison is essential to the firm's long-term well-being. If a firm consistently fails to achieve reasonably established target rates of return on investment, that firm should perhaps diversify into a different line of economic activity.

Other parties involved in pricing

Managers responsible for pricing decisions must consider a variety of other people concerned with price. Oxenfeldt lists seven parties: those responsible for sales promotion, the ultimate customers for the product, rival sellers, potential rivals, wholesalers, suppliers, and the government.[6] Although economic theory usually stresses only two of these parties—buyers and sellers—the pricing process must take all of them into account, for they are all involved in the pattern of communication and influence that determines the final outcome.

The case of the wholesaler brings out the complexity of the pricing environment. Most manufacturers distribute their products through wholesalers rather than directly. The mutual interests of the manufacturer and the wholesaler are obscure. The manufacturer would like the wholesaler to carry the product at a minimum markup, but the margin

---

[6] Alfred R. Oxenfeldt, *Pricing for Marketing Executives,* (Belmont, Calif.: Wadsworth, 1961).

must be large enough to stimulate a desire to carry and push the product. The manufacturer would like a variety of wholesalers to provide a wide coverage of the market, but wholesalers often want to handle products on an exclusive basis. The manufacturer may wish to control prices charged to retailers and even control the retail price, but wholesalers may wish to expand sales by cutting the price or wish to obtain a larger margin than the suggested price provides. A reduction of price by the manufacturer may reduce the value of the wholesaler's inventories, a fact that may lead to resentment unless some adjustment is made. Many of these issues are resolved by reference to trade policies and customs.

The relation of the government to pricing decisions is an especially painful one to many businesses. Especially difficult is the problem of avoiding price discrimination of the sort deemed illegal under the Robinson-Patman Act. Most multiproduct firms, especially those with widespread markets, engage in price discrimination in a broad sense. The problem is to determine when such discrimination becomes illegal in the sense of the statutes. The criteria of legality require a determination of whether the pricing practices injure rivals or tend to lessen competition. They also require consideration of whether or not price differences reflect cost differences—for example, the lower costs made possible by supplying large quantities to certain customers. Similar difficulties arise in the interpretation of statutes and court decisions governing resale-price maintenance, sales below cost, basing-point systems of pricing, and a variety of other pricing practices.

Virtually all large firms pay some attention to target rates of return on investment when establishing prices, but the literature indicates little evidence of rigid adherence to mechanical implementation of prices that would assure realization of those targets. Firms in the private section of the U.S. economy appear to favor price stabilization.

Price stabilization

Return on investment (ROI) is determined by expressing earnings as a percent of sales and multiplying that quotient by the turnover of investments. The turnover factor is determined by dividing the firm's sales by its total investment. Many firms prefer to charge a price that is relatively stable over a long period of time. These firms may increase ROI by increasing the number of times they turn over their investment. Such firms do not object to a low profit margin on each unit sold, provided they sell a large number of units.

Apparently, A&P pursues a pricing policy that allows it to receive a low profit margin per unit sold but allows the sale of a large number of units. The Ma and Pa type grocery store, by comparison, insists upon a high profit margin. When associated with a low inventory turnover, such a policy may cause a relatively low return on investment (ROI).

A corporation's profit is affected, adversely or otherwise, by its pricing policy. During the early months of an expansionary phase of the business cycle, corporate profits increase at a rate more rapid than increases in other economic variables. Generally speaking, the category called corporate profits is a leading economic indicator. During the downward, or contractionary, stage of the business cycle, corporate profits generally decline at a rate more rapid than other economic variables. Expressed in terms of corporate profitability, the firms do well during expansions and are hurt badly during contractions. An oligopolistic firm, acting alone, cannot eliminate this situation but can alleviate the situation by charging a constant price throughout the contraction and expansionary stages of all business cycles. Stabilization of price in this manner allows the firm to do the following:

1. Retain the goodwill of all customers during the recessionary periods.
2. Smooth some of the peaks and valleys that occur otherwise in its profitability picture.
3. Reinforce the theory of "sticky" oligopolistic prices at some point A, as in Figure 8–12. (This reinforcement of the theory is beneficial to the firm if it helps explain that price is not influenced by cartels, unwritten agreements, or other forms of collusive activity but is, instead, based on sound economic principles.)
4. Earn a relatively stable rate of return on investment.

A multiplicity of corporate policies and procedures go into the price-making decision for any company. No single executive at the oligopolistic firm is charged with the overall responsibility of the pricing decision. Many firms rely more heavily on one pricing practice than others, but most firms use a combination of all factors in determining price. Some firms determine the price they will charge for a product before they produce it.

Price-cost pricing

A characteristic of the oligopolistic product market is that entry into the industry is difficult, if not all but impossible. When was the last time a new firm entered the U.S. steel, automobile, glass, or cigarette-manufacturing industry? Oligopolists tend to belong to one particular industry more than to any other industry but can have heavy commitments in more than one industry. For example, the B. F. Goodrich Company is considered to be a member of the rubber industry; yet, it is heavily engaged in the chemical industry. A similar statement could be made for many diversified, multiproduct, multiplant oligopolistic firms.

General Electric manufactures refrigerators at the Kelvinator plant on the south side of Chicago. The plant makes harvest gold, avocado green, and white refrigerators plus many different sizes of freezers, requiring different kinds of insulation. Some units have automatic ice-makers, and some are without; but separate pricing arrangements must be established for each finished product. The method of price determination depends upon how long a product has been in the corporate line.

If the product to be priced is one the corporation has been selling for a relatively long time, the price will be sticky at or near some point (as with point A in Figure 8–12). The prices of these established products tend to move in the same direction by about the same amount and at the same time, as explained previously. But what about the pricing of new products?

When a corporation decides to enter a new line of economic activity by producing, distributing, and selling a new product, price may be determined first, and then engineers, industrial managers, cost accountants, and so on are told to produce a product that will yield a satisfactory profit margin when sold at the predetermined price. These firms try not to engage in cost-plus pricing.

When General Motors decided to enter the small car field several years ago with its Vega, it established a price level at which the Vega would be expected to compete. At that time GM engineers and others were told to produce a car that would be priced competitively with Volkswagon and other foreign imports. The price range of Volkswagen and other vehicles with which the Vega would be expected to compete was well known to even the most casual observers in the automobile market. GM established the price of Vega and then committed itself to the task of keeping unit cost, on average, lower than unit price of the finished product. This pricing technique is heavily relied upon by many large oligopolists.

Cost-plus pricing

Cost-plus pricing is assumed by some economists to be the primary method of actual business pricing. Presumably, business firms determine the overall cost of manufacturing a particular product, mark up that cost by some predetermined profit margin, and use the resulting figure as the price for which the product will be sold in the open market. If firms have a good knowledge of per-unit costs of products and can be oblivious to competitive factors in the open market, this cost-plus pricing technique has considerable merit. Otherwise, it does not.

This method assumes the firm is able to determine a standard cost per unit of output. It assumes a predetermined target rate of return on investment exists and is known to the corporation. This standard cost is supposed to be marked up by a specified amount, and the resulting figure becomes market price. *Standard cost* as used in this procedure is synonymous with the firm's *full cost of operations*. This is a full-cost system of pricing, and most firms should not rely upon full-cost pricing procedures, even if the firm is capable of determining with some degree of precision what the actual unit costs are. (Exact unit cost data are almost always unavailable.) Reasons for not wanting to follow a full-cost pricing process evolve mostly around capacity. Only when excess capacity exists should a company attempt to recover full costs in price.

Full-cost pricing is assumed by some businesspeople to be the normal technique, but it is not. However, individual firms often contribute to the confusion with respect to cost-plus pricing. Consider the oligopolist who has entered into an employment contract with a union requiring, say, a 6 percent raise to become effective at some specified future date. Since the oligopolist employs a relatively large number of persons, the wage agreement is of interest to the general public and appears in the press. Company officials might say that since a 6 percent increase has been granted in wages, it will be necessary to increase prices by 6 percent. In other words, since costs have risen by 6 percent, prices will have to rise by a like amount. Would such a statement be valid? Did costs go up by 6 percent? No!

If wages go up by 6 percent and the firm is following a cost-plus pricing policy and wants to pass these costs on to the consumer, prices will have to increase only by the amount of the increase in wages, not the percentage increase in wages. Assume wages account for 60 percent of the total cost of doing business for this firm. The firm would have to increase prices, on average, by 3.6 percent (6 percent of 60 percent) to pass to the ultimate consumer no more than the increased cost of the wage package. The only time prices should go up by an amount equal to the percentage increase in the wage agreement is if 100 percent of all costs were for wages. What oligopolistic firm operating within the confines of the domestic American economy is that labor intensive? When corporations complain publicly that they must pass the cost of wage increases on to the consumer, they lend support to the cost-plus theory of pricing.

Full-cost pricing

One difficulty in discussing full-cost pricing is the absence of a generally accepted definition. In this book full-cost pricing means pricing at a level covering total costs, including overhead, plus a predetermined markup. The view that full-cost pricing must assure profitable business operations is widespread. Some writers and trade associations consider the method to be a "scientific approach" to pricing, presumably because it substitutes a formula for subjective judgments. Other writers claim that the method is a reasonable way of dealing with uncertainty and ignorance.

If managers do not know the shape or position of their firms' demand curves, they may find it convenient to adopt a technique that does not require such knowledge. If they are strongly motivated by questions of fairness and justice in pricing, they may adopt a formula that treats all categories of customers alike at all times, regardless of market conditions. Full-cost pricing may help assure prices that are related to long-run cost in such a way as to discourage the entry of new competition into the industry. Last, full-cost pricing may, if adopted by all members of the industry, help protect the firms against price wars and cutthroat price competition, at the same time providing some flexibility in adjusting prices to cost changes.

It might be contended that overhead allocations and profit markups of full-cost pricing help assure that facilities are not allocated to products that fail to carry their share of overhead and produce their share of profit. If firms always operated at full capacity, the logic of this argument would be more appealing. In a world of cyclical change, of seasonality in demand, of varying price elasticities, and of complementary relations in demand, it is diffucult to see how full-cost pricing can approach optimal profits.

In addition, it should be noted that full-cost pricing accepts the accountant's definition of costs, with its stress on original costs, its questionable treatment of opportunity costs, and its arbitrary allocations of overhead. It seems unlikely that a price formula based on an inflexible and (for economic purposes) erroneous view of costs can lead to profitable operations.

This discussion of full-cost pricing does not state that the method is entirely without merit, but it does suggest that managers should carefully consider whether or not it meets the needs of a particular situation before accepting it.

Pricing checklist[7]

To determine its needs, a firm should consider several factors before arriving at a pricing policy:

1. Consideration of price-volume relationships (elasticities of demand) to determine what happens to total revenue at various prices.
2. Comparison of those price-volume relationships with incremental costs to determine the most profitable price on each item.
3. Estimation of the contribution to overhead and profits on each product that can be produced with the given facilities.
4. Selection of those products and sales at those prices that will assure the largest contributions to overhead and profits.
5. Investment in new facilities according to the estimated profits in the future of alternative products at optimum prices, taking costs into account.

---

[7] This list is based upon the following works: Dean, Joel, *Managerial Economics* (Englewood Cliffs, N.J.: Prentice-Hall, 1951); Oxenfeldt, Alfred R., *Pricing for Marketing Executives* (Belmont, Calif.: Wadsworth, 1961); Haynes, W. Warren, *Pricing Decisions in Small Business* (Westport, Conn.: Greenwood, 1973).

6. Flexibility of prices over time to meet changing market and cost conditions, unless there are strong arguments against flexibility (possible retaliation, high costs of changing decisions, etc.).

7. Consideration of the impact of price changes on the image of the company in the market, on customer goodwill, and on the firm's reputation for fair prices.

8. Consideration of the impact that price changes in one commodity may have on the sales of other items.

9. Experimentation with price changes, when this is not too costly to determine what customer responses are likely to be.

10. Determination of how much customers will benefit from price reductions, for this will give some clues as to the response to price changes.

11. Comparison of the long-range implications of price changes with the immediate impact of those changes.

12. Consideration of the life cycle of the product, with different price strategies for new products than for mature products facing a decline in demand.

13. Consideration of competitors' reactions to price changes.

14. Evaluation of the impact of price changes on the entry or exit of competitive rivals.

15. Coordination of price policies with other marketing policies, so that these are consistent and complementary.

16. Determination of the incremental costs or marginal costs of each product, even when full-cost pricing is applied, in order to evaluate the impact of full-cost pricing from time to time.

17. Avoidance of overestimating how much can be accomplished by pricing alone; it is only one phase of management and cannot guarantee profitable operations.

Overall, reliance at some point upon incremental reasoning is beneficial.

Incremental reasoning in pricing

Neither the traditional theory of the firm, with its high level of abstraction and generalization, nor the widely known shortcut formulas, with their inflexibility, provide the complete answer to the pricing problem. Economic theory, for example, reveals in imperfectly competitive product markets that production occurs at the point at which the marginal revenue and marginal cost curves intersect. Price is determined by guiding off the demand or average revenue function. In pure competition, price is the marginal revenue curve. As a practical matter, the typical oligopolist finds it virtually impossible to change output by only one unit.

With output measured on the horizontal axis and price on the vertical, assume that the horizontal axis represents the revenue-ton-miles flown by United Airlines. If United has a flight that leaves Chicago for Miami and bases its decision of the number of miles to be flown on the point at which the marginal revenue and marginal cost curves intersect on an oligopolistic demand function (as in Figure 8–12), it is conceivable profit would be maximized somewhere south of Atlanta. How would the airplane, its crew, passengers, and freight make it the rest of the way to Miami?

Marginal revenue and marginal cost help to establish price and output levels within one or more of four theoretically sound market models. The degree of preciseness with respect to output implied by these marginal curves is neither desired nor possible in the real world. Yet, the concepts are sound and must be applied in the real world if the firm is to maximize its position, however defined. Oligopolistic firms maximize their position in the market if they price a project in a manner that will allow incremental revenue to be greater than or equal to incremental cost. Incrementalism is the same as marginalism except that it refers to the change in revenue and/or cost per project (or per airline run in this case), instead of per unit of output or per mile.

In the Chicago to Miami flight, for example, marginal revenue would have been a rate of change in total revenue per revenue-ton-mile flown. Incremental revenue would simply be the change in total revenue to United Airlines as a result of putting on the Chicago to Miami run. United's incremental costs are the changes in total costs incurred by the airlines as a result of flying from Chicago to Miami—the total cost of all the fuel consumed, meals served, tires purchased, landing fees paid, maintenance crews employed, salaries paid to crew members, and other direct costs associated with the flight. If the change of total revenue from the flight is equal to or greater than the change in total costs of the flight, if incremental revenue exceeds incremental cost, incremental profit is positive and the flight should be made. Moreover, all short-run pricing decisions should be made on this kind of incremental basis by oligopolistic firms, provided excess capacity exists within the firm.

The incremental approach considers only the increases in out-of-pocket costs associated with the project and compares these costs with the increases in revenues that will result from the project. The difference, by definition, is incremental profit. (Note: No overhead costs are included in the incremental analysis. Fixed costs are "sunk" in the short run and need not be covered on the incremental basis if the firm is to function profitably). In this United Airlines example in which excess capacity exists, depreciation on the aircraft itself and other fixed costs that may exist in connection with the overall operation of United Airlines Company, Inc. should not be considered when the decision is made to go or not go from Chicago to Miami.

Corporate executives are reluctant to acknowledge that fixed costs are in fact sunk in the short run and for that reason often prefer to follow a price-cost method of pricing or, as indicated earlier, some form of cost-plus pricing procedure. The cost-plus pricing procedure is, in effect, a full-cost process and is one that, if followed, allows profit maximization to the firm only if that firm is operating at capacity in the short run. Virtually no oligopolistic firm operates normally at anything greater than 80 to 85 percent of capacity; consequently, most oligopolists have some excess capacity. If a firm finds itself operating at 90 to 95 percent of capacity, it expands its production capabilities, and it reverts to a condition of excess capacity.

Incremental reasoning leans heavily on economic theory, but it reformulates the theory in a form more suitable for decision making.

Incremental reasoning in its most general form states: If a pricing decision leads to a greater increase in revenue than in costs, it is sound; if it leads to a greater reduction in costs than in revenues, it is favorable. What incremental reasoning amounts to, therefore, is the comparison of the impact of decisions on revenues and costs. Such reasoning does not, however, require a restriction of attention to revenues, costs, and profits; it permits, indeed it requires, consideration of the extent to which the decision contributes to or detracts from other goals. Recognition of multiple goals requires weighing of objectives and, at the present state of knowledge, considerable subjective judgment. One way of handling this difficulty is to concentrate first on the impact of the decision on profits and later to adjust for other considerations.

Applying incremental reasoning to pricing decisions requires a full play of the imagination to make certain that all repercussions of the decision are taken into account. The following should be helpful:

1. In evaluating the cost of impact of the pricing (and output) decision, the stress should be on the changes in total revenue and total cost rather than on average costs. Overhead allocations are irrelevant and should be ignored. Incremental reasoning requires statistical measurement of incremental costs or judgment about which costs are affected and by how much.

2. The method requires attention to the long-run as well as the short-run impact of the decision. A decision to increase prices now may increase immediate profits, but it may gradually undermine the firm's reputation for low prices and destroy customer goodwill. It may even attract new competition.

3. The method requires consideration of possible complementary relations in demand between one product and another. The major reason for loss leaders in retailing is that they attract customers who will purchase other items. Any time the price decision on one item has an impact on the sale of other items, these additional effects on revenue must be equated.

4. The incremental method takes into account demand elasticities or, more simply, price-volume relationships. The decision maker must have

some way of determining the impact of price change on volume. Sometimes a statistical or experimental approach to measuring demand may be justified. Other times the manager may estimate responsiveness of sales to price by evaluating past experience and by considering various factors that might influence demand for this particular product.

5. The method requires attention to market structure. In some cases the closeness of a large number of substitutes may mean that the firm has little control over price. In other cases differentiation of the product may provide some scope for price policy, though it may require a careful coordination of pricing with sales promotion activity. In still other cases the possible retaliation of competitors should be taken into account.

6. The method requires some way of dealing with uncertainty. The manager never knows the exact consequences of his or her pricing decisions. The degree of uncertainty may vary from one decision to another. No general rules govern optimal behavior in such circumstances, for attitude toward risk varies from one individual to the next. In a large, impersonal corporation, individual attitudes toward uncertainty may be ignored; decisions can be based on the aim of maximizing expected profits (average profits). In small firms the greater willingness of some managers than others to take chances is often a perfectly reasonable reflection of different attitudes toward possible gains or losses. Thus, it is impossible to generalize that a manager should always say yes to a decision that offers a 0.7 probability of adding $100,000 to profits with a 0.3 probability of losses of $120,000. One manager may be attracted by the fact that this is a better than fair gamble. Another manager may be concerned that it offers the possiblity of complete bankruptcy.

7. Incremental reasoning requires attention to changing business conditions. Instead of a mechanical application of formulas through good times and bad, it suggests the possibility of price flexibility to meet changing markets. This is not to say that flexibility is always wise, but rather to stress that it is always worthy of consideration.

8. Incremental reasoning implies individualization of pricing on the various products of a multiproduct concern. It is true that mechanical formulas simplify pricing decisions. In a firm with thousands of products, such a simplification may cut managerial costs. But demand and competitive conditions facing the products are likely to be diverse; rigid pricing formulas prevent adjustment to that diversity. This is again a question of benefits versus costs. Will the firm gain enough in added profits or in furtherance of its other goals to justify the added management costs?

Note that incremental reasoning implies both cross-sectional flexibility and flexibility over time. Cross-sectional flexibility is the willingness to adapt prices to the special conditions of demand and cost that face each product. Flexibility over time has to do with the ability to adapt pricing to changing market conditions, to shifts in demand, to changes in price elasticities, and to the availability of excess capacity.

It is more important to develop a way of reasoning about pricing than it is to learn specific rules. Correct reasoning can be tailor made to particular circumstances; rules frequently are applied when they no longer fit.

The extent to which price-cost pricing, full-cost pricing, incrementalism (marginalism), and so on are followed by any particular firm is unknown. The degree of price flexibility, the extent of trial-and-error types of pricing behavior, and the appropriate classification by market structure of firms that pursue one particular kind of pricing policy as opposed to other kinds is likewise unknown. Yet, knowledge of these matters is of importance to the allocation of scarce resources within the economy. These issues remain unresolved at this writing. To say that full-cost pricing should be the exception rather than the rule and that incremental costing, pricing, and profitability should be the rule and not the exception is theoretically sound. Yet, some individual firms continue at times to make pricing decisions based on (1) subjectively determined market conditions (2) the desire to imitate the pricing behavior of other firms, (3) the acceptance of suggested prices handed down by manufacturers, (4) the desire to experiment with a price, and even at times (5) the notion that collusive activity is a necessary part of price determination.

Summary

Market structure affects the firm's decisions about pricing, quality improvement, and promotion. In the structure of pure competition, there are many sellers of a homogeneous product, and entry into the industry is easy. The firm's average and marginal revenue curves are horizontal at the general market price, so the firm must act as a price taker; the firm can choose an output-sales rate. In a purely competitive market structure, long-run expansion of capacity and output pushes prices down and squeezes out profits of marginal firms; a well-managed firm may keep costs low enough to continue to earn good rates of return on capital.

In monopoly there is one seller of a unique product, and entry into the industry is precluded. Barriers to entry may be temporary or more enduring. They include restricted access to low-cost raw material, patents, franchises, and economies of scale so great in relation to market demand that a single firm has a decisive cost advantage. In monopoly, the firm's demand and marginal revenue functions slope down and to the right, and it can select a combination of price and output-sales rate that is most profitable.

In monopolistic competition, there are many sellers of differentiated products, and entry is easy. Monopolistic competition allows the firm to determine short-run pricing and output-sales rate in the manner of a monopoly, but the competitive aspect of the industry enters through long-run capacity and output expansion that pushes each product's demand curve to the left. Profits of marginal firms are eliminated by market forces. Nevertheless, a well-managed firm may be able to keep costs down and demand up, so that it maintains good returns on investment.

Deliberate demand shifting (through quality changes and changes in promotion) can be profitable for firms that have differentiable products. Decisions related to demand shifting include: selecting least-cost combinations of inputs for production of quality changes and increased promotion, determining least-cost combinations of quality and promotion for any given shift of demand, deciding whether additional shifting of demand will be profitable, and determining whether price change is advantageous after a demand shift. Concepts and techniques of production economics can be used in managing demand shifts.

In oligopoly, a few sellers account for a large part of total industry output. Products may be either homogeneous or differentiated. Entry into oligopolistic industries is difficult. Production at competitive costs requires output that is large in relation to total market demand and must be sold in competition with established firms that have entrenched positions in distribution channels plus, for differentiated products, already-developed consumer preferences. The distinguishing characteristics of oligopoly is that actions of one firm may perceptibly affect profits of rivals, leading to immediate and direct reactions as the other firms attempt to protect their market positions. Thus, possible reactions of rivals should be taken into account in making decisions about prices, quality, and promotion.

If an oligopolist believes other firms will not follow a price increase but will follow a price reduction, the demand curve is kinked at the current price, and the marginal revenue function has two sections separated by a vertical gap. If the average and marginal cost functions run through the vertical gap (as is likely), the oligopolist will stand to lose by price change in either direction, and prices will be sticky in the face of sizable changes in either cost or demand. Shifts in cost or demand eventually make price changes advantageous. Output is immediately responsive to demand shifts but not to changes in cost, unless these lead to price adjustments.

Other patterns of oligopoly pricing behavior include:

1. Price leadership. (The leader cannot raise price above the level desired by the lowest-cost firm.)
2. Collusion. (This is difficult to maintain because of conflicts of interest about market sharing that lead to cheating and is illegal in the United States.)
3. Price wars. (Wars are usually local and short.)
4. Nonprice competition. (The reaction of competitors to demand shift-

ing is not immediate and may not be head on; this is not an alternative for firms in homogeneous oligopolies.)

Decision trees may be useful in an oligopoly firm's decisions about marketing tactics. They are composed of decision points, action branches, chance-event points, and event branches for which probabilities and payoffs are specified. If the payoffs are total results for a firm for an operating period, risk adjustment of the decision tree may be advisable. Risk adjustment requires estimates of management's preference function, so that preference values are substituted in the place of the payoffs on the decision tree.

CASES

Price and nonprice competition

Great Northern Nursery

The Great Northern Nursery was the second largest garden nursery and landscaping firm in Charlottetown, Prince Edward Island, Canada, a city of about 150,000. A family concern founded in about 1910, the company had a continual reputation for quality and service. In 1981, four partners cooperated in managing the firm.

The firm grew most of its own materials on 500-acre plot but purchased a few plants from wholesalers. It also sold a small fraction of its materials at wholesale; the local climate and soil conditions gave it an advantage on some plant varieties. Most of the sales were at retail at the company's garden center. The mail-order business was relatively small. One of the partners was in charge of the landscaping service as well as service work and spraying, another in charge of growing and propagation, and a third in charge of the garden center.

Pricing policies and practices The firm did not appear to have a definite policy on pricing. The officials, skeptical of systematic approaches to pricing, did not maintain a cost accounting system and doubted that it would be useful. In fact, one of the partners stated that most experiments in cost accounting in other nurseries had failed and had been abandoned. He claimed that uncertainty about the weather, plant diseases, and soil conditions made it impossible to predict the cost of growing a particular plant variety. The long period it took to produce plants also made cost estimating difficult.

The same official stated that the firm's plants were priced "according to the market, just as wheat and corn are priced." The firm's prices were a little higher than prices of nurseries to the south, where labor costs were lower, but lower than prices in the large metropolitan areas. The firm did not maintain systematic records of what other firms were charging, though it did have a file of catalogs of other nurseries. This file was not kept up to date, and it was apparently not used often. In fact, the company officials appeared to know only vaguely what the price differentials from firm to firm were. Thus, if the firm's prices were based on the market, it was on a subjective evaluation of market forces rather than on any kind of statistical analysis.

The officials believed that the firm's prices were slightly on the low side in the local market, if one excluded the prices at some of the large chain groceries. They pointed to some advertisements in the local newspaper showing higher prices at a competitive firm.

Changes in prices   Price changes on plants were infrequent. Prices were established in the summer for the coming year, and these prices were published in a September catalog. The partners believed that price changes during the year were undesirable; they did not even revise their mimeographed wholesale-price list during the season. The main exception to this rule was pricing for the end-of-season sale in May, at which time two categories of plants were marked down:

1. Dormant materials that had been dug up the previous fall and winter. These materials—including fruit trees, hedges, and shrubs—would have to be destroyed if not sold in May.

2. Block clearance items, mostly evergreens. If a few evergreens are occupying a block of land, it is desirable to sell them off at reduced prices to clear the land. Some of these materials may be of lower quality, but usually this is not the case.

The partners revised prices from one season to the next. In 1979, for example, they took into account an increase in labor costs and raised their prices.

Round-number pricing and promotional pricing   The company officials have traditionally preferred round numbers in pricing, such as $6 or $7 per plant, though they often used such prices as $6.50 and $8.25. In 1979, they broke away from this policy when they adjusted prices for labor cost changes. For example, they increased one price from $6.75 to $6.95, believing that a $7 price would develop customer resistance. In 1980, the firm returned to such prices as $7.25 and $9.25. A plant's price was the same regardless of how the plant was sold—by telephone, by purchase at the garden store, or by mail order.

The partners believed that round-number pricing was consistent with the atmosphere of quality and dignity the company tried to maintain. They did not want to be classified with the chain stores and mass-mail-order firms, which sometimes had a poor reputation. In 1981, however, the firm experimented with prices of $1.11, $2.22, and $4.44 on distress items in oversupply. In 1981, the partners also experimented with two-for-one sale, which permitted customers to purchase a second plant for $1 upon purchase of the first plant at the regular price. In addition, bulbs, fertilizers, and other items purchased on the outside were being sold at odd prices in 1981. Expert merchandisers and speakers at trade meetings had convinced the partners that some experimentation with promotional pricing might be desirable in building up volume. But the catalog prices were kept on a round-number basis; the promotional odd prices were the exception rather than the rule.

In 1982, the partners were not yet certain that the experiments with promotional pricing had been successful, but they were planning several new traffic builders. For example, they planned to offer one popular rose bush free to the purchaser of five rose bushes. The trend appeared to be toward more specials of this sort, but these specials were still the exception.

Pricing of particular plants   The firm did not have control over all of its prices. Some plants were patented; the firm holding the patent set the price and collected a royalty from individual nurseries. The markups on such plants were usually higher than the Great Northern Nursery's markups on plants of similar size and variety.

In spite of the general inflation in costs and prices in the 1970s, the prices on some plants were lower than in earlier years. For example, *Juniperus excelsa stricta* (15–18 inches) was selling at $8.50 instead of the $10 of a decade earlier. The reasons for the price decline were the reduction in demand for this variety and the fact that it was more readily available. Company officials were uncertain whether or not they were making money on this variety at such low prices, but they continued to grow it. One partner, however, stated that the company would not continue to grow a plant that did not return a profit in the long run.

Another plant that had fallen in price was *Taxus cuspidata browni*. This plant was in short supply in 1972–73, but supply had caught up with demand by 1980, and prices had reached a more normal level.

Some of the company's prices were 25 percent or even 50 percent below prices in the larger metropolitan markets. The company grew some plants especially adapted to the local climate in large blocks, with resultant economies of scale.

The prices of some plants at first appeared to be out of line with plant size. An example was globe *Taxus*. The officials explained that this plant requires special shearing to give it the desired shape. Thus, the labor costs were higher, and it took more years for the plant to grow to a given size. The officials doubted that they were making as great a profit on these plants as on the same variety left unsheared.

1. How does cost appear to relate to the nursery's pricing?
2. How does demand appear to relate to the nursery's pricing?
3. How does the contribution concept appear to relate to the nursery's pricing?
4. How does the opportunity-cost concept appear to relate to the nursery's pricing?
5. What changes, if any, in pricing do you recommend?

Atlantic Printing Company[1]

Mr. Prescott, president of the Atlantic Printing Company, believed that few printers had an accurate method of determing the cost of an individual job. He believed that the result was price cutting and deterioration of industry profits, which in 1979 averaged 2.5 percent of sales. The Atlantic Printing Company had installed a modern cost system, which combined forecasting and actual costs and developed data to serve as a basis for pricing. Prescott believed that other firms should adopt a similar system.

Background   The Atlantic Printing Company, one of more than 100 firms in the Greater Miami metropolitan area of greater than 800,000 population, employed more than 300 workers and was located in a modern, air-conditioned plant. Competition was intense, though printers tended to specialize in particular kinds of work. On some kinds of printing, the Atlantic company competed with printers in other cities. The company was a commercial printer, producing a wide variety of jobs but avoiding short runs and small volumes that were of interest to smaller firms. Exhibit 1 illustrates the production process of job-order print shops and is applicable to the Atlantic Printing Company.

The company's cost system: Hourly machine rates   The budgeted-cost system required the estimation of hourly machine costs for the coming

Exhibit 1
Production flow diagram for job-order printing

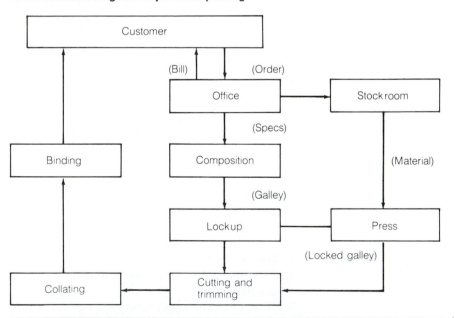

---

[1] This case is an altered version of material presented as "Fulgrave Printing Company," William R. Henry, Ph.D. and W. Warren Haynes, *Managerial Economics* (Plano, Tex.: Business Publications, 1978); pp. 507–513.

period. The company accountants estimated total labor and overhead costs for the next year; they also estimated the volume of sales and the number of machine-hours required for those sales. These cost and hour estimates became the basis for the hourly machine rate on each machine, group of machines, and other cost centers in the plant. The hourly machine rates included overhead costs, which were distributed to the various machines. Exhibit 2 shows how hourly costs were estimated for one press.

The budgeted-cost system required 45 different hourly machine rates. These rates were sometimes revised during the year to bring them in line with actual experience. In theory the rates might be revised slightly every 60 or 90 days. In the 12 months preceding June 1980, however, only 10 rates had been revised. In June 1980, Mr. Green, company vice president, revised 14 additional rates. Mr. Green had the primary responsibility for rate revisions.

In the establishment of the hourly machine rates, seasonal fluctuations in sales were ignored. The objective was to set rates for the year as a

Exhibit 2
Determination of hourly cost for vertical press

Investment: $10,000
Floor area: 300 square feet
52 weeks × 40 hours = 1 full-time worker = 2,080 hours to be paid for
  52 weeks × 40 hours = 2,080 maximum possible working hours.
Less: 10 days vacation = 80 hours (10 days × 8 hours)
Less: 6 days holidays = 48 hours (6 days × 8 hours)
100 percent production = 2,080 hours − 128 hours = 1,952 hours

1. Direct costs:

Labor: 2 workers at $1.75 × 2,080 hours *	$ 7,280.00
F.O.A.B. unemployment (percent of labor)	254.80
Worker's compensation	21.84
Power (1,600 K.W.H. at $.04)	64.00
Depreciation (10% of investment)†	1,000.00
Repairs (1% of investment)	100.00
Total direct costs	$ 8,720.64

2. Indirect Costs

Warehouse rent (300 sq. ft. × $3)	$ 900.00
Insurance (½% of investment)	50.00
Taxes (1% of investment)	100.00
Administrative costs (80% of direct costs)	6,976.51
Total indirect costs	$ 8,026.51

3. Total cost for one year (next 12 months) $16,747.15

4. Hourly rates

100% production (1,952 hours)	$ 8.58
80% production (1,562 hours)	10.72
60% production (1,171 hours)	14.30
40% production (781 hours)	21.44
20% production (390 hours)	42.94

* The difference between this wage rate and minimum wage to be paid by CETA.
† Equipment put in use prior to Economic Recovery Act of 1981.

whole. Mr. Green stated that it did not make sense for the company to set higher rates in the low season simply because the fixed costs had to be distributed over a smaller volume; nor was it reasonable to compute lower hourly machine rates in the peak seasons.

Costing individual jobs   The hourly machine rates were the chief factors but not the only factors in pricing individual jobs. In estimating the cost of a job, specialized estimators accumulated the costs on a job for each machine or other cost center through which it would pass. For this purpose time standards were required. In 1980, the company was engaged in estimating time standards on the basis of its own experience. Prior to this time, it had relied on time standards or norms published by national agencies. Even when internal time standards were established, the company maintained records showing comparisons with the outside norms to see how its own experience measured up.

Thus, the estimated cost in each cost center consisted of the time standard multiplied by the predetermined hourly cost. The full cost of the total job was the sum of such costs on every process used in the production of the order plus the cost of materials. The charge for materials depended on the quantity used in the individual order. The company usually did not pass on to the customer any savings resulting from consolidating orders in the purchase of materials, and quantity discounts were not passed on to the customer unless the order was large enough in itself to result in such a discount. An estimated price for a job is illustrated in Exhibit 3.

Pricing individual jobs   In principle the company followed the practice of pricing on the basis of full cost plus a predetermined markup. A special markup was applied to outside materials before their inclusion in the total cost of the work to which the profit markup was added. However, a certain amount of judgment entered into pricing; it was not merely a mechanical procedure. The authority over pricing was delegated to the sales department, though Green sometimes had an influence over pricing decisions.

Exhibit 3
Price estimate for an individual job

Materials (including the markup on materials):	
1,000 sheets 17 × 22, 20 lb. white Howard Bond 50 lbs. @ $0.30	$ 15.00
½ lb. Bronze blue ink @ $1.90	0.95
Production:	
Composition—2 hours × $7.86 hourly cost	15.72
Lockup—½ hour × $8.15 hourly cost	4.08
Press, vertical—5 hours × $10.72 hourly cost	53.60
Cutting—1 hour × $5.60 hourly cost	5.60
Total cost	$ 94.95
Markup on total cost (20%)	19.00
Selling price	$113.95

The company officials believed firmly in pricing on the basis of full costs. They believed the failure of some companies to adhere to this practice accounted for the severe competition in the industry. In fact, they believed other pricing procedures were unethical and referred to price-cutters as chiselers.

The predetermined markups varied from one category of business to another. The Atlantic company divided its business into five categories, each with a different markup percentage as indicated by Exhibit 4.

Company officials did not apply the markups mechanically. They used judgment in modifying the estimates. Sometimes the estimators themselves had an influence over the final price; they might estimate a low machine cost on a particular job because a fast worker would be assigned to it. Green, the vice president, did not approve of this practice, which was based on the estimators' misunderstanding of company policy. He argued that the time standards on any job should be based on average performance, not on the speed of the particular employee who might work on a job. He believed that the sales force sometimes put pressure on the estimators to come up with low estimates. In some cases judgment on the part of the estimators was justified. For example, they might know that a particular customer's job would flow expeditiously through the plant and that a reduction in actual cost would result.

Higher markups on brokering Class I, with the highest markups, included what is known in the printing business as brokering. This consisted of jobs that were produced largely on the outside, with only a minority of the work done by the Atlantic Company. Not all printing companies charged a higher markup on such jobs; in fact, some companies reduced their markups to get such jobs. Green was certain that the Atlantic policy was sound, even though the higher markup was applied

Exhibit 4
Markup schedule

Type of job	Markup on cost
Class I: The first run of any job requiring speculative creative work. Any job requiring outside purchases of more than 60 percent of the final price.	20 percent markup on outside materials plus 20 percent markup on the total cost including outside materials.
Class II: Reruns of jobs originally in class I; first runs of jobs not requiring speculative creativity.	15 percent markup on outside materials plus 20 percent markup on total cost.
Class III: Reruns of jobs originally in class II.	15–15 percent.
Class IV: Jobs that are part of a total program and that will result in additional business.	10–15 percent.
Class V: Magazines and other special publications.	10–10 percent.

to the entire job and not merely to the "value added." He gave the following reasons for this position:

1. Since brokering jobs require a relatively small amount of machine time, they absorb only a small amount of overhead. (As noted earlier, the overhead is allocated through the hourly machine rates.) A high markup was needed to assure that the sales commissions were covered.
2. Brokering jobs usually require more work on design and more special contact with the customer.
3. Brokering jobs are frequently speculative; an extra charge would help compensate for the extra risk.

Price competition versus nonprice competition Green stated that a high proportion of printing costs were fixed for short-run changes in volume. For example, labor costs did not vary greatly in proportion to volume because of the difficulty of retaining printers if they were laid off during the lulls in business. Green estimated that only 45 or 50 percent of the costs were variable. He recognized that the low level of variable costs created a temptation to cut prices; in fact, this was one reason for the cutthroat competition in the industry. Nevertheless, the Atlantic Company resisted pricing below full cost. Green stated several reasons for this policy:

1. Prices below full cost depress the market and result in low industry profits. Such prices are unethical.
2. Regular customers might be offended by special prices on irregular business. They preferred to deal with a company with consistent and stable price policies.
3. Although it might seem desirable to get fill-in business to make use of idle capacity, there was no assurance that the capacity would in fact be idle when the jobs were ready to be run. Delays in starting jobs were frequent and unpredictable. Low-price jobs might interfere with the flow of regular work.

Green also stated that if the volume of business were down for a considerable period, it would be possible to pare some of the so-called fixed costs. For example, the labor force would be contracted. It was true that other costs, such as depreciation, would run on anyway, but these made up a small percentage of the total. The president of the company, Prescott, admitted that the company might have to adjust to competition if idle capacity became a serious problem. In the 1960s and 1970s, however, there had been no prolonged periods of substantial idle capacity.

The company preferred to rely on nonprice competition to win customers, and the company stressed good customer relations. For example, if a customer's order turned out to be for a larger volume than was originally intended, the company would pass on half of the savings in unit costs. Green believed that such a practice helped retain customers. Sometimes the company provided special services to the customer without charge. For example, Green spent part of his evenings doing editorial work on a customer's manuscript.

1. Does the company use full-cost pricing? Discuss.
2. What is the significance of the high proportion of fixed costs in the company's operations?
3. Should the hourly rates be higher, lower, or the same in low seasons? Use Exhibit 2 to prove your points.
4. Would the company be better off to transfer attention from hourly machine rate to incremental costs?
5. Evaluate the reasons for not pricing below full costs.

PROBLEMS
Price and non-price competition

8–1   What are the unique (or distinguishing) characteristics of each of the following industry structures: (*a*) pure competition, (*b*) pure monopoly, (*c*) monopolistic competition, and (*d*) oligopoly?

8–2   Why is a decision about price precluded for a firm under pure competition?

8–3   A monopolistically competitive industry can be regarded as monopolistic from the short-run perspective but competitive from the long-run perspective. Explain.

8–4   What is meant by the assertion that a monopoly firm is the industry in which the firm operates?

8–5   Assuming product price is held constant, explain the determination of optimum demand shifting and final rate of sales. What complications arise if the firm attempts to treat pricing and demand shifting as variables to be determined simultaneously?

8–6   Could full-cost prices be close to optimal prices? Explain.

8–7   Could a firm that uses full-cost pricing have an operating loss? Explain.

8–8   A leading manufacturer of blue jeans is planning to sell a new line of vests to retail outlets. The cost to each retailer will be $28. The manufacturer attaches a price tag to each vest. What price should be on the tag if the retailer is to allow a 25 percent discount to all buyers during special retail sales events while allowing herself a 20 percent profit above the cost?

8–9   Rigoh Electronics manufactures a commercial electronic fishing
device that is in high demand along the east coast of the United
States. Each unit costs $248. Rigoh sells the units to a ware-
house distributor who, in turn, sells them to retail outlets. Rigoh
prints a retail price tag on each unit at the point of manufacture.
The wholesaler gets a 15 percent discount; the retailer, an 18
percent profit. What price should Rigoh print on each price tag?

8–10   The Star Fish Shop sells red snapper in large quantity to a
wholesaler-distributor. The cost to the distributor is $2.25 per
pound. Star Fish suggests the price at which the wholesaler
should sell the product to the retailer and prints this suggestion
on its packaged fish. If the wholesaler is to allow a 20 percent
discount to all retail purchasers and, simultaneously, retain a 15
percent profit for himself, what price per pound should Star Fish
suggest as a retail price?

8–11   St. Ormond's Key Record Shop buys off-brand name records
and tapes at $4.25 each. It wants to give a 15 percent discount
to all tourists and still make a 20 percent profit on all records
and tapes sold. What price should be stamped on the tapes and
records?

8–12   In a purely competitive industry that produces Product X, the
equations for annual market supply and market demand are,
respectively:

$$Q(\text{millions of units}) = 25{,}000\ P_x + 20P_x^2$$
$$Q(\text{millions of units}) = 100{,}000 - 2{,}000P_x + 6P_x^2$$

a. Determine the industry's equilibrium price and quantity
(P_x is price in dollars).
b. Use a graph to show what you have just done. It should
resemble Figure 8–1.

8–13   For one small firm in the purely competitive industry of problem
8–1, the total cost function can be approximated in the relevant
range by the following equation:

$$TC = \$4{,}800 + \$2.40Q_x + \$0.06Q_x^2$$

in which Q_x is the annual output rate in thousands.

a. Use marginal analysis to determine the rate of output that
will maximize the firm's profit. Calculate the amount of the
profit.

b. Use a graph to illustrate what you have just done.
c. Use the method of maximizing the value of the profit function to determine the firm's optimal rate of output. Compare with the result of part *a* above.
d. Draw a graph depicting what you have just done.

8–14   A pure monopoly has estimated the following demand and cost functions:

$$\text{Demand: } Q = 4{,}000 - 0.8P$$

where

P = Price in dollars.
Q = Annual sales in units.

$$\text{Cost: } TC = \$240{,}000 + \$3{,}600Q$$

where Q = Annual output in units.

a. Using marginal analysis, determine the profit-maximizing output-sales rate and price. Calculate the amount of profit.
b. Draw a graph to illustrate what you have just done.
c. Employ the technique of maximizing the value of the firm's profit function to determine the firm's optimum output-sales rate. Compare the result with the solution to part *a* above.
d. Use a graph to depict what you have just done.

8–15   Given the short-run curves below, what do OAD_q, OBC_q, and $ABCD$ represent? What does the area under the MC curve from O to q represent? Is the industry in equilibrium? Explain.

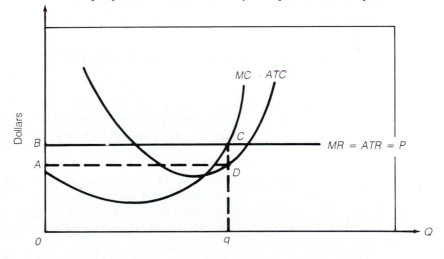

8–16   Given the short-run curves, what do *OACq, OPBq, APBC,* and the area under the *MR* curve from 0 to *q* represent? Is the industry in equilibrium? Explain.

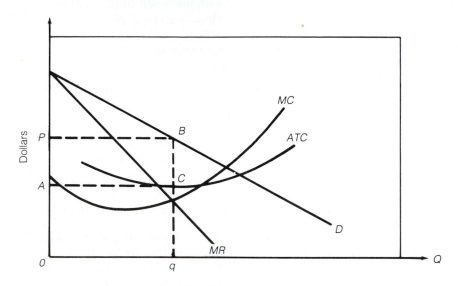

8–17   The manager of a firm producing rope for a perfectly competitive market is presently having the firm produce 50 units of rope for sale at $50 a unit. He determines the following schedule:

Units of rope	Total cost
48	$2,395
49	2,450
50	2,500
51	2,545
52	2,585
53	2,630
54	2,680
55	2,735
56	2,795

Determine his best production level, and draw a graph to show the cost and revenue situation.

8–18   A monopolist has two separate plants, both capable of producing widgets for sale in a single market. The cost and revenue schedules are as follows. How much does each plant produce, and what is the price at which the total output is sold?

P	Q	TC_1	TC_2
$24	1	$ 50	$ 35
23	2	55	43
22	3	59	49
21	4	62	53
20	5	64	55
19	6	65	60
18	7	67	69
17	8	77	79
16	9	92	90
15	10	110	102
14	11	130	115
13	12	151	129
12	13	173	144
11	14	196	160

8–19   An oligopoly firm has estimated the following demand for its single differentiated product:

$$\text{Above the present price: } P = \$50 - \$0.0025Q$$
$$\text{Below the present price: } P = \$80 - \$0.01Q$$

where

P = Price in dollars.
Q = Weekly sales in tons.

The firm's cost function is:

$$TC \text{ (in dollars per week)} = \$40,000 = \$28Q$$

a. Determine the firm's optimal rate of output-sales, price, and profit.
b. Draw a graph showing what you have just done.
c. Assume that the firm's variable cost per unit increases $4 per unit because of a new labor contract. Other firms in the industry are not currently facing comparable cost increases. Determine the firm's optimal output-sales, pricing, and profit.
d. Construct a graph depicting what you have just done.
e. Returning to part *c,* assume that *all* firms in the industry are confronted by the same cost increase of $4 per unit, where all firms have a similar construction of costs, revenues, and profits. Now, determine the one firm's optimal output, pricing, and profit.
f. Make a graph illustrating what you have just done.

Selected references

Aaronovitch, S., and Malcolm C. Sawyer. "Price Change and Oligopoly." *Journal of Industrial Economics* (UK) 30, no. 2 (December 1981), pp. 137–47.

Amihud, Yakov, and Haim Mendelson. "Dealership Market: Market-Making with Inventory." *Journal of Financial Economics* (Netherlands) 8, no. 1, pp. 31–53.

Amit, Eilon. "On Quality and Price Regulation under Competition and under Monopoly." *Southern Economic Journal* 47, no. 4 (April 1981), pp. 1056–62.

Baron, D. "Limit Pricing, Potential Entry, and Barriers to Entry." *American Economic Review* 63 (September 1973).

Bass, Frank M. "A Simulataneous Equation Regression Study of Advertising and Sale of Cigarettes." *Journal of Marketing Research,* August 1969.

Clarke, Frank H.; Massako N. Darrough; Heinke, John M. "Optimal Pricing Policy in the Presence of Experience Effects." *Journal of Business* 55, no. 4 (October 1982), pp. 517–30.

Cowling, Keith and A. J. Raynes. "Price, Quality, and Market Share." *Journal of Political Economy* 73 (November–December 1970).

Dolan, Robert J., and Abel P. Jeuland. "Experience Curves and Dynamic Demand Models: Implications for Optimal Pricing Strategies." *Journal of Marketing* 45, no. 1 (Winter 1981), pp. 52–62.

Douglas, G., and J. Miller. "Quality Competition, Industry Equilibrium, and Efficiency in the Price-Constrained Airline Industry." *American Economic Review* 64 (September 1974).

Gronberg, Timothy J., and Jack Meyer. "Spatial Pricing and Its Effect On Product Transportability." *Journal of Business* 55, no. 2 (April), pp. 269–80.

Hammond, John S. "Better Decisions with Preference Theory." *Harvard Business Review* 45 (November–December 1967).

Hartman, Raymond S. "A Probability Model of Oligopoly Pricing." *Applied Economics* (UK) 14, no. 3 (June 1982), pp. 219–34.

Harris, Milton, and Artur Raviv. "A Theory of Monopoly Pricing Schemes with Demand Uncertainty." *American Economic Review* 71, no. 3 (June 1981), pp. 347–65.

Hirshleifer, Jack. "Where Are We in the Theory of Information?" *American Economic Review* 63 (May 1973).

Kaserman, David L., and Patricia L. Rice. "A Note on Predatory Vertical Integration in the U.S. Petroleum Industry." *Journal of*

Economics & Business 33, no. 3 (Spring–Summer 1981), pp. 262–266.

Koenigsberg, Ernest. "Uncertainty, Capacity, and Market Share in Oligopoly: A Stochastic Theory of Product Quality." *Journal of Business* 53, no. 2 (April 1980), pp. 151–64.

Maccini, Louis J. "The Impact of Demand and Price Expectations on the Behavior of Prices." *American Economic Review* 68, no. 1 (March 1978), pp. 134–45.

Marino, Anthony M. "Optimal Departures from Marginal Cost Pricing: The Case of a Rate of Return Constraint." *Southern Economic Journal* 48, no. 1 (July 1981), pp. 37–49.

McCallum, Bennett T. "Monetarism, Rational Expectations, Oligopolistic Pricing, and the MPS Econometric Model." *Journal of Political Economy* 87, no. 1 (February 1979), pp. 57–73.

Means, Gardiner C. "The Administered Price Thesis Confirmed." *American Economic Review* 62 (June 1972).

de Menil, George. "Aggregate Price Dnyamics." *The Review of Economics and Statistics* 56, no. 2 (May 1974), pp. 129–40.

Meyer, Robert A., and Hayne E. Leland. "The Effectiveness of Price Regulation." *Review of Economics & Statistics* (Netherlands) 62, no. 4 (November 1980), pp. 555–66.

de Meza, David. "Generalized Oligopoly Derived Demand with an Application to Tax Induced Entry." *Bulletin of Economic Research* (UK) 34, no. 1 (May 1982), pp. 1–16.

de Meza, David, and Thomas von Ungern Sternberg. "Market Structure and Optimal Stockholding: A Note." *Journal of Political Economy* 88, no. 2 (April 1980), pp. 395–99.

Miller, D. "Getting the Price Right." *British Telecom Journal* (UK) 3, no. 2 (Summer 1982), pp. 8–9.

Roberts, Kevin W. S. "Welfare Considerations of Nonlinear Pricing." *Economic Journal* (UK) 89, no. 353 (March 1979), pp. 66–83.

Sahling, Leonard. "Price Behavior in U.S. Manufacturing: An Empirical Analysis of the Speed of Adjustment." *The American Economic Review* (December 1977), pp. 911–25.

Salop, Steven C. "Monopolistic Competition with Outside Goods." *Bell Journal of Economics* 10, no. 1 (Spring 1979), pp. 141–56.

Scherer, F. M. "Research and Development Resource Allocation Under Rivalry." *Quarterly Journal of Economics* 81 (August 1967).

Schnabel, Morton. "An Oligopoly Model of the Cigarette Industry." *The Southern Economic Journal* 38, January, 1972.

Silberston, Aubrey. "Surveys of Applied Economics: Price Behavior of Firms." *The Economic Journal* 80 (September 1970).*

Smith, Stanton D., and Walter C. Neale. "The Geometry of Kinky Oligopoly: Marginal Cost, the Gap, and Price Behavior." *Southern Economic Journal* 37 (January 1971).

Stigler, George. "Price and Non-Price Competition." *Journal of Political Economy* 76 (January–February 1968).

Waterson, Michael. "Vertical Integration, Variable Proportions and Oligopoly." *Economic Journal* (UK) 92, no. 365 (March 1982), pp. 129–144.

Weston, J. Fred, Steven Lustgarten; Namci Grottke; and J. Peter Matlila, "The Administered Price Thesis Denied: Note." *American Economic Review* 64 (March 1974).

Weston, J. Fred, "Pricing Behavior of Large Firms." *Western Economic Journal* 10 (March 1972).

Wilder, Ronald P.; C. Glyn Williams; and Davinder Singh; "The Price Equation: A Cross-Sectional Approach." *The American Economic Review,* September 1977, pp. 732–40.

---

* This article is included in Thomas J. Coyne, *Readings in Managerial Economics,* 3d ed. (Plano, Tex.: Business Publications, 1981).

CHAPTER

9

Profitability analysis

A primary justification for the existence of a privately owned corporation is profitability. In fact, a firm must generate profits in the long run if it is to remain in business. Since profits are a cost of doing business, these costs must be recovered. Recovery of costs is made easier if top management understands the mechanisms by which a capitalistic system allows profits to be made, and attempts to structure its pricing practices in a manner unique to each of its products. This chapter discusses these concepts.

The preceding chapter said the market structure in which a firm finds itself has much to do with the firm's ability to administer the price of its product. Another purpose of this chapter, therefore, is to discuss pricing problems and techniques facing multiproduct, multinational, oligopolistic firms. The manner in which these firms recognize pricing problems—and adjust price and output accordingly—has a direct bearing on profits. Before proceeding it is essential to understand fully that two institutions must exist if a firm is to function profitably in a mixed capitalistic economy: (1) private property and (2) a price system. Let us take a brief look at each institution.

Private property

Private property may be defined as real or personal property that is not publicly owned. If it is private, it belongs to one person. Inasmuch as corporations, by definition, are legal entities and therefore "persons," they may own property privately. This property may be in the form of land and/or capital equipment—two of the factors of production necessary for the profitable operation of a firm.[1]

---

[1] Ownership of a third factor of production, labor, became illegal in the United States as a result of the American Civil War.

A firm may generate profits if it allocates scarce resources efficiently. These profits may be retained by the firm. They represent part of a company's personal property. The firm may do with these earnings as it pleases provided, of course, the monies are not used illegally. Consequently, profits accruing to a firm in this manner may accumulate in what is known to the firm as its retained earnings account.

If profitability declines, the retained earnings account does not expand. Future investment from retained earnings becomes difficult, if not impossible, to finance. If new investments cannot be made from earnings retained (from past profitable operation), the probability is high that financial intermediaries in general and commercial banks in particular, will be unwilling to extend loans to the firm for expansionary purposes. With reduced or no external sources of funds available for investment purposes, and with its retained earnings account dwindling or dry, new investment by the firm becomes difficult if not impossible to make. Under such circumstances, employment, output, and income may be expected to decline.

To the extent that monies are made available through the retained earnings accounts of the various firms and industries within an economy, the economy can easily find itself in a self-reinforcing upward spiral in terms of employment, output, and income—an upward spiral that allows the firm to recover its costs, an expansion made possible primarily because of the institution of private property. Economic systems that protect the integrity of private property are ones that stand the best chance of creating an environment conducive to the best possible allocation of scarce and costly resources.

Common property ownership

"What is usually called socialism was termed by Marx, the 'first,' or lower phase of Communist society. Insofar as the means of production become common property, the word 'communism' is also applicable, providing we do not forget that this is not complete communism."[2] A primary distinction between the mixed capitalistic economy of the United States and that of the socialist or communist nations of the world has to do with the principle of private property. The current Communist Party of the Soviet Union (CPSU) considers the elimination of private property to be the most important characteristic of their system. "Private ownership of the means of production is abolished in the very first stages of the rise to Socialist society. . . . Public ownership makes possible the equality of all citizens, national economic planning, crisis-free economic development, full employment."[3] Economic systems that prefer common

---

[2] Vladimir Lenin, *Collected Works, English Edition,* vol. 25 (Moscow: Progress Publishers, 1966), p. 471.

[3] "Socialism and Communism," *Soviet Life,* September, 1975, p. 50.

ownership of corporations, however, may find their net new investment needs impossible to meet from internally generated funds. They may have to seek investment monies from abroad.

Firms operating in a socialistic environment often measure their contribution to society by the magnitude of the deficit incurred by the firm. The larger the deficit, the greater the contribution to society. This kind of unclear thinking with respect to prices and profitability within a firm or industry located in a socialistic society may result in that firm's being unable to provide the monies necessary for initial investment or expansion. In contrast, firms operating within one of the four basic market structures defined in the preceding chapter must earn a normal profit if they are to exist in the long run. Normal profit is a cost of doing business, and firms must recover all costs in the long run.

Currently, socialistic societies prefer to do without certain creature comforts rather than introduce the notion of private property, which would allow profitability. A subsidiary of Pan-American Airlines, the Inter-Continental Hotel, entered into an agreement in principle with the Soviet travel agency, Intourist, to construct a 1,500-bed motel in Moscow, a 2,000-bed motel in Leningrad, and an 800-bed motel in Kiev. The Pan-American subsidiary has had some experience in this kind of activity; in fact, it runs a large hotel in Budapest, Hungary. When Intourist realized that Inter-Continental expected a management fee, which would serve as its share of the "profits", Intourist cancelled the agreement. The CPSU would prefer to do without the badly needed hotel space rather than allow total costs of the hotels to be recovered. Actions of this sort are to be expected whenever and wherever the decision makers do not understand that profits are a cost of doing business. In the United States, some publicly owned schools (including state universities), rapid-transit systems, and electric and other utilities are often mismanaged in the same way and for the same reason.

The price system

Profit is made possible in a capitalistic economy because of the institution of private property. Various kinds of profitability may be made, dependent upon (1) the market structure in which the firm is located and (2) the time frame about which one is speaking.[4] But of primary importance to a firm's ability to generate profits, regardless of market structure, is that the economy functions within the confines of a price system.

A price system is an economic system wherein all factor inputs (i.e., land, labor, and capital) and all products produced (i.e., automobiles, television sets, ladies' dresses, and so on) are distributed in exchange for a precise amount of money. Scarce goods and services are allocated to

---

[4] Economic profits are possible in each of the four market structures in the short run. Only normal profit may be earned by them in the long run.

those persons who are ready, willing, and able to pay the price. Food stamp activities, surplus butter and cheese programs, and other federal and state governmental give-away programs notwithstanding, the mixed capitalistic system that functions in the United States operates within the confines of the price system. When combined with the institution of private ownership of real and personal property, the price system enables profitability to exist. Socialist systems, by contrast, rely less heavily upon the price system for allocative functions. They keep wage rates low and supply a worker with as much as an additional $33\frac{1}{3}$ percent of wage rate in educational, medical, dental, housing, and other welfare subsidies. Since the socialist worker needs fewer dollars for purposes of handling daily transactions, the price system is circumvented somewhat.[5]

Profit theories

In the domestic American economy, profitability is a major reason for a firm's existence. The most common theory of profitability may be the so-called residual theory. This theory—known also as the businessperson's theory or the accountant's theory—refers to the amount of money remaining when total costs are subtracted from total revenues.

The residual theory of profitability has the advantage of being easy to understand and relatively easy to calculate. Included in the firm's total revenues are all monies received by the firm during the specific period of time being reviewed. Included in total costs are all explicit expenses incurred by the firm plus depreciation allowances.[6] Total costs may be increased or decreased by changing the method of depreciation. Obviously, when costs change and revenues stay constant, residual profitability is affected.

As has been indicated, the institutions of (1) private property and (2) the price system combine to allow the generation of profits by private enterprise. The residual theory of profit explains how the firm retains that portion of its total revenues not expended as part of explicit costs. For example, if total revenues equal $100, and total costs including depreciation equal $80, the residual profit before tax would be the remaining $20. Assuming a tax rate of 50 percent, the corporation could retain $10 profit after tax (PAT). From PAT the firm might designate $4 to $6 for dividends (40 to 60 percent is normal), the remainder to be placed in the retained

---

[5] These welfare measures are used often to encourage the mobility of labor within the Soviet Union. By granting extra food rations, somewhat larger apartments, television sets, radios and so on, the Communist Party of the Soviet Union (CPSU) was able to work toward completion of important projects during the 1970s, such as the Baikal-Amur Railroad. These kinds of "extras," plus slightly higher wage rates, were used by the Soviet Union for development of virgin lands during the 1950s and 1960s. In the United States, similar extras are packaged in what are known as fringe benefits.

[6] Depreciation is not an out-of-pocket expense. It is included among the costs as though it were an out-of-pocket expense so as to minimize the firm's income tax payments. Depreciation is a tax shield for the company.

earnings account. We have seen that this latter point is important! It is out of retained earnings that most monies for new investment originate.

Large, publicly owned firms must pay dividends if they expect to float additional issues of common stock. All firms must hold some profit in retained earnings if they are to have a source of funds from which positive new investment may originate during subsequent periods. New investment is necessary for the continued existence of all firms, and it is not reasonable for a firm to assume that 100 percent of net new investments needs could be (1) borrowed via long-term loans at commercial banks or through bonded indebtedness in the capital markets or (2) obtained in equity markets at each time of need. Since dividends and transfers to the retained earnings account must be paid, the economist considers these payments to be a cost of staying in business. Anything that must be paid while conducting business is a cost. Normal, residual profits, therefore, are a cost of doing business.

Frictional theory of profit

If most firms in an industry are earning a profit expressed, perhaps, as 10 percent of sales ($10/100) and calculated as explained on a residual profitability basis, all costs are covered in the long run. This is so because all factors of production receive their opportunity cost; no factors are overpaid; and none are exploited. But the real world does not operate that way according to the frictional theory of profitability. Under this theory, profits accrue in the short-run to some firms in excess of normal. These larger profits are known as economic profits and may exist in any one of the four market structures. These economic profits represent an unearned income to the firm. The firm is thought to be able to gain and then maintain these levels of economic profits due to inflexibility in (1) the resource markets, (2) the product markets, or (3) some combination of the two. Immobile factors of production exist and generate friction within an economy, thereby creating opportunities for economic profit. Frictional profits were made by some firms in the 1970s because of the situation in Iran.

Shortly after the Arab oil boycott of the early 1970s huge quantities of foreign exchange poured into the country of Iran. American and European business and professional persons moved to the country in relatively large numbers, on temporary assignment. Rental rates of relatively small apartment complexes soared. Rents changed from about $300 per month for a two-bedroom unit to some figure in excess of $1,700 per month for the same apartment. This rapid transformation in price gave rise to abnormally high profits for landowners because (1) residential real estate for rental purposes was fixed in total supply in the short run, and (2) demand for rental property of this nature exceeded by a large amount the available supply of rental units.

Frictional profits are not possible in the long run so long as (1) entrance into the industry is not prohibited, and (2) other imperfections with respect to factor and product markets disappear. Frictional profits disappeared in Iran as the Shah's regime collapsed and government policies almost simultaneously changed. New government policies reflected leadership that deplored at least two institutions: (1) private property and (2) the price system.

Innovation theory of profits

Unearned surplus (economic profits) may be earned by innovators because of the unique position they occupy in the economy. The innovative theory of profitability explains that profits in excess of normal may be made by those firms who invent a new product or who change the physical appearance of an old product at a time when demand is high and the innovator is able to limit supply. The innovator will continue to make economic profits until and unless his or her particular tehcnique of product differentiation is made available to competitors or until additional research by the innovator or a competitor causes the current innovation to appear insignificant in the minds of the buyers relative to an even newer, better product.

Examples of profitability accruing to innovators are not difficult to find. Kodak film and film-processing techniques have allowed average rates of return in excess of normal to be taken by the Rochester, New York, company. Innovative profits have gone to Xerox, IBM, and perhaps General Motors and Mercedes Benz. Few observers would argue that billionaire Howard Hughes did not reap innovative profits as a risk-taking entrepreneur. During the early days of the automobile industry, Henry Ford and others accumulated huge economic profits. Innovation and invention allowed these men to occupy a position in factor and product markets that, quite simply, was unavailable to lesser mortals.

The prominent Austrian-born economist Joseph Alois Schumpeter explained that innovations of this sort come in clusters. The clustering of innovations has the advantage of stimulating employment, output, and income in the short run. Clustering has the disadvantage of contributing to the magnitude of business cycles. Innovations occur because the combined impact of private property and the price system allow the innovator to retain a substantial profit. Another institution, personal freedom, allows the innovator the time necessary to simply sit and think about innovations.

Other profit theories

Theories of profitability exist that claim profit to be the compensation that must be paid to owner/managers if they are (1) to continue with their services and (2) to retain whatever other factors of production they have allocated for purposes of running a particular business. Theories of this sort assume that certain factors of production exist and perform certain functions. These functions must be continued if the business is to prosper. Factor inputs, (i.e., labor, capital) will continue only so long as they are compensated. Certain of these theories may, at times, appear more valid than others. Regardless of the theory upon which a firm places primary reliance, in a mixed-capitalistic society, these things remain true in the mid-1980s: (1) A profit must be made if all costs are to be recovered, and (2) profits cannot be generated if the institutions of private property and the price system are dissolved.

Factors important to understanding profitability include financial and operating leverage, present value, net present value, and internal rate of return. These and other financial measurements are included in Part 5. Break-even and profit-volume analyses are techniques more immediately applicable to the subject of profitability and are covered in this chapter. In addition, this chapter discusses profitability analysis for several types of production involving distinct runs that come to planned ends. Production of product types or models is considered first and then production that takes the form of projects. Particular attention is given to the impact of learning curves on variable costs, analysis of new-product profitability, effects of changes in rates and lengths of production runs, analysis of profitability of model changeover, and the critical-path method of estimating project "crashing" cost.

The chapter then moves into an analysis of intermittent purchasing and intermittent production. These activities result from economies of producing at instantaneous rates in excess of sales or usage rates.

Let's take a look first at break-even analysis.

Break-even charts

Figure 9–1 illustrates a conventional break-even chart. Rate of output, Q, or perhaps sales quantity, is measured along the horizontal axis. Total revenue, TR, and total cost, TC, are measured along the vertical axis. The total revenue function in the figure is drawn as a straight line through the origin. Underlying the use of this linear revenue function is an assumption that price, b_1, is constant regardless of the rate of sales. This assumption is appropriate under conditions of pure competition, a condition wherein a firm can sell any rate of output within its capacity at the going or market price, a price determined by forces beyond the firm's control. The assumption of constant price is not appropriate if the firm has a demand curve that slopes down and to the right. Break-even analysis for the case of sloping demand is explained later in this chapter.

The total cost function in Figure 9–1 is revealed as a straight line from an intercept on the vertical axis. The intercept, b_0, is fixed cost per period, and the slope, b_2, of the cost function is a constant value of

Figure 9–1
Typical break-even chart

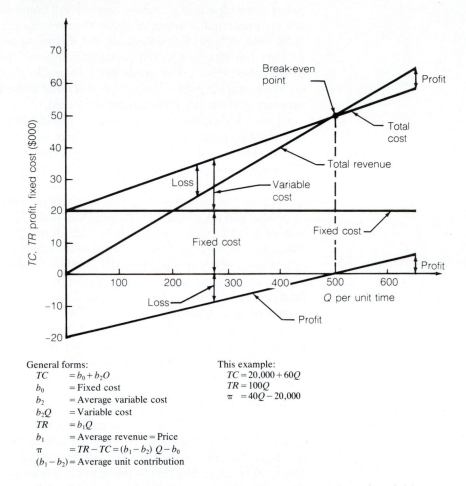

General forms:

TC	$= b_0 + b_2 O$
b_0	$=$ Fixed cost
b_2	$=$ Average variable cost
$b_2 Q$	$=$ Variable cost
TR	$= b_1 Q$
b_1	$=$ Average revenue $=$ Price
π	$= TR - TC = (b_1 - b_2)\ Q - b_0$
$(b_1 - b_2)$	$=$ Average unit contribution

This example:

$TC = 20{,}000 + 60Q$
$TR = 100Q$
$\pi = 40Q - 20{,}000$

variable cost per unit of output or sales. A constant value of variable cost per unit assumes: (1) Variable inputs have constant marginal productivity; (2) input prices do not change with changes in the quantities used; and (3) rates of use of inputs can be changed in a smooth, continuous way—there are no ''lumpy'' variable inputs. Break-even analysis for cases in which assumption 1 or 2 does not hold is explained later in the chapter.

The primary purpose of break-even analysis is not to determine the break-even point—the point at which total revenue equals total cost. This break-even point is of interest, but the analysis shows something of much greater use to the manager—what happens to profits (or losses) at various rates of output greater and less than the break-even quantity. The primary purpose of break-even analysis is to determine the effects of changes in output and sales upon total costs, total revenue, and profit.[7]

Information contained in a break-even chart can be summed up by a profit function, such as the one depicted in the lower portion of Figure 9–1. Profit, π, is $TR - TC$, so it is $b_1Q - (b_0 + b_2Q)$, or $(b_1 - b_2)Q - b_0$. In words, profit for the period is the unit contribution (price minus variable cost per unit) times the rate of output or sales, less fixed cost.

Sometimes the information on a break-even chart is presented in an alternative form like the one illustrated in Figure 9–2. In this alternative

Figure 9–2
Break-even chart: Contribution to profit form

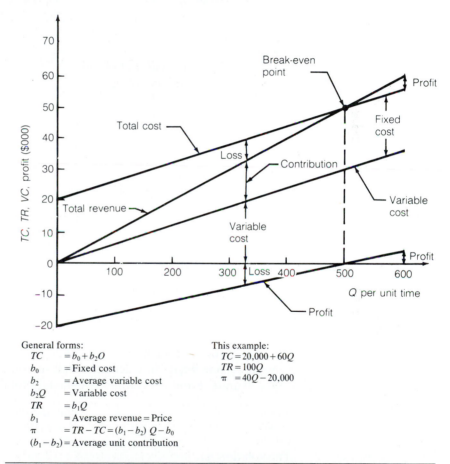

General forms:

$TC \quad = b_0 + b_2O$
$b_0 \quad = \text{Fixed cost}$
$b_2 \quad = \text{Average variable cost}$
$b_2Q \quad = \text{Variable cost}$
$TR \quad = b_1Q$
$b_1 \quad = \text{Average revenue} = \text{Price}$
$\pi \quad = TR - TC = (b_1 - b_2)Q - b_0$
$(b_1 - b_2) = \text{Average unit contribution}$

This example:

$TC = 20,000 + 60Q$
$TR = 100Q$
$\pi = 40Q - 20,000$

---

[7] The term *total revenue* usually means realized revenue from sales during the production period. However, break-even analysis can also be used in cases in which part or all of the production is to go to a deliberate buildup of finished goods inventory. In the latter case, *total revenue* means value of output as derived from expected revenue of future periods.

form, the variable cost function is drawn as a straight line from the origin, and fixed cost is added to obtain a total cost function that parallels variable cost. This "contribution to profit" form of break-even analysis has the advantage that contributions, if any, to overhead and profit are very easy to see.

Algebraic form of break-even analysis

Algebraic execution of break-even analysis is illustrated in Figure 9–1. The total revenue and total cost functions in this figure are:

General form:

$$TR = b_1 \cdot Q$$
$$TC = b_0 + b_2 \cdot Q$$

This example:

$$TR = \$100 \cdot Q$$
$$TC = \$20,000 + \$60 \cdot Q$$

where

TR is total revenue per unit of time.
TC is total cost per unit of time.
Q is output per unit of time.
b_1 is price of the product.
b_0 is fixed cost per unit of time.
b_2 is marginal (and average variable) cost per unit of output.

To determine the break-even level of output, set the expression for revenue equal to the expression for total cost, as follows:

General form:

$$b_0 + b_2 \cdot Q = b_1 \cdot Q$$

This example:

$$\$20,000 + \$60 \cdot Q = \$100 \cdot Q$$

The solution is:

General form:

$$Q = \frac{b_0}{b_1 - b_2}$$

This example:

$$Q = 500$$

In words, break-even output is fixed cost divided by unit contribution.

Suppose one wants to calculate profit at some stated level of output, say, 650 units. Profit (π) is total revenue less total cost, as follows:

General form:

$$\pi = (b_1 \cdot Q) - (b_0 + b_2 \cdot Q)$$

This example:

$$\pi = (100 \cdot Q) - (\$20,000 + \$60 \cdot Q)$$

The solution is:

General form:

$$\pi = -b_0 + Q (b_1 - b_2)$$

This example:

$$\pi = \$6,000$$

In words, profit is the product of output and unit contribution minus fixed cost.

Construction of break-even charts

Where does one obtain the information used in plotting a break-even chart? There are two common methods of deriving the necessary information from the income statement.

1. One approach, which we shall call the classification approach, is to take a single income and expense statement and use judgment in classifying items of cost into those that are fixed and those that are variable. Line managers and plant accountants, who have initmate knowledge of the role of each cost item in relation to production, should have little difficulty with such classificaiton. Some careful work may be necessary in separating the fixed and variable components of those items of cost that contain both. If there are lumpy variable inputs, there may be jumps in cost that produce a stairstep effect at each point where input is increased. The slope of the cost function is the sum of the variable costs per unit of output over the various items of cost in this category. The fixed cost is the sum of costs per period over the various items in this category. The final chart might look like Figure 9–3 if there were a lumpy input in the structure of costs.

2. A second approach, which we shall call the historical approach, is to compare a series of income and expense statements for a sequence of periods in which the management unit had varying levels of output or sales. By plotting the output-cost combinations, the analyst obtains a

Figure 9–3
A complex break-even chart

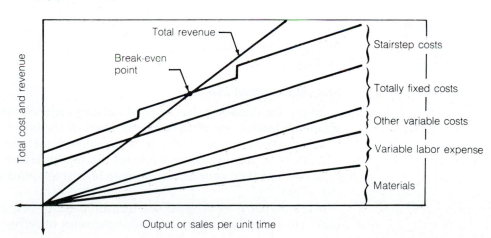

Figure 9–4
Estimating the total cost line from a scatter diagram

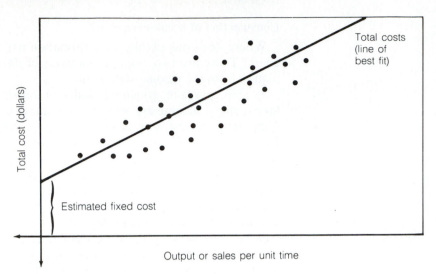

scatter diagram similar to the one shown in Figure 9–4. Each dot shows the combination of output and total cost for a particular period. The dots will not fall exactly on a single line because influences other than output have also affected costs. Often, however, the dots will have a pattern, and a line of best fit may be located. The slope of this line is an estimate of marginal cost (or average variable cost if the line is straight). The intercept of the line is an estimate of fixed cost. More refined methods are possible. For example, one may correct the data for changes over time in prices of materials or other inputs or for changes over time in labor per unit of output and other conversion ratios. Also, a fit of the cost function to the data can be made by statistical techniques, as explained in Chapter 6.

Scale of the output axis

So far, the discussion has avoided defining precisely what is measured on the horizontal axis of a break-even chart. If the firm produces a single standard product, one simply uses the amount of physical output (in pounds, tons, cubic yards, or whatever the appropriate unit may be). The total cost line then provides an estimate of cost at various rates of physical output.

If the output is heterogeneous, measurement of output is more complex. How can General Electric add quantities of refrigerators to quantities of kitchen ranges? One possibility is to assign weights, such as hours of direct labor used, to each of the products and then to measure the total output as an index number. Another possibility is to measure output as a percent of plant capacity. A simpler and more widely used method is to measure output in sales dollars (i.e., dollar value of kilowatt-hours of electricity generated). Using sales dollars weights the various products by their respective prices. None of these approaches completely overcomes the conceptual problems involved in relating total cost to heterogeneous output. Suppose the labor content of products is used as a weighting factor, and labor efficiency changes for one product compared with another. Does it follow that the relative costs of the products have changed in the same proportion? Or suppose prices are used as weights, and the price of one product changes. Has the relative cost of this product changed in the same proportion?

Appraisal of break-even analysis

Since break-even analyses are widely used in decision making and in projecting financial results of business operations, let us consider some of the limitations of the technique.

1. In conventional charts, the price of the output is taken as given. If one wishes to handle a case in which price is a variable that affects sales quantity, one way is to draw a series of total revenue lines on the chart, one for each price to be considered. One can then estimate sales quantity at each price, determine profit if that quantity is actually sold, and look at the sensitivity of profit to changes in prices and the corresponding quantities. This approach is illustrated in Figure 9–5.

2. Cost functions developed by the historical approach may be erroneous if there were changes over time in prices of inputs. If production records are available that show physical amounts of inputs used, cost data can be standardized to a specified set of input prices, and the error can be avoided.

3. Cost functions developed by the historical approach may be erroneous if there were changes over time in production technology, effectiveness of supervision, legislation and regulation, or other influences on conversions of input to output.

4. When break-even charts are based on accounting data, as they usually are, the cost functions may be in error because of data limitations: omissions of imputed cost, arbitrary estimates of depreciation, and inappropriate allocations of overhead cost.

5. Selling costs are difficult to handle. Selling costs are not so much a result of output as they are a cause of changes in sales quantities. Furthermore, the relationship of selling costs to output is especially unstable over time.

Figure 9–5
Break-even chart with alternative revenue lines for alternate prices

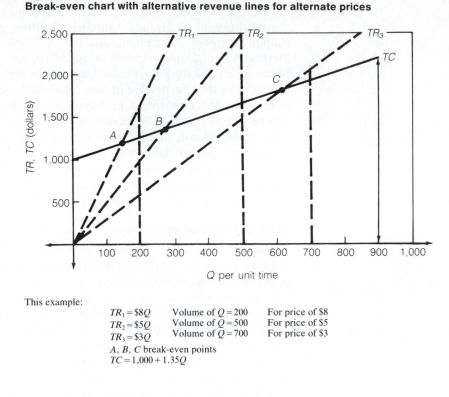

This example:

$TR_1 = \$8Q$	Volume of $Q = 200$	For price of \$8
$TR_2 = \$5Q$	Volume of $Q = 500$	For price of \$5
$TR_3 = \$3Q$	Volume of $Q = 700$	For price of \$3

A, B, C break-even points
$TC = 1,000 + 1.35Q$

6. Some of the costs of a particular period may not be the result exclusively of output in that period. Maintenance expenses of a given period may be the result of hard use of a past period or preparation for hard use in a future period.

7. Taxes must be considered. One may develop the chart to show part of profit going to the government in taxes. However, if the company has alternating years of profit and loss, with recovery of taxes during loss years, the adjustment for taxes is somewhat difficult to show on the chart.

It is easy to build up a formidable list of limitations of break-even charts. Some writers are skeptical of their usefulness unless they are made more complex than is usual. At the same time, break-even analysis is simple, easy to understand, and inexpensive.

Usefulness of break-even charts undoubtedly varies from industry to industry. Those industries experiencing frequent changes in input prices, rapid improvements in technology, and many shifts in product mix will profit little from break-even analysis. In other industries, break-even analyses may be quite useful to managers who are familiar with their limitations and simplifications, Management depends heavily on analytic tools that cut through the complexity of reality and focus attention on fundamental relationships.

The Manitoba Hydro-Electric Company, Manitoba, Canada

The shorter the short run, the more likely it is that virtually all costs are fixed; in the long run all costs are variable. Generally, the short run may be considered a period of time sufficiently long to allow a plant (firm) to change its rate of output (e.g., a production facility assembly line may be speeded or slowed) but not enough time to change the capacity of the plant.

The long run is a period of time sufficiently long to allow the plant (firm) to change not only its rate of output, but also the size and, therefore, the capacity of that plant. It is often true that the long-run adjustment, if made, may not be noticed until some period after it is too late to avoid having the event take place. As was seen in Chapter 6, Studebaker-Packard Corporation made its long-run adjustment when it left South Bend, Indiana, and set up operations in Canada. The Penn-Central Railroad made its long-run adjustment when it declared bankruptcy. Penn-Central knew when it signed the bankruptcy papers that it had made its long-run adjustment; Studebaker-Packard presumably did not.

Under no circumstances should one think of the short run or long run in connection with some specified period of time—one year, for example. Changes in costs over time are too subtle for that kind of thinking. By the same token, it is inconsistent with the definition of short run and is an overstatement to suggest that all costs are fixed rigidly in the short run. It is recognized that variable costs, such as direct labor charges to the firm, may be reduced by laying off workers if and when demand for the finished product and/or service of the organization declines; therefore, total short-run direct labor costs may be flexible in a downward direction at times. This condition existed and was noticeable during 1982, when the unemployment rate climbed toward 12 percent of the labor force. If these reductions in cost take place, they do so at irregular intervals and do so over the course of a business cycle.

Direct labor is referred to often as a variable cost (VC). This cost plus all other variable costs, such as certain raw material purchases, must be subtracted from the firm's total costs (TC) to determine its fixed costs (FC); that is, $TC - VC = FC$. Determination of a firm's break-even point assumes that total costs can be broken into these two distinct components: fixed costs and variable costs. If substantially all costs are fixed in the short run, no meaningful distinction between these two kinds of costs can be made; consequently, any calculation of a firm's break-even point in terms of the number of dollars of sales needed to break even, or in terms of the number of units the firm needs to produce in order to break even, may be subject to a considerable degree of error. Nevertheless, some authors continue to provide break-even examples. The concept is sound, but it is often difficult to get agreement within a firm concerning what fixed cost is and what it is not. With these limitations in mind, consider the following break-even example.

The Manitoba Hydro-Electric Board and Subsidiary Companies are located in the province of Manitoba, Canada. This firm operates approximately 9 hydroelectric plants, 2 thermoelectric and almost 30 diesel-electric plants—all with interconnecting generating stations. If the major operating plants of this Canadian facility have total revenues approximating $89,882,000 from the sale of power and about $1,415,000 from other sources, revenues and expenses for the year 1984 could be expressed as follows:

Revenues:
    Sale of power $89,882,000
    Other revenue   1,415,000
                                               $91,297,000
Expenses:
Administrative and general
        operating expenses . . . $33,103,000
Depreciation 19,153,000
Net interest expense   36,175,000
                                                88,971,000
Gross returns $2,326,000

Calculation of the break-even point for the firm in dollars may be expressed as:

$$B.E._{\text{Dollars}} = \frac{FC}{1 - \dfrac{VC}{S}}$$

where

FC = Total fixed cost of the firm.
VC = Total variable cost.
S = Total sales.

In order to determine the break-even point in dollars, total costs of the firm must be broken into two distinct components, namely, fixed costs and variable costs. For this calculation Manitoba Hydro-Electric Company top management would have to agree to the portion of general and administrative expenses representative of direct labor and variable costs. Once this determination is made, one can calculate the firm's break-even point. For purposes of this presentation, assume about 20 percent of the $88,971,000 total cost is variable in the short run. Consequently, $71,176,800 represents fixed cost, and $17,794,200 is variable cost. A break-even point expressed in dollars is equal to:

$$B.E._{\text{Dollars}} = \frac{FC}{1 - \dfrac{VC}{S}}$$

$$= \frac{\$71,176,800}{1 - \dfrac{\$17,794,200}{\$91,297,000}}$$

$$= \frac{\$71,176,800}{1. - .20}$$

$$= \frac{\$71,176,800}{.80}$$

$$= \$88,970,000$$

The astute observer will notice that the $88,970,000 break-even point is $2,326,000 less than the $91,297,000 gross revenue generated by this Canadian firm.

A break-even point in terms of dollars may be calculated for any firm of any size—organized for profit or nonprofit—provided the information concerning total costs is available and these costs can be broken into their fixed and variable component parts.

The break-even point for the Manitoba Hydro-Electric Board and Subsidiary Companies in terms of units (in this case kilowatt-hours produced) and for the segment of business estimated here may be calculated as follows:

$$B.E._{\text{Units}} = \frac{FC}{(p - v)}$$

where

FC = Fixed costs.
p = Price per kilowatt-hour generated.
v = Variable cost per kilowatt-hour generated.

In a manufacturing firm, price (p) would represent the money charged per unit of output. For the Manitoba Hydro-Electric Board, the break-even point in terms of kilowatt-hours produced can be estimated by assuming average revenue charges per month are synonomous with price of the product and by estimating the variable costs per kilowatt-hour. Approximately 23 percent of total revenue generated is assumed to come from residential users and 77 percent from commercial users of electricity. Price (p) is approximated from this distribution between users at $39.11, and variable cost per unit (v) is estimated to be $7.11.[8]

[8] Variable cost per kilowatt-hour = $\dfrac{\$17,794,000, \text{ variable cost}}{2,501,473, \text{ kilowatts at capacity}}$ = $7.11.

$$B.E._{\text{Units}} = \frac{FC}{(p-v)}$$

$$= \frac{\$71,176,800}{\$39.11 - \$7.11}$$

$$= \frac{\$71,176,800}{\$32.00}$$

$$= 2,224,275 \text{ kilowatt-hours}$$

Using these assumptions, the firm would break even when operating at 88.91 percent of rated capacity.

$$\left(\frac{2,224,275}{2,501,473} = 88.91\% \right)$$

Capacity is assumed to be 2,501,473 kilowatts.

It is highly desirable to calculate one's break-even point in terms of units as well as dollars to be sure the break-even point does not occur at some output greater than the ability of the firm to produce. Without calculating the break-even point in units, one might find belatedly that the capacity of the firm is not great enough to break even, given its cost and price structure.

Profit-volume analysis

Many authors have adapted break-even analysis to the situation of the multiproduct firm. They construct break-even charts for the individual product, individual department, or sector. One variation is what Bergfeld, Earley, and Knobloch call the profit-volume (P/V) technique, or cost-volume-profit analysis.[9] The main concepts used in the P/V technique are:

P/V income = Sector's sales volume in dollars minus sector variable costs.

Profit contribution = P/V income minus specific programmed costs.

Specific programmed costs = Costs of selling the output of the sector or other costs of promoting that sector (as opposed to programmed cost for the firm as a whole).

P/V ratio = The ratio between the unit P/V income and unit price; that is, unit contribution or slope of the P/V line.

This variation on the break-even chart is shown in Figure 9–6. The function begins at a specific programmed cost, below the zero contribution line. The upward-sloping line shows the profit contribution; its slope is

---

[9] Albert J. Bergfeld, James S. Earley, and William R. Knobloch, *Pricing for Profit and Growth,* (New York: McGraw-Hill, 1957). Modern cost accounting books frequently include a chapter on this type of analysis.

the P/V ratio or contribution per dollar of sales. Here, output is heterogeneous and is being measured in sales dollars. One moves along the
sloping line to the point representing the expected sales volume. The
vertical distance between this point and the zero line is the profit contribution for the sector. Such a chart ignores overheads that cannot be
definitely allocated to this sector. It reveals whether or not a product is
covering its variable and programmed costs; it reveals what contribution
the product is making to overall company overhead and profit. The chart
permits an evaluation of product profits at varying levels of sales and
provides information for the comparison of contributions from one product to another.

Algebraic form of profit-volume analysis

Profit-volume analysis by the algebraic technique is explained with the
aid of Figure 9–6. The profit-contribution function is determined as follows:

General form:

$$P/V = S - SVC = b_1 Q - b_2 Q = (b_1 - b_2)Q$$

$$PC = P/V - SPC = \frac{b_1 - b_2}{b_1} S - SPC$$

where

P/V	$= P/V$ income.
S	$=$ Sales volume or total revenue.
SVC	$=$ Sector's variable cost.
b_1	$=$ Product price.
b_2	$=$ Sector's average variable cost.
$b_1 - b_2$	$=$ Contribution per unit of Q.
$(b_1 - b_2)/b_1$	$=$ Contribution per dollar of sales or P/V ratio.
PC	$=$ Profit contribution.
SPC	$=$ Specific programmed costs.

To determine the sector's break-even sales volume, set the expression
for *PC* equal to 0, as follows:

$$\frac{b_1 - b_2}{b_1} S - SPC = 0$$

The solution is:

$$S = \frac{SPC}{\frac{b_1 - b_2}{b_1}}$$

Figure 9–6
Profit-contribution chart

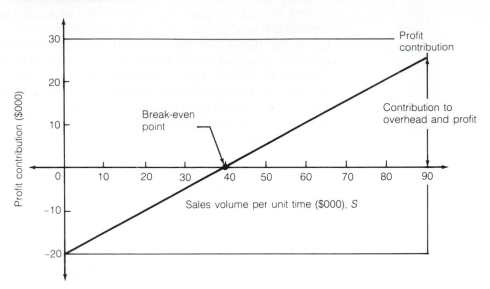

Profit contribution = $0.5 \, S - \$20,000$.

In words, sector break-even volume is obtained by dividing specific programmed costs by sector contribution per dollar of sales. For the example
of Figure 9–6: Price is $100; sector's average variable cost is $50; and
SPC is $20,000;

$$P/V = \frac{100 - 50}{100} S = 0.5S$$
$$PC = 0.5S - 20,000$$

Break-even points:

$$0.5S - 20,000 = 0$$
$$S = 40,000$$

To determine results at any given sales volume, simply substitute that
level of sales into the *PC* equation.

Curvilinear functions

Break-even analysis and profit-volume analysis are often concerned
with results over relatively short ranges of output. Maximum sales expected at a given price and minimum sales expected at the same price
may set the upper and lower limits, respectively, to the relevant range of
output. In another setting, sharply rising costs beyond the designed capacity of a plant may set the upper limit to output, and a break-even point
that is not far away may set the lower limit. In such cases as these, the

assumption that cost and revenue are linear functions of output may be quite close to the true relationships.

On the other hand, if a relatively wide range of output is to be considered, the total cost function will often be curvilinear. A firm with a curvilinear total cost function would face a linear total revenue function if product price were independent of output of the firm (perfect competition). This situation produces a break-even chart like the one depicted in Figure 9–7. Note that there are two break-even points. Note also that profit is maximum at that particular level of output where the vertical distance between the cost and revenue curves is greatest.

If the firm faces a demand curve that slopes down and to the right (monopoly or monopolistic competition), the total revenue function rises to a peak and then declines. In this case, both the cost curve and the revenue curve are curvilinear, and the break-even chart is similar to Figure 9–8. As before, there are two break-even points, and a particular level of output that produces maximum profit.

Figure 9–7
A break-even chart with curvilinear total cost function

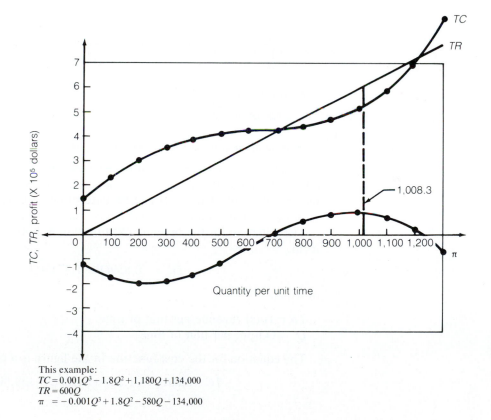

This example:
$TC = 0.001Q^3 - 1.8Q^2 + 1,180Q + 134,000$
$TR = 600Q$
$\pi = -0.001Q^3 + 1.8Q^2 - 580Q - 134,000$

Figure 9–8
A break-even chart with curvilinear total cost and total revenue functions

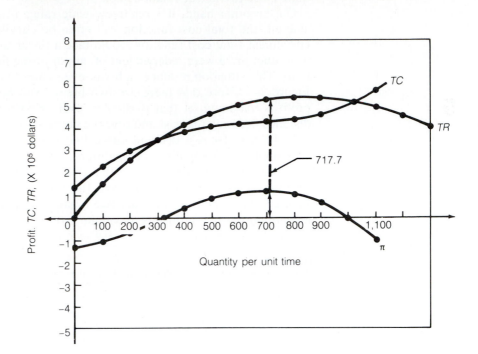

This example:
$TC = 0.001Q^3 - 1.8Q^2 + 1,180Q + 134,000$
$TR = -0.859Q^2 + 1,374.4Q$
$\pi = -0.001Q^3 + 0.941W^2 + 194.4Q - 134,000$

Algebraic determination of optimum output

If there is a curvilinear form of the cost function (or of both the cost and the revenue functions), there is a particular level of output that yields maximum profit. This level can be determined analytically by algebraic techniques. The method is explained by reference to Figure 9–8.

The equation for the revenue (R) function in Figure 9–8 is a quadratic form:

$$TR = -0.859Q^2 + 1,374.4Q$$

in which

$TR =$ Total revenue per unit of time.
$Q \ \ =$ Output per unit of time.

The equation for the cost function in the figure is a cubic form:

$$TC = 0.001Q^3 - 1.8Q^2 + 1,180Q + 134,000$$

The equation for profit (π) is the expression for total revenue less the expression for total cost:

$$\pi = -0.859Q^2 + 1{,}374.4Q - 0.001Q^3 + 1.8Q^2 - 1{,}180Q - 134{,}000$$

Combining terms:

$$\pi = -0.001Q^3 + 0.941Q^2 + 194.4Q - 134{,}000$$

At its maximum point, the slope of the profit function is zero. Since the slope of this function is its first derivative with respect to Q, a general expression for the slope can be found as follows:

$$\frac{d\pi}{dQ} = -0.003Q^2 + 1.882Q + 194.4$$

Let this expression be set equal to 0:

$$0 = -0.003Q^2 + 1.882Q + 194.4$$

The resulting equation can be organized in the general quadratic form:

$$0 = aQ^2 + bQ + c$$

The general quadratic form has two solutions, the two values of Q. These two roots are determined by the general equation:

$$Q = \frac{-b \pm \sqrt{b^2 - 4ac}}{2a}$$

For the example, the equation for the roots of Q and two solution values are:

$$Q = -90.33$$
$$Q = 717.7$$

The negative value cannot be the solution, so the second value is the answer sought.

In words, in the case of a curvilinear cost function, the quantity corresponding to maximum profit can be obtained by:

1. Subtracting the cost function from the revenue function to obtain the profit function.
2. Determining the first derivative of the profit function with respect to Q.
3. Setting the expression for the first derivative equal to zero.
4. Solving the resulting equation for the value of Q.[10]

---

[10] Determining the maximum value of the profit function (as explained in this chapter) and determining the point at which marginal cost equals marginal revenue (as explained in Chapter 6) are alternative ways of solving the same problem: What is the optimum rate of output/sales?

Although the above procedure pinpoints a particular value for "optimum" output, two cautions should be kept in mind. First, the expected value of profit may not change much over a considerable range of values for output (i.e., profit may not be very sensitive to changes in output in the vicinity of optimum). Second, cost and revenue functions used in analysis are estimates; the true functions may be shaped and positioned somewhat differently.

Either the linear or the curvilinear form could describe the relationship of cost to changes in output over a specified range in a particular firm. However, analyses based on these forms do not have the same results. In the case of curvilinear cost and/or revenue functions, profit reaches a peak at a particular level of output; this output is optimum.

Implications for decision making

One should avoid oversimplified generalizations about the relationship of cost to output in the short run. It appears that short-run cost functions approach quite close to linear over the usual range of output in many industries. On the other hand, rising marginal costs are sometimes encountered.

A reasonable way for managers to estimate the effects of alternative actions upon cost is to use their own judgment in determining how the different categories of cost will be affected by these actions. Changes in cost for the various items can then be aggregated to provide cost information relevant to the decision. This flexible approach can be applied to decisions about product information and abandonment as well as to choices of level of output with plant regarded as given.

Managers should be especially careful not to overlook the possibility of rising marginal costs as output per unit of time is increased. Causes of rising marginal cost can be subtle: gradual declines in labor productivity as the work force is increased, creeping managerial inefficiency as the ratio of supervisors to workers falls, and increases in waste of materials and user cost as production presses harder against the designed capacities of machinery and equipment.

Profitability analysis for discrete production runs includes consideration of production that takes the form of one run. As this section is read, one should assume that product types—certain models of certain products—have limited lives. Such projects are undertaken on a one-shot basis. It is not always known in advance or intended that the model be a single run. The Edsel by Ford Motor, for example, was a project having a limited life, although the planners at Ford had hopes of bigger and better things for the Edsel when it was introduced. Let's take a closer look at a successful product.

Terminating production: Product types (or models) and projects

Initially, deal with production that takes the form of one run. The first case considered is that of products, product types, or models that have limited lives. It is followed by an analysis of production that takes the form of projects—construction, system installation, research and development, and others.

Product life cycles

The pattern of a product's sales rates over time is called the life cycle of the product. Consider first the total sales of a general product (ice-cooled household refrigerators, kerosene lamps, CB radios, personal calculators). Marketing specialists conceive the life of a successful product as consisting of four recognizable stages, illustrated in Figure 9–9 and defined as follows:

Introduction   Potential customers are just becoming aware of the product. Demand is created; the marketing objective is to get some buyers to try the product. Sales rates are low and slowly rising.

Growth   Customers become gradually aware of the product. Acceptance begins to spread rapidly. Sales zoom upward and strain the productive capacities of the industry. More producers enter the industry. The marketing objective is to develop brand preferences.

Maturity   Most potential customers have made their initial purchases. The market becomes saturated and demand is limited to replacement and population growth. Price and nonprice competition becomes intense.

Decline   The product begins losing its appeal as lifestyles change and products based on new technologies become available. Excess capacity builds up, even though one producer after another drops out of the market.

**Figure 9–9
A product's life cycle**

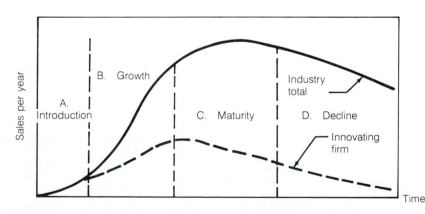

The life cycle depicted in Figure 9–9 is a generalized pattern; many products do not follow the pattern exactly. As with the Edsel, some are failures and are abandoned during the introduction stage, causing heavy losses for the unsuccessful innovator. Others have a slow, prolonged growth stage rather than the sharp rise in sales rates shown in Figure 9–9. The maturity stage of some products lasts for many years (gelatin desserts, innerspring mattresses, gasoline-powered automobiles), whereas other products may be quickly passing fads (hula hoops, miniskirts, most hit records). The decline stage may be gradual (black-and-white television receivers) or abrupt and rapid (mechanical desk calculators). Despite the many deviations from the generalized pattern, the concept of a product life cycle is useful because most general products do pass through these recognizable stages with their wide variations in sales rates. Awareness of a product's location in its life cycle is of extreme importance to one interested in maximizing profitability of that product. Obviously, if a product that is currently profitable is also declining rapidly, a decision to pump *x* millions of additional dollars into it

Figure 9–10
Sales over time—three very familiar products*

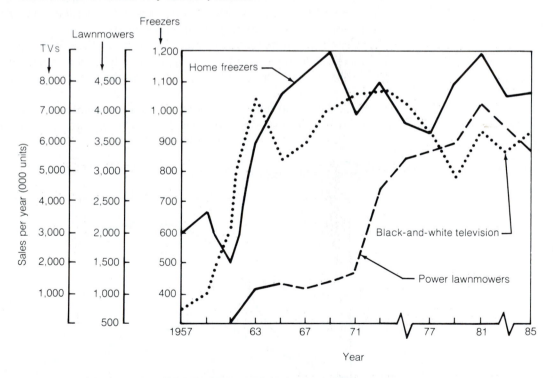

* Figures 9–10 through 9–14 are adapted from S. G. Sturmey "Cost Curves and Pricing in Aircraft Production," *Economic Journal* (December 1964).

might be more than a little risky. Figure 9–10 shows sales rates for three familiar products that appear to have entered their maturity stages.

An individual firm's sales over time are that firm's share of the industry's total sales.[11] During the early introduction stage, a firm that is the first innovator may have all sales of the product, but the company's output will ordinarily be a steadily decreasing share of the industry total as other firms enter during the growth stage (see Figure 9–9). Sales rates of any given model may level off, or even begin to decline, long before the onset of the maturity stage of the general product. A producer may be able to lengthen the period of profitable production by introducing a series of improved models or product types, as depicted in Figure 9–11. Each such model or type has a life cycle of its own, which may be as short as a single year (1984 Ford Mustang) or may run several years (IBM's personal computer model).

In managing products that have life cycles, special attention must be given to deciding (1) whether or not to introduce new products, (2) alternative strategies for introduction, (3) economic effects of variations in rate of production and lengths of production run, and (4) when to shut down production and end the lives of old products. Economic analyses appropriate to these decisions are discussed in the sections to follow.

Figure 9–11
Life cycles of a series of models

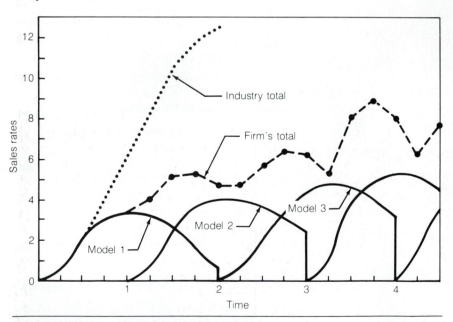

---

[11] When initially accepting employment with a firm, it is good to know where that company is located on its growth cycle. Declining firms in declining industries are not known for their high salaries and/or opportunity for advancement.

New-product profitability analysis: An overview

In deciding whether to introduce a new product, management must estimate profits over the whole potential life of the product. Losses may be unavoidable during the introductory stage but may be more than offset by subsequent profits. The firm's planning objective is to maximize the present value of expected future net cash flows over a period extending as long as the life of any product under consideration.

Projecting a new product's sales and revenue   The time path of sales rates for a type or model of a product depends upon (1) the underlying pattern of local industry sales for the general product class and (2) the firm's share of industry total, which will depend partially upon the firm's pricing and promotion. Since the company cannot be certain about the success of a new product, it is advisable to make alternative forecasts. For example, the Cessna aircraft manufacturer might make three forecasts of sales patterns for a new type of plane, as illustrated in Figure 9–12. Management's subjective probability estimates for each of the three sales patterns may be different for alternative pricing strategies, as shown in Table 9–1.

Table 9–1
Cessna forecasts for a new plane

Degree of success	Total number of planes	Management's subjective probability estimates	
		Price—$10 million	Price—$9.5 million
Low	50	.30	.05
Moderate	100	.45	.55
High	200	.25	.40

Figure 9–12
Cessna forecasts for a new plane

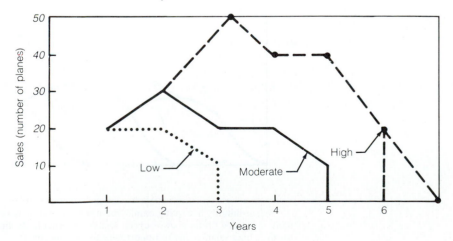

Projecting a new product's costs In making a new product, some costs will be fixed and, perhaps, sunk for the production run: detailed product design and styling, construction and testing of a prototype, detailed planning of production processes, purchase of specialized jigs and tools, selection and training of a work force, and cost of positioning and starting up. As the total volume of the production run is increased, there are more units to share the fixed cost of the run, and the amount prorated to each unit is reduced.

Total variable cost of the production run (labor, materials, power, direct overhead) increases with total volume. However, the additions to variable cost are usually less than proportional to expansion of total production because of a phenomenon called the learning curve.

Effects of learning curves on variable costs per unit

It has been observed that a labor force working on a new product becomes more efficient as the length of the production run is increased. Skills improve, more specializations are developed, coordination gets better, and innumerable adjustments are found to make the work easier and faster. The resulting patterns of declining labor cost per unit over successive units of output are called learning curves. Learning curves are apparent in building a series of similar structures (houses, industrial plants, bridges), in assembling complex products (computers, automated machine tools, naval vessels, aircraft), and in carrying out a series of difficult process start-ups (metal refining, paper making, chemical synthesis, container manufacturing).

A common form of the learning curve is based on reduction of labor per incremental unit of output by a constant fraction each time the total output to date is doubled. For example, suppose the labor requirement is reduced by 10 percent with each doubling of output. Incremental labor required for the ith unit is 0.9 times the incremental labor needed for the $\frac{i}{2}$th unit. The factor 0.9 is called the learning rate for the particular work process. The equation for the learning curve in the above example is $L_i = 0.9L_{i/2}$, in which L is incremental labor per unit. If the first unit produced (the prototype) requires 1,000 units of labor, the second is projected to take 900 units, the fourth to need 810 units, the eighth to require 729 units, and so on. On long production runs, learning curves can produce very sizable reductions in labor used per unit, as may be seen in Figure 9–13.

Learning rates may vary from one work process to another. The proportion of labor used in tasks that are not machine-paced is an important determinant of the learning rate. Learning curves are particularly impressive in aircraft manufacturing, where most labor is used in manual tech-

Figure 9–13
Effects of learning on labor used

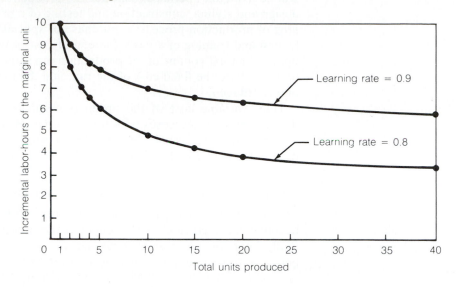

niques. The following rules of thumb have been developed for estimating learning rates prior to any experience with a new work process:

If the proportion of direct labor not paced by machines is	The expected learning rate is
0.75	0.80
0.50	0.85
0.25	0.90

The rate of improvement in labor efficiency tends to be greater (value of the learning-rate coefficient tends to be smaller) than the above values if the product is a completely new design. However, if the product is a slight modification of one that has already been run by the same work force, the initial unit will have labor costs reflecting some of the learning from the previous production run, and subsequent improvement will be smaller (the learning-rate coefficient will be larger) than the values above.

The effects of learning curves upon labor costs make it imperative for new product profitability to be analyzed over the whole life cycle of the product. It is often necessary to take losses in early periods, when labor costs are high, in order to reach those points on the learning curve at which labor costs become low enough that profits can be made.

Deciding whether or not to introduce a new product

An example of Cessna aircraft's assumed decision regarding whether or not to introduce a new plane illustrates the interaction of the learning-curve effect upon costs and the pricing effect upon revenue.

Cost analysis   This structure of costs is hypothetical but representative of costs of manufacturing a moderate-size passenger plane.

1. Variable costs.
    a. Direct labor, primarily assembly labor—a learning rate of 0.8 is assumed.
    b. Materials and components. Materials cost per unit stabilize early in the production run and are assumed constant. Components (landing gear, engines, radios, instruments, seats, etc.) are standard items used in a number of other aircraft and have a constant cost per unit.
    c. Indirect labor and power—assumed to have a constant cost per unit.
2. Fixed costs for the production run.
    a. Research, engineering, styling.
    b. Purchase of specialized jigs, dies, and tools.
    c. Selling and promotion.

Total and unit costs at various levels of total output are similar to those listed in Table 9–2 and illustrated in Figure 9–14. As total output increases, cost per unit decreases in the fixed-cost category because the fixed total cost is prorated over more units, and cost per unit decreases in the variable-cost category because of the effect of the learning curve upon direct labor cost per unit.

Profitability analysis, using a decision tree   Profitability analysis requires comparisons of costs and revenues at the various levels of output for which management has made subjective probability estimates. Assume management's sales and probability forecasts for the new plane are the seven-year projections in Table 9–1, and the cost estimates for the plane are those listed in Table 9–2. A decision tree provides an efficient organization of the alternative outcomes of the new product venture and their probabilities, since these depend upon pricing strategies. A tree for this example is shown in Figure 9–15.

A decision tree is composed of nodes and branches and runs from left to right. At the extreme left, the square node represents a decision point

Table 9–2
Average and total costs for a new plane (in $millions)

Output	Direct labor	Other variable costs	Variable cost per unit	Fixed cost per unit	Average total cost per unit	Total cost at this output
10	$1.54	$6.20	$7.74	$30.00	$37.74	$ 377.40
20	1.28	6.20	7.48	15.00	22.48	449.60
30	1.15	6.20	7.35	10.00	17.35	520.50
40	1.05	6.20	7.25	7.50	14.75	590.00
50	0.98	6.20	7.18	6.00	13.18	659.00
100	0.80	6.20	7.00	3.00	10.00	1,000.00
200	0.65	6.20	6.85	1.50	8.35	1,670.00

Figure 9–14
Cessna total cost and total revenue for a new plane

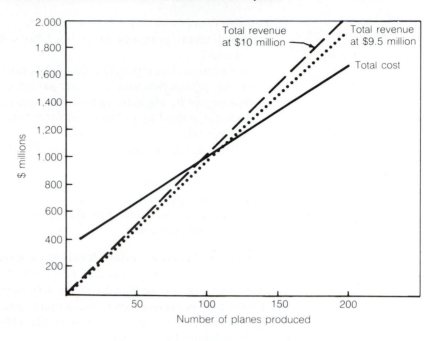

from which there are two action branches representing the firm's alternative pricing strategies. The action branches lead to round nodes standing for chance-event points. Chance events are alternative states of nature that are beyond the firm's control (here the alternative states of nature are sales volumes that depend upon customer acceptance and actions of competitive firms). On each chance-event branch one posts the estimated probability of the event and the firm's expected outcome or payoff (revenue minus cost).

Calculate the mathematical expectation of payoff for each of the pricing strategies. Calculations begin at the payoffs at the extreme right of the decision tree. The expected value of the strategy of pricing at $10 million per unit, on the top action branch, is the sum of the products of the payoffs times their probabilities and is determined as follows (all values in $millions):

Probability	Times	Payoff	Equals	Expected value
.30	×	− $159	=	− $47.7
.45	×	0	=	0.0
.25	×	330	=	82.5
Expected value of strategy				$34.8

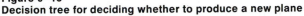

Figure 9–15
Decision tree for deciding whether to produce a new plane

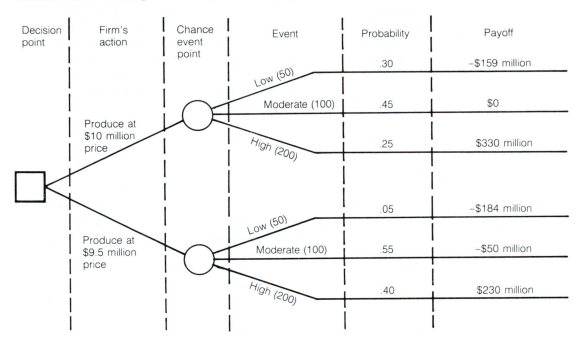

The expected value of the strategy of pricing at $9.5 million per unit can be calculated for the lower action branch as follows:

Probability	Times	Payoff	Equals	Expected value
.05	×	−$184	=	−$ 9.2
.55	×	−$ 50	=	− 27.5
.40	×	$230	=	92.0
Expected value of strategy				$55.3

Based on expected values, the new product is profitable, and the strategy of pricing at $9.5 million produces a greater expected value than pricing at $10 million per plane. Note: The expected value of a decision is the average outcome that it would have if it could be carried out a great number of times with probabilities of payoffs as estimated by management for the particular decision. The outcome of any one decision will, of course, be some specific payoff—a payoff that may differ from the decision's expected value. It is reasonable to base all decisions on expected values if the firm's total activities and financial base are large enough that the firm's overall value cannot be substantially reduced by the outcome of any one of the decisions. If possible downside variations in outcomes are large in relation to the firm's total income and wealth, management may wish to adjust payoffs for risk by substituting the corresponding preference values into the decision tree.

Skimming versus penetration pricing In the example above, results of alternative constant prices over the product's life cycle were projected. Pricing strategies that involve changes in prices over the life cycle could be more profitable. One such strategy is skimming, in which the product is initially offered at a relatively high price, and the price is gradually reduced to tap a wider and wider market. The objective is to maximize total revenue from eventual saturation of the market. Skimming is most suitable for products that have relatively inelastic demand at the high introductory prices and relatively elastic demand at the subsequently lowered prices. Skimming is often used in introducing a new product that is unique or very much differentiated (Polaroid innovations, personal pocket-size calculators, electronic wristwatches).

An alternate strategy for new-product pricing is penetration pricing, in which the price at introduction is lower than the level that will be maintained after the product is established in the market. The objective is a rapid buildup of sales rate. Penetration is most suitable for products that have relatively elastic demand at the low introduction prices, economies of scale that give substantial reductions in unit costs at greater rates of output, and a potential for early imitation that makes it advisable to price low to discourage entry of competitors. Penetration has often been used in introducing new food products and toiletries (two packages for the price of one, a coupon worth 50 percent off the regular price). Tang, an orange juice substitute, and Pringles, chips made from dehydrated potatoes, are examples of products that first appeared as special offers.

Ways of changing a production run that is under way

As a firm observes sales of a product, it can revise its plans for output of the current production run. In decisions about changes in output of a run that is under way, costs already incurred or obligated are treated as sunk. Only those costs that vary with changes in production rate or length of the run are relevant.

Although total output must be matched to total sales over the product's life cycle, output can be greater than sales in a given period (with a buildup of finished goods inventory), or sales can exceed production in a period (with depletion of inventory and/or an accumulation of back orders). Over a product's life, the firm may set up a series of production runs in the manner illustrated in Figure 9–16. If we focus attention on any one production run, we see that its own volume can be varied in four different ways:

1. With rate of production held constant, total output of the run can be increased (decreased) by adding to (subtracting from) the length of the run, as depicted in part A of Figure 9–17. For example, a manufacturer

Figure 9–16
Sales and production over product's life cycle

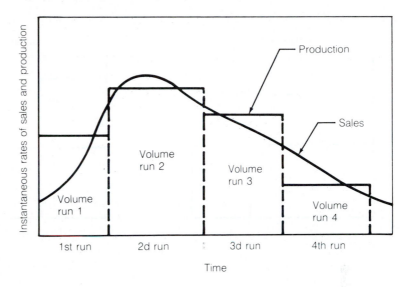

who has a greater sales rate than expected can build up an order backlog, maintain the original planned rate of production, and increase the planned length of the production run.

2. With planned total output of the run held constant, the length of the run can be cut (or stretched out) by accelerating (or slowing down) the rate of production, as shown in part B of Figure 9–17. For example, a manufacturer or contractor may be asked to speed up the delivery rate of an order or the completion date of a contract (for a given number of aircraft of a particular type, for a series of similar structures, for a large building, for an elaborate data processing system, and so on).

3. With length of the run held constant, the instantaneous rate of production and the planned total volume can be varied in the same proportion as illustrated in part C of Figure 9–17. This kind of change in volume is appropriate when a change in sales rate is viewed as permanent, or at least indefinite.

4. Rate of production, length of run, and planned total output can all be varied simultaneously, as in part D of Figure 9–17.

Method 4 is an amalgam of the first three methods. It will not be analyzed as such, since a clearer understanding can be gained by studying its components. Method 3, in which instantaneous rate and planned total volume are varied in the same proportion, is simply that change in rate of output of a continuative production process that has been analyzed at some length in earlier chapters. It will not be given further attention in this chapter. Thus, we shall analyze only method 1 (change in length of

Figure 9–17
Changes in output of production runs

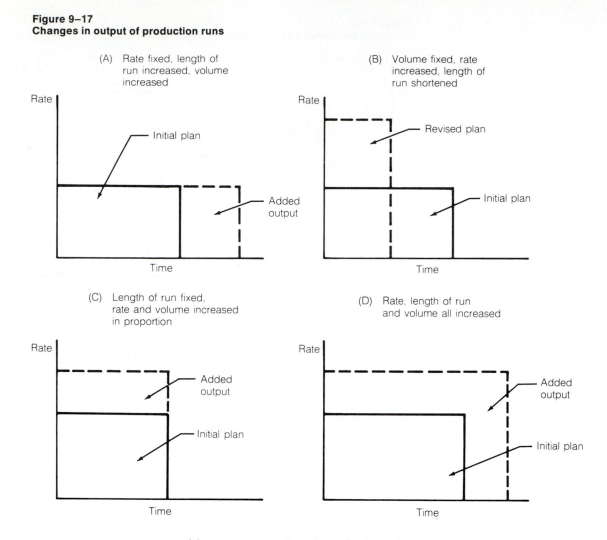

(A) Rate fixed, length of run increased, volume increased

(B) Volume fixed, rate increased, length of run shortened

(C) Length of run fixed, rate and volume increased in proportion

(D) Rate, length of run and volume all increased

run with rate constant) and method 2 (change in rate with total output constant) in the sections to follow.

Analyzing profitability of a change in length of run

With a production run under way, is it profitable to accept additional orders and lengthen the run? The decision depends on a comparison of incremental costs of the added output with the corresponding incremental revenue. The incremental costs resulting from stretching a production run are of two types: (1) incremental production costs and (2) opportunity costs of any limited resources required during the stretch (if the use of these resources means foregoing contribution that could be earned from other products or a new model of the same product). Analyze first a case in which the firm has no alternative uses for its fixed inputs, so there are no opportunity costs associated with the increase in the length of the run.

First example: Opportunity costs are zero Suppose Sohio has built eight identical gasoline service stations and is considering four more stations to be built from the same plan. The effect of the learning curve upon incremental unit cost should be taken into account. The company's records show that its variable costs in building the first, second, fourth, and eighth stations (restated in current, or inflation-corrected, dollars) were as listed in Table 9–3. Although costs of materials and indirect labor appear to have stabilized early in the production run, there is evidence of a learning curve in the direct labor column. As a check on this hypothesis, Sohio's management calculates direct labor costs for several *i*th units as a percentage of the corresponding ½th units, with the following results:

Number of unit (i)	$i/2$	Cost of ith unit/Cost of $i/2$th unit
2	1	0.860
4	2	0.849
8	4	0.849

Based upon the above results, management concludes that the learning rate is approximately 0.85.

To estimate the direct labor cost of the next four units, the following approach is used. The formula for a learning curve of this type is:

$$L_m = L_m \left(\frac{n}{m}\right)^2$$

in which

L_n = Direct labor required for the *n*th unit.
L_m = Known labor used in the *m*th unit.
x = Log of the learning-rate coefficient divided by the log of the number 2.

Table 9–3
Production costs—construction

Job	Direct labor	Indirect labor	Materials cost	Total cost
1	$62,200	$4,000	$50,200	$116,400
2	51,800	3,900	49,700	105,400
4	44,000	3,900	49,800	97,700
8	37,300	3,900	49,600	90,800

Values of x for selected learning rates are listed below:

Learning rate	Value of x
0.75	-0.4150
0.80	-0.3219
0.85	-0.2345
0.90	-0.1520
0.95	-0.0740

For the estimates that Sohio needs, m is 8; n is 9, 10, 11, and 12; x is -0.2345; and L_m is \$37,300.

Direct labor costs of the ninth unit can be estimated as follows:

$$L_9 = \$37,300 \times \left(\frac{9}{8}\right)^{-0.2345}$$

$$= \$37,300 \times \left(\frac{8}{9}\right)^{0.2345}$$

$$= \$36,284$$

Assume materials costs are constant at \$49,700, and indirect labor costs are constant at \$3,900. Adding in the direct labor cost just estimated, the total incremental production costs of the 9th unit can be projected at \$89,884. Incremental costs of the 10th, 11th, and 12th units can be estimated in the manner described above, and the projected costs of all four units are as listed in Table 9–4. The total incremental production costs are estimated at \$354,616. Any revenue in excess of this amount is expected to be a contribution toward the company's overhead cost and possible profits.

Second example: Opportunity costs exist   Suppose Sohio does have alternative uses for its fixed inputs, in which uses the company would earn contributions. These alternative contributions can be viewed as opportunity costs of the fixed inputs for the service station construction project; these contributions, which must be sacrificed if the company builds the stations, are costs that should be added to incremental production costs.

For example, assume that if the firm did not build the stations, it could take on two smaller jobs—one having an estimated contribution of

Table 9–4
Estimated future costs—XYZ Construction

Job	Direct labor	Indirect labor and materials	Total cost
9	\$36,284	\$53,600	\$89,884
10	35,399	53,600	88,999
11	34,616	53,600	88,216
12	33,917	53,600	87,517

$15,000 and the other having an estimated contribution of $25,000. In this case the opportunity costs of the fixed inputs is $40,000, and the total incremental economic cost of the service station project is the incremental production cost of $354,616 plus the opportunity cost of $40,000—or $394,616.

Third example: Analyzing profitability of model changeover   Opportunity costs are particularly important for a firm that is deciding whether to continue production of a current model or to switch to a new model. For example, suppose a firm is at the end of a third production year of the current model and is considering whether to make a major styling change or to simply face lift by substituting a few bolt-on items. Further, assume that pricing will be the same with or without the major change in the product, but the new model would be expected to have sales of 500,000 units during the next year compared with 350,000 units expected to sell if the firm continues the current model. However, of the 150,000 units of sales foregone by continuing the current model, it is estimated that perhaps 90,000 will be recouped during the subsequent year when the delayed change in styling is finally introduced. So the net loss in sales during the next year is reduced to 60,000 units. The opportunity cost of delaying the major model changeover is the contribution the company would expect to earn on the net loss of 60,000 units, and this opportunity cost should be compared with the incremental increase in contribution that can be earned on 350,000 units of the current model (as a result of being far out on the learning curve instead of passing through the first 350,000 units of a new curve for the new model) plus the value of the income from one year's investment of the postponed fixed cost associated with a new production run (detailed engineering and styling, purchase of specialized tools and dies, selection and training of the work force, etc.).

Model for analysis of profitability   A model to analyze the profitability of increasing the rate of production for a given total volume can be derived. All of the above increases in value of the firm's output are viewed as opportunity costs that are reduced as the production rate is increased. On the other hand, cost of the firm's tangible production inputs (labor, materials, power, etc.) goes up as the production rate is increased. The model appears as shown in Figure 9–18. If there were no opportunity costs to consider, cost would be minimized by choosing a rate such that the cost of tangible inputs is minimized, illustrated by point X in Figure 9–18. But where there are opportunity costs, the total cost of the production run is lowest at a saddle point corresponding to a faster production rate, as illustrated by point Y in Figure 9–18.

Summary

Corporate profitability is made possible by the institutions of (1) private property and (2) the price system. Interference with either institution will

Figure 9–18
Minimizing economic cost (maximizing profitability) by choosing an optimal rate of production

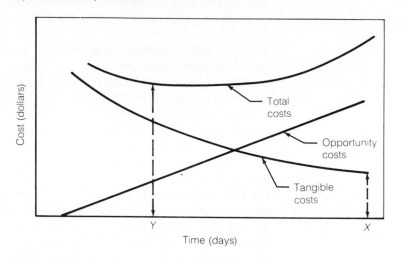

adversely affect corporate profits. Corporate profits are essential to the creation and continuation of retained earnings, the accounting category from which most net new investment (plus employment, output and additional income) originates.

This chapter has revealed that "normal" profit is a cost of doing business. Any firm failing to recover its total costs, which include normal profits, will be depriving itself of a large source of funds for future investment purposes. A firm without profit after tax to transfer into its retained earnings account would have to look for future investment funds in the capital markets (i.e., bonds or common stock). But, new long-term debt and equity issues may not be possible for a company that has failed to generate profits.

Profit theories are numerous but may be broken into four broad classifications: (1) residual theory of profitability, (2) frictional theory of profitability, (3) innovation theory of profitability, and (4) compensatory and/ or functional theories. Regardless, if a firm is to be profitable it must break even.

Break-even analysis is a technique used in comparing the total cost of output or sales to the corresponding value at various rates of output or sales. It can be applied in decisions about production for deliberate buildup of inventory or about production matched by sales in the same period. Break-even analysis can reveal the sensitivity of profit to changes in rate of output, prices of inputs or of the product, or input-to-output conversion ratios (such as labor per unit of output). It can be carried out algebraically or by graphing.

Cost functions used in break-even analysis can be estimated from an income and expense statement for a single period by using a classifications approach, or the functions may be statistically derived from a series of statements over various periods in which the firm had differing rates of output. The scale of the output or sales axis may be in physical units if the firm has a single homogeneous product. If the firm has a mix of products, output or sales can be measured in one of the following: an index (such as hours of direct labor used), percent of plant capacity used in production, dollar value of output.

Profit-volume analysis focuses on contribution of a product, department, or sector toward the overhead costs and profit of the firm. The P/V technique can also be used to compare contributions of different products or to compare contributions of the same product at differing prices. The algebraic method of P/V analysis is easy to complete.

If the firm has a curvilinear total cost curve, faces a sloping demand curve, or both, it has an optimum rate of output that can be determined by two mathematical approaches: (1) Determine rate of output at which dTC/dQ (the slope of total cost, which is marginal cost) is equal to dTR/dQ (the slope of total revenue, which is marginal revenue), or (2) determine the rate of output at which dP/dQ (the slope of the profit function) is zero and the function is maximum.

The chapter also discussed the profitability analysis of production runs that have planned termination or interruption. The first section was concerned with production that takes the form of a single run. The first kind of terminating production considered was production of models or types that pass through life cycles. New-product profitability analysis should extend over the whole life cycle, since it may be necessary to take early losses in order to get to the profitable range of production at low unit costs. Learning curves decrease variable unit cost as more units are added to the total of a run. Skimming pricing is sometimes used on new products—the objective is to increase total revenue from the amount of product that eventually saturates the market. Penetration pricing is an alternative approach—the objective is to get a rapid buildup of sales and output rates to levels that allow low unit costs.

After a production run is under way, the firm can change either the length of the run (and its total output) or the rate (leaving total output constant). Changes in length of run were analyzed first. The profitability of such a change can be determined by comparing incremental costs of the additional output with incremental value. Incremental costs include added costs of tangible production inputs. If the increase in length of run requires services of the firm's fixed inputs that have alternative uses, incremental costs also include opportunity costs of the fixed inputs. In deciding whether to make model changeovers, special attention must be given to comparison of (1) contribution that must be foregone on any net loss in sales if the changeover is not made with (2) cost reduction on the units produced in a longer production run of the old model—as compared with cost for the same number of units in the first year of a new model.

Profitability of a change in the rate of production for a fixed total output can be analyzed by comparing the resulting increased cost of production with increased value because the result of production is available sooner. A convenient model for determining the optimum rate treats foregone value because of delayed completion as an opportunity cost. The approach is to minimize the sum of tangible production cost (which increases with rate) and opportunity cost (which decreases with rate).

CASES

Profitability analysis

How to break even*

Accountant: Karen, you said you put in these peanuts because some people ask for them, but do you realize what this rack of peanuts is costing you?

Karen: It is not going to cost. It is going to generate a profit. Sure, I paid $25 for a fancy rack to hold the bags, but the peanuts cost only 6 cents a bag, and I sell them for 10 cents. I calculate that if I sell 50 bags a week to start, it will take 12½ weeks to cover the cost of the rack. After that, I clear 4 cents a bag profit. The more I sell, the more I make.

Accountant: That is an antiquated and completely unrealistic approach, Karen. Fortunately, modern accounting procedures permit a more accurate picture, which reveals the complexities involved.

Karen: Huh?

Accountant: To be precise, those peanuts must be integrated into your entire operation and be allocated their appropriate share of business overhead. They must share a proportionate part of your expenditures for rent, heat, light, equipment depreciation, decorating, salaries for your waiters, cook. . . .

Karen: The cook? What's he have to do with the peanuts? He doesn't know I have them!

Accountant: Look Karen, the cook is in the kitchen; the kitchen prepares the food; the food is what brings people in here; and the people ask to buy peanuts. That's why you must charge a portion of the cook's wages as well as a part of your own salary to peanut sales. This sheet contains a carefully calculated cost analysis, which indicates the peanut operation should pay exactly $1,278 per year toward these general overhead costs.

Karen: The peanuts? Pay $1,278 a year for overhead? The nuts?

---

* Not completely original with the author; initial source unknown.

Accountant: It's really a little more than that. You also spend money each week to have the windows washed, to have the place swept out in the mornings, keep soap in the washroom, and provide free cokes to the police. That raises the total to $1,313 per year.

Karen: [Thoughtfully] But the peanut sales rep said I would make money . . . put them on the end of the counter, he said . . . and get 4 cents a bag profit. . . .

Accountant: [With a sniff] He's not an accountant. He's a marketing major. Do you actually know what the portion of the counter occupied by the peanut rack is worth to you?

Karen: It's not worth anything. There's no stool there . . . just a dead spot at the end.

Accountant: The modern cost picture permits no dead spots. Your counter contains 60 square feet, and your counter business grosses $15,000 a year, Consequently, the square foot of space occupied by the peanut rack is worth $250 per year. Since you have taken that area away from general counter use, you must charge the value of the space to the occupant.

Karen: You mean I must add $250 a year more to the peanuts?

Accountant: Right. That raises their share of the general operating costs to a grand total of $1,563 per year. Now then, if you sell 50 bags of peanuts per week, theses allocated costs will amount to 60 cents per bag.

Karen: What?

Accountant: Obviously, to that must be added your purchase price of 6 cents per bag, which brings the total to 66 cents. So you see, by selling peanuts at 10 cents per bag, you are losing 56 cents on every sale.

Karen: Something or someone is crazy!

Accountant: Not at all! Here are the figures. They prove your peanuts operation cannot stand on its own feet.

Karen: [Brightening] Suppose I sell a lot of peanuts . . . thousands and thousands of bags a week, instead of 50?

Accountant: [Tolerantly] Karen, you don't understand the problem. If the volume of peanut sales increases, our operating costs will go up. . . . You'll have to handle more bags with more time, more depreciation, more everything. The basic principle of accounting is firm on that subject: ''The bigger the operation, the more general overhead costs that must be allocated.'' No, increasing the volume of sales won't help.

Karen: Okay, if you are so smart, you tell me what I should do.

Accountant: [Condescendingly] Well . . . you could first reduce operating expenses.

Karen: How?

Accountant: Move to a building with cheaper rent. Cut salaries. Wash the windows biweekly. Have the floor swept only on Thursday. Remove the soap from washrooms. Decrease the square-foot value of your counter. For example, if you can cut your expenses 50 percent, that will reduce the amount allocated to peanuts from $1,563 to $781.50 per year, reducing the cost to 36 cents per bag.

Karen: [Slowly] That's better?

Accountant: Much, much better. However, even then you would lose 26 cents per bag if you only charge 10 cents. Therefore, you must also raise your selling price. If you wanted a net profit of 4 cents per bag, you would have to charge 40 cents.

Karen: [Flabbergasted] You mean even after I cut operating costs 50 percent I still must charge 40 cents for a 10-cent bag of peanuts? Nobody's that nuts about nuts! Who'd buy 'em?

Accountant: That's a secondary consideration. The point is, at 40 cents you'd be selling at a price based upon a true and proper evaluation of your then-reduced costs.

Karen: [Eagerly] Look! I have a better idea. Why don't I just throw the nuts out and put them in the trash can?

Accountant: Can you afford it?

Karen: Sure. All I have is about 50 bags of peanuts . . . cost about three bucks . . . so I lose $25 on the rack, but I'm out of this nutsy business and no more grief.

Accountant: [Shaking his head in disbelief] Karen, it isn't that simple. You are in the peanut business! The minute you throw those peanuts out you are adding $1,563 of annual overhead to the rest of your operation. Karen . . . be realistic. . . . can you afford to do that?

Karen: [Completely crushed] This is unbelievable! Last week I was going to make money. Now I'm in trouble . . . just because I think peanuts on a counter could bring me some extra profit . . . just because I believe 50 bags of peanuts a week is easy.

Accountant: [With raised eyebrow] That is the object of modern cost studies, Karen . . . to dispel those false illusions.

1. What is the incremental cost per bag of peanuts?
2. What is the weekly contribution of the peanut rack?
3. How would the case be changed if there were an alternate use for the space, such as a chewing gum display?

4. Does management need full cost including allocated overhead for some purposes, or can all management decisions be based on contributions above incremental cost?

5. Comment on the accountant's principle: "The bigger the operation, the more general overhead costs that must be allocated." Are there better criteria for allocating overhead costs?

National Cash Register's critical-path method to profitability

Under the residual theory of profitability, one can improve his/her profits by increasing revenues or decreasing costs, or some combination of these two things. Always, but particularly during recessionary times, it is desirable to minimize cost. When production takes the form of projects (construction, system installation, research and development), the work process consists of a great many different activities and tasks. Some of these must be completed before others can be undertaken. The cost of each must be minimized if profit is to be maximized.

Assume that construction project Y consists of the following five tasks:

Activity	Hours required
A. Procure materials	0.5
B. Make part 1	3.0
C. Make part 2	2.0
D. Assemble part 1 to part 2	1.0
E. Paint the assembly	1.0

One should calculate the least time in which project Y can be completed. Prepare a diagram showing the activities that must be performed in sequence and the ones that can be carried out simultaneously. The diagram is to be made up of arrows representing each of the activities plus nodes representing points at which one activity must be finished before another activity can be started. The diagram for project Y is shown in Exhibit 1.

The minimum time for project completion is the greatest total time

Exhibit 1
Diagram for project Y

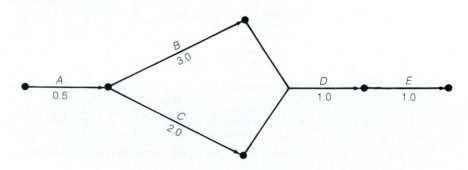

required to travel any path from the beginning to the end of the project. In project Y there are two possible paths: *A–B–D–E*, requiring 5.5 hours, and *A–C–D–E*, requiring 4.5 hours. The first path may be called the critical path, since it is the one that determines minimum time. The project could be speeded by doing task *b* in less time, but there would be no gain from shortening the time for task *c*. In general, a project can be finished earlier only by speeding up, or "crashing," the activities along the critical path.

The critical-path method (CPM) is a technique used to identify the critical and noncritical activities in a large project. Only about 10 percent of all activities will usually be found to be critical. Project completion time can be shortened by carrying out the critical activities at a greater-than-normal rate—with higher-than-usual cost. The cost of cutting a day from time required varies from one critical activity to another. There is some point along the critical path at which one day can be cut at the least cost, then another point at which a day can be cut at the next least cost, and so on. Thus, the critical-path method can be used to determine the least-cost ways of cutting successively greater and greater amounts of time so as to obtain the function in Figure 9–18, which relates cost of tangible inputs to project time.

National Cash Register's direct-mail campaign called for sending literature to potential buyers of computers and data systems. The project was divided into the 16 separate tasks listed in Exhibit 2. As shown in the exhibit, costs and times were estimated on both a normal basis and a

Exhibit 2
NCR Century direct-mail campaign

	Activity duration in days		Activity dollar cost		Rate of cost increase ($ per day)
Activity	Normal	Crash	Normal	Crash	
A. Rough copy	8	3	$ 400	$ 650	$ 50
B. Copy for announcement	2	1	125	225	100
C. Layout	10	5	600	1,200	120
D. Approval	3	3	—	—	—
E. Research mailing lists	5	1	100	540	110
F. Final art	12	7	750	1,500	150
G. Approval—announcement	2	2	—	—	—
H. Final copy	6	2	250	400	38
I. Type set	3	1	350	525	88
J. OK mailing lists	1	1	—	—	—
K. Printing—announcement	4	2	150	400	125
L. Printing	18	12	2,150	3,350	200
M. Order mailing lists	14	6	500	620	15
N. Deliver to mailing center announcement	1	1	—	—	—
O. Deliver to mailing center	2	2	—	—	—
P. Mail material	5	1	1,150	1,650	125

Source: Edward J. Feltz, "The Costs of Crashing," *Journal of Marketing*, July 1970, p. 66.

Exhibit 3
Network for the NCR project

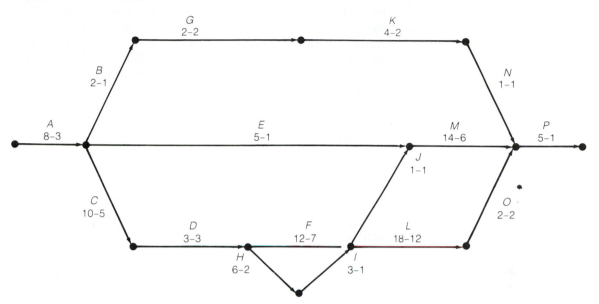

Source: Edward J. Feltz, "The Costs of Crashing," *Journal of Marketing,* July 1970, p. 65.

crash basis for each of the tasks. The final column in the table is based on the assumption that for any one activity, the cost per day cut from the time requirement is a constant.

The CPM network for this project is shown in Exhibit 3. The letters correspond to the tasks listed in Exhibit 2, and the numbers show the normal and crash times, respectively. There are six possible paths from the start of the project to the finish. The one that takes the longest and in which all activities are carried out on a normal basis is the path *A–C–D–F–L–O–P*. This path requires 58 days and is the initial critical path for the project.

1. How would you improve profitability (reduce the project time at least cost) for National Cash Register's direct-mail program?
2. Reveal your answer(s) in graphical and in tabular format.

PROBLEMS
Profitability analysis

9–1   A newly constructed high school is owned and operated by the Diocese of Houston. This diocesan high school, as with public and private schools everywhere, has direct labor charges budgeted on a contractual basis. The teachers are paid a specified amount of money for the school year, regardless of the number of hours worked or the number of students in attendance. A situation of direct labor on a contractual basis is often beneficial for both management and labor. In the case of this high school, the advantages are twofold: (1) The arrangement provides the teachers with the security of knowing that a certain amount of money will be forthcoming, and (2) it allows the school board to budget for payment of a particular sum of money. The disadvantages are also twofold: (1) The number of students per classroom could be increased by the central administration, and the teacher would have little or no control over the heavier teaching load; and (2) if enrollment were to decline significantly, the school board would be stuck paying for services it did not want and could not use. In terms of break-even analysis, this latter point is very important; it may mean all costs are fixed rigidly in the short run. Fixed costs are $572,000. Tuition, on average, is not quite $500 per student, per year. Calculate the high school's break-even point.

9–2   A porcelain figurine is made and sold by Berkeley Enterprises at a variable cost of $500 per unit. The fixed costs per period are $1,000. Each unit is sold at a price of $750.

a. Draw a break-even chart, labeling all lines, the axes, profit (loss), and the break-even point.
b. Redraw the graph with a fixed cost of $2,000 per year.
c. "The dividing line between fixed and variable cost depends upon the particular decision involved." Explain.

9–3   Cost and related data are shown below for the McDonald's and Wendy's locations near Santa Cruz, California.

	McDonald's	Wendy's
Fixed costs	$800,000	$400,000
Discretionary costs	120,000	240,000
Variable costs/unit (family unit)	3	7
Sales price/unit (family unit)	8	10

a. Compute the break-even point for each company.
b. The McDonald's Company is thinking of increasing advertising expenditures by $100,000. Recompute the break-even point. If the increased expenditure yields 25,000 more units of sales, is it wise?
c. Which company is more susceptible to adverse economic conditions? Why?

9–4   *a.* Why might unit cost (as determined by conventional accounting) differ from the incremental cost per unit (as needed for decision making)?

b. What is meant by "the opportunity cost basis" of the economist's concept of depreciation?

9–5   Radio Shack has recently purchased a plant to manufacture a new computer module. The following data pertain to the new operation:

Estimated annual sales	24,000 units
Estimated costs:	
Material	$4/unit
Direct labor	$0.60/unit
Overhead	$24,000 per year
Administrative expenses	$28,800 per year
Selling expenses	15% of sales

a. If profit per unit is to be $1.02, what will be the selling price?

b. Compute the break-even point, both in dollars and in units.

9–6   The Sun Corporation has the following budget for the coming year:

Fixed costs	$40,000
Subcontracting costs (variable)	$2 per unit
Other variable costs	$1 per unit
Sales price	$5
Budgeted production and sales	30,000 units

As an alternative to subcontracting, a plant can be leased for the year for $51,200. Total variable cost under this arrangement would be $1.20 per unit.

a. Find the break-even point under the initial budget.

b. Compute the break-even point under the lease arrangement.

c. Should the lease of plant be undertaken?

d. How sensitive is the Sun Corporation's profit figure to sales volume under each alternative?

9–7   Ford Motor Co. makes an assembly that attaches to an ordinary dump truck and converts the truck into a snow dozer with a hydraulically controlled blade. Assume this product is sold on an experimental basis to highway departments and city governments in Ohio and Michigan for use in clearing highways and city streets. The company's sales department has estimated that annual sales in units (Q) will vary with price in dollars (P) as follows: $Q = 15,000 - 1.25P$. Ford's accounting department projects annual fixed costs of \$6,750,000 and variable production costs at a constant \$7,600 per dozer assembly.

a. Derive the function relating the company's annual profit to sales.
b. Determine optimum production and sales rate, maximum profit, and best price.

9–8   With the data from problem 9–7, carry out an alternative approach to the determination of optimal output, maximum profit, and best price. Base this alternative approach on marginal cost and marginal revenue.

a. Derive Ford's functions relating marginal cost and marginal revenue to sales.
b. Determine the sales rate at which marginal cost equals marginal revenue.
c. How does the optimal sales rate just obtained compare with the rate determined in problem 9–7? What is your conclusion about profit and price as determined by the method of equating marginal cost to marginal revenue?

9–9   Gulfcraft Corporation of Clearwater Beach, Florida, has designed a jet-powered hydrofoil that will be the fastest craft afloat. Its intended use is in marine pursuit and interception by law enforcement officers. Total sales of the product during the expected five-year life cycle will partially depend upon management's pricing and partially depend upon the uncertain behavior of competing firms. Unit costs will fall at higher total sales levels because of spreading fixed costs of the production run and the effect of learning upon labor costs.

In considering just two of the possible prices for the hydrofoil, Gulfcraft's management made the following estimates of the probabilities of various sales levels and the total unit costs at each of the sales levels.

Sales (units)	Probabilities Price \$1 million	Price \$0.9 million	Unit cost (\$millions)
20	0.20	0.10	\$1.55
50	0.50	0.30	1.00
100	0.30	0.60	0.82

a. Construct a decision tree to assist in the choice of price.
b. Calculate expected values of the alternative pricing strategies.

c. Would it be appropriate to base the decision on the expected values, or should some adjustment be made for risk?

9–10   What is a critical path? What is crashing?

Selected references

Arndt, Johan, and Geir Gripsrud. "Exploring Price Dealing Behavior among Food Retailers." *European Journal of Marketing* (UK) 15, no. 7 (1981), pp. 23–35.

Beckenstein, Alan R., and H. Landis Gabel. "Experience Curve Pricing Strategy: The Next Target of Antitrust?" *Business Horizons* 25, no. 5 (September-October 1982), pp. 71–77.

Coyne, Thomas J. "Commercial Bank Profitability by Function." *Financial Management* 2 (Spring 1973).*

———. "Oil Industry Profitability: An Interindustry Comparison of Returns to Equity." *Business Economics* 15, no. 3 (1980), pp. 59–64.

Damus, Sylvester. "Two-Part Tariffs and Optimum Taxation: The Case of Railway Rates." *American Economic Review* 71, no. 1 (March 1981), pp. 65–79.

Darden, Bill R. "An Operational Approach to Product Pricing." *Journal of Marketing* 32 (April 1968).

Enns, J. D. "Markets, Property Markets and Market Failures." *Appraisal Institute Magazine* (Canada) 24, no. 4 (December 1980), pp. 11–15.

Feinberg, Robert M. "The Lerner Index, Concentration, and the Measurement of Market Power." *Southern Economic Journal* 46, no. 4 (April 1980), pp. 1180–86.

Joskow, Paul L., and Alvin K. Klevorick. "A Framework for Analyzing Predatory Pricing Policy." *Yale Law Journal* 89, no. 2 (December 1979), pp. 213–70.

McFarland, Floyd B. "Markup Pricing and the Auto Industry: A Partial Explanation of Stagflation in an Oligopolistic Economy." *American Journal of Economics & Sociology* 41, no. 1 (January 1982), pp. 1–15.

Mirman, Leonard J., and David Sibley. "Optimal Nonlinear Prices for Multiproduct Monopolies." *Bell Journal of Economics* 11, no. 2 (Autumn 1980), pp. 659–670.

Sherman, Roger. "Pricing Inefficiency under Profit Regulation." *Southern Economic Journal* 48, no. 2 (October 1981), pp. 475–89.

Sherman, Roger. "On Multiproduct Sales Maximization." *International Economic Review* 23, no. 1 (February 1982), pp. 79–82.

Straszheim, Donald H., and Mahlon R. Straszheim. "An Econometric Analysis of the Determination of Prices in Manufacturing Industries." *Review of Economics and Statistics* 58, no. 2 (May 1976), pp. 191–201.*

---

* This article is included in Thomas J. Coyne, *Readings in Managerial Economics,* 3d ed. (Plano, Tex.: Business Publications, 1981).

CHAPTER

10

Selected topics in pricing

This chapter is concerned with advanced topics in pricing. It begins with a discussion of price discrimination, in which differences in prices of a product in its various markets do not match differences in costs. It then takes up the subject of peak-load pricing, in which the price of a nonstorable good is increased and decreased with changes in demand over short periods of time. Public utility rate regulation is also discussed. This is a situation in which particular attention is given to the choice between average cost and marginal cost pricing of output of what traditionally has been a decreasing cost industry. The chapter moves on to price and output determination for joint products (i.e., products that are technically interdependent in production). A final topic, transfer pricing in large, multiple-product, multiple-process companies, concludes the chapter.

Price discrimination

Two definitions of price discrimination are necessary for our purposes. One is a tight, rather narrow definition that is useful for analytic purposes. The other is a looser, broader definition, but it might be closer to the realities of business.[1] The two definitions are:

1. The practice of charging different prices to different segments of the same market for the same commodity or service.
2. The practice of charging prices with differences that do not correspond to differences in marginal costs of slightly differentiated goods or services.

---

[1] *Price discrimination* is a neutral, technical term describing a particular business practice rather than something that is evil by definition.

The first definition presumes a homogeneous commodity. The second definition recognizes that differentiation of price is likely to accompany differentiation in characteristics of the commodity. To determine whether price discrimination exists, one must compare price differentials with cost differentials. The absence of price differentials may be discriminatory, as is the case when the same commodity is sold at the same price over a wide territory throughout which transportation costs vary. Or the existence of price differentials may be nondiscriminatory, as is the case if price differences match differences in transportation costs.

Numerous pieces of legislation have been passed to deal with the issue of price discrimination. For example, to protect consumers against certain chain-store pricing practices and other practices, specific forms of price discrimination were declared illegal in 1936. The Robinson-Patman Act of 1936 defined price discrimination and outlined penalties for violators. Initially, violators were to be "fined not more than $5,000 or imprisoned more than one year, or both."[2] Whether a $5,000 potential fine was ever deterrent enough to discourage price discrimination may be questionable. The top penalty for corporate violators is currently $1 million; for individuals it is $100,000 and three years in prison.

Price discrimination by large corporations is possible and profitable (1) if they sell their products in widely divergent geographic areas of the country and (2) if each geographic area provides the company with a demand curve unique to that particular section of the country. If the demand curve for the same product differs in and among several separate sections of the country, the elasticity of demand coefficient of its demand and marginal revenue curves will be different. Consequently, different prices could be charged.

If total costs are the same regardless of the section of the country in which the finished product is sold, but the slope of the demand curve in each section is different, total profit may be maximized by charging a price in each section of the country consistent with that section's demand curve.

Due to the relative inability of certain customers to substitute alternative modes of transportation, railroads (the Chessie System, for example) are provided with a relatively inelastic demand curve in some parts of the country for certain freight and commodities hauled. The demand curve they face for a commodity in one part of the country may be different than that in another part of the country; it may be more inelastic. If customers have virtually no alternative to using the railways for transportation of certain bulk commodities, the railway may face several different demand curves for the same service. Each curve would have a different elasticity of demand coefficient. These differences would allow the railroad to charge different prices to different customers for an iden-

---

[2] 74th Congress, Session No. 2, pp. 1526–1528.

tical service, even though costs to the railway might be the same in each case.

Part *a* of Figure 10–1 reveals the price and output behavior of a good or service sold when demand is relatively price inelastic. Part *b* reveals the price and output behavior of the company for the same product. The differences in price elasticities between parts *a* and *b* cause the price in part *a* to be higher than the price charged in part *b*.[3] Segmentation of the market into two components causes this difference in elasticity. Part *c* depicts the price and output behavior of the combined markets. The downward-sloping demand and marginal revenue functions in part *c* are obtained by adding horizontally the demand and marginal revenue curves depicted in parts *a* and *b* of the figure.

Note that the marginal cost curve is assumed to be constant and equal in each market segment; therefore, the differences in price between parts *a* and *b* in Figure 10–1 cannot be explained by differences in cost. The only explanation for the difference is price discrimination on the part of the firm. This discrimination is made profitable because of the different demand curves.

Of course, Figure 10–1 is presented for illustrative purposes only. There is no reason to assume that firms discriminate in price whenever and wherever possible. Moreover, for those firms who engage in price discrimination, there is no reason to assume that markets would be broken neatly into only two component parts. The Chessie System, for example, may want to establish freight rates based upon the commodity

Figure 10–1
Price discrimination: Segmented markets

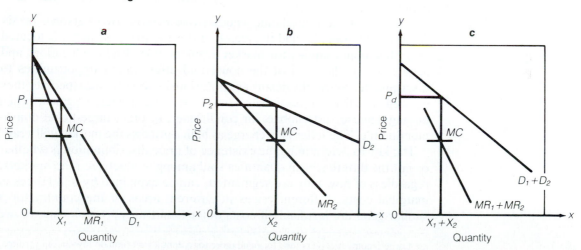

---

[3] Marginal costs for the combined operation of the corporation are set equal to the marginal revenue in each of the segmented markets. Price per unit of output is not equal. It is determined by guiding off the demand function in each market.

being hauled as opposed to basing the rate on the number of revenue-ton-miles hauled. Railroad rates for hauling anthracite coal, for example, may be higher than rates for bituminous coal, even though the number of miles over which the coal must be hauled is the same. The freight rate for cantaloupe may exceed that for lettuce; wheat rates may differ from rye rates. Coke, iron ore, steel, and so on may each have a rate that differs from other rates charged. These differences are almost always statistically significant and cannot be traced to changes in railroad costs associated with handling and/or potential liability of the various commodities.

Various regulatory agencies attempt to minimize the economic impact of price discrimination. It is the Interstate Commerce Commission that is charged with primary responsibility for trucks and railroads. But one should not assume that price discrimination opportunities are limited to the nation's railroads. Virtually any oligopolistic firm able to sell in different markets could discriminate. In addition to the segmenting of final markets, discrimination could be based upon the buyer's age or sex, or whether or not the buyer serves as the head of household. Discrimination can be based upon income. The federal and many state income taxes discriminate in this manner.

Marital status is important in price discrimination matters and is often related to the discrimination cases that may develop in connection with the head of household. If the head of household is married, but the spouse is absent (perhaps in military service), a furnace repair bill can easily be two or three times greater than otherwise might be the case. Widowed, divorced, separated, and never-married persons are segments into which many markets can be divided for similar applications of price discrimination.

The size of the household, whether one person, two persons, or six persons, for example, and the region of the country in which it is located also offer opportunities for market segmentation. Race, education, and occupation of the head of the household offer similar opportunities to discriminate. Since physicians are notoriously poor businesspeople, they as well as other professionals tend to be discriminated against when buying a house, automobile, air conditioner, or other large-ticket consumer durable. The seller may charge as high a price as the market will bear.[4]

The key to determining the existence of price discrimination is whether or not the differences in quantities sold among and between the markets, regardless of how they are segmented, can be explained by differences in marginal costs. Different prices in different areas of the country for a similar good are justifiable if costs other than transportation charges are

---

[4] Large-income receivers tend to spend more for a dental visit than do low-income groups. The exception to this statement is the dentist who charges welfare patients an amount equal to or greater than the amount charged to the richest of patients. The dentist may figure the probability is high that the Health and Human Services Office (welfare) will pick up the bill. If not, he or she may try writing off the uncollectible account to bad debts.

such that a higher and/or lower price can be justified. If marginal costs are the same and prices are different, price discrimination exists.

Examples of situations wherein differences in price cannot be explained by differences in cost include:

Contingency fees charged by attorneys throughout the United States   The attorney retains a percent of all monies collected from an insurance company in a wrongful death accident, for example. If the case is settled for $400,000, she/he may take a $200,000 fee; if it is settled for $300,000, the fee may be $150,000. The costs incurred by the attorney would be identical in either event.

Out-of-state tuition   Government-owned colleges and universities charge a higher tuition for persons enrolled who are not residents of the state. Once again, the costs incurred by the university while educating an out-of-state student do not differ from the costs incurred by educating an in-state student. The difference in price (tuition) is justified on the basis that neither the out-of-state student nor the student's parents have paid taxes to the state in which he/she is enrolled. For that reason the student should not be given the advantages accruing to those who have paid state taxes. This argument overlooks the fact that much land and money for state universities originated with the federal government and, presumably, both the parent and the student have paid or will pay federal income and other taxes.

Fees for utilities   Electric utility companies charge a lower price per kilowatt-hour to industrial users than to household users. The cost per kilowatt-hour generated is the same in both cases.

Automobile tires   Automobile tires sold to automobile manufacturers as original equipment are sold at significantly lower prices than are automobile tires in the replacement market to households and businesses. Also, in the replacement tire market, the identical tire is available to different classes of buyers at different prices—for example, those who buy replacement tires for large fleets get a fleet discount unavailable to private car owners.

Recreation   Motion picture houses charge rates to children that are lower than the rates charged to adults. This kind of behavior follows an ability-to-pay principle. Obviously, the younger person is less able to incur the cost of a movie ticket or an amusement park ride than is an adult. Ability to pay is the principle behind the progressive income tax rate and is the one pursued principally by the United States government. Its purpose is to redistribute income in a somewhat more equal and equitable manner than otherwise might be the case. As a total population, we voted to give this power to the federal government. At no time did we vote to give a group of amusement park operators, motion picture operators, physicians, or attorneys who may charge on the basis of ability to pay, a similar right. Until and unless U.S. citizens vote to give individual businesses and occupations the right to redistribute wealth in a manner similar to that of the federal government, this pricing practice will be considered by some observers to be discriminatory.

Mental hospitals   Federal and state governments are opposed to price discrimination, yet find themselves practicing it. Many mental hospitals, often those organized and operated by individual state agencies, charge for mental care on the basis of patient's family's ability to pay. Even a wealthy family could be expected to deplete its resources quickly. Many families pay nothing.

From this discussion the reader should understand that price discrimination is only possible when (1) groups of buyers are separable, (2) their elasticities of demand differ, and (3) resale between groups is impossible.

Nature of gains from price discrimination

Price discrimination increases net revenue from any given total amount of product. An example demonstrates the nature of the gains from the practice. Suppose B&W is selling an identical product in two markets, market A and market B, at the same price of $1,000 per unit. It learns that the price elasticity of demand (e_p) is -2.0 in market A and has the less-elastic value of -1.5 in market B. B&W calculates the marginal revenue of the product in each of the markets:

$$\text{In any market, } MR = \text{Price}\left(1 + \frac{1}{e_p}\right)$$

$$\text{In market A, } MR = \$1,000\left(1 + \frac{1}{-2.0}\right) = \$500$$

$$\text{In market B, } MR = \$1,000\left(1 + \frac{1}{-1.5}\right) = \$334, \text{ approximately}$$

In the example, if one unit of the current total sales rate is reallocated from market B to market A, with price being raised in market B and reduced in market A by appropriate amounts, the total revenue of the firm is increased by approximately $500 - $334, or $166. Transferring additional units from market B to market A would give similar but steadily decreasing gains. With additional transfers, the marginal revenues of the two markets would be coming closer and closer together, falling in market A and rising in market B, until the marginal revenues became equal in the two markets. At this point, the potential gains from quantity reallocation and price discrimination would be fully realized.

Choosing pricing and output to maximize profits

The technique for profit maximization under price discrimination will be introduced by the case of a product with the same marginal cost for two markets, each having a different demand elasticity. After this basic problem is understood, the technique can be extended to the case of differentiated products with marginal costs that vary among the different markets. A seller facing an opportunity to practice price discrimination needs to know the following things:

1. How much total output and sales?
2. How should total sales quantity be allocated among the various markets?
3. What prices should be charged in each of the markets?

Figure 10–2 shows how answers to the above questions can be obtained. The firm has two market segments, market 1 and market 2. Each has its own demand and marginal revenue function as before. The aggregate marginal revenue function is MR_{1+2}, as obtained by horizontal summation of the quantities found on MR_1 and MR_2 at each value of marginal revenue (in practice, summation at close intervals may be satisfactory). For example, take the value of $5 for marginal revenue. At this value, how many units can be sold in market 1? How many in market 2? The answers are 21 and 22 units, respectively. If the firm always allocates total sales between two markets so as to maximize total revenue, the marginal revenues of the two markets will always be equal, and the total sales quantity at any given value of marginal revenue will be the sum of the quantities in the respective markets at that value of marginal revenue. In the example, the total quantity at a marginal revenue of $5 is 21 plus 22, or 43.

On the cost side of the analysis, only the marginal cost is relevant. In the example of Figure 10–2, there is no difference in cost whether the

Figure 10–2
Price discrimination—an identical product, two markets

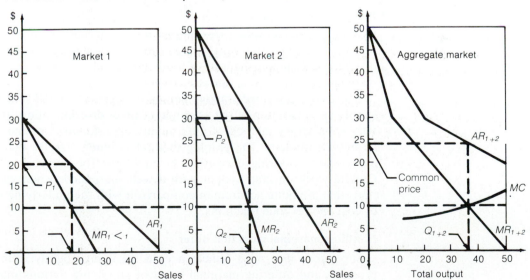

product sells in market 1 or market 2. Therefore, the firm has one marginal cost function showing the relation of cost to rate of total output.

Optimum total output is found where marginal cost becomes equal to aggregate marginal revenue. In Figure 10–2, this point is found at $10, corresponding to a total output of 36 units. The optimum allocation of output among the markets is found by extending a horizontal line at the optimum value of marginal revenue—a line running back to the individual marginal revenue functions. In the example of Figure 10–2, the horizontal line runs at $10 and intersects market 2's marginal revenue function at a sales rate (Q_2) of 20 units; the line intersects market 1's marginal function at a rate (Q_1) of 16 units. Optimum market prices are found by extending vertical lines up to the individual demand curves from the optimal market quantities just determined. In Figure 10–2, Market 1's price (P_1) is $20; the price in market 2 (P_2) is $30.

If all 36 units were sold at the same price in both markets, the price that would clear the market is found on the aggregate demand function and is $24. Gains from price discrimination in the example of Figure 10–2 can be calculated as follows.

Revenue per period with price discrimination:
Market 1, price of $20 times quantity of 16	$320
Market 2, price of $30 times quantity of 20	600
	$920

Revenue per period without price discrimination:
Market 1, price of $24 times quantity of 10	$240
Market 2, price of $24 times quantity of 26	624
	$864

Price discrimination maximizes total revenue from any given amount of total output by allocating this output among markets in such a way that marginal revenues are equalized in the various markets and maximizes profit by determining that rate of total output and sales at which aggregate marginal cost is equal to aggregate marginal revenue.

The above-described graphic method of aggregation and solution is not simply an illustration of the principle of price discrimination. It is also a very satisfactory method of determining approximate optimal values in an actual problem. The graphic method is much simpler than analytic approaches requiring derivation of equations for aggregate functions. Careful work on graph paper with a well-sharpened pencil yields solutions that are quite accurate in comparison with the underlying estimates of cost and revenue functions.

Handling marginal costs that differ

Suppose a firm must handle a case involving slightly differentiated products and differing marginal costs of supplying various markets. In this case, the product's marginal costs should be separated into two categories. One is basic cost—cost that applies to all output regardless of its market destination. The second category is market-specific cost—cost that depends upon the particular market segment. Each market-specific marginal cost, which may be constant or may be a function of sales rate, is subtracted from the particular market's marginal revenue function. The (cost-adjusted) aggregate marginal revenue function is then formed by horizontal summation of quantities on the cost-adjusted marginal revenue functions at each value of marginal revenue (or at close intervals). Optimum total output is found where aggregate marginal revenue is equal to marginal cost on the product's basic marginal cost function. Each market's quantity allocation is found on its adjusted marginal revenue function at the optimum value of marginal revenue determined in the previous step, and each market's price is found on its demand function at the optimum quantity allocation to that market.

Social and legal issues

Price discrimination's social effects are not necessarily harmful. The practice may be beneficial. Although it raises prices to some buyers, it lowers them to others. When price differentiation is used in monopolistically competitive industries and differentiated oligopolies, the long-run effect is to increase total output and, if envelope curves are L shape, to reduce average prices as capacity is increased by entry and expansion. On the other hand, price differentiation by a pure monopolist may increase profits that would be excessive even under ordinary pricing. Of course, many pure monopolies are regulated so that average prices are held close to average cost; in such cases, price discrimination allows greater total output and lower average prices if the monopoly has decreasing average costs. To sum up, price discrimination may be socially beneficial (on balance, the gains to some outweighing the losses to others) provided it is carried out by regulated monopolies or by firms in monopolistically competitive industries in which profits are held in check by entry and expansion.

It is not always possible to determine whether observed price differences are explained by price discrimination. The first difficulty is in determining whether two or more products are really differentiated versions of the same product or two different products on which price comparisons are inappropriate. A second difficulty is in measuring marginal costs of the various products, which requires some way of dealing with common costs.

The legal status of differential pricing is uncertain. This book avoids many of the legal intricacies of antitrust and price discrimination legislation and rulings. In general, the Federal Trade Commission and the courts have permitted price differentials that reflect differences in cost; our earlier discussion of costs should explain why this criterion has been so troublesome in such cases. The courts tend to rely on average costs rather than marginal costs in measuring cost differentials, with consequent difficulties in the treatment of overhead. The courts have upheld quantity discounts that could be justified by cost differentials but have ruled against quantity discounts that may injure or suppress competition. A major criterion of illegality is injury to competitors.

The position of managers in this area of differential pricing is a complex one. They are challenged to use imagination in finding more profitable ways of adjusting prices to market conditions, but they may be concerned with their obligations to the public and with avoidance of price differentials that might be considered unfair or harmful to competition. Managers must also consider the legal consequences of their pricing behavior, including the possibility that their ideas of equity in this complex area may not always conform to those of the Federal Trade Commission or the courts.

Price discrimination illustrations

Many illustrations of price discrimination could be presented, for it is a widespread practice. To save space, it seems appropriate to restrict attention to price discrimination in the public utilities. The utilities usually sell services that cannot be economically resold by the buyers, and thus they are particularly likely to use price discrimination.

Water supply   An outstanding study of water supply indicates that price discrimination is widely practiced by municipal water companies, both private and public.[5] In New York City some users at this writing have no water meters, which means they pay a flat rate with no extra charge for heavy water use. Obviously, there is discrimination between such users and those who pay according to volume of consumption. This discrimination encourages the waste of water. In Los Angeles lower rates are charged for irrigation water than for water in urban use, and the rate differentials are clearly not in proportion to marginal costs. The result is a subsidy to farm production.

Some of the water-rate differentials are in line with cost differences and thus are not discriminatory in the strict definition of price discrimination. For example, most water systems charge less per unit for greater volumes, a fact that may reflect the lower cost of delivering and metering the increments in volume. In Los Angeles (and in many other cities) a rate differential exists between noninterruptible service and service that the water department may curtail at its convenience. Since the cost of water delivered at peak periods is greater than that delivered at other times, this differential is not necessarily discriminatory—it is a way of charging for the extra load that peak users place on the system. There will be more information on peak-load pricing shortly.

---

[5] See J. Hirshleifer, J. C. DeHaven, and J. W. Milliman, *Water Supply: Economics, Technology and Policy* (Chicago: University of Chicago Press, 1960).

Gas and electricity   Gas and electricity rates of the Consolidated Gas, Electric Light, and Power Company of Baltimore are probably representative of those in the gas and electricity industries in general. The rate schedules incorporate several kinds of price discrimination, all with the approval of regulatory agencies.[6] One kind of discrimination, "peak-off-peak," involves a failure to relate rates to the differentials in costs between peak and off-peak periods. The simplest form of such discrimination is charging the same rate in both peak and off-peak periods. Even when higher rates are charged to peak energy users, the methods of allocating costs often fail to apply as high a proportion of capacity costs to the peak periods as is warranted, resulting in a subsidy of peak production by off-peak sales.

Peak-load pricing   The electric power industry provides one example of a peak-load problem. If electric service is offered at constant prices, hourly sales quantities vary during the day and over seasons of the year due to changes in demand. Electricity cannot be economically stored in significant quantities, and the production-transmission-distribution system fails under sustained overload. Thus, peak hourly sales quantity, or peak load, determines necessary capacity of the system. Figure 10–3 shows an actual hourly load curve for one utility on a day it reached peak load.

If the sales peak is high and narrow, capacity adequate to handle peak load may be substantially greater than that needed most of the time. By increasing prices in peak periods, sales quantities (and necessary capacity) can be reduced. At the same time, quantities in off-peak periods can be increased through shifting of demand. The problem in peak-load pricing is to determine, simultaneously, the best prices in both peak and off-peak periods and best capacity. Similar problems are found in distribution of natural gas and water and provision of telephone services.

One kilowatt-hour of electricity may be considered no different than any other one, but 100 hours of electricity does not have the same value to apartment dwellers on Fifth Avenue in Manhattan at 10 A.M. that 100 hours of electricity would have at 10 P.M. on the same winter day. Electricity is a homogenous product only (1) if the use to which it is put remains unchanged during the time it is being used and (2) if the value of the product remains unchanged during the same period. If what appears to be a homogenous product (a kilowatt-hour of electricity) is differentiated in the mind of the consumer or if the product has a greater value during a certain period of the day than during a different period, a company may wish to charge a price for the good that reflects these differences.

---

[6] See R. K. Davidson, *Price Discrimination in Selling Gas and Electricity* (Baltimore: The Johns Hopkins Press, 1955).

Figure 10–3
Load curve for December 19

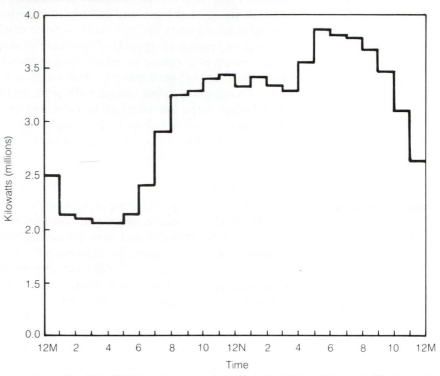

Source: Donald N. DeSalvia, "An Application of Peak-Load Pricing," *Journal of Business,* October 1969, p. 460.

The 9, 10, and 11 A.M. and 1 and 2 P.M. classrooms on Mondays, Wednesdays and Fridays at many state universities are filled to capacity. During the same hours on Tuesdays and Thursdays, empty classrooms are not as noticeable. Students place heaviest demand on university facilities during certain peak hours. In order to accommodate these students, universities find themselves taxing households and businesses to construct additional classroom facilities to meet peak demands. Classroom space is relatively abundant during the afternoon hours between 2 and 5 P.M. Many evenings, Saturdays, and sometimes for weeks between semesters the university classrooms are almost empty. On Sunday no classes are scheduled, all classrooms are unused. Yet, students enrolling in a course offered late on Tuesday and Thursday afternoons or Saturday morning incur the same tuition charges as those students sign up for peak periods. Would a leveling of peak demands be obtainable by offering a lower fee to those students willing to use the facilities during off-peak hours?

Local bartenders learned long ago that a happy hour helped to bring in customers during off-peak hours.

The Long Lines department of AT&T experimented with after-6 P.M. and after-9 P.M. telephone rates, which are lower than rates charged for calls made during the normal working day. These lower rates are traceable to the company's desire to reduce demands on it for additional services and equipment. Alleviation of peak demand is possible if some calls are postponed to later in the day. As the AT&T example illustrates, peak-load pricing has been in existence for a relatively long time. However, to date it has been implemented on a relatively small scale by relatively few multinational firms. Introduction of peak-load pricing by firms having large fixed-cost components may (1) make acquisition of additional capital equipment unnecessary, (2) provide some additional contribution toward existing overhead expenses, and (3) increase profitability.

A disadvantage associated with peak-load pricing has to do with price discrimination in general and antitrust laws in particular. If the same product is sold to different customers at different prices, some observers may argue that one or more provisions of the Robinson-Patman Act have been violated.[7] Remember, price discrimination exists if differences in price for similar goods or services cannot be explained by differences in marginal costs. It may be reasonable to assume the marginal cost per unit of output for a kilowatt-hour generated at 10 A.M. is lower than marginal cost incurred at 10 P.M. if the lowering of price in off-peak periods allows the firm increased use of fixed assets while helping it postpone or eliminate the need for new, costly equipment. Economists generally agree on the following two propositions:

1. Peak prices should be higher than off-peak prices for two reasons: (a) to allocate the limited capacity available at the peaks to those who are willing to pay most for it and (b) to help cover the cost of providing additional capacity required to meet that peak consumption that remains at the higher prices.

2. The only relevant costs in determining both peak and off-peak prices are the marginal costs. (Unfortunately, some difference of opinion remains on how to measure the marginal costs.)

Some general principles

Electric power companies must have the capacity to meet peak loads. The question is: Should they vary rates from peak to off-peak periods? Almost all economists who have studied the question say the companies should charge higher rates at the peaks, since the cost of producing for the peak includes cost of some capacity used only during the peak and is clearly greater than the cost for other periods. Failure to charge higher rates in peak periods causes peak consumption to be higher than it would

---

[7] Section 2(a) of the Clayton Act as amended by the Robinson-Patman Act, 15 U.S.C. *13(a).

be otherwise. When the utility must construct extra capacity to meet the peak, cost of extra capacity is subsidized by necessarily higher rates for off-peak use. In the absence of such capacity, the utility must engage in "load shedding" (cutting off the electricity supply of some customers), a practice that is arbitrary and inefficient.

Economists have developed what appears to be a logical solution to peak-load pricing. The solution is to equate each period price with its marginal cost. Figure 10–4 shows the solution for both peak and off-peak periods. This solution is based on an assumption of constant marginal cost.[8]

Assume for purposes of simplicity that for half of each day, demand is constant as D_1D_1' and the other half constant at D_2D_2'. The kilowatt-hour charge in the low-demand period should include only the energy cost, since there is no need to add to capacity for this period. The kilowatt-hour charge in the high-demand period is equal to the energy cost plus the capacity cost. Capacity cost per kilowatt-hour is total capacity cost per day divided by total kilowatt-hours sold during the peak period. The capacity cost per kilowatt-hour is part of the marginal cost in the peak period, since capacity must be added to meet this demand.

The above solution might be called the long-run equilibrium solution in which the capacity has already been adjusted to the level of demand. At first, capacity may be short or in excess of this equilibrium, so that the

Figure 10–4
Long-run peak and off-peak pricing: The firm peak case

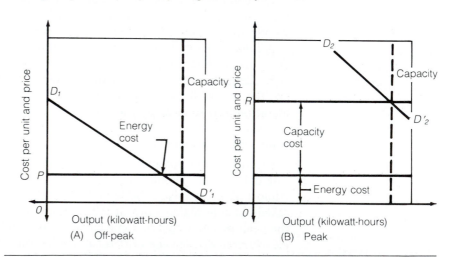

---

[8] A solution for the more realistic case of increasing marginal cost is more complex but is developed according to the same principles. See P. O. Steiner's "Peak-Loads and Efficient Pricing," *Quarterly Journal of Economics* (November 1957), pp. 585–610; see also, J. Hirshleifer's "Comment" in the August, 1958 issue, pp. 51–62.

Figure 10–5
Short-run peak-load pricing: The firm peak case

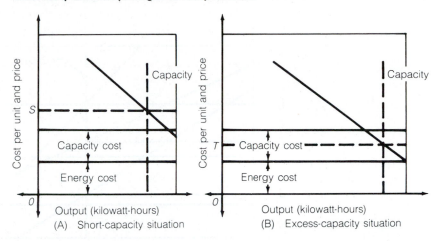

rule must be restated: In the short run the price at the peak should be such as to equate sales quantity with the available capacity. If capacity is in short supply, the price should be set at a level higher than the sum of the per kilowatt-hour capacity and energy costs to discourage consumption by those who place low marginal values on electricity and to allocate the supply to those with high marginal values. Part A of Figure 10–5 illustrates that *OS* is the appropriate price. In an excess capacity situation, the price should be at *OT,* as shown in part B of the figure.

The short-run prices for the peak period are not based on full cost, but they allocate available capacity efficiently. In the first case the utility should add capacity. In the second case it should fail to replace capacity as it wears out. In both cases it should set the rate on off-peak consumption to cover only the energy cost. In the long run, after capacity adjustment, pricing at marginal cost in both periods can be such that it just covers full cost.

A more complete discussion would consider the possibility (some economists would say the inevitability) of curvilinear costs, with rising marginal costs.

Shifting peaks

Increases in peak-period prices flatten the peak and may shift some sales to adjacent periods. Sales in other periods may then equal or even exceed those at the peak. In this case it is necessary to plot both demand curves (the high demand and low demand) on the same graph. Figure 10–6 illustrates. This time we add the two demands vertically to get D_c. This combined demand curve provides estimates of how much buyers will pay for one unit of off-peak energy plus one unit of peak energy. The utility should expand capacity to the point at which D_c intersects the sum of the

Figure 10–6
Peak and off-peak pricing: The shifting peak case

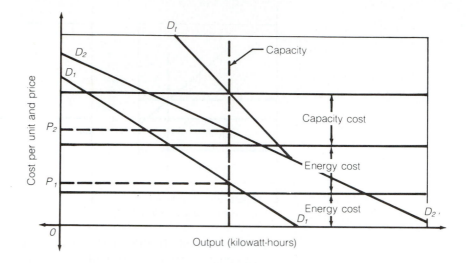

capacity cost (as defined in the preceding section) plus twice the energy cost. At this point the prices will cover marginal cost of energy plus marginal capacity cost (the capacity will be fully used in both periods). The prices OP_1 and OP_2 are again set to "clear the market" (use up the capacity). The result is that the capacity is fully utilized in both periods.

This analysis can be generalized to more than two periods and to periods that are unequal in length. The theoretical literature on peak-load pricing has also been extended to cover a wider range of considerations, such as indivisibilities in production and differences in plant costs.[9]

Some practical problems

A number of obstacles stand in the way of actual application of the preceding analysis.

1. Demands in different periods cannot be predicted accurately.

2. Measurement of the marginal energy and capacity costs is no simple problem. Marginal costs of generation are increasing with level of output in a typical power system, due to differences in ages, locations, and types of power plants. Figure 10–7 shows DeSalvia's estimates of the relationship of marginal costs to cumulative output of an actual system in 1963.[10] In this figure, the most efficient generation is used first, then the next

[9] O. E. Williamson, "Peak-Load Pricing and Optimal Capacity under Indivisibility Constraints." *American Economic Review* (September 1960), pp. 810–27; see also, M. A. Crews' "Comment," March 1968, pp. 168–70.

[10] Donald N. DeSalvia, "An Application of Peak-Load Pricing," *Journal of Business,* October 1969, p. 467.

Figure 10–7
Cumulative capacity in order of incremental fuel cost

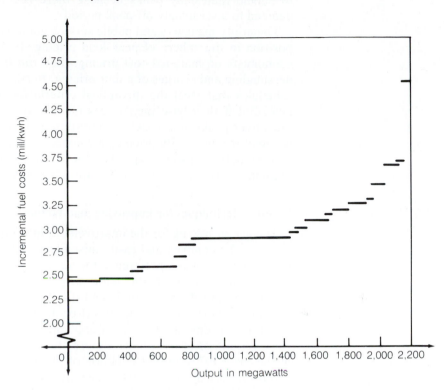

Source: Donald N. DeSalvia, "An Application of Peak-Load Pricing," *Journal of Business*, October 1969.

most efficient, and so on. Off-peak rates equal to marginal or energy costs that increase with cumulative output would make some contribution toward capacity cost, since these rates would exceed energy costs of the most efficient sources.

3. The proposed scheme involves flexible prices over time. This results from the necessity of using trial and error in searching for appropriate prices and from shifts in demand that cannot be exactly matched at all times by shifts in capacity. This poses serious problems for the administration of rate changes—problems compounded by the requirement of approval of changes by regulatory commissions.

4. The public might react unfavorably to prices that seem discriminatory even though they may not be.

5. The public might also react unfavorably to the instability of prices the pricing scheme, in an extreme form, would require. They might prefer to know in advance the rates they would pay rather than be subject to sharp shifts in such rates.

6. Some electric companies find that seasonal peaks are more difficult to handle than daily peaks because there is little opportunity to shift demand to a seasonally off-peak period.

The utility managers and public service commissioners are in a difficult position in the sphere of peak-load pricing. If they heed the advice of economists on marginal-cost pricing, they run the risk of public misunderstanding and charges of unfair pricing. Furthermore, constructing rate schedules that meet the theoretical criteria for optimization is no easy task. But if they base their prices on full costs and try to average out rates over peaks and troughs in consumption, they are responsible for a waste of resources. By pricing peak-load consumption at its real cost and thereby deferring some capacity growth, they could reduce resource requirements (primarily investment) by substantial amounts.

Nonprice techniques for improving load factors

The use of pricing for the improvement of utility load factors has been shown to be complex and easily misunderstood. As a result, many companies have shown a preference for marketing and other nonprice techniques that accomplish the same purpose. These consist of increased advertising in off-peak periods and the development of new markets or new products to use facilities in off-peak periods. Electric utilities have engaged in promoting the use of appliances that consume energy in off-peak periods or at least have a more stable demand. After the shortage of the early 1970s and introduction of price decontrols in the 1980s, gas companies are again advertising heavily for business.

Nonprice devices have the advantage of flexibility. Customers appear to resent frequent changes of price but are tolerant of varying promotional activity. When advertising pushes consumption toward capacity, it is easy to diminish the effort, but it is not so easy to take away a low price that has been used to promote a particular type of consumption.

Public utility rate regulation

Pricing (rate mixing) in the public utilities presents a special problem in economic analysis. The electricity, gas, water, telephone, and public transportation utilities are natural monopolies. In any one locality a single firm tends to drive out competing firms. These are industries in which technology of production and distribution results in substantial economies of scale, which means that one large firm can more economically produce than can several firms. Legislatures have recognized these economies of scale and tendencies to monopoly by granting franchises protecting utility companies from competition but subjecting them to rate control by regulatory commissions.

Basic pricing

Three alternative policies for pricing in the public utilities are possible: monopoly pricing, full-cost pricing, and marginal cost pricing. All are illustrated in Figure 10–8, which depicts a decreasing-cost firm. Price *OA* is the monopoly price—the price that maximizes profit. Almost all observers agree that this price is intolerable to the public, since it provides a monopoly profit at the expense of consumers. It results in a misallocation of resources, since the value to consumers of additional output would exceed the value of resources such additional output would use up.

Price *OB* is the price sought in the usual utility regulation. It is based on full cost—it covers fixed as well as variable costs and includes a normal return on investment. Price *OB* is set to provide a fair rate of return on the investment in the utility. The history of rate regulation is a history of controversy over what rates of returns are fair and conducive to the growth and financial strength of the utilities. It is also a history of controversy over the "rate base"—value of the property on which the rate of return should be allowed. In periods of inflation the utilities have a strong preference for valuation at reproduction cost. They argue that the original costs, or "book costs," do not reflect the true value of the property and that returns on property valued at such costs are confiscatory. Some regulatory commissions, on the other hand, favor original cost or a variation of original cost known as prudent investment, not only

Figure 10–8
Alternative levels of public utility rates

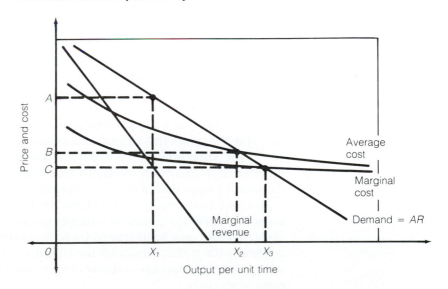

because this practice holds down utility rates, but also because original cost is easier to objectively determine. Considerable litigation often results from estimates of reproduction cost; accounting conventions reduce the amount of litigation that is possible over original cost.

The issue of original cost, reproduction cost, or other variations, such as fair value, is still not settled. The state regulatory commissions have not standardized their practices in establishing the rate bases; a full discussion of this issue must be left to books on public utility economics. It is necessary to note, however, that the exact level of *OB* (the price at full cost) depends somewhat on the particular regulatory agency having jurisdiction over the utility.

Marginal cost pricing

Price *OC* in Figure 10–8 is the price at marginal cost. Much of the literature on welfare economics expresses a preference for this price. The discussion of marginal cost pricing tends to become rather involved, but the argument can be summarized in nontechnical language. It is claimed that the welfare of society is increased if the price is lowered below *OB* because of the value of the added service exceeds the marginal cost of added output. The recommended price is *OC,* the point at which the demand curve intersects the marginal cost curve. At *OC,* the value to the marginal user (measured by the price the user pays for the last unit, which is also the price for all units) is equal to the value of the resources used up to produce the last unit. Any higher price and lower consumption, it is argued, means a failure to maximize welfare.

Price *OC* has the disadvantage that it does not cover total costs in a decreasing-cost firm. The economists who favor marginal cost pricing recommend that the government pay a subsidy to the utility so that it can cover all costs. Some of them even recommend public ownership on the grounds that the government is not required to cover all costs out of revenues.

If the utility is subject to increasing costs, as may be true of the telephone, electric, and gas companies of the 1980s, marginal cost pricing may result in prices that exceed total costs. This result is shown in Figure 10–9. The firm earns excess profits in this case, but not as high as the profits that would be possible without regulation. Special taxes could siphon off a large part of the excess profit.

Marginal cost pricing is objectionable on several grounds. Subsidies mean the loss of the control advantages of rules that revenues must cover costs. Utilities may be distracted from their main business if they have to contend with political agencies for subsidies. Their profits may depend more upon their success in demonstrating the need for subsidies than in controlling costs.

Figure 10-9
Marginal cost pricing in an increasing-cost industry

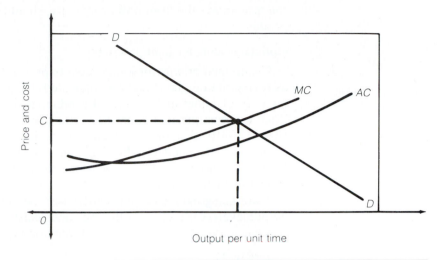

Multiple-product
pricing

Multiple-product price and output determination must cope with product interdependency in production. Interdependency can take the form of joint products, a situation in which the production of one product necessitates the production of another. Similac and Pream were joint products.

Similac is produced and marketed in both powder and liquid form. Each product is available in retail stores everywhere. The technology needed to produce Similac is such that the liquid product is off-white or somewhat yellow in color; the cans of Similac powder are pure white, free of spots or blemishes. Powdered Similac reminds one of pure, newly fallen snow. The ultimate use of Similac is the same regardless of whether it is purchased in liquid or powdered form—it is a baby food. In essence, liquid and powdered Similac are joint products.

Joint products, by definition, are interdependent in the production process. A decrease in the quantity produced of powdered Similac causes a change in the total cost curve for the corporation. If the total production of this infant food is to remain constant at a time when the quantity supplied of powdered Similac declines, that portion of the total cost that must be borne by liquid Similac increases.

If a young mother considered liquid Similac to be a perfect substitute for powdered Similac, an increase in the price per can of powdered Similac would cause an increase in demand (shifting of the demand function to the right) for the liquid infant food. The degree of substitutability by mothers from liquid to powdered or vice versa becomes known to the corporation as a result of testing the product in numerous hospitals, listening to the advice of hundreds of obstetricians and pediatricians, and carefully noting the comments of satisfied users of the products. In time, the firm knows the fixed proportions that should be produced of the joint product.[11]

Optimal pricing for joint products

The optimal pricing for joint products produced in fixed proportions is as reviewed in Figure 10–10. As indicated, the horizontal axis reveals the quantity of liquid and powdered product that would be manufactured. Price and cost per unit is on the vertical (y) axis. Profit is maximized in Figure 10–10 in a manner identical to that used in earlier chapters; namely, at the point at which marginal revenue equals marginal cost. However, earlier market models of imperfectly competitive firms assumed a single product, whereas Figure 10–10 assumes two joint products are being manufactured. Otherwise, the determination of price and output levels is the same. Difference does exist, however, in the marginal revenue curve. MR_t is the vertical summation of MR_l and MR_p.[12]

Figure 10–10
Quantity of liquid and powdered Similac

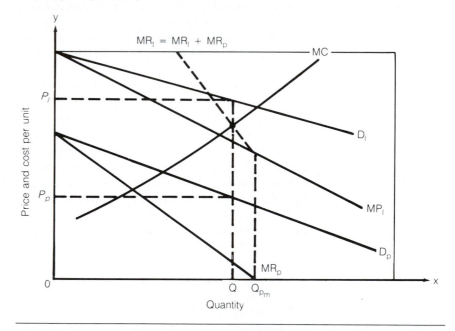

[11] Similac is the registered trade name of a high-quality infant food manufactured by Ross Laboratories, Columbus, Ohio.

[12] For joint products produced in fixed proportions, the overall costs to the firm remain fairly stable. Changes in output are due primarily to changes in demand and marginal revenue curves. This statement is true even if each product is produced in a separate plant. Liquid Similac, for example, may be produced in Columbus, Ohio, and powdered Similac, in Sturgis, Michigan.

The profit maximizing point is determined by equating MR_t and MC. Price for the powdered Similac is determined by guiding off the demand curve and arriving at P_p; the liquid Similac is priced accordingly at P_l.

MR_t is equal to MR for all levels of output to the right of Q_{pm}. No quantity of powdered Similac would be produced beyond this point because of the negative condition of MR_p at all points to the right of Q_{pm}. Some economists might advise destruction of all powdered Similac to the right of this point. Most certainly, additional factor inputs should not be employed to produce quantities greater than Q_{pm}, for to do so would be to invite lower prices, lower revenues, lower profits. On the other hand, should the demand for liquid Similac increase, or should conditions be such that the marginal revenue and marginal cost curves for the liquid Similac would intersect at points to the right of Q_{pm}, the corporation would increase its output of liquid Similac but hold constant its production of the powdered product.

Pream: The extract of Similac

When manufacturing any product, a certain amount of waste, or extract, is unavoidable. In making powdered, pure white Similac from cow's milk, a certain amount of extract develops. The extract could be (1) destroyed, (2) sold on the open market (but as indicated above, this action could depress prices, total revenue, and profits), or (3) converted to a new use. Ross laboratories decided upon the third option.[13]

Pream, a powdered coffee creamer originally containing milk fat, was developed to (1) provide a profitable use for the extra milk fat (extract) remaining after the production of Similac, a joint product, and (2) to provide an additional entry into the consumer products field. Development of Pream provided the firm with an outlet for profitable use of all extract from powdered Similac. Heavy national advertising helped Pream become profitable. However, this profitable product caused certain questions to be raised with respect to the price at which the Similac extract should be transferred internally to the product Pream. As the company solved the problem of what to do with its extract from Similac, it created a transfer-pricing problem for itself.

Joint costs and joint products

A classic example of joint costs is that of meat production. Meat packers sell products to both food chains and leather tanners. Prices are

---

[13] Pream has been sold to Early California Corporation, Los Angeles, California; Ross Laboratories in Columbus, Ohio, synthetically manufactures the product for them. In the early stages of Pream development, cow milk was used.

governed by demand and not by individual product costs. The objective is to set prices at levels that will clear the market for both meat and hides. Output will be at levels that will equate the marginal revenue from both meat and hides to the marginal cost of producing both.

The grocery, in turn, must determine what price to charge for the different cuts of meat obtained from the carcass. As Holdren states, "The elasticity of demand rather than carcass cost dominates the determination of the relative prices of different cuts of meat." [14] In some stores hamburger and chuck roast may be sold below the average cost of the carcass. As beef prices rise, the range of prices on different cuts narrow, and the customer substitutes cheaper cuts for more expensive ones. Such substitution relations in demand complicate the determination of the most profitable prices.

Holdren found that the individual store managers tended to keep their prices on chuck, hamburger, and round steak competitive with prices in other stores. They followed a "get rid of" principle in pricing the other cuts. They bought enough carcasses to fill the demand for round steak and chuck roast and altered the prices of other cuts (except hamburger) until the market was cleared. In other words, the stores did not use anything approaching a mathematical model reflecting the demand and cost conditions. They instead followed a series of decision-making rules: Imitate the price of other stores on some cuts; purchase quantities according to the demand for those cuts at the imitative prices; and price the other cuts to get rid of the quantity that results for the previous rules. These rules do not reveal how the imitative prices are established, a question that cannot be answered by studying one or a few stores at a time.

Figure 10–11 represents a slight alteration from the situation in Figure 10–10. Here MR_2 becomes negative before MR_{1+2} reaches the marginal cost curve. The firm will not maximize profits if it keeps on reducing the price on product 2 to get rid of it; the negative marginal revenue means a loss in total revenue. Product 2 will be sold up to the point at which its marginal revenue is zero, with P_2 the appropriate price. But it is profitable to produce more packages, until MR_1 equals the marginal cost. The excess units of product 2 will be destroyed, since their appearance on the market will depress prices.

Other variations in the situation may be worked out by the reader. These could include a case in which one of the products is sold in a purely competitive market or one in which both are sold in such a market. Another interesting variation is the case in which there is a cost of destruction.

[14] Bob R. Holdren, *The Structure of a Retail Market and the Market Behavior of Retail Units* (Englewood Cliffs, N.J.: Prentice-Hall, 1960), pp. 121–22.

**Figure 10–11
Maximization of profits—joint products with destruction of part of one product**

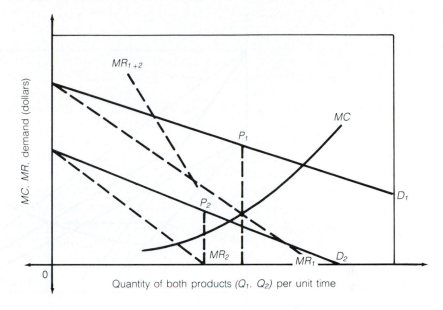

Alternative products

Figure 10–12 illustrates output and price determination for alternative products. Both of these products require services of some facility that will be fully utilized. Therefore, output of any one product can be increased only by cutting back output of the other product.[15]

The quantity axis in Figure 10–12 measures total use of the facility (i.e., hours per week). The demand and marginal revenue curves for the several products have been restated in terms of equivalent demand and marginal revenue product curves for hours of facility use per week. The marginal cost curve in Figure 10–12 assumes that variable cost depends only on hours of plant operation and does not change as the plant is switched from product to product. The firm maximizes profit if it selects a product mix such that the marginal revenues (per unit of facility use) are equal across the various products and are also equal to marginal cost (per unit of facility use) at total output. Amounts of facility use for various products can be converted into equivalent outputs and market prices for the products.

The above analysis can be extended to cases in which variable costs differ from product to product (demands must be net of product-specific variable costs), in which marginal cost is constant up to some limit of

---

[15] See Eli W. Clemens, ''Price Discrimination and the Multiple-Product Firm,'' *Review of Economic Studies* 19 (1950–51), pp 1–11.

Figure 10–12
Maximization of profit—alternative products

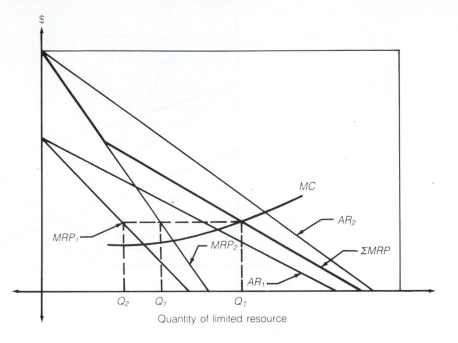

plant use. (In this latter case, marginal "rents"—differences between marginal revenues and marginal costs—are equated.) The analysis can also be extended to a special case in which there is excess (economically redundant) plant capacity.

Decisions on multiple products are relatively unsophisticated in most firms. The construction of models that reflect the important interrelationships is a difficult and costly task. Therefore, most managers rely mainly on experience and trial and error. One might assume that such a rough-and-ready approach will often provide approximations to the theoretical optima. At any rate, let's get back to Similac and their transfer-pricing problem.

Transfer pricing

Ross Laboratories almost always had a surplus of milk fat, which they sold in eastern cream markets each year during the summer months. This fat went primarily to New York, Pennsylvania, and New Jersey. Surplus milk solids, at times, were dried and sold in bulk at the then-current market prices as powdered skim milk.

Various methods of arriving at a cost for skim milk solids and milk fat solids derived from purchased whole milk proved to be unsatisfactory. Commodity profits and/or losses from the sale of these products depended upon (1) price fluctuations caused by weather changes, (2) the month of the year in which the sale was made, and (3) variations in government-imposed storage regulations and conditions.

Efforts to resolve the transfer-pricing problem were made by making a detailed study of the previous 10 years' data concerning whole milk prices, butter fat market prices, skim powdered milk prices, in-house condensing and powdering expenses, and the resulting commodity profit and loss on the sale of the products. In addition, determination was made of the relative valuations of milk fat and skim solids at any given whole milk price. If the values were high enough, the firm could break even on the purchase and sale of these commodities.

From these data, the corporation derived the relative valuations for milk fat and skim solids at any given whole milk price. Based on the study, the firm elected to value butter fat solids at 75 percent of the cost of 4 percent whole milk purchased during the period. They valued skim milk solids at 25 percent of whole milk costs.[16] The expenses attributable to receiving, processing, separating, and pasteurizing whole milk to the point at which the milk took the form of 40 percent cream and fluid skim milk were allocated to fat and skim solids on the same 75/25 percent basis.[17]

The extract of Similac clearly had a price that could have been obtained on the open market had the corporation offered it for sale. Intermediate products of this sort could, and perhaps should, be transferred from one wholly owned subsidiary of the corporation to another at the price the firm could have received externally had the product been sold. In other words, profit is maximized for the firm when it uses transfer prices that are opportunity costs in nature.[18]

Ross Labs is not alone in attempting to determine a proper transfer price. In fact, the toughest pricing problem of the 1980s might be determination of an appropriate business-to-business price when each business involved is owned by the same owner or holding company. Most large multiple-product, multiple-plant companies develop complex prices and patterns of intracompany transfers of goods. For example, an integrated international petroleum company acquires vast amounts of crude oil from hundreds of sources, allocates the heterogeneous raw material to dozens

---

[16] Letter from R. W. Brust, Treasurer, Ross Laboratories, Columbus, Ohio.

[17] An alternative approach to the problem could have been to develop a single value for all milk solids rather than development of a break-even point for surplus commodities, by product.

[18] This statement assumes an in-house pricing policy that is based directly or indirectly on costs, at least one of which is raw materials cost. In the case of Pream, no directly competitive product existed at the time of its introduction to the market. The price per unit would not be influenced necessarily by its cost of production. Price could be whatever the market would bear. With hindsight, one knows the product was well received by the American public. The probability is high that economic profits accrued to this innovator in the short run.

of refineries that produce industrial goods and consumer products in varying proportions, and routes output through complex marketing channels that include thousands of retail outlets. In any week, a great many decisions must be made within such a firm. These include level of output, product mix, input combinations, pricing, scheduling, routing, and inventory accumulation and depletion. These decisions must be made at many plants and for many products.

A huge firm must be organized into numerous divisions that are allowed considerable autonomy in day-to-day decision making. The divisions transfer goods among themselves. The prices at which these goods are transferred affect divisional decision making, and wrong decisions (relative to overall company objectives) can be expected if transfer prices understate or overstate values and costs.

For purposes of decision making, intracompany transfers should be priced at marginal cost. Marginal cost is the market price (opportunity cost) if there is an external market for the good. Otherwise, it is explicit marginal cost as determined within the supplying division.

Transfer pricing: Intermediate products

The extract of Similac could have been sold in eastern cream markets each year. The price that could have been received from the sale is the minimum cost per pound of extract the parent, Ross Laboratories, should charge its subsidiary division, Pream. To charge a price less than that which can be obtained in competitive markets is (1) to understate the costs of raw material inputs for Pream, (2) to overstate the profitability of the finished Pream product, and (3) to subsidize, generally, the entire Pream operation.

To charge a price greater than that obtainable for the raw materials needed to manufacture the powdered coffee creamer would have just the opposite effects; namely, (1) raw material costs would be overstated, (2) profitability would be understated, and (3) Pream would be subsidizing the overall Similac operation. It is neither desirable nor necessary that either product be subsidized if the intermediate product (butter fat in this example) can be sold competitively on the open market.

If the intermediate product is produced in quantities greater than those needed to manufacture the subsidiary product, one of two things should occur: (1) One hundred percent of the extract of Similac can be transferred to Pream, and whatever the Pream division does not use can be sold at competitive prices on the open market; or (2) Similac can sell its extract in competitive markets at the prevailing market rate and, quite simply, allow the Pream division to purchase whatever quantity it needed at those rates. Either of the approaches might seem to be suitable, but the probability is high that the second alternative will generate larger profits and/or lower costs for the combined Similac-Pream operation. The second alternative creates a "profit center" atmosphere. The concept of a profit center is well established and requires that responsibility for profits or losses be assigned whenever possible to individual product lines.[19] There will be more on this subject shortly.

Quite simply, if the intermediate product is available in surplus quantities, the unused portion of that product may be sold in competitive markets. If the intermediate product is not produced in large enough quantities, the subsidiary division will have to purchase its additional needs on the open market.

Intermediate product pricing: No external market

The transfer pricing problem is minimized if an external market exists for the intermediate product. In the absence of a market for the intermediate product, the transfer price can be determined by (1) negotiations between the parties[20] or (2) marginal cost pricing.

Negotiation Negotiation works well if the subsidiary to whom the intermediate product is being transferred is independent of the company or division providing the product. Too much independence between the parties may result in no agreement regarding the proper transfer price.

Marginal cost pricing Marginal cost pricing assumes the quantity supplied is a function of the cost of manufacturing an additional unit of output. The change in total cost per unit of output caused by having to produce the intermediate product is the price at which the product is transferred to the subsidiary. In the case of Similac, butter fat transferred to the Pream division would be at a price equal to the marginal cost curve of manufacturing powdered Similac.

In the absence of a negotiated transfer price, the firm maximizes profit and/or minimizes cost by relying upon a transfer price equal to its marginal cost, as explained above.

The practice of transferring intermediate products to a manufacturing division at their marginal cost is appropriate when no external market exists for the good and when negotiating transfer prices between the parties is not workable. It is not the preferred method of transfer pricing. The preferred method, in the absence of competitive markets, is negotiation. Marginal cost pricing has the following disadvantages:

1. Assigning a cost to the subsidiary manufacturer in an arbitrary manner.

---

[19] Joel Dean, "Decentralization and Intracompany Pricing," *Harvard Business Review,* July–August, 1955, pp. 65–74.

[20] As indicated elsewhere, a student of managerial economics should understand that almost everything is negotiable, except grades. After all, there seems to be an exception to almost every rule.

2. Assigning a cost over which the subsidiary plant manager has virtually no control.
3. Assigning a cost so rigid in structure that it might distort the profitability of the subsidiary operation.
4. Assigning a cost that allows the subsidiary to claim, "I could have done better had I been allowed to exert greater operating control over my raw material input costs."

Profit centers

Joel Dean has provided insight into a method by which firms can resolve transfer pricing problems via creation of profit centers.[21] The profit center, by definition, refers to the assignment of responsibility for all profits and/or losses to the management of a particular operation. If Pream Division were to function as a profit center, it would be characterized by (1) independence of operation and (2) flexibility and freedom to make decisions.

The multiproduct, multinational firm that establishes profit centers affects, adversely or otherwise, the profit condition of the firm and serves two purposes: (1) It provides the best possible mechanism for solution to the transfer-pricing problems, and (2) it allows the profit center manager's performance to be evaluated more succinctly than is the case if the manager's job description, responsibilities, and authority were less clearly defined.

To the greatest extent possible, multiproduct firms should establish profit centers. These centers should be managed by a person who is responsible for all profits or losses incurred by the center. Such a manager must have control over his/her budget, be responsible for all hiring and firing, and (of particular importance to this discussion) be free to buy all raw material inputs wherever and from whomever offers the best price. This latter statement implies: (1) Managers should negotiate the transfer price of raw materials into or out of their particular area of responsibility; (2) in the absence of a negotiated price, managers should not be reluctant to establish the price at marginal cost; and (3) regardless of the outcome of steps (1) and (2), profit center managers should be free to buy or not buy the raw materials in question.

Profit maximization via transfer pricing

Prior to, during, and after the oil embargo of the early 1970s, the major oil companies operated profit centers. These profit centers proved to be very advantageous for a number of reasons, one of which may be traced directly to President Nixon's wage-price freeze of August 15, 1971.

---

[21] Dean, "Decentralization and Intercompany Pricing," pp. 65–74.

Included in Nixon's wage-price freeze was the notion that firms could pass to the ultimate consumer any increases in costs the firm could document. Certain "economies of being established" were realized at that time. Although individual oil company profit centers were owned by the same corporate giants located in New York, they did have autonomy. Consider, for example, the firm that owned a profit center in Saudi Arabia where the oil is drilled, call this A; a profit center in England where the oil is refined, call this B; and a profit center in the United States where the oil is marketed, call this C.

The parent company allows profit center A to increase its price in response to changing world conditions in oil. A transfers its output to B. At the higher price, B has a noticeable increase in raw material input costs. B transfers these increased costs to C when the oil is shipped from the refinery to the marketing division, from England to the United States Profit center C is permitted by the U.S. government to pass to the ultimate consumer the increases it incurred as a result of doing business with B. Inasmuch as B is an autonomous agent, one over which profit center C has no control, the wage and price board allows C to increase its price in line with the increased costs received from B. Note: The whole transfer pricing process is made possible by the corporate structure of the parent company.

Summary

The chapter discussed several topics in pricing. Price discrimination increases revenue from any given amount of product. Profit maximization under price discrimination requires selection of a total output that equates marginal cost with aggregate marginal revenue and allocation of this output among the various markets in such a way that their marginal revenues are equal to aggregate marginal revenue. Prices of the individual products are found on their demand curves at the optimal quantities. The aggregate marginal revenue function is formed by horizontal aggregation of quantites at each value of marginal revenue. To engage in profitable price discrimination, the firm must (1) have two or more markets in which price elasticities of demand are different under nondiscriminatory pricing and (2) have the ability to prevent arbitrage. Price discrimination may be socially beneficial (though some buyers do pay higher prices) if it is carried out by a properly regulated monopoly or by firms in industries in which excess profits are wiped out by long-run entry and expansion. Selective price discrimination that undercuts a competitor's price may be illegal.

Peak-load pricing requires higher prices in peak-load periods and reduced prices in off-peak periods. The long-run solution in the firm-peak case is to set price at marginal cost in both periods—where marginal cost in the off-peak period includes only variable cost, but marginal cost in the peak period also includes an allocation of capacity cost to each unit sold.

Public utility rate regulation requires the regulated firms to charge prices below the monopoly level. The rate structure, or price level, usually sought is at the full-cost level. Recovery of full cost may encourage a utility to misallocate resources. The greater the misallocation, the higher the so-called rate base goes. Some economists argue that social welfare would be increased by regulating rates of natural monopolies down to the marginal cost level, although subsidies to the regulated firms (from general tax revenues) might be necessary.

In pricing joint products produced in fixed proportions, marginal revenues from both producers are summed vertically at each rate of output of one of the products. The optimum rate of output is found where marginal cost is equal to aggregate marginal revenue, and the prices of the two products are found on the individual demand curves at the optimum rate of output. In pricing alternative produts, the marginal revenue product functions are aggregated horizontally, with units of the scarce resource or facility being used as measures of rate of production. Optimum total production is found where marginal cost per unit of scarce resource is equal to aggregate marginal revenue product. Individual product uses of the scarce resource are found on their marginal revenue product functions at the solution value, and their prices are found on their demand curves at outputs corresponding to the amounts of scarce resource used.

Transfer pricing requires transfers at marginal cost for purposes of decision making. Marginal cost is the market price (opportunity cost) for an intermediate product that has an external market, or it is the explicit marginal cost of production within the supplying division when this is higher or when the intermediate product has no outside market. Negotiations between profit center managers often result in the best possible transfer price for a given good or service.

CASES

Selected topics in pricing

Birch Paper Company[1]

"If I were to price these boxes any lower than $480 a thousand," said James Brunner, manager of Birch Paper Company's Thompson division, "I'd be countermanding my order of last month for our salespeople to stop shaving their bids and to bid full-cost quotations. I've been trying for weeks to improve the quality of our business, and if I turn around

---

[1] This case was prepared by William Rotch under the direction of Neil E. Harlan of the Harvard University Graduate School of Business Administration as a basis for classroom discussion rather than to illustrate either effective or ineffective handling of administrative situations. Copyright 1956 by the President and Fellows of Harvard College. Used by specific permission.

now and accept this job at $430 or $450 or something less than $480, I'll be tearing down this program I've been working so hard to build up. The division can't very well show a profit by putting in bids which don't even cover a fair share of overhead costs, let alone give us a profit.''

Birch Paper Company was a medium-size, partly integrated paper company, producing white and kraft papers and paperboard. A portion of its paperboard output was converted into corrugated boxes by the Thompson division, which also printed and colored the outside surface of the boxes. Including Thompson, the company had four producing divisions and a timberland division, which supplied part of the company's pulp requirements.

For several years each division had been judged independently on the basis of its profit and return on investment. Top management had been working to gain effective results from a policy of decentralizing responsibility and authority for all decisions but those relating to overall company policy. The company's top officals believed that in the past few years the concept of decentralization had been successfully applied and that the company's profits and competitive position had definitely improved.

Early in 1957 the Northern division designed a special display box for one of its papers in conjunction with the Thompson division, which was equipped to make the box. Thompson's staff for package design and development spent several months perfecting the design, production methods, and materials that were to be used; because of the unusual color and shape, these were far from standard. According to an agreement between the two divisions, the Thompson division was reimbursed by the Northern division for the costs of its design and development work.

When the specifications were all prepared, the Northern division asked for bids on the box from Thompson division and from two outside companies. Each division manager was normally free to buy from whatever supplier he or she wished; and even on sales within the company, divisions were expected to meet the going market price if they wanted the business.

In 1957 the profit margins of converters such as the Thompson division were being squeezed. Thompson, as did many other similar converters, bought its paperboard and its function was to print, cut, and shape it into boxes. Although it bought most of its materials from other Birch divisions, most of Thompson's sales were made to outside customers. If Thompson got the order from Northern, it probably would buy its linerboard and corrugating medium from the Southern division of Birch. The walls of a corrugated box consist of outside and inside sheets of linerboard sandwiching the fluted corrugating medium. About 70 percent of Thompson's out-of-pocket cost of $400 for the order represented the cost of linerboard and corrugating medium. Though Southern had been running below capacity and had excess inventory, it quoted the market price, which had not noticeably weakened as a result of the oversupply. Its out-of-pocket costs on both linear and corrugating medium were about 60 percent of the selling price.

The Northern division received bids on the boxes of $480 a thousand from the Thompson division, $430 a thousand from West Paper Company, and $432 a thousand from Eire Papers, Ltd. Eire Papers offered to buy from Birch the outside linerboard with the special printing already on it, but would supply its own inside liner and corrugating medium. The outside liner would be supplied by the Southern division at a price equivalent of $90 a thousand boxes and would be printed for $30 a thousand by the Thompson division. Of the $30, about $25 would be out-of-pocket costs.

Since this situation appeared to be a little unusual, William Kenton, manager of the Northern division, discussed the wide discrepancy of bids with Birch's commercial vice president. He told the vice president, "We sell in a very competitive market, where higher costs cannot be passed on. How can we be expected to show a decent profit and return on investment if we have to buy our supplies at more than 10 percent over the going market?"

Knowing that Brunner had on occasion in the past few months been unable to operate the Thompson division at capacity, it seemed odd to the vice president that Brunner would add the full 20 percent overhead and profit charge to his out-of-pocket costs. When asked about this, Brunner's answer was the remark that appears at the beginning of the case. He went on to say that having done the developmental work on the box, and having received no profit on that, he felt entitled to a good markup on the production of the box itself.

The vice president explored further the cost structures of the various divisions. He remembered a comment that the controller had made at a meeting the week before to the effect that costs that for one division were variable, could be largely fixed for the company as a whole. He knew that in the absence of specific orders from top management, Kenton would accept the lowest bid, which was that of the West Paper Company for $430. However, it would be possible for top management to order the acceptance of another bid if the situation warranted such action. And though the volume represented by the transactions in question was less than 5 percent of the volume of any of the divisions involved, other transactions could conceivably raise similar problems later.

1. How does the theory of transfer pricing relate to this case?
2. Is there a conflict in the case between the needs of decisions on pricing and the needs of profit determination? Explain.
3. What price should be set on the special display boxes? Discuss.

Utah Pie Company v. *Continental Baking Co. (et al.)*[1]

This case was argued January 17, 1967; decided April 24, 1967; a rehearing was denied June 5, 1967. Mr. Justice White delivered the opinion of the Court.

This suit for treble damages and injunction under § § 4 and 16 of the Clayton Act, 38 Stat. 731, 737, 15 U.S.C. § § 15 and 26 was brought by petitioner, Utah Pie Company, against respondents, Continental Baking Company, Carnation Company, and Pet Milk Company. The complaint charged a conspiracy under § § 1 and 2 of the Sherman Act, 26 Stat. 209, as amended, 15 U.S.C. § § 1 and 2, and violations by each respondent of § 2(a) of the Clayton Act as amended by the Robinson-Patman Act, 49 Stat. 1526, 15 U.S.C. § 13(a). The jury found for respondents on the conspiracy charge and for petitioner on the price discrimination charge. Judgment was entered for petitioner for damages and attorneys' fees and respondents appealed on several grounds. The Court of Appeals reversed, addressing itself to the single issue of whether the evidence against each of the respondents was sufficient to support a finding of probable injury to competition within the meaning of § 2(a) and holding that it was not. We reverse.

The product involved is frozen dessert pies—apple, cherry, boysenberry, peach, pumpkin, and mince. The period covered by the suit comprised the years 1958, 1959, and 1960 and the first eight months of 1961. Petitioner is a Utah Corporation which for 30 years had been baking pies in its plant in Salt Lake City and selling them in Utah and surrounding states. It entered the frozen pie business in late 1957. It was immediately successful with its new line and built a new plant in Salt Lake City in 1958. The frozen pie market was a rapidly expanding one: 57,060 dozen frozen pies were sold in the Salt Lake City market in 1958, 111,729 dozen in 1959, 184,569 dozen in 1960, and 266,908 dozen in 1961. Utah Pie's share of this market in those years was 66.5 percent, 34.3 percent, 45.5 percent, and 45.3 percent, respectively, its sales volume steadily increasing over the four years. Its financial position also improved. Petitioner is not, however, a large company. At the time of the trial, petitioner operated with only 18 employees, nine of whom were members of the Rigby family, which controlled the business. Its net worth increased from $31,651.98 on October 31, 1957, to $68,802.13 on October 31, 1961. Total sales were $238,000 in the year ending October 31, 1957, $353,000 in 1958, $430,000 in 1959, $504,000 in 1960, and $589,000 in 1961. Its net income or loss for these same years was a loss of $6,461 in 1957, and net income in the remaining years of $7,090, $11,897, $7,636, and $9,216.

Each of the respondents is a large company and each of them is a major factor in the frozen pie market in one or more regions of the country. Each entered the Salt Lake City frozen pie market before petitioner began freezing dessert pies. None of them had a plant in Utah. By the end of the period involved in this suit Pet had plants in Michigan, Pennsylvania, and California; Continental in Virginia, Iowa, and California; and Carnation in California. The Salt Lake City market was supplied by respondents chiefly from their California operations. They sold primarily on a delivered price basis.

The "Utah" label was petitioner's proprietary brand. Beginning in 1960, it also

---

[1] United States Reports, October Term 1966, vol. 386 (Washington D.C.: U.S. Government Printing Office, 1967), pp. 685–706.

sold pies of like grade and quality under the controlled label "Frost 'N' Flame"
to Associated Grocers and in 1961 it began selling to American Food Stores under
the "Mayfresh" label. It also, on a seasonal basis, sold pumpkin and mince
frozen pies to Safeway under Safeway's own "Bel-air" label.

The major competitive weapon in the Utah market was price. The location of
petitioner's plant gave it natural advantages in the Salt Lake City marketing area
and it entered the market at a price below the then going prices for respondents'
comparable pies. For most of the period involved here its prices were the lowest
in the Salt Lake City market. It was, however, challenged by each of the respondents at one time or another and for varying periods. There was ample evidence
to show that each of the respondents contributed to what proved to be a deterio-
rating price structure over the period covered by this suit, and each of the respondents in the course of the ongoing price competition sold frozen pies in the
Salt Lake market at prices lower than it sold pies of like grade and quality in
other markets considerably closer to its plants. Utah Pie, which entered the
market at a price of $4.15 per dozen at the beginning of the relevant period, was
selling "Utah" and "Frost 'N' Flame" pies for $2.75 per dozen when the instant
suit was filed some 44 months later. Pet, which was offering pies at $4.92 per
dozen in February 1958, was offering "Pet-Ritz" and "Bel-air" pies at $3.56 and
$3.46 per dozen respectively in March and April 1961. Carnation's price in early
1958 was $4.82 per dozen but it was selling at $3.46 per dozen at the conclusion
of the period, meanwhile having been down as low as $3.30 per dozen. The price
range experienced by Continental during the period covered by this suit ran from
a 1958 high of over $5 per dozen to a 1961 low of $2.85 per dozen.

We deal first with petitioner's case against the Pet Milk Company. Pet entered
the frozen pie business in 1955, acquired plants in Pennsylvania and California
and undertook a large advertising campaign to market its "Pet-Ritz" brand of
frozen pies. Pet's initial emphasis was on quality, but in the face of competition
from regional and local companies and in an expanding market where price
proved to be a crucial factor, Pet was forced to take steps to reduce the price of
its pies to the ultimate consumer. These developments had consequences in the
Salt Lake City market which are the substance of petitioner's case against Pet.

First, Pet successfully concluded an arrangement with Safeway, which is one
of the three largest customers for frozen pies in the Salt Lake market, whereby it
would sell frozen pies to Safeway under the latter's own "Bel-air" label at a price
significantly lower than it was selling its comparable "Pet-Ritz" brand in the
same Salt Lake market and elsewhere. The initial price on "Bel-air" pies was
slightly lower than Utah's price for its "Utah" brand of pies at the time, and near
the end of the period the "Bel-air" price was comparable to the "Utah" price
but higher than Utah's "Frost 'N' Flame" brand. Pet's Safeway business
amounted to 22.8 percent, 12.3 percent, and 6.3 percent of the entire Salt Lake
City market for the years 1959, 1960, and 1961, respectively, and to 64 percent,
44 percent, and 22 percent of Pet's own Salt Lake City sales for those same years.
Second, it introduced a 20-ounce economy pie under the "Swiss Miss" label and
began selling the new pie in the Salt Lake market in August 1960 at prices ranging
from $3.25 to $3.30 for the remainder of the period. This pie was at times sold at
a lower price in the Salt Lake City market than it was sold in other markets.

Third, Pet became more competitive with respect to the prices for its "Pet-
Ritz" proprietary label. For 18 of the relevant 44 months its offering price for

"Pet-Ritz" pies was $4 per dozen or lower, and $3.70 or lower for six of these months. According to the Court of Appeals, in 7 of the 44 months Pet's prices in Salt Lake were lower than prices charged in the California markets. This was true although selling in Salt Lake involved a 30- to 35-cent freight cost.

The Court of Appeals first concluded that Pet's price differential on sales to Safeway must be put aside in considering injury to competition because in its view of the evidence the differential had been completely cost justified and because Utah would not in any event have been able to enjoy the Safeway custom. Second, it concluded that the remaining discriminations on "Pet-Ritz" and "Swiss Miss" pies were an insufficient predicate on which the jury could have found a reasonably possible injury either to Utah Pie as a competitive force or to competition generally.

We disagree with the Court of Appeals in several respects. First, there was evidence from which the jury could have found considerably more price discrimination by Pet with respect to "Pet-Ritz" and "Swiss Miss" pies than was considered by the Court of Appeals. In addition to the seven months during which Pet's prices in Salt Lake were lower than prices in the California markets, there was evidence from which the jury could reasonably have found that in 10 additional months the Salt Lake City prices for "Pet-Ritz" pies were discriminatory as compared with sales in western markets other than California. Likewise, with respect to "Swiss Miss" pies, there was evidence in the record from which the jury could have found that in five of the 13 months during which the "Swiss Miss" pies were sold prior to the filing of this suit, prices in Salt Lake City were lower than those charged by Pet in either California or some other western market.

Second, with respect to Pet's Safeway business, the burden of proving cost justification was on Pet and, in our view, reasonable men could have found that Pet's lower priced, "Bel-air" sales to Safeway were not cost justified in their entirety. Pet introduced cost data for 1961 indicating a cost saving on the Safeway business greater than the price advantage extended to that customer. These statistics were not particularized for the Salt Lake market, but assuming that they were adequate to justify the 1961 sales, they related to only 24 percent of the Safeway sales over the relevant period. The evidence concerning the remaining 76 percent was at best incomplete and inferential. It was insufficient to take the defense of cost justification from the jury, which reasonably could have found a greater incidence of unjustified price discrimination than that allowed by the Court of Appeals' view of the evidence.

With respect to whether Utah would have enjoyed Safeway's business absent the Pet contract with Safeway, it seems clear that whatever the fact is in this regard, it is not determinative of the impact of that contract on competitors other than Utah and on competition generally. There were other companies seeking the Safeway business, including Continental and Carnation, whose pies may have been excluded from the Safeway shelves by what the jury could have found to be discriminatory sales to Safeway. What is more, Pet's evidence that Utah's unwillingness to install quality control equipment prevented Utah from enjoying Safeway's private label business is not the only evidence in the record relevant to that question. There was other evidence to the contrary. The jury would not have been compelled to find that Utah Pie could not have gained more of the Safeway business.

Third, the Court of Appeals almost entirely ignored other evidence which provides material support for the jury's conclusion that Pet's behavior satisfied the statutory test regarding competitive injury. This evidence bore on the issue of Pet's predatory intent to injure Utah Pie. As an initial matter, the jury could have concluded that Pet's discriminatory pricing was aimed at Utah Pie; Pet's own management, as early as 1959, identified Utah Pie as an "unfavorable factor," one which "d[u]g holes in our operation" and posed a constant "check" on Pet's performance in the Salt Lake City market. Moreover, Pet candidly admitted that during the period when it was establishing its relationship with Safeway, it sent into Utah Pie's plant an industrial spy to seek information that would be of use to Pet in convincing Safeway that Utah Pie was not worthy of its custom. Pet denied that it ever in fact used what it had learned against Utah Pie in competing for Safeway's business. The parties, however, are not the ultimate judges of credibility. But even giving Pet's view of the incident a measure of weight does not mean the jury was foreclosed from considering the predatory intent underlying Pet's mode of competition. Finally, Pet does not deny that the evidence showed it suffered substantial losses on its frozen pie sales during the greater part of the time involved in this suit, and there was evidence from which the jury could have concluded that the losses Pet sustained in Salt Lake City were greater than those incurred elsewhere. It would not have been an irrational step if the jury concluded that there was a relationship between price and the losses.

It seems clear to us that the jury heard adequate evidence from which it could have concluded that Pet had engaged in predatory tactics in waging competitive warfare in the Salt Lake City market. Coupled with the incidence of price discrimination attributable to Pet, the evidence as a whole established, rather than negated, the reasonable possibility that Pet's behavior produced a lessening of competition proscribed by the Act.

Petitioner's case against Continental is not complicated. Continental was a substantial factor in the market in 1957. But its sales of frozen 22-ounce dessert pies, sold under the "Morton" brand, amounted to only 1.3 percent of the market in 1958, 2.9 percent in 1959, and 1.8 percent in 1960. Its problems were primarily that of cost and in turn that of price, the controlling factor in the market. In late 1960 it worked out a co-packing arrangement in California by which fruit would be processed from the trees into the finished pie without large intermediate packing, storing, and shipping expenses. Having improved its position, it attempted to increase its share of the Salt Lake City market by utilizing a local broker and offering short-term price concessions in varying amounts. Its efforts for seven months were not spectacularly successful. Then in June 1961, it took the steps which are the heart of petitioner's complaint against it. Effective for the last two weeks of June it offered its 22-ounce frozen apple pies in the Utah area at $2.85 per dozen. It was then selling the same pies at substantially higher prices in other markets. The Salt Lake City price was less than its direct cost plus an allocation for overhead. Utah's going price at the time for its 24-ounce "Frost 'N' Flame" apple pie sold to Associated Grocers was $3.10 per dozen, and for its "Utah" brand $3.40 per dozen. At its new prices, Continental sold pies to American Grocers in Pocatello, Idaho, and to American Food Stores in Ogden, Utah. Safeway, one of the major buyers in Salt Lake City, also purchased 6,250 dozen, its requirements for about five weeks. Another purchaser ordered 1,000 dozen. Utah's response was immediate. It reduced its price on all of its apple pies to $2.75 per dozen. Continental refused Safeway's request to match Utah's price, but renewed its offer at the same prices effective July 31 for another two-week period. Utah filed suit on September 8, 1961. Continental's total sales of frozen pies increased from 3,350 dozen in 1960 to 18,800 dozen in 1961. Its market share increased from 1.8 percent in 1960 to 8.3 percent in 1961. The Court of Appeals concluded that Continental's conduct had had only minimal effect, that it had not injured or weakened Utah Pie as a competitor, that it had not substantially lessened competition and that there was no reasonable possibility that it would do so in the future.

We again differ with the Court of Appeals. Its opinion that Utah was not damaged as a competitive force apparently rested on the fact that Utah's sales volume continued to climb in 1961 and on the court's own factual conclusion that Utah was not deprived of any pie business which it otherwise might have had. But this retrospective assessment fails to note that Continental's discriminatory below-cost price caused Utah Pie to reduce its price to $2.75. The jury was entitled to consider the potential impact of Continental's price reduction absent any responsive price cut by Utah Pie. Price was a major factor in the Salt Lake City market. Safeway, which had been buying Utah brand pies, immediately reacted and purchased a five-week supply of frozen pies from Continental, thereby temporarily foreclosing the proprietary brands of Utah and other firms from the Salt Lake City Safeway market. The jury could rationally have concluded that had Utah not lowered its price, Continental, which repeated its offer once, would have continued it, that Safeway would have continued to buy from Continental and that other buyers, large as well as small, would have followed suit. It could also have reasonably concluded that a competitor who is forced to reduce his price to a new all-time low in a market of declining prices will in time feel the financial pinch and will be a less effective competitive force.

Even if the impact on Utah Pie as a competitor was negligible, there remain the consequences to others in the market who had to compete not only with Continental's 22-ounce pie at $2.85 but with Utah's even lower price of $2.75 per dozen for both its proprietary and controlled labels. Petitioner and respondents were not the only sellers in the Salt Lake City market, although they did account for 91.8 percent of the sales in 1961. The evidence was that there were nine other sellers in 1960 who sold 23,473 dozen pies, 12.7 percent of the total market. In 1961 there were eight other sellers who sold less than the year before—18,565 dozen or 8.2 percent of the total—although the total market had expanded from 184,569 dozen to 226,908 dozen. We think there was sufficient evidence from which the jury could find a violation of § 2(a) by Continental.

The Carnation Company entered the frozen dessert pie business in 1955 through the acquisition of "Mrs. Lee's Pies" which was then engaged in manufacturing and selling frozen pies in Utah and elsewhere under the "Simple Simon" label. Carnation also quickly found the market extremely sensitive to price. Carnation decided, however, not to enter an economy product in the market, and during the period covered by this suit if offered only its quality "Simple Simon" brand. Its primary method of meeting competition in its markets was to offer a variety of discounts and other reductions, and the technique was not unsuccessful. In 1958, for example, Carnation enjoyed 10.3 percent of the Salt Lake City market, and although its volume of pies sold in that market increased substantially in the next year, its percentage of the market temporarily slipped to 8.6 percent. However, 1960 was a turnaround year for Carnation in the Salt Lake City market; it more than doubled its volume of sales over the preceding year and thereby gained 12.1 percent of the market. And while the price structure in the market deteriorated rapidly in 1961, Carnation's position remained important.

We need not dwell long upon the case against Carnation, which in some respects is similar to that against Continental and in others more nearly resembles the case against Pet. After Carnation's temporary setback in 1959 it instituted a new pricing policy to regain business in the Salt Lake City market. The new policy involved a slash in price of 60¢ per dozen pies, which brought Carnation's price to a level admittedly well below its costs, and well below the other prices prevailing in the market. The impact of the move was felt immediately, and the two other major sellers in the market reduced their prices. Carnation's banner year, 1960, in the end involved eight months during which the prices in Salt Lake City were lower than prices charged in other markets. The trend continued during the eight months in 1961 that preceded the filing of the complaint in this case. In each of those months the Salt Lake City prices charged by Carnation were well below prices charged in other markets, and in all but August 1961 the Salt Lake City delivered price was 20¢ to 50¢ lower than the prices charged in distant San Francisco. The Court of Appeals held that only the early 1960 prices could be found to have been below cost. That holding, however, simply overlooks evidence from which the jury could have concluded that throughout 1961 Carnation maintained a below-cost price structure and that Carnation's discriminatory pricing, no less than that of Pet and Continental, had an important effect on the Salt Lake City market. We cannot say that the evidence precluded the jury from finding it reasonably possible that Carnation's conduct would injury competition.

Section 2(a) does not forbid price competition which will probably injure or lessen competition by eliminating competitors, discouraging entry into the market, or enhancing the market shares of the dominant sellers. But Congress has established some ground rules for the game. Sellers may not sell like goods to different purchasers at different prices if the result may be to injure competition in either the sellers' or the buyers' market unless such discriminations are justified as permitted by the Act. This case concerns the sellers' market. In this context, the Court of Appeals placed heavy emphasis on the fact that Utah Pie constantly increased its sales volume and continued to make a profit. But we disagree with its apparent view that there is no reasonably possible injury to competition as long as the volume of sales in a particular market is expanding and at least some of the competitors in the market continue to operate at a profit. Nor do we think that the Act only comes into play to regulate the conduct of price discriminators when their discriminatory prices consistently undercut other competitors. It is true that many of the primary line cases that have reached the courts have involved blatant predatory price discriminations employed with the hope of immediate destruction of a particular competitor. On the question of injury to competition such cases present courts with no difficulty, for such pricing is clearly within the heart of the proscription of the Act. Courts and commentators alike have noted that the existence of predatory intent might bear on the likelihood of injury to competition. In this case there was some evidence of predatory intent with respect to each of these respondents. There was also other evidence upon which the jury could rationally find the requisite injury to competition. The frozen pie market in Salt Lake City was highly competitive. At times Utah Pie was a leader in moving the general level of prices down, and at other times each of the respondents also bore responsibility for the downward pressure on the price structure. We believe that the Act reaches price discrimination that erodes competition as much as it does price discrimination that is intended to have immediate destructive impact. In this case, the evidence shows a drastically declining price structure which the jury could rationally attribute to continued or sporadic price discrimination. The jury was entitled to conclude that "the effect of such discrimination," by each of these respondents, "may be substantially to lessen competition . . . or to injure, destroy, or prevent competition with any person who either grants or knowingly receives the benefit of such discrimination. . . ." The statutory test is one that necessarily looks forward on the basis of proven conduct in the past. Proper application of that standard here requires reversal of the judgment of the Court of Appeals.

Since the Court of Appeals held that petitioner had failed to make a prima facie case against each of the respondents, it expressly declined to pass on other grounds for reversal presented by the respondents. 349 F.2d 122, 126. Without intimating any views on the other grounds presented to the Court of Appeals, we reverse its judgment and remand the case to that court for further proceedings. It is so ordered. Reversed and remanded.

The Chief Justice took no part in the decision of this case. Mr. Justice Stewart and Mr. Justice Harlan joined in dissenting:

I would affirm the judgment, agreeing substantially with the reasoning of the Court of Appeals as expressed in the thorough and conscientious opinion of Judge Phillips.

There is only one issue in this case in its present posture: Whether the respondents engaged in price discrimination "where the effect of such discrimination may be substantially to lessen competition or tend to create a monopoly in any line of commerce, or to injure, destroy, or prevent competition with any person who either grants or knowingly receives the benefit of such discrimination. . . ." Phrased more simply, did the respondents' actions have the anticompetitive effect required by the statute as an element of a cause of action?

The Court's own description of the Salt Lake City frozen pie market from 1958 through 1961, shows that the answer to that question must be no. In 1958 Utah Pie had a quasi-monopolistic 66.5 percent of the market. In 1961—after the alleged predations of the respondents—Utah Pie still had a commanding 45.3 percent, Pet had 29.4 percent, and the remainder of the market was divided almost equally between Continental, Carnation, and other, small local bakers. Unless we disregard the lessons so laboriously learned in scores of Sherman and Clayton Act cases, the 1961 situation has to be considered more competitive than that of 1958. Thus, if we assume that the price discrimination proven against the respondents had any effect on competition, that effect must have been beneficial.

That the Court has fallen into the error of reading the Robinson-Patman Act as protecting competitors, instead of competition, can be seen from its unsuccessful attempt to distinguish cases relied upon by the respondents. Those cases are said to be inapposite because they invovled "no general decline in price structure," and no "lasting impact upon prices." But lower prices are the hallmark of intensified competition.

The Court of Appeals squarely identified the fallacy which the Court today embraces:

". . . a contention that Utah Pie was entitled to hold the extraordinary market share percentage of 66.5, attained in 1958, falls of its own dead weight. To approve such a contention would be to hold that Utah Pie was entitled to maintain a position which approached, if it did not in fact amount to a monopoly, and could not exist in the face of proper and healthy competition."

I cannot hold that Utah Pie's monopolistic position was protected by the federal antitrust laws from effective price competition, and I therefore respectfully dissent.

1. Did the competitors engage in price discrimination? Were these practices illegal? Should they be considered illegal?
2. Does the fact that Utah Pie Company is a small independent firm, facing large competitors, influence your appraisal of the case?
3. Is the market structure competitive, monopolistically competitive, or oligopolistic?
4. Did the ruling in the case reduce competition or protect it?

PROBLEMS
Selected topics in pricing

10–1   What conditions would make it certain that price discrimination is being practiced by a seller? How does price discrimination make the seller better off? What conditions make price discrimination illegal?

10–2   A firm produces product q and sells it in a perfectly competitive market for $10 per unit. Its total cost function is $C = q^3 - 9q^2 + 25q + 10$. What should its production be? What is its *ATC, MC, MR,* and profit at this point?

10–3   Does marginal cost pricing yield some contribution toward a firm's fixed cost if the firm's long-run marginal cost function is rising with increases in the rate of output? What happens if the long-run marginal cost is falling with increases in the rate of output?

10–4   A monopolist sells a homogeneous product in two distinct markets. The estimated demand relations are:

$$P_1 = 300 - 2.5Q_1$$
$$P_2 = 500 - 15Q_2$$

The cost relation is:

$$TC = 2,500 + 45Q + 0.5Q^2$$

If the monopolist is a profit maximizer, determine the price and quantity in each market and the total profit.

10–5   For purposes of managerial decision making, a supplying division's transfer price should be quoted to using divisions at the division's internal marginal cost or at the externally determined marginal opportunity cost, whichever is greater. What is meant by "the division's internal marginal cost"? By the "externally determined marginal opportunity cost"?

10–6   Overseas Industries serves both a domestic and a European market from New York City. The demand in the two markets differs:

For domestic it is $P = 500 - 8Q$
For Europe it is $P = 400 - 5Q$

All sales of Overseas' product are on an f.o.b. New York basis. The total cost function for the company is:

$$TC = \$10,000 + 20Q$$

a. If the markets can be kept segmented, what quantities and prices are applicable to each market?
b. If the markets were not separable, what should the overall quantity be? At what price?
c. Compare the total profit under part *a* to that under part *b*. Is price discrimination profitable?

10–7   The International Nickel Company (INCO) produces two products from a single raw material. Product X is considered to be the by-product of the manufacture of product Y. The demand equation of the two products are:

$$Q_y = 500 - 5P_y$$
$$Q_x = 2,500 - 10P_x$$

Three units of X are produced for every unit of Y. Total cost is:

$$TC = 200 + Q_y$$

a. What quantity of Y should be produced? At what price should it be offered for sale?
b. What percent of X production will be sold if it is priced appropriately?

c. How would the answer in part *b* change of the production ratio of X to Y were 6 to 1?

d. If the production ratio were flexible, what would be the optimal ratio?

10–8   Kellogg Incorporated maintains its own farms for the production of cereal grains used in the company's breakfast products. Recently Kellogg was divisionalized by the board of directors in an effort to eliminate coordination problems within the corporation. A problem has arisen, however, as to what prices the farming division will charge the breakfast foods division for cereal grains. Wheat, for example, could be sold to the outside market in virtually any quantity for $2.10 a bushel. Assume wheat may also be purchased for $2.10 per bushel. The cost function of the wheat farming operation is:

$$TC = 90,000 + 0.0005Q^2w$$

The breakfast foods division can process wheat into a product that will cost $3.30 per bushel, exclusive of the cost of the wheat. Assume one bushel of wheat goes into each bushel of finished product. The demand equation for this product is:

$$P = 6.50 - 0.0000115Q_p$$

a. What price should the farming division charge the breakfast foods division for wheat?

b. How much wheat should Kellogg produce? To whom should it be sold?

c. How much breakfast product should be produced? At what price should it be offered for sale?

10–9   North Coast Foundry is divisionalized into the foundry division and the machine shop division. The machine shop division produces and sells a patented part for which it needs a custom casting. The demand equation for the final product is:

$$P = 15.40 - 0.0035Q_p$$

Finished operations on the casting cost $3.10 per unit. The foundry division has estimated its cost for producing the casting as:

$$TC = 420 + 0.0015Q^2c$$

a. What quantity of the final product should be produced? At what price?

b. What should the foundry division charge for the castings?

10–10 Goodyear sells a product in two separate markets. Given the following price and cost structures, what are the prices and quantities it will choose for each market? What is the total quantity produced?

Market 1		Market 2		Costs	
Q	P	Q	P	Q	TC
1	10.0	1	15	1	6
2	9.5	2	14	2	7
3	8.0	3	13	3	9
4	7.0	4	12	4	18
5	6.0	5	11	5	28
				6	40

Selected references

Baumol, William J. "Quasi-Permanence of Price Reductions: A Policy for Prevention of Predatory Pricing." *Yale Law Journal* 89, no. 1 (November 1979), pp. 1–26.

Benke, Ralph L., Jr.; James Don Edwards; and Alton R. Wheelock. "Applying an Opportunity Cost General Rule for Transfer Pricing." *Management Accounting* 63, no. 12 (June 1982), pp. 43–51.

Carlton, Dennis W., and Jeffrey M. Perloff. "Price Discrimination, Vertical Integration and Divestiture in Nature Resource Markets." *Resources and Energy* (Netherlands) 3, no. 1 (March 1981), pp. 1–11.

Coyne, Thomas J. "Financial Returns to Equity: The Profitability of the Electric Utility." *Public Utilities Fortnightly* 109, no. 4 (1982), pp. 19–28.

Crew, Michael A., and Paul R. Kleindorfer. "Regulation and Diverse Technology in the Peak-Load Problem." *Southern Economic Journal* 48, no. 2 (October 1981), pp. 335–43.

Dean, Joel. "Decentralization and Intracompany Pricing." *Harvard Business Review* (September–October 1966).*

Donaldson, David, and B. Curtis Eaton. "Patience, More than its Own Reward: A Note on Price Discrimination." *Canadian Journal of Economics* 14, no. 1 (February 1981), pp. 93–105.

Fowler, D. J. "Transfer Prices and Profit Maximization in Multinational Enterprise Organizations." *Journal of International Business Studies* 9, no. 3 (Winter 1978), pp. 9–26.

French, Warren; Jan Henkel; and James Cox III. "When the Buyer Is the Object of Price Discrimination." *Journal of Purchasing & Materials Management* 15, no. 1 (Spring 1979), pp. 2–7.

Griffin, James M. "The Econometrics of Joint Production: Another Approach." *Review of Economics and Statistics* 59, no. 4 (November 1977), pp. 389–97.

Haddock, David D. "Basing-Point Pricing: Competitive versus Collusive Theories." *American Economic Review* 72, no. 3 (June 1982), pp. 289–306.

Hollas, Daniel R., and Thomas S. Friedland. "Competition, Regulation, and Second-Degree Price Discrimination in the Municipal Electric Industry." *Quarterly Review of Economics & Business* 20, no. 3 (Autumn 1980), pp. 41–59.

Kamerschen, David R. "An Economic Approach to the Detection and Proof of Collusion." *American Business Law Journal* 17, no. 2 (Summer 1979), pp. 193–209.

Keller, Edmund R. "Price Discrimination and the Law: The Inflation Dilemma." *Antitrust Law & Economics Review* 11, no. 4 (1979), pp. 17–26.

Lovell, C. A. Knox, and Kenneth L. Wertz. "Price Discrimination in Related Markets." *Economic Inquiry* 19, no. 3 (July 1981), pp. 488–94.

Saving, T. R., and Arthur S. De Vany. "Uncertain Markets, Reliability and Peak-Load Pricing." *Southern Economic Journal* 47, no. 4 (April 1981), pp. 908–23.

Spulber, Daniel F. "Spatial Nonlinear Pricing." *American Economic Review* 71, no. 5 (December 1981), pp. 923–33.

Straszheim, Donald H., and Mahlon R. Straszheim. "An Econometric Analysis of the Determination of Prices in Manufacturing Industries." *Review of Economics and Statistics* 58, no. 2 (May 1976), pp. 191–201.

Wenders, John T. "Peak-Load Pricing in the Electric Utility Industry." *Bell Journal of Economics* 7 no. 1 (Spring 1976), pp. 232–41.*

Wilson T. "The Price of Oil: A Case of Negative Marginal Revenue." *Journal of Industrial Economics* 27, no. 4 (June 1979), pp. 301–15.

---

* This article is included in Thomas J. Coyne, *Readings in Managerial Economics,* 3d ed. (Plano: Business Publications, 1981).

5

Financial management

C H A P T E R

11

Capital budgeting

Capital budgeting (capital-expenditure planning) is allocation of capital among alternative investment opportunities. Capital budgeting procedures and techniques must be understood if a company is to plan successfully for its long-term investment needs. It is a process that requires an understanding of the time value of money and the cost of capital. The procedure assumes in its application that the user is ready, willing, and able to attempt a forecast of net cash inflows and outflows from a specific investment. Capital budgeting has profound effects upon the competitive position of the firm, the rewards it can provide, and the managerial responsibilities it imposes. Capital-expenditure planning is regarded as one of the important functions of financial management.

The capital budgeting process requires knowledge, skills, and judgment of people in various functional occupations, such as engineering, production, marketing, personnel, accounting, risk, transportation, and real estate as well as finance and economics. Thus, these specialists should also understand how business investment planning is done. Indeed, everyone intending to make a managerial career in business or in nonprofit organizations needs competence in capital budgeting.

Capital budgeting incorporates many concepts introduced in earlier chapters. Demand, cost, and pricing concepts are essential tools in forecasting investment results. Incremental reasoning is used in separating projected cash flows that would be associated with each of the various opportunities. Investment in a project is justified only if it provides a return equal to or greater than the firm's opportunity cost of capital.

Importance to the aggregate economy

Capital budgeting procedures and techniques appear at times to be mechanical in nature; yet, they serve the purpose of helping management

474

select from among numerous competing and/or conflicting proposals. Investment proposals are presented because someone within the firm believes a profit could be made if additional monies were provided for the purpose of funding a particular investment. If the use of funds is limited within a firm, management decides among and between financial proposals. It may decide, say, between a $1 million investment in a small computer installation needed by the production department and investment of the same $1 million for a fleet of new automobiles wanted by the sales manager. As the firm goes through the time-consuming and expensive process of determining precisely how its money will be invested and what the rate of return on that investment should be, it is, in effect, also helping to determine the total dollar volume of gross private domestic investment within the aggregate economy.

As will be indicated in Chapter 13, gross private domestic investment (GPDI) is comprised of residential and nonresidential construction, production of durable equipment, and changes in business inventories. It is changes in the business inventories component that many observers believe to be the primary factor responsible for all of the recessions experienced by the domestic economy since the Great Crash of 1929–1934. However, expansion of the broader category, GPDI, may be the single most important requirement we have in the 1980s if the United States is to continue for an additional 200 years or more as a progressive industrial economy. GPDI is, in effect, the summation of all business investment decisions made within an individual department, firm, or industry. Ultimately, summation of investments made by all industries in the nation is GPDI.

Many current members of top and uppermiddle management in the United States completed their formal academic training in the late 1940s or 1950s—at which time they may not have studied economics and/or financial management. Even if these leaders had been exposed to financial management in college, the firm with which they took employment after graduation may not have been using the technique and would have provided no on-the-job training. What the managers had learned in college may have been quickly forgotten. Besides, capital budgeting has changed significantly within the past few years. This chapter and the one that follows contains materials that should be an integral part of every manager's tool kit.

Central role of corporate strategy

Many investment opportunities are uncovered in the ordinary course of business.[1] Needs to replace machinery that is wearing out and to expand departments that are overworked seem obvious and urgent. Numer-

[1] See H. Igor Ansoff, *Corporate Strategy* (New York: McGraw-Hill, 1965).

ous suggestions for using capital can be expected to come from operating levels of the firm. Without deliberate effort, most firms discover more capital expenditure proposals than can be accepted. Indeed, there is usually a backlog of apparently worthy projects.

An entrepreneurial management is not content simply to select among investment proposals arising in the spontaneous manner described above. Instead, it stimulates, directs, and coordinates capital budgeting by formulating an explicit statement of the corporate strategy. Corporate strategy includes delineation of the business or businesses in which the firm intends to engage, a statement of its attitudes toward business and financial risks, and a plan for achieving competitive advantages. As has been revealed earlier in this text, strategy is not frozen; as time passes and circumstances change, strategy evolves.

At any given time, strategy is management's concept of the best future use of the firm's resources and competences in the light of opportunities and hazards expected to result from general economic, social, and political trends. Strategy delineates the set of "businesses to be in" in terms of various product-market specializations. It lists specific objectives by periods extending to the planning horizon. The objectives include numbers and kinds of customers, product mix, market share, product development, rate of growth, flexibility of production and marketing posture, level and stability of return on capital, and nature of intended competitive advantages.

Corporate strategy is also an implicit statement of "businesses that the firms will not be in." By foregoing allocations of capital and management to projects that are incompatible with strategy, the firm concentrates its capital and know-how into critical masses. Scale of effort and depth of resources are kept sufficient to carry the firm across the thresholds of business success: It is able to develop products, penetrate markets, endure start-up costs, and so forth.

For present purposes, the following relationships of corporate strategy to capital budgeting should be kept in mind.

1. Although many opportunities for investment are uncovered in the ordinary course of business, this spontaneous discovery process has no sense of direction. In contrast, corporate strategy stimulates a deliberate search for opportunities and directs the growth of the firm along a desired path.

2. Projects that are clearly not compatible with corporate strategy are rejected, and projects that are clearly essential in implementing the strategy receive priority. Decisions about these two groups of projects do not require forecasts of profitability of the individual projects.

3. Many other projects will be proposed that are compatible with strategy but not essential to it. Capital budgeting is concerned with choices among projects in this group, and these decisions do require forecasts of individual project costs and returns.

An overview of capital budgeting

Capital budgeting can be conceived as planning for profit maximization over several periods—from the present to some planning horizon—over all activities of a firm, and subject to restraints imposed by the availability and cost of capital and the firm's corporate strategy. From this point of view, in which capital is a resource that needs to be allocated among alternative uses, useful insight about the nature of capital budgeting can be gained by considering how the principles of resource allocation explained in Chapter 6 might be applied.

Any given amount of capital should be allocated among alternative uses (that is, among programs and among projects within programs) according to the priority principle: Allocate capital first to that use in which it has the greatest marginal revenue productivity, then to the next best use, and so on, until all of the given amount of capital is used. The firm should expand the total amount of capital in use so long as capital's marginal revenue product is greater than the firm's marginal resource cost of capital.

Capital's marginal revenue product in any given program (receivables, inventories, plants, research and development, expansion of markets, and so forth) is the addition to the firm's future cash flows (future excess of incremental income over incremental expense) per unit of capital used at the margin of that program (that is, in the worst project). Capital's marginal resource cost is the addition to the firm's future performance for capital suppliers (interest payments, dividend distributions, current earnings retentions on behalf of stockholders) that is made necessary at the margin of capital acquisition (by the last increments added to the firm's capital base) per unit of capital obtained.

Capital's marginal revenue product and capital's marginal resource cost are consequences of the presence of capital over some period of time. Both can be expressed as rates: monetary amounts per dollar of capital per year of its presence. Annualized returns and costs of capital are decimal fractions of a dollar, and it is convenient to express them as percentages of the dollar. For example, we might say, ''The marginal cost of capital is 8 percent,'' or ''The marginal project has a 10 percent rate of return.''

A somewhat different point of view must be established in order to understand the specific techniques used in capital budgeting. The alternative perspective is as follows. Each of the possible uses of capital (projects) has incremental effects on the firm's revenues and costs over a series of future periods. From the incremental net cash inflow(s) of any given project in any given period, subtract the corresponding incremental net cash outflows. The result (which may be positive or negative) is called the project's net cash flow. Most projects produce a multiperiod series of cash flows.

A project's net cash flow in any given period can be discounted period by period from the time of receipt back to the present, obtaining the present value of that period's net cash flow. The discount factor to be used over any one of the intervening periods corresponds to that period's marginal cost of capital expressed as an annual percentage rate. Summing the discounted cash flows of all future periods for any one project yields the present value of all future incremental effects of that project; the sum may be called the present value of the project.

When the initial outlay on a project (the outlay at the outset) is subtracted from the project's present value, the result is called net present value of the project. Net present value may be positive or negative; if it is positive, the project is thought to be profitable. Roughly, the net present value method of testing a project for profitability is a method of determining whether the project's rate of return is greater than the corresponding marginal cost of capital. If the firm accepts all profitable projects, the method simultaneously determines the total amount of capital that the firm will use and the allocation of this capital among projects.

It is clear that a plan for profit maximization over all of the firm's activities from the present to some planning horizon, subject to restraints imposed by the availability and cost of capital and the firm's strategy, is also a plan for maximizing both the firm's terminal value (the value at the planning horizon) and its present value.

Forecasting cash flow of a project

Incremental revenues are the relevant values in comparing investment proposals. Engineering methods can be used to forecast technical input-output relationships. These technical estimates can be combined with economic forecasts of input and product prices to obtain expected incremental impacts of the project upon the firm's future expenses and revenues. Careful analysis is needed to overcome effects of arbitrary factors for overhead allocations and historical asset valuations upon any accounting data used in capital-expenditure planning.

Keep in mind that a project's cash flow is the amount by which the project's incremental effect on cash inflows exceeds the project's incremental effect on cash outflows. Cash flow is calculated for each project, period by period.

It is useful to distinguish between two types of investments. The first type is the cost-reducing project. An example is replacement of one machine by a more productive machine that decreases required labor. Cash flow produced by such a project consists of expected net reductions in operating expenses of future periods.

Another type of investment is the revenue-increasing project. An example is an increase in advertising expected to allow a price increase.

Cash flow resulting from such a project would be the expected net increases in revenues of future periods.

Some projects combine elements of cost reduction and revenue expansion. An example would be simultaneous modernization and expansion of a plant, expected to yield future reductions in unit cost as well as allowing increased rate of output.

Depreciation is not subtracted from revenue in estimating cash flow for a project. The objective is to estimate net cash inflow in each period subsequent to the initial outlay at the outset of the project. Note that if a project should provide total cash inflow just equal to total depreciation, we would say that the project provides a return of cash over a period of years but that it provides no return on capital while it is tied up in the project.

A simple numerical example will help clarify the process of estimating net cash flow. Assume the existence of a neighborhood Dairy Queen—not the complete store, with its menu of soft drinks, hot dogs, hamburgers, french fries, and soft cone (custard) ice cream. This store has just the ice cream machine, one machine only. In addition, it has one 16-year-old operator. No one else. All sales are for cash (50¢ per cone). There is no debt on the machine or the business. The cash flows are as follows:

Sales		$1000
Operating and administrative		
expenses	$800	
Depreciation	100	900
Profit before tax		100
Tax (50%)		50
Profit after tax		$ 50

Net cash flow (NCF) is profit after tax (PAT) plus depreciation (dep.), or:

$$NCF = PAT + \text{dep.}$$
$$= \$\ 50 + \$100$$
$$= \$150$$

Net cash flow is $150, or 15 percent of sales in this example. Note two things: (1) Net cash flow is three times greater than profit after tax, and (2) this ice cream business could incur negative profit aftertax figures (losses) while simultaneously generating positive net cash flows.

Time value of money

Capital budgeting procedures and techniques rely upon the time value of money; moreover, time value of money is easily understood if one considers it in connection with the value of a "consol." A consol, by definition, is a debt instrument, the maturity date of which is so far in the future that for all practical purposes it might just as well never mature. An example of a consol might be a 99-year railroad bond; the buy and sell decisions entered into by the holder of this consol rarely have much to do with the expectation on the part of the holder that she/he will hold the debt instrument until its maturity date.

What is the value of a consol having a coupon redeemable yearly and valued at $50, with an interest rate of 5 percent? The value is:

$$V = \frac{R}{i}$$
$$= \frac{\$50}{.05}$$
$$= \$1,000$$

where

V = Value of the consol.
R = Equal annual payment that exists for the lifetime of the asset.
i = Riskless interest rate.

Assuming that over time, and for whatever reasons, the interest rate changes to, say, 10 percent, the value of the asset falls. The R, of course, remains at $50 as V declines.

The new value of the consol is:

$$V = \frac{R}{i}$$
$$= \frac{\$50}{.10}$$
$$= \$500$$

A 100 percent increase in the rate of interest caused a 50 percent decrease in the value of the asset.

Quite clearly, there is an inverse relationship between the value of such financial assets as consols and the interest rate. This relationship almost always exists. If it is understood properly it has many uses.

The "proper" approach(s)

Two theoretically sound methods exist for evaluating a capital budgeting proposal: the net present value approach and the internal rate of return approach. Each method requires the user to consider the amount of time that expires while cash from the project is flowing into the firm. A relatively popular, yet unsound, method of evaluating capital budgeting is known as the payback method. Its lack of soundness is explained by the manner in which it overlooks the time value of money in its calculation. Moral: No capital budgeting method is sound if it ignores the time value of money in its calculation. Proper application and utilization of capital budgeting requires an understanding of compounding, present value, and annuities. Let's take a closer look at each.

Compound value

Promises to receive money at a later date have a value today that is less than the amount to be received at that later date. How much less depends on the effective interest rate. For example, a promise to receive $108 one year from today is worth $100 today if the interest rate is 8 percent, and $100 invested today at 8 percent would be worth $108 one year from today.

$$P_1 = R_o (1+i)$$
$$= \$100 (1+.08)$$
$$= \$108$$

where

R_o = Amount of money available for investment initially, in this case $100.

i = Interest rate (riskless).

P_1 = Amount of money available to the investor after one period of time. This factor could just as easily have been revealed as P_n, where n is equal to the number of periods during which the money is assumed to be invested.

Had the $100 been invested at the stated rate of interest, 8 percent, for a period of nine years, the value to the investor at the end of the ninth year would be $199.90:

$$P_9 = R_o (1+i)^9$$
$$= \$100 (1+i)^9$$
$$= \$100 \times 1.999$$
$$= \$199.90$$

In the above equation, $(1+i)^9$ is equal to what may be known as an interest factor amounting to 1.999. The interest factor may be calculated, as above, or obtained by referring to the Appendix (the Appendix includes a table for computing the compound sum of a dollar. In that table the interest factor 1.999 is determined at the intersection of the 8 percent column and the ninth period of time. The compound value of a dollar for different periods and interest rates can be found in a similar fashion.)

Present value

The process of discounting a future stream of cash to its present-day value (*PV*) over time, is done by taking the reciprocal of the compound sum times the amount of money to be obtained at the end of some period of time (*P_n*). The reciprocal of any number is one over that number; consequently, the reciprocal of the compound sum of a dollar invested at 8 percent for nine years is $\dfrac{1}{1.999}$ or, more simply, .50025. The interest factor is .50025. This interest factor times the amount of money to be received at the end of some specified period, nine years, and amounting to $199.90 has a present-day value of $100.

$$PV = R \left(\frac{1}{(1+i)^9} \right)$$
$$= \$199.90 \times .50025$$
$$= \$100$$

The present value of a promise to receive a lump sum of $199.90 that had been invested at 8 percent for nine years is $100. Interest-factor tables have been calculated revealing the present-day value of a dollar for various interest rates, and a table is presented in the Appendix.

Present value of an annuity

By definition, an annuity is a promise to receive or pay (whichever the case may be) a specified sum of money for a specified period of time at a specified rate of interest. The present-day value of an annuity may be determined by the following equation:

$$\text{Present value of annuity} = R\,\frac{1 - v^n}{i}$$

where

R = Specified sum of money available each period.
v^n = Present-day value of a dollar.
i = Riskless interest rate.

A promise to receive $100 per year for nine consecutive years at 8 percent has this value today:

$$\text{Present value of annuity} = R\,\frac{1 - v^n}{i}$$
$$= R\,\frac{1 - v^9}{i}$$
$$= \$100 \left(\frac{1 - .5002}{.08} \right)$$

$$= \$100 \left(\frac{.4998}{.08} \right)$$
$$= \$100 \ (6.2475)$$
$$= \$624.75$$

Instead of calculating the value for each time period, one may refer to a present value of an annuity table as presented in the Appendix. Go to the 8 percent column, ninth row, and find the present value of an annuity interest factor 6.2475; multiply R ($100 in this example) by that factor, and arrive at the present value of an annuity, $624.75.

Lotteries

As with many other states, Ohio has a state lottery. One of the larger prizes to be won by having the correct number on a $.50 ticket is $300,000. However, at no time does the winner receive a lump-sum payment of $300,000. The $300,000 prize is awarded in 20 annual payments of $15,000 each. Is a promise to receive $15,000 yearly for 20 years worth $300,000 today? Certainly not!

Since the state of Ohio is offering a specified sum of money for a specified period of time, the present-day value of a $300,000 prize can be calculated by using the present value of an annuity formula. The value of a promise to receive $15,000 at the end of each year for 20 years is worth today only $147,272, if the interest rate averages approximately 8 percent over the upcoming 20-year period:

$$\text{Present value annuity} = R \ \frac{1 - v^n}{i}$$
$$= \$15,000 \left(\frac{1 - v^{20}}{i} \right)$$
$$= \$15,000 \left(\frac{1 - .2145}{.08} \right)$$
$$= \$15,000 \left(\frac{.7855}{.08} \right)$$
$$= \$15,000 \ (9.818)$$
$$= \$147,270$$

or obtain an interest factor from the Appendix and calculate as follows:

$$\text{Present value annuity} = R \left(\frac{1 - v^n}{i} \right)$$
$$= \$15,000 \ (9.818)$$
$$= \$147,270$$

Only about $64,500 would have to be invested today at a compound rate of 8 percent in order to accumulate $300,000 at the end of the 20th year.

$$\text{Compound value} = P_1 = R_o\ (1+i)^n = \$64,500\ (4.661) \approx \$300,000$$

One knows this statement is true because:

Present value $= (\$300,000) \times$ (interest factor taken from the present value of a dollar Appendix for 20 years)
$$= \$300,000 \times .215$$
$$= \$64,500$$

In other words, if $64,500 were set aside today with the assurance that it would earn 8 percent per year at the end of each year, it would grow to about $300,000 in 20 years.

If the state of Ohio would award a lump-sum payment of $300,000 (as opposed to remitting it over a 20-year period at $15,000 per period) and if the recipient of that $300,000 prize could deposit it in debt instruments (bonds) that would yield with certainty 8 percent per year, the winner and/or the winner's heir would become a millionaire; $300,000 invested today would grow to approximately $1,395,349 by the end of the 20th year. This can be seen by:

$$\text{Compound value} = (PV)\ (1+i)^n$$
$$= (\$300,000)\ (4.661)$$
$$= \$1,398,300$$

Or the calculation may be made:

$$= \frac{\text{Amount to be awarded today}}{\text{(interest factor for the present value of a dollar to be received at the end of the 20th year at 8 percent)}}$$
$$= \frac{\$300,000}{.215}$$
$$= \$1,395,349 \text{ [2]}$$

As interest rates rise, the present-day value of a $300,000 promise from the state of Ohio would decline, since it requires less initial capital to produce the $300,000.

A $300,000 prize paid over 20 years has a present-day value of only $112,042 if interest rates over the score of years average 12 percent. State officials do not know with certainty what the current dollar value of a

---

[2] These two answers do not equal due to rounding.

lottery winner's winnings are, but the probability is quite high that the value is not less than $112,042 (12 percent), nor greater than $186,933 (5 percent). All of these winnings to the ticket holder are, of course, before taxes.

In order to make use of the present-value concept, it is essential that all returns to the firm be expressed as cash flows; the numerator (R) in the consol equation should be the net cash flow to be received by the firm over some specified period of time. When returns to the firm are considered in terms of their net cash flow, present-day value may be calculated as explained, and the only adjustment necessary to convert this present-value figure to a net present-value amount is to subtract the total dollar cost of the project from the present-value statistic:

$$NPV = PV - C$$

where C = Total cost of the project.

No major capital outlay should be made by any section, department, division, or subsidiary of any corporation, public or private, until some effort is made to determine the net present value of the future stream of cash that will flow to the firm as a result of that investment. This statement is valid for all organizations, profit and nonprofit alike. It is as applicable to hospitals, universities, and so on as it is to the bluest of the blue-chip corporations. Return for a look at a specific project.

Suppose Economic Consultants Incorporated (ECI) is considering installation of a new computer. The price to ECI is $23,000, and there is a $2,000 installation cost; the initial outlay totals $25,000. Suppose the machine provides a faster and higher-quality print-out on which price can be increased. Annual revenue is expected to increase by $1,500. The machine is expected to reduce annual direct labor expenses by $5,500 a year, but maintenance labor expenses will be increased by $500.

Suppose that in its cost accounting ECI normally estimates indirect labor at 30 percent of direct labor and overhead at 110 percent of direct labor. In the case of the new machine, direct labor will be reduced, but indirect labor and overhead will not be affected. Therefore, the factors normally used for overhead allocation must be disregarded. Forgetting the Economic Recovery Act of 1981 for a minute, assume for sake of simplicity a straight-line depreciation on the machine over a five-year period of $5,000 per year. Depreciation is not a cash expense and is not deducted in projecting pretax cash flow.

There are tax considerations. Assume taxes are 50 percent of profits. The new machine will increase profits and thus increase taxes, and the increase in taxes must be deducted in determining incremental cash flow. Depreciation is subtracted from pretax net cash flow in determining taxable income and the amount of taxes.

Suppose the machine is expected to last for seven years and to have no salvage value. A disposal cost of $1,160 (remove and haul away) is projected. The cash flows of the seven years would be projected as shown in Table 11–1.

The estimated project results are a net aftertax cash inflow of $5,750 in each of the first five years, $3,250 in the sixth, and $2,670 in the seventh year. Total estimated cash inflow is $34,670, which is more than the initial outlay of $25,000. Clearly, there is some return on capital tied up in the project as well as a recovery of the entire initial outlay. However, the total cash inflow is not directly comparable with the initial outlay. As they stand, these numbers ignore the time value (opportunity cost) of money. This opportunity cost must be taken into account in determining whether it is desirable to exchange the initial outlay for an expectation of receiving a larger total amount in installments distributed over a period of seven years. The technique of measuring profitability of multiperiod projects, with proper consideration given to capital's opportunity costs, must be understood.

Table 11–1
Cash flows from ECI's computer

Period 1:	
Incremental revenue	$1,500
Net labor savings	5,000
Pretax net cash inflow	$6,500
Less: Taxes at 50% ($6,500 – $5,000)	750
After tax net cash inflow	$5,750
Period 2, 3, 4, and 5:	
Same as period 1	
Period 6:	
Incremental revenue	$1,500
Net labor savings	5,000
Pretax net cash inflow	$6,500
Less: Taxes at 50% ($6,500)	3,250
After tax net cash inflow	$3,250
Period 7:	
Incremental revenue	$1,500
Net labor savings	5,000
	$6,500
Less: Disposal cost	1,160
Pretax net cash inflow	$5,340
Less: Taxes at 50%	2,670
After tax net cash inflow	$2,670

(handwritten annotation: 5 yr depr. exp)

Measuring project profitability

Present value of the entire future cash flow expected from an investment—or present value of the project—can be determined by summing discounted cash flows of the individual periods. Profitability of the project can then be measured by comparing its present value with the required initial outlay. Various present values can be calculated for any given project, depending on the rate or rates used in discounting. Opportunity costs of capital are the appropriate discount rates, since the objective is to determine whether the project has returns to capital that are equal to or greater than the capital's cost.

Discounting cash flows

The formula for determining present value of a stream of cash flow is:

$$V = \frac{R_1}{(1+i)} + \frac{R_2}{(1+i)_2} + \ldots + \frac{R_N}{(1+i)^N} + \frac{S}{(1+i)^N}$$

where

V	= Present value.
i	= Interest rate or, more generally, cost of capital expressed as an annual rate.
$R_1, R_2 \ldots R_N$	= aftertax cash flows in years 1, 2 . . . N.
N	= Project duration (conventionally tied to life of asset).
S	= Salvage value of the asset in year N.

For the illustration given in Table 11–1, computations would be set up as follows, assuming a constant 6 percent discount rate:

$$V = \frac{\$5,750}{(1.06)} + \frac{\$5,750}{(1.06)^2} + \frac{\$5,750}{(1.06)^3} + \frac{\$5,750}{(1.06)^4} + \frac{\$5,750}{(1.06)^5} + \frac{\$3,250}{(1.06)^6} + \frac{\$2,670}{(1.06)^7} = \$28,288$$

The arithmetic involved in the above calculations would be simple in principle but time-consuming. Fortunately, discount tables (compound interest tables) can be used to simplify the calculations. Discount tables are widely available in banks and other lending institutions, and a partial set of tables is provided in the appendix at the back of this book. Use of discount tables is explained below.

Internal rate of return

Discount the cash flows of Table 11–1 at a 10 percent rate. (The factors for present value of $1 received at the end of various future periods are in the Appendix.) The project's cash flow of $5,750 in year 1 is discounted to present value by multiplying the cash flow by the present value factor of 0.90909, found in column (1) on the line corresponding to period 1. Present value (rounded to the nearest whole dollar) is $5,227.

Results for cash flows of the various periods and for the project as a

Table 11–2
Discounted cash flows (10 percent)

Period	Cash flow	Times	Factor for present value	Equals	Present value
1	$5,750	×	0.90909	=	$ 5,227
2	5,750	×	0.82645	=	4,752
3	5,750	×	0.75131	=	4,320
4	5,750	×	0.68301	=	3,927
5	5,750	×	0.62092	=	3,570
6	3,250	×	0.56447	=	1,834
7	2,670	×	0.51316	=	1,370
					$25,000

whole are summarized in Table 11–2. Note that the total present value of the project's cash flows is $25,000, an amount just equal to the project's required initial outlay. If discounted at 10 percent, the project has no net present value, where net present value is defined as present value minus initial outlay. A discount rate that produces zero net present value (by making present value equal to initial outlay) is called the project's internal rate of return. Each project has its own internal rate. The nature of internal rate of return is displayed below by decomposition of the hypothetical project's cash flows.

Cash flow decomposition at the internal rate   Table 11–3 shows the separation of each period's cash flow into two parts: (1) returns on the project balance at 10 percent and (2) partial recovery of initial outlay. The project balance is defined as initial outlay less cumulative recovery. It is helpful to think of a positive project balance as an amount that the company's treasury has lent to the project. During period 1 there is $25,000 in the project. Cash flow is $5,750, of which $2,500 is required to provide a 10 percent return on the project balance. The remaining $3,250 can be viewed as a partial return of the treasury's initial outlay, or a reduction of the project balance. Thus, the new project balance is $21,750.

By similar reasoning, cash flows of periods 2 through 6 can be decomposed into interest (returns on capital still tied up) and partial return of initial outlay (reductions of project balance). By the end of period 7, the project balance has finally been reduced to zero (except for the small rounding error). The initial outlay has been fully recovered, and the project has provided a 10 percent rate of return on capital tied up in the project. Note that the column in Table 11–3 titled "Partial return of initial outlay" divides the initial outlay into seven parts. The amount of $3,250 at the top of the column is in the project for only one year; the amount of $3,575 in the second row is invested for two years; and so on. The amount of $2,428 at the bottom of the column is the only part of initial outlay that is invested in the project over the whole seven-year period.

Table 11–3
Decomposition of cash flows (10 percent)

Period	Project balance	Cash flow	Interest at 10 percent	Partial return of initial outlay	New project balance
1	$25,000	$5,750	$2,500	$3,250	$21,750
2	21,750	5,750	2,175	3,575	18,175
3	18,175	5,750	1,818	3,932	14,243
4	14,243	5,750	1,424	4,326	9,917
5	9,917	5,750	992	4,758	5,159
6	5,159	3,250	516	2,734	2,425
7	2,425	2,670	242	2,428	-3

Present value equals the initial outlay (net present value is zero) if the cash flows of a project are discounted at the project's internal rate of return. To calculate a project's internal rate when it is unknown, a trial-and-error approach is used. In the first step, a guess at the rate is used in discounting. If the resulting present value is greater than initial outlay, the project's internal rate is higher than the rate that has been used in discounting, so another trial should be made with a higher rate. If present value is less than initial outlay, the internal rate is lower than the rate used in discounting, so another trial can be made with a lower rate. The trial-and-error process is continued until a rate is found that makes present value equal to or very close to initial outlay; such a rate is a close approximation of the project's internal rate of return. The trial-and-error process can be speeded by interpolation. (Most computer centers have programs for rapid determination of internal rates of return.)

Net present value

If a project's internal rate of return is above the firm's cost of capital, the project is profitable. A test of profitability can be made by discounting the project's cash flows at expected cost of capital rates over the relevant periods. To illustrate such tests of profitability, assume that cost of capital is expected to be at a constant rate of 6 percent over the next seven years. The following example, based on the project of Table 11–1, shows how the present values of the project's cash flows and of the project as a whole can be calculated.

Refer to the table for 6 percent rate of interest in the Appendix. The cash flow of $5,750 of period 1 is discounted to present value by multiplying it by the present-value factor of 0.94340, which is found in column 1 of the 6 percent discount table, opposite period 1. The result, rounded to the nearest dollar, is $5,425. Results for all seven years are summarized in Table 11–4.

Table 11–4
Discounted cash flows (6 percent)

Period	Cash flow	Times	Factor for present value	Equals	Present value
1	$ 5,750	×	0.94340	=	$ 5,424
2	5,750	×	0.89000	=	5,117
3	5,750	×	0.83962	=	4,828
4	5,750	×	0.79209	=	4,555
5	5,750	×	0.74726	=	4,297
6	3,250	×	0.70496	=	2,291
7	2,670	×	0.66506	=	1,776
	$34,670				$28,288

Note that the total present value of the project's cash flows is $28,288, much less than their total of $34,670 before discounting. However the reduced amount of $28,288 is greater than the initial outlay. Subtracting the $25,000 of initial outlay from the $28,288 present value of the project, we obtain $3,288, the project's net present value. The nature of net present value can be clarified by looking closer at the project's cash flows and the rate (or rates) used in discounting.

Cash flows and the discount rate   Assume the firm's opportunity cost of capital is a constant 6 percent. This is the rate the firm can earn on funds invested outside the project in question, either in other projects inside the firm or in outside investments. The cash flow results of the hypothetical project can be decomposed as shown in Table 11–5.

During period 1, the project balance is $25,000. Again, think of a positive project balance as the amount the company treasury has lent to the project. The first year's cash flow is $5,750; subtracting $1,500 for interest (cost of capital) leaves $4,250, which can be viewed as a partial return of the treasury's initial outlay, or a reduction of the project balance. Thus, the new project balance is $20,750.

By similar reasoning, cash flows of period's 2 through 6 can be broken into interest (cost of capital) and reductions of project balances by partial returns of initial outlay. At the end of period 6, the project balance is

Table 11–5
Decomposition of cash flows (6 percent)

Period	Project balance	Cash flow	Interest at 6 percent	Partial return of capital	New project balance
1	$25,000	$5,750	$1,500	$4,250	$20,750
2	20,750	5,750	1,245	4,405	16,245
3	16,245	5,750	975	4,775	11,470
4	11,470	5,750	688	5,062	6,408
5	6,408	5,750	385	5,365	1,043
6	1,043	3,250	63	3,187	−2,144
7	−2,144	2,670	−129	2,799	−4,943

−$2,144; the project has returned $2,144 over and above the initial outlay. It is helpful to think of a negative project balance as a deposit the project has made into the company treasury.

In period 7 the negative project balance is put to other uses so as to yield a return of 6 percent or annual earnings of $129; this amount can be credited to the project as an additional deposit in the company treasury. The $2,670 cash flow in period 7 is also an additional deposit, so the project balance is −$4,943 at the end of period 7 and the end of the project. The final project balance, discounted at 6 percent, has a net present value of $3,287 as viewed from the outset of the project. This amount is (except for rounding error) identical with the net present value of $3,288 calculated by subtracting the initial outlay of $25,000 from the project's present value of $28,288.

Why does the project have a net present value? Because it has an internal rate of return greater than the cost of capital that was used in discounting. Thus, it can pay the cost of capital on the project balance and can return more than the initial outlay to the company treasury. Concerning the example above, one could say that a decision to go into the project increases the present value of the firm by approximately $3,288. This gain in present value is one measure of the project's profitability.

Profitability index (*P*1)   The ratio of present value to initial outlay, called profitability index (or benefit-cost ratio), is sometimes used as a measure of relative profitability of projects. For the example in Table 11–4, the profitability index is $28,288/$25,000, or 1.13. The profitability index measures results per dollar of initial outlay, which is desirable in comparing projects of different sizes. For the example used here, the profitability index says that there is a gain of 13 cents in present value for each dollar that goes into the project at the outset.

Discounting period by period, with rates varying   Cost of capital may vary from period to period. If it is expected to vary over the life of a project, the project's cash flows should be discounted, using the appropriate rate in each period. To illustrate, using the cash flows from Table 11–1, assume that management has estimated the firm's cost of capital over the next few periods as follows:

Period 1	12%
Period 2	10%
Period 3 and 4	8%
Period 5, 6, and 7	6%

Table 11–6 shows how present values should be calculated for the cash flows of various periods and for the project as a whole.

For example, the amount of $2,670 estimated for period 7 is assumed to be received at the end of the year, so it is discounted back to the

Table 11–6
Discounting period by period, with rate changes

Period received (at end)	Present value (dollars)	Period discounted (rate of discount used)*						
		1(12%)	2(10%)	3(8%)	4(8%)	5(6%)	6(6%)	7(6%)
1	$ 5,134	$5,750						
2	4,667	5,227	$5,750					
3	4,321	4,840	5,324	$5,750				
4	4,002	4,482	4,930	5,324	$5,750			
5	3,775	4,228	4,651	5,023	5,425	$5,750		
6	2,012	2,254	2,480	2,678	2,892	3,066	$3,250	
7	1,560	1,747	1,922	2,076	2,242	2,376	2,519	$2,670
	$25,471							

Net present value = $25,471 − $25,000 = $471.
Profitability index (benefit-cost ratio) = $25,471/$25,000 = 1.02.
* Values in table are dollars at ends of periods.

beginning of period 7 (or the end of period 6) at period 7's 6 percent cost of capital by multiplying by 0.9434 (the discount factor for one year at 6 percent), yielding the value of $2,519. This value of $2,519 is discounted back to the end of period 5 at period 6's percent cost of capital, resulting in $2,376, and so on until the present value of $1,560 is finally obtained for the seventh period's cash flow. Cash flows of earlier years are discounted in a similar manner.

Costs of capital

Costs of capital, as annual rates, are needed in discounting cash flows to test a project's profitability. This section explains what is meant by *cost of capital* and how cost of capital may vary from period to period. In this section it is assumed that management has selected a ratio of debt to equity that is expected to minimize the total cost of capital and that this ratio is to be held constant as the firm makes changes in total capital employed. This assumption is made in many tests, even though the theoretical relationship of average cost of capital to debt-equity ratio remains controversial. Empirical determination of optimal capital structure of firms of a given risk class appears to be very difficult. Average cost of capital probably varies only slightly with gradual changes in the debt-equity ratio over a fairly wide range.

The interest rate needed for purposes of discounting the future stream of net cash to the firm is known as the firm's cost of capital. Each firm must determine for itself the interest factor, rate, or more correctly, the cost of capital it should use. The calculation requires utilization of the firm's balance sheet. Remember two things: (1) The cost of capital is different for each firm, and it changes as often as the amount of money needed to operate the firm changes; and (2) monies invested at rates in excess of the firm's cost of capital serve to increase the net present value of the firm's assets.

The simulated lower right-hand side of a balance sheet for the Joseph Schlitz Brewing Company as of December 31, 1983, is assumed to be as presented in Table 11–7. These figures are used for calculation of a cost of capital. Ideally, a firm should equate its IRR, once calculated, with its marginal cost of capital (MCC) in a manner similar to that reflected in Figure 11–1. In practice, it is the weighted cost of capital (average cost) that is used.

Only the lower right-hand side of the balance sheet is used for this calculation, since we are dealing with long-term commitments on the part of, or equity positions in, the firm.

Table 11–7
Weighted cost of capital

	Capital component available—par value for bonds and common stock and present market value for retained earnings	Aftertax rate* (percent)	Aftertax total dollar cost
Bonds (7.2%)	$ 50,000,000	3.60%	$ 1,800,000
Long-term notes payable (8%)	15,500,000	4.00	620,000
Other long-term notes (6%)	3,183,000	3.00	95,490
Common stock †	76,379,000 §	7.85	5,995,752
Retained earnings ‡	247,314,000 §	17.32	42,834,785
	$392,376,000		$51,346,026

$$\text{Weighted cost of capital} = \text{WCC} = \frac{\$\,51,346,026}{\$392,376,000} = .13086 = 13.09 \text{ percent}$$

* A 50 percent tax rate is assumed.

† Assumed value as appropriate. One could use paid-in surplus, if any, plus par value or market value. Authorized 30 million shares, issued 29,373,654 shares. Total cost of common shares as used here is expressed as the quotient of net earnings to net sales. If one assumes net sales approximated $700 million and net earnings $55 million, the inexact cost of common shares is almost 8 percent.

$$\frac{\$55,000,000}{\$700,000,000} = .07857 \times 100 = k_e = 7.857 \text{ percent}$$

‡ The cost of equity capital may be calculated also by solving for k, where k equals the cost of equity capital:

$$k = D/P_o + g$$

where D is 1982 dividends paid of $0.68; price ($P_o$) equals the average price of the common stock traded on the market and assumed to be $22; and growth ($g$) is the average rate of change in earnings per share. For example, if EPS were $0.72 in 1977 and $1.60 in 1983, growth ($g$) averaged 14.23 over the six-year period; consequently, the cost of equity may be stated as:

$$k = D/P_o + g$$
$$= \frac{.68}{22} + .1423$$
$$= .0309 + .1423$$
$$= .1732 = 17.32$$

§ The cost of common stocks and the cost of retained earnings could have been combined into one formulation using the procedure in note ‡ above, but that process is no more accurate. When used for forecasting, it assumes the future will behave in a manner similar to the past, and such an assumption is naive.

Figure 11–1
Equilibrium point for IRR and MCC: The desired condition

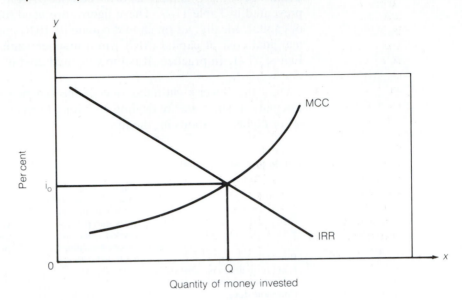

Weighted cost

Estimation of the marginal cost of capital for the firm begins by calculating its present weighted cost of capital (WCC) as shown in Table 11–7.

Cost of debt

As revealed in Table 11–7, average cost of capital for use in any given year is a weighted average of the percentage annual cost of funds obtained by borrowing and the percentage annual cost of equity (funds obtained by retaining earnings or by selling additional shares of common stock). First examine the cost of borrowed funds. The before-tax cost of debt is the nominal interest rate. If the firm has long-term and short-term debt at differing interest rates, the pretax cost of debt is the weighted average of these rates. Aftertax cost of the firm's debt is reduced by the deductibility of interest payments as expenses when the firm's taxable income is being calculated. Thus, aftertax cost of debt is the nominal interest rate times one minus the firm's marginal tax rate expressed as a decimal. For example, if the firm's before-tax interest rate is 8 percent, and the firm's marginal tax rate is 50 percent, the aftertax cost of debt is $8 \times (1 - 0.50)$, or 4 percent. It is appropriate to put the cost of capital on an aftertax basis, since this cost is to be compared with internal rates of return that are derived from aftertax cash flows of projects. Both the returns on capital and the costs of capital are on an aftertax basis. The relevant cost of capital is the expected future marginal cost, period by period, but as implied by footnote § in Table 11–7, this figure is difficult to obtain.

Cost of equity

Cost of equity is the percentage that expected earnings per share must be of the stock's current price in order to maintain the current stock price unchanged. This value is derived from management's estimate of earnings per share required to provide the combination of dividends and capital gains expected by marginal holders of the common stock. Marginal shareholders are those persons just willing to hold the stock at its current price in the light of their expectations of dividends and capital gains.

An approximation of cost of equity that may be useful in some instances can be calculated by adding the stock's current percentage yield to the projected average annual percentage increase in earnings per share and stock price over the next few years. (In using this approach, it is assumed that the marginal stockholders and management have similar information and are projecting similar rates of growth.) For example, if the stock's current price is $50 per share, the current dividend is $3 per share, and the projected rate of gain in earnings per share and stock price is 8 percent annually, the cost of equity is $3/$50 + 0.08, or 0.14, or 14 percent. This is the approach used in footnote ‡ of Table 11–7.

Weighted average of debt cost and equity cost

A useable approximation of the cost of capital for a given period is the weighted average of the cost of debt and the cost of equity, where the debt and equity are sources of funds for new investment in that period. Suppose the following things were true: (1) The firm is maintaining a ratio of 40 percent debt to 60 percent equity; (2) aftertax cost of marginal debt is 4 percent annually; and (3) cost of marginal equity is estimated to be 14 percent annually. The weighted average cost of capital would be 0.40 × 0.04 + 60 × 0.14, or about 10 percent.

The weighted cost of capital (WCC) to the firm changes if, say, a new debenture is sold. Suppose the brewing company sells a new series of debentures amounting to $75 million, carrying a before-tax cost of 10 percent, and maturing in 25 years. The capitalization of the firm after sale of the new debt issue would appear as shown in Table 11–8.

WCC would decrease 9.93 percent, from 13.09 to 11.79, if the $75 million in new monies needed by the brewing company were obtained from the sale of new debentures costing 10 percent per annum before tax. A decision to sell new bonds costing that amount of money would be sound so long as the internal rate of return (IRR) on the new monies invested ≥ than the cost of capital, the marginal cost of capital, MCC.

The new WCC will always serve to lower the old WCC if the new debt

Table 11–8
Weighted cost of capital

	Capital component available—par value for bonds and common stock; present market value for new debentures and retained earnings	Aftertax rate (percent)	Aftertax total dollar cost
Bonds (7.2%)	$ 50,000,000	3.60%	$ 1,800,000
Long-term notes payable (8%)	15,500,000	4.00	620,000
Other long-term notes (6%)	3,183,000	3.00	95,490
New debentures (10%)	75,000,000	5.00	3,750,000
Common stock	76,379,000	7.85	5,995,752
Retained earnings	247,314,000	17.32	42,834,785
	$467,376,000		$55,096,027

$$\text{Weighted cost of capital} = \text{WCC} = \frac{\$\ 55,096,027}{\$467,376,000} = .11788 = 11.79 \text{ percent}$$

issue has a cost that is less than the old WCC; inasmuch as 5 percent after tax, the cost of the newly raised $75 million, is less than 13.09 percent, the WCC prior to flotation of the new issue, the new WCC must decline. The amount by which it declines is dependent upon the weight and tax status of each component within the capitalization of the company.

Marginal cost of capital

One could assume that the marginal cost of capital eventually rises with increases in the firm's planned total new investment in the current period. Curve WCC in Figure 11–2 shows a theoretical relationship of average cost of capital to amount of investment. Increments of capital are positioned along the curve from left to right in order of ascending cost. Increment OB is that portion of the firm's total cash flow from old projects, which can be called return of capital; amount OB is approximately equal to the accounting valuation of total depreciation. Although the stream of funds corresponding to partial recovery of initial outlay in old projects could be used for reduction of debt and distributions to owners (thereby returning the capital to its original sources and cutting down the firm's capital base), it is usually retained and invested in new projects. Cost of capital over the range OB is a weighted average opportunity cost. In retaining these funds, the firm foregoes opportunities to reduce debt (thus decreasing required interest payments) and to reduce equity (thus cutting back the earnings "required" to support expected dividends and capital gains per share).

The second increment of capital, amount BD in Figure 11–2, is the sum of the current period's retained earnings plus the proceeds of new bor-

Figure 11–2
Cost of capital

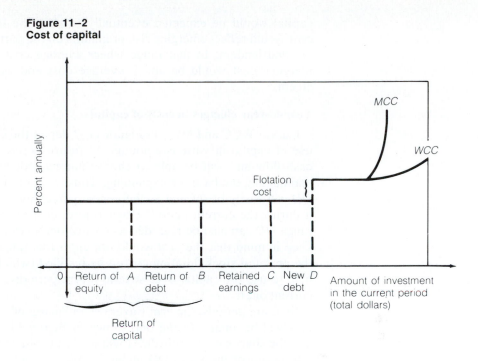

rowing that keeps debt and equity in the desired ratio. Increment BD is an expansion of the firm's capital base. Cost of capital over the range BD is also a weighted average opportunity cost, since the firm is foregoing opportunities to avoid borrowing (which would decrease interest cost) and to distribute some current earnings (which would cut back the needed rate of growth in earnings per share and in stock price).

If management so decides, the firm can acquire any of the various amounts of capital along function WCC to the right of increment BD in Figure 11–2. However, these further increments can only be obtained by going to the capital market to sell additional shares of common stock and to engage in new borrowing that maintains the selected debt-equity ratio. Cost of the first increments of capital to right of range BD is above the cost in range BD because of transactions charges (flotation costs) on the new common stock. If the firm does sell new common stock, cost of capital (as annual percentage rates) will be quite high unless the funds are to be retained and reinvested over several periods and perhaps all the way to the planning horizon, so that the transactions charges can be prorated over several periods.

Curve WCC is a schedule of alternatives. Management can choose any one of these combinations of total investment and average cost, but the choice for the current period must be only one of the points on the curve. As management increases planned total investment, the marginal cost of capital would be expected eventually to rise; the increase in marginal cost would reflect emerging risk premiums on the parts of both stockholders and lenders. In that range where average cost of capital is rising, marginal cost would be above average cost and would be rising more steeply.

Year-to-year changes in costs of capital

Curves WCC and MCC in Figure 11–2 depict the costs of one period's use of capital in various amounts. In future periods the firm will have cash flow and will be able to choose among reducing the capital base, maintaining the base, or expanding. Thus, cost of capital over the range *OD* can easily be viewed as the annual percentage rate of cost for using it during the current period. Furthermore, cost of capital to the right of range *OD* can also be regarded as cost of one period's use, provided we keep in mind that the firm would not enter this range unless it expected the prorated stock flotation cost to be justified (which may involve planning to use the capital over several future periods as well as during the current one).

In future periods, the firm's average and marginal cost of capital schedules will be similar to the one shown in Figure 11–2, but the positions and the shapes of the schedules will likely change from period to period. The height of the range OD along the WCC curve shifts from period to period with changes in supply and demand conditions in the general money market, and the length of range OD in any particular period depends upon the amount of cash flow produced by old projects during that period. The shape of the WCC and MCC curves to the right of range OD depend upon lender and stockholder attitudes toward the firm's riskiness and probable success in expanding at various rates, and these attitudes could change from period to period.

In any given period, the amount of investment (and that period's average and marginal costs of capital) depends upon the nature of that period's set of investment opportunities, the height and form of that period's cost of capital schedules, and management's estimates of marginal costs of capital in future periods. The nature of investment opportunities changes from period to period with the outlook for general economic conditions, competitive conditions, and the firm's success in product and market development. It is clear that a firm's marginal cost of capital can be expected to vary from period to period.

The theoretically correct way to test the profitability of a project is to discount its cash flows, period by period, at varying rates, as illustrated in Table 11–6. The rates to be used for discounting are forecasts of marginal costs of capital in future periods and, for the first period only, the estimated marginal cost of capital in the current period. Although most managers have difficulty in estimating future marginal costs of capital, assumptions about these rates are necessary. Much of the present literature of corporate finance takes it for granted that management is willing to assume that capital's marginal cost will be constant over future periods at the current period's value. More attention should be given to the managerial implications of costs that vary from period to period.

Mutually exclusive projects

It is sometimes necessary to choose between two mutually exclusive projects. In such cases, it is possible for the larger of the two projects to be the best choice, even if it has a slightly lower internal rate of return. The larger project can be regarded as the equivalent of the smaller one plus an incremental project. If both the smaller project and the incremental project are profitable, then the larger project should be selected.

An example of mutually exclusive projects is the case in which management can choose between two technologies and two sets of machines and equipment for a given production process. Since production must be done one way or the other, the investment proposals are mutually exclusive. The following example shows how such a case can be analyzed.

Table 11–9, compares two mutually exclusive projects. The smaller project, project A, is already familiar to readers of this chapter because of its use in earlier examples. Project B is larger, has longer life, and has a different pattern of cash flows. Project B-A is the incremental project, with initial outlay and each cash flow calculated as the amount for project B less the corresponding amount for project A. The incremental initial outlay is project B's $55,000 less project A's $25,000, or $30,000. Similarly, the incremental first-year cash flow is project B's $2,000 less project A's $5,750, or −$3,750.

Assume that marginal costs of capital over future periods have been forecast as follows: period 1, 10 percent; period 2, 8 percent; all subsequent years, 6 percent. Present value calculations for project A and project B-A, after discounting period by period, are shown in Table 11–9. It can be seen that project A is profitable with a net present value of $1,758. However, project B-A is also profitable with a net present value of $1,020. Therefore, project B, which is equivalent to a combination of the smaller project and the incremental project, should be selected.

Summary

Capital budgeting is allocation of capital among alternative investment opportunities and determination of the total amount of investment in the current period. It is concerned with choices among projects that are compatible with corporate strategy but not clearly essential to it. Corporate strategy is a delineation of the businesses in which the firm is to be engaged, a statement of attitudes toward business and financial risks, and a plan for achieving competitive advantages.

Table 11–9
Incremental analysis of mutually exclusive projects

	Cash flows		
Period	**Project A**	**Project B**	**Project B-A**
1	$ 5,750	$ 2,000	$ – 3,750
2	5,750	4,000	– 1,750
3	5,750	12,000	6,250
4	5,750	16,000	10,250
5	5,750	14,000	8,250
6	3,250	12,000	8,750
7	2,670	10,000	7,330
8	0	8,000	8,000
9	0	4,000	4,000
Initial outlay	$25,000	$55,000	$ 30,000

Present value of project B-A:

Period received (at end)	Present value (dollars)	Period discounted (rate of discount used)*		
		1(10%)	**2(8%)**	**All others (6%)**
1	$ – 3,409	$ – 3,750		
2	– 1,473	– 1,620	$ – 1,750	
3	4,963	5,449	5,896	$ 6,250 at end of Period 3
4	7,678	8,446	9,122	10,250 at end of Period 4
5	5,831	6,414	6,927	8,250 at end of Period 5
6	5,834	6,418	6,931	8,750 at end of Period 6
7	4,610	5,071	5,477	7,330 at end of Period 7
8	4,747	5,222	5,640	8,000 at end of Period 8
9	2,239	2,463	2,660	4,000 at end of Period 9
	$ 31,020			

Net present value = $31,020 – $30,000 = 1,020.
Profitability index (benefit-cost ratio) = $31,020/$30,000 = 1.034.

* Values in body of table are dollars at ends of periods.

Capital budgeting procedures and techniques are mechanical in nature, yet contribute significantly to the overall decision-making ability of the firm. In using the two theoretically sound approaches to evaluating proposals, the firm is attempting to assure itself that investments will make money for the firm.

Proponents of capital budgeting procedures and techniques often overstate their case badly. At times they claim too much for the technique. Therefore, as with all business decision-making activities, one should apply extremely large doses of common sense when applying either the net present value approach or the internal rate of return calculation to a particular project or proposal.

The evaluation of a consol and the concepts associated with it are simple to master, yet essential to an overall understanding of the time value of money in general and the present-day value of a stream of net cash to be received at some future date in particular. A project's cash flows must be estimated as the first step in testing or measuring the project's profitability. Cash flows of a cost-reducing project are the expected net reductions in costs of future periods, and cash flows of a revenue-increasing project are the net increases in revenues of future periods. Depreciation, a cost that is, in effect, prepaid at the time of the initial outlay for the project, is not a cash cost in subsequent periods and is not subtracted from revenue in estimating cash flows. However, depreciation is subtracted from the pretax cash flow in determining taxable income and the amount of taxes that are to be subtracted to put the project's cash flows on an aftertax basis.

A project's profitability can be tested by comparing its present value with the initial outlay. Any excess of present value over initial outlay is called net present value and is a measure of profitability. A project's present value is the sum of future cash flows discounted back to the present at rates corresponding to costs of capital over the various periods.

A project can have a positive net present value only if the project's internal rate of return is greater than the project's marginal cost of capital. Internal rate of return is that constant rate of discount that makes the project's present value just equal to the initial outlay. Each project has its own internal rate of return.

Costs of capital may vary from period to period. In such instances, each project's cash flows should be discounted period by period, at varying rates. Costs of capital in any given period are weighted averages of the aftertax cost of debt and the cost of equity. Cost of equity is the expected rate of return (an annual percentage rate) that makes marginal (most reluctant) stockholders just willing to hold the common stock at its current price.

It is sometimes necessary to choose between two mutually exclusive projects where the larger of the projects could be the best choice even though the smaller has a somewhat higher internal rate of return. To analyze mutually exclusive projects, the larger project is treated as the equivalent of the smaller one plus an incremental project. The profitabilities of the smaller project and the incremental project are tested by the net present value approach. If both projects are profitable, the larger project (which is the equivalent of the two projects combined) is selected.

CASES

Capital budgeting

Seiberling, Inc.[1]

Seiberling Rubber was a well-established company engaged in the manufacture of various rubber and plastic goods. The products were generally inexpensive, and a high volume of sales had to be maintained to enable the company to recover its fixed costs. The management consciously avoided taking on any products that could be characterized as novelties

---

[1] This case is an altered version of material presented as "Avella, Inc.," William R. Henry, Ph.D. and W. Warren Haynes, *Managerial Economics* (Plano, Tex.: Business Publications, 1978), pp. 613–618.

or fads likely to have a relatively brief period of prosperity. Seiberling had been fortunate in maintaining a stable pattern of sales over the years and had developed a strong customer loyalty. The company had gained a reputation through its production of a relatively complete line of quality products. There was some competition from the producers of specialties, but no other business in the industry offered competition with such a complete line.

Edgar A. Gordon, who had recently retired as chairman of the board, was firmly convinced that the company should maintain a strong working capital position and finance its resources primarily with equity capital. This policy, he believed, would place the company in a favorable position to exploit opportunities when they arose and would have the further advantage of providing protection during prolonged periods of general economic decline.

This policy was being carefully reviewed. Many of the officers and directors believed that a restrictive policy had checked the growth of the company and had resulted in the loss of many favorable opportunities for profitable investment. There was no desire, however, to make rapid changes. The position of the firm and its policies and procedures were being examined.

The company had maintained a minimum cash balance of approximately $1.5 million at all times. Throughout the year, cash needs were carefully budgeted and plotted on a broken-line graph as shown in Exhibit 1.

Any cash flow in excess of what was required in order to finance current operations was invested in short-term government securities. This investment was adjusted up or down according to the seasonal needs for cash. Careful budgeting had resulted in stabilizing the cash balance at about the desired level.

During 1983 Seiberling increased its working capital by $1,310,000. The statement of financial position at December 31, 1983, and the condensed operating statement for the year 1983, as given in Exhibit 2, were considered by the controller to be typical. The gross cost of the plant and equipment at the end of the fiscal year was $24,362,130. After deducting the accumulated depreciation of $16,740,630, there was a remaining net book value of $7,621,500.

The controller of the company, Charles A. Penberthy, was in the process of reviewing the way in which business investment opportunities were evaluated to determine their economic feasibility. Penberthy was well acquainted with the various activities of the company through his long years of service in production, sales, and financial administration.

Investment proposals were initiated by a new-products committee, which worked closely with the director of research. Possible projects were carefully screened as to market potential, their relationship to existing product lines, and production possibilities. The controller and his staff

Exhibit 1
Cash position budget (as of September 20)

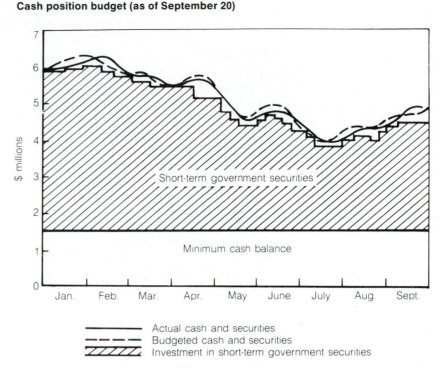

Actual cash and securities
Budgeted cash and securities
Investment in short-term government securities

assisted in this screening process. As a general rule, a project was not accepted unless analysis revealed that the project would probably yield a rate of return upon investment of at least 30 percent before taxes. The 30 percent rate of return had been established as a guide on the basis that the company had been earning approximately that rate on its investment in machinery and equipment over the years. For example, the company earned $4,686,073 before taxes during 1983. The total cost of the machinery and equipment (without allowance for depreciation) at the end of the year was $15,654,257. Relatively insignificant acquisitions or replacements and obvious cost-saving possibilities did not go through such a rigorous screening process.

After the project had been accepted by the new-products committee, it was reviewed by the marketing committee of the board of directors. Source of net working capital:

Net income before depreciation charges of $1,302,994	$3,510,050
Uses of net working capital:	
Dividend payments	$1,250,100
Fixed-asset additions	959,950
Total	$2,200,050
Net increase in working capital	$1,310,000

Exhibit 2

SEIBERLING, INC.
Statement of Financial Position
For the Year Ended December 31, 1983

Current assets:
Cash.. $ 1,707,269
U.S. government securities at cost including accrued
    interest 3,111,398
Accounts receivable 7,818,592
Inventories 8,616,133
Prepaid expenses.. 309,380
    Total current assets 21,562,772

Current liabilities:
Accounts payable 1,141,834
Accrued taxes, wages, and miscellaneous expenses 1,788,636
Estimated federal income tax liability less U.S. Treasury
    notes of $1,080,000 183,301
    Total current liabilities 3,113,771

Net working capital 18,449,001
Other assets:
Miscellaneous investments 590,417
Real estate, machinery, and equipment at cost less
    depreciation 8,420,152

Net assets $27,459,570

Capital:
Common stock... $ 7,413,480
Capital in excess of par value 2,527,242
Reinvested earnings 17,518,848
                                 $27,459,570

Statement of Earnings
For the Year Ended December 31, 1983

Sales and other income $48,654,260

Cost and expenses:
Cost of products sold 30,232,458
Selling, administrative and general expenses..................... 13,535,720
Federal income tax, estimated 2,479,017
    Total cost and expenses................................. 46,447,204

Net earnings.. $ 2,207,056

Both the net additional revenue and the direct cost savings to be derived from the project were considered in arriving at the net dollar advantage before taxes. The net additional revenue was the gross revenue
anticipated from the project as reduced by the cost of goods sold and
estimated selling and administrative expenses. The cost of goods sold
was computed in the conventional manner, including the cost of direct
materials, direct labor, and manufacturing overhead. Manufacturing
overhead, including depreciation, was applied to the products on a pre-

determined rate basis as a percentage of direct labor cost. An allowance of 17 percent of the estimated gross revenue was deducted for selling and administrative expenses. This percentage had been established from past experience studies, which showed that the selling and administrative expenses that should be identified with a product were approximately 17 percent of sales. Finally, depreciation computed on a straight-line basis on the facility cost and on what was called the capital corollary was deducted to arrive at the net dollar advantage before taxes, using the *format* below:

1. Direct cost savings before depreciation $
2. Increased revenue
    Sales $
    Cost of goods sold   _____
    Gross profit
    17 percent allowance for selling and administrative
    expenses   _____
    Net revenue addition   _____
3. Gross dollar advantage [(1) + (2)]
4. Less depreciation of facility cost and capital corollary   ════════
5. Net dollar advantage before taxes [(3) − (4)] $

The capital corollary represented the allocated investment in floor space used. Penberthy maintained that each machine had to absorb a portion of the cost of space used. If the allocated plant costs, such as depreciation, taxes, and insurance, were not considered, the building expansion required to accommodate additional equipment would be unfairly charged against the last piece added—when in reality all additional pieces helped bring about the need for building expansion. The corollary investment was estimated to amount to 70 percent of the cost of the equipment. Some time in the past a study had been made over a period of time to determine the relationship between plant costs and investment. As a result of this study, it was found that the allocated plant costs would amount to about 70 percent of the investment in equipment.

The total average annual investment was then computed. The cost of the equipment itself was divided in half to arrive at an average. The capital corollary cost amounting to 70 percent of the equipment cost was similarly averaged. Furthermore, a provision was made for the increase in working capital that would be required to support the project.

A study had been made showing that approximately 9 percent of the estimated gross revenue was held as accounts receivable, 21 percent of the estimated cost of goods sold was invested in inventories, and 5 percent of the estimated cost of goods sold was held as a minimum cash balance.

Accordingly, these percentages were applied to the expected gross revenue and cost of goods sold resulting from the project to arrive at the additional investment held in the form of working capital, using this *format*.

One-half facility estimated cost	$
One-half capital corollary	
Total working capital	
Total average annual investment	$

As an example, an evaluation of a proposal to manufacture a certain type of air mattress to be used in swimming pools is given in Exhibit 3.

Projects that were accepted were subject to a postcompletion audit. If the results did not come close to expectations, a decision was reached as to whether or not an additional audit was to be made. In certain cases it

Exhibit 3
Economic evaluation of facility acquisition proposal (net dollar advantages before taxes)

Increased revenue:		
Sales	$793,278	
Cost of goods sold	558,774	
Gross profit	234,504	
Allowance for selling and administrative expenses—17%	134,857	
Net revenue increase		$ 99,647
Gross dollar advantage		99,647
Less depreciation of facility cost and capital corollary		25,730
Net dollar advantage before taxes		$ 73,917
Investment		
One half facility estimated cost		$ 75,675
Capital corollary:		
One half other fixed assets		52,973
Total working capital		216,677
Total average annual investment		$345,325

$$\frac{\text{Net dollar advantage before taxes—\$73,917}}{\text{Total average annual investment—\$345,325}} = 21.4\% \text{ rate of return}$$

Explanatory notes:		
Total facility cost (est. life of 10 years, no residual salvage value)	$151,350	
Capital corollary (70% of $151,350)	105,945	
Sales	793,278	
Cost of goods sold	558,774	
Selling and administrative expenses (17% of $793,278)		$134,857
Working capital:		
Accounts receivable (9% of $793,278)	71,395	
Inventories (21% of $558,774)	117,343	
Cash (5% of $558,774)	27,939	
Total working capital		216,677
Depreciation [10% of ($151,350 + $105,995)]	$ 25,730	

was believed that if more time were allowed, the project would eventually meet the requirements. On the other hand, some projects might show that there was little opportunity for improvement and that additional audits would not be justified. An unsuccessful project might be liquidated, or it might be continued as a sort of necessary evil that had to be tolerated. For example, even though it did not justify itself, a project might be maintained in order to round out the product line.

Penberthy and his staff were actively investigating the possibility of improving the method by which business investment proposals were evaluated. Both Penberthy and his staff had been reading then-current literature on the subject and had attended various conferences dealing with this topic.

1. Evaluate the capital budgeting procedures of the Seiberling Company, including the following specific considerations:
   a. The amount of working capital on hand.
   b. The cutoff rate.
   c. The cost of capital to the company.
   d. The formula for computing the rate of return.
   e. The treatment of overhead in the computations.
   f. The treatment of depreciation in the computations.
   g. The use of the capital corollary concept.
   h. The provision for working capital.
2. Would the capital budgeting procedures described in this case be equally applicable to replacement investments and to investments in entirely new facilities? Discuss.

Kathy, Karen, and Kevin

Kathy, Karen, and Kevin are partners in a duplication machine rental business known as Kopy Kwik. They own Xerox and other duplicating equipment. Locations for these machines are often relatively easy to obtain, but more often than not, potentially profitable locations must be purchased. Each partner has other business interests, and the firm is a sideline for all of them. In 1976, they started buying and otherwise acquiring small locations for their duplicating machines in towns of populations under 15,000. This venture proved highly successful, as shown in Exhibit 1. A comparison of Exhibits 1 and 2 indicates an extremely high return on the original investment (most of the capital consisted of plowed-back earnings). Exhibits 3 and 4 provide additional information on company operations.

In 1983 and 1984, several major decisions were required of the partners. One concerned the purchase of additional locations in several towns scattered in nearby states. The partners knew that such locations were available at prices of from five- to six-times earnings. On the basis of past

Exhibit 1

Kopy Kwik
Comparative Statement of Income and Expense
For the Years Ended December 31, 1979 to 1983

	1983	1982	1981	1980	1979
Income:					
Gross sales.............	$109,790	$114,163	$104,212	$79,124	$68,675
Other income............	3,068	742	340	0	1,139
Capital gains	396	5,046	2,210	658	0
Total income	113,254	119,951	106,762	79,782	69,814
Operating expenses:					
Cost of material..........	4,385	2,698	4,264	4,066	4,329
Wages and salaries	20,043	25,698	19,878	13,467	12,142
Agency commissions	12,830	13,591	11,060	10,106	9,042
Transportation expenses ..	4,823	5,050	5,433	4,059	3,806
Insurance	7,049	1,719	1,306	915	934
Depreciation	13,237	14,223	10,148	8,309	7,920
Rent....................	6,240	4,894	4,509	2,827	2,268
Office supplies...........	2,338	2,066	918	834	849
Maintenance	1,442	2,116	2,429	1,919	1,890
Taxes and licenses	2,960	2,275	1,814	1,202	901
Professional services	366	6,123	804	200	249
Travel expenses	346	303	6,316	3,036	2,546
Other expenses	8,360	13,446	12,093	6,532	2,893
Total material cost and expense	$ 84,419	94,202	80,972	57,472	49,769
Net profit before manager's salary	28,835	25,749	25,790	22,310	20,045
Manager's salary...........	4,800	4,800	4,213	4,160	4,160
Net profit	$ 24,035	$ 20,949	$ 21,577	$18,150	$15,885

experience, the partners had established a rule of thumb that they would not pay more than five-times earnings, and they had never paid more than this amount.

The partners knew of one small store that would be perfect and available at a price of five times earnings. The company had some of its own equipment and had allowed it to run down, so that considerable repairs might be necessary. Kathy believed that the profits could be increased by immediately raising rentals from the existing level by 20 percent and by another 20 percent at a later date. For example, the company might raise the rate on its smallest duplicating machine from $100 per month to $120 per month and eventually to $150 per month. The firm's experience in the past was that improved maintenance and service would permit increased rates.

In establishing rates the company was influenced somewhat by the rates in other small towns. The prevailing rate on the size machine already discussed was $150 per location, although some rates went as low as $120. Rates were almost double in cities of 50,000 population or greater.

Exhibit 2

Kopy Kwik
Comparative Balance sheets
January 1, 1979–March 31, 1983

	1983	1982	1981	1980	1979
Assets					
Cash	$ 4,756	$ 4,630	$ 2,182	$ 3,337	$ 1,626
Accounts receivable	11,384	8,446	12,366	6,150	7,419
Notes receivable	824	0	0	0	0
Inventories	2,450	2,711	3,349	3,359	2,698
Total current assets	19,414	15,787	17,897	12,846	11,743
Fixed assets	77,819	77,546	88,334	45,854	43,084
Other assets	1,333	1,995	1,748	1,257	477
Total assets	$98,566	$95,328	$107,978	$59,957	$55,304
Liabilities and capital					
Current liabilities:					
Notes payable	$14,293	$14,088	$ 20,800	$ 5,000	$10,000
Accounts payable	2,718	3,382	3,730	1,692	474
Accrued expenses....	780	989	1,162	178	142
Federal tax withheld	311	311	264	130	154
Other	45	21	827	12	155
Total current liabilities	18,147	18,791	26,777	7,012	10,925
Long-term notes	4,400	8,800	17,688	0	0
Total liabilities...	22,547	27,591	44,465	7,012	10,925
Capital					
Kevin	25,350	22,579	21,171	17,648	14,793
Kathy	25,339	22,579	21,171	17,648	14,793
Karen	25,339	22,579	21,171	17,648	14,793
Total capital	76,018	67,737	63,514	52,945	44,378
Total liabilities and capital	$98,566	$95,328	$107,978	$59,957	$55,304

Exhibit 3
Additions to fixed assets for Kopy Kwik

	1982–83	1981–82	1980–81	1979–80
Land	$ 0	$ 0	$ 3,800	$ 0
Duplicating machines	12,800	10,860	48,608	9,770
Trucks	902	820	1,720	1,142
Buildings	0	101	142	214
Machinery	356	0	1,039	302
Office equipment	97	337	558	118
Total additions	$14,154	$12,118	$55,867	$11,546

Before purchasing a new location for its duplicating equipment, the partners did research into its potential volume and costs. Outside organizations provided probable demand data, which could be used to establish average daily use. It was necessary to obtain cost and profit data from the potential seller or from an analysis based on the experience of Kathy, Karen, and Kevin.

Kathy expressed the view that six-times earnings was too much to pay

Exhibit 4
Fixed assets and reserves for depreciation for Kopy Kwik

	Balance 4–1–82	Additions	Retirements	Balance 3–31–83
Assets:				
Land	$ 6,193	$ 0	$ 0	$ 6,193
Duplicating machines	104,182	12,800	10,148	106,834
Autos and trucks	8,281	902	2,400	6,783
Buildings	8,316	0	0	8,316
Machinery and other equipment	2,338	356	0	2,694
Office equipment	2,155	97	62	2,190
Totals	$131,465	$14,155	$12,610	$133,010
Reserves for depreciation:				
Duplicating machines	$ 43,274	$11,273	$ 9,620	$ 44,926
Autos and trucks	6,149	713	2,300	4,563
Buildings	2,023	438	0	2,461
Machinery and other equipment	1,325	538	0	1,863
Office equipment	1,148	274	46	1,376
Totals	$ 53,919	$13,236	$11,966	$ 55,189

for duplicating locations in small towns. She knew of some shopping center leases and other prime locations that might be available at that price but wasn't much interested in following up on such opportunities.

In 1984, another issue arose. Kevin wished to sell his interest in the firm to the other partners. The partners wanted to set a price that was fair and that recognized Kevin's one-third financial contribution to the firm.

1. Is the rule of buying companies at five-times earnings but not at six-times earnings a reasonable one? Discuss.
2. The partners were able to borrow large sums of money for new ventures by selling municipal bonds at 6 percent. Assuming this to be the cost of capital and assuming a 15-year life of the business beyond the time of the case, estimate the present value of Kathy, Karen, and Kevin's firm. Compare this value with a price of five-times earnings.
3. The partners had access to investment opportunities that in recent years had returned more than 20 percent profit (before taxes). Assuming the opportunity cost of capital to be 20 percent, estimate the present value of the firm. Compare this value with a price of five-times earnings.
4. Which cost of capital estimate (6 percent or 20 percent) is appropriate? Discuss.
5. Discuss the way in which you handled depreciation in your computation.
6. Should Kathy, Karen and Kevin buy the small location mentioned in the case? Discuss.

7. What would be a fair price to pay Kevin for his one-third interest in the company?

PROBLEMS
Capital budgeting

11–1 Why is an explicit statement of corporate strategy needed in carrying out capital expenditure planning?

11–2 What is the appropriate test of profitability for a proposed project?

11–3 What is a project balance?

11–4 Is a project's net present value the same as the present value of the project's terminal value? Explain.

11–5 Industrial Products, Inc. invested a total sum of $100,000 in two business ventures, I and II. At the end of the first period, I and II yielded returns of 7 percent and 6 percent, respectively. How had Industrial Products invested the $100,000 if the total amount earned was $6,500? (How much money was invested in each venture?)

11–6 Why might a firm's marginal costs of capital vary from period to period? How does period-to-period variation in capital's marginal cost affect the techniques used in testing the profitability of proposed projects?

11–7 If a firm's marginal cost of capital is increasing with expansion of investment in a given period, what problem is thereby introduced into capital expenditure planning?

11–8 The Longboat Key city council is considering imposition of a tax on motel construction. Representative of the motels in this resort area is one held by a holding company—in fact, the particular motel being studied is one of two units owned by the holding company whose total investment is $25 million. Unit I is located on Longboat Key; unit II is in another city. The holding company has not supplied precise cost and/or revenue data to city council. It is known by council that 9½ percent was earned last year on the combined investment. Unit I earned 6 percent; unit II earned 14 percent. Before preparing the first draft of this proposed legislation, council asked its finance committee to estimate the holding company's investment in unit I. What is it?

11–9   Suppose a firm is operating under capital rationing (it will not go outside for funds, even though these could be profitably used). What is the nature of the resulting difficulty in carrying out rational capital allocation?

11–10   Sears Roebuck & Co. is considering installing a new conveyor for materials handling in a warehouse. The conveyor will have an initial cost of $75,000 and an installation cost of $7,200. Expected benefits of the conveyor are the following: (*a*) Annual labor cost will be reduced by $17,200, and (*b*) breakage and other damages from handling will be reduced by $400 per month. Some of the company's costs are expected to increase as follows: (*a*) Electricity cost will rise by $100 per month, and (*b*) annual repair and maintenance of the conveyor will amount to $900. Assume that the company uses five-year, straight-line depreciation, the conveyor has an expected useful life of eight years and a projected salvage value of $5,000, and Sears expects marginal income to be taxed at a 48 percent rate.
   a. Estimate future cash flows for the proposed project.
   b. Determine the project's internal rate of return.
   c. Present the capital project's cash flows by using the internal rate of return as cost of capital.

11–11   Assume the following expected marginal costs of capital in future periods for Sears in problem 11–10 above:

Period	Marginal cost (percent annually)
1	20%
2	15
3	12
4–8	10

   a. Determine the project's net present value.
   b. Decompose the project's cash flow using the costs of capital listed above. (Assume reinvestment of negative project balances at the firm's marginal cost of capital.)
   c. Calculate the benefit-cost ratio for the project.

11–12   Assume the engineering department at Sears has developed an alternative design for a conveyor. The alternate design has lower initial cost, but it will not save as much labor, and there are other minor differences. The initial cost would be $60,000 and the annual reduction in labor cost would be approximately $13,000. Reduction in damage in material handling would be

$400 per month, and electricity cost would be increased $100 per month (both amounts are in comparison with present conditions in which there is no conveyor). Annual maintenance and repair are projected at $750 for the alternate-design conveyor; it is expected to have a useful life of six years; and the salvage value is estimated to be $1,000.

a. Determine the cash flows for use in an incremental analysis to aid the choice between the $75,000 conveyor and the $50,000 conveyor.

b. Using the marginal costs of capital listed in problem 11–11, carry out the incremental analysis by calculating the net present value of the incremental project and its benefit-cost ratio. What would you recommend that the firm do?

11–13   "In adjusting for a project's risk, the manager should consider possible effects of the project on the firm's overall profitability rather than just the variance of the expected outcome of the project as such." Explain.

11–14   "Although only one project will actually be the marginal project accepted during the current period, each project must be tested as if it were the marginal project by discounting its cash flows at marginal cost of capital rates." Explain.

Selected references

Coyne, Thomas J. "Present Value of Future Earnings: A Sensible Alternative to Simplistic Methodologies." *Insurance Counsel Journal* 49, no. 1 (1982), pp. 25–31.

Coyne, Thomas J.; M. Goulet Waldeman and Mario J. Picconi. "Residential Real Estate versus Financial Assets." *Journal of Portfolio Management* 7, no. 1 (1980), pp. 20–24.

Dean, Joel. "Measuring the Productivity of Investment in Persuasion." *Journal of Industrial Economics* 15 (April 1967).*

Donaldson, Gordon. "New Framework for Corporate Debt Policy." *Harvard Business Review* 56, no. 5 (September–October 1978), pp. 149–64.*

Doyle, P. "Economic Aspects of Advertising: A Survey." *Economic Journal* 73 (September 1968).

---

* This article is included in Thomas J. Coyne, *Readings in Managerial Economics*, 3d ed. (Plano, Tex.: Business Publications, 1981).

Elliott, J. Walter. "The Cost of Capital and U.S. Capital Investment: A Test of Alternative Concepts." *Journal of Finance* 35, no. 4 (September 1980), pp. 981–99.

Flath, David, and Charles R. Knoeber. "Taxes, Failure Costs, and Optimal Industry Capital Structure: An Empirical Test." *Journal of Finance* 35, no. 1 (March 1980), pp. 99–117.

Gupta, Vinod K. "Factors Determining Interindustry Differences in Advertising Intensity: Canadian Manufacturing." *Quarterly Review of Economics & Business* 20, no. 3 (Autumn 1980), pp. 60–76.

Irvine, F. Owen, Jr. "Merchant Wholesaler Inventory Investment and the Cost of Capital." *American Economic Review* 71, no. 2 (May 1981), pp. 23–29.

Mao, James C. T. "Survey of Capital Budgeting: Theory and Practice." *Journal of Finance* 25 (May 1979).*

Mehta, Dileep R.; Edward A. Moses; Benoit Deschamps; and Michael C. Walker. "The Influence of Dividends, Growth, and Leverage on Share Prices in the Electric Utility Industry: An Econometric Study." *Journal of Financial & Quantitative Analysis* 15, no. 5 (December 1980), pp. 1163–196.

Mishan, Ezra J. "Evaluation of Life and Limb: A Theoretical Approach." *Journal of Political Economy,* July–August 1971.

Schmitz, Robert E., Jr. "The Delayed Application Method of Research Apportionment: Determining the Discount Rate." *International Tax Journal* 6, no. 3 (February 1980), pp. 208–21.

Smith, Pierce R. "A Straightforward Approach to Leveraged Leasing." *The Journal of Commercial Bank Lending,* July 1973, pp. 40–47.

Stanley, Marjorie Thines. "Capital Structure and Cost-of-Capital for the Multinational Firm." *Journal of International Business Studies* 12, no. 1 (Spring–Summer 1981), pp. 103–120.

12

Risk and uncertainty

In Chapter 11 the discussion of capital budgeting treated the cash flows of projects as if they were certain. However, each projected cash flow is actually the mean of the expected values in a subjective probability distribution. If these subjective distributions take the normal form, variability of project results can be quantified by calculating coefficients of variation, where each such coefficient is the ratio of the standard deviation of expected cash flows to the mean of these expectations. The greater the coefficient of variation, the greater the riskiness of the project.

The possibility of differences in riskiness among projects must now be dealt with. An example of a comparison of project variability is shown in Figure 12–1, in which two projects have the same means of the probability distributions of expected internal rates of return, but the distribution of expected results for Project B has a larger standard deviation than that of Project A. Since most stockholders are risk averse (i.e., prefer less risk to more risk, other things being equal), management should choose Project A over Project B. In this example, it is easy to see that some kind of risk adjustment is being made in comparing the results of Project B with those of Project A.

For most managers, the easiest approach to risk adjustment is to increase or decrease costs of capital to be used in discounting, depending on how risky the project looks. If the project appears to have higher risk than average, something can be added to cost of capital as a risk premium. On the other hand, if the project is thought to have lower risk than average, something can be subtracted from costs of capital.

Some companies establish classes of risk and develop a managerial consensus as to the cost of capital adjustments that are appropriate for each class. Risk classification of projects can be assisted by sensitivity

515

Figure 12–1
Comparison of project variabliity

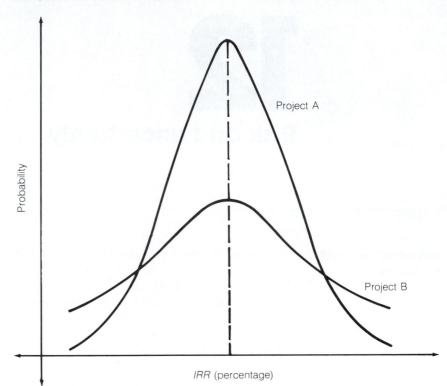

analysis using optimistic, most likely, and pessimistic assumptions about such planning data as equipment life, prices of inputs and products, and rates of output and sales.

Note that the risk evaluation for any given project should be in terms of how that project, as an addition to the firm's total activity, could affect the firm's overall profitability. A project that has a large variance of expected outcome may not be classified as a high-risk project if the initial outlay is small compared with the firm's total capital base. On the other hand, a project that has moderate variance of expected outcome may be regarded as high risk if it requires an initial outlay that is large in relation to total capital used.

Using decision trees in capital planning

Capital planning often involves decision-event-decision chains. The nature of such chains is illustrated by the following hypothetical example.[1]

---

[1] The example cited and discussion presented is based on John F. Magee, "Decision Trees for Decision Making," *Harvard Business Review* (July–August 1964), pp. 126–38.

A company has developed a new product that cannot be manufactured in present facilities. Management must decide whether to build a small plant or a large one. There is uncertainty about future demand for the product.

If the company builds a large plant, it must live with it whatever the size of market demand. If it builds a small plant, the plant can be expanded if demand is found to be high during the introductory period. However, total investment and cost of operating an expanded plant will be greater than the outlay and cost of production for a plant built for large-scale operation at the outset.

Demand may be low initially and continue low for the expected 10-year life of the product. There is a small chance that demand will be high initially and then fall back to a low level after many initial users find the product unsatisfactory. Or demand may be high initially and continue high for the product's expected life.

Here is the decision-event-decision chain: If the firm decides to build a small plant initially, it can observe the first chance event—the size of initial demand—and then make a second decision on whether or not to expand the plant. On the other hand, if the firm decides to build a large plant initially, the flexibility of a subsequent decision about expansion is precluded. But if demand is high initially and continues high, building a large plant at the outset results in greater cash flow during the first years and less total investment.

Suppose the following estimates of demand have been made:

Nature of demand	Probability	
High initial demand, high subsequent demand	.60	} .70
High initial demand, low subsequent demand	.10	
Low initial demand, low subsequent demand	.30	
Low initial demand, high subsequent demand	.00	

If demand is high initially, the chance that it will continue high is .86, calculated as the ratio of .60 to .70, where .70 is the total probability that initial demand will be high. If demand is high initially, the chance that it will be low subsequently is .14, calculated as the ratio of .10 to .70. And, if demand is low initially, the chance that it will continue low is 1.00, calculated as the ratio of .30 to .30. Comparing .86 to .60, it is clear that knowledge of high initial demand increases the probability that subsequent demand will be high. Similarly, comparing 1.00 to .40, it can be seen that knowledge of low initial demand increases the probability that subsequent demand will be low. Uncertainty about subsequent demand is decreased by knowledge of initial demand.

Assume that management has made the following estimates of annual cash flow under various conditions:

Plant size	Demand	Annual cash flow	Explanation
Large	High	$1,000,000	Capacity matched to demand and no room for competitors.
Large	Low	100,000	High fixed cost, low sales.
Small	Low	200,000	Small capacity matched to low demand, no room for competitors.
Small	High	400,000 initially 300,000 thereafter	After two years, competition would become keen.
Expanded	High	700,000	Capacity matched to demand, but not as efficient as plant designed for large volume from the outset.
Expanded	Low	50,000	Highest fixed cost, low sales.

Assume, finally, that a large plant would require $3 million of initial outlay, a small plant would require $1.3 million, and expansion of a small plant would cost an additional $2.2 million.

A decision tree that organizes the hypothetical firm's alternatives, the chance events and their probabilities, and the firm's outcomes (or payoffs) is shown in Figure 12–2. The tree structure is helpful in determining

Figure 12–2
Using a sequential decision tree and discounted payoffs

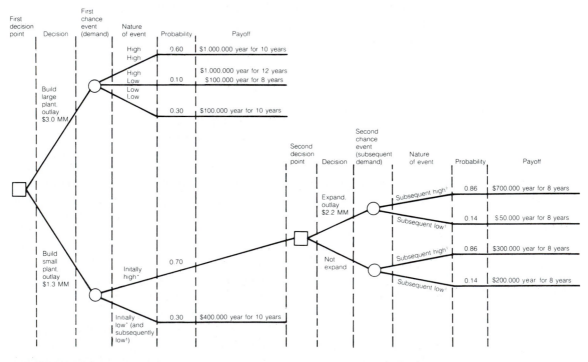

* Initial demand (first two years).
† Subsequent demand (next eight years).

which of the current alternatives (large plant or small plant) has the greatest expectation of payoff.

Analysis of the tree begins at the second decision point in Figure 12–2. We must determine a monetary value—called the position value—for this decision. The position value of a decision is simply the expected value of the decision, or the mathematical expectation of monetary outcome for the preferred action branch of that decision. An expected value is the average result that would be obtained if the decision could be repeated a great number of times under the same conditions.

The position value of the second decision can be calculated as shown in Table 12–1. In discounting the cash flows, a constant marginal cost of capital at 10 percent is assumed for simplicity (in a real problem, it would likely be desirable to discount period by period, at varying rates). The cash flows are treated as if received at the end of the various years, and Table 12–1A shows their present values as of the time that Decision 2 must be made. Table 12–1B shows how the position value of Decision 2 is determined. The expected discounted value of a decision to expand is $3,248,954; subtracting the $2.2 million of additional outlay for plant leaves a net expected value (as of the time Decision 2 is made) of $1,048,954. On the other hand, the expected discounted value of a decision not to expand is $1,525,781. Therefore, if the firm were in the position of Decision 2, having observed high initial demand, the preferred action branch would be not to expand. The expected discounted value of the preferred action, which is the position value of Decision 2, is $1,525,781.

Table 12–1
Expected value of Decision 2, with discounting
(Decision 2 is not effective until beginning of year 3)

A. **Present values of cash flows**

Decision	Chance event	Outcome (cash flow)	Present value (at time of Decision 2)
Expansion	High subsequent demand	$700,000 for 8 years	$3,734,430
	Low subsequent demand	$ 50,000 for 8 years	266,745
No expansion	High subsequent demand	$300,000 for 8 years	1,600,470
	Low subsequent demand	$200,000 for 8 years	1,066,980

B. **Expected discounted values of the alternatives**

Decision	Chance event	Probability of event	×	Present value of outcome	=	Expected value of decision
Expansion	High subsequent demand	0.86	×	$3,734,430	= $3,211,610	
	Low subsequent demand	0.14	×	$ 266,745	= 37,344	
						$3,248,954
	Less initial outlay					2,200,000
	Expected net present value					$1,048,954
No expansion	High subsequent demand	0.86	×	$1,600,470	= $1,376,404	
	Low subsequent demand	0.14	×	$1,066,980	= 149,377	
	Expected net present value					$1,525,781

The preferred action at the time of Decision 1 can now be determined as shown in Table 12–2. Table 12–2A lists the present values of the cash flow outcomes as of the time Decision 1 must be made, and Table 12–2B provides the comparison that allows the preferred action to be selected. The expected discounted value of the outcome of building a large plant is $4,088,744; subtracting the initial outlay leaves an expected net present value of $1,089,744. On the other hand, the expected discounted value of the outcome of building a small plant is $1,798,046; subtracting the initial outlay of $1.3 million leaves an expected net present value of $498,046. Thus, the preferred action alternative, for a management basing all decisions on comparisons of expected values, is to build the large plant at the outset, before initial demand is known.

Note that the decision to build a large plant has a 30 percent probability of low initial and low subsequent demand, resulting in an outcome with a

Table 12–2
Expected value of Decision 1, with discounting

A. **Present values of cash flows**

Decision	Chance event	Outcome (cash flow)	Present value (at time of Decision 1)
Large plant	High initial and high subsequent demand	$1 million for 10 years	$6,144,600
	High initial and low subsequent demand	$1 million for 2 years and $100,000 for 8 years	$1,735,500 440,910
			2,176,410
	Low initial and low subsequent demand	$100,000 for 10 years	$ 614,460
Small plant	High initial demand	$450,000 for 2 years plus the Decision 2 position value of $1,525,781	$ 780,975 1,260,982
			2,041,957
	Low initial demand	$200,000 for 10 years	$1,228,920

B. **Expected discounted values of alternatives**

Decision	Chance event	Probability of event	×	Present value of outcome	=	Expected value
Large plant	High initial and high subsequent demand	0.60	×	$6,144,600	=	$3,686,760
	High initial and low subsequent demand	0.10	×	$2,176,410	=	217,641
	Low initial and low subsequent demand	0.30	×	$ 614,460	=	184,338

	$4,088,739
Less initial outlay	3,000,000
Net present value	$1,089,739

Decision	Chance event	Probability of event	×	Present value of outcome	=	Expected value
Small plant	High initial demand	0.70	×	$2,041,957	=	$1,429,370
	Low initial demand	0.30	×	$1,228,920	=	$ 368,676

	$1,798,046
Less initial outlay	1,300,00
Net present value	$ 498,046

net present value of $2,385,540 (present value of $614,460 less the initial outlay of $3 million). On the other hand, the decision to build a small plant has an outcome with a net present value of $71,080 (present value of $1,228,920 less the initial outlay of $1.3 million), not nearly so bad an outcome for this condition of low initial and low subsequent demand. If the new plant involves a sizable part of the firm's total capital, the outcome of the decision may have a very noticeable effect upon the firm's overall profitability and value. In such a case, management might wish to make risk adjustments. In making risk adjustments, a project should be treated as an addition to the firm's other activities, and risk should be viewed in the light of the project's possible effects upon the whole-firm outcome.

Risk adjustment, of course, is largely subjective and varies from one management to another. Risk evaluation for any given project should take into account the possible effects upon the firm's overall profitability and value of the possible variations in that project's outcome. Some companies establish classes of project risk and a consensus as to the risk premiums and discounts that should be applied to the costs of capital used in discounting each class of project.

Capital projects may involve decision-event-decision chains. In such instances, decision trees are useful in organizing the relevant information and selecting the preferred initial action. If there are wide variations in the project's possible outcomes, and the project is a substantial part of the total capital base, it may be desirable to adjust for risk by substituting preference values for the monetary outcomes in the decision tree.

Uncertainty and planning

All business decisions are made under conditions of some uncertainty. Management does not know and cannot know all the future events that will affect the outcome of each alternative. It cannot know how consumer tastes and demands will change in the future. It cannot know what new competition will enter the market, how the present competitors will behave, what new substitutes will appear, or what new technological developments will alter the environment. It cannot predict exactly the impact of political changes that may result in changes in regulations, subsidies, fiscal policies, or international trade policies. It cannot even be certain of its own internal cost structure, for it does not have control over raw material prices, wage changes, or rates of obsolescence of equipment. Rates of productivity may respond to improvements in management and working conditions, but not by precisely predictable amounts.

Most of this book has proceeded as though management does have perfect information about the outcome of decisions, though it has faced up to the implications of uncertainty at several points. One has noted that decisions on prices are frequently the outcome of reasoning or experimentation, which might be called partial marginalism—management accommodates to uncertainty by going only part way in incremental reasoning. One has also commented that the shortcuts that are widespread in actual capital budgeting are reasonable adjustments to uncertainty. This text has taken the position that it is often useful to ignore uncertainty, at least in the early stages of analysis.

In recent years the analytical tools for dealing with uncertainty have been refined and sharpened. The problem in an introductory book in managerial economics is to determine how far to go into this analysis. The following discussion is an attempt to avoid two extremes: on the one hand, the attempt to boil a whole course in probability and Bayesian statistics into one chapter; on the other hand, the mere repetition of the cliché that risk and uncertainty are important without saying anything significant about them.

| **A variety of approaches to uncertainty** | It is well to recognize that management can deal with uncertainty in a variety of ways. The choice of the appropriate approach is itself an important business decision. Information varies in degree from the situations at one extreme, in which uncertainty is so insignificant that it is convenient to ignore it, to the situations at the other extreme, in which it is so great that choices can be little more than random selections. The analysis of uncertainty becomes more profitable between those extremes. |

Some writers make a distinction between risk and uncertainty.[2] Risk refers to relatively objective probabilities that can be computed on the basis of past experience or some a priori principle. Examples of the use of past experience are the actuarial probabilities in the insurance business that certain proportions of fires of various magnitudes will take place or that certain numbers of people of various ages will die. Examples of the a priori type are the odds that a coin will turn up heads or that an ace will be drawn from a deck of cards. In any of these cases the probability of the outcomes can be computed with considerable precision. In risk situations experience is repetitive and provides a frequency distribution about which inferences can be drawn by objective statistical procedures. Some business adjustments for risk are covered shortly in this chapter. Uncertainty, on the other hand, is relatively subjective, there being insufficient past information or insufficient stability in the structure of the variables to permit exact prediction.

Most business decisions take place under conditions of uncertainty, for each decision is made in somewhat a different environment. Sometimes

---

[2] Frank H. Knight, *Risk, Uncertainty and Profit* (Boston: Houghton Mifflin, 1921), p. 233.

the term *objective probability* is used in connection with risk and *subjective probability* in connection with uncertainty.

A few writers have taken the position that risk and uncertainty are completely different phenomena and require completely different treatments. Where risk is involved, it is convenient to compute the whole probability distribution. In cases of uncertainty, the parameters of the probability distribution itself are unknown. In such instances it is common to simplify the problem and focus on only a few of its elements. The recent tendency, however, is to treat subjective probabilities as different from objective probabilities only in degree. There is a continuum from high uncertainty to low uncertainty. What is called risk is toward one end of the continuum; complete ignorance is at the other. Most problems in management fall between. In the remainder of this chapter we shall use the term *uncertainty* to refer to the whole continuum and to include risk as part of uncertainty.

What are the alternative methods for dealing with uncertainty? There are at least nine approaches:

1. Avoidance of analysis by following rules of thumb, tradition, or external suggestions.
2. Simplification of the problem through break-even analysis.
3. Application of the insurance principle.
4. Hedging.
5. The search for additional information;
6. Sampling.
7. The stress on flexibility.
8. The stress on diversification.
9. Increased control over the future.

Avoidance of analysis by following rules of thumb, tradition, or external suggestions

One way to deal with uncertainty is to escape from it by avoiding analysis as much as possible. Rules of thumb provide a way of making decisions without much thought. The adherence to traditional "decision rules," such as those on markups and markdowns in department stores, can convert decision making into mechanical routine requiring little analysis. Many retail store managers prefer to stock commodities on which prices have been suggested by manufacturers, for they can thus avoid making pricing decisions. (They still must make decisions on which items to stock.) Still another way of avoiding analysis is through the simple imitation of the prices of others.

It is wrong to conclude that these rules of thumb and shortcuts are devoid of any economic meaning. In a competitive society firms do not survive unless they make some kind of adjustment to market forces. The decision rules that do survive must represent ways of dealing with cost, demand, and competitive factors. For example, manufacturers' suggested prices are undoubtedly based on experience with what retailers can live with. Imitative prices may enable a firm to learn from the experience of others, or it may be a kind of price followership that cuts down on cutthroat competition in the industry.[3]

Break-even analysis and similar simplifications

The break-even charts we have seen, the ones that reveal total cost and total revenue curves, represent only one of a family of similar devices to simplify analysis. A payback criterion is quite similar to the break-even chart, for it focuses attention on the probability of doing better than a certain predetermined standard or criterion. Although the earlier discussion of break-even charts argued that management should concern itself with the whole cost-revenue relationship and not merely a single point, it is clear that many managers do take great interest in the break-even point itself. Their reasoning seems to be as follows: It is impossible under conditions of uncertainty to determine the exact volume that will be attained. It is possible, however, to determine roughly the chance that the future volume will exceed that at the break-even point. If the probability of exceeding the break-even volume is extremely high, the manager may be satisfied without knowing the probabilities of specific volumes. If, however, the chances of falling below the break-even point are too high, the manager may reject the proposal outright. Such a use of the break-even point may seem unreasonable, since it places a proposal that may provide a 90 percent expected return on the same level as one with a 10 percent expected return if both have about the same probability of being above the break-even point. Looking at the matter in another way, this approach ignores the desirability of risking losses if the chances for large gains are great. If the manager is extremely conservative—if his/her marginal utility of income falls sharply—this approach may make sense, for the large gains result in a smaller proportional change in utility than in dollars.

The payback criterion is similar to the break-even point as a way of avoiding a full analysis of uncertainty. Managers who use the payback criterion are satisfied with determining that the probability of the investment paying for itself in less than the predetermined time is extremely high, but they avoid the hard work of determining the probabilities that the rates of return will be 10 percent, 20 percent, and so on. They are satisfied with a strong assurance that the investment will pay off without knowing exactly how profitable it might be.

The two approaches to uncertainty discussed so far are consistent with a "satisficing theory," which argues that business people are often satis-

---

[3] See Armen A. Alchian, "Uncertainty, Evolution and Economic Theory," *The Journal of Political Economy* (Chicago: University of Chicago Press, 1950), pp. 211–21.

fied with less than the optimum. As long as results come up to predetermined ideas of what is satisfactory, these businesspeople will look no further for better solutions. High degrees of uncertainty increase this temptation to "let well enough alone," or at least not to spend a great deal of effort in finding the very best. In fact, under conditions of uncertainty, the concept of the "best," "most profitable," or "optimum" becomes fuzzy, since managers must choose among probability distributions that overlap, rather than among single-point estimates.

The insurance principle

In the case in which it is possible to compute "objective" probabilities on the basis of past experience (the case some economists have labeled "risk"), the insurance principle may be applicable. Even in this situation there is high uncertainty about the event faced by each individual firm. No one knows which worker will suffer an injury. No one knows which buildings will burn in fires. But by pooling these uncertainties, it is possible to compute the probabilities for the mass, if not for the individuals. Insurance converts the high uncertainty about individual losses into a high degree of certainty about pooled losses.

The "law of large numbers" helps explain this conversion of high uncertainties about individual events into objective probabilities for the mass of events. The law observes that certain mass phenomena have a tendency toward regularity in behavior. Examples are the number of aces that will be drawn from complete decks of cards if the draws are repeated many times, the numbers of houses that will burn down in a year nationally, the number of deaths in each age category, and so on.

Only when the law of large numbers applies is a sound insurance program possible. The regularity in mass phenomena makes it possible to transfer risks. An individual can pay premiums to an insurance company in return for a promise to compensate for losses. Sometimes self-insurance is feasible. A firm owning 1,000 trucks might, instead of paying premiums to an outside insurance firm, establish a reserve for covering the losses in accidents that will inevitably occur. The predictability of accidents would be stable enough so that the reserve would absorb the losses without much danger of an unusual financial drain in a single year.

Insurance differs from the methods of dealing with uncertainty discussed so far in that it actually reduces uncertainty for the individual. The insured replaces a high degree of uncertainty about the occurrence of a particular event with the certainty of a definite premium. The insurance company reduces uncertainty by pooling risks and applying the law of large numbers.

Hedging

The traditional definition of *hedging* has been the "matching of one risk with an opposing risk." The Chicago Board of Trade with its futures markets excel in this area of activity. By holding two opposite positions, a person can avoid the risk of loss, though simultaneously losing part of the opportunity for gain. If, for example, one holds a large inventory of raw materials as an incident to doing business, she/he may wish to avoid the danger of declining prices. In some industries a decline in the prices of raw materials might more than wipe out any profits that might be earned through normal operations. An opposite example is the firm that operates in a short rather than a long position, as would be the case if it has made a contract to deliver a commodity at a future date at a predetermined price. By the time such a firm is ready to manufacture and deliver, it may find that raw material prices have risen, wiping out any profit that might be earned.

Futures markets provide one means of hedging against price increases or decreases. Such markets permit the purchase or sale of contracts for future delivery, especially in the case of such storable commodities as grain, cotton, and metals. The buyers of futures contracts normally do not actually want to take delivery on the contracts, nor do the sellers want to make the delivery. Some of the buying and selling of these contracts is done by speculators who are betting on rising prices or falling prices in the future. Such speculation is somewhat the opposite of hedging, for it involves the assumption of risk rather than its avoidance.

More specifically, the hedging operation could proceed as follows. A flour-milling firm is worried that prices may change before it has processed and delivered its flour. It holds large inventories of wheat and a decline in the price of wheat and flour could wipe out the processing profits. Since it is long on wheat, the firm might sell futures on wheat for delivery about the time the flour would be ready for delivery. If the price of wheat and flour goes down, the firm loses on the flour it delivers, but it gains from buying wheat at "spot" (current cash) prices to fulfill the futures contract.[4] If the price of wheat and flour go up, the margin on the flour actually milled increases, but this increased profit is offset by a loss in the futures market.

Another illustration involves the purchase of futures. A manufacturer may make a contract to deliver finished goods six months later at specified prices. The danger is that rising prices will wipe out the profit. The purchase of futures will enable a firm to profit on the price rise in the futures market at the same time it loses on the higher prices it must pay on the materials actually used in manufacture. If the prices fall, the firm loses in the futures market but earns a higher profit margin in manufacture.

A fuller discussion of hedging is unnecessary here, except to note that

---

[4] The firm normally would never see the wheat bought and sold in the hedging transactions. The discussion considers only the simplest type of hedging and neglects some of the complications that exist in practice.

it can take many forms. The "put and call" options on the stock market may take the form of hedges. Some writers even classify insurance as a type of hedge. But research suggests that the use of the futures market for risk avoidance is not common practice at this time. Perhaps hedging does not deserve the central position in discussions of uncertainty it has traditionally received.

The search for additional information

Another way to reduce uncertainty is to gather more information. If a firm is uncertain about price-volume relationships (the elasticity of demand) it may collect more data about the past response of purchases to price. It may refine its analysis, taking a large number of variables into account. If it is uncertain about the marginal cost of increased output, it may install better accounting methods for separating costs into appropriate categories. It may run statistical correlations between cost and output.

The methods of forecasting discussed in Chapters 13 and 14 contribute to better information for decision making. General economic forecasts, industry forecasts, and forecasts of the demand for individual products should reduce the uncertainty about future sales. Econometric studies of the variables affecting the sales of individual products along with analyses of the psychological and sociological determinants of consumer behavior should contribute to more accurate predictions of demand. One of the great needs at the present time is for follow-up studies that would show how successful the forecasting and statistical studies have been in actual practice in improving decisions.

The collection of information is costly. Like any other managerial activity, it produces benefits that must be weighed against the added expenses. The improvement and growing use of computers is making it possible to process larger quantities of data economically. The growing knowledge of operations research, statistics, and managerial economics is increasing skills in making better use of information, but there will always be a point at which added information will no longer pay for itself.

Sampling

Sampling provides a way of cutting costs in the collection of information. Instead of attempting to obtain complete information about a problem, management may make use of systematic sampling techniques to obtain sufficient information for the purposes at hand. The theory of sampling provides a basis for inferring characteristics of the total population of data from selected observations. The arguments in favor of sampling are several: It reduces the cost of data collection; it reduces the time to make the study required as background for the decision; and sometimes the systematic collection of samples will result in more accurate information than the haphazard collection of more information. In cases in which the collection of information requires the destruction of the product—as might be the case in testing radio tubes—sampling is the only feasible approach. When the information sought concerns a continuing process, the collected observations are necessarily a sample taken from this infinite, continuing population.

Economic considerations should govern decisions on sampling. Let us consider the problem of controlling quality in manufacturing. Suppose we are interested in holding down the proportion of defects. Sometimes the cost of defects is so high and the cost of observations so low that complete measurement is desirable. Such is the case in the inspection of parachutes—no one would advocate that management rely on sampling to determine the proportion of defects, since no level is tolerable. As the benefits from the information decrease or the costs of sampling increase, it becomes economical to reduce the size and frequency of the samples.

Sequential sampling provides a way of reducing the cost of sampling. Suppose the problem is one of accepting or rejecting some tires; say, the Firestone 500. One approach would have been to take a single sample from the lot and make a decision on the basis of the number of defects in the sample. This particular tire, of course, is no longer in production. An alternative would have been to take a smaller sample the first time, with three possible outcomes.

In such sampling, if the number of defects in the sample is small enough, management will accept the lot without further investigation. If the number of defects is larger than some predetermined level, management should reject the lot. If the defects lie somewhere in between, management should take another sample (with possibly a third or fourth sample if the number of defects still lies in the intermediate zone). The advantage of sequential sampling is that it may require a smaller sample size, on the average, to reach a decision on acceptance of a lot.

The notion of sequential decision making is much broader than the use of sequential samples in quality control. Management has a certain amount of information pertinent to a decision at hand. It must make a choice between deciding now on the basis of the limited information available or collecting additional information. For example, management may decide to introduce a new product now on the basis of limited information, or it may decide to hire a marketing research firm to collect data on the demand for the product. When it receives the marketing research findings, it may still be dissatisfied and may experiment with trial runs before making the final decision. At each step the value of the added information in reducing uncertainty and providing better estimates must be weighed against the costs of research and the costs of delay. In the past managers have used rough judgments in determining whether they should act now or wait for added data; in the future more systematic users of probability theory may replace such broad judgments, but some subjective judgment will always remain.

Flexibility

Flexibility provides another way of reducing the unfavorable effects of uncertainty. Rather than build facilities that will minimize costs at the mean expected level of demand or for some other specified level, it may be better to adopt more flexible methods that are more costly at the mean level but less subject to rising costs away from the mean.

A break-even chart can also portray the comparison between a high-fixed-cost plant (which produces high profits beyond the break-even point and high losses if sales fall short) and a more flexible plant (which may be more moderate on both the profit and loss sides). The specialized plant may mean a higher break-even point, which is a sensible choice if the certainty of being beyond that point is high enough.

Illustrations of flexibility are numerous. A digital computer is more flexible than the more specialized analog computer but is sometimes a more costly way to handle a specialized computing task. Mid-1980 versions of the IBM, TI, Burroughs, Radio Shack, Digital, Wang, and numerous other personal and/or professional computers offer a degree of flexibility that was considered pie-in-the-sky thinking only a few short years ago. Assembly-line production techniques are less flexible than functional plant layouts but are more productive in turning out a predetermined product. (Methods have been found to combine some of the advantages of the specialization of the assembly line with some of the flexibilities of functional layouts.) A bowling alley may involve construction of a specialized building little-suited for any other purpose or may make use of a general-purpose building that could be converted to a grocery store if the bowling enterprise failed. A firm may choose to maintain a high level of current assets to fixed assets to be able to meet changing economic conditions, at the sacrifice of higher earnings on more fixed assets. A farmer may select a type of barn easily converted from the storage of hay to a shed room for feeding cattle or to dairying. Some breeds of cows are better suited to switching back and forth from milk and beef products but produce less milk than do other breeds.

Diversification

Still another way of preparing for uncertainty is by diversifying activities. The ancient warning against putting all of one's eggs in one basket shows that this principle has a long history, though it is only in recent years that a systematic theory of diversification has appeared. The principle of diversification is well known among stock purchasers, who tend to combine stocks from a variety of industries with different economic characteristics. It is also known in manufacturing, in which some firms wish to avoid being tied to the vicissitudes of one or two product lines. Especially when the firm is interested in the stability of earnings as well as the magnitude of earnings, it looks to diversification to average out the impacts of uncertain changes in particular markets. For example, Goodyear Tire & Rubber Company acquired Celeron (oil and gas) in 1983 as part of an effort to sever its heavy, almost total reliance on the automotive industry. Also the stress on survival of the firm rather than on maximum short-run profits leads to a search for variety.

Control over the future

Still another way of dealing with uncertainty is to try to control the variables that bring it about. Many, if not most, large firms maintain expensive offices in Washington, D.C., as well as in appropriate state capitols for purposes of lobbying. Lobbyists are able to obtain special treatment, control, and/or favors that are simply unavailable to the non-lobbyist taxpayer. Management has no direct control over government regulations and other external events and must take the consequences. However, if the firm is large enough, it may be able to bring outside economic forces into some kind of order. For example, collusion among oligopolists has as its aim not only the monopoly profits that may result from price control but also the reduction of uncertainty. The perennial attempts by trade associations to win acceptance of pricing formulas and accounting systems is similar. Price leadership is a way of reducing uncertainty about the reactions of rivals to a firm's price changes. And it is possible that a firm may manipulate advertising and other promotional devices to reduce the instability and uncertainty of sales and production volumes.

Basic tools for the analysis of uncertainty

The analysis of uncertainty is a major topic in itself—one that could easily take up this full volume. Nevertheless, it is desirable to introduce the basic concepts in the language of management. Most managers cannot be experts in statistical analysis, but they can develop skills in identifying situations where expert advice is appropriate. More important, managers must identify risky investments and attempt to make an appropriate comparison of them to less-risky uses of a similar amount of money. Consider the riskiness of Treasury bills.

Treasury bills are sold by the Federal Reserve Banks. Application to include payment for a Treasury bill may be made on Thursday of any week at the Federal Reserve Bank of Chicago, or at one of the eleven other Federal Reserve Banks. The Monday following a decision by the large institutional buyers establishing a price and a yield on T bills, the relatively small purchaser is able to take advantage of that yield. She or he receives a check representing interest income on the T bill. In other words, a $10,000 Treasury bill applied for on Thursday is awarded the following Monday, at which time a check for, say, $346.90 may be sent to the purchaser as interest income on the $10,000 paid for the bill; consequently, the actual cost of the T bill is $9,653.10, and the yield is $346.90. Under the assumption that conditions would behave in the future as they did in the past, this yield could be expressed in terms of a 7.187 percent annual yield (2×3.594). Regardless of yield, the return on the Treasury bill is a certain event and, by definition, is one in which no risk or uncertainty is associated. Such a situation does not exist when a business firm makes an investment. Consider the beer business.

The Joseph Schlitz Brewing Company produces and sells beer and malt liquor in the domestic American economy. On a particular local beer, for example, it has net earnings approximating (in thousands) $45,700 on net sales of $788,360, for a return on sales of 5.797; the return on assets for the period was about 10 percent, ($\frac{\$45,700}{\$456,353} = .10014$). For a given nine-month period, this beer company could have a return on sales of about 6 percent and a return on assets of about 10.5 percent. However, beer drinkers are thought to be a fickle lot, and forecasting demand for a given brand of beer is difficult and risky. The fourth fiscal quarter of activity of any given year might provide dramatically different results.

Schlitz Brewing might employ approximately 7,000 workers, approximately 71 percent of whom could belong to labor unions. The company could be affected by one or more of 27 separate labor agreements in existence within the company. The price, cost, and output behavior of this firm (which give rise to the returns on sales and assets as indicated above) involves a supervisory function that must operate at times under conditions of uncertainty. Decisions made by management affect, adversely or otherwise, the profitability of the overall operation. To say the operation of any plant owned by Schlitz is riskier than having an equivalent dollar amount of assets invested in Treasury bills is to seriously understate the case. It is quite clear that the operation of any business within or outside the continental limits of the United States is riskier than an equivalent amount of money placed in Treasury bills.

Certainty equivalents

The position often taken by some analysts is that if a riskless investment can yield with certainty an annual return of 7.187 percent and a riskier investment of the same amount of money could return 10.014 percent over the same period, a certainty equivalent can be calculated by dividing the certain return (C_t) by the riskier return (R_t).

$$\text{Certainty equivalent} = \frac{C_t}{R_t}$$

$$7.187/10.014 = .7177 \text{ (Multiply by 100}$$
$$\text{to convert to percent.)}$$
$$.7177 \times 100 = 71.77 \text{ percent}$$

This certainty equivalent, once obtained, may be used in the present value and net value approaches when evaluating capital budgeting proposals. In calculating the present value of an annuity, the equation is:

$$\text{P.V.}_{\text{annuity}} = T\,\frac{1 - v^n}{i}$$

In Chapter 11, an example of this formulation provided a total dollar value of \$624.75. If the \$100 equal annual flow in that example were to be adjusted by a certainty equivalent (*CE*, known also as α_t), the present value of the annuity would be:

$$\text{P.V.}_{\text{annuity}} = (\alpha_t T)\left(\frac{1 - v^n}{i}\right)$$

where

$T = $ Equal annual payment of \$100 per year.
$n = $ Nine years.
$i \ = 8$ percent.
$\alpha_t = 71.77$.

We have:

$$\text{P.V.}_{\text{annuity}} = (\alpha_t T)\left(\frac{1 - .50002}{.08}\right)$$
$$= (\alpha_t T)\ \ (.4998/.08)$$
$$= \$71.77\ \ \ (6.2475)$$
$$= \$448.38$$

The certainty equivalent method used here assumes the Joseph Schlitz Brewing Company would consider adjusting its net cash flow forecast by a factor that had considered in its calculation, the opportunity cost of a riskless security. It should be recognized that the same quantities of money made available for investment in capital equipment could not be made available for investment in Treasury bills. Commercial banks do not lend monies for speculative purposes in the money market. It is unlikely that stocks, bonds, and/or retained earnings would be used for the purchase of T bills by a manufacturing firm interested in long-run returns.

This certainty equivalent method, if considered by a firm like Schlitz, might be used in connection with a decision to enlarge its Tampa, Florida, annual barrel capacity beyond 1.4 million per year or to install a new production facility in Syracuse, New York. If used in this manner, the approach to the problem might be one of accepting whichever proposal tends to have the highest mean expectation in terms of the additional number of barrels of beer capable of being produced. The approach is based on the assumption that the probability distribution of sales for enlargement of the Tampa, Florida, plant differs from the probability distribution of the sales forecast from a potential Syracuse, New York, plant; columns 3 and 5 of Table 12–3 confirm the differences in probability distributions of assumed data for the company.[5]

Masses of data that at first appear chaotic can often be arranged by grouping them into frequency distributions. This is done by tabulating the numbers of observations that fall into certain class intervals. Table 12–4 provides an illustration of arrivals of vehicles at a toll booth on the Pennsylvania turnpike.

One way of communicating such data is to present them graphically, as in Figure 12–3. Many kinds of data show a gradual increase of frequencies up to a peak and then a gradual decline as is true of the data in that diagram.

If there were some reason to assume that the observations were representative and highly likely to repeat themselves, one might use these past observations as the basis for estimates in the future. Thus, one might say that the probability of the number of arrivals being from 8 A.M. to

Table 12–3
Mean expectation of beer sales (units)
Syracuse, New York, and Tampa, Florida

(1) x_i Number of Barrels (millions)	(2) $p(x_i)$ Syracuse	(3) $x_i \cdot p(x_i)$	(4) $p(x_i)$ Tampa	(5) $x_i \cdot p(x_i)$
4.0	.10	400,000	.50	2,000,000
4.5	.15	675,000	.20	900,000
5.0	.25	1,250,000	.15	750,000
5.5	.25	1,375,000	.10	550,000
6.0	.15	900,000	.05	300,000
6.5	.10	650,000		
	1.00		1.00	
Mean expectation $= \mu =$ average $= 5,250,000$				4,500,000

[5] The decision to enlarge the Tampa, Florida, plant versus the breaking of ground in Syracuse, New York, would be based upon many factors other than the number of units (barrels) to be sold as the result of that particular plant's production. Yet, if one assumes for the moment that location would be based upon this one criterion only, the preferred location is Syracuse, New York.

Table 12–4
Frequency distribution: Arrivals at toll booth per hour

Number of vehicles arriving each hour	Frequency of occurrences	Percent of total occurrences
0– 3.9	2	4
4– 7.9	7	13
8–11.9	12	22
12–15.9	17	31
16–19.9	10	18
20–23.9	6	11
24–27.9	1	2
	55	101*

* Not 100 because of rounding.

11:59 A.M. was .22, or 22 percent. The probability of 24 or more arrivals would be .02 or 2 percent.

Unfortunately, most problems of interest to a manager do not present themselves in such a simple form. Past data do not serve so easily as a basis for establishing probabilities for the future, although inferences can be drawn from past observations. In fact, many decisions must be based on a heterogeneous collection of information of great variety—last period's beer sales, the average seasonal pattern of beer sales, surveys of buyers' attitudes, forecasts of business conditions, and the manager's own assessment of the situation. Still, it is convenient to summarize the

Figure 12–3
Histogram of arrivals at toll booth

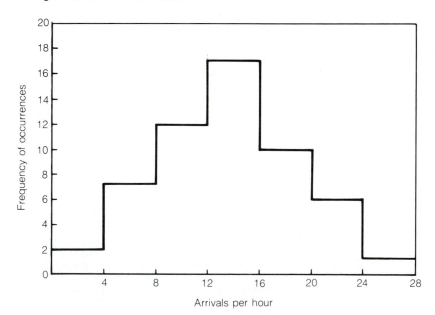

final estimates of what may happen in the form of a probability distribution. This forces the manager to think systematically about estimates rather than to become overwhelmed by emotions. The election forecaster who thought in 1948 that the probability of a Truman defeat was 80 percent had probably not done more homework than those few souls who were certain of a Truman victory, though neither was as well informed as those who were analyzing the actual results as they came in from the polls. (The ability of the analysts to be almost 100 percent confident of the outcome in a particular state on the basis of data from a few precincts is based, of course, on a sophisticated use of sampling and probability analysis.)

The normal distribution and other distributions

Most readers will be familiar with the fitting of a normal curve to a frequency distribution like that shown in Table 12–4 and Figure 12–3. The normal curve is a bell-shaped curve with well-defined mathematical properties. Many actual distributions in industry and nature approximate the normal distribution, but not all. The arrival of vehicles at toll booths is, in fact, not to be expected to follow a normal pattern for theoretical reasons developed in books on queuing theory. Actual observations of vehicle arrivals do not follow the normal distribution. The actual distributions tend toward the theoretical distributions, which are Poisson at lower volumes and normal at higher volumes.

The fact is that several different theoretical distributions are available to deal with a variety of problems. Among them are the exponential distribution, the gamma distribution, the binomial distribution, and the Pascal distribution. In the following discussion attention is concentrated on normal distributions, or cases in which normal distributions provide close approximations to reality.

A frequency distribution can be specified by the identification of its parameters. A normal distribution is specified if the central valve (the mean) is given along with a measure of dispersion (such as the standard deviation). The arithmetic mean $\bar{y}$ is computed from the formula:

$$\bar{y} = \frac{\sum_{i=1}^{n} y_i}{n} = \frac{y_1 + y_2 + y_3 + \cdots + y_{n-1} + y_n}{n}$$

The standard deviation σ is given by the formula:

$$\sigma = \sqrt{\frac{\sum_{i=1}^{n} (y_i - \bar{y})^2}{n-1}}$$

This is roughly the square root of the average deviations of observations from the means squared. One point of significance about the standard deviation is that we can use it to generalize about the probabilities of occurrences at certain ranges from the mean, as indicated in Figure 12–4.

Figure 12–4
Areas under the normal curve

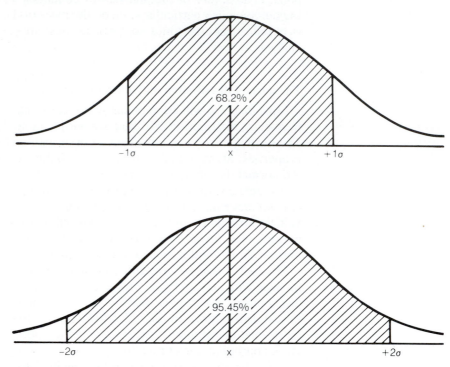

Applications of normal distributions

The break-even analysis in earlier chapters tended to gloss over the problem of uncertainty. The fact is, however, that the sales volume plotted along the horizontal axis of a break-even chart is almost always uncertain. Indeed, the costs themselves may be uncertain. Let us assume here that the cost estimates are dependable enough to use in the form of certainty equivalents and concentrate on the uncertainty of sales volume.

Suppose the two beer factories encounter the same cost functions and the same mean estimates of sales. It might appear that the optimum decision for one also applies to the other. But if the dispersion (standard deviation of sales) for one is greater than that for the other, this is not true. If the costs are at all curvilinear or if they include discrete "stairsteps," it is by no means clear that the gains at high sales will exactly compensate for lower sales at the lower end of the probability distribution. The corporate income tax also brings a degree of complexity into the analysis; losses are not treated precisely as negative profits for tax purposes. Last, attitudes toward risk vary within a firm and from firm to firm. A highly uncertain sales situation might be avoided if the disutility of losses is considered high.

Uncertainty becomes a more important consideration in the area of capital budgeting, but it is seldom given specific attention in the usual discussions of capital budgeting. Sometimes higher cutoff rates (costs of capital) are applied to riskier investments, but this procedure is rather subjective. Still another approach is to apply sensitivity analysis. Such analysis attempts to determine how much difference to profits or other objectives a shift in cash flows will make. However, this analysis fails to examine the probabilities of such shifts in sufficient detail. It may be useful to apply probability analysis more directly. The procedures for doing so using standard deviation analysis have been developed.

Adjustments for risk

If Schlitz is a risk averter and the data in Table 12–3 are accurate, and assuming further that desired increases in existing capacity approximate 4 million barrels per year or less, a cursory review of the table might cause one to select enlargement of the Tampa facility. The probability distribution is such that there appears to be a better chance of selling 4 million barrels from Tampa than of doing approximately the same thing if new ground is broken in Syracuse. Also at first glance, the Syracuse operation may appear somewhat more risky by some standards of measure, but it is capable of producing a 16⅔ percent greater output, on average, than can be had with an enlargement at Tampa. If this larger output could be sold and if the price per unit of output would be the same at both plants, while cost conditions did not vary from plant to plant, obviously, the total revenue and, subsequently, the total profitability to the firm would appear to be greater at the Syracuse location.

Many business economists consider *standard deviation* to be a synonym for the word *risk*. One project or investment proposal is thought to be riskier than another if the measure of dispersion around its mean is greater. In other words, the greater the dispersion, the higher the standard deviation, and consequently, the greater the risk.

Standard deviations of beer sales (barrels) for plants to be located in Syracuse (715,891) and Tampa (612,372) are presented in Table 12–5. The Syracuse location standard deviation indicates that investment there is riskier than investment of a like amount of money in Tampa.

Assuming an identical cost and revenue structure(s) and a break-even point of 4.2 million barrels of beer at each plant, an approximation of the

Table 12–5
Standard deviations of beer sales (barrels) Syracuse, New York vs. Tampa, Florida

(1) Potential beer sales (number of barrels) (x_i) (millions)	(2) $(x_i)^2$ (millions)	(3) Syracuse, New York $p(x_i)$	(4) $x_i^2\, p(x_i)$	(5) Tampa, Florida $p(x_i)$	(6) $(x_i)^2\, p(x_i)$
4.0	16.00	.10	1,600,000	.50	8,000,000
4.5	20.25	.15	3,037,500	.20	4,050,000
5.0	25.00	.25	6,250,000	.15	3,750,000
5.5	30.25	.25	7,562,500	.10	3,025,000
6.0	36.00	.15	5,400,000	.05	1,800,000
6.5	42.25	.10	4,225,000		
		1.00	28,075,000	1.00	20,625,000

$$
\begin{aligned}
\sigma_S^2 &= x_i^2\, p_{\text{Syracuse}}\,(x_i) \quad -(\mu_{\text{Syracuse}})^2 \\
&= 28{,}075{,}000{,}000{,}000 - 27{,}562{,}500{,}000{,}000 \\
&= 512{,}500{,}000{,}000 \\
\sigma_S &= 715{,}891
\end{aligned}
\qquad
\begin{aligned}
\sigma_T^2 &= \Sigma\, x_i^2\, p_T\,(x_i) - (\mu_T)^2 \\
&= 20{,}625{,}000{,}000{,}000 - 20{,}250{,}000{,}000{,}000 \\
&= 375{,}000{,}000{,}000 \\
\sigma_T &= 612{,}372
\end{aligned}
$$

Schlitz's probability of losing money could be made by assuming a normal distribution and solving for Z, where Z is a normal random variable ($\mu = 0$; $\sigma = 1$).

If
$X =$ Mean (average) expectation of production.
$\mu =$ Mean (average) of the total population.
$\sigma =$ Standard deviation.

then

$$
\begin{aligned}
Z_{\text{Syracuse}} &= \frac{x - \mu}{\sigma} \\
&= \frac{4{,}200{,}000 - 5{,}250{,}000}{751{,}891} \\
&= \frac{-1{,}050{,}000}{715{,}891} \\
&= -1.4667 \\
&= -1.47 \\
P[Z < -1.47] &= .07^{[6]}
\end{aligned}
$$

There is a 7 percent chance the Syracuse plant will operate at an output less than its break-even point, as indicated in Figure 12–5.

Inasmuch as the Z value is negative, the figure taken from the "Areas Under the Normal Curve" Appendix is less than 4.2 million barrels of

---

[6] Areas under the normal curve are provided in the Appendix; .0708 is located at the intersection of the .07 row and the 1.4 line.

Figure 12–5
Probability of loss: Syracuse

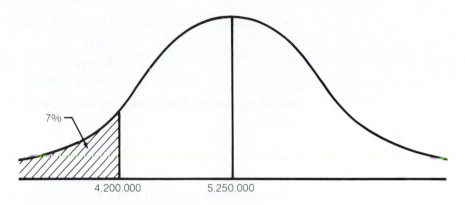

beer (break even) for Schlitz; just the opposite would have been true had the *Z* value been positive.

The probability of not breaking even at the Tampa location is about 31 percent:

$$P[Z<-.4899]=.31 \text{ (again, as taken from the Appendix)}$$

$$Z_{\text{Tampa}}=\frac{x-\mu}{\sigma}$$

$$=\frac{4,200,000-4,500,000}{612,372}$$

$$=\frac{-300,000}{612,372}$$

$$=-.4899$$

By this standard of measurement, the Tampa expansion would be too risky relative to the Syracuse location.

Coefficient of variation

Determination of the probability of not breaking even on one project or another is always worthwhile, but one must be careful with proper interpretation of the result. Inasmuch as the standard deviation is higher for the Syracuse data than for that data assumed for the Tampa location, economists might consider Syracuse to be the riskier location. Yet, if the distribution turns out to be normal, the probability of not breaking even in Tampa is greater than in Syracuse. A solution to the problem is often calculation of the coefficient of variation.

The coefficient of variation is the standard deviation divided by the mean expectation:

$$v = \frac{\sigma}{\text{ME}}$$

For the potential Schlitz Brewing Company investment in Syracuse, it is:

$$v = \frac{715,891}{5,250,000}$$
$$= .14, \text{ or } 14 \text{ percent}$$

and for the potential investment in Tampa, it is:

$$v = \frac{612,372}{4,500,000}$$
$$= .14, \text{ or } 14 \text{ percent}$$

The coefficient of variation is a worthwhile tool when the values differ among and between various investment proposals; moreover, textbook examples aside, these values almost always differ. When they do not differ, the best approach is the one mentioned earlier: Assume risk to be synonymous with standard deviation σ; and the larger it is, the greater the risk if, and only if, break-even estimates are unavailable. In this example, and in spite of a higher standard deviation in Syracuse, the location in Tampa is riskier when a normal bell-shaped curve is assumed.

Decision trees

Decisions involving uncertainty are not usually as simple as implied earlier in this text. In many cases the decision about what is to be done now will determine the options that will be open at the next stage. The initial decision cannot be made until these later options are evaluated. The decision tree is a useful device for analyzing this kind of problem.

Suppose Goodyear has an opportunity to purchase one of two other firms, but cannot buy both. If the first purchase is highly successful in producing a sufficient cash inflow, the second purchase might be possible at a later date, unless the firm is sold elsewhere in the meantime. The tree diagram would resemble Figure 12–6.

At first glance the purchase of A may appear best because it produces the highest cash inflow. However, if the probability of the cash inflow of $100,000 is low, not only may the purchase of A be less satisfactory on its own merits, but it may also limit the chances of making the second purchase.

Assume that a cash inflow of $40,000 is sufficient to finance a second purchase. Let us also assume that the objective is to maximize the net cash inflow over the first three years without regard to discounting, the cost of capital, or other considerations stressed by sophisticated capital budgeters.

Figure 12–6
Tree diagram

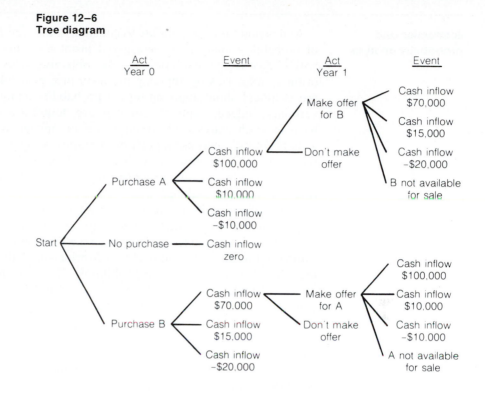

The probabilities for purchase A are as follows:

Cash inflow	$100,000	–	Probability 0.8
Cash inflow	10,000	–	Probability 0.1
Cash inflow	10,000	–	Probability 0.1

For purchase B:

Cash inflow	$ 70,000	–	Probability 0.7
Cash inflow	15,000	–	Probability 0.2
Cash inflow	20,000	–	Probability 0.1

If the purchase of A is delayed one year, the probability that it will not be available the next year is .5. If the purchase of B is delayed, this probability of nonavailability would be .2.

The analysis requires working backward, from the right-hand side to the left-hand side. It requires attaching probabilities to all events. Even with this structuring of the problem, some ambiguities remain, for it is not really rational to allow undiscounted cash inflows to govern the decision.

Economics and
probability analysis

At this point it is appropriate to consider some well-known applications of probability analysis to managerial problems. One is now concerned with subjective probabilities, for the objective risks can be treated as ordinary expenses by applying the insurance principle. Many managers are skeptical about applying formal probability analysis to cases of uncertainty; indeed, many statisticians are doubtful about the theoretical basis for such analysis. The trend, however, appears to be moving toward a more formal analysis; a growing literature supports the use of payoff tables, Bayes's theorem, tree diagrams, Monte Carlo simulation methods, queuing theory, and other techniques for making use of probability theory in decision making.

In the following discussion the mathematics of probability are avoided. Neglected also are the methods used to obtain particular probability distributions—for example, glossing over the ways in which newly acquired sample information is combined with prior subjective probabilities and reaching revised subjective probabilities. These are problems better left for more formal courses in statistics. It is assumed the reader knows what is meant by a statement that the probability of a particular event is .15 or that the cumulative probability that a magnitude exceeds a particular level is .63. Such terminology is part of the language of business and should be familiar to all.

The effort here is to demonstrate that the economic concepts developed throughout this book can be combined with probabilities in a variety of managerial problems. It is best to consider a variety of examples; unfortunately the illustrations must be kept simple to make the discussion clear. In real business situations a number of complications are likely to appear.

Inventory control models

The simplest probability model goes under the name of "Cookie Maker," a chocolate chip cookie-making operation with locations in many shopping malls throughout the nation. The owner-baker is faced with the decision of how many chocolate chip cookies to stock at the beginning of the day. Assume each small cookie sells for five cents but costs the owner-baker two cents. Every sold cookie results in a profit of three cents; every unsold cookie results in a loss of two cents. How many cookies should the baker stock? The baker cannot make a decision without having some notion of demand, and these notions of demand are likely to be in the form of probabilities. Let us suppose that the baker's subjective probability distribution for sales on this particular day are as shown in Table 12–6. Note that the probabilities in Table 12–6 are cumulative probabilities.

Table 12–6
Subjective probabilities of various
levels of cookie sales

Level of Sales	Probability that sales will exceed or equal that level
0	1.00
50	1.00
100	.99
200	.90
300	.75
350	.40
400	.25
500	.10
600	.02
700	.01
800	.00

One way of gaining insight into this simple problem is to think of it in terms of incremental costs and incremental gains. The incremental gain from stocking one more cookie is three cents multiplied by the probability that sales will equal or exceed the amount carried in stock. The incremental cost of adding that cookie is the two cents multiplied by the probability that sales will fall below the amount carried in stock.

If we start with zero cookies, the incremental gain must be three cents, for there is no doubt that the cookie will sell. The incremental cost is zero, for the probability that the cookie will not sell is nil. The baker should increase the size of stocks up to the point at which the incremental cost equals the incremental gain. Equation 12–1 presents the condition for the optimum:

$$mP(d \geq s) = cP(d < s) \tag{12–1}$$

in which

m	= Margin per cookie.
d	= Demand (quantity of sales).
s	= Amount stocked.
c	= Cost of each cookie.
$P(d \geq s)$	= Cumulative probability that demand will exceed or equal stocks

Since the two probabilities in equation (12–1) must add to unity, the equation may be rewritten in this form:

$$mP(d \geq s = c\ 1 - P(d \geq s) \tag{12–2}$$

The left-hand side of this equation is the incremental gain, and the right-hand side is the incremental cost. The equation is often rewritten in this form:

$$P(d \geq s) = \frac{c}{m+c} \tag{12-3}$$

which indicates that the baker should keep increasing stocks up to the point at which the cumulative probability that sales will exceed or equal the stocks declines to the ratio of the unit cost to the sum of the unit cost and the unit margin.[7]

Let us apply this reasoning to the probability schedule in Table 12–6. Since the ratio of c to $m+c$ is .40, it follows that the baker should stock 350 chocolate chip cookies. At this point the incremental gain is $0.12 (the probability of .40 that sales will equal or exceed 350 multiplied by the margin of $0.3) and the incremental cost is also $.012 (the probability of .60 that the cookie sales will be less than 350 multiplied by the unit cost of $.02).

Unfortunately, most inventory problems are more difficult than the one described. Even the baker might want to take other factors into account, such as the loss of customer goodwill that would be caused by very often running out of stock of a certain cookie (i.e., raisin, chocolate chip, and so on). In manufacturing the problem is often one of maintaining an inventory continuously over time and of weighing the carrying costs (interest, storage space, insurance, obsolescence, deterioration, and so on) against the cost of stockouts. The problem is complicated by the need to determine the economic lot size (or economic purchase quantity).

Scrap allowances

The analysis of scrap allowances is similar to that in some inventory control models. The problem is one of producing a specified quantity of nondefective pieces. The uncertainty arises from not knowing how many defects to expect. The firm may build up a probability distribution on the number of defects, making use of past experience or of current knowledge about the production process. An increase in the size of the production run reduces the risk of running short and of having to set up the process to fill out requirements. On the other hand, the increased production run increases the chances of producing too many units, with the loss of the labor and materials that go into the excess production.

The scrap allowance problem differs from the cookie problem in that the cost of running short is a lump-sum cost—the cost of setting up for a second run.[8] The cost of overages is proportional to the number of units of overage (or can be assumed to be so in most cases).

---

[7] The full derivation of the formulas cited here appears in most books on operations research.

[8] We shall ignore the possibility of a third or subsequent setup.

The optimum scrap allowance is given by the equation

$$K_u P(n=j) = k_o P(n<j) \tag{12-4}$$

in which

n = Serial number of the required last good piece.

j = Specified number of units planned in a run.

k_o = Unit cost of overages.

K_u = Lump-sum cost of setting up a second run.

The left-hand side of this equation is the expected gain from scheduling the jth unit. The right-hand side is the expected cost of the jth unit. The variable that can be manipulated by management is j, the number of units to be scheduled in the first run. As j is increased, the probability of overages (the probability that n is less than j) increases, and the expected cost of overage rises. Eventually, the expected cost of overages will catch up with the expected gain from scheduling the jth unit. At this point the incremental profit of increasing j by one unit is zero; beyond this point the incremental profit becomes negative.[9]

The formula for the economical scrap allowance can be rewritten:

$$\frac{P(n=j)}{P(n<j)} = \frac{k_o}{K_u} \tag{12-4}$$

which is a simpler form for practical use, although it is less easy to interpret in incremental terms. In this formula the ratio of the probabilities is made equal to the ratio of the costs. Note that $P(n=j)$ is the probability that the number of units scheduled is exactly the number of units required—the probability that this particular level of j will be the one to preclude having to set up a second time.

A bidding model

This book has devoted considerable space to pricing but no space, up to this point, to the special form of pricing known as bidding. Bidding takes place when several sellers compete for a given contract, each establishing a bid without communication with the others.[10] This problem is necessarily probabilistic in character; each bidder must somehow evaluate the probability of winning the contract at various bids. In the past bidders have no doubt relied on informal evaluations of the probabilities.

---

[9] These statements depend on a smooth, single-humped probability distribution, which is what one would normally expect in practice.

[10] Other forms of bidding, such as auction bidding, require an entirely different analysis.

In the future the formal application of probability theory may become more widespread.

The first step in the analysis is to determine the probabilities that the lowest opponent bid will involve various percentage markups. For the sake of simplicity, let us assume that the markup must be in discrete jumps of 5 percent and that the probabilities are as follows:

Markup on cost	Probability that lowest opponent bid will be at this markup
0%	.05
5	.10
10	.20
15	.30
20	.20
25	.10
35	.05
40	.00

The manufacturer could use past experience in setting up this probability distribution. The manufacturer might also make use of current knowledge as to how desperate opponents are to win the bid and how many opponents are likely to enter bids. The discussion here assumes that the opponents' bidding habits will not change. It also assumes that the bids are not fixed—written with such great specificity that only the one bidder, chosen in advance, can meet the specifications. If the manufacturer sets the markup low enough, the probability that of winning the bid becomes high, but the manufacturer sacrifices profits on the job. Maximization of expected profit involves a compromise between getting the most profit out of each job and increasing the chances of getting the job.

Let us consider a job that will cost $20,000. Let z represent the decision variable (the markup on the manufacturer's bid) and x, the markup on the lowest bid. Let π represent the profit in dollars. Then:

$$E(\pi) = \$20,000zP(x>z)$$

which means that the expected profit is equal to the $20,000 multiplied by the markup and by the probability that the lowest opponent bid will exceed the markup. The objective is to maximize $E(\pi)$. As we increase the markup from 0 percent and to 5 percent, the expected profit increases from $0 to $20,000 × .05 × .85, or $850.[11] As we increase the markup to 10

---

[11] Assume that a bid equal to that of opponents will mean loss of the contract. Also assume that the cost is the same for all bidders. More sophisticated models can overcome the limitations of these assumptions.

percent, the expected profit increases to $20,000 \times .10 \times .65$, or $1,300. The results are summarized below:

z	$E(\pi)$
0%	$ 0
5	850
10	1,300
15	1,050
20	600
25	250
30	0

The bid with the highest expected profit is at 10 percent, which means that the bid should be at $22,000. If the manufacturer were to quote bids with fractional markups, a markup of 14.99 percent would be preferable, but our model should then also recognize fractional bids by the opponents. (Calculus and continuous probability distributions would be more appropriate in this more realistic case.)

Oil-drilling decisions

A somewhat different problem presents itself when the alternatives open to management are limited in number but are substantially different in character. In the cookie and scrap allowance problems the decision is about a magnitude—the number of cookies to stock or the number of units to schedule for production. Frequently, however, management is concerned with a choice among a small number of alternatives. Such might be the case when the choice is between drilling and not drilling for oil. The decision maker does not know whether or not the outcome will be successful; he or she must face up to uncertainty. The decision maker might do better to resort to some formal analysis of probabilities than to depend on intuition or rough guesses.

The first step is to determine the probabilities of the outcomes.[12] At this point the decision maker will want to use as much information on past experience and geological data as possible. Suppose that the subjective probabilities are:

Dry hole	.70
100,000 barrels	.20
500,000 barrels	.10

Suppose that the incremental net revenues (after discounting and after the deduction of all expenses, including the initial drilling costs of $50,000) are: [13]

---

[12] This illustration is based on C. Jackson Grayson, Jr., *Decisions Under Uncertainty: Drilling by Oil and Gas Operators* (Boston: Harvard Business School, Division of Research, 1960).

[13] Assume the decision maker owns one third of a well that will cost $150,000 to drill.

Dry hole	$-\$\ 50,000$
100,000 barrels	$\$\ 50,000$
500,000 barrels	$\$450,000$

It is now possible to compute the expected monetary value of drilling or not drilling. The expected monetary value of drilling is:

$$.70 \times (-\$50,000) + .20 \times (\$50,000) + .10 \times (\$450,000) = \$20,000$$

The expected monetary value of not drilling is \$0. The analysis indicates that it is profitable to drill. It is true that this particular hole might well turn up dry, but in the long run the losses will more than offset the gains if this type of analysis is followed consistently.

The oil-drilling illustration provides an opportunity to introduce two modifications that are receiving considerable attention in the literature. The first has to do with personal risk preferences. The expected monetary value does not take such personal attitudes toward risk into account and might lead to the wrong conclusion. For example, one oil driller might place a lower marginal utility on added income than on reduced income. A loss of \$50,000 might mean bankruptcy and disgrace; a gain of \$450,000 might be worth much less than it seems because of the driller's diminishing marginal utility of income. Thus, although the expected monetary value of drilling in the illustration just described is \$20,000, the expected utility might be negative. For a different decision maker with a greater fondness for risk, the chance of profits of \$450,000 might be most attractive, and the person might be willing to drill under even less favorable conditions. Before a sound decision is possible, the drillers must measure their marginal utility of income at various income levels. (The feasibility of such utility measurements is still a matter of controversy.) In large corporations, in which the utilities of thousands of stockholders might be involved, the expected monetary value would probably be an adequate measuring stick.[14]

The other modification is concerned with the value of additional information. The decision maker is not required to make a choice between drilling and not drilling on the basis of the probabilities with which he or she starts. The driller can collect additional information that will allow revision of his/her probabilities—for example, employing someone to make seismographic soundings. Figure 12–7 is a tree diagram showing alternative acts and the probabilities of various events. The seismographic recordings show whether or not subsurface structure usually associated with oil pools exists. If the structure does exist, the probability of dry holes is reduced.

We already know the value of no action is \$0. We know that the expected monetary value of drilling is \$20,000. A small amount of arith-

---

[14] Even if a firm uses expected monetary value as the criterion, it still might want to investigate the risk preferences of individual managers within the firm to determine whether those preferences can be reconciled with the objectives of the firm.

Figure 12–7
Tree diagram for oil-drilling problem

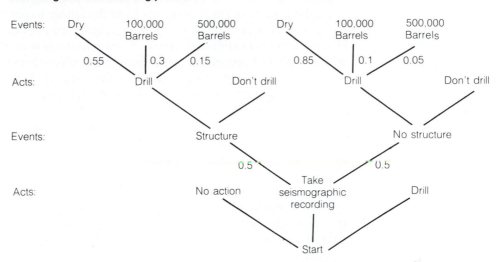

metic will show that the expected value with the seismographic sounding is $32,500 minus the cost of the sounding. Thus the value of the sounding is $12,500. It is in this way that the value of additional information can be determined.

The practicality of probability models

Some managers may have difficulty reconciling the requirements of practicality with the theoretical models under discussion. They may object that the models are too general and overly simple. One answer to the objection of overgenerality is that management must develop models to fit specific problems. The simple models are valuable in giving insight into a problem, but they must be adapted to each specific situation. Another reply is that analysis always requires simplification, for the human mind (even with the aid of computers) is incapable of dealing with all of the factors bearing on a problem. The whole history of science is one of deriving simple generalizations about a complex world. The whole history of management is one of focusing on the key variable, the manipulation of which will achieve practical results.

In some applications the usefulness of probability analysis is well established. Statistical quality control has shown its worth for several decades. Queuing models have produced savings that are known to be substantial. But there is a shortage of systematic, scientific studies that have evaluated the results of the great variety of models that have been proposed. Some researchers are careful to estimate in advance the dollar savings that will result from their proposals, but fewer take the trouble to present studies of the savings that have actually materialized. In many cases the absence of follow-up studies is a result of managerial secrecy —there is no reason to let one's competitors in on a good thing. In other cases the paucity of findings results from the failure to put the recommendations into effect, at least not in the original form. Human resistance to change, failures of educating the work force to the new methods, conflicts with established procedures, and many other obstacles stand in the way of application. Even more serious is the general failure of managers throughout industry to study the results of decisions systematically.

Sensitivity analysis is one way of bridging the gap between probability theory and the practical needs of management. Management can use the models to measure the sensitivity of the results to errors in the estimates. For example, it has been found that the present value of a chain of trucks is relatively insensitive to variations in the replacement period.[15] For one type of truck, a replacement period anywhere between 2.2 years and 4.4 years will produce approximately the same results in minimizing costs. In such a situation, errors in estimates are not likely to result in seriously unprofitable decisions. Similarly, the use of queuing theory in decisions on the number of work stations to install are not likely to be greatly affected by the usual errors of estimate that result from uncertainty. Formal models for determining such sensitivities of profits or costs to errors will help management focus attention on areas in which it will pay to accumulate more information to reduce the errors. Sensitivity analysis is merely one of a number of ways of making it easier for management to cope with uncertainty.

Summary

This chapter has presented only a few of the simplest models of combining probability and economic analysis. Probability analysis has been applied to a great variety of management problems: determining the optimal number of toll collectors at a toll bridge or tunnel, analyzing brand loyalty and brand switching, analyzing the work load on various employees, determining an economic sampling plan for the inspection of purchased parts or for manufactured parts, evaluating the results of industrial experimentation, and many others.

It should be clear that the formal analysis of probabilities has come first in cases in which a fairly steady flow of information is available. Applications are more common in production than in marketing, presumably because information from within the firm on production costs is more accessible and reliable than information on external consumer demands. Management seldom applies formal probability theory to relatively nonrepetitive decisions, such as plant expansions or the employment of new top executives.

---

[15] See Vernon L. Smith, "Economic Valuation Policies: An Evaluation," *Management Science,* October 1957.

It seems likely that managers will make greater use of probability and statistical analysis in the future, even under conditions of high uncertainty. The intuitions on which managers have relied so heavily in the past are susceptible to wide margins of error. It is too easy for managers to make errors in calculation when a complex chain of probabilities is at issue. The student who wishes to progress to more advanced work in managerial economics should obtain a thorough training in mathematics and statistics, for the models that are likely to be important in the future will require considerable sophistication in the use of quantitative methods. Mathematical and statistical methods are needed in addition to the applied economic theory stressed throughout this book.

CASES

Risk and uncertainty

Liggett & Myers

"Warning: The Surgeon General Has Determined That Cigarette Smoking Is Dangerous to Your Health." However, tobacco products continue to sell well, and Liggett & Myers Tobacco Co., Inc. is a leader in its field. Its products are sold within the domestic American economy as well as abroad. The company's cigarette brands include Lark, L&M, and Chesterfield. Pipe tobacco brands include such well-known names as Sterling Blend and Harmony; in addition, the company makes Red Man chewing tobacco.

As with many other large companies, Liggett & Myers has diversified into such products as J & B Rare Scotch Whiskey, pet food (Liv-A-Snaps), and certain cereal products. The firm employs about 7,000 people.

This company has all the benefits and problems associated with any firm that must pay federal excise taxes in the United States and abroad, liquor import duties, federal and state liquor taxes, and federal, state, and local income taxes.

This firm can be expected to operate at times under conditions of capital constraint. In other words, it makes investment decisions that, *en toto,* do not exceed a specified sum of money. Assume the company has $15 million to invest in its smoking and chewing tobacco operations and must decide between expanding its St. Louis, Missouri, and Toledo, Ohio, facilities versus allowing these two plants to continue as they are and building a new facility to be located in Owensboro, Kentucky. What analysis would they employ?

Assume modernization in St. Louis and Toledo, combined, would cost $15 million and this figure is the precise amount necessary to construct a new facility in Owensboro. Also assume that top management must decide upon one project or the other. Assume new construction is riskier from a net cash flow standpoint in the immediate short run than is expansion of existing facilities. Cost of capital figures are as follows: to the

Owensboro proposal, 16 percent; for expansion in St. Louis and Toledo, 12 percent. The project can break even with $2 million in net cash flows.

Exhibit 1 reveals the probability distribution and annual net cash flows assumed from the St. Louis and Toledo operation along with the probability distribution and annual net cash flows assumed for investment in Owensboro. Using the data assumed in this table, which of these two mutually exclusive investments should Liggett & Myers management decide upon? Assuming all factors constant other than those indicated:

1. Calculate the mean expectation, standard deviation and probability of loss for each project.
2. Determine the present value of the net cash flows for each project.
3. Calculate the net present value (NPV) of the net cash flows for each project.
4. Calculate the internal rate of return (IRR) for each project.
5. Accept the investment that has the highest NPV and/or IRR consistent with a low probability of loss. Explain your work fully.

Exhibit 1
Tobacco company probability distribution of net cash flows, by location

(1)	(2)	(3)
	Probability	**Net cash flows**
Location	**distribution**	**($ millions)**
St. Louis and	.10	$2.0
Toledo	.15	2.5
	.25	3.0
	.25	3.5
	.15	4.0
	.10	4.5
	1.00	
Owensboro	.50	$3.0
	.20	3.5
	.15	4.0
	.10	4.5
	.05	5.0
	—	5.5
	1.00	

The uncertain director

In December 1981, Pete Karcheck agreed to become a director of the Madusa Barber and Beauty Supply Company, which is located in a northeastern suburb of Baltimore, Maryland. He was a cousin of three majority stockholders in the company—Sarah Captain, the company vice president, and her sister and brother, both of whom were inactive. Karcheck understood that one of his responsibilities was to represent the interests of these stockholders.

Background   The Madusa Barber & Beauty Supply Company was founded in 1931 by Bob Captain, father of the three major stockholders just mentioned. The company engaged in supplying hair and beauty products of a high quality. The company had a citywide reputation for fine service, dependability, and strong managerial ethics. The firm did considerable work for local high schools and colleges. In addition, it serviced one professional football team. Its main customers were barber shops and beauty salons, whose owner-operators would drive to Madusa's warehouse to purchase their towels, hair dyes and sprays, and similar products. The firm never reached a large size; maximum employment was 30.

Bob Captain maintained several policies that undoubtedly limited the profits of the firm. He refused to deliver anything, anywhere, even though opportunities to do so were numerous. He tried to maintain employment for most of his employees during the Depression of the 1930s despite the low level of business, a fact that weakened the financial structure of the company at the start.

Upon Bob Captain's death in 1977, his daughter Sarah Captain took over management of the company as president. It was her intention to serve as president until she could find a candidate with more industry experience than she had at the time. She was unable to find a successor until 1979. The company was not particularly profitable during her presidency.

In October 1979, Sarah Captain succeeded in employing a new president, Richard Questel, who was thoroughly familiar with the industry. Questel received a salary and was to share in the company profits on a prearranged basis. One of Questel's first acts was to sign a contract with a junior college near Baltimore, resulting in a 40–50 percent increase in sales (see Exhibit 1).

In 1981 when Peter Karcheck became a director, the firm was still located in an antiquated four-story building not entirely suited to clean, modern inventory-handling techniques. The building had been largely written off—most of the balance sheet item "Building and building improvements" represented land and a new elevator installed in conformance with safety requirements. The building was located near the center of the city and was undoubtedly worth more than $40,000 only because of its location.

Developments in 1980, 1981, and 1982   In spite of the improvement in profits from 1979 to 1980 (see Exhibit 1), the company prospects did not appear favorable to Karcheck. He found that a serious difference had arisen between Questel, the president, and the vice president, Sarah Captain. Captain believed that Questel was not living up to certain agreements made orally when he was employed and that he was not carrying out some of the long-standing policies of the firm. Furthermore, she

Exhibit 1

MADUSA BARBER AND BEAUTY SUPPLY COMPANY
Comparative Profit and Loss Statement for the Years Ended September 30,
1979, 1980, 1981 and the First Six Months of 1982

	1979		1980		1981		For the 6 months ended March 31, 1982	
	Amount	Percent to net sales	Amount	Percent to net sales	Amount	Percent to net sales	Amount	Percent to net sales
Net sales:								
Junior College	$ 0	0%	$ 64,712	27.55%	$100,058	36.60%	$ 25,530	20.08%
Other	174,625	100.00	170,141	72.45	173,306	63.40	101,594	79.92
Total net sales	174,625	100.00	234,853	100.00	273,364	100.00	127,124	100.00
Cost of sales:								
Materials cost	72,228	41.36	87,591	37.30	102,677	37.56	50,867	40.01
Change in work in process	(508)	(0.29)	(735)	(0.31)	46	0.02	(1,039)	(0.82)
Direct department expenses	2,030	1.16	4,552	1.94	4,618	1.69	2,664	2.10
Wages—direct	44,970	25.75	61,823	26.32	64,866	23.73	32,074	25.23
Wages—indirect	15,266	8.74	14,244	6.07	15,383	5.63	7,454	5.86
Wages—maintenance	3,449	1.98	3,234	1.37	3,469	1.27	1,878	1.48
Spoilage	1,155	0.66	2,409	1.03	1,794	0.66	720	0.57
Payroll taxes	1,594	0.91	2,043	0.86	2,356	0.86	895	0.70
Power and light	1,256	0.72	1,108	0.47	1,141	0.42	624	0.49
Insurance—general	699	0.40	765	0.33	278	0.10	—	—
Water	81	0.05	130	0.06	105	0.04	36	0.03
Fuel	747	0.43	1,097	0.47	991	0.36	870	0.68
Building maintenance	460	0.26	1,377	0.59	833	0.30	147	0.12
Depreciation—building	655	0.38	655	0.28	655	0.24	480	0.38
Depreciation—machinery	5,015	2.87	5,256	2.23	6,124	2.23	3,045	2.40
Total cost of sales	149,097	85.38	185,550	79.01	205,336	75.11	100,715	79.23
Gross profit	25,528	14.62	49,303	20.99	68,028	24.89	26,409	20.77
Expenses:								
Administrative, general	22,339⎫		25,896⎫		31,382⎫		13,388⎫	
Selling	12,295⎭	19.84	12,807⎭	16.48	19,570⎭	18.64	11,450⎭	19.54
Operating profit (loss)	(9,106)	(5.22)	10,600	4.51	17,075	6.25	1,571	1.23
Other income	1,640	0.94	8,999	3.83	1,377	0.50	533	0.42
Total	(7,466)	(4.28)	19,599	8.34	18,452	6.75	2,104	1.65
Other deductions	+1.748	+1.00	−2,071	−0.88	−2,068	−0.75	−913	−0.71
Profit (loss) before provision for taxes on income	(9,214)	(5.28)	17,528	7.46	16,384	6.00	1,191	0.94
Provision for taxes—estimated	0	0	−2,561	−1.09	−5,356	−1.96	−389	−0.31
Net profit (loss)	$ (9,214)	(5.28)%	$ 14,966	6.37%	$ 11,028	4.04%	$ 802	0.63%

believed that he was limiting her authority to much narrower confines than was originally intended. Questel apparently believed that Captain was interfering with his management of the business and that she was cutting across organizational channels. There was evidence of the formation of factions at lower levels in the firm.

The board of directors met once a month. In 1981 and 1982, it consisted of five members: Questel, Karcheck, two members who represented the Industrial Foundation (which held mortgage bonds in the company), and

Whalen (a minority stockholder). Sarah Captain preferred not to hold a position as a director, but she attended meetings. The majority of the directors appeared to be satisfied with the new presidency, partly because of the improved profit position, which offered greater protection to the creditors.

The approximate division of the common stock in the company was as follows:

Sarah Captain	25%
Sarah's sister	18
Sarah's brother	17
Questel	10
Whalen	20
Others	10

The company had paid no dividends to the stockholders for more than 10 years when in late 1981 the board voted a dividend of $1 per share. Karcheck had at first favored a larger dividend but was convinced that this would be unwise after examining a cash budget for the near future. The payments due on the mortgage, the accrued taxes, the bonus due the president, and other obligations seemed to preclude a larger dividend at that time.

Captain had always worked at a low salary, both as president and vice president. In 1982, the board approved an increase in her salary from $23,500 to $25,000. She had felt an obligation to her family to keep her father's business going. She also felt the same responsibility to the company employees that her father had exhibited in earlier years. Besides, she thought keeping her salary low might discourage other workers from pushing for higher wages and/or salaries. In addition to salary, she had an unlimited expense account and the possibility of dividends.

The situation in 1982 Karcheck became increasingly concerned with the company's situation as the year 1982 passed. The profit position had deteriorated after 1981. The company appeared to be too dependent on a single customer, the junior college, and sales to that customer had showed evidence of declining early in 1982 (see Exhibit 1). The tension between the president and vice president continued, and disharmony spread through the company. For example, the superintendent spoke rudely to Captain and refused to let her "interfere" even when it seemed necessary to her to check on the progress of some orders for which she was responsible. Several employees resigned, including one who had displayed considerable promise as a manager.

Karcheck was concerned about several possibilities facing the company: (1) losing the junior college dormitory business and the resulting loss of profits, (2) declines in other sales, (3) resignation of the president, which would probably mean loss of the junior college business; and (4) greater inefficiency and higher costs caused by internal friction. Karcheck believed that most of the stockholders had long before assumed that their stock was almost worthless, and there was a possibility that Questel (who owned about 10 percent of the stock) might eventually be able to buy up a majority interest at low prices.

Several alternatives occurred to Karcheck as he thought about the problems of the company:

1. The company might lower prices to get fuller use of its idle capacity and labor force. Karcheck suspected that a high proportion of the costs were fixed, especially wage costs. Beauty supply firms did not normally hire and fire workers as business increased and decreased; they found it necessary to maintain the small work force during the lulls, which resulted in idle labor during a substantial part of the year.

2. The company might raise prices to improve its margins, though Karcheck noted that there were at least 50 competitors in the city, some of whom might win customers away if prices were raised.

3. The company might invest in improved equipment in order to cut costs. Karcheck knew little about warehouse equipment and even less about computerized inventory control procedures.

4. There was a 75 percent chance the company would build or lease a new one-floor plant, which would result in 20 percent lower handling costs. Karcheck did not know what this building would cost, but he learned from an acquaintance in the supply business that simply moving and rewiring certain equipment might cost $60,000.

5. There was a 50–50 chance the company would add to its sales force, which consisted in 1982 of the part-time efforts of the president and the vice president and the efforts of the sales manager. The sales manager was paid a 10 percent commission on sales.

Karcheck was not completely satisfied with any of these alternatives. But he believed that inaction could result in complete failure for the company.

Exhibit 2 presents a comparative balance sheet for the years 1980 through 1982.

1. Do the profit and loss statements in Exhibit 1 show the economic profits of the firm? Do they reflect the full opportunity costs? Explain.
2. Break the expenses in Exhibit 1 into fixed and variable categories. (It may be necessary to split some categories. It will be necessary to use rough judgments in some of the separation of costs.)
3. What is the ratio of incremental cost to revenue (sales) according to your fixed-variable cost breakdown? What is the significance of this fact?
4. Does the capital stock and surplus category on the balance sheet show the economic worth of the firm? Explain.

Exhibit 2

MADUSA BARBER AND BEAUTY SUPPLY COMPANY
Comparative Balance Sheet

Assets	Year ending March 31		
	1980	1981	1982
Current assets:			
Cash	$ 15,028	$ 19,073	$ 4,152
Accounts receivable	16,188	18,467	29,995
Inventories:			
Materials	10,598	10,361	9,682
Other goods	329	537	189
Supplies	2,038	1,041	1,962
Materials in process	4,329	5,183	5,322
Total current assets	48,511	54,662	51,302
Other:			
Cash surrender value—life insurance (pledged)	4,518	4,750	4,750
Accounts receivable—officers and employees	119	739	44
Claim for refund of federal income taxes	—	892	892
Total other	4,637	6,381	5,686
Property, plant, and equipment (mortgaged):			
Building and building improvements	23,637	24,291	24,291
Machinery and equipment	121,285	118,916	119,168
Delivery equipment	53	53	53
Office furniture and fixtures	6,544	6,667	6,707
Total depreciable assets	151,517	149,927	150,219
Less reserve for depreciation	104,818	111,491	115,161
	46,699	38,436	35,059
Land	9,115	9,115	9,115
Deferred charges	2,623	1,561	1,643
	$111,586	$110,155	$102,805

Liabilities and capital			
Current liabilities:			
Notes payable (due within one year)			
Industrial Foundation	$ 3,000	$ 3,000	$ 3,000
For equipment purchased	7,400	3,125	2,192
Accounts payable	21,310	20,534	21,062
Accrued expenses	1,084	1,363	1,861
Provision for taxes on income—estimated	2,688	5,523	401
Provision for bonuses—estimated	—	—	433
Total current liabilities	35,482	33,545	28,950
Deferred indebtedness:			
Mortgage notes payable maturing subsequent to September 30, 1980			
Industrial Foundation	17,000	12,750	10,500
For equipment purchased	3,200	—	—
Founders, Inc.	—	806	—
Capital stock and surplus:			
Common stock authorized and issued (500 shares—no par value)	48,480	48,480	48,480
Surplus	7,423	14,573	14,875
	$111,586	$110,155	$102,805

5. What is the major issue in this case? (Beware of ignoring issues that are not listed in the case.)
6. Sarah Captain continued to insist on the policy of refusing to deliver products. Do you agree with her? Why or why not?
7. What action should Karcheck recommend?

PROBLEMS
Risk and uncertainty

12–1   The general sales manager of a Canadian wine merchant is considering opening a territory somewhere in Alberta. His marketing research people claim monthly sales of about 400 cases, on average, of the numerous wines handled by the firm could be achieved anywhere in Canada. These sales estimates are normally distributed and have a standard deviation of 200 cases. In the provinces of Saskatchewan, Manitoba, or British Columbia, what is the probability that a randomly selected city would have sales of less than 100 cases per month? Draw a figure depicting an understanding of your answer. (Hint: Use "The Area under the Normal Curve" in the Appendix).

12–2   If the marketing research people to whom reference is made in problem 12–1 are correct with their sales estimates, what is the probability of randomly selecting a city in the province of Alberta and selling more than 600 cases of wine in that city in a given month? Draw a graph or figure depicting an understanding of the answer.

12–3   Attorney Pearl Barker has been asked by the New Brunswick, New Jersey, Board of Education to negotiate a contract with its teachers union. The negotiations could be consummated very quickly or could drag on for weeks. She can have a fixed price or a cost–plus fixed-fee contract. Net of all costs to her, Barker thinks there is a 50 percent chance of making $12,000, a 30 percent chance of making $18,000, and a 20 percent chance of making $20,000 if she accepts the fixed-price contract. These differences in expected returns are based upon her estimates of the number of negotiation sessions necessary to obtain a contract. All estimates are based primarily on her previous negotiating experiences in other school districts.

Under the cost–plus fixed-fee arrangement Barker thinks there is a 50 percent chance of making $10,500; a 30 percent chance of making $16,000; and, a 20 percent chance of making $18,000.

How much money could Barker earn (*a*) under the fixed-rate contract? (*b*) under the cost-plus contract? Use a decision tree to explain your answer.

Which contract should Barker select? Why?

12–4   Under what circumstances is a business decision made under conditions of risk or uncertainty?

12–5   If probabilities of success versus failure of a certain business decision are thought to exist, can these probabilities be improved upon and, if so, how?

12–6   During his term of office, a U.S. senator from Ohio has supported antibusiness legislation 90 percent of the time when the President was a Democrat, and 60 percent of the time when the President was a Republican. Suppose there is a 50 percent chance that a Republican will win the next presidential election. The public relations department of United States Steel is interested in knowing how this senator will vote on the MX missile. Members of the department believe that rejection of the missile would be harmful to business. What is the probability of this senator supporting antibusiness legislation? How uncertain of this senator's vote do you think U.S. Steel executives should be?

Selected references

Abel, Andrew B. "Empirical Investment Equations: An Integrative Framework." *Carnegie-Rochester Conference Series on Public Policy* 12 (Spring 1980), pp. 39–91.

Birch, Eleanor M., and Calvin D. Siebert. "Uncertainty, Permanent Demand, and Investment Behavior." *American Economic Review* 66, no. 1 (March 1976), pp. 15–27.

Coyne, Thomas J. "Electric Utility Profitability in Ohio (When Risk Is Compared with Reward)." *Public Utilities Fortnightly* 110, no. 6 (1982), pp. 44–48.

Doherty, Neil A. "Is Rate Classification Profitable?" *Journal of Risk & Insurance* 48, no. 2 (June 1981), pp. 286–95.

Dowell, Richard S. "The Distribution of Occupational Asset Risk." *Southern Economic Journal* 47, no. 2 (October 1980), pp. 463–76.

Hilliard, Jimmy E. "Asset Pricing under a Subset of Linear Risk Tolerance Functions and Log-Normal Market Returns." *Journal of Financial & Quantitative Analysis* 15, no. 5 (December 1980), pp. 1041–61.

Lee, Sang M. "Decision Analysis through Goal Programming." *Decision Sciences* 2 (April 1971).

Miline, Frank. "Borrowing, Short-Sales, Consumer Default, and the Creation of New Assets." *Journal of Financial & Quantitative Analysis* 14, no. 2 (June 1979), pp. 255–73.

Mullins, David W., Jr. "Does the Capital Asset Pricing Model Work?" *Harvard Business Review* 60, no. 1 (January-February 1982), pp. 105–114.

Rappaport, Alfred. "Sensitivity Analysis in Decision Making." *Accounting Review,* July 1967.

Reinhardt, U. E. "Break-Even Analysis for Lockheed's Tri Star: An Application of Financial Theory." *Journal of Finance* 28, no. 4 (September 1973), pp. 821–38.*

Wu, C. C. "Price-Output Uncertainty and Allocative Efficiency: An Empirical Study of Small-Scale Farms." *The Review of Economics & Statistics* 61, no. 2 (May 1979), pp. 228–33.

---

* This article is included in Thomas J. Coyne, *Readings in Managerial Economics,* 3d ed. (Plano, Tex.: Business Publications, 1981).

6

Forecasting, corporate strategy, and long-range planning

C H A P T E R

13
Forecasting

The forecasting challenge

Some practicing business economists spend approximately 60 percent of their time forecasting. Agreement is not commonplace among these forecasters about the relative merits of different methodological approaches to forecasting problems. However, there are two factors about which most economists agree: (1) Economic forecasts are almost always wrong. (2) Even when a forecast is reasonably accurate, more often than not, it may be correct for reasons other than those related by the forecaster. This chapter explains some of the more common approaches to economic forecasting and provides an insight into each method.

Forecasting changes in the economy is about as hazardous an undertaking as forecasting changes in the weather. Nonetheless, economic forecasts, even when not as accurate as one would like, are crucially important to planning within the firm.

No forecasting technique stands alone. One or more techniques are used in conjunction with other methods. This systematic marshalling of methods is not obvious to the uninitiated who read often of a general business condition forecasting method and assume, wrongly, that this method is the one used for arriving at a specific set of conclusions. The real world does not operate that way. One must be careful, therefore, not to expect too much from any one approach to the forecasting problem—some cynics have come to expect nothing of any method.

The objective of this chapter is not to produce a sophisticated general business forecaster but to provide a survey of commonly used forecasting methods that will be helpful in evaluation and application of forecasts made by others. Few businesses make their own general business forecasts. On the other hand, many managers do make forecasts of demands for particular products that are partially based upon business conditions analyses carried out by others.

564

Forecasters may start with a forecast of the smallest conceivable unit within a firm—say, a department or a division. Next, they may forecast activities of the plant in which that department is located, then forecast for all plants in the firm, all firms in the industry, all industries in the economy and, subsequently, forecast aggregate domestic economic activity. On the other hand, the forecaster could start with a broad measure of economic activity—say, gross national product. She/he could next calculate the forecast for an industry or a series of industries and work downward into the smaller components of the economy (into the firm, for example). The approach used in this chapter is to start with the broader approach, a presentation of gross national product (GNP).

Starting as we are with statistics and approaches unique to calculation and interpretation of the nation's GNP, one is tempted to assume the price and output behavior of the typical firm can be explained in full or in part by GNP. Nothing could be further from the truth. Gross national product, by definition, is the total dollar value of all goods and services produced in an economy during a given period of time. For about 60 years, the U.S. Department of Commerce, through its Office of Business Economics (OBE), has produced a publication entitled *Survey of Current Business*. This publication is considered by many forecasters to be important reading for each month. It contains much of the statistical data needed for application of the analytical tools used by the forecaster.

One shortcoming of GNP is that it fails to calculate what one might call gross social product. At this writing, the economics profession has not accepted a technique or method of analysis, along the lines of calculation of GNP, that quantifies the quality of life within the economy. Consequently, practicing business economists are unable to forecast whether changes in GNP, in real or in nominal terms, are capable of contributing to the betterment of society. Of greater importance to our discussion here is the inability of forecasts to determine whether changes in GNP will always relate well to changes of specific variables within a particular company. Wouldn't it be nice, for example, if the forecaster could relate anticipated changes in GNP to anticipated changes in the quality of life and determine whether a firm or industry would be better off in quality as well as in quantity if its rate of employment, output, and/or income could be adjusted by some specified rate?

Not only do the national income accounts fail to calculate gross social product, but some observers say they have not provided the kinds of statistics needed for better explanation of the input-output coefficients needed for microeconomic analysis, planning, and forecasting.

A look to the future

Generally, six approaches to economic forecasting may be cited:

1. Leading, lagging, coincident indicator approach.

2. Surveys of plans to spend or save, consensus forecasts, and so on.
3. Simple extrapolation of trend lines.
4. Mathematical and/or econometric models.
5. Input-output analysis.
6. Judgmental methods.

Judgmental method

The last method of economic forecasting mentioned is the one with which people have the most difficulty. It may be the method possessing the least academic respectability but may also be the most heavily used in practice. The method is relied upon heavily for decision-making purposes by a large number of corporate executives who have had just enough background in economics and finance to have picked up some of the jargon. Academic economists look down from their ivory towers at users of this approach, considering it to be a horrible example of forecasting. They consider the approach of use primarily to an imaginary forecaster who takes "some pleasure in thinking of himself as a model builder."[1] This person "expresses his outlook judgments in the form of a gross national product breakdown. But his would be strictly a laundry list style of forecasting. He would simply go down the sector list, making up forward estimates, one by one, by some intuitive process out of whatever mix of past data, current gossip, and recent comments in the business press he happened to have at hand."[2] This kind of forecaster would ignore the National Bureau of Economic Research leading indicators, would avoid economic surveys, might not even extrapolate a trend line, and abhors the idea of having to learn enough arithmetic (mathematics?) for implementation of even the simplest form of econometric model.

Academicians are probably too critical of judgmental approaches to economic forecasting. It works, at times better than any other method; and a business executive is not about to exchange a workable, usable method of economic forecasting for a simulation model, or something similar, when the simulation and/or econometric methods have not been as successful for that particular firm as has reliance upon judgmental methods.

Aggregative data: GNP and national income

Gross national product (GNP) by the product approach is the summation of: (1) personal consumption expenditures, (2) gross private domestic investment, (3) government purchases of goods and services, and (4) net exports; therefore, one measure of the value of the nation's output is

---

[1] John P. Lewis, "Short-Term General Business Conditions Forecasting: Some Comments on Method," *Journal of Business,* October 1962, p. 354.
[2] Ibid.

GNP. In addition, the total dollar cost of factor inputs to the economy may be determined in what is known as national income statistics. The Office of Business Economics provides these data.

National income is the summation of (1) wages, salaries, and supplements; (2) the income of unincorporated businesses and their inventory valuation adjustment; (3) rental income; (4) interest income; and (5) corporate income and inventory valuation adjustment. Gross national product for the United States as of December 31, 1980, 1981, with 1982, with projections for 1983, 1984, and 1985 are revealed in Table 13–1.

The table reveals that approximately 63 percent of GNP is spent by households for durables, nondurables, and services, whereas about 14 or 15 percent is accounted for by gross private domestic investment and 20 percent of the total goes to the combined bureaus of the federal, state, and local governments. Net exports account for about 2 or 3 percent of GNP. Numerous assumptions must be made for some of these data. GNP statistics in Table 13–1 for the years 1983, 1984, and 1985, for example, assume yearly percentage changes in nominal consumer expenditures of about 2.5 in 1983; 4.5 in 1984; and 3.5 in 1985. Similar judgments have been made for each year for all other variables in the table.

Table 13–1
Gross national products: Product approach ($ billions)

	1980	1981	1982	1983	1984	1985
GNP (1972 dollars)	$1,474	$1,503	$1,476	$1,510	$1,580	$1,639
Consumer expenditures	931	948	957	987	1,026	1,052
Durables	137	140	139	149	163	165
Nondurables	356	362	365	373	382	391
Services	438	445	453	465	481	496
Gross private domestic investment	208	226	197	208	232	252
Producers durable equipment	118	120	112	106	114	126
Nonresidential construction	49	52	53	49	49	51
Residential construction	47	45	40	48	58	61
Inventory change	−5	9	−9	6	12	13
Net exports	51	42	30	19	21	25
Government purchases of goods and services	285	287	291	296	300	310
Federal	107	110	116	120	122	129
State and Local	178	177	175	176	179	181
GNP (current dollars)	$2,633	$2,938	$3,058	$3,280	$3,589	$3,913

Keynes' general theory of employment

Of use to forecasters is the economic impact on real employment, output and income of changes in personal consumption allowances; changes in business spending; and changes in federal, state, and local government spending. Insofar as impact upon the aggregate economy is concerned, government and business spending are often the same. It does not matter to the economy whether the U.S. Government buys a blue, four-door Chevrolet for the Government Accounting Office in St. Louis or whether that same blue car is purchased by United States Steel as part of its sales fleet in San Francisco. The same quantity of steel, paint, plastic, rubber, glass, aluminum, tin, and so on, is involved. Also, employment in the firms and industries that manufacture these inputs is not different. Therefore, Keynes' theory of employment treats government and investment spending as synonymous insofar as economic impact is concerned. This Keynesian theory has been reduced to one side of one sheet of paper by Dillard. Once mastered, it is very useful in judgmental forecasting.[3] The theory is presented in Figure 13–1, which describes the causal relationships in existence within the economy. The theory also helps analysts to think more deeply than they otherwise might about interactions upon and changes in such variables as money, interest rate,

Figure 13–1
Keynesian economics: Casual relationships*

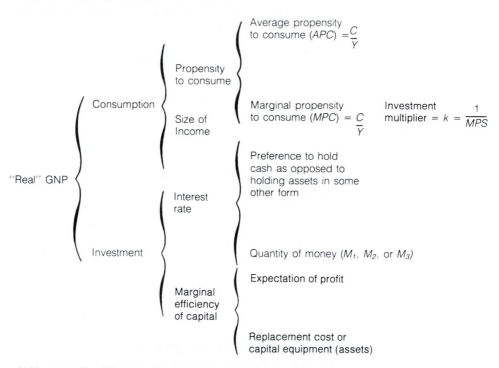

* *C* is consumption; *Y* is income, and *MPS* is marginal propensity to save.

---

[3] J. Dudley Dillard, *The Economics of John Maynard Keynes* (Englewood Cliffs, N.J.: Prentice-Hall, 1947), p. 49.

income, propensities to consume and save, expectations of profit, and replacement costs of necessary capital assets.

Figure 13–1 explains that real GNP is dependent upon effective demand, which by definition, is one's readiness, willingness and, ability to buy at prevailing prices those goods offered for sale within the economy. Effective demand is affected, adversely or otherwise, by (1) the propensity to consume and (2) the size of the economy's total dollar investment. Employment depends, therefore, on investment which, in turn, is dependent upon the rate of interest firms must pay when they borrow money and the efficient use to which that money is put, the so-called marginal efficiency of capital.

Interest rates represent prices charged by financial intermediaries (i.e., banks) for the use of money. These rates are administered, fixed at times in the short run, by the actions of the Federal Reserve System.

Opportunistic forecasting with a GNP model

The basic assumption in GNP model building is that demand governs business activity. If total spending increases, business activity increases. The problem of forecasting is thus one of forecasting components of aggregate demand. For this purpose it is desirable to break GNP into several parts, each of which represents an important segment of total expenditure as presented in Table 13–1. This basic assumption of changes in demand causing change in real output differs significantly with the supply-side economics of President Reagan's earlier views. The presentation here, however, is a time-tested, theoretically sound approach that should be mastered by the student.

The time spent on analyzing a component may not be proportional to its dollar magnitude; inventory investment and consumption of durable consumer goods are more volatile than other components and require attention out of proportion to their share of the total.

The problem of consistency   The procedure is to forecast the components of the GNP and to sum. But because the components are interdependent, cross-checking and adjustment are required. The level of consumption, for example, depends in large part on the level of the gross national product itself. Purchases of plant and equipment depend on many factors, but among them is the rate at which the GNP is increasing and the extent to which demand is exerting pressure on capacity. Inventory investment depends on the rate of current purchases as well as on the accuracy with which this rate has been anticipated. Net foreign investment depends in part on the rate of growth in the domestic gross national product as compared with that of foreign national products.

It might be objected that the problem is circular and insoluble. If each component depends on others or on the total, where does one start? Mathematicians would find no difficulty with such a situation; they could construct a series of simultaneous equations to reflect the kinds of inter-dependence under discussion. In fact, this is exactly what economists do. Even without the system of equations, it is possible to make adjustments in one component to bring it in line with a forecast of another and to make a series of adjustments of this sort until the forecast as a whole appears consistent.

Federal government expenditures   The forecaster usually starts with es-timates of government expenditures because they are more likely to be independent of other components. Although it is true that the government sometimes adjusts some spending according to the level of business activ-ity, most of it is planned in advance; the forecaster can make use of the budgets, proposed legislation, and presidential messages that indicate the direction of federal spending.

The simplest procedure is to start with the latest figure on federal government expenditures and to concentrate on probable increases or decreases from that figure. What are the sources of information about future government spending? The President's budget message and state of the union message early in the year provide information on what he proposes for the next budget period. The Bureau of the Budget publishes more detailed reports on spending plans. Newspapers and weeklies pro-vide information on how the President's program is progressing in Con-gress and on other changes in expenditure that may emanate from Congress. Commentators try to evaluate the probabilities of certain pro-grams succeeding in getting through the legislative mill and others' fail-ing. Again, it should be stressed that the forecast must be in terms of spending on current production. Appropriation of funds by Congress does not assure that those funds will be spent in the period under consid-eration.

Forecasting federal government spending requires both political and economic astuteness. One major difficulty is in predicting shifts in mili-tary requirements. But, as demonstrated in the Vietnam War, even under crisis conditions shifts in military spending may be slow. The Department of Commerce publication *Defense Indicators* is a useful source of data about military spending.

State and local government expenditures   The task of aggregating the expenditures of thousands of separate state and local governments is beyond the resources of most forecasters. The simplest solution is to deal with probable changes in the aggregate. Since World War II, state and local government expenditures have exhibited an upward trend so consis-tent from year to year that many forecasters simply project the trend into the future. Extrapolation of trends is normally a risky venture; structural forces that accounted for the trend in the past may not endure in the future. In the case of state and local government expenditures, however, continually increasing demands for such public programs as education and police services appear to ensure continued annual increments in spending. The increments in state and local spending tend to grow over the years—a trend that should be taken into account in the forecast.

Expenditures on plant and equipment If one knew nothing about recent levels of spending, forecasting expenditures on new plant and equipment would be extremely hazardous. It is simpler to forecast changes in the total based on knowledge of current attitudes, plans, and conditions. However, it is vital to remember that this category of spending has gone through rather dramatic fluctuations in the past. Investment is based on expectations of future sales and profits, and expectations are prone to change sharply. Investment is also sensitive to rates of change in other categories of spending and in current or expected pressures on capacity. Fortunately, several surveys of business plans for investment are available to assist the forecaster.

The forecaster of investment must be aware of a wide variety of influences. Current profits and stock prices no doubt influence future expectations. Current monetary conditions partially determine the ability of firms to finance expansions (although heavy reliance on plowed-back earnings blunts this influence). Relationships of production rates to designed capacities (operating ratios) help form expectations of the need for a new plant and equipment. The rate of technological change determines obsolescence of old equipment and thus influences the rate of replacement. It is no use pretending that analysis of such diverse influences is easy, and a high degree of accuracy is not to be expected. Fortunately, the supply of data for investment forecasting is constantly increasing. The *Survey of Current Business,* for example, now publishes data on anticipated changes in sales, on manufacturers' evaluations of their capacity, and on the carryover of plant and equipment projects.

Residential construction An evaluation of monetary conditions—the availability of credit, interest rates, and the terms on which mortgage loans may be obtained—is more important in forecasting residential construction than in forecasting for any other sector. Changes in financial conditions lead to changes in construction expenditures. The size of down payments required in purchasing new homes and the length of time for repayment influences the magnitude of construction. Pegged Federal Housing Administration (FHA) and Veterans Administration (VA) interest rates have been major factors in fluctuations in new housing. When those rates are far below current market rates, availability of FHA and VA loans diminishes sharply. Privately financed housing starts have been more stable. Among the other influences are the following: the level of vacancies in homes and apartments already built; the rate of formation of new families, which depends on the age structure of the population; and consumer attitudes toward future income prospects.

The forecaster of residential construction should give attention to several statistical series. The F. W. Dodge Corporation publishes data on construction contract awards, which give an idea of prospective building about five months in the future. Data are also available in the *Surveys of Current Business* and elsewhere on housing starts and on construction already under way. Since it takes a number of months to complete buildings that have been started, figures on housing starts provide some insight into the future level of construction. The problem of seasonal variations is a handicap in interpretation of data on construction awards and starts. A rise in one of these indexes may merely reflect the usual spring and summer increase in building activity. It is desirable to correct data for seasonal variations, but the methods used for such corrections have difficulty when separating cyclical from seasonal influences.

Inventory investment   Inventory investment is highly volatile, sometimes rising to a positive $30 billion (annual rate) in prosperity and falling to a negative $25 billion in recession. Since World War II no other sector has had a greater influence in determining the pace of expansion or contraction in short-run business activity. The recession of the early 1980s was a so-called inventory adjustment.

One important influence on inventory investment is the ratio of inventory levels to sales. In short-run forecasting it is reasonable to assume that businesses intend to maintain a certain ratio of stocks to sales, or to production rates in the cases of raw materials and goods in process. Inventories below these levels are inadequate to meet production and customer requirements. Inventories above this level involve unnecessary interest, storage expenditures, and risks of obsolescence. Over long periods technological change and improvements in inventory management may permit changes in these ratios, but in short-run forecasting such trends can be ignored.

The level of inventory investment also depends on expectations of people in business. If they expect sales to increase, they will build up inventories, and vice versa. Thus, the forecasting of inventory investment must rest on an evaluation of business expectations, which in turn depends on expected changes in the other sectors. *Fortune* magazine and other publications attempt to evaluate inventory-sales ratios and sales expectations and to convert these into estimates of inventory changes.

Some forecasters find it useful to distinguish between voluntary and involuntary investment or disinvestment. Inventories may increase because businesses want them to take care of anticipated improved business. In such a case a present rise in inventory investment is a favorable indicator of future levels of investment. An increase in inventories may, however, result from a failure of sales to reach anticipated levels, in which case an eventual contraction of the inventory buildup may be expected as firms cut back their orders for replacements. Similarly, inventories may contract because of managers' planning or because of an unexpected increase in sales; the one cause has the opposite significance of the other. It is true that data on inventory investment do not reveal whether or not the investment or disinvestment is voluntary, but it is not difficult in practice to determine whether the present inventory expansion or contraction is one planned by business or, instead, one that is likely to experience a reversal in the near future.

The big problem in estimating inventory investment is timing. One may know that a present expansion of inventories is temporary but may be unable to specify exactly when the reversal will take place. One may be aware that a present inventory disinvestment results from a desire to bring stocks back in line with sales but may not know how long the correction will continue, especially if a continued decline in sales means a continued failure in the restoration of the desired ratio.

The excess of exports over imports The prospect for the excess of exports over imports is extremely complex, involving an evaluation of both the import and export situations, which requires an investigation of the progress of foreign economics as well as the domestic scene, international comparisons of price and wage changes, revisions in tariffs and other policies affecting trade, and the study of the markets for particular commodities important in international trade. Of particular concern to a forecaster in the 1980s are the value of the U.S. dollar abroad (i.e., exchange rates) and the attitudes of foreign governments toward allowing U.S. dollars to return home.

Such developments as oil price increases by the Organization of Petroleum Exporting Countries (OPEC) and the opening of trade with the Soviet Union and China have increased the importance of this sector in recent years. An understanding of international affairs would be helpful in analyzing the foreign trade sector.

Consumption The Keynesian tradition is to consider consumption to be relatively passive. If the main determinant of consumption is income, then the forecast of the other segments should lead to the required forecast of consumption. One need merely apply the multiplier theory, which says that given change in the other segments (investment and government spending) should result in an induced change in consumption because of the changes in income that result. We do not yet have a precise idea of the magnitude of the multiplier, although we are quite certain that it is less for decreases in nonconsumption spending than it is for increases in such spending.

The judgmental forecaster knows that when consumption or investment as defined in connection with Figure 13–1 increases, GNP will increase by an amount greater than the increased spending. When spending takes place, regardless of whether it originates as consumption or investment, new employment, output, and income follow. The increases in employment are associated with increases in income. It is out of this newly generated income that a certain amount of new consumption and new savings takes place. As the newly employed persons spend a portion of their newly earned income, additional investment becomes necessary and, literally, a self-reinforcing series of expenditures takes place, each creating an additional round of employment, output, and income.

Figure 13–1 reveals the investment multiplier to be the reciprocal of the marginal propensity to save. A comment with respect to this calculation is in order. All changes in income ($\triangle Y$) must represent 100 percent of themselves or, more simply, 1.0. Changes in income, by definition, may be accounted for only by changes in consumption—the marginal propensity to consume (MPC)—or changes in savings—the marginal propensity to save (MPS). In other words, out of changes in income, all monies that are not consumed must be saved.

It is generally thought that the marginal propensity to consume for most households in the domestic American economy is something less than the average propensity to consume (APC). For example, if the APC is 90 percent, the MPC may be 75 percent. The value of MPC is important because $\triangle Y$ minus MPC is equal to MPS. The reciprocal of MPS is the multiplier (k) in Figure 13–1.

The magnitude of future changes in income is thought to be affected by the size of the investment multiplier, k, where k is equal to the reciprocal of the marginal propensity to save. Symbolically this condition may be stated also as follows:

$$k = \frac{1}{1-b}$$

where b is the marginal propensity to consume (MPC). If MPC = .666666, the multiplier is 3; that is, a \$1 increase in spending raises the level of income by \$3. If MPC = .50, the multiplier is 2. If MPC = 0, the multiplier is 1. As indicated earlier, however, experience in the American economy reveals propensities to consume and save that result in investment multipliers greater than 1. Assuming the investment multiplier, k, to be 3, an exogenous change in spending—say, a federal government deficit approximating only \$70 billion could ultimately give rise to changes in GNP of three times \$70 billion, or \$210 billion.

The notion of a multiplier was an important component of Keynesian economic theory and remains today a matter of serious importance to the economic forecaster, judgmental and otherwise. As with many theories in economics, the concept is sound, but actual calculation of the multiplier presents problems for the forecaster. Investment multipliers are applicable to economic forecasts using aggregative-type data for the national economy and remain valid for regional, and smaller, geographical locations. Also, the probability is high that the magnitude of the multiplier remains fairly constant in the short run. Nevertheless, about the best one can do for implementation of this theory in empirical research is to acknowledge its existence and be careful not to claim too much for the results acquired by its application.

One simple rule that provides fairly accurate forecasts of consumption is as follows: In normal recoveries from mild recessions, the increase in consumption is approximately equal to the increase in non-consumption spending; in mild recessions, consumption remains at the pre-recession level or increases slightly. This rule requires modification for more severe recessions or depressions and for inflationary periods or periods when shortages are expected. In any case the forecaster should modify estimates for special influences on consumption in the period under study. In particular he or she should make a separate study of the demand for durable consumers' goods, which tends to be more volatile and more subject to special influences that will be discussed shortly.

A more sophisticated approach makes the forecast of consumption a part of the solution of at least two simultaneous equations that reflect the relations between disposable personal income and the GNP, between consumption and disposable personal income, and that might treat the increase or decrease in nonconsumption spending as an independent variable. This approach begins to move in the direction of the econometric models to be discussed shortly.

No one (and certainly not Keynes himself) ever really believed that forecasting of consumption was a simple matter of estimating income. The forecasting must contend with autonomous and induced changes in consumption. There is reason to believe that consumers' attitudes and expectations influence their expenditures, and a multitude of factors help determine spending on particular types of commodities and services.

The forecaster may forecast consumption of durable goods separately, for durable goods more than nondurables are subject to special influences. In fact, the careful forecaster will break durable goods into such subcomponents as purchases of automobiles, household appliances, and furniture. In forecasting consumption of durable consumer goods, one should take into account the present levels of installment debt. High debt may mean a reluctance of lenders to permit future increases in indebtedness and also a reluctance of consumers to obligate themselves further. One should also evaluate present holdings of consumer durables.

Individual components: Sources and suggestions   The sketch of gross national product model building presented so far provides a framework for the forecaster. Filling in the detail requires a knowledge of sources of information, supported by skills in using that information to the best effect. Table 13–2 lists some of the most common sources of data and indicates their uses.

Table 13–2
Sources and uses of key forecasting information

Component of GNP	Type of information	Source and date	Uses of the information
Federal government spending	President's budget message to Congress.	Newspapers carry summaries in January. Also published by government.	Provides the most important information on federal expenditures for the next fiscal year, starting on July 1. Is subject to revision by Congress.
	Summary of the budget message.	*The Budget in Brief* (government publication in January).	Presents a summary of the budget message.
	Review of the economic situation with emphasis on the federal budget.	President's *Economic Report* (government publication in late January).	Presents an interpretation of the budget and its economic implications.
	Review of the economic situation with emphasis on the federal budget.	*Midyear Budget Review* (government publication in August).	Presents a review of the federal spending program for the current fiscal year, reflecting congressional revisions of the budget.
	Reports on congressional action on presidential spending plans.	Newspapers and weekly magazines throughout the sessions of Congress.	Provides information on the success or failure of the President's program in Congress, as well as predictions of future plans both of the President and Congress.
State and local government spending	Data on the levels of state and local government spending in recent periods.	The national income accounts in the *Survey of Current Business* (monthly).	The usual procedure is to extrapolate the recent trend into the future, with possible revisions based on newspaper reports on expedited programs or on financial difficulties.
Investment in plant and equipment	Surveys of intentions to invest.	McGraw-Hill (*Business Week* in November); also Department of Commerce and SEC (*Survey of Current Business,* November, March, and other issues).	These surveys provide excellent information in business investment plans for the coming year (or quarter). The past record of these surveys is good for most periods.

Table 13–2 (continued)

Component of GNP	Type of information	Source and date	Uses of the information
	New orders for durable goods.	*Survey of Current Business* (monthly).	Since orders usually lead actual production and sales, this series provides suggestions on future changes in investment.
	Nonresidential construction contracts (F. W. Dodge Index).	*Survey of Current Business* (monthly) and *Business Conditions Digest* (monthly).	Since construction awards should normally lead actual construction, this series suggests potential changes in the building of factories, office buildings, stores, etc.
Residential construction	Family formation.	Intermittent projections by the Bureau of the Census.	Provides information of a key segment of the potential market for new housing.
	Residential construction contracts awarded or housing starts.	*Survey of Current Business* (monthly) and *Business Conditions Digest* (monthly).	Provides an indication of potential changes in housing construction before those changes take place.
	Mortgage terms and ease of securing loans (down payments, interest rates, monthly payments).	Newspapers provide intermittent reports. *Federal Reserve Bulletin* (monthly).	Information on the terms of FHA, VA, and regular mortgages indicates the financial restraints on the purchase of new homes.
	Vacancy rate.	Bureau of Labor Statistics.	Indicates the extent of saturation of the housing market.
	Home-building survey.	*Fortune* magazine (monthly).	Indicates developments in residential construction.
Inventory investment	Ratios of inventories to sales on the manufacturing, wholesaling, and retailing levels (requires computations involving series on inventories and series on sales).	*Survey of Current Business* (monthly).	Indicates whether inventories are high or low in relation to a "normal" ratio. Must be interpreted with caution in the light of recent changes in final sales and the attitude of business toward inventories.
	Manufacturers' inventory expectations.	*Survey of Current Business* (monthly).	Indicates extent to which businesses expect to expand or contract inventories.

Table 13–2 (*concluded*)

Component of GNP	Type of information	Source and date	Uses of the information
	Inventory surveys.	*Fortune magazine* (monthly).	On the basis of sales expectations and assumed inventory-sales ratios, estimates amount of inventory change.
Consumer durable goods	Surveys of consumers' intentions to spend and save (including intentions to buy automobiles).	Survey Research Center, University of Michigan and Federal Reserve Board. *Federal Reserve Bulletin* (quarterly).	Indicates intentions to purchase durable goods. There is considerable correlation between these intentions and actual purchases.
	Rate of housing construction.	*Survey of Current Business* (monthly).	The building of new houses has an important influence on sales of furniture and appliances.
	Installment credit outstanding (in relation to the disposable personal income).	*Federal Reserve Bulletin* (monthly).	A high level of installment credit already outstanding may mean a lower willingness to incur new debt or a lower willingness to lend.
	Buying-plan surveys.	National Industrial Conference Board *Business Record*.	Suggests potential changes in the purchase of consumer goods.
	Projected consumer outlays on durable goods and housing.	*Consumer Buying Indicators* (quarterly).	Covers surveys of plans of consumers to purchase automobiles, appliances, furniture, and housing.
Nondurable consumer goods and services	Regression lines relating the past consumption of nondurable goods and services to the past disposable personal income.	Past issues of the *Survey of Current Business* provide the necessary data. Special articles in the *Survey of Current Business* review findings on such relationships.	Past relationships to disposable personal income show considerable stability, though the rate of sales to income rises in recession.
Comprehensive collection of indicators	Charts covering most of the best-known indicators.	*Business Conditions Digest* (monthly).	A compact collection of charts covering indicators of income, production, prices, employment, and monetary conditions.

Some awkward problems   In using the gross national product model, the forecaster must face some difficulties mentioned here only briefly. The two most serious problems are those related to price changes and to induced effects of changes in one segment of the economy on other segments.

Forecasting would be much simpler if one could assume stability in prices. However, in some years the increase in the GNP in current dollars may be as much a result of inflation as of changes in real product. The forecaster should provide separate estimates of changes in production and changes in prices.

One simple procedure is to make an initial forecast using the framework already described, giving no attention to potential price changes but temporarily making the assumption of stable prices. The forecaster can then examine the implications of the initial forecast, making adjustments where necessary. If, for example, the initial forecast is one of a great increase in aggregate demand that will place considerable pressure on capacity, the forecaster may anticipate considerable inflation resulting from the competition for scarce resources. In any case the forecaster must take care in separating analysis in real terms from that in terms of current dollars. An extrapolation of past increases in state and local government spending that reflects both inflation and increases in volume does not make sense if one is forecasting only the physical increase in output.

As already noted, various segments of the GNP are interdependent. Forecasted changes for one segment may have important implications for another. The econometrician gets around the problem by using simultaneous equations reflecting these interdependencies. The forecaster using the more qualitative model under discussion must somehow make adjustments in the initial forecasts that will perform, at least roughly, the function served by the simultaneous equations. Suits provides a good (and simple) way of dealing with multiplier-accelerator effects.[4]

Checks for consistency   The final step in GNP model building is to check the various components for consistency. Among the questions that are appropriate are the following:

1. Is the forecast level of government expenditure consistent with the total forecast? If the overall forecast indicates heavy unemployment, a reduction in taxes or an increase in public works might be in prospect. If the overall forecast indicates inflationary pressures, an increase in taxes or curtailment of spending might be imminent.

2. Are the assumptions on the monetary sector consistent with the overall forecast? If the overall forecast indicates heavy unemployment, an easing of money by the Federal Reserve System may be imminent, with possible repercussions on residential construction or other sectors.

3. Are prospective profits consistent with other parts of the forecast? The forecasting of profits has not been discussed, but the thorough forecaster will check to see that prospective profits are in line with estimates of investments.

---

[4] Daniel B. Suits, *Principles of Economics* (New York: Harper & Row, 1970), pp. 193–209.

4. Is the level of personal saving consistent with the rest of the forecast? The forecast of personal saving has not been developed, although it is directly related to the forecast of consumption. A complete forecast would devote special attention to the savings forecast. Actual savings always equals actual investment. When the level of savings is thought to be too low, as in 1981 and 1982, it is cause for concern on the part of all economic forecasters.

5. What magnitude of government surplus or deficit is likely under the conditions indicated? Some forecasters pay particular attention to the prospective deficit or surplus. They believe that deficits or surpluses in the government sector are more important than the simple changes in public expenditures. If government spending is increasing, but tax collection is increasing even faster, the stimulating effect of expenditures will be much smaller than would be the case with taxation lagging behind spending. When government deficits are large, as in 1984, the managerial economist must determine the impact of such deficits on employment, output, income and, of course, price inflation.

Judgmental-type forecasters need to know some theory; conversely, some academic-type forecasters could use some business experience. "Theoretical types often intermingle with hard-nosed technicians," but not often enough to satisfy some business chiefs and, given a choice, the business experience is hard to beat. For example, officials at Exxon are quick to note "a person intuitive at macro-assessment is really important . . ."[5] A good judgmental forecaster is in demand.

Forecasting without macro models

Indicator forecasts

Just as one can obtain observed levels of GNP or national income over time, many other time-series of economic measurements are available. Some of these series have been found to have timing differences in relation to changes in general business activity. There is particular interest in those series with movements that precede (lead) changes in GNP. Searching for such series has been a major interest of the National Bureau of Economic Research, especially of Wesley C. Mitchell, Arthur Burns, Geoffrey Moore, and Julius Shiskin.[6]

The basic idea of the indicators approach is that certain types of measured behavior usually begin to slow *before* the general level of economic activity turns downward. If such a type of behavior also usually increases

---

[5] *Business Week,* April 28, 1975, p. 50.

[6] The National Bureau of Economic Research is a private nonprofit research organization with the object to "ascertain and to present to the public important economic facts and their interpretation in a scientific and impartial manner." The four individuals mentioned constitute the nucleus of the group at the national bureau, which has been studying business cycles for about 50 years.

before the level of economic activity turns upward, the data series measuring the behavior is called a *leading indicator*. It reaches a peak before GNP does, and it goes through a trough before GNP turns up. To the extent that such indicators are accurate, they may be useful in forecasting. Economists, politicians, and (perhaps) voters were concerned about the leading indicators during the election campaigns of 1984, when the indicators appeared to be forecasting an upturn in economic activity. Relationships of leading, lagging, and coincident indicators to the peak and trough of the business cycle are shown in Figure 13–2.

Economists at the National Bureau of Economic Research (NBER) have devoted much effort to the classification of large numbers of series into these general categories. Further, they have compiled lists of series easily accessible to the forecaster. A long list includes 88 U.S. series— 72 monthly and 16 quarterly. Of these, 36 can be classified as leading indicators, 25 roughly coincident, 11 lagging, and 16 unclassified by timing.[7] A short list is a subset of the long list and can include 25 U.S. series

Figure 13–2
Leading, lagging, and coincident indicators

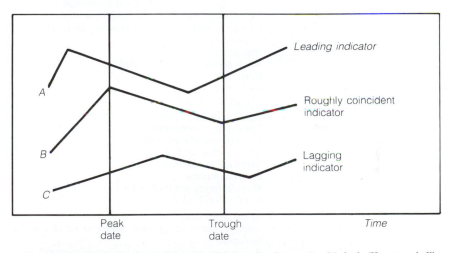

Source: Roger K. Chisholm and Gilbert R. Whitaker, Jr., *Forecasting Methods* (Homewood, Ill.: Richard D. Irwin, 1971), p. 42.

---

[7] In their book, *Indicators of Business Expansions and Contractions,* Geoffrey H. Moore and Julius Shiskin (New York: Columbia University Press for the National Bureau of Economic Research, 1967) briefly review previous efforts in classifying series and note that Mitchell and Burns studied nearly 500 monthly or quarterly series in preparing *Statistical Indicators of Cyclical Revivals,* Bulletin 69 (New York: National Bureau of Economic Research, 1938). They also report that Moore investigated about 800 such series in preparing his book, *Statistical Indicators of Cyclical Revivals and Recessions,* Occasional Paper 31 (New York: National Bureau of Economic Research, 1950).

—12 leading, 7 coincident, and 6 lagging. Four of these are quarterly; the remainder are monthly. A short list including median leads (−) or lags (+) in months is shown in Table 13–3.[8]

A set of 36 leading indicators, or even the short group of 12 leaders, usually contains conflicting signals. A method of summarizing their net indication is needed. NBER has developed such a method, called the diffusion index. The diffusion index is the percentage of members of a set of series that is moving upward. It ranges from 0 (when all are moving downward) to 100 (when all series are moving upward).

Table 13–3
A "short-list" of economic indicators

Classification and series title	First business cycle turn covered	Median lead (−) or lag (+) in months
Leading indicators (12 series)		
Average work week, production workers, manufacturing	1921	− 5
Nonagricultural, placements, BES	1945	− 3
Index of net business formation	1945	− 7
New orders, durable goods industries	1920	− 4
Contracts and orders, plant and equipment	1948	− 6
New building permits, private housing units	1918	− 6
Change in book value, manufacturing and trade inventories	1945	− 8
Industrial materials prices	1919	− 2
Stock prices, 500 common stocks	1873	− 4
Corporate profits after taxes, Q*	1920	− 2
Ratio, price to unit labor cost, manufacturing	1919	− 3
Change in consumer installment debt	1929	−10
Roughly coincident indicators (7 series)		
Employees in nonagricultural establishments	1929	0
Unemployment rate, total (inverted)	1929	0
GNP in constant dollars, expenditures estimate, Q*	1921	− 2
Industrial production	1919	0
Personal income	1921	− 1
Manufacturing and trade sales	1948	0
Sales of retail stores	1919	0
Lagging indicators (6 series)		
Unemployment rate, persons unemployed 15+ weeks (inverted)	1948	− 2
Business expenditures plant and equipment, Q*	1918	+ 1
Book value, manufacturing and trade inventories	1945	+ 2
Labor cost per unit of output, manufacturing	1919	+ 8
Commercial and industrial loans outstanding	1937	+ 2
Bank rates, short-term business loans, Q*	1919	+ 5

* Q means quarterly.
Source: G. H. Moore, and J. Shiskin, *Indicators of Business Expansions and Contractions* (New York: National Bureau of Economic Research, 1967).

---

[8] Moore and Shiskin, *Indicators of Business Expansions and Contractions,* p. 34. Note that this book revised the lists of indicators to include new series. It includes an appendix and the 862 series they examined as well as the sources for each.

Individual indicators of economic activity may be of interest not only because they have uses in general economic forecasting, but also because they directly provide some information about specific business conditions that can possibly be related to demand shifts for particular goods or services. For current information on these indicators, a good source is *Business Conditions Digest* (BCD), published monthly by the Commerce Department. Data can also be obtained monthly from the Commerce Department's *Survey of Current Business* and the Federal Reserve Board's *Federal Reserve Bulletin,* mentioned previously. Before using these series, especially the various leading indicators, the forecaster may find it helpful to consult the various NBER publications.

Substantive criticisms can be made of the indicators approach. Four weaknesses cited by Lewis are: (1) the indicators give no indication of the magnitude of future changes in economic activity; (2) they are very short range with probably only six months' advance warning; (3) the individual series seldom move together, whereas the diffusion index hides specific series; and (4) for leading series to be useful there must be no major structural changes in the economy which might shorten or lengthen their lead time.[9]

Various empirical investigations of predictive accuracy of the indicators approach have been made. Evans sees the NBER approach as providing a good picture of the economy and as a valuable collector and verifier of data, but he concludes that leading indicators cannot be used effectively or accurately as the core of a practical method of forecasting.[10] Nevertheless, economic indicators may be useful in conjunction with other methods.[11]

Diffusion indexes

A diffusion index is an indicator of the extensiveness of an expansion or contraction. Further, it may provide information about forthcoming changes in direction of the set. For example, if during an expansionary period the diffusion index for all leading indicators stands near 90 for several months but then begins to fall, it warns the forecaster that some of the leading series are beginning to turn downward; a general decline in economic activity may be forthcoming. It is calculated by determining the percent of the time series that is rising. If, for example, 9 of 12 time series are rising, the diffusion index stands at 75 percent.

The diffusion index is a device used successfully by many economists

---

[9] John P. Lewis, "Short-Term General Business Conditions Forecasting, Some Comments on Method," *Journal of Business,* October 1962, pp. 347–48.

[10] Michael K. Evans, *Macroeconomic Activity* (New York: Harper & Row, 1969), p. 460.

[11] David M. McKinley, Murray G. Lee, and Helene Duffy, *Forecasting Business Conditions* (New York: American Bankers Association, 1965), p. 176; Leonard H. Lempert, "Leading Indicators," in *How Business Economists Forecast,* ed. William F. Butler and Robert A. Kavesh (Englewood Cliffs, N.J.: Prentice-Hall, 1966).

in business, labor, and government. It is often presented on a two-dimensional graph and depicts the percent of, say, all leading indicators that are rising at some particular time. BCD publishes in its "Analytical Measures" section diffusion indexes for many time series. In its simplest possible form, the diffusion index has the advantages of (1) allowing the analyst to see at a glance if most series are rising or falling and (2) providing information on which series are changing, in what direction, and by about what rate of change.

The characteristics of the diffusion index are such that no allowance is made for magnitudes of change within and between series. For example, the index may be a composite of all leading indicators on the NBER short list only. The index also serves as a way to compare different time series. The diffusion index based on NBER's short list provides the analyst with a representation of what is expected to be a normal situation during a given period of time. The index, from a conceptual standpoint, allows that at any particular time everything in the economy is not in step; some series are moving up while others are moving down. The index lets one know whether on net balance the time series are moving in an upward or downward direction. Figure 13–3 presents a diffusion index using explanatory hypothetical data. Six points are plotted in this figure. The vertical axis (y) reveals the percent of the time series that are rising. Its range is from 0 to 100 percent. On the horizontal axis (x), time is used.

The diffusion index lets one know the overall trend of economic activity that may be represented by the time series included in the index. Moreover, it is of significant value for one attempting to pinpoint turns, upper and/or lower, within the business cycle. It often has the disadvantage of leading the analyst to assume all component parts of the index to be of equal weight or value.[12] The importance of specific time-series data used within the short list of indicators is enough justification for heavy use of this economic forecasting tool, but it must be used with caution.

Special indicators

As we have seen, the barometric measures rely heavily upon time-series data, many of which are provided in BCD on a monthly basis. In addition to using these statistics provided by the U.S. Department of Commerce, many corporations have found it desirable to develop leading, lagging, or coincident indicators that are unique to their particular firm and/or industry. These indicators are developed along lines of the NBER approach as described in *Measuring Business Cycles*.[13] They have

---

[12] Weights are used by the Department of Commerce for all time-series data included in its diffusion indices.

[13] Arthur F. Burns and Wesley C. Mitchell, *Measuring Business Cycles* (New York: National Bureau of Economic Research, 1964); see also *Business Cycles: The Problem and Its Setting* (New York: National Bureau of Economic Research, 1927).

Figure 13–3
Diffusion index: Explanatory data

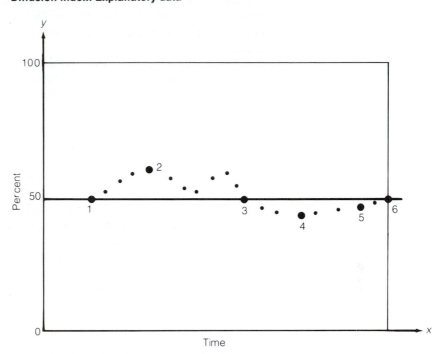

where

(1) Trough, or lower turn,
(2) Expansionary phase of the business cycle because most series are rising.
(3) Peak, or upper turn, one half of the series are rising and one half of the series are falling.
(4) Contractionary phase.
(5) Near the lower turn.
(6) Trough, or lower turn. Note: (*a*) One half of the series is declining, and (*b*) they may not be the same series that declined before.

proven to be of significant use to the firm creating the indicators. They provide a tool to be used in solving individual forecasting problems that this observor recommends strongly if a separate department of economic planning and/or forecasting exists within the company. For firms developing their own indicators, the question is: What criteria for testing a series should be used? Some suggestions to the forecaster concerning specific time-series data include the following:

1. *Measure use of resources.* The time-series should measure the use of resources in units or in dollars. Because of price inflation, data presented in dollars is difficult to adjust and, therefore, often is less than reliable.
2. *Broad coverage.* The time series should be broad enough to reveal meaningful changes within the indicator and between the indicator

and another with which it will be compared; however, the indicator should not be so broad as to conceal more than it reveals.

3. *Detailed material*. The raw data of the time series should be in a condition good enough for individual components to be studied in great detail.

4. *Data available frequently*. For economic indicator purposes, the frequency with which the data are available is of utmost importance; consequently, data should be available on a monthly basis or more often if possible. Quarterly data are not misleading, per se, and are often the only data available, but a monthly or weekly time series is preferred. Annual data should be avoided, if possible.

5. *Timeliness*. The figures to be used in the time series should be available promptly. In this manner, the analyst operating for a specific firm has an edge over a counterpart who may be working for the federal government. The economist working for private enterprise or a not-for-profit organization has the figures on sales, production, employment, and so on for the firm many months in advance of similar data that may be published by the government.

6. *Accuracy*. In addition to having detailed material made available frequently and in a prompt manner, one needs to know whether the data are estimates or actual figures. National income accounting statistics including GNP are estimates. There is nothing inherently wrong with this kind of statistic, but analysts need to know the degree of confidence they can place in the data obtained. How accurate are the estimates?

7. *Amplitude fluctuations*. Some time-series data contain very wide amplitude fluctuations, and the economist needs to know whether these fluctuations are as one might expect within a particular business cycle. Is there a sound theoretical reason to explain whatever amplitude fluctuations there may be in the data?

8. *Sensitivity*. If at all possible, the economist should obtain a time series that is supersensitive to general business conditions. The more sensitive the time series is to the aggregate economy, the more reliance one will be able to place in that series as an indicator of aggregate activity.

9. *Timing*. The timing criterion differs from timeliness, above, and requires the series to be one that behaves consistently from cycle to cycle.

10. *Representative*. The data may not be as broad in coverage as the analyst would like, but she/he must nevertheless be assured it is representative of the firm and/or industry in which she/he is interested.

11. *Adjustments*. Whenever necessary, all data used in the series should be adjusted for changes in season, population, and so on.

12. *Indexed.* If the series is an index based on some kind of sampling procedure or technique, one must be careful to weigh it properly. Only properly weighted indexes should be used.

13. *Continuity.* If an economist working for private enterprise is to establish an economic indicator for a firm or industry that is to be of some significance to that firm in the long run, the time-series data must be available and comparable over long periods of time. It is of little value to prepare a time series for economic indicator purposes only to find later that additional data either will not or cannot be made available to the analyst.

Even a cursory review of these criteria of a good series reveals that no time series would be used by the NBER, *BCD,* or similar agencies and publications if the series had to gain and then maintain passing scores in each of the 13 suggested areas. Some time-series data published in *BCD* on a monthly basis measure up to these tests better than others; none of them is perfect. The individual firm cannot expect its criteria to be perfect. *BCD* and NBER continue to test new indicators while discarding others. Economists working for U.S. Steel, the U.S. Manufacturers Association, labor unions, and Chambers of Commerce should expect to do the same.

Surveys of attitudes and plans

Among the leading indicators noted in Table 13–3 are new orders in durable goods industries and new building permits for private housing. These orders and permits represent earlier plans and intentions that are in the process of being carried out. Information about attitudes toward the future and plans for the future may have relatively long leads compared with actual producer or consumer behavior. One method of measuring attitudes and plans is to ask managers or consumers what they expect the future to bring. This is the survey method.

Do you expect to buy a new car next month? Do you expect to buy a new refrigerator, stove, television set, centralized air conditioner, and so on next month, or next summer, or next year? Questions like these often result in answers indicative of what the homemaker would like to be able to buy next month or next year. Responses to such questions are not as reliable as questions dealing with the recent past. For example, did you buy a new automobile last month? Did you buy a new refrigerator, stove, television set, or centralized air-conditioning unit last month or last year? Answers to questions concerning the future are not as reliable as those to questions concerning the past. Nonetheless, attempts to forecast changes in economic activity often rely upon surveys of households, business executives, and/or government officials; these surveys seek information concerning plans to consume, plans to invest, or plans to save.

Opinion polling of this sort is part of the business economist's forecasting tool kit.

Economists attempting to do forecasts in firms or industries concerned primarily with supplying consumer durable and nondurable goods are inclined to place heavier reliance on opinions of potential customers than are those economists attempting to forecast the potential market demand for durable equipment. Economic forecasters at General Motors, for example, are more concerned with the opinions of potential buyers of new domestic passenger cars than are the economists employed by American Car Foundry (ACF), who need to know the number of new freight cars that will be demanded by all railroads and private car lines for domestic use during the upcoming calendar months.

Many firms, operating usually through their research departments, rely heavily upon opinion sampling and often conduct the surveys themselves. Just as often they farm out this kind of activity to independent research organizations. The makers of Kraft cheeses and Hoover vacuum cleaners should be expected to rely more heavily upon consumer opinions than would the makers of Timken Roller Bearings or officials at the Norfolk and Western Railway. Those companies that undertake their own consumer research compare their results with the published reports made available by the U.S. government, the publishing houses, commercial banks, and numerous university-based research studies.

Sources of survey information

In addition to the enumerable private surveys conducted and often published for general consumption, some sources of survey information are as follows:

1. The series compiled and made available by the F. W. Dodge Division, McGraw-Hill Information Systems Company, New York, New York. These data report the total dollar value of contracts within the United States for new construction, major alterations, and/or additions. Moreover, F. W. Dodge provides an insight into the following (*a*) residential construction—for example, one- and two-family housing, apartment buildings, hotels, motels, dormitories, and other forms of shelter; (b) nonresidential construction, such as commercial, manufacturing, educational, scientific, health and hospital treatment facilities, public buildings, religious institutions, and recreation facilities; (c) nonbuilding construction, such as highways, bridges, dams, river development and harbor facilities, missile and space facilities, and engineering projects of somewhat massive proportions (e.g., missile sites and airports).

2. *Fortune* magazine, the National Industrial Conference Board, the Office of Business Economics of the U.S. Department of Commerce, the early fall and spring surveys of the McGraw-Hill Corporation, the Secu-

rities and Exchange Commission, the National Association of Purchasing Agents' surveys, the National Association of Homebuilders' surveys, the "Occasional Papers" of the National Bureau of Economic Research—these sources provide the researcher with an abundance of survey-based opinions concerning the condition of the aggregate economy and its component parts.

These sources of survey information include plans for new plant and equipment, personal consumption expenditures, and government spending at the federal, state, and local level. They are available to the general public at very modest prices. In fact, survey information made available through the 12 Federal Reserve Banks in their numerous economic research publications is free.

Attitudinal variables may explain changes in demand for goods and services by households, business, and government purchases within the economy, but questions pertaining to the future result in almost hopeless answers. Nonetheless, key consumer anticipations supplement the alternative methods of economic forecasting. More complete information can be found in Lansing and Morgan's book *Economic Survey Methods* and the many references they cite on specific techniques—including designing the survey, sampling the population, collecting the data, and analyzing the results.[14] Basically, there are two areas for use of survey method —producer behavior and consumer behavior; these will be taken up in order. However, first consider a sometimes neglected area of survey forecasting—plans of governments.

Since government expenditures approximate 20 percent of GNP, planned activity in this sector must always be considered in business forecasting. Governments' intentions are available earlier than reliable information about consumer or producer plans for activities during the corresponding period. For example, in January 1984 the proposed budget of the United States for the fiscal year October 1, 1984–September 30, 1985 is presented to Congress by the President.[15] Similarly, state governments publish their full-year spending intentions well in advance of the fiscal year. Budgets of governments can be surveyed to determine what the public sector of the economy is planning to do. Determining the level of government spending in the United States is relatively easy. The federal government and each unit of government at the state and local level spends at least 100 percent of what is made available to it.

---

[14] John B. Lansing and James N. Morgan, *Economic Survey Methods* (Ann Arbor, Mich.: Survey Research Institute, 1971).

[15] The timing and the procedures underlying approval of the budget have been altered by the Congressional Budget Reform and Impoundment Control Act of 1974. For a discussion, see C. William Fischer, "The New Congressional Budget Establishment and Federal Spending: Choices for the Future," *National Tax Journal,* March 1976, pp. 9–14.

Producer expectations regarding investment expenditures, sales, and inventory levels are all subjects of survey research. There are three major surveys of investment anticipations: the Commerce Department-Securities and Exchange Commission (SEC) survey, the McGraw-Hill survey, and the National Industrial Conference Board survey. In the Commerce-SEC survey, firms are asked about their previous quarter's investment and also their anticipated investment during the next quarter. Anticipations and realizations can be compared quarter by quarter. The results of this survey are published the third month of each quarter in the *Survey of Current Business*.

The McGraw-Hill survey appears twice yearly in *Business Week* and concentrates on investment plans, especially of larger firms. The first survey is taken in October; the results are published early in November and cover the following year. A resurvey is taken in early spring and published in April.

The National Industrial Conference Board survey concentrates on capital appropriations of 1,000 manufacturing firms. Because of the focus on appropriations, this source of "anticipatory data" is likely to be firmer than simple expectations, as measured in the two surveys mentioned above.

In addition to investment anticipations, the Commerce-SEC survey also obtains sales and manufacturing inventory expectations. The results of these surveys appear quarterly in the *Survey of Current Business*.

Turning to consumer expectations surveys, several groups compile such data. Perhaps the best known of these was the Survey Research Center at the University of Michigan. The approach taken by this group was more complicated than simply asking individuals whether or not they plan to purchase an automobile or appliance sometime during the next six months, although questions about buying plans were a part of the survey. In addition, there were several queries into the attitudes of consumers, which advocates of this forecasting method believe to be as important as actual plans. An example of an attitudinal question is: "Now, about things people buy for their house—I mean furniture, house furnishings, refrigerator, stove, TV, and things like that—do you think now is a good or bad time to buy such large household items?" [16] Answers to attitudinal questions were then classified as being optimistic, neutral, or pessimistic, and should be used in an index of general attitudes. The results of these surveys were reported annually in the Survey Research

---

[16] See, for example, Eva Mueller, "Ten Years of Consumer Attitude Surveys: Their Forecasting Record," *Journal of the American Statistical Association*, December 1963; or I. Friend and F. G. Adams, "The Predictive Ability of Consumer Attitudes, Stock Prices and Nonattitudinal Variables," *Journal of the American Statistical Association*, December 1964.

Center's *Survey of Consumer Finances* and in business news outlets, such as *The Wall Street Journal*.

Predictive accuracy of consumer surveys is subject to much dispute. Forecasters directly related to institutions conducting such surveys claim good accuracy and have provided evidence to show the strength of their position. These advocates point out that consumer purchase action requires more than just ability, as might be suggested by a simple relationship of personal consumption to income. In addition, there must be willingness to buy; this is what the surveys purportedly measure.

Those who do not agree with the surveying method of forecasting usually argue that directly measurable variables, such as credit conditions, are the root cause of the behavior. Therefore, in their view surveys add nothing to ordinary econometric models of the economy.

A more moderate view may be advisable. The forecaster may decide that it is better to utilize additional information about attitudes than to ignore it completely.

Simple extrapolation of trend lines

Simple extrapolation of trend lines may be the most naive of several naive approaches to forecasting. Nonetheless, it is a method often used in business and economic situations. It assumes the future will behave in a manner very similar to the past.

Applied to federal government defense spending expressed in $billions, for example, using simulated quarterly data from 1981 through 1984 and making projections for each quarter of 1985, an extrapolation of the trend line would project such spending for 1985 to be $322.7 billion in the first quarter, $329.2 billion in the second quarter, $335.7 billion in the third quarter, and $342.2 billion in the fourth quarter. Table 13–4 reveals these figures and the historical data upon which the projection is made. In addition, it provides the *Y* intercept at $232.15 billion and a slope of the trend line at 6.47.[17]

The trend line presented in Figure 13–4 is determined by the method of least squares and is based upon data from Table 13–4. Suppose economists at Douglas Aircraft used this method to project total governmental defense spending in the fourth quarter of 1984 and for each calendar quarter of 1985, based on data provided in Table 13–4; they would have underestimated governmental outlays somewhat for each quarter. Their naive approach would be based entirely on the historical data and on the assumption that the future would behave in a manner similar to the past. In this instance, the historical data began with the fourth quarter of 1981.

---

[17] The *Y* intercept and slope have no economic meaning except when used in context with the material provided in Table 13–4.

**Table 13–4
Federal governmental
defense spending—
total (simulated data)**

Year	$ billions
1981.4	242.1
1982.1	251.1
1982.2	253.8
1982.3	255.1
1982.4	262.6
1983.1	269.0
1983.2	273.3
1983.3	276.9
1983.4	286.4
1984.1	296.3
1984.2	304.4
1984.3	312.3
1984.4	323.8
1985.1	322.74
1985.2	329.21
1985.3	335.68
1985.4	342.15

Y intercept = 232.15
Slope of line =   6.47

Source of raw data: *Survey of Current Business,* or similar reliable source.

Had the Douglas forecasters selected the fourth quarter of 1983 as their point of departure for extrapolating the trend line, they would have projected very accurately the governmental spending for the first quarter of 1985. But, how does one know when projecting trend lines what data, with 20–20 hindsight, will prove ultimately to be most accurate?

An alternative approach used in this kind of projection is to assume that some constant rate of change will take place from quarter to quarter. In reviewing U.S. federal government purchases of goods and services as presented in Table 13–4, one might be tempted to assume the rate of spending increases by 2–3 percent per calendar quarter. Consequently, using a 2½ percent growth factor, total spending in billions of dollars for the first quarter of 1985 could have been calculated at:

$$\text{U.S. government spending for } 1985.1 = \text{U.S. government spending as of } 1984 \times (1 + \text{interest rate})$$
$$= \$323.8 \text{ billion} \times 1.025$$
$$= \$331.89 \text{ billion.}$$

Remember: First quarter 1985 government purchases amounted to $331.6 billion—probably close enough as a short-term approximation technique.

Figure 13–4
Simulated U.S. government defense spending, total (quarterly data—fourth quarter 1981 through fourth quarter 1984, with projection for each quarter of 1985)

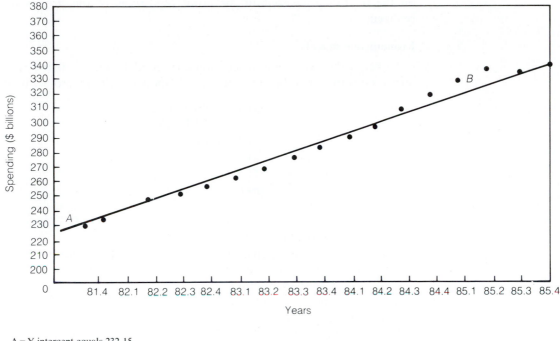

A = Y intercept equals 232.15
Note: Slope of curve is 6.47
B = Preliminary actual, 1985.1

Econometric models —simple equations

The idea of measuring changes in economic variables is not new. Even Adam Smith, in his much celebrated *The Wealth of Nations,* written in 1776, used mathematical models of sorts to explain changes in the rate of output that he theorized would take place in his pin factory if certain specialization of labor techniques were followed. Modern-day econometrics is somewhat more sophisticated than the measurements suggested by Smith and his followers, but its intent is the same: to explain or describe past economic activities and to project anticipated changes in economic variables for upcoming short- and/or long-term periods of time.

Econometric models, whether they be simultaneous or single equation in nature, provide the economist with rather precise quantitative results. Preciseness of answer is the greatest advantage accruing to the analyst who uses econometrics. But this precision can serve as a severe handicap if the limitations and results of all equations are not understood clearly and explained thoroughly. Thorough understanding with respect to the limitations of the equations and interpretation of the results is mandatory. Business executives, government officials, and labor leaders must analyze the results of econometric models very carefully if favorable impact on the overall price, output, or profit objectives of the firm is to be realized.

Econometric models

To begin the discussion of econometric models and to define several terms, consider the following very simple model of the macro economy.

$$(1)\ Y = C + I + G + X$$
$$(2)\ C = a + bY + dC_{-1}$$
$$(3)\ I = e + fi$$
$$(4)\ G = G'$$
$$(5)\ X = X'$$
$$(6)\ i = i'$$

where

Y is gross national product.

C is consumption expenditures, with C_{-1} denoting consumption expenditures in the previous period.

I is investment expenditures.

G is government expenditures.

i is an interest rate.

X is net foreign exports.

a, b, d, e, and f are unknown parameters or constants (i.e., unknown numbers).

The above equations are either behavioral equations or identities. The behavioral equations are those that contain unknown parameters (i.e., Equations 2 and 3). The term *behavioral* stems from the fact that these equations specify how economic groups, such as consumers and producers, behave. The remaining equations are identities, either equilibrium conditions (1) or definitional identities (4, 5, and 6). Variables within the set of equations can be classified as endogenous or exogenous. Values of endogenous variables are determined within the system of equations. In this example, they include GNP, consumption expenditures, and investment expenditures. Values of exogenous variables are specified from outside the system by the forecaster. These latter variables include expected government spending, net exports, and interest rate. C_{-1} is a predetermined variable.

Steps in forecasting with an econometric model consist of the following. First, a model such as the one indicated above must be specified. Economic theory determines the appropriate functional relationships (specification becomes a point of contention when the basic theory differs among forecasters). In the above example, a simple "consumption function'' hypothesizes that current consumption depends upon current income and also upon consumption in the previous period. Each equation is an explicit statement of how the forecaster believes some of the sectors of the economy are interrelated. As a group these equations compose what are believed to be the important behavioral characteristics of the economy (i.e., they specify the model).

The second step in the forecasting process is estimation of the unknown parameters—the values of a, b, c, d, e, and f. This requires two bits of expertise: knowledge of data and their sources and intimate knowledge of statistical estimation methods. The most commonly used form of estimation is some type of regression technique. Of course, this technique must take into account the fact that the model is an interdependent one; that is, consumption is a major portion of income (Y) but is, in turn, affected by the level of income.

The third step in forecasting is simulation. The forecaster plugs in values for the exogenous variables to get forecasts of the endogenous ones. For instance, assume that the following behavioral equations had been estimated.

$$C = 44 + 0.35Y + 0.7C_{-1}$$
$$I = 400 - 9{,}620i$$

Further assume that the forecaster is willing to assume the following values for the exogenous variables:

$$C_{-1} = 510$$
$$G = 300$$
$$X' = 30$$
$$i' = 0.05$$

The forecaster would then predict the level of gross national product to be 1,000.

Note that the structure of the above simple model includes an interperiod feedback effect through lagged consumption that would keep this model going if initial values of G', X', and i' were assumed to hold constant for several periods into the future. Or a more interesting simulation could be carried out by plugging in expected changes in these predetermined variables. Projections more than one period into the future may be of much interest, even though they become less and less reliable as the horizon is extended.

In appraising the basic four-step procedure for forecasting—constructing a model, estimating the parameters, choosing values for the exogenous variables, and simulating the future—several possible weak links are obvious. First, there is the possibility of incorrectly specifying the model. For example, perhaps interest rates actually have little bearing upon investment expenditures, whereas profits of earlier periods are a good predictor of investment. In such a case, predictions will not be very accurate, and the forecaster needs to modify the model.

A second possible weakness relates to any attempt to extrapolate into the future based on past experience. A change in the structure of the economy cannot be measured immediately, even though it may be having important effects on the level of income and employment. This problem can be encountered even in short-run forecasts. Therefore, it would involve really heroic assumptions to project GNP as much as 15 years into the future using a quarterly model of the U.S. economy tested for the period 1945–1985.[18]

A third possible weak link in the procedure involves choice of values for exogenous variables. In the more complex models discussed below, these guesses about the future can be crucial.

Perhaps the most important positive feature of econometric model forecasting is that it requires the forecaster to completely specify the assumptions underlying the forecasts. This allows thorough examination of all aspects of the model and may lead to improvements in the approach.

Another strength of econometric models is their capability for simulation of a great variety of possible environments. For example, the impact of a possible major railway strike can be predicted. Such information can possibly lead to more intelligent policymaking than would otherwise be possible.

Of course, practical econometric models are much more sophisticated than the naive model presented above. During the past 35 years, econometric model building and forecasting has been a growth industry. One of the early models of the U.S. economy was constructed and estimated by Lawrence Klein.[19] It was followed by the Klein-Goldberger model, which in turn, led to the 32–equation forecasting model used in the early 1960s at the University of Michigan.[20]

Another early model, constructed during the 1960s, was that of the Office of Business Economics of the Department of Commerce.[21] The

[18] An analogous procedure would be to "backcast" GNP for 1930 based on the same model and compare predicted with observed values.

[19] *Economic Fluctuations in the United States, 1921–1941* (New York: John Wiley & Sons, 1950).

[20] Lawrence R. Klein and Arthur S. Goldberger, *An Econometric Model of the United States, 1929–1952* (Amsterdam: North Holland Publishing, 1955). For a discussion of the University of Michigan model used in the early 1960s as well as a very lucid description of the techniques of forecasting from econometric models, see Daniel Suits, "Forecasting and Analysis with an Econometric Model," *American Economic Review,* March 1962, pp. 104–32. A more up-to-date discussion of the Michigan model is in Michael D. McCarthy, *Wharton Mark III Quarterly Economic Forecasting Model* (Philadelphia: Wharton Series on quantitative Economics, 1972).

[21] M. Liebenberg, A. H. Hirsch, and J. Popkin, "A Quarterly Econometric Model of the United States: A Progress Report," *Survey of Current Business,* May 1966, pp. 13–20.

structure of this model, often called the OBE model, is shown in Figure 13–5. Note the basic relationships and the classification of variables into exogenous, endogenous, and lagged endogenous categories.

In the late 1960s, several major econometric models were produced by university and nonprofit organizations. Among these were the very large Brookings Institution model,[22] the Wharton Model at the University of

Figure 13–5
Condensed flow diagram

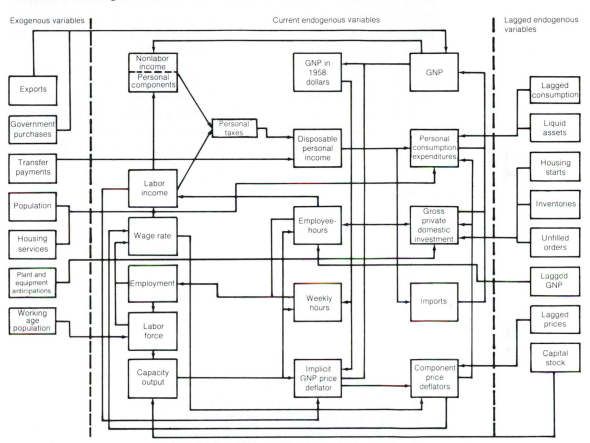

Source: U.S. Department of Commerce, Office of Business Economics.

[22] James S. Duesenberry, Gary Fromm, Lawrence R. Klein, and Edwin Kuh, *The Brookings Quarterly Econometric Model of the United States* (Chicago: Rand McNally, 1965). Further results are found in a book edited by the same authors entitled *The Brookings Model: Some Further Results* (Amsterdam: North Holland Publishing Co., 1969). For critiques of the Brookings Model, see Z. Griliches, "The Brookings Model Volume: A Review Article," *Review of Economics and Statistics,* May 1968, pp. 215–34; or R. J. Gordon, "The Brookings Model in Action: A Review Article," *Journal of Political Economy,* May–June 1970, pp. 489–525.

Pennsylvania,[23] and a monetary-oriented model developed jointly by the Board of Governors of the Federal Reserve System and Massachusetts Institute of Technology.[24]

Although there is continuing academic interest in econometric forecasting models, the decades of the 1970s and 1980s have been and will be notable for model building in the private sector. Reports on the major forecasts produced by the private sector models are made public from time to time, but the principal work of these organizations, forecasts for particular clients, and the documentation of the models are not available for examination. Among firms producing forecasts from econometric models are these: Data Resources Incorporated, Chase Econometrics, Townsend-Greenspan and Company, and several major banks.

The results of numerous econometric and opportunistic forecasts are annually summarized by at least two organizations—The Federal Reserve Banks of Richmond and of Philadelphia. To gain insight into possible short-run developments in the national economy during the coming year, one would do well to study these summaries along with the leading indicators and then possibly undertake some opportunistic forecasting for oneself. (Additionally, for the producer selling in a regional market, several local or regional econometric models are currently being developed.)

Single-equation models

To say the quantity of football tickets demanded in New York is dependent upon (1) the percent of total games won last year, (2) the population of the New York metropolitan area, and (3) the disposable personal income of households in the area would, in effect, establish a single-equation, unspecified model, which could be stated symbolically as follows:

$$Q_d = f(P_{t-1}, p, I)$$

where

P_{t-1} = Percent of games won last year.

p = Population of the New York metropolitan area.

I = Effective buying power per household.

Were one to assume the relationship to be linear and should she/he want to know what percent of the variation in quantity demanded can be explained by the three variables, one might use regression analysis and alter the model as follows:

---

[23] Evans, *Macroeconomic Activity*, describes the structure of the original Wharton Model, while McCarthy, *Wharton Mark III Quarterly Economic Forecasting Model*, documents the updated version of this model.

[24] Frank de Leeuw and Edward M. Gramlich, "The Channels of Monetary Policy: A Report on the Federal Reserve-MIT Model," *Journal of Finance* May 1969, pp. 265–90.

$$Y = a + bP_{t-1}, + cp + dI + e_t$$

where

$$a = \text{The constant term.}$$
$$b, c, \text{ and } d = \text{Parameters to be estimated.}$$
$$e = \text{The error or disturbance term.}$$

Presumably, e represents the random distribution of influences that affect the dependent variable, the average home game attendance of the New York Jets. This e term is a residual that is supposed to account for all factors affecting the quantity of tickets demanded not included in the independent variables. It may also include the effects of variables omitted from the equation.

Multiple-equation models

Single-equation models are easy to calculate and apply, but they are often too limiting. Under such circumstances a more elaborate set of data are assembled.

Business conditions analysis and forecasting by utilization of simultaneous equations used to be a tedious and troublesome process, but the modern computer has alleviated the task considerably. Yet, the problem has not been eliminated, and the simultaneous-equation model retains its rigid structure. This rigidity is necessary even though it may cause the analyst to overlook variables that are, perhaps, more important than ones included initially in the analyst's equation (model). The respective weight of the variables to one another and to the equation are assumed by the analyst to be constant and, as with the simple equation model, this assumption proves often to be invalid. Nonetheless, let's take a closer look.

The model could be a relatively simple one of the total economy. It could be presented as:

$$Y = C + I + G$$

where

$$Y = \text{The net national product.}$$
$$C = \text{Personal consumption expenditures.}$$
$$I = \text{Net new investment on the part of businesses.}$$
$$G = \text{Federal, state, and local government expenditures.}$$

In this simplified model, Y (net national product, by definition) could also be considered as a residual that results from subtracting capital consumption allowances (CCA)[25] from gross national product (GNP); in other words,

$$Y = GNP - CCA$$

---

[25] CCA is a synonym for *depreciation allowances*.

Personal consumption expenditures (C) could be thought of as a function of income. The income figure could be thought of as national income, personal income, or disposable personal income. The income statistic used would be dependent upon the theory of the consumption function relied upon by the analyst.[26] In addition, personal consumption expenditures (C) could be determined at least in part by reliance upon personal consumption expenditures made last period. For example:

$$PCE = a_o + a_1 DPI_{t-1} + a_2 \Delta DPI_t + a_3 PCE_{t-1}$$

where

PCE = Personal consumption expenditures.

DPI_{t-1} = Disposable personal income last period.

ΔDPI_t = Change in disposable personal income this time period.

PCE_{t-1} = Personal consumption expenditures last period.

a_o = Some constant.

a_1, a_2, and a_3 = Regression coefficients.

Dealing with time periods 1929 through 1940 and 1946 through 1965 in constant dollars, the *Survey of Current Business* published results of the above equation. Selected demand and supply equations are as follows.[27]

Demand equations

(1) Personal consumption expenditures, 1929–40 and 1946–65 (constant dollars):

$$PCE_t = 1.5229 + 0.4953\ DPI_{t-1} + 0.6600\ \Delta DPI_t + 0.4676\ PCE_{t-1}$$
$$\quad (2.7222)\ (0.1859) \qquad (0.2949) \qquad (0.2105)$$

$$R^2 = 0.99$$

(2) Investment in residential structures, 1929–40 and 1946–65 (constant dollars):

$$I_{r_t} = -24.237 - 4.6328 i_{3-5t} + 7.052\frac{DPI_t}{P} + 0.9437\ H_t$$
$$\quad (4.6342)\ (0.718) \qquad (4.23) \qquad (0.2300)$$
$$\qquad\qquad - 2.6284\ D_k - 8.3270\ D_{30-50}$$
$$\qquad\qquad (1.3635) \quad (2.1936)$$

$$R^2 = 0.96$$

---

[26] The absolute income hypothesis, the relative income hypothesis, and other somewhat lesser known theories of the consumption function should be investigated by the reader. Milton Friedman's *Theory of the Consumption Function* (National Bureau of Economic Research: Princeton University Press, 1958) is recommended.

[27] Variables for these demand and supply equations are measured in $billions. See Lester C. Thurow, "A Fiscal Policy Model of the United States," *Survey of Current Business,* June, 1969, pp. 45–64.

(3) Change in business inventories, 1947–65 (constant dollars):

$$\Delta IV_t = -29.943 + 0.1321 \ GNP_{p_t} - 0.9930 \ IV_{t-1} + 40.644\frac{1}{UR'} + 1.7183 \ T_t^{46}$$

$$(6.990) \ (0.0337) \qquad (0.1227) \qquad (10.470) \qquad (0.6945)$$

$$R^2 = 0.85$$

(4) State and local government purchases of goods and services per capita (excluding compensation), 1947–65 (constant dollars)

$$\frac{G_{3t}}{P} = -0.10494 + 0.02601\frac{GNP_{t-1}}{P} + 0.5665\frac{S_t}{P} + 0.3543\frac{GAC_t}{P}$$

$$(0.018578) \ (0.01703) \qquad (0.1967) \qquad (0.3970)$$

$$R^2 = 0.95$$

(5) Demand-side estimate of GNP (constant dollars)

$$GNP_t^d = PCE_t + I_{s_t} + I_{e_t} + I_{r_t} + \Delta IV_t + EX_t - M_t + G_{s_t} + G_{f_t} + GGP_t$$

Supply equations:
(1) Gross flow of corporate funds, 1948–65 (current dollars)

$$CPCCA_{c_t} = -3.6723 - 1.5649 \ UR_t + 0.2045 \ GNP_t$$

$$(3.7943) \ (0.6638) \qquad (0.0090)$$

$$+ 1.3852 \sum_{i=0}^{t} (D_{pbt} - UL_i)$$

$$R^2 = 0.98$$

(2) Corporate capital consumption allowances, 1947–65 (constant dollars)

$$CCA_{c_t} = -10.993 + 0.0569 \ K_{t-1} + 0.0045 \ K_{t-1}^{54} + 0.0050 \ K_{t-1}^{62};$$

$$(1.450) \ (0.0036) \qquad (0.0010) \qquad (0.0006)$$

$$R^2 = 0.99$$

(3) Corporate profits (book value) before taxes (current dollars)

$$CP_t = CPCCA_{c_t} - (CCA_{c_t}) \ (DF_{it})$$

(4) Gross government product (constant dollars)

$$GGP_{s_t} = 3.916E_{s_t}$$
$$GGP_{f_t} = 3.997E_{m_t} + 4.913E_{f_t};$$
$$GGP_t = GGP_{s_t} + GGP_{f_t}$$

(5) Supply-side estimate of GNP (constant dollars)

$$GNP_t^3 = GGP_t + GNP_{pt}$$

An econometric model attempts to present in mathematical symbols, equations and identities, an abstraction of the so-called real world. These models have been very successful in describing relationships that exist within the economy, but they have been somewhat less than successful when used as predictive devices. The models attempt to establish relationships the anlyst considers to be sound, based upon a priori reasoning that, when subjected to empirical statistical tests, allows the analyst to confirm or reject any preconceived notions held about the relationships.

Some economic variables within the model are exogenous, whereas others are endogenous. Exogenous variables are ones produced outside of the model and may include, for example, birth rates, immigration rates, changes in city income tax rates, and so on. Endogenous variables are determined within the model and may include such information as personal consumption expenditures, gross private domestic investment, government purchases of goods and services, and so on.

These findings imply that econometric forecasting is still both an art and a science. Indeed, a major aspect of econometric forecasting involves fine tuning of models and using judgment. The usual method of fine tuning is to make adjustments in the constant terms of various equations. It appears that there is a certain amount of opportunism, even in the use of completely specified econometric models. In fact, it may not be correct to regard opportunistic and econometric forecasting as mutually exclusive categories. Although econometric forecasters continually fine tune, opportunistic forecasters often buy services of major private forecasting models and then adjust these forecasts to reflect their own judgments. Thus, although business conditions analysis is becoming more and more sophisticated, the judgmental role of the economist-forecaster continues to be important.[28] Judgment is important also in forecasting via utilization of input-output analysis.

Input-output analysis   Input-output analysis as a tool in economic forecasting is available to us primarily because of the pioneering effort of Nobel Prize-winning laureate, Wassily Leontief.[29]

Leontief is considered by most observers to be the father of input-

---

[28] This point is argued in Otto Eckstein, ''Econometric Models and the Formation of Business Expectations,'' *Challenge* March–April 1976, p. 14.

[29] Wassily Leontief, ''Input-Output Economics,'' *Scientific American,* October 1951, pp. 15–21. See also *The Structure of American Economy,* 1919–1939 (New York: Oxford University Press, 1951).

output analysis. His pioneering work relates the production of each industry to its consumption from every other industry. As a result of Leontief's work, input-output tables are provided for the entire economy by the U.S. government. These tables differ in a statistical sense from those provided initially by Leontief.

The Department of Commerce has published benchmark input-output tables for the years 1947, 1958, and 1963; in addition, the 1958 table was updated to 1961, and the 1963 table was updated to 1966. The federal government's most recent input-output presentation is in terms of constant 1967 dollars. It is a valuable forecasting device.[30]

Gross national product may be calculated by summing personal consumption expenditures, gross private domestic investment, net exports of goods and services, and government purchases of goods and services. In addition, national income comprises wages, salaries, and supplements plus income of unincorporated businesses, rental income, interest income, corporate profits, business transfer payments, indirect business taxes and subsidies less (plus) current surplus of government-owned and -operated businesses. Table 13–5 reminds the reader of these two approaches to calculation of GNP. Another approach exists: gross national product in input-output format. Table 13–6 depicts this format in rows and columns. The sum of the rows and/or the columns is equal to GNP.

Table 13–6 contains one shaded box, which represents the sales of goods and services from, among others, agriculture, mining, construc-

Table 13–5
The gross national product by national income and gross product approach

Income approach	Product approach
Compensation of employees	Personal consumption expenditures
Proprietors' income	Gross private domestic investment
Rental income of persons	Net export of goods and services
Corporate profits and inventory valuation adjustment	Government purchases of goods and services
Net interest	
Business transfer payments	
Indirect business tax and nontax liability	
Less: Subsidies less current surplus of government enterprises	
Capital consumption allowances	
Gross national product	Gross national product

---

[30] The Input-Output Structure of the U.S. Economy: 1967," *Survey of Current Business*, February, 1974, pp. 24–56. See also: "Input-Output Structure of the U.S. Economy: 1967," vol. 3, "Total Requirements for Detailed Industries," a supplement to the *Survey of Current Business* (1974), published by U.S. Department of Commerce; in addition, see vol. 1, "Transactions Data for Detailed Industries," and vol. 2, "Direct Requirement for Detailed Industries."

Table 13–6
The gross national product: In Input-output format

	Producers	Persons	Investors	Foreigners	Government	
Producers		Personal consumption expenditures item 10	Gross private investment item 11	Net exports of goods and services item 12	Government purchases of goods and services item 13	Gross national product
Employees	Employee Compensation item 1					
Owners of Business and capital	Profit-type income and capital consumption allowances items 2,3, 4,5,6,8,9					
Government	Indirect business taxes item 7					
	Gross national product					

tion, manufacturing, trade, transportation, services, and all others, in effect, to themselves. In other words, some manufacturing firms produce a product that is sold to other manufacturing firms. Table 13–7 is similar to Table 13–6, with the exception that the shaded area for producers in Table 13–6 is expanded into a matrix of 8×8 so as to account for the economic activity of this "producers" shaded box. When used in conjunction with the input-output tables provided by the Department of Commerce, the total value expressed in 1967 constant dollars of raw materials, semifinished products, and intermediate services may be revealed separately for each industry located in the shaded area. The reader will note there is nothing sacred about the size of the shaded area depicted in Table 13–7. This matrix could have as many rows and columns as there are producers within the economy. In fact, the latest Department of Commerce tables used 82 distinct industrial classifications for purposes of determining the flows necessary for calculation of GNP.

Input-output analysis serves the dual purpose of (1) describing the complex relationships between and among producers within the economy

Table 13–7
Input-output flow table

		Producers								Final Market			
		Agriculture	Mining	Construction	Manufacturing	Trade	Transportation	Services	Other	Persons	Investors	Foreigners	Government
Producers	Agriculture									Personal consumption expenditures	Gross private domestic investment	Net exports of goods and services	Government purchaser of goods and services
	Mining												
	Construction												
	Manufacturing												
	Trade												
	Transportation												
	Services												
	Other												
Value added	Employees	Employee compensation								Gross national product			
	Owners of business and capital	Profit-type income and capital consumption allowances											
	Government	Indirect business taxes											

and (2) establishing quantitative relationships among these variables in a manner that allows one to make forecasts of changes in demand. Mostly, it allows one to measure changes in demand, employment, output, and income in a large number of industries simultaneously. For example, by using the input-output tables, one can determine the effects of a decrease in demand of domestic-made automobiles on overall economic activity.

During the recent recession most observers were concerned with the condition of the American automobile industry. At that time and by any standard of measurement, the industry had exceedingly high levels of unsold inventory. Even a casual observer could have noted quickly that corporate profits in the automobile industry would suffer badly. But what about the peripheral industries? A decrease in demand for autos initially leads to a decrease in the production of cars and an increase in unemployed auto workers. But the economic impact of a downturn in demand for automobiles causes decreases in steel production, chemicals, iron ore, limestone, and coal. In addition, the demand for upholstery fabrics declines; synthetic fibers are more difficult to sell; plastics, tin, aluminum, glass, and rubber products suffer also. Moreover, the trucking, rail, and airline industries are affected adversely. Input-output analysis allows one to determine the degree of hurt in each of these industries.

If the forecaster has information available concerning the geographic location of industries, the economic impact of changes in GNP upon specific regions of the country can be made. In addition, input-output is useful in cost/price analysis. It allows the economist to determine the direct and/or indirect impact on each industry of changes in price. One has reason to believe this method of analysis will be relied upon heavily by firms, industries, trade associations, and federal, state, and local governments interested in determining the economic impact of energy shortages on the total dollar value of all goods and services produced within the economy—the impact of changes in energy availability (supply) upon GNP.

Use of tables

Table 13–8 reveals the total dollar value of the transactions among all industries in the matrix. Each row in this table reveals the distribution of output to each industry or user; each column reveals the value of the industries' inputs in terms of raw materials, semifinished products, and/or services. The table describes the level of economic activity by industry within the nation in constant 1967 dollars.

Table 13–8 reveals the flows of dollars in producers' prices. These are the flows needed to document the transactions that occur between and among the industries cited. The importance of the consumer to the economy becomes evident in this table. Food and kindred products (14) sold about 94 percent of its total output in final consumer markets (line 14 of Table 13–8, $60,974 \div $64,911). Changes in these markets should be expected to cause changes in food industry. As the population increases in size, it changes its composition and alters its tastes and preferences. Food producers will be affected, adversely or otherwise. On the other hand, farm machinery and equipment (44) sold about 76 percent of its total output to intermediate consumers (line 44 of Table 13–8, $2,942 \div $3,868 = 76\%$). Meanwhile, the metal container industry (39) sold 59 percent of its total output to the food and kindred products industry (14) (line 39 of Table 10, $1,980 \div $3,355 = 59\%$).

The relative importance of different industries to the aggregate economy and their importance to one another can be studied in greater detail by making use of the complete table, available where U.S. Government periodicals are maintained.

Table 13–8 reveals the flows of dollars in constant 1967 producers' prices necessary to accumulate the transactions between and among in-

Table 13–8
Interindustry transactions, 1967 ($millions at producers' prices)

Industry No.	For the distribution of output of an industry, read the row for that industry. For the composition of inputs to an industry, read the column for that industry.	Livestock and livestock products	Food and similar products	Final demand		Total final demand	Total	Industry No.
				Personal consumption expenditures	Gross private fixed capital formation			
		1	14					
1	Livestock and livestock products							1
14	Food and similar products			60,974		64,911		14
			1,980					
39	Metal containers						3,355	39
44	Farm machinery and equipment				2,942	3,868		44

dustries that result in GNP. Table 13–9 is a follow-up of Table 13–8 in that it relates each of the inputs of industry to its total output. That is, it lets one know the direct requirements of each industry. The columns in Table 13–9 reveal the inputs needed from each industry named in the rows. For example, to produce $1 of output, the coal-mining industry (7) requires about 13 cents of its own production, 16 cents of output from the chemicals and selected chemical products industries (27), 2 cents from the electric, gas, water and sanitary industries (68), and so on. Table 13–9 is illustrative; a more complete table is available from the Superintendent of Documents in Washington, D.C.

Assuming the proportions assigned in Table 13–9 by the Department of Commerce remain constant, demand for a good or service upon an industry can be calculated. Assume the crude petroleum and natural gas

Table 13–9
Direct requirements per dollar of gross output, 1967 (producers' prices)

Industry No.	For the composition of inputs to an industry, read the column for that industry.	Livestock and livestock products		Coal mining	Crude petroleum and natural gas		Scrap, used and secondhand goods	Industry No.
		1		7	8		83	
1	Livestock and livestock products							1
7	Coal mining			0.12636				7
8	Crude petroleum and natural gas				0.02487			8
27	Chemicals and selected chemical products			0.01591				27
68	Electric, gas, water and sanitary services			0.02172				68
71	Real estate and rental				0.16161			71

industry (8) finds new sources of its product and wants to produce $1 million worth of new energy to its users. Column 8 of Table 13–9 reveals that the crude petroleum and natural gas industry would need more than $24,870 ($1 million × 0.02487) from itself. To obtain $1 million dollars worth of new sales, the industry would have to produce $1,024,870 worth of energy. This amount of new energy production would require more than $165,629 ($1,024,870 × 0.16161) from the real estate and rental industry (71). The total amount of money to be made available to the crude petroleum and natural gas industry could be determined by proceeding down column 8 and multiplying $1,024,870 by each of the factors listed in that column. Individual firms located within the crude petroleum and natural gas industry may then determine the change in sales volume that will accrue to them. This estimate of the individual firm's change in demand will be based upon the share of total market held by that firm. Similar calculations may be made for each industry.

Table 13–10 reveals the total requirements, by industrial classification, of finished product delivered to each industry. As with Tables 13–8 and 13–9, it is illustrative; the reader is asked to see a more complete table.

Table 13–10
Total requirements (direct & indirect) per dollar of delivery to final demand, 1967 (producers' prices)

Industry No.	Each entry represents the output required, directly and indirectly, from the industry named at the beginning of the row for each dollar of delivery to final demand by the industry named at the head of the column.	Livestock and livestock products	Coal mining	Office supplies	Industry No.
		1	7	82	
1	Livestock and livestock products				1
7	Coal mining		1.14708		7
37	Primary iron and steel manufacturing		0.03985		37
45	Construction, mining, and oil field machinery		0.04101		45
65	Transportation and warehousing		0.02610		65

It is because of the data in this table that one is able to calculate the economic impact on industries of a specified change in demand. Using a full version of Table 13–10, for example, one should be able to determine the economic impact of an increase (decrease) in radio, television, and communication equipment on the radio, television, and communication equipment industry, as well as on all of the other industries specified in the table. Each industry listed across the top of the page reveals the output required from each industry listed down the page.

To provide demand with $1 million of coal mining (7), about $1,147,080 ($1 million × 1.14708) is required in total from industry 7; about $41,010 ($1 million × .04101) from industry 37, primary iron and steel manufacturing; about $39,850 ($1 million × .03985) from industry 45, construction, mining, and oil field machinery; about $26,100 ($1 million × .02610) from industry 65, transportation and warehousing; and so on. The reader should make similar calculations for this industry and others so as to become familiar with the data.

A word of caution

Before Tables 13–9 or 13–10 can be used for purposes of determining the economic impact on the various industries caused by changes in demand for various goods and services, a certain amount of additional information is necessary. It is beyond the scope of this presentation to deal in great depth with that data, except to indicate that easy-to-read, readily available tables have been provided for this purpose by the Department of Commerce in one or more of its many publications.[31] The supplemental data needed concerns such matters as the transportation costs involved in the delivery to final markets of the goods produced and trade margins on each item specified as a set of final demands.

Summary

This chapter discussed analysis and short-range forecasting of business conditions—levels of activity for the economy as a whole and for its major sectors. Activity for the economy is commonly measured by Gross National Product, which is the market value of all final goods and services. The main components of GNP are consumption, investment, government purchases, and net exports.

In the indicators approach, interest centers on a group of 12 leading indicators and the diffusion index (percent of indicators rising) which summarizes their net indication. Surveys of attitudes and plans related to the future may be of particular interest in relation to the outlooks for producer and consumer durables. Neither the indicators approach nor

---

[31] For example, see *Survey of Current Business,* February, 1974, pp. 28–33.

the surveys approach appear to be satisfactory for use as the core of a business forecasting system.

Opportunistic forecasting takes a list of sectors of the economy and forecasts future changes from current values, using all available information. The opportunistic approach appears to be more successful when it is used with partially specified models of the economy. In such models, the values of some variables are regarded as functions of others. The values of the independent, or exogenous, variables are forecast first, and the values of the dependent, or endogenous, variables can then be determined. In a partially specified model, particular importance is attached to the multiplier, which is the ratio of change in disposable personal income to changes in investment or government purchases.

Over the decades, forecasting with fully specified macroeconomic models has been increasing rapidly and the models used have become more sophisticated. This kind of forecasting uses the econometric approach in estimating the structural equations of the models. Results from these models, for the economy and its major sectors, are periodically summarized by the Federal Reserve Banks of Richmond and Philadelphia.

No method of economic forecasting stands alone! Some business economists devote 60 per cent or more of their working time to the building and interpretation of various forecasting models, methods and devices. Each method mentioned in this chapter has advantages and disadvantages which cause individuals to support it more strongly than they might support other methods; yet, when the chips are down and a deadline must be met, economists tend to do the best they can with what they have at the time. All they know with certainty is that they will be wrong, and the degree of error can be expected to increase in proportion to the time span covered by the forecast.

No serious student would argue that the methods of analysis presented here are perfect. However, they are the best we have at this time. And, used in conjunction with one another, they can provide the kinds of insight into business problems that are necessary for proper allocation of scarce resources within the firm.

CASES

Forecasting

The United States Football League: The Cleveland Downs

The United States Football League is considering a franchise in Cleveland, to be known as the Cleveland Downs. Prospective owners think the new team could do as well financially as did the Cleveland Browns in the 1960s and early 1970s.

A professional football team has existed in Cleveland for many years. Presumably, as with professional athletic clubs elsewhere, the Cleveland

Browns were managed in a manner that provided a satisfactory profit for the owner(s). In addition to television royalties, commercials, concessions sold at home games, and so on, profitability depends in large part on the average number of persons attending the home games. To determine the Browns total revenue, and ultimately total profit, answer the following questions:

1. What part of the variation in the number of tickets demanded each year for home game attendance is explained by the percent of games won last year, the population in the Cleveland metropolitan area, and the effective buying power (disposable personal income) per household in the Browns' market area? An answer may be calculated by using the information provided in Exhibit 1.
2. Assuming the Browns' experience is a valid indicator of potential financial success for the Downs, use the coefficients obtained for question 1 to project (*a*) whether and (*b*) why the Cleveland Downs will succeed. By assumption, the Downs of 1984 should attract about the same number of people as the Browns of 1974.[1] You are being asked to apply and interpret your equation from question 1.

Exhibit 1
Factors affecting average home game attendance: The Browns in Cleveland

(1)	(2)	(3)	(4)	(5)
	Average home game attendance	Percent of games won last year	Population of Cuyahoga County (000)	Effective buying income/ household
Year				
1959	56,397	75.0	1,654.0	7,754
1960	56,329	58.3	1,670.3	8,035
1961	60.984	72.7	1,695.4	8,087
1962	60,335	61.5	1,715.2	8,356
1963	69,490	53.8	1,737.3	8,475
1964	78,476	71.4	1,719.3	8,891
1965	79,612	76.9	1,752.1	9,678
1966	77,750	78.6	1,763.0	10,159
1967	77,830	64.3	1,746.5	10,668
1968	75,301	64.3	1,766.7	11,389
1969	82,623	71.4	1,769.7	12,159
1970	81,054	76.9	1,728.1	12,570
1971	77,358	50.0	1,764.4	13,292
1972	75,513	64.3	1,763.9	13,156
1973	70,058	71.4	1,673.9	14,442

Source: Columns 2 and 3 provided by *Akron Beacon Journal* newspaper records. Columns 4 and 5 obtained from *Sales Management.*

---

[1] This may be a heroic assumption. The Downs experience may turn out to be quite different from that of the Browns, at least in part because of the different level of interest in the new football league.

An exercise in business conditions analysis

Forecast for 1970: Leading indicators[1]   Twelve leading indicators shown in *Business Conditions Digest* appeared as in Exhibits 1 and 2. In the mid-1980s, mechanical, barometric, and econometric models of aggregate

Exhibit 1
Cyclical indicators: Selected indicators by timing (leading indicators)

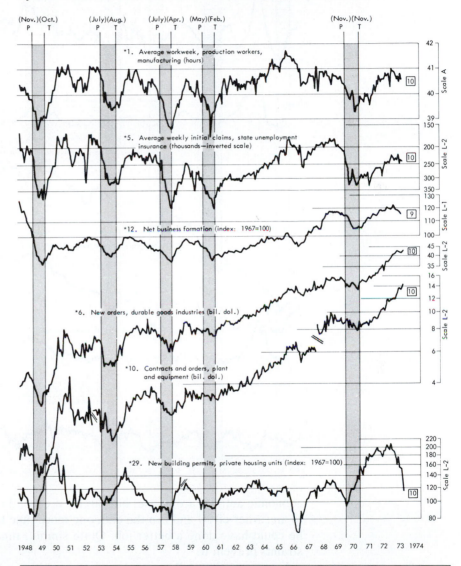

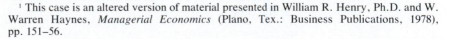

[1] This case is an altered version of material presented in William R. Henry, Ph.D. and W. Warren Haynes, *Managerial Economics* (Plano, Tex.: Business Publications, 1978), pp. 151–56.

Exhibit 2
Cyclical indicators: Selected indicators by timing

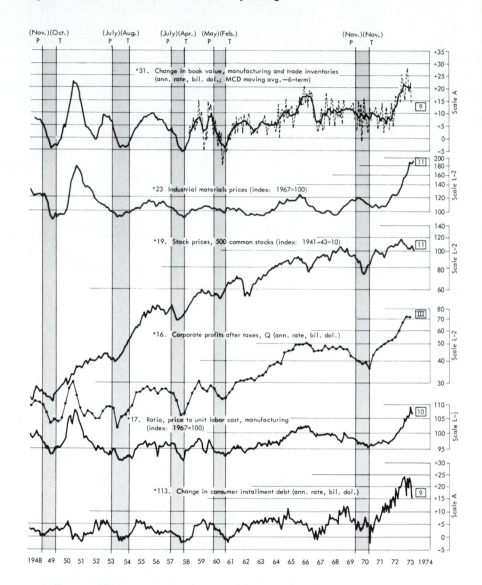

economic activity are in use; but rarely, if ever, does a forecaster return
to an earlier effort and run the data one more time to determine how she/
he could have done a better job. Quite simply, time and budgetary constraints prevent it.

Forecast 1970 GNP, using data that would have been available to you
at the time.

1. What kind of forecast for 1970 would you have made on the basis of movements in these indicators in 1969?
2. How much confidence would you have in this forecast?
3. Were you to do a similar forecast for 1986, what would you do differently?

GNP Forecast for 1970: Mechanical Model

PART I

Prepare a forecast of the GNP and its principal components for each quarter through 1970, using the data for 1969, third quarter (*Survey of Current Business,* July 1971) as follows:

	Billions
Gross national product	$940.2
Change in GNP from previous period	18.4
Personal income	759.3
Disposable personal income	643.2
Personal outlays	600.9
Personal consumption expenditures	584.1
Interest paid by consumers and transfer payments to foreigners	16.8
Change in business inventories	10.4
Corporate profits before tax (adjusted)	78.0
Corporate profits taxes	38.2
Corporate profits after taxes	39.8
Capital consumption allowances (depreciation)	82.1
Indirect business taxes, etc.	87.1
Contributions for social insurance	54.7
Transfer payments, etc.	95.7
Dividends	24.7
Changes in dividends from previous period	0.5

It is important to know the following relationships:

Net national product	= GNP − Capital consumption allowances.
National income	= Net national product − Indirect business taxes.
Personal income	= National income − Corporate profits + Dividends − Contributions for social insurance + Transfer payments.
Disposable income	= Personal income − Personal income taxes.
Gross private domestic investment	= Fixed investment + Net change in inventory investment.

Assume that the following data are given:

	Annual rates ($ billions)				
	1969:4	1970:1	1970:2	1970:3	1970:4
Government expenditures on goods and services:					
Total	$213.0	$217.3	$216.5	$220.1	$223.7
Federal	99.5	100.2	96.8	96.1	95.9
Defense	78.4	78.9	75.1	74.2	73.2
Nondefense	21.2	21.3	21.6	21.9	22.7
State and local	113.5	117.1	119.7	124.0	127.9
Fixed investment	132.3	130.8	132.1	133.5	133.6
Nonresidential investment	102.2	100.8	102.1	104.8	100.8
Residential investment	30.1	30.0	29.9	28.7	32.8
Net exports	2.7	3.5	4.2	4.0	2.7

Source: *Survey of Current Business* (July 1971).

Assume also that:

1. Personal outlays in each quarter are equal to 0.95 of disposal income in the preceding quarter. The portion of personal outlays represented by interest paid by consumers and personal transfer payments by foreigners increases by $0.3 billion in each quarter, and the balance represents consumer expenditures on goods and services. Personal consumption expenditures are personal outlays less such transfers.

2. Examine past inventory behavior and make your own estimates, taking into account what you know, or can find out, about current conditions in the economy.

3. The quarter-to-quarter change in corporate profits before taxes in $billions is equal to:

$$.04 \, (\Delta GNP)_t + 0.3 \, (\Delta \, Inv)_t - 0.2 \, (\Delta GNP)_{t-1} - 1.0 \text{ billion}$$

4. The change in corporate profits taxes equals 45 percent of the current change in the corporate profits before taxes.

5. Dividends change by 30 percent of the current change in corporate profits after taxes plus 50 percent of the change in dividends in the previous quarter.

6. The change in contributions to social security (payroll taxes) amounts to 10 percent of the change in GNP.

7. The change in indirect business taxes is equal to 15 percent of the change in GNP.

8. The change in transfer payments by government and certain interest payments increases $1.3 billion per quarter.

9. The change in personal income taxes is equal to 15 percent of the change in personal income.

10. Capital consumption allowances increase by $1.5 billion in each quarter.

PART II

After you have completed mechanical projections based on the above assumptions, consider how reasonable they seem in the light of all other information you have at your disposal. What assumptions do you believe should be changed? How, how much, and for what reason? What would be the order of magnitude of the changes induced in your first projection? Has this approach given adequate attention to the multiplier? Explain the basis for your conclusion.

PART III

Compare your forecast for 1970 with the actual changes in the GNP and its components during that year. How great was the error in your forecast? What are the apparent reasons for those errors?

(Note: Statistical data will be found in issues of the *Survey of Current Business* and in *Economic Indicators*. Current business literature—such as *Business Week, Fortune,* monthly letters of the leading commercial banks and Federal Reserve Banks, the monthly issues of *Economic Indicators,* and the publications of the leading investment services—will supply information that may enable you to form an opinion on the reasonableness of the given assumptions and data to be used in the mechanical projections.)

PROBLEMS
Forecasting

13–1   In measuring GNP, sales of products or services that will be used as production inputs by another business firm are not included. Why not?

13–2   How does depreciation enter into the determination of NNP (net national product)?

13–3   What, exactly, is the difference between an endogenous and an exogenous variable? Give several examples of each.

13–4   What is the multiplier? How does it enter into GNP forecasting?

13–5   Where could you find current information about the following: government spending, investment, residential construction, inventories, consumer durables, consumption of nondurables?

13–6   A diffusion index is to be calculated for the "short group" of 12 leading indicators. Of this group, eight are moving up and four are moving down. What is the value of the diffusion index?

13–7   Suppose the value of the multiplier for positive changes is taken to be 2.0. Given that consumption in a recent period was $973 billion, investment was $184 billion, and government purchases were $339 billion, assume investments in the following period were expected to be $193 billion and government purchases were expected to be $359 billion (with the tax collections unchanged). What is the forecast of consumption in the next period?

13–8   Assume you are using a simple partially specified GNP model as follows:

$$GNP = I + G + C$$
$$C = 0.552 GNP$$

Using the data for the recent period from problem 13–7 above, calculate the forecasts of *GNP* and *C* for the next period.

Selected references

Armstrong, J. Scott. "Forecasting with Econometric Methods: Folklore versus Fact." *Journal of Business* 51, no. 4 (1978), pp. 549–63.*

Bellante, Don. "The North-South Differential and the Migration of Heterogeneous Labor." *American Economic Review* 69, no. 1 (March 1979), pp. 166–75.

Bopp, Anthony E., and John A. Neri. "The Price of Gasoline: Forecasting Comparisons." *Quarterly Review of Economics and Business* 18, no. 4 (1978), pp. 23–32.*

Burch, S. W., and H. O. Stebler. "The Forecasting Accuracy of Consumer Attitude Date." *Journal of the American Statistical Association* 64 (December 1969).

Christ, Carl F. "Judging the Performance of Econometric Models of the U.S. Economy." *International Economic Review* 16, no. 1 (February 1975), pp. 55–74.

Chow, Gregory C. "Are Econometric Methods Useful for Forecasting?" *Journal of Business* 51, no. 4 (1978), pp. 565–68.

Cohen, Morris. "Forecasting Capital Goods: The Eclectic Approach." *Business Economics,* September 1970, pp. 66–72.

Conference Board, *Business Outlook 1973.* New York: The Conference Board Economic Forum, 1973.

Cooper, Ronald L. "An Econometric Forecasting Model of the Financial Sector of U.S. Households." *Applied Economics,* 1973, pp. 101–17.

* This article is included in Thomas J. Coyne, *Readings in Managerial Economics,* 3d ed. (Plano, Tex.: Business Publications, 1981).

Dederick, Robert G. "Economic Outlook Questionnaire." *Business Economics,* January 1974, pp. 74–80.

DePamphilis, Donald M. "Forecasting Expenditures on Consumer Durable Goods." *Business Economics,* May 1974, pp. 56–59.

————. "Forecasting Medical Care Expenses." *Business Economics* 11, no. 4 (September 1976), pp. 21–31.

Eckstein, Otto. "Econometric Models and the Formation of Business Expectations." *Challenge* 19 (March–April 1976).

Federal Reserve Bank of Boston, *New England Economic Review* (September–October 1973) pp. 4–29.

Feinberg, Phyllis. "Forecasting the Merger and Acquisition Game." *Institutional Investor* 14 (Fall 1980), pp. 43–47.

Gerking, Shelby D. "Input-Output as a Simple Econometric Model." *Review of Economics and Statistics* 58, no. 3 (August 1976), pp. 274–82.

Gols, A. George. "The Use of Input-Output in Industrial Planning." *Business Economics,* May 1975, pp. 19–27.

Gronau, Reuben. *The Value of Time in Passenger Transportation: The Demand for Air Travel.* New York: National Bureau of Economic Research, 1970.

Haitovsky, Yoel; George Treyz; and Vincent Su. *Forecasts with Quarterly Macroeconometric Models.* New York: National Bureau of Economic Research 1974.

Hawkins, Lawrence P. "Residential Electricity Sales—The Economics of Forecasting." *Public Utilities Fortnightly,* September 1976, pp. 31–35.

Heller, Peter S. "Diverging Trends in the Shares of Nominal and Real Government Expenditure in GDP: Implications for Policy." *National Tax Journal* 34, no. 1 (March 1981), pp. 61–74.

"Input-Output Structure of the U.S. Economy, 1963." *Survey of Current Business* 49 (November 1969).

Kosobud, Richard F. "Folklore into Fact: Appraising Forecasting Methods." *Journal of Business* 51, no. 4 (1978), pp. 569–71.

Lanford, H. W., and L. V. Imundo. "Approaches to Technological Forecasting as a Planning Tool." *Long Range Planning* (August 1974).

Leontief, Wassily W. "Input-Output Economics." *Scientific American* 185, no. 4 (October 1951), pp. 15–21.*

Lewis, John P. "Short-Term General Business Conditions Forecasting: Some Comments on Method." *Journal of Business* 35, no. 4 (October 1962), pp. 343–56.*

McNees, Stephen K. "The Forecasting Performance in the Early 1970s." *New England Economic Review* (July-August 1976).

_____. "Are Econometricians Useful? Folklore versus Fact." *Journal of Business* 51, no. 4 (1978), pp. 573–77.

Miernyk, W. H. "Long-Range Forecasting with a Regional Input-Output Model." *Western Economic Journal* 6 (June 1968).

Miller, Preston J. "Forecasting with Econometric Methods: A Comment." *Journal of Business* 51, no. 4 (1978), pp. 579–84.

Moore, Geoffrey H. "The Analysis of Economic Indicators." *Scientific American* 232, no. 1 (January 1975), pp. 17–23.

Norton, Curtis L., and Ralph E. Smith. "A Comparison of General Price Level and Historical Cost Financial Statements in the Prediction of Bankruptcy." *Accounting Review,* January 1979, pp. 72–87.

Okun, Arthur M. "The Predictive Value of Surveys of Business Intentions." *The American Economic Review,* May 1967.

Simon, Nancy W., and Phillip M. Ritz. "Producers Durable Equipment in the 1963 and 1967 Input-Output Studies." *Survey of Current Business,* February 1975, pp. 25–32, 36.

Suits, Daniel B. "Forecasting and Analysis with an Econometric Model." *American Economic Review* 52 (March 1962).

Thomas, C. Hamshaw. "Product Forecasting—The BAC 3–11 Airliner." *Long Range Planning* (June 1970).

Thompson, Russell G., and H. Peyton Young. "Forecasting Water Use for Policy-Making: A Review." *Water Resources Research* (August 1973), pp. 792–99.

U.S. Department of Commerce. "The Input-Output Structure of the U.S. Economy: 1963." *Survey of Current Business Supplement,* November 1969. See also, "The Input-Output Structure of the U.S. Economy: 1967." *Survey of Current Business Supplement,* February 1974, pp. 33.

Wecker, William E. "Comments on 'Forecasting with Econometric Methods: Folklore versus Fact.' " *Journal of Business* 51, no. 4 (1978), p. 585.

CHAPTER

14

Competitive strategy and long-range planning

Strategy has a long-run perspective. It extends beyond the expected useful life of much of the firm's plant and equipment. Strategic planning can select a future "business to be in," specified in terms of product mix, markets in which the products will be sold, and competitive advantages the firm may expect to achieve.

The chapter begins with a brief description of goals, objectives, and the process of formulating strategy. Presented also is an overview of uses of long-range forecasts in strategic planning. The chapter discusses social forecasting, technological forecasting, and resource forecasting. It concludes with examples of economic analyses in strategic planning by business and nonprofit organizations.

Goals, objectives, and strategy

Long-range planning and strategy formulation is relatively new to the American business scene, having been introduced to large firms for the first time in a formalized sense in the early 1950s. By the mid-1980s, formal strategic planning has matured to the point that firms of all sizes in the profit as well as the not-for-profit area make use of it routinely. At this writing a very large body of knowledge exists in the area of competitive strategy and long-range planning. This chapter introduces the art with the expressed hope that the student will pursue the subject more deeply elsewhere.

Long-range forecasting and strategy formulation take place at the highest levels within the organization. For strategy within the organization to be successfully implemented, the firm must have goals and objectives. These two words have different meanings. Suppose a professor had as her objective the notion of gaining and maintaining national leadership in her field. Such an objective is so broad and expressed in such a general manner that it may never be achieved. Specific goals can be achieved. To reach her objective this same professor might decide to publish a refereed article in a particularly noteworthy journal every so often. As the professor achieves her goals, she sets new ones, striving always to reach the objective. Once objectives are set and the need for goals is realized, the professor in this example and, of course, the business firm in the real world, develop a specific strategy for reaching specified goals. Time allotments are made, budgets are established, equipment is obtained and put in place, and everything else thought necessary by the planner is synchronized in an overall strategy that is thought workable at the time. Long-range forecasting comes into being as executives attempt to determine how well and how promptly their goals will be met. It is through the forecasting process that one can determine the efficiency and effectiveness of the firm's overall corporate strategy.

Most professionals in the field agree that for corporate strategy to be effective in the long run, the strategic plan (i.e., budgets, equipment, and so on) must be devised and put in place by the manager responsible for the overall performance of a particular profit center, plant, portfolio, or whatever. In addition, the manager charged with overall responsibility for carrying out the strategic plan is almost always the person best qualified to make necessary changes as the need for change becomes obvious over time. Therefore, the art of strategic planning is one of setting or establishing a long-term objective that may, at the time it is set, be thought to be unreachable.

John Kennedy, when he was serving as President of the United States, set as an objective the notion that the United States would gain and maintain international leadership in science; he set as a goal the placing of a person on the moon during the decade of the 1960s. The next step was to establish very specific goals that would help reach the objective. Certain earth-orbiting-missile programs came into existence. Plans were made for astronauts to orbit the earth in space vehicles. Designing suits to wear in space, building earth stations, and similar goals came into being—all to help achieve the broader objective. Managers of the various and sundry space projects and programs established strategies that were considered necessary to achievement of the various goals. Economic forecasters and other forecasters kept track of the quantities of money necessary to launch the space program and from time to time issued long-range forecasts as to the probability of reaching certain goals by specified dates.

Goals, objectives, and strategies are all interrelated, and the manager in charge must understand this interrelationship. He or she must then develop a cohesive statement that can be readily understood by stockholders as well as corporate managers, up and down the traditional lines of authority. This process undoubtedly sounds simple enough although, perhaps, somewhat abstract. It is a process that requires constant attention and a proper sense of direction, without which scarce and costly resources almost definitely will be misallocated. Proper communications keeps division managers, functional department heads, and subordinates on track. A process that has proved most useful is periodic issuance of formalized written statements, often no longer than two pages in length. Such a statement reveals what is taking place with respect to a particular goal. It contains seven steps:

1. *Subject*. The manager specifies precisely what it is that she/he is dealing with at the time.
2. *Object*. The object being pursued is precisely stated. This is not to be confused with the overall objective. It is, instead, the goal that is being worked on at the time.
3. *Present*. The manager states as succinctly as possible the present situation as she/he sees it. How close the department is to achieving a particular goal, for example.
4. *Proposal*. The manager precisely proposes what must be done to reach the goal, in full and on time.
5. *Advantages*. The manager reveals the advantages associated with pursuing the proposal. Such things as how much more quickly and, perhaps, more cheaply and better the goal could be reached if a particular series of events were to take place.
6. *Disadvantages*. With any proposal and despite its numerous advantages, there are bound to be some drawbacks. Costs and other considerations might be of such a nature that the disadvantages of the proposal outweigh the advantages. Regardless, the report needs to address the disadvantages at this point.
7. *Action*. What action does the manager recommend? Whatever it is, it needs to be stated. In this last section of the statement, the manager puts her/his ideas on the line, in writing, and either sinks or swims with them. As the reader might guess, this is the hardest step in the report, since it opens the manager widest to potential criticism. Once this report is read by superior and subordinate persons, extensive planning revisions may be necessary. It is here that the negotiations process, the feedback, and the reviews take place. It is also at this point that major progress can be made in formulation of the best possible strategic plan for the firm at that particular time.

The smaller the firm, the greater the probability that strategic planning is relatively simple and does not occupy large quantities of the chief executive's time. Nonetheless, the planning and the process is the same and is no less important to realization of the firm's objectives. The process laid forth here is, therefore, as important to the ma-and-pa organization as it is to AT&T.

**Formulation of
strategy**

The game of chess provides an example of a need for strategy. Success (i.e., winning) requires planning ahead for at least a few plays. One chess player may have an offensive strategy requiring concentration of powerful pieces for a thrust down the middle of the board. Another may have a defensive strategy requiring early "castling," with a buildup of a deep defense in front of the king's castle. Strategy suggests most of the early moves of each player. Further, every move, even an opportunistic play, is evaluated in terms of its contribution toward the player's overall objective: to checkmate the other player's king.

Businesses are formulating strategy when they make decisions about the general direction and scope of their desired growth, assuming growth at some specified rate or to a certain absolute size is the firm's objective. Delineation of a future business-to-be-in suggests priorities for present resource allocations to technological research, market development, management recruiting and training, plant and equipment expenditures, and mergers and acquisitions. Many contemporary decisions of line managers and staff specialists are or should be formed by their relationships to the firm's long-term strategy.

The ongoing, never-ending process of strategy formulation includes specification of objectives, establishment of goals, evaluation of the firm's strengths and weaknesses, a forecast of trends in the environment, delineation of economic threats and opportunities, and a search for synergy (economic complementarity among potential activities of the firm).[1]

Objectives and goals

Conventional microeconomic theory asserts that a business firm often attempts to act in ways that allow it to maximize profits. Some writers have suggested that firms attempt to maximize sales rather than profits.[2] Others have hypothesized that firms simply attempt to "satisfice"— reach some satisfactory level of profits and sales.[3] Still others have hypothesized that the primary objective of the firm is survival,[4] or that the firm is primarily interested in growth in order to survive.[5]

A broadly stated goal, such as long-run profit maximization, is not very

---

[1] The concept of strategy follows the concept of H. Igor Ansoff, *Corporate Strategy* (New York: McGraw-Hill, 1965). Ansoff's book contains many important concepts and techniques not mentioned here.

[2] William J. Baumol, *Economic Theory and Operations Analysis,* 3d ed. (Englewood Cliffs, N.J.: Prentice-Hall, 1972), p. 320.

[3] Richard M. Cyert and James G. March, *A Behavioral Theory of the Firm* (Englewood Cliffs, N.J.: Prentice-Hall, 1963).

[4] Peter Drucker, "Business Objectives and Survival Needs: Notes on a Discipline of Business Enterprise," *Journal of Business* 31 (1958), pp. 81–90.

[5] John Kenneth Galbraith, *The New Industrial State,* 2d ed. (Boston: Houghton Mifflin, 1971), pp. 171–72.

helpful in the strategy formulation process. Goals must be more specific. For example, a firm may establish some target rate of return on total assets used over the next 3 to 10 years. Ansoff says that even this specific goal must be decomposed into a set of subsidiary objectives relating to external competitive strengths and internal operating efficiency. Figure 14–1 illustrates an operationally useful set of long-range objectives. Note the goals are quantifiable, so that the firm can measure and, perhaps, forecast the extent to which its objectives are being met.

In addition and related to the profitability objective, the firm has a set of objectives related to flexibility. Internal flexibility is provided by liquidity; external flexibility is attained through diversification.[6] Both methods help ensure that the business will not have its profits overcome by a

Figure 14–1
A set of long-range objectives

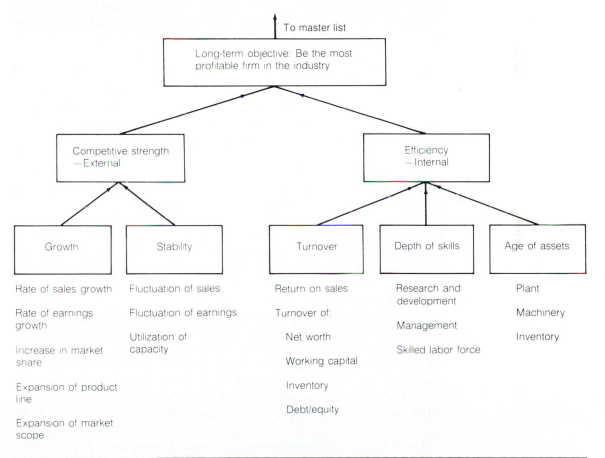

---

[6] Ansoff, *Corporate Strategy*, pp. 50–53.

single adversity. A business with reserve borrowing power can meet the threat of an unexpected product improvement by a competitor. A firm that is diversified across several product lines is not dependent upon the buying power of any one group of customers.

The objectives of profitability and flexibility are typically conflicting, so that trading off less of one for more of the other is necessary. Serious in-house negotiations and trade-offs may be necessary in order to obtain agreement regarding these objectives. For example, a reduction in plant and equipment expenditure will allow an increase in assets that are quickly convertible to cash. Both objectives are subject to self-imposed responsibilities and institutional constraints. In some instances management may feel responsible for provision of steady employment and job security to long-time employees, to the detriment of profitability. Other firms might have less noble reasons. For example, General Motors might not pursue growth or profitability within a single product line—say, Chevrolet—to the point that competition is wiped out and countervailing actions by the Antitrust Division of the Justice Department are stimulated.

Selecting the "business to be in"

The firm selects an evolving product mix and a corresponding set of markets that appear to offer the best prospects for achieving its objectives. It compares various possible deployments of its limited (but possibly in part unique) set of resources and organizational competences. Strategy formulation requires appraisal of the firm's strengths and weaknesses, determination of the particular business competences that are essential for success in various avenues of expansion, and forecasts of the results of successful operation in each line of activity.

The firm's relative strengths and weaknesses can be appraised by (1) an examination of past performance to locate patterns of success or failure and (2) direct comparison of the firm's skills and capacities with those of major competitors. In the words of Quinn, "The purposes of such exercises should be: to identify and exploit the comparative weaknesses of competitors, to marshal sufficient resources into specific subareas of the company's operations to dominate them, to recognize where competitive strengths allow the company wider latitude in pricing or product policies than competitors, and to pinpoint the company's own weaknesses for more aggressive action or purposeful withdrawal."[7] Appraisal of the firm's strengths and weaknesses should cover all of the resources and competences required in its present business, plus any other capabilities that it has or can reasonably expect to acquire. Table

---

[7] John B. Quinn, "Technological Strategies for Industrial Companies," in *Technological Forecasting and Corporate Strategy*, ed. Gordon Wills, David Ashton, and Bernard Taylor (New York: American Elsevier Publishing, 1969), p. 58.

14–1 lists a few examples of the kinds of organizational characteristics that are considered.

Requirements for business success in various industries are determined through (1) listing the technological, marketing, financial, and management capabilities required by the nature of each industry and (2) developing competitive profiles of the most successful firms in each industry. Then, in Ansoff's words, "Superposition of our firm's competence profile with the competitive profiles measures the 'fit' with each new industry and hence the chances of a successful entry."[8]

Table 14–1
Outline for internal appraisal and industry analysis

1. Product-market structure:
   a. Products and their characteristics.
   b. Product missions.
   c. Customers.

2. Growth and profitability:
   a. History.
   b. Forecasts.
   c. Relation to life cycle.
   d. Basic determinants of demand.
   e. Averages and norms typical of the industry.

3. Technology:
   a. Basic technologies.
   b. History of innovation.
   c. Technological trends-threats and opportunities.
   d. Role of technology in success.

4. Investment:
   a. Cost of entry and exit—critical mass.
   b. Typical asset patterns in firms.
   c. Rate and type of obsolescence of assets.
   d. Role of capital investment in success.

5. Marketing:
   a. Means and methods of selling.
   b. Role of service and field support.
   c. Roles and means of advertising and sales promotion.
   d. What makes a product competitive.
   e. Role of marketing in success.

6. Competition:
   a. Market shares, concentration, dominance.
   b. Characteristics of outstanding firms and of poor firms.
   c. Trends in competitive patterns.

7. Strategic perspective:
   a. Trends in demand.
   b. Trends in product-market structure.
   c. Trends in technology.
   d. Key ingredients in success.

Source: H. Igor Ansoff, *Corporate Strategy* (New York: McGraw-Hill, 1965), p. 146.

---

[8] Ansoff, *Corporate Strategy*, p. 101.

Forecasts of results of successful business operations in the various industries are obviously needed in choosing a "portfolio" of businesses-to-be-in. The firm needs estimates of growth prospects, return on assets used, and year-to-year variability in sales and income, assuming a competent organization, in each line of business. Such estimates cannot be made without projections and analysis of trends affecting demand for products and services, competition, the institutional and legal environment, timing and nature of technological changes, availability and relative cost of resources, and increases in industry capacity.

An overview of long-range forecasting

Long-range forecasting is still a primitive art. It deals with dimly perceived forces that interact in complex ways. Consider the effect of the birthrate on the economy. Changing cultural values could lower birth rates; reduced birth rates diminish prospective future demands for goods and services used in the public schools; in the more distant future, the reduced number of new workers entering the labor market may tend to lift wages and thus increase the demand for capital goods. On the other hand, illegal immigrants by the millions exist today in the United States. Their presence may diminish the economic impact of lower birth rates; in addition, changing cultural values could eventually reduce the institutional pressure for complete retirement at age 65. The increase in older workers continuing part-time employment could tend to depress wages and thus decrease the demand for capital goods.

There are no adequate formal models around which the whole process of long-range forecasting can be organized. However, the forecasting process can be broken into phases and carried out in a logical sequence:

1. Projecting, extrapolating, or constructing trends and potential breakthroughs and developments in the principal environmental influences, one at a time.
2. Assessing the potentials for interaction (reinforcement or interference) among the various trends and adjusting the forecasts to take interactions into account.
3. Considering the probable ecological ramifications of simultaneous environmental changes resulting from the adjusted trends.
4. Appraising potential social feedback upon progress of the trends and control of their ecological ramifications.
5. Developing the apparent range of alternative states of the future business environment.[9]

---

[9] Adapted from the statement by Otis D. Duncan, "Social Forecasting—the State of the Art," *The Public Interest,* Fall 1969, p. 115.

Social planning   Three areas have been selected for attention here. Boundaries of these areas are not well defined, but using them facilitates discussion and allows emphasis of key interrelationships among the areas. These areas, or groupings, are: cultural trends, political trends, and demographic trends.

Cultural trends

Culture consists of beliefs, values, customs, and attitudes exhibited by members of a society. Culture is learned by these members. Over time, culture changes and so does the behavior of the people—both as consumers of goods and services and as suppliers of personal services and capital needed by businesses. Thus, changes in culture can have profound effects upon the demand for products and suppliers of inputs. Some discernible trends in American culture and their implications for long-range planning are discussed below.

The easy life.   Puritan and frontier virtues—hard work, thrift, and individualism—are on the decline. In Philip Kotler's apt phrases, Americans want the "soft life," the "sweet life," the "social life," and the "safe life." [10] This condition appears similar to that of the Romans, prior to the decline and fall of their empire. Demands in the future can be expected to burgeon for products that increase convenience and leisure time (e.g., convenience foods), provide luxury and recreation (e.g., motor homes), mark the user as a person of "good taste" and conventional opinions (e.g., memberships in social clubs), and increase confidence and security (e.g., variable annuity forms of life insurance). Simultaneously, native workers appear less willing to endure jobs that are dirty, noisy, dangerous, monotonous, and physically arduous.

A secular, this-world, here-and-now attitude   Americans are placing less relative value on deferred satisfactions. Even the religious concept of eternal life is receiving decreased emphasis in some denominations. Thus, a sales appeal that reminds consumers they "only go around once in life" and should, therefore, make the most of it (with the assistance of a particular product) has been effective. Many consumers are willing to build up heavy loads of debt rather than defer purchases until they can pay cash. In most cases, if a person cannot afford to pay cash for a consumer durable or nondurable, that person or family cannot afford the item.

Broader perspective—living in a "larger world"   Faster transportation and better communication broaden the perspective of the relevant

---

[10] Philip Kotler, *Marketing Management: Analysis, Planning & Control (Englewood Cliffs, N.J.: Prentice-Hall, 1967)*, pp. 82–87.

world.[11] Consider how quickly Concorde crosses the Atlantic, and think of the millions of Americans watching the live broadcasts of moon walks and foreign wars. Simultaneously, there is increasing interdependence and competition among people and their activities. Effects of a firm's actions upon the environment of other firms and persons (external effects) are becoming more important and better understood. There is an increasing tendency to look to government agencies for protection of the environment and of the interests of various groups through regulation of privately owned businesses and through directly providing goods and services. Kotler lists several problem areas that make high-growth markets for direct sales to state and local governments: population growth (e.g., contraceptives and birth control literature to children), poverty (e.g., subsidized housing), urbanization (e.g., law enforcement equipment), air and water pollution (e.g., pollution measurement devices), congested transportation (e.g., rapid transit systems), and agriculture (e.g., supplies for disease and pest eradication programs).[12]

Decreased importance of values associated with the traditional concept of family   There is a decline in the relative authority and influence of parents compared with children, an increasingly permissive attitude toward sexual interests and activities, and decreased delineation of male and female roles. These trends bring greater emphasis upon products designed for young people or designed to make consumers look or feel younger. Large markets for pornographic materials have been opened. There is a move toward unisex looks in men's and women's clothing. In the labor market, sexual rigidity is breaking down; there are now more female airline pilots and lawyers and more male telephone operators and registered nurses.

Cultural values of individuals affect their behavior as consumers, producers, and voters. Thus, changing cultural values propel and shape the trends in political institutions. How a business should or could forecast these trends accurately is uncertain at this writing.

Political trends

Futuristic books stress the increasing importance of the role of government in daily life of the population as a major theme. General trends in the role of government include: (1) increased absolute size of government budgets and employment, (2) increased use of public planning and regulation, (3) increased emphasis on income redistribution, (4) increasing

---

[11] Daniel Bell, "The Study of the Future," *The Public Interest* Fall 1965, pp. 120–21.

[12] Kotler, *Marketing Management*, pp. 146–49.

importance of international affairs, and despite the verbiage of presidents Carter and Reagan, (5) increased governmental control over the daily affairs of consumers and businesses.

Size and composition of budgets Expenditures by federal, state, and local governments in the United States amount to hundreds of billions of dollars annually. The federal deficit alone for each year during the mid-1980s and beyond also amounts to hundreds of billions of dollars. Senator Ted Kennedy and Representative "Tip" O'Neil continue to call for more government spending. They say additional deficits are needed, in 1983, to "get the economy moving again." Changes in the composition of these expenditures can cause large shifts in demand and in the cost of various inputs. For example, the decision to build the interstate highway system had enormous impact upon builders of earth-moving equipment, such as Caterpillar, and upon producers of cement. A future political decision to subsidize large-scale expansion of rapid transit would have similar impact upon a different set of suppliers.

Planning and regulation. To date, the United States has not used public economic planning as much as have France and some other European countries. However, there has been increasing use of such powers as stockpiling of materials for later resale to stabilize prices. Antitrust and labor legislation and the manner of their enforcement have important bearings upon the nature and result of business behavior. Consumer and environmental protection legislation also affect business practices and opportunities.

Income redistribution Programs designed to provide minimum incomes, or even those intended to provide minimum requirements for food and health care, affect private firms on the demand side through consumption changes and on the production cost side through their effects on work attitudes.

International affairs Government policy concerning international trade and finance has tremendous effects upon firms with substantial participation in importing or exporting. Diplomatic recognition of the People's Republic of China and the opening of trade with the Soviet Union allow American firms some opportunity to compete for product exporting and importing and raw material purchases in two large economies that have enormous potential for the future. OPEC price and output decisions, the continued wars in the Middle East (i.e., the 1982 invasion of Lebanon by Israel, the Iran-Iraq War), and the situation in El Salvador and other Latin American states serve to increase the degree of risk and uncertainty associated with long-term business strategies. Tariffs, quotas, subsidies, rates of exchange, and loan guarantees are examples of government policies and activities that determine the potential for exporting and the intensity of competition from imports. Many firms in Mexico, for example, borrowed heavily from banks in the United States and by mid-1983 could not repay these loans.[13]

Demographic trends

Demography is the study of changes in population, its composition by age groups and various other classifications, and the spatial distribution of population groupings. Demography is concerned with changes in such factors as death rates, birth rates, marriage rates, and geographic mobility. Demographic forecasts are helpful in projecting demand for products and availability of labor.

After individuals are born, their progress through the schools and into the labor force can be projected with considerable confidence. Babies born after the Vietnam War, for example, need jobs, housing, automobiles, and other durable goods. The "most probable" forecasts must be made for all products.

Estimates of the number of people who will be born in future years are subject to extremely wide errors. Zero population growth was at one time a widely accepted objective. Without immigration, a fall in birth rates would be felt by manufacturers of children's clothing and school equipment, by textbook publishers, by teachers, and by educational institutions. Then would come the successive impacts upon producers of teenage goods, the residential construction industry, and producers of durable goods needed after family formation.

Projected locations of population groups are of much interest in business planning. In any given year, about one fifth of the population moves. In general, the population is becoming increasingly concentrated in large urban areas. The 100 largest metropolitan areas contain almost 60 percent of the total population and more than 60 percent of the total purchasing power. However, major metropolitan areas grow at different rates, and this increases the usefulness of demographic studies in projecting sales by product mixes. It is also helpful in identifying markets and in planning plant sizes and locations.

An example: Social forecasting at the General Electric Company

"If . . . sociopolitical forecasting is done comprehensively and successfully, on both a short- and long-term basis, a business is not so likely to be taken by surprise by shifting public needs, changing aspirations of employees or customers and legislative or administrative action by government." These words are from a sociopolitical forecast originally pre-

---

[13] At this writing, Mexican concerns owe almost $100 billion to U.S. banks. Economic, social, and military consequences of the greatest nature may exist in the very near future if this debt remains unpaid.

pared for the General Electric Company.[14] The methodology of this study included:

1. Interviews with more than 60 prominent educators, representatives of business, research administrators, members of the press, and government officials.
2. A review of a considerable amount of futurist literature.
3. A synthesis that takes into account at least part of the interactions among the individual ideas and predictions.

This study forecasted that social change in the United States during the 1970s would result from interaction of eight forces. The process involved in the study is equally applicable to the 1980s and beyond. The following is a list of the long-term variables considered and the forecaster findings in each area.

Increasing affluence   Real income would double from 1965 to 1980. Increasing percentages of income would be spent on travel, leisure, culture, and self-improvement. General Electric forecasted developing public impatience with circumstances leading to individual hardships—poverty, unemployment, expenses of sickness and accidents, meager income after retirement, and strikes. Money would be more and more taken for granted and less and less useful as a motivator.

Economic stabilization   GE expected that the swing in unemployment during the 1970s would be kept in the range 3–4.5 percent and that recession cutbacks in industrial production would be no greater than 5 percent. Greater stability was expected from more use of contracyclical monetary and fiscal policy and certain structural changes in the economy. The forecasters badly misjudged the behavior of this variable, as witnessed by the devastating recession that was in place during the last two years of the forecast period, 1979 and 1980.

Rising tide of education   The forecasters expected spending on education to increase from about 6 percent of 1970 GNP to about 10 percent of the greater 1980 GNP. Two or three years of college, provided free to the student, would become the norm. Content of education would shift in the direction of preparation to accept change. The better-educated population would become less tolerant of authoritarianism and develop higher expectations for its work experience. The basic shift away from advanced studies in the liberal arts and sciences and toward business and engineering was not included as an important part of the forecast.

Changing attitudes toward work and leisure.   General Electric thought the character of work would be changing (from manufacturing to services, from blue-collar to white-collar, from tools to automation) and that

---

[14] Earl B. Dunckel, William K. Reed, and Ian H. Wilson, *The Business Environment of the Seventies* (New York: McGraw-Hill, 1970), pp. 44–47.

the structure of work would also be changing (more work/study programs, more sabbaticals, more part-time work). They suggested the opportunity for an increase in modular work scheduling to allow employees greater flexibility in selecting the number of hours to work.

Growing interdependence of institutions   The United States is becoming a national, rather than a regional, economy and society. Local problems have national importance because of communication that brings them to the attention of people in other places. There is an expansion of the government role and greater meshing of all levels of government activity because of the awareness of these problems. At the same time, there is increasing willingness to use private enterprise in solving social problems. The authors expected traditional boundaries between the public and the private sector to continue to become blurred.

Emergence of the postindustrial society   More and more of GNP were expected to be produced in education, professions such as law and medicine, governments, and nonprofit institutions. With the relative decline in profit-making, consumer-oriented operations, new measures of social output would be needed.

Pluralism and individualism.   There is growing realization that the federal government cannot by itself cope with such problems as poverty and pollution. The authors forecast a strengthening of local and state governments, along with growth of regional authorities to deal with such problems as rapid transit and metropolitan zoning. They thought that social and organizational patterns would be shaped in the 1970s by a wave of individualism that would emphasize equality, personal worth, and the supremacy of individual rights over those of the organization.

The urban-minority problem   The authors expected urban minorities to press for power over their own services and institutions. Particular targets would be schools, welfare, police and fire services, sanitation, recreation, banks, supermarkets, and lending agencies.

The study went on to project effects of the above trends upon institutions in the socioeconomic-political system and upon the value system of the population. With respect to the effects upon business, the study forecast the following:

1. Increased concern for continuing education and development of employees.
2. Increased expectations of safety and other qualities of products.
3. Increased insistence that business pay more of the social cost of problems it helps create (pollution, congestion).
4. Increased expectations that business will have long-range goals that are consistent with the national interest.
5. Increased opposition to conglomerate forms of business.
6. Increased pressure for consumer protection, extending to packaging and advertising and possibly to quality and utility of products.

7. Increased governmental regulation of plant location.
8. Increased governmental regulation of hiring, testing, and training, to promote national personnel policies.
9. Stricter control of mergers by large companies.
10. Increased involvement of private business in the social needs markets, with business and government cooperating in organizational patterns similar to those of National Aeronautics and Space Agency and Atomic Energy Commission.
11. Increased use of project task force organization in business.
12. Increased participation in effective decision-making in business by professional and technical experts.
13. Increasing difficulty in motivating individuals toward organizational goals.
14. Increasing emphasis on autonomy, creativity, and inherently gratifying work.[15]

Future social trends will be propelled and formed partially by technological changes. For example, present attitudes toward sexual behavior have been deeply affected by availability of effective and inexpensive oral contraceptives and abortion—which has prompted a large number of unanswered legal and moral questions. On the other hand, many future technological changes will be brought into place in response to changing private and social needs. For example, food needs will likely lead to a technology of ocean farming. Thus, social forecasting and technological forecasting are closely related.

Technological planning

Although technological forecasting must have been attempted throughout the industrial era, formal methods of forecasting have been developed only very recently. Most of the techniques have been introduced since the early 1960s.

General approaches to technological forecasting

There are two views of technological change. The ontological view sees inventions as coming on the scene independently of external circumstances or needs. This view leads to exploratory forecasting, in which one begins with existing technology, projects potential progress, and then considers how these changes may affect the nontechnical business environment. In other words, exploratory forecasting is started by mapping technological possibilities out toward their limits.

The contrasting teleological view of technological change sees it as a response to external social forces that create new demands. This view

---

[15] Dunckel et al., *The Business Environment* pp. 75–79.

leads to normative forecasting, in which forecasters start by predicting the future needs and objectives of society. They then work back to the current state of technology to determine the gaps that must be closed to permit meeting social aspirations.[16]

Normative forecasts have been criticized on the basis that even widely recognized needs do not necessarily call forth an invention, but they extend further into the future than do exploratory methods. On the other hand, exploratory forecasters have been criticized for their refusal to take into account the probable future desires of society, but exploratory forecasts are simpler and do focus on technological issues. The most reasonable approach appears to be a combination of the two methods.[17] Jantsch says, "A complete technological forecasting exercise . . . always constitutes an interactive process between exploratory and normative forecasts . . . it constitutes a feedback cycle in which both opportunities and objectives are treated as adaptive inputs."[18]

Specific techniques for technological forecasting

The purpose of technological forecasting is not to predict specific forms that technology will take at some exact date in the future. Instead, the primary interest is in determining the probability that selected end results will be achieved and to evaluate their significance. Quinn points out that technology is knowledge systematically applied; this knowledge improves in small increments and what appears to be a breakthrough is often simply an accumulation of small advances that add up to a significant change.[19] If and when cancer is conquered the cure will probably occur in this manner. It should also be kept in mind that there may be several technologies that can accomplish a given mission.

Intuitive forecasting techniques include the Delphi method and scenario writing. The Delphi method was developed by Olaf Helmer at Rand Corporation.[20] It develops forecasts based on a consensus of experts without permitting personal interactions. Bandwagon effects, halo effects, and ego involvements with publicly expressed positions are reduced. At the outset, several experts respond to a written questionnaire. Summaries of the forecasts are returned to the experts with a request to modify or defend deviating forecasts. Modifications and defenses are

---

[16] These concepts are taken from Robert V. Ayres, *Technological Forecasting and Long-Range Planning* (New York: McGraw-Hill, 1969).

[17] John P. Dory and Robert J. Lord, "Does TF Really Work?" *Harvard Business Review*, November–December 1970, p. 20.

[18] E. Jantsch, "Technological Forecasting in Corporate Planning," in *Technological Forecasting and Corporate Strategy*, ed Wills et al., p. 21.

[19] John B. Quinn, "Technological Forecasting," *Harvard Business Review*, March–April 1967, p. 99.

[20] Olaf Helmer, *Social Technology* (New York: Basic Books, 1966).

returned to the panel until a relative consensus develops, or the issues causing disagreement are clearly defined. Figure 14–2 illustrates a Delphi consensus on the timing of selected technological end results.

Scenario writing produces narrative, time-ordered, logical sequences of events. Each such scenario is a description of a possible evolving future environment. Scenarios can be used as inputs to a forecasting technique or as vehicles for communication among forecasters. Scenarios are, strictly speaking, predictions rather than forecasts, since each scenario takes the form "If (some set of things), then (some other set)." Among the prominent practitioners of scenario writing are Herman Kahn and his associates at Hudson Institute.[21]

More analytic techniques of technological forecasting include morphological analyses, several forms of trend fitting (S curves, envelope forecasting, correlations) and system approaches. Morphological analysis is an attempt at identification and enumeration of all possible means of arriving at a given objective. The analyst tries to find new and feasible methods that do not violate scientific principles. For example, given the objective "propel a vehicle," Ayres enumerates possible energy sources ranging from kinetic to nuclear with numerous intermediate steps in energy conversion.[22] Since the purpose of morphological analysis is to find previously overlooked solutions to problems, it is not, strictly speaking, a forecasting device but rather a method of generating inputs for the forecasting process.

Trend fitting is especially suited to forecasting future capabilities, such as the human ability to transmit information or rate of travel. Several kinds of curves may be used; perhaps most common are S curves. These show slow growth until the potential of a technology is recognized, rapid growth as this potential is exploited, and then deceleration of growth as the curve approaches a limiting value for the particular technology.

Envelope forecasting is based on a smooth curve drawn tangential to a family of S curves, as illustrated in Figure 14–3. The implicit assumption of the envelope method is that some new technology will allow the technological trend to continue until some absolute limit, such as speed of sound or speed of light, is approached.

Correlation relates a trend in one technical parameter to a trend or trends in one or more other variables. For example, the speed of commercial air transport tends to increase (with a time lag) as speeds of military aircraft are increased, since research and development for the

---

[21] Herman Kahn and A. J. Weiner, "The Next Thirty-Three Years: A Framework for Speculation," in *Business Strategy,* ed. H. Igor Ansoff (Middlesex, England: Penguin Books Ltd., 1969), pp. 75–106. Also by the same authors, *The Year 2,000* (New York: Macmillan, 1967).

[22] Ayres, *Technological Forecasting,* pp. 75–77.

Figure 14–2
A Delphi consensus of scientific breakthrough

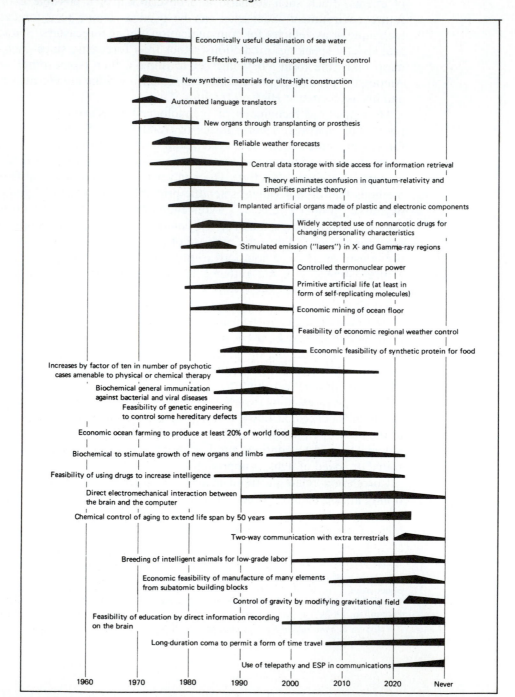

Source: R. J. Gordon and O. Helmer, *Report on a Long-Range Study,* Report P–2982, Rand Corporation, September 1964.

Figure 14–3
Trend fitting (S curves)

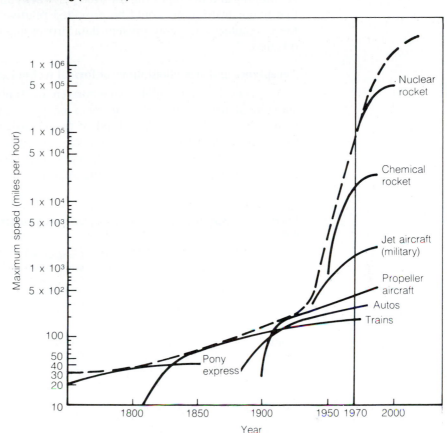

Source: Robert V. Ayres, *Technological Forecasting and Long-Range Planning* (New York: McGraw-Hill, 1969); reprinted in Arthur Gerstenfeld, "Technological Forecasting," *Journal of Business* 44, no. 1 (1971), pp. 10–18.

military sector spill over into the design of commercial equipment. Thus, one trend leads and forecasts the other.

Systems analyses put entire operating systems under scrutiny to pinpoint weaknesses in present technology. For example, an analysis of railroad passenger travel revealed, among other problems, that the rail cars weighed 2,000 pounds per passenger and that passengers were uncomfortable in high-speed turns. Existing technology could be used to lighten cars to 600 pounds per passenger and to bank the cars in turns. Another form of systems analysis assumes new technology and asks what its affect would be on present systems. For example, what would be the effect of a time-shared computer system with 200 terminals, 20,000-character program capacity, virtually unlimited memory, and $300 per hour total user cost? Some consequences: Small businesses could handle all accounting and tax reporting for $100 per week; all interested students in five major institutions could be provided relatively unlimited access to the computer; and many present data processing installations would be obsolete.[23]

Acceptance and some limitations of formal technological forecasting

A survey by Gerstenfeld, summarized in Table 14–2, revealed that substantial percentages of firms responding to the questionnaire were using at least one specific method of technological forecasting and that the mean of their forecast horizons was approximately seven years into the future.[24] Although corporate planners must use some form of technological forecasting, they should avoid engaging in science fiction fantasies

Table 14–2
Number of companies, by industry, using technological forecasting, as related to growth

Industry	Number of company respondents per industry	Companies using at least one specific forecasting method — Number	Percent of industry	Industry growth rate*	Mean number of years into the future
Transportation equipment	13	8	61.5%	5.0%	7.15 $(N=8)$
Chemicals and allied products	27	18	66.6	8.3	6.52 $(N=17)$
Electrical machinery, equipment, and supplies	21	15	71.5	6.4	7.75 $(N=15)$
Fabricated metals	10	7	70.0	4.7	5.50 $(N=7)$
Primary metals	7	1	14.3	3.6	5.00 $(N=1)$
Food and kindred products	27	14	52.0	3.2	7.15 $(N=13)$
Paper and allied products	8	5	62.5	4.9	7.00 $(N=5)$
Scientific instruments	5	4	80.0	5.5	5.25 $(N=4)$
Machinery, except electrical	18	11	61.0	5.8	7.69 $(N=11)$
Petroleum refining and related industries	14	7	50.0	3.2	10.00 $(N=7)$
Stone, clay, and glass	4	2	50.0	3.5	7.50 $(N=2)$
Textile mill products	8	3	37.5	3.5	5.00 $(N=3)$
Total	162	95			7.06†$(N=93)$

* Annual percent, 1957–60 to 1960–65. Growth rates based on *Federal Reserve Production Indexes for Industries*, U.S. Department of Commerce, Bureau of the Census.
 † Average years.
 Source: Bureau of the Census, U.S. Department of Commerce, Long-Term Economic Growth (Washington, D.C.: Government Printing Office, October 1966); reprinted in Arthur Gerstenfeld, "Technological Forecasting," *Journal of Business* 44, no. 1 (1971), p. 16.

[23] Examples are from Quinn, "Technological Strategies," p. 94.

[24] Arthur Gerstenfeld, "Technological Forecasting," *Journal of Business* 44, no. 1 (1971), pp. 10–18.

that involve technological developments beyond the relevant planning horizon. Furthermore, it should be kept in mind that there are unavoidable pitfalls in forecasting. Quinn lists: (1) unexpected interactions of several coincidental and apparently unrelated advances; (2) unprecedented demands, such as the "need" for atomic energy for military purposes; (3) major discoveries of entirely new phenomena, such as lasers, and (4) inadequate data concerning scientific resources committed to various lines of research and development.[25]

Technological developments are sensitive to changes in relative prices of natural resources. If some resources begin rising in price because of relative scarcity, a search for substitutes and for other methods of reducing requirements for the scarce inputs is set in motion. If other resources begin to have falling prices because of abundance, a search for new technological uses of the plentiful inputs is undertaken. Thus, resource forecasting is complementary to technological forecasting.

Resource planning

In resource forecasting, it is necessary to consider both needs and availabilities or, in economic terms, demands and supplies. These are the forces that will determine the relative prices of inputs and thereby affect choices of production techniques and relative prices of products. For example, costs of many products include substantial proportions of energy. Expected future availability and relative prices of oil, coal, gas, electricity, and nuclear energy at various places will affect choices of plant locations, production techniques, and product mixes.

Only the largest business firms will make original studies of resource prospects, since these investigations are complex and expensive. Most firms will adapt projections from outside sources to fit their own needs and circumstances. This section describes one of the generally available resource forecasts and discusses some considerations in evaluating and adapting the results of the study.

Resources in America's Future: methods and findings

Resources in America's Future and other publications by the organization called Resources for the Future, Inc., are the products of a large-scale, continuing study of economic growth of the United States with emphasis on the role of natural resources.[26] *Resources* contains projec-

---

[25] Quinn, "Technological Strategies," pp. 101–3.

[26] Hans H. Landsberg, Leonard L. Fischman, and Joseph L. Fisher, *Resources in America's Future* (Baltimore: Johns Hopkins University Press, 1963). Other RFF publications include: Sam H. Schurr, et al., *Energy in the American Economy 1850–1955;* Marion Clawson, et al., *Land for the Future;* Harold J. Barnett and Chandler Morse, *Scarcity and Growth: The Economics of National Resource Availability;* Harvey S. Perloff, et al., *Regions, Resources, and Economic Growth.*

tions of demand and supply of natural resources to the year 2000 for the United States.

The authors of *Resources in America's Future* emphasize that their numerical results are projections rather than forecasts. These projections are based on a set of assumptions, most of which are carefully specified. These are some of the principal methods:

1. Trends in consumption are extrapolated with some modification to reflect informed judgment—these changes usually have the effect of flattening the consumption growth curves.
2. Substitutions among materials and more efficient materials use through expected technological changes were incorporated if the implications of such changes could be quantified.
3. Sector inter-relationships, along the lines emphasized in the discussion of input-output, were taken into account to some extent, although input-output analysis as such was not used.
4. Three projections were usually made—these included a probable or medium level plus a low projection and a high projection.

The forecasts were also based on an implicit assumption that the future cultural-political environment would be similar to that of the early 1960s. The book includes virtually no consideration of possible future concerns about pollution. There were explicit assumptions about advances in technology, world trade, and public policy affecting the search for and the use and conservation of natural resources.

The outcome of the study was "the prospect of sustained economic growth supported by an adequacy of resource materials." Although no general shortage of materials was expected, some particular resources were projected to become relatively scarce. This would imply relatively higher prices for these resources as the years pass, although the book does not get into the outlook for prices. Obviously, the study did not anticipate the runaway inflation of the late 1970s, the oil problem of the early 1970s, nor the very slow recovery of the early 1980s.

Evaluating and adapting resource forecasts

A user of the resource projections in *Resources in America's Future* could begin by examining the explicit and implicit assumptions about future technological change, future world-trade conditions, and future social and political trends. His or her assumptions might be different from those in the book, and these differences could suggest modifications in the resource forecasts. Business planners could be especially interested in forecasts of changes in relative prices of inputs. The task of price forecasting is left for the reader of the book.

Resource forecasting requires consideration of sector interrelationships. For example, it is obvious that as the demand for automobiles increases or decreases, demand for steel (thus, iron ore, coal, coke and heat) will change. Less obvious, there will be an economic impact upon demand for electric power from such sources as hydroelectric generators, coal, and nuclear energy. Steel production requires huge quantities of power. When steel production declines, the demand for electricity and for electric power-generating plants declines. The Ohio Edison Company and other utilities in the Midwest would have saved their customers tens of millions of dollars throughout the 1980s and beyond, had proper evaluation and adaptation of resources been understood and made in the late 1960s and 1970s.

The relative impact of changes in demand upon each of several sources depends upon the relative price of each source. Relative prices are determined largely by other demands for the same resources. As indicated in the previous chapter in the discussion of input-output analysis, intersector relationships are of particular interest to most users of resource forecasts. This is because most firms must look to other sectors for product demands and supplies of inputs.

Mergers and acquisitions process

Using competitive strategy and long-range planning enables a firm to determine the proper "business to be in."[27] This decision is heavily influenced by two factors: (1) the maturity of the industry and/or (2) the maturity of the particular product being produced.

Industry maturity

Every industry goes through four distinct phases: (1) embryonic, (2) growth, (3) mature, and (4) aging. As exhibited in Figure 14–4, the maturity of the industry is calculated by comparing the cash throw-off relative to the cash generated, expressed as a percent. This figure is called a Ronagraph and is presented in more generalized fashion as Figure 14–5. It is an extremely important concept, since it calls attention to the fact that everything goes through an aging process. Products that at one time were exceedingly valuable to the company, one day enter a period in which they are no longer very valuable. Copyrights and patents are the most obvious examples of very profitable, or at least potentially profitable, items that have a limited life cycle insofar as profitability is concerned. Figure 14–6 is illustrative of a firm that has traditionally done quite well in terms of profitability but finds itself in the latter phase of the mature stage or the beginning phase of the aging stage, as indicated in Figures 14–4 and 14–5.

Assume a corporation has as its long-term objective the notion of being the most profitable firm in the industry. In addition, assume it has established a corporate goal of obtaining a corporate growth rate of 15 percent

---

[27] This discussion benefitted from presentation made by Howard Tracy, Vice President, Sherwin-Williams, at INROADS seminar, Oberlin College, August 1982.

Figure 14–4
Return on net assets over time

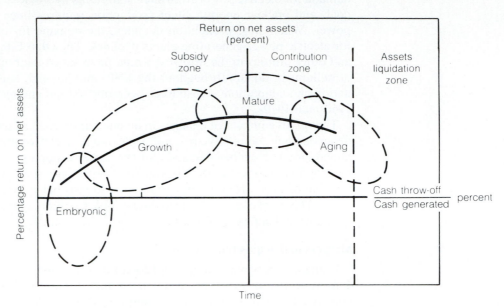

Figure 14–5
Industry maturity

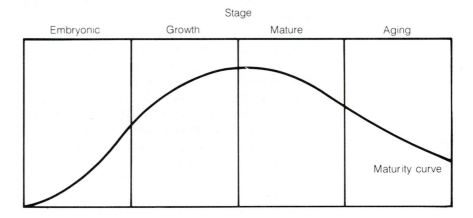

annually expressed in earning per share. If the product of the firm is in the mature or aging stage of its growth cycle, the current business for the firm might be expressed from 1979 through 1985 as it is in the shaded area in the bottom right-hand corner of Figure 14–6. Regardless of the firm's continued operating efficiency and production of products of high quality, the earnings per share must decline due to the stage of the product or

Figure 14–6
The strategic gap

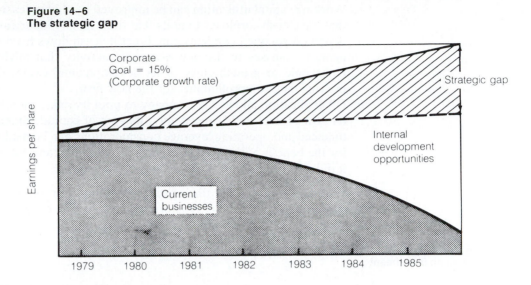

service being produced. In an effort to alleviate this situation, the corporation can develop certain minimal development opportunities internally. Figure 14–6 assumes this internal development exists and takes place to the maximum ability of the firm. Notice, however, that a strategic gap develops despite this effort. Almost automatically, the gap arises because of the corporate goals of a 15 percent corporate growth rate. Quite often, the most powerful tool available to management in such a situation is to acquire or merge with another firm. Mergers and/or acquisitions are principal ways of increasing returns to the corporation, thereby closing the strategic gap.

The acquisition may or may not be in the same industry. As we will see shortly, diversification is often quite effective as part of the corporation's overall strategic plan. Regardless, returns to the firm may be increased through acquisition by one or more of the following ways:

1. Productivity of capital is improved if merger and/or acquisition brings with it special skills and knowledge of the industry by one partner who can apply this knowledge and these skills to the competitive problems and opportunities facing the other partner.
2. If additional dollar investments are made in markets closely related to the current fields of operation of the dominant partner, a reduction can be noticed in the long-run average total cost curve.
3. A corporation can significantly outperform the competition if expansion in an area of competence leads to development of a critical mass of resources—a mass that is simply overwhelming when viewed by the competition in a cold, dispassionate objective manner.

4. Working capital utilization can be improved by shifting cash from units that have cash surpluses to units that traditionally incur cash deficits.
5. A new, diversified company can direct its cash flows from mature and aging businesses to the new economic activity that might be in the embryonic or growth stage of its developmental cycle, thereby improving long-run profitability for the new firm.
6. Diversification allows the company to pool its risks, thereby lowering its cost of debt and, conceivably, its cost of capital. Simultaneously, financial and operating leverage considerations can be made to operate for the benefit of the diversified company to an extent far greater than it did while the firm was in its nondiversified state.

Assuming all goes well, the traditional system of profitability analysis as depicted in Figure 14–7 is improved. As returns on investment rise,

**Figure 14–7
Return on investment**

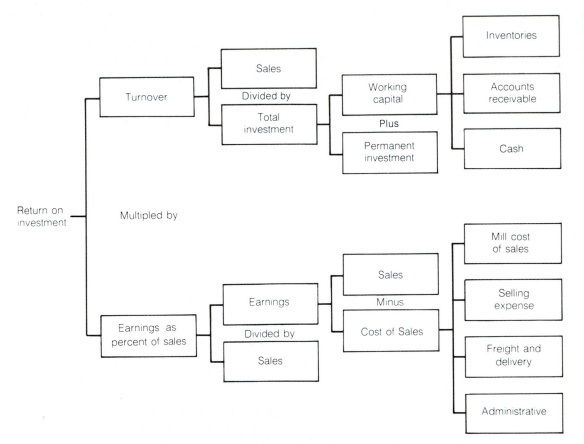

and if the dividend policy of the firm is not materially and adversely affected, the earnings per share of the now-diversified firm can be expected to improve. The strategic gap in Figure 14–6 can be closed.

Diversification

Diversification is the process of expanding the business activity into related, or previously unrelated, areas. Diversification should serve to create additional value for the shareholders. It can be accomplished via vertical or horizontal integration, as depicted in Figure 14–8. The combined resources of two companies should give rise to a net cash flow and/or income stream for the combined company that is significantly greater than the flows or income that could be realized from the two companies if viewed separately. In addition, amplitude fluctuations in net cash flow or income for the combined company should be significantly less than for the companies viewed individually.

The combined company should allow utilization of its net working capital to such an extent that contraseasonal or contracyclical activity in business is minimized; that is, a substantial reduction in risk takes place within the new firm. At times, of course, redeployment of capital to higher growth markets that generate higher net operating margins is necessary. Net operating margins are expressed in Figure 14–7 as "earnings as percent of sales." When multiplied by turnover the net operating margin changes the return on investment for the firm.

Theoretically, a corporate acquisition program results from the corporate strategic planning effort. It might look like the depiction in Figure

Figure 14–8
Diversification

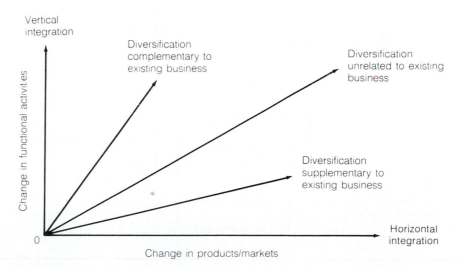

14–9. Several different approaches exist and may be pursued by a firm as it attempts to fill its strategic gap.

When the strategic gap is filled through the process of acquisition and diversification, the acquiring company analyzes possible acquisition target candidates by studying several variables as follows:

1. *Corporate structure.* Does the to-be-acquired firm have a strong management team? Does the team have similar support functions that can be centralized? *Support functions* refers here to accounting, computer operations, legal departments, public relations departments, research and development activities, and so on.
2. *Marketing.* Is the marketing structure basically strong or weak? If the to-be-acquired firm has had a marketing department that has not been able to realize its sales potential, the acquiring firm will want to know why. The acquiring firm might have very strong, well-established channels for its own product line. In such a situation, the acquiring firm can turn a marketing organization that was thought to be quite weak into an effective, profitable unit.
3. *Management team.* Is the management team poorly motivated in the to-be-acquired firm, or is it simply untalented? If motivation has been

Figure 14–9
The acquisition process

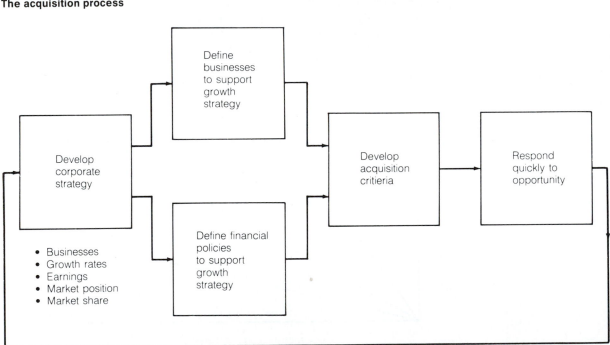

the problem in the past, the acquiring firm might be able to turn the situation around to its benefit.

4. *Manufacturing.* A characteristic to look for in an acquisition-target candidate is one of excess operating capacity, in place and ready to go. If this excess capacity is of an appropriate type and if the marketing team can be turned into a strong organization, additional sales growth in the product line to be manufactured can be expected with relatively few delays.

5. *Copyrights, patents, trade, and/or brand names.* Does the possible acquisition target have trade names that have not been exploited to the fullest? If so, the strategic gap can be closed by proper exploitation of previously under-utilized assets.

Strategic gaps such as the one depicted in Figure 14–6 have been closed by the process of mergers and acquisitions a large number of times during the 1970s. Figure 14–10 reveals the number of mergers and acquisitions of U.S. companies during that time. The dollar value of those acquisitions is depicted in Figure 14–11. As one can readily see, the total dollar volume and the number of mergers increased significantly subsequent to 1975.

As with products and the so-called product cycle, mergers appear to go through periods. Figure 14–12 provides the economic scenario and resulting merger/acquisition activity from 1968 through 1980. Quite

Figure 14–10
Successful acquisitions (number of mergers and acquisitions of U.S. companies, completed transactions*)

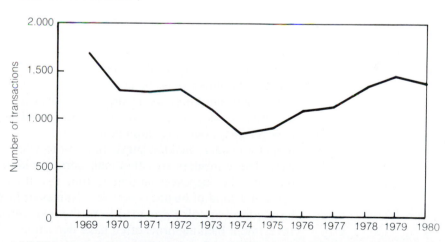

* Publicly announced/completed mergers and acquisitions with purchase price greater than $750,000 or 5 percent of acquired company.
  Data source: H. W. Ebeling, Jr. and T. L. Doorley, "A Strategic Approach to Acquisitions," *Journal of Business Strategy*, vol. 3, pp. 44–54.

Figure 14–11
The journal of business strategy (Mergers and acquisitions over $200 million, completed transactions*)

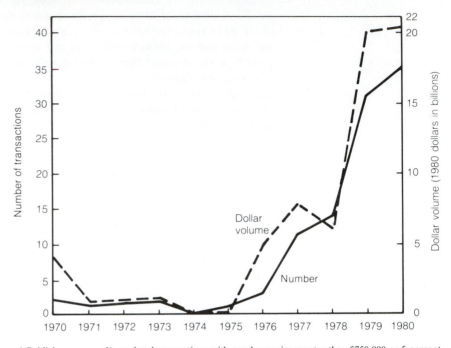

* Publicly announced/completed transactions with purchase price greater than $750,000 or 5 percent of acquired company; 1980 estimate based on announced transactions.
    Data source: "A Strategic Approach to Acquisitions," H. W. Ebeling, Jr. and T. L. Doorley, *Journal of Business Strategy* vol. 3, pp. 44–54.

clearly, when interest rates are high and rising, interest in mergers and acquisitions, likewise, rises.

In situations wherein the strategic gap is to be filled by the acquisition process, attention must be given to the potential acquisition candidates. How does one know as a corporate manager or director what firm to acquire and under what set of circumstances? The answer to this question is never easy, but close attention to the need to fill the gap often results in many insiders making suggestions as to what the company should do next. These insiders are often managers at middle or lower levels within the firm who suggest from time to time that the company should begin a particular kind of business activity. Names of firms that could or should be acquired are also provided from the investment banking community. Investment banking firms often have departments devoted exclusively to the merger and acquisition process. Investment bankers are anxious to serve as negotiators and mediators in the process of acquisition and, of course, they receive a handsome fee for this activity. Consequently, they

Figure 14–12
The journal of business strategy (Four distinct acquisitions periods)

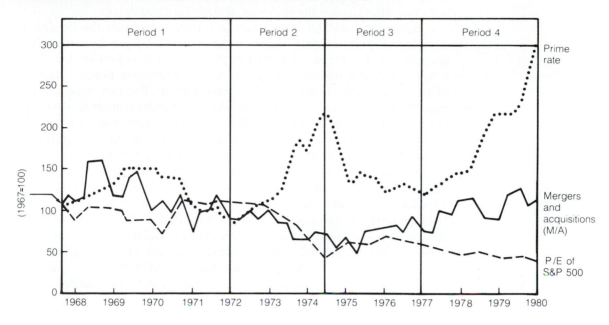

Period 1—1967–1972

Economic scenario:
  High economic growth.
  Low inflation.
  Low interest rates.
  P/E and P/E spreads are
    high.
  Corporate solvency
    declining.

Resulting M/A activity:
  M/A at record levels.
  Mergers/acquisitions use
    P/E leverage of stock.
  Acquisition emphasis is
    on diversification and
    growth companies.

Period 2—1972–1974

Economic scenario:
  Economic crisis.
  Inflation surge.
  High interest rates.
  P/E and P/E spreads
    collapse.
  Corporate solvency crisis.

Resulting M/A activity:
  Collapse of M/A boom.
  Decline in using stock
    acquisitions.
  Reevaluation of past M/A
    strategies and targets.
  Disposition activity
    increases.

Period 3—1974–1977

Economic scenario:
  Economic recovery.
  Continued high inflation.
  Continued high interest
    rates.
  P/E and P/E spreads stay
    depressed.
  Corporate solvency
    recovery.
  U.S. dollar declines.

Resulting M/A activity:
  M/A activity recovers.
  Cash is major method of
    payment.
  Oil companies and large
    companies initiate giant
    M/A era.
  Foreign M/As in the
    United States surge.

Period 4—1977–1980

Economic scenario:
  Economic cycle matures.
  Inflation surges.
  Interest rates peak.
  P/E and P/E spreads
    decline.
  Corporate solvency crisis
    for some.
  Solvency spread
    increases.

Resulting M/A activity:
  M/A activity approaches
    record levels.
  Cash remains major
    method of payment.
  Acquisition of real,
    inflation-protected, and
    undervalued assets
    emphasis.
  New target industries.
  Foreign M/As in the
    United States continue
    to increase.

are more than anxious to cooperate with a firm seeking a merger. To a lesser extent stockbrokers, accountants, and others interested in the corporation often suggest the names of acquisition candidates.

It takes approximately two years to properly evaluate the candidate once the corporation that intends to fill its strategic gap by acquisition decides that a particular firm just might be what it is looking for. Two years worth of research on a firm is a very expensive process, and as often as not results in no acquisition taking place. For this reason, firms must be extremely cautious. The acquiring firm must temper its desire to close its strategic gap with the rather cold realization that earnings per share might be further depleted by a series of investigations of potential candidates if none of the candidates are found to be acceptable.

In addition to in-house costs associated with investigating a potential candidate, the firm will almost definitely incur an investment bankers fee. This fee is normally calculated on what is known in the trade as the Lehman formula. The Lehman formula means the finder of a firm for the company shall be paid 5 percent of the first $1 million spent on the firm; 4 percent on the second million dolars; 3 percent on the third million dollars; 4 percent on the fourth million dollars; and, 1 percent on the fifth and subsequent millions of dollars spent on the firm to be acquired.

Summary

The chapter discussed competitive strategy and long-range planning. Strategic planning selects a product or product mix and a market or a set of markets, establishes specific profitability objectives related to competitive strength and operating efficiency, and determines the degrees of liquidity and diversification to provide flexibility. The company's strategic plan is an attempt to make the best possible match of the firm's competences with the opportunities projected for the future. Long-range forecasting aids strategic planning by providing the outlook for profitability of a well-managed firm in each of the industries that are to be considered.

Although long-range forecasting is more of an art than a science, it can be carried out in a logical sequence: (1) projecting trends and major developments in the principal environmental influences, taking these one at a time; (2) assessing the potentials for interaction among the various trends and developments and adjusting the forecasts to accommodate the interactions; (3) considering the ecological ramifications of the adjusted trends as they evolve simultaneously; (4) appraising potential social feedback aimed at controlling the ecological consequences of the various trends and developments; and (5) developing the range of alternative states of the future business environment.

Social forecasting is concerned with cultural, political, and demographic influences upon the future environment of business firms. Technological forecasting focuses upon future possibilities for conversions of inputs into desired goods and services. Resource forecasting looks at prospects for future changes in supplies and requirements of land, minerals, and energy and pays particular attention to possible changes in the relative prices of resources.

After forecasts have been made for the economy's broad aggregates—such as demands for final products, changes in input-output conversion rates, and available supplies of resources—input-output analyses may be useful in estimating derived demands for intermediate goods.

A strategic gap exists or will exist for most firms. This gap can be filled often via the merger or acquisition route. Proper selection of the acquisition candidate(s) and the costs related thereto are of major importance to the continued, long-term profitability of the firm.

**PROBLEMS
Competitive strategy
and long-range
planning**

14–1   *a.* Actual balance sheet data, 1976–1981, are provided in Exhibit 1; pro forma balance sheet data are provided in Exhibit 2; actual income statement data are provided in Exhibit 3; pro forma income statement data are provided in Exhibit 4. For each year, 1976 through 1986, calculate and/or construct:

   (1) Annual growth rate as a percent of sales. As a percent of net income.
   (2) Earnings per share.
   (3) Net profit margin (percent).
   (4) Gross profit margin (percent).
   (5) Return on equity (percent).
   (6) Current ratio.
   (7) Quick ratio.
   (8) Long-term debt to capitalization (percent).
   (9) Working capital to sales (percent).
   (10) SGAE to sales ratio (percent).
   (11) Cost of goods sold to sales ratio (percent).
   (12) Inventory turnover to cost of goods sold.
   (13) Fixed asset turnover.
   (14) Times interest earned.
   (15) Inventory/sales (percent).
   (16) Receivables/sales (percent).
   (17) Payables /sales (percent).
   (18) Inventory + receivables − payables/sales (percent).

Exhibit 1

Balance Sheet
$ millions
Actual Data through 1981

Assets	1976	1977	1978	1979	1980	1981
Current Assets:						
Cash + S–T investments	$ 21.0	$ 21.0	$ 15.0	$ 25.0	$ 30.0	$ 33.0
Accounts receivable	68.0	74.0	103.0	112.0	122.0	133.0
Inventory	68.0	66.0	82.0	103.0	111.0	121.0
Other current assets	14.0	12.0	18.0	22.0	19.0	21.0
Total current assets	171.0	173.0	218.0	262.0	282.0	308.0
Gross plant	127.0	133.0	159.0	198.0	228.0	253.0
Less: Accumulated Depreciation	59.0	61.0	72.0	82.0	93.0	106.0
Net plant	68.0	72.0	87.0	116.0	135.0	147.0
Long-term investments	5.0	5.0	2.0	2.0	6.0	6.0
Intangibles	N/A	N/A	3.0	3.0	3.0	3.0
Other assets	3.0	4.0	4.0	8.0	8.0	8.0
Total assets	$247.0	$254.0	$314.0	$391.0	$434.0	$472.0

Liabilities						
Current liabilities:						
Notes payable	$ 6.0	$ 5.0	$ 9.0	$ 21.0	$ 12.0	$ 7.0
Current portion of L–T debt	3.0	2.0	4.0	3.0	6.0	11.0
Accounts payable	30.0	29.0	43.0	52.0	55.0	61.0
Taxes payable	13.0	8.0	8.0	10.0	9.0	10.0
Other current liabilities	23.0	23.0	36.0	47.0	51.0	56.0
Total current liabilities	74.0	67.0	100.0	133.0	133.0	145.0
Other liabilities	7.0	9.0	14.0	13.0	17.0	17.0
Long-Term Debt:						
Convertible	—	—	—	—	—	—
Senior	21.0	20.0	21.0	41.0	61.0	63.0
Subordinated	—	—	—	—	—	—
Total long-term debts	21.0	20.0	21.0	41.0	61.0	63.0
Minority interest	—	N/A	N/A	N/A	—	1.0
Owners' equity:						
Preferred equity	—	—	—	—	—	—
Convertible preferred	—	—	—	—	—	—
Capital stock	34.0	34.0	35.0	37.0	37.0	37.0
Retained earnings	110.0	124.0	144.0	167.0	186.0	209.0
Total equity	144.0	158.0	179.0	204.0	223.0	246.0
Total liability and owners' equity	$247.0	$254.0	$314.0	$391.0	$434.0	$472.0

b. For each year, 1981 through 1986, construct a sources and uses of cash statement:

(1) Present the discounted net cash flows in terms of present value. (Use a 20 percent discount rate).

(2) Assume the terminal or salvage value of the assets amount to $454.00.

   (*a*) What is the total value of the net cash flows?

   (*b*) What is the discounted value of the net cash flows (use a 20 percent discount rate)?

Exhibit 2

Balance Sheet
($ millions)
Pro Forma Data, 1982 through 1986

Assets	1982	1983	1984	1985	1986
Current assets:					
Cash + S–T investments	$ 37.0	$ 40.0	$ 44.0	$ 47.0	$ 51.0
Accounts receivable	148.0	162.0	176.0	190.0	204.0
Inventory	134.0	147.0	160.0	173.0	185.0
Other current assets	23.0	25.0	27.0	29.0	32.0
Total current assets	342.0	374.0	407.0	439.0	472.0
Gross plant	283.0	315.0	349.0	384.0	421.0
Less: Accumulated depreciation	121.0	137.0	155.0	175.0	196.0
Net plant	162.0	178.0	194.0	209.0	225.0
Long-term investments	6.0	6.0	6.0	6.0	6.0
Intangibles	2.0	2.0	2.0	2.0	1.0
Other assets	8.0	8.0	8.0	8.0	8.0
Total assets	520.0	568.0	617.0	664.0	714.0

Liabilities	1982	1983	1984	1985	1986
Current liabilities:					
Notes payable	9.0	11.0	14.0	21.0	15.0
Current portion of L–T debt	11.0	11.0	10.0	—	0.0
Accounts payable	67.0	73.0	80.0	86.0	93.0
Taxes payable	12.0	13.0	14.0	16.0	18.0
Other current liabilities	61.0	67.0	73.0	79.0	85.0
Total current liabilities	160.0	175.0	191.0	202.0	211.0
Other liabilities	17.0	17.0	17.0	17.0	17.0
Long-term debt:					
Convertible	—	—	—	—	—
Senior	69.0	72.0	72.0	72.0	72.0
Subordinated	—	—	—	—	—
Total long-term debts	69.0	72.0	72.0	72.0	72.0
Minority interest	2.0	3.0	4.0	5.0	7.0
Owners' equity:					
Preferred equity	—	—	—	—	—
Convertible preferred	—	—	—	—	—
Capital stock	38.0	38.0	38.0	38.0	38.0
Retained earnings	234.0	263.0	295.0	330.0	369.0
Total equity	272.0	301.0	333.0	368.0	407.0
Total liability and owners' equity	520.0	568.0	617.0	664.0	714.0

c. Assuming no additional monies are available to the firm beyond 1986, would the total market value (sales price) of this firm have been excessive in 1981 if it had sold at $300.00?

14–2   Explain the extent to which diversification helps close the so-called strategic gap.

Exhibit 3

Income Statement
Actual Data through 1981
($ millions)

	1976	1977	1978	1979	1980	1981
Net sales	$377.0	$420.0	$494.0	$592.0	$695.0	$759.0
Less: Cost of goods sold	259.0	296.0	343.0	426.0	510.0	558.0
Gross profit	118.0	124.0	151.0	166.0	185.0	201.0
Less:						
Depreciation	8.0	8.0	9.0	10.0	13.0	13.0
Selling, general and administrative	68.0	77.0	92.0	100.0	115.0	125.0
Operating profit	42.0	39.0	50.0	56.0	57.0	63.0
Add: Other net income	(1.0)	4.0	4.0	3.0	7.0	8.0
Less:						
Interest	4.0	5.0	6.0	8.0	14.0	13.0
Amortization	—	—	—	—	—	—
Pretax income	37.0	38.0	48.0	51.0	50.0	58.0
Less:						
Income tax	17.0	17.0	20.0	19.0	20.0	24.0
Minority interest	—	—	—	1.0	1.0	1.0
Extraordinary items	—	—	—	—	—	—
Net income	20.0	21.0	28.0	31.0	29.0	33.0
Less: Preferred dividends	—	—	—	—	—	—
Income available for common	20.0	21.0	28.0	31.0	29.0	33.0
Less:						
Common dividends	6.0	7.0	8.0	9.0	9.0	10.0
Adjustment to retained earnings	—	—	—	—	—	—
Change in retained earnings	$ 14.0	$ 14.0	$ 20.0	$ 22.0	$ 20.0	$ 23.0
Shares outstanding (000s)	7,500	7,523	7,557	7,690	7,716	7,716
Shares convertible (000s)	243	188	452	433	407	407
Earnings per share (primary)	2.67	2.79	3.71	4.03	3.76	4.30
Earnings per share (F.D.)	2.59	2.71	3.45	3.81	3.57	4.09
Dividends per share	0.73	0.90	1.05	1.13	1.20	1.37
Price per share	20.67	19.00	23.00	20.88	21.13	24.18
PE ratio	7.74	6.81	6.20	5.18	5.62	5.62

Exhibit 4

Income Statement
Pro Forma Data, 1982 through 1986
($ millions)

	1982	1983	1984	1985	1986
Net sales	$840.0	$921.0	$1,002.0	$1,083.0	$1,164.0
Less: Cost of goods sold	616.0	676.0	735.0	794.0	854.0
Gross profit	224.0	245.0	267.0	289.0	310.0
Less:					
Depreciation	15.0	16.0	18.0	20.0	21.0
Selling, general and administrative	139.0	152.0	165.0	179.0	192.0
Operating profit	70.0	77.0	84.0	90.0	97.0
Add: Other net income	8.0	9.0	10.0	10.0	11.0
Less: Interest	13.0	13.0	12.0	10.0	9.0
Amortization	0.0	—	—	—	—
Pretax income	65.0	73.0	82.0	90.0	99.0
Less: Income tax	26.0	29.0	33.0	36.0	40.0
Minority interest	1.0	2.0	2.0	2.0	2.0
Extraordinary items	—	—	—	—	—
Net income	38.0	42.0	47.0	52.0	57.0
Less: Preferred dividends	—	—	—	—	—
Income available for common	38.0	42.0	47.0	52.0	57.0
Less:					
Common dividends					
Adjustments to retained earnings	12.0	13.0	15.0	17.0	18.0
	—	—	—	—	—
Change in retained earnings	$ 26.0	$ 29.0	$ 32.0	$ 35.0	$ 39.0
Shares outstanding (000's)	7,716	7,716	7,716	7,716	7,716
Shares convertible (000's)	407	407	407	407	407
Earnings per share (primary)	4.90	5.44	6.09	6.73	7.39
Earnings per share (F.D.)	4.61	5.18	5.77	6.38	6.99
Dividends per share	1.55	1.74	1.93	2.14	2.34
Price per share	27.29	30.65	34.11	37.76	41.33
PE ratio	5.57	5.63	5.60	5.61	5.59

Selected references

Czamanski, Daniel Z. "Some Considerations Concerning Industrial Location Decisions." *European Journal of Operational Research* (UK) 6, no. 2 (February 1981), pp. 227–31.

Day, Lawrence H. "Long-Range Planning in Bell Canada." *Long Range Planning* (September 1973).

Earnest, Kenneth R. "Applying Motivational Theory in Management Accounting." *Management Accounting* 61, no. 6 (December 1979), pp. 41–44.

Easterbrook, Frank H. "Predatory Strategies and Counterstrategies." *University of Chicago Law Review* 48, no. 2 (Spring 1981), pp. 263–337.

Fisher, G. H. "The World of Program Budgeting." *Long Range Planning* (September 1969).

Oster, Sharon. "Industrial Search for New Locations: An Empirical Analysis." *Review of Economics and Statistics* 61, no. 2 (May 1979), pp. 288–92.

Rosen, Stephen. "The Future from the Top: Presidential Perspectives on Planning." *Long Range Planning* (August 1974).

Smalter Donald J. "Anatomy of a Long-Range Plan." *Long Range Planning* (March 1969).

Taylor, Bernard. "Strategic Planning for Resources." *Long Range Planning* (August 1974).

A P P E N D I X

Tables useful for capital budgeting and areas under the normal curve

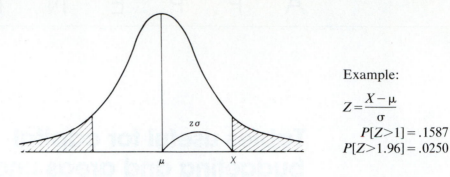

Example:

$$Z = \frac{X - \mu}{\sigma}$$

$$P[Z>1] = .1587$$
$$P[Z>1.96] = .0250$$

Normal deviate z	.00	.01	.02	.03	.04	.05	.06	.07	.08	.09
0.0	.5000	.4960	.4920	.4880	.4840	.4801	.4761	.4721	.4681	.4641
0.1	.4602	.4562	.4522	.4483	.4443	.4404	.4364	.4325	.4286	.4247
0.2	.4207	.4168	.4129	.4090	.4052	.4013	.3974	.3936	.3897	.3859
0.3	.3821	.3783	.3745	.3707	.3669	.3632	.3594	.3557	.3520	.3483
0.4	.3446	.3409	.3372	.3336	.3300	.3264	.3228	.3192	.3156	.3121
0.5	.3085	.3050	.3015	.2981	.2946	.2912	.2877	.2843	.2810	.2776
0.6	.2743	.2709	.2676	.2643	.2611	.2578	.2546	.2514	.2483	.2451
0.7	.2420	.2389	.2358	.2327	.2296	.2266	.2236	.2206	.2177	.2148
0.8	.2119	.2090	.2061	.2033	.2005	.1977	.1949	.1922	.1894	.1867
0.9	.1841	.1814	.1788	.1762	.1736	.1711	.1685	.1660	.1635	.1611
1.0	.1587	.1562	.1539	.1515	.1492	.1469	.1446	.1423	.1401	.1379
1.1	.1357	.1335	.1314	.1292	.1271	.1251	.1230	.1210	.1190	.1170
1.2	.1151	.1131	.1112	.1093	.1075	.1056	.1038	.1020	.1003	.0985
1.3	.0968	.0951	.0934	.0918	.0901	.0885	.0869	.0853	.0838	.0823
1.4	.0808	.0793	.0778	.0764	.0749	.0735	.0721	.0708	.0694	.0681
1.5	.0668	.0655	.0643	.0630	.0618	.0606	.0594	.0582	.0571	.0559
1.6	.0548	.0537	.0526	.0516	.0505	.0495	.0485	.0475	.0465	.0453
1.7	.0446	.0436	.0427	.0418	.0409	.0401	.0392	.0384	.0375	.0367
1.8	.0359	.0351	.0344	.0336	.0329	.0322	.0314	.0307	.0301	.0294
1.9	.0287	.0281	.0274	.0268	.0262	.0256	.0250	.0244	.0239	.0233
2.0	.0228	.0222	.0217	.0212	.0207	.0202	.0197	.0192	.0188	.0183
2.1	.0179	.0174	.0170	.0166	.0162	.0158	.0154	.0150	.0146	.0143
2.2	.0139	.0136	.0132	.0129	.0125	.0122	.0119	.0116	.0113	.0110
2.3	.0107	.0104	.0102	.0099	.0096	.0094	.0091	.0089	.0087	.0084
2.4	.0082	.0080	.0078	.0075	.0073	.0071	.0069	.0068	.0066	.0064
2.5	.0062	.0060	.0059	.0057	.0055	.0054	.0052	.0051	.0049	.0048
2.6	.0047	.0045	.0044	.0043	.0041	.0040	.0039	.0038	.0037	.0036
2.7	.0035	.0034	.0033	.0032	.0031	.0030	.0029	.0028	.0027	.0026
2.8	.0026	.0025	.0024	.0023	.0023	.0022	.0021	.0021	.0020	.0019
2.9	.0019	.0018	.0018	.0017	.0016	.0016	.0015	.0015	.0014	.0014
3.0	.0013	.0013	.0013	.0012	.0012	.0011	.0011	.0011	.0010	.0010

* Interpretation of the example: The probability of Z being greater than 1.96 is 2.5 percent. Plus Z or minus Z refers to the number of standard deviations to the right or left of the mean (μ). $Z = \frac{x - x}{\sigma}$ and entries in this table represent one of the shaded areas, and equals the probability of that area.

2% PER PERIOD

Period	(1) Present Value of $1	(2) Amount to Which $1 Will Accumulate	Present Value of $1 per Period		Amount to Which $1 per Period Will Accumulate	
			(3) Received at End	(4) Received Continuously	(5) Received at End	(6) Received Continuously
1	98039E 00	10200E 01	98039E 00	99016E 00	10000E 01	10100E 01
2	96117E 00	10404E 01	19416E 01	19609E 01	20200E 01	20401E 01
3	94232E 00	10612E 01	28839E 01	29126E 01	30604E 01	30909E 01
4	92385E 00	10824E 01	38077E 01	38457E 01	41216E 01	41627E 01
5	90573E 00	11041E 01	47135E 01	47604E 01	52040E 01	52559E 01
6	88797E 00	11262E 01	56014E 01	56573E 01	63081E 01	63710E 01
7	87056E 00	11487E 01	64720E 01	65365E 01	74343E 01	75084E 01
8	85349E 00	11717E 01	73255E 01	73985E 01	85830E 01	86685E 01
9	83676E 00	11951E 01	81622E 01	82436E 01	97546E 01	98518E 01
10	82035E 00	12190E 01	89826E 01	90721E 01	10950E 02	11059E 02
11	80426E 00	12434E 01	97868E 01	98844E 01	12169E 02	12290E 02
12	78849E 00	12682E 01	10575E 02	10681E 02	13412E 02	13546E 02
13	77303E 00	12936E 01	11348E 02	11461E 02	14680E 02	14827E 02
14	75787E 00	13195E 01	12106E 02	12227E 02	15974E 02	16133E 02
15	74301E 00	13459E 01	12849E 02	12977E 02	17293E 02	17466E 02
16	72845E 00	13728E 01	13578E 02	13713E 02	18639E 02	18825E 02
17	71416E 00	14002E 01	14292E 02	14434E 02	20012E 02	20212E 02
18	70016E 00	14282E 01	14992E 02	15141E 02	21412E 02	21626E 02
19	68643E 00	14568E 01	15678E 02	15835E 02	22841E 02	23068E 02
20	67297E 00	14859E 01	16351E 02	16514E 02	24297E 02	24540E 02
21	65978E 00	15157E 01	17011E 02	17181E 02	25783E 02	26040E 02
22	64684E 00	15460E 01	17658E 02	17834E 02	27299E 02	27571E 02
23	63416E 00	15769E 01	18292E 02	18475E 02	28845E 02	29132E 02
24	62172E 00	16084E 01	18914E 02	19102E 02	30422E 02	30725E 02
25	60953E 00	16406E 01	19523E 02	19718E 02	32030E 02	32350E 02
26	59758E 00	16734E 01	20121E 02	20322E 02	33671E 02	34006E 02
27	58586E 00	17069E 01	20707E 02	20913E 02	35344E 02	35697E 02
28	57437E 00	17410E 01	21281E 02	21493E 02	37051E 02	37420E 02
29	56311E 00	17758E 01	21844E 02	22062E 02	38792E 02	39179E 02
30	55207E 00	18114E 01	22396E 02	22620E 02	40568E 02	40972E 02

4% PER PERIOD

Period	(1) Present Value of $1	(2) Amount to Which $1 Will Accumulate	Present Value of $1 per Period		Amount to Which $1 per Period Will Accumulate	
			(3) Received at End	(4) Received Continuously	(5) Received at End	(6) Received Continuously
1	96154E 00	10400E 01	96154E 00	98064E 00	10000E 01	10199E 01
2	92456E 00	10816E 01	18861E 01	19236E 01	20400E 01	20805E 01
3	88900E 00	11249E 01	27751E 01	28302E 01	31216E 01	31836E 01
4	85480E 00	11699E 01	36299E 01	37020E 01	42465E 01	43308E 01
5	82193E 00	12167E 01	44518E 01	45403E 01	54163E 01	55239E 01
6	79031E 00	12653E 01	52421E 01	53463E 01	66330E 01	67648E 01
7	75992E 00	13159E 01	60021E 01	61213E 01	78983E 01	80552E 01
8	73069E 00	13686E 01	67327E 01	68665E 01	92142E 01	93973E 01
9	70259E 00	14233E 01	74353E 01	75831E 01	10583E 02	10793E 02
10	67556E 00	14802E 01	81109E 01	82721E 01	12006E 02	12245E 02
11	64958E 00	15395E 01	87605E 01	89345E 01	13486E 02	13754E 02
12	62460E 00	16010E 01	93851E 01	95715E 01	15026E 02	15324E 02
13	60057E 00	16651E 01	99856E 01	10184E 02	16627E 02	16957E 02
14	57748E 00	17317E 01	10563E 02	10773E 02	18292E 02	18655E 02
15	55526E 00	18009E 01	11118E 02	11339E 02	20024E 02	20421E 02
16	53391E 00	18730E 01	11652E 02	11884E 02	21825E 02	22258E 02
17	51337E 00	19479E 01	12166E 02	12407E 02	23698E 02	24168E 02
18	49363E-00	20258E 01	12659E 02	12911E 02	25645E 02	26155E 02
19	47464E-00	21068E 01	13134E 02	13395E 02	27671E 02	28221E 02
20	45639E-00	21911E 01	13590E 02	13860E 02	29778E 02	30370E 02
21	43883E-00	22788E 01	14029E 02	14308E 02	31969E 02	32604E 02
22	42196E-00	23699E 01	14451E 02	14738E 02	34248E 02	34928E 02
23	40573E-00	24647E 01	14857E 02	15152E 02	36618E 02	37345E 02
24	39012E-00	25633E 01	15247E 02	15550E 02	39083E 02	39859E 02
25	37512E-00	26658E 01	15622E 02	15932E 02	41646E 02	42473E 02
26	36069E-00	27725E 01	15983E 02	16300E 02	44312E 02	45192E 02
27	34682E-00	28834E 01	16330E 02	16654E 02	47084E 02	48020E 02
28	33348E-00	29987E 01	16663E 02	16994E 02	49968E 02	50960E 02
29	32065E-00	31187E 01	16984E 02	17321E 02	52966E 02	54019E 02
30	30832E-00	32434E 01	17292E 02	17636E 02	56085E 02	57199E 02

6% PER PERIOD

Period	(1) Present Value of $1	(2) Amount to Which $1 Will Accumulate	Present Value of $1 per Period		Amount to Which $1 per Period Will Accumulate	
			(3) Received at End	(4) Received Continuously	(5) Received at End	(6) Received Continuously
1	94340E 00	10600E 01	94340E 00	97142E 00	10000E 01	10297E 01
2	89000E 0C	11236E 01	18334E 01	18879E 01	20600E 01	21212E 01
3	83962E 00	11910E 01	26730E 01	27524E 01	31836E 01	32782E 01
4	79209E 00	12625E 01	34651E 01	35680E 01	43746E 01	45046E 01
5	74726E 00	13382E 01	42124E 01	43375E 01	56371E 01	58046E 01
6	70496E 00	14185E 01	49173E 01	50634E 01	69753E 01	71825E 01
7	66506E 00	15036E 01	55824E 01	57482E 01	83938E 01	86432E 01
8	62741E 00	15938E 01	62098E 01	63943E 01	98975E 01	10192E 02
9	59190E 00	16895E 01	68017E 01	70038E 01	11491E 02	11833E 02
10	55839E 00	17908E 01	73601E 01	75787E 01	13181E 02	13572E 02
11	52679E 00	18983E 01	78869E 01	81212E 01	14972E 02	15416E 02
12	49697E-00	20122E 01	83838E 01	86329E 01	16870E 02	17371E 02
13	46884E-00	21329E 01	88527E 01	91157E 01	18882E 02	19443E 02
14	44230E-00	22609E 01	92950E 01	95711E 01	21015E 02	21639E 02
15	41727E-00	23966E 01	97122E 01	10001E 02	23276E 02	23967E 02
16	39365E-00	25404E 01	10106E 02	10406E 02	25673E 02	26435E 02
17	37136E-00	26928E 01	10477E 02	10789E 02	28213E 02	29051E 02
18	35034E-00	28543E 01	10828E 02	11149E 02	30906E 02	31824E 02
19	33051E-00	30256E 01	11158E 02	11490E 02	33760E 02	34763E 02
20	31180E-00	32071E 01	11470E 02	11811E 02	36786E 02	37878E 02
21	29416E-00	33996E 01	11764E 02	12114E 02	39993E 02	41181E 02
22	27751E-00	36035E 01	12042E 02	12399E 02	43392E 02	44681E 02
23	26180E-00	38197E 01	12303E 02	12669E 02	46996E 02	48392E 02
24	24698E-00	40489E 01	12550E 02	12923E 02	50816E 02	52325E 02
25	23300E-00	42919E 01	12783E 02	13163E 02	54865E 02	56494E 02
26	21981E-00	45494E 01	13003E 02	13389E 02	59156E 02	60914E 02
27	20737E-0C	48223E 01	13211E 02	13603E 02	63706E 02	65598E 02
28	19563E-00	51117E 01	13406E 02	13804E 02	68528E 02	70564E 02
29	18456E-00	54184E 01	13591E 02	13994E 02	73640E 02	75828E 02
30	17411E-00	57435E 01	13765E 02	14174E 02	79058E 02	81407E 02

8% PER PERIOD

Period	(1) Present Value of $1	(2) Amount to Which $1 Will Accumulate	Present Value of $1 per Period		Amount to Which $1 per Period Will Accumulate	
			(3) Received at End	(4) Received Continuously	(5) Received at End	(6) Received Continuously
1	92593E 00	10800E 01	92593E 00	96249E 00	10000E 01	10395E 01
2	85734E 00	11664E 01	17833E 01	18537E 01	20800E 01	21621E 01
3	79383E 00	12597E 01	25771E 01	26789E 01	32464E 01	33746E 01
4	73503E 00	13605E 01	33121E 01	34429E 01	45061E 01	46840E 01
5	68058E 00	14693E 01	39927E 01	41504E 01	58666E 01	60983E 01
6	63017E 00	15869E 01	46229E 01	48054E 01	73359E 01	76256E 01
7	58349E 00	17138E 01	52064E 01	54120E 01	89228E 01	92751E 01
8	54027E 00	18509E 01	57466E 01	59736E 01	10637E 02	11057E 02
9	50025E 00	19990E 01	62469E 01	64936E 01	12488E 02	12981E 02
10	46319E-00	21589E 01	67101E 01	69750E 01	14487E 02	15059E 02
11	42888E-00	23316E 01	71390E 01	74209E 01	16645E 02	17303E 02
12	39711E-00	25182E 01	75361E 01	78337E 01	18977E 02	19726E 02
13	36770E-00	27196E 01	79038E 01	82159E 01	21495E 02	22344E 02
14	34046E-00	29372E 01	82442E 01	85698E 01	24215E 02	25171E 02
15	31524E-00	31722E 01	85595E 01	88975E 01	27152E 02	28224E 02
16	29189E-00	34259E 01	88514E 01	92009E 01	30324E 02	31522E 02
17	27027E-00	37000E 01	91216E 01	94818E 01	33750E 02	35083E 02
18	25025E-00	39960E 01	93719E 01	97420E 01	37450E 02	38929E 02
19	23171E-00	43157E 01	96036E 01	99828E 01	41446E 02	43083E 02
20	21455E-00	46610E 01	98181E 01	10206E 02	45762E 02	47569E 02
21	19866E-00	50338E 01	10017E 02	10412E 02	50423E 02	52414E 02
22	18394E-00	54365E 01	10201E 02	10604E 02	55457E 02	57647E 02
23	17032E-00	58715E 01	10371E 02	10781E 02	60893E 02	63298E 02
24	15770E-00	63412E 01	10529E 02	10945E 02	66765E 02	69401E 02
25	14602E-00	68485E 01	10675E 02	11096E 02	73106E 02	75993E 02
26	13520E-00	73964E 01	10810E 02	11237E 02	79954E 02	83112E 02
27	12519E-00	79881E 01	10935E 02	11367E 02	87351E 02	90800E 02
28	11591E-00	86271E 01	11051E 02	11487E 02	95339E 02	99103E 02
29	10733E-00	93173E 01	11158E 02	11599E 02	10397E 03	10807E 03
30	99377E-01	10063E 02	11258E 02	11702E 02	11328E 03	11776E 03

10% PER PERIOD

Period	(1) Present Value of $1	(2) Amount to Which $1 Will Accumulate	Present Value of $1 per Period		Amount to Which $1 per Period Will Accumulate	
			(3) Received at End	(4) Received Continuously	(5) Received at End	(6) Received Continuously
1	90909E 00	11000E 01	90909E 00	95382E 00	10000E 01	10492E 01
2	82645E 00	12100E 01	17355E 01	18209E 01	21000E 01	22033E 01
3	75131E 00	13310E 01	24869E 01	26092E 01	33100E 01	34729E 01
4	68301E 00	14641E 01	31699E 01	33258E 01	46410E 01	48694E 01
5	62092E 00	16105E 01	37908E 01	39773E 01	61051E 01	64055E 01
6	56447E 00	17716E 01	43553E 01	45696E 01	77156E 01	80953E 01
7	51316E 00	19487E 01	48684E 01	51080E 01	94872E 01	99540E 01
8	46651E-00	21436E 01	53349E 01	55974E 01	11436E 02	11999E 02
9	42410E-00	23579E 01	57590E 01	60424E 01	13579E 02	14248E 02
10	38554E-00	25937E 01	61446E 01	64469E 01	15937E 02	16722E 02
11	35049E-00	28531E 01	64951E 01	68147E 01	18531E 02	19443E 02
12	31863E-00	31384E 01	68137E 01	71490E 01	21384E 02	22437E 02
13	28966E-00	34523E 01	71034E 01	74529E 01	24523E 02	25729E 02
14	26333E-00	37975E 01	73667E 01	77292E 01	27975E 02	29352E 02
15	23939E-00	41772E 01	76061E 01	79803E 01	31772E 02	33336E 02
16	21763E-00	45950E 01	78237E 01	82087E 01	35950E 02	37719E 02
17	19784E-00	50545E 01	80216E 01	84163E 01	40545E 02	42540E 02
18	17986E-00	55599E 01	82014E 01	86050E 01	45599E 02	47843E 02
19	16351E-00	61159E 01	83649E 01	87765E 01	51159E 02	53676E 02
20	14864E-00	67275E 01	85136E 01	89325E 01	57275E 02	60093E 02
21	13513E-00	74003E 01	86487E 01	90743E 01	64003E 02	67152E 02
22	12285E-00	81403E 01	87715E 01	92031E 01	71403E 02	74916E 02
23	11168E-00	89543E 01	88832E 01	93203E 01	79543E 02	83457E 02
24	10153E-00	98497E 01	89847E 01	94268E 01	88497E 02	92852E 02
25	92296E-01	10835E 02	90770E 01	95237E 01	98347E 02	10319E 03
26	83905E-01	11918E 02	91609E 01	96117E 01	10918E 03	11455E 03
27	76278E-01	13110E 02	92372E 01	96917E 01	12110E 03	12706E 03
28	69343E-01	14421E 02	93066E 01	97645E 01	13421E 03	14081E 03
29	63039E-01	15863E 02	93696E 01	98306E 01	14863E 03	15594E 03
30	57309E-01	17449E 02	94269E 01	98908E 01	16449E 03	17259E 03

12% PER PERIOD

Period	(1) Present Value of $1	(2) Amount to Which $1 Will Accumulate	Present Value of $1 per Period		Amount to Which $1 per Period Will Accumulate	
			(3) Received at End	(4) Received Continuously	(5) Received at End	(6) Received Continuously
1	89286E 00	11200E 01	89286E 00	94542E 00	10000E 01	10589E 01
2	79719E 00	12544E 01	16901E 01	17895E 01	21200E 01	22448E 01
3	71178E 00	14049E 01	24018E 01	25432E 01	33744E 01	35730E 01
4	63552E 00	15735E 01	30373E 01	32161E 01	47793E 01	50607E 01
5	56743E 00	17623E 01	36048E 01	38170E 01	63528E 01	67268E 01
6	50663E 00	19738E 01	41114E 01	43534E 01	81152E 01	85929E 01
7	45235E-00	22107E 01	45638E 01	48324E 01	10089E 02	10683E 02
8	40388E-00	24760E 01	49676E 01	52601E 01	12300E 02	13024E 02
9	36061E-00	27731E 01	53282E 01	56419E 01	14776E 02	15645E 02
10	32197E-00	31058E 01	56502E 01	59828E 01	17549E 02	18582E 02
11	28748E-00	34786E 01	59377E 01	62872E 01	20655E 02	21870E 02
12	25668E-00	38960E 01	61944E 01	65590E 01	24133E 02	25554E 02
13	22917E-00	43635E 01	64235E 01	68017E 01	28029E 02	29679E 02
14	20462E-00	48871E 01	66282E 01	70183E 01	32393E 02	34299E 02
15	18270E-00	54736E 01	68109E 01	72118E 01	37280E 02	39474E 02
16	16312E-00	61304E 01	69740E 01	73845E 01	42753E 02	45270E 02
17	14564E-00	68660E 01	71196E 01	75387E 01	48884E 02	51761E 02
18	13004E-00	76900E 01	72497E 01	76764E 01	55750E 02	59032E 02
19	11611E-00	86128E 01	73658E 01	77994E 01	63440E 02	67174E 02
20	10367E-00	96463E 01	74694E 01	79091E 01	72052E 02	76294E 02
21	92560E-01	10804E 02	75620E 01	80072E 01	81699E 02	86508E 02
22	82643E-01	12100E 02	76446E 01	80947E 01	92503E 02	97948E 02
23	73788E-01	13552E 02	77184E 01	81728E 01	10460E 03	11076E 03
24	65882E-01	15179E 02	77843E 01	82426E 01	11816E 03	12511E 03
25	58823E-01	17000E 02	78431E 01	83048E 01	13333E 03	14118E 03
26	52521E-01	19040E 02	78957E 01	83605E 01	15033E 03	15918E 03
27	46894E-01	21325E 02	79426E 01	84101E 01	16937E 03	17934E 03
28	41869E-01	23884E 02	79844E 01	84544E 01	19070E 03	20192E 03
29	37383E-01	26750E 02	80218E 01	84940E 01	21458E 03	22721E 03
30	33378E-01	29960E 02	80552E 01	85294E 01	24133E 03	25554E 03

15% PER PERIOD

Period	(1) Present Value of $1	(2) Amount to Which $1 Will Accumulate	Present Value of $1 per Period		Amount to Which $1 per Period Will Accumulate	
			(3) Received at End	(4) Received Continuously	(5) Received at End	(6) Received Continuously
1	86957E 00	11500E 01	86957E 00	93326E 00	10000E 01	10733E 01
2	75614E 00	13225E 01	16257E 01	17448E 01	21500E 01	23075E 01
3	65752E 00	15209E 01	22832E 01	24505E 01	34725E 01	37269E 01
4	57175E 00	17490E 01	28550E 01	30641E 01	49934E 01	53592E 01
5	49718E-00	20114E 01	33522E 01	35977E 01	67424E 01	72363E 01
6	43233E-00	23131E 01	37845E 01	40617E 01	87537E 01	93950E 01
7	37594E-00	26600E 01	41604E 01	44652E 01	11067E 02	11877E 02
8	32690E-00	30590E 01	44873E 01	48160E 01	13727E 02	14732E 02
9	28426E-00	35179E 01	47716E 01	51211E 01	16786E 02	18015E 02
10	24718E-00	40456E 01	50188E 01	53864E 01	20304E 02	21791E 02
11	21494E-00	46524E 01	52337E 01	56171E 01	24349E 02	26133E 02
12	18691E-00	53503E 01	54206E 01	58177E 01	29002E 02	31126E 02
13	16253E-00	61528E 01	55831E 01	59921E 01	34352E 02	36868E 02
14	14133E-00	70757E 01	57245E 01	61438E 01	40505E 02	43472E 02
15	12289E-00	81371E 01	58474E 01	62757E 01	47580E 02	51066E 02
16	10686E-00	93576E 01	59542E 01	63904E 01	55717E 02	59799E 02
17	92926E-01	10761E 02	60472E 01	64901E 01	65075E 02	69842E 02
18	80805E-01	12375E 02	61280E 01	65769E 01	75836E 02	81392E 02
19	70265E-01	14232E 02	61982E 01	66523E 01	88212E 02	94674E 02
20	61100E-01	16367E 02	62593E 01	67178E 01	10244E 03	10995E 03
21	53131E-01	18822E 02	63125E 01	67749E 01	11881E 03	12751E 03
22	46201E-01	21645E 02	63587E 01	68245E 01	13763E 03	14771E 03
23	40174E-01	24891E 02	63988E 01	68676E 01	15928E 03	17094E 03
24	34934E-01	28625E 02	64338E 01	69051E 01	18417E 03	19766E 03
25	30378E-01	32919E 02	64641E 01	69377E 01	21279E 03	22838E 03
26	26415E-01	37857E 02	64906E 01	69660E 01	24571E 03	26371E 03
27	22970E-01	43535E 02	65135E 01	69907E 01	28357E 03	30434E 03
28	19974E-01	50066E 02	65335E 01	70121E 01	32710E 03	35107E 03
29	17369E-01	57575E 02	65509E 01	70308E 01	37717E 03	40480E 03
30	15103E-01	66212E 02	65660E 01	70470E 01	43475E 03	46659E 03

18% PER PERIOD

Period	(1) Present Value of $1	(2) Amount to Which $1 Will Accumulate	Present Value of $1 per Period		Amount to Which $1 per Period Will Accumulate	
			(3) Received at End	(4) Received Continuously	(5) Received at End	(6) Received Continuously
1	84746E 00	11800E 01	84746E 00	92163E 00	10000E 01	10875E 01
2	71818E 00	13924E 01	15656E 01	17027E 01	21800E 01	23708E 01
3	60863E 00	16430E 01	21743E 01	23646E 01	35724E 01	38351E 01
4	51579E 00	19388E 01	26901E 01	29255E 01	52154E 01	56719E 01
5	43711E-00	22878E 01	31272E 01	34009E 01	71542E 01	77803E 01
6	37043E-00	26996E 01	34976E 01	38037E 01	94420E 01	10268E 02
7	31393E-00	31855E 01	38115E 01	41451E 01	12142E 02	13204E 02
8	26604E-00	37589E 01	40776E 01	44344E 01	15327E 02	16668E 02
9	22546E-00	44355E 01	43030E 01	46796E 01	19086E 02	20756E 02
10	19106E-00	52338E 01	44941E 01	48874E 01	23521E 02	25580E 02
11	16192E-00	61759E 01	46560E 01	50635E 01	28755E 02	31272E 02
12	13722E-00	72876E 01	47932E 01	52127E 01	34931E 02	37988E 02
13	11629E-00	85994E 01	49095E 01	53392E 01	42219E 02	45914E 02
14	98549E-01	10147E 02	50081E 01	54464E 01	50818E 02	55266E 02
15	83516E-01	11974E 02	50916E 01	55372E 01	60965E 02	66301E 02
16	70776E-01	14129E 02	51624E 01	56142E 01	72939E 02	79323E 02
17	59980E-01	16672E 02	52223E 01	56794E 01	87068E 02	94688E 02
18	50830E-01	19673E 02	52732E 01	57347E 01	10374E 03	11282E 03
19	43077E-01	23214E 02	53162E 01	57815E 01	12341E 03	13421E 03
20	36506E-01	27393E 02	53527E 01	58212E 01	14663E 03	15946E 03
21	30937E-01	32324E 02	53837E 01	58549E 01	17402E 03	18925E 03
22	26218E-01	38142E 02	54099E 01	58834E 01	20634E 03	22440E 03
23	22218E-01	45008E 02	54321E 01	59075E 01	24449E 03	26588E 03
24	18829E-01	53109E 02	54509E 01	59280E 01	28949E 03	31483E 03
25	15957E-01	62669E 02	54669E 01	59454E 01	34260E 03	37259E 03
26	13523E-01	73949E 02	54804E 01	59601E 01	40527E 03	44074E 03
27	11460E-01	87260E 02	54919E 01	59725E 01	47922E 03	52116E 03
28	97119E-02	10297E 03	55016E 01	59831E 01	56648E 03	61606E 03
29	82304E-02	12150E 03	55098E 01	59920E 01	66945E 03	72804E 03
30	69749E-02	14337E 03	55168E 01	59996E 01	79095E 03	86017E 03

20% PER PERIOD

Period	(1) Present Value of $1	(2) Amount to Which $1 Will Accumulate	Present Value of $1 per Period		Amount to Which $1 per Period Will Accumulate	
			(3) Received at End	(4) Received Continuously	(5) Received at End	(6) Received Continuously
1	83333E 00	12000E 01	83333E 00	91414E 00	10000E 01	10970E 01
2	69444E 00	14400E 01	15278E 01	16759E 01	22000E 01	24133E 01
3	57870E 00	17280E 01	21065E 01	23107E 01	36400E 01	39929E 01
4	48225E−00	20736E 01	25887E 01	28397E 01	53680E 01	58885E 01
5	40188E−00	24883E 01	29906E 01	32806E 01	74416E 01	81632E 01
6	33490E−00	29860E 01	33255E 01	36480E 01	99299E 01	10893E 02
7	27908E−00	35832E 01	36046E 01	39541E 01	12916E 02	14168E 02
8	23257E−00	42998E 01	38372E 01	42092E 01	16499E 02	18099E 02
9	19381E−00	51598E 01	40310E 01	44218E 01	20799E 02	22816E 02
10	16151E−00	61917E 01	41925E 01	45990E 01	25959E 02	28476E 02
11	13459E−00	74301E 01	43271E 01	47466E 01	32150E 02	35268E 02
12	11216E−00	89161E 01	44392E 01	48697E 01	39580E 02	43418E 02
13	93464E−01	10699E 02	45327E 01	49722E 01	48497E 02	53199E 02
14	77887E−01	12839E 02	46106E 01	50576E 01	59196E 02	64936E 02
15	64905E−01	15407E 02	46755E 01	51288E 01	72035E 02	79020E 02
16	54088E−01	18488E 02	47296E 01	51882E 01	87442E 02	95921E 02
17	45073E−01	22186E 02	47746E 01	52376E 01	10593E 03	11620E 03
18	37561E−01	26623E 02	48122E 01	52788E 01	12812E 03	14054E 03
19	31301E−01	31948E 02	48435E 01	53131E 01	15474E 03	16974E 03
20	26084E−01	38338E 02	48696E 01	53417E 01	18669E 03	20479E 03
21	21737E−01	46005E 02	48913E 01	53656E 01	22503E 03	24664E 03
22	18114E−01	55206E 02	49094E 01	53855E 01	27103E 03	29731E 03
23	15095E−01	66247E 02	49245E 01	54020E 01	32624E 03	35787E 03
24	12579E−01	79497E 02	49371E 01	54158E 01	39248E 03	43054E 03
25	10483E−01	95396E 02	49476E 01	54273E 01	47198E 03	51775E 03
26	87355E−02	11448E 03	49563E 01	54369E 01	56738E 03	62239E 03
27	72796E−02	13737E 03	49636E 01	54449E 01	68185E 03	74797E 03
28	60663E−02	16484E 03	49697E 01	54515E 01	81922E 03	89866E 03
29	50553E−02	19781E 03	49747E 01	54571E 01	98407E 03	10795E 04
30	42127E−02	23738E 03	49789E 01	54617E 01	11819E 04	12965E 04

Index to cases

671

Index

This book has been set Linotron 202 n in 10 and 9 point Times Roman, leaded 2 points. Part numbers are 24 point Avant Garde Book and part titles are 27 point Avant Garde Bold. Chapter numbers are 24 point Avant Garde Book and chapter titles are 20 point Avant Garde Bold. The size of the type page is 36 by 46½ picas.